The
ECONOMY
of
PUERTO
RICO

RENEWALS 458-4574
DATE DUE

WITHDRAWN
UTSA LIBRARIES

The
ECONOMY
of
PUERTO RICO

Restoring Growth

SUSAN M. COLLINS
BARRY P. BOSWORTH
MIGUEL A. SOTO-CLASS
Editors

CENTER FOR THE NEW ECONOMY
San Juan, Puerto Rico

BROOKINGS INSTITUTION PRESS
Washington, D.C.

Copyright © 2006
THE BROOKINGS INSTITUTION
CENTER FOR THE NEW ECONOMY

All rights reserved. No part of this publication may be reproduced or transmitted
in any form or by any means without permission in writing from the
Brookings Institution Press, 1775 Massachusetts Avenue, N.W.,
Washington, DC 20036
www.brookings.edu.

Library of Congress Cataloging-in-Publication data
The economy of Puerto Rico : restoring growth / Susan M. Collins,
Barry P. Bosworth, and Miguel A. Soto-Class, editors.
    p.   cm.
Includes index.
ISBN-13: 978-0-8157-1554-2 (hardcover : alk. paper)
ISBN-10: 0-8157-1554-4
ISBN-13: 978-0-8157-1553-5 (pbk. : alk. paper)
ISBN-10: 0-8157-1553-6
   1. Puerto Rico—Economic policy. 2. Puerto Rico—Economic
conditions—1952– I. Collins, Susan Margaret II. Bosworth, Barry,
1942– III. Soto-Class, Miguel A.   IV. Title.
HC154.5.E275 2006
338.97295—dc22   2006010533

Library
University of Texas
at San Antonio

9 8 7 6 5 4 3 2 1
The paper used in this publication meets minimum requirements of the
American National Standard for Information Sciences—Permanence of Paper
for Printed Library Materials: ANSI Z39.48-1992.

Typeset in Adobe Garamond

Composition by Circle Graphics
Columbia, Maryland

Printed by R. R. Donnelley
Harrisonburg, Virginia

Contents

v

Foreword

Thnis book is the culmination of a collaborative effort between the Brookings Institution and the Center for the New Economy (CNE). Building on CNE's initial vision to develop a growth strategy for Puerto Rico, the two institutions undertook a research project pairing researchers from the island and the mainland. The resulting papers incorporate empirical analyses and distill policy implications of particular relevance to Puerto Rico at the outset of the twenty-first century.

The Brookings Institution first became involved in the analysis of the Puerto Rican economy in 1930 with the publication of *Porto Rico and Its Problems*. That publication was followed by a period of remarkable economic progress that continued up to the 1970s. More recently, the rate of economic progress has slowed and there has been little or no further convergence of living standards in Puerto Rico with those on the mainland. In particular, rates of poverty are unacceptably high. At the seventy-fifth anniversary of the 1930 report, it is appropriate to undertake a critical re-evaluation of the island's economy and to seek means of re-invigorating growth.

The editors wish to thank a number of individuals for their extremely valuable contributions to this project. In particular, we are grateful to

Deepak Lamba Nieves and Sergio M. Marxuach Colón of the Center for the New Economy, as well as Starynee Adams, Gabriel Chodorow-Reich, and Kristin Wilson of the Brookings Institution for their assistance in organizing the project and preparing the volume. Also at Brookings, Eric Haven verified the chapters. Katherine Kimball edited the manuscript, while Carlotta Riba assisted with proofreading, and Julia Petrakis prepared the index. At CNE, we would like to thank Carla Alonso, Ana Sofía Allende, Sofía Stolberg, and Michelle Sugden for their support and assistance.

The views expressed in this book are solely those of the authors, and should not be ascribed to the organizations or persons acknowledged above (or on the acknowledgements page) or to the trustees, officers, or staff members of either the Center for the New Economy or the Brookings Institution.

STROBE TALBOTT
Brookings Institution

MIGUEL A. SOTO-CLASS
Center for the New Economy

Preface

Puerto Rico has been the subject of numerous studies throughout the past three hundred years. Since very early in its history, both foreign and local observers have recorded their interpretations of, and judgments about, the island. Marshal Alejandro O'Reilly, who arrived in San Juan in April 1765, was one of the earliest. He identified three key elements of the island's economy that continue to play a role to this day: the large informal economy, the fragility of public finances, and the dependence on foreign transfers.

In the nineteenth century two reports stand out. First is the extensive survey conducted by Colonel George Dawson Flinter in the early 1830s, which describes trends that still resonate today, such as the remarkable openness of the Puerto Rican economy to international trade and the incidence of large-scale tax evasion. The other significant report from this period is the *Report on the Island of Porto Rico* by Henry K. Carroll, published in 1899 just after the change of sovereignty. Carroll, President McKinley's special commissioner for Puerto Rico, identified poverty and education as two of the principal issues affecting Puerto Rican social development. Both continue to be areas of concern.

The twentieth century brought a stream of studies and reports on Puerto Rico's economy and society. Two of these reports are particularly noteworthy for their comprehensiveness and importance in guiding policy. The first is *Porto Rico and Its Problems*, published by the Brookings Institution in 1930. This study, prompted by various groups of Puerto Rican private citizens, was a thorough examination of the island's social and economic landscape. Its coverage included education, public debt, public health, agriculture, trade, and the state public works. It contained a long list of recommendations, many of which were eventually implemented by the Puerto Rican government. The authors identified two distinct problems affecting the island, one economic, the other political. The economic one was "how to raise the incomes and standards of living of her people to something approaching parity with those prevailing in continental United States." The political one was "how to establish mutually satisfactory public relations between the Island and the mainland." Today, both issues remain at the very core of the island's political economy.

The other important study from this period was Harvey Perloff's *Puerto Rico's Economic Future: A Study in Planned Development*, published by the University of Chicago Press in 1950. This study, conducted at the request of the University of Puerto Rico, is a sobering assessment of the economic development of the island at mid-century. It signaled the potential of export-led growth for Puerto Rico that came to be known as the "industrialization by invitation" program. Its recommendations, which dominated economic policy in Puerto Rico during the second half of the twentieth century, focused on attracting foreign capital, matching it with the excess pool of local labor, and exporting the resulting products to the rest of the world. By most accounts this model was relatively successful in jump-starting the Puerto Rican economy.

However, the Puerto Rican economy began to falter in the 1970s, as evidenced by the Tobin Report of 1975 and the Krepps Report of 1979. At the close of 2005, its performance presented an economic conundrum. From some perspectives, it has been quite successful. Living standards exceed those in the rest of Latin America, and some quality of life measures are comparable to those in the most highly developed countries. At the same time, after fifty years of intense social change and economic growth, close to half of the Puerto Rican population still lives under the U.S. poverty line, and this number shows no sign of declining.

By most criteria, Puerto Rico has created the conditions for strong sustained growth. It has increased educational attainment to OECD levels and made extensive investments in physical capital and infrastructure. In addition, Puerto Rico is one of the world's most open economies; and it has a strong institutional framework, built around protection of property rights and respect for the rule of law. By these standards, Puerto Rico should be growing much more rapidly. Why did growth slow down?

This question is the principal subject of the project that resulted in this book. Both Brookings and the Center for the New Economy (CNE) have strived to produce a balanced and fair assessment of the Puerto Rican economy, based on empirical data and independent analysis. In addition to critically examining the record of economic growth, this study also seeks to provide policy recommendations that can and should be implemented by the Puerto Rican and U.S. governments.

DEEPAK LAMBA NIEVES
SERGIO M. MARXUACH COLÓN
MIGUEL A. SOTO CLASS

Center for the New Economy
San Juan, Puerto Rico
April 2006

Acknowledgments

This project was entirely financed by the contributions of private citizens and enterprises in Puerto Rico. We are grateful to the following contributors who have provided financial support to this endeavor and encouraged an atmosphere of complete academic freedom for the project:

Churchill G. Carey, Jr.
Ángel Collado-Schwarz
José Enrique Fernández
Antonio Luis Ferré

Jaime Martí
Enrique Vila del Corral
Joaquín Viso
Triple S, Inc.

1

Introduction and Summary

SUSAN M. COLLINS, BARRY P. BOSWORTH,
AND MIGUEL A. SOTO-CLASS

A t the close of the millennium, Puerto Rico was a tale of two economies. It had achieved some impressive economic milestones. Per capita income was substantially higher than in the rest of Latin America. In terms of quality of life measures such as literacy rates, years of schooling, and life expectancy, it ranked close to the most highly developed countries. But in other key dimensions, Puerto Rico appeared stuck under an economic glass ceiling. Although Puerto Rican residents have been American citizens since 1917, nearly half of them still lived under the U.S. poverty line, and the income gap relative to the mainland was widening.

As a territory of the United States, Puerto Rico shares key U.S. institutions; in particular, the region operates under U.S. judicial, monetary, and tariff systems. It is one of the world's most open economies, with free mobility of goods, services, capital, and labor to the large, prosperous U.S. market. One might expect these conditions to pave the way for rapid economic development in Puerto Rico, with living standards converging steadily with those enjoyed in the rest of the nation. Indeed, in the decades following World War II, Puerto Rico was hailed as a success story, sustaining impressive rates of economic growth and significantly raising domestic living standards. Its gross domestic product (GDP) per worker rose from 30 percent of the U.S. average in 1950 to 75 percent in 1980, a remarkable achievement.

But over the past twenty-five years, the economic situation on the island has deteriorated.[1] Growth in GDP has slowed substantially, and no further progress has been made in narrowing the gap with the U.S. mainland. Gross national income per capita, a more appropriate measure of living standards, yields an even less favorable picture. While income per capita doubled from just over 20 percent of the U.S. average in 1950 to roughly 40 percent in the early 1970s, it has drifted back down to only about 30 percent more recently. Living standards in Puerto Rico are farther from the U.S. average today than they were in 1970, and per capita income is only about half that of the poorest state.

Why did Puerto Rico's economic progress stall? More important, what can be done to restore growth? These are the questions that motivated the Center for the New Economy and the Brookings Institution to undertake this collaborative research project. The objective was to examine Puerto Rico's economy and propose strategies for sustainable growth. Although it necessarily touches on political issues at times, no assessment of the alternative political options for the region was intended. Indeed, our economic analyses and proposed growth strategy are status neutral and will be relevant regardless of political regime.

The issues raised by Puerto Rico's puzzling economic performance are both important and interesting. Many Americans are unaware that the incomes of a large group of fellow citizens have been far below the average. More broadly, it is critical to understand why an economy with so many of the characteristics economists deem key to growth should not perform better. And as economic integration expands and deepens in Europe and elsewhere, it is ever more essential to understand which policy levers remain available for a small but open peripheral economy to ensure that it does not fall behind.

A preliminary analysis of Puerto Rico's economic situation highlighted a set of overlapping concerns that appeared to be at the heart of Puerto Rico's economic difficulties. These included dimensions of labor supply and demand, entrepreneurship, the fiscal situation, financial markets, and trade. In selecting authors to study each of these topics, we paired Puerto Rican and mainland experts so as to ensure that the analysis was appropriately grounded in the relevant historical context. The authors met for an initial conference in San Juan in May 2004. Drafts of all the papers, as well as commentary by invited discussants, were presented at a second, academic conference in March 2005, also in San Juan. The revised analyses and discussant remarks are presented in this volume.

The volume consists of nine substantive chapters—each summarized briefly in the remainder of this chapter. Chapter 2 provides an empirical overview of Puerto

---

1. We sometimes follow common parlance in using the phrases "on the island" and "on the mainland" to distinguish developments in Puerto Rico from those in the rest of the United States. In addition to the principal island of Puerto Rico, the Commonwealth also includes Vieques, Culebrita, Palomino (know by some as the Spanish Virgin Islands), Mona, Monito, and various other isolated islands.

Rico's growth experience, setting the stage for subsequent chapters. Motivated by the island's extremely low employment rates, the next two chapters study labor supply from two different perspectives. Chapter 3 focuses on the effects of public transfers on labor supply, and chapter 4 examines the influence of a broader range of determinants. Chapter 5 addresses the quality of the labor supply, looking at the educational system and its performance. Private sector development, a critical component of labor demand, is the focus of chapter 6. Chapter 7 examines fiscal policy, an area of considerable local autonomy but growing difficulties. Puerto Rico has much less control over its monetary and trade policies than it would if it were an independent country. Nonetheless, financial markets and cross-border interactions are central to the island's economic performance. These issues are the subject of chapters 8 and 9. The final chapter of the volume pulls together the lessons from these analyses and sets out a growth strategy for Puerto Rico.

IN THE SECOND CHAPTER, Barry P. Bosworth and Susan M. Collins examine the level and growth of production and income in Puerto Rico. Pulling together data from a variety of sources, they analyze why economic performance faltered, identify the main characteristics of the current economy, and highlight the key challenges to restoring sustained growth.

The analysis uncovers three main sets of findings. First, official statistics substantially overstate production of goods and services on the island. The problem arises from section 936 of the U.S. tax code, which provided strong incentives for U.S. corporations to use transfer pricing to shift reported income to Puerto Rico. Profits earned in Puerto Rico are effectively exempt from U.S. taxation. These provisions were introduced in 1976 and remained in force until they were repealed in 1995, with a ten-year phase-out. The authors document the magnitude of the distortion in a number of ways and then construct "adjusted" GDP estimates. Their preferred measure cuts the level of Puerto Rican GDP by about 20 percent in 2003 and that of output growth by 0.7 percent a year since 1975. The tax distortion explains much of the growing gap between Puerto Rico's measured production and national income, and the adjusted data highlight the sluggishness of recent economic performance. Bosworth and Collins conclude that U.S. tax policy has done a disservice to Puerto Rico by providing U.S. corporations incentives for investments with few or no employment or local linkages.

Second, their examination of the relationship between GDP per worker (productivity) and income per capita (living standards) highlights the reasons why Puerto Rico's income per capita has fallen relative to the U.S. level since 1970. Using the adjusted GDP data, they find that labor productivity in Puerto Rico stalled and employment as a share of its working-age population declined to just two-thirds of the U.S. level.

Third, they undertake a growth-accounting analysis that decomposes growth in Puerto Rico's output per worker into the contributions from increased physical and human capital per worker and those from a residual measure of total factor productivity. This analysis clearly distinguishes two periods in Puerto Rico's economic performance. In the early period (roughly 1950–75), the island sustained growth rates in output per worker near 5 percent a year, comparable to rates achieved in the rapid growth phases for Ireland and East Asia and well above the Latin American average. With growth rates more than double those on the mainland, this was a period of significant catch-up for Puerto Rico and was characterized by both capital deepening and increased efficiency of factor usage. In contrast, since 1975 Puerto Rico has fallen behind. The authors estimate that Puerto Rican growth in output per worker dropped to just over 1 percent a year, below that of the mainland.

The growth accounts uncover two reasons for Puerto Rico's slow growth in labor productivity. One is that capital accumulation did not keep pace with increases in employment. Although investment rates have recovered somewhat, they are insufficient to support long-term growth at the level achieved in the earlier period. In contrast, Puerto Rico stands out for relatively high contributions of increased human capital to growth, owing to continued gains in educational attainment. Indeed, the island has largely caught up with the mainland in terms of average years of schooling. The other is a sharp, persistent slowing of growth in total factor productivity. Again using the adjusted output measure, the authors find that total factor productivity growth fell after 1970, turning negative in the 1990s. This pattern suggests a secular deterioration, which is more worrisome than the typical Latin American experience of sharp cyclical fluctuations in economic growth.

PUERTO RICO'S PER CAPITA INCOME is less than one-third that of residents of the U.S. mainland. Much of this difference can be traced to employment rate differences—and ultimately to labor force participation rate differences—between the two economies. Furthermore, these differences have increased substantially over time. The labor force participation rate of Puerto Ricans between the ages of twenty and sixty-four is currently just 85 percent of the equivalent participation rate on the U.S. mainland for men and 62 percent for women.

In chapter 3, Gary Burtless and Orlando Sotomayor examine reasons for the trend toward lower relative employment rates in Puerto Rico. Their analysis focuses on implications of the generosity and structure of government transfer benefits available to Puerto Rico residents. The chapter presents empirical evidence, including the timing of changes in policy versus employment rates and differences in trends across differentially affected groups. Although other developments, including a minimum-wage hike and two severe recessions after 1973, account for part of the slump in Puerto Rican labor supply, the authors conclude that changes in the generosity of transfer benefits played a crucial role.

Burtless and Sotomayor document that government transfer payments account for a large percentage of the total income received by Puerto Rico residents. This percentage rose steeply in the 1970s and 1980s. Since 1990, government transfer benefits have provided 25 to 28 percent of Puerto Rico's personal income, twice the equivalent percentage on the U.S. mainland.

The authors examine the effects of five transfer programs in detail: Puerto Rico's equivalent of the food stamp program, unemployment insurance, Social Security retirement and disability benefits, government-provided health insurance, and Temporary Assistance for Needy Families. All of these programs has important work-discouraging effects because they reduce benefit payments to recipients who find employment. The chapter documents cases in which an increase in earned income may be more than offset by reductions in various public assistance payments.

Burtless and Sotomayor also note that, because average incomes are lower in Puerto Rico than on the mainland, the U.S. Social Security program offers significantly more attractive retirement and disability benefits to Puerto Rican workers. In view of the generosity of disability insurance pensions for low-wage Puerto Rican workers, for example, it is not surprising that the disability rate in Puerto Rico is well above the U.S. average. The authors document differences that may account for 2 to 3 percentage points of the lower labor force participation rate in Puerto Rico relative to the United States.

Burtless and Sotomayor argue that policymakers should aim to increase employment and labor force participation rates on the island so they approach or match those on the U.S. mainland. To reform social protection programs so they encourage rather than discourage work, the authors call for modifications in current benefit schedules and new eligibility rules for assistance that would redesign transfer programs to increase incentives to work and encourage workers to earn higher wages.

The authors emphasize the importance of linking program benefits with incentives to seek employment or to increase the hours of work. An example of such a program is the earned income tax credit in the United States, which provides a supplement to earnings. In contrast, a typical assistance program, such as Puerto Rico's Nutritional Assistance Program, discourages work among recipients by reducing benefits to those who find employment. To reduce program costs and encourage bigger increases in workers' weekly earnings, Burtless and Sotomayor propose a Puerto Rican wage supplement program that requires participating workers to hold jobs with minimum hours conditions. Such restrictions would allocate larger subsidy payments to those workers who make the biggest increases in their monthly hours of work.

MARÍA ENCHAUTEGUI AND RICHARD FREEMAN also focus on Puerto Rico's strikingly low employment rates. Their analysis concentrates on men, because they find that it is the low male employment rate that is "off the map" in comparison with other countries. A unifying theme of their work is the "rich uncle (Sam) hypothesis": the primary reason for the low employment, the authors posit, is that Puerto Rico's

unique relationship with the United States has produced an economic environment that discourages work on both the supply and demand sides of the market.
This hypothesis suggests that the close tie between the island and the mainland has
been double edged, offering Puerto Ricans many of the benefits of living in a
highly advanced economy but also contributing to the employment problem.

The authors begin by documenting what has happened to male labor force
participation and employment, using measures of labor force activity from the
census and household surveys. They conclude that at the turn of the twenty-first
century, Puerto Rican men had an exceptionally low involvement in the labor
market by global standards. This resulted from both a downward trend in participation in the 1970s, which produced a permanent detachment of many men
from the workforce, and a rising proportion through the 1990s who reported
themselves disabled. The remainder of the chapter attempts to answer the question, "Why don't more Puerto Rican men work?"

Enchautegui and Freeman identify and examine a number of interacting factors that may play a role. One is the distorted relationship between aggregate
demand and employment. The authors show that employment in Puerto Rico has
been more closely related to the slower-growing GNP than to the faster-growing
GDP. Furthermore, the tax incentives for investing in capital-intensive activities
may have also distorted the pattern of GDP and employment in Puerto Rico.

Second, like Burtless and Sotomayor, they argue that transfer programs—
especially the Social Security Disability Insurance and the Nutritional Assistance
Programs—are likely to have had large disincentive effects on male employment.
A third potential factor is the option for workers to migrate to the mainland. The
authors explain that this has both direct effects—such as reducing labor force
participation if those most willing to work are more likely to migrate—and indirect effects—such as raising the reservation wage of those on the island.

Finally, the authors focus on Puerto Rico's wage structure in comparison
with that on the mainland. Surprisingly, the highest relative earnings are for less
educated workers—in contrast with the normal pattern in cross-country earnings
differences, whereby the earnings of the most educated workers in developing
and high-income countries are more similar because of their greater opportunities for emigration.

Three possible explanations are examined. Puerto Rico's adoption of the
U.S. minimum wage has limited downward wage flexibility. Income transfers
may have created a reservation wage considerably above the minimum and
above the full employment wage rates. Finally, potential migration to the
United States may have created a wage floor above the minimum.

There is a widespread belief that many jobless Puerto Rican men work in the
informal sector and are therefore not measured by standard labor force surveys.
Thus Enchautegui and Freeman undertook a small pilot study to find out what
men in communities with potentially low employment were doing. Their

results suggest that the official Department of Labor data understate employment considerably but understate labor force participation only modestly.

Their chapter concludes with a discussion of policy implications. The authors note that it is the federal government—not the commonwealth—that controls many of the factors affecting employment. These include the level of benefits of Social Security and eligibility into this program, the minimum wage, federal tax incentives, the amount of transfer to the poor, and border control. Enchautegui and Freeman argue that Puerto Rico needs to work with the U.S. government to redesign these programs to encourage work. They also advocate the introduction of an earned income tax credit or a program of tax credits to firms on the basis of the number of jobs created. They also suggest that a shift in compensation toward deferred benefits such as pensions or health insurance could reduce the rate of withdrawal of older men from the workforce.

PUERTO RICO HAS HAD a remarkable record of educational development during the past forty years. In chapter 5, Helen Ladd and Francisco Rivera-Batiz document Puerto Rico's gains in education and identify areas requiring further improvement. They conclude that significant increases in the quality of schooling are now necessary if the island is to continue to use education as an engine of economic development. They also express concern about evidence of large educational inequities.

Beginning in the mid-1940s, the Puerto Rican government committed itself to dramatically increasing education funding. The result has been considerable gains in student enrollments. The average years of schooling of Puerto Rican workers increased from 2.7 years in 1940 to 11.0 years in 2000, and in this respect Puerto is now comparable to the United States and many other high-income countries. Puerto Rico is also in the top tier of world nations ranked by their proportion of college-educated adults.

Measuring educational quality in Puerto Rico has proved more difficult because of the limited availability of systematic testing in schools. One approach is to look at the rates at which students are switching to private schools. Indeed, the private sector has grown from a relatively small sector providing elite education to a much larger and diverse system serving 25 percent of all students.

Ladd and Rivera-Batiz find a dropout rate of 21 percent, which, though higher than the rate in the United States, is far lower than previous estimates for Puerto Rico. Dropout rates for students from low-income families are particularly high. Combining the dropout rate and the school delay rate (which reflects retention in grade), they estimate that almost half the youth aged eighteen to twenty-four residing in the poorest 30 percent of households of Puerto Rico confront severe educational challenges.

During the 1990s Puerto Rico undertook a major overhaul of its education system with the purpose of decentralizing the Department of Education and increasing the autonomy of community schools. In addition to these governance changes, Puerto Rico significantly increased its public spending on elementary and secondary education. However, Puerto Rico still spends only about half the U.S. average per pupil and significantly less than Utah and Mississippi, the two lowest-spending states.

Ladd and Rivera-Batiz conclude that the reforms have not yet yielded the intended benefits of a smaller bureaucracy and less centralization. Their analysis highlights the lack of accountability as a major problem. The system now is facing the worst of both worlds: a large and politicized bureaucracy and a failed program of decentralization of authority to the school level, with little or no accountability at either level.

Puerto Rico is now subject to the test-based accountability provisions of the 2001 No Child Left Behind Act and therefore must test all students annually in grades 3 to 8. While certain parts of this federal legislation should be helpful to Puerto Rico, the failure of many low-performing schools to meet annual performance standards could further discredit the public school system and lead to a greater movement of students to the private sector. Increasing the level of support for failing schools, expanding funds to improve teaching quality, and generating enhanced parental involvement through better integration of schools into social and community service programs constitute three areas in which the government can help public schools.

Tertiary education enrollments in Puerto Rico have also risen sharply. However, in 2002–03 only 39 percent of the students currently enrolled in higher education were male. The prospect of creating an underclass of Puerto Rican men whose lack of college education prevents entry into mainstream labor markets may have potentially problematic social implications.

Although the initial expansion of tertiary education was primarily in the public sector, enrollment in private institutions has been growing more rapidly and now accounts for 62.7 percent of all students in higher education. Paradoxically, the public sector universities tend to be more selective and cater to students from more affluent backgrounds than private institutions, even while the private schools charge much higher tuition.

Despite rising enrollments, the island's public institutions of higher education have significantly increased spending per student over time. The result is that Puerto Rico spends about the same amount per student in its public universities as does the United States. In terms of student outcomes, however, Puerto Ricans take far longer to graduate than their counterparts in the United States. Research productivity in Puerto Rican universities also appears to be lower.

Finally, Ladd and Rivera-Batiz find that the return to an additional year of schooling has been basically unchanged since 1970.[2] This contrasts with a rising

2. Bosworth and Collins, in chapter 2, find that the wage premium for college graduates in Puerto Rico has been either flat or increasing, depending on definitions and methodology.

wage premium on the mainland over the same period. The difference may reflect a variety of factors. One is the rapidly rising supply of higher-educated labor. On the demand side, the authors note that almost all the decline in the wage premium occurred in the public sector. In 2000 almost 40 percent of all employed workers with a college degree or more in Puerto Rico were working for the government.

STEVEN J. DAVIS AND LUIS A. RIVERA-BATIZ analyze some of the demand-side dimensions of what they label an "employment shortfall of stunning dimensions" in Puerto Rico. Their work focuses on the relatively underdeveloped state of the commonwealth's private sector, its implications, and what might be done to invigorate it.

The chapter begins by empirically examining the structure of employment in Puerto Rico. Two features stand out. First, the authors show that the employment shortfall is concentrated in the private sector—or, more specifically, in the free enterprise segment, which they define as businesses that operate in the formal economy without large subsidies, special regulatory advantages, or extensive oversight by government bureaucracies. Less than one-quarter of working-age Puerto Ricans holds a job in the free enterprise segment of the economy, compared with more than half of the working-age population on the mainland. These findings support the view that Puerto Rico suffers from an inhospitable business climate.

Second, the authors argue that Puerto Rico's industry structure is misaligned with the human capital mix of its population and has been for decades. The average schooling level of working-age persons in Puerto Rico is below that of any U.S. state. Yet Puerto Rico ranks among the top third of states in terms of the schooling intensity of its industry structure. This implies that the missing jobs in Puerto Rico are concentrated in labor-intensive industries that rely heavily on less educated workers. They argue that this feature is testament to the need for substantial revisions to domestic industrial and employment policies.

Davis and Rivera-Batiz identify seven key factors that they argue have jointly contributed to Puerto Rico's huge employment shortfall, underdeveloped private sector, and misaligned industry structure:

—Large government transfer payments undermine work incentives and contribute to a deficit of work experience and marketable skills.

—Minimum-wage laws discourage the hiring of less skilled workers and diminish opportunities to acquire experience and training on the job.

—High public sector employment and production has softened competitive pressures on the island and discouraged the emergence of a vibrant private sector.

—Section 936 of the U.S. tax code and other federal tax incentives have helped create an industry structure that is poorly aligned with the job opportunities needed by Puerto Rico's population.

—Puerto Rico's own tax code is replete with provisions that benefit special business interests at the expense of the general welfare.

—Puerto Rico's regulatory environment deters business entry, hampers job creation, and erodes competitive pressures in many ways. Like many provisions of the tax code, these reflect and promote a business culture focused on rent seeking.

—The permitting process suffers from several serious problems that raise the costs of doing business, undercut the drive for employment growth, and retard economic development.

Although their analysis focuses on implications of each for employment, the authors stress that these factors also lower real incomes and living standards by undermining labor productivity.

In the final section of their chapter, Davis and Rivera-Batiz undertake a detailed study of the permitting process, informed by interviews of more than one hundred persons with expertise or firsthand experience. Widely shared views are that the permitting process is excessively slow and costly, fraught with uncertainty, subject to capricious outcomes, prone to corruption, and susceptible to manipulation by business rivals, politicians, and special interest groups. Independent evidence from public sources supports these claims. The authors discuss efforts to reform the permitting process but conclude that these efforts have met with limited success.

JAMES ALM assesses Puerto Rico's fiscal situation. Although he addresses the role of fiscal deficits and some features of public expenditure, he focuses on the tax side, emphasizing weak tax administration and the overuse of tax incentives in undermining government effectiveness in promoting development.

Puerto Rico's public debt grew more rapidly than GNP between 1990 and 2004. Deficits have been especially large in recent years, reaching $3 billion in 2004, and they are compounded by growing unfunded pension liabilities. In response, two credit agencies lowered their ratings on Puerto Rican bonds in May 2005, making debt service payments more expensive. Much of the new debt has gone to the financing of current expenditures and will therefore provide few benefits to future generations tasked with paying off the debt. Persistent fiscal imbalance threatens Puerto Rico's welfare in the near and the long term, suggesting a need for structural changes in expenditure and taxation.

Despite the fiscal deficits, public sector expenditure as a percentage of GNP has not risen in the past few years. Indeed, central and municipal spending is relatively lower today than it was thirty years ago (even if state enterprises are included) and below that in most developed countries. In terms of composition, central government spending is comparable to the "average" U.S. state; however, Puerto Rico spends a smaller share on education and higher shares on health and welfare. Discontent with government spending thus seems to stem from something other than the size of outlays. Noting that government's share of total employment has not declined as rapidly as government's share of consumption, Alm hypothesizes that public sector productivity may have decreased.

Alm finds much to criticize in Puerto Rico's tax system. Commonwealth status means its residents do not pay federal income taxes, though the island receives some revenue from the federal government. The Puerto Rican government has full autonomy in designing a collection mechanism for internal revenue ~~~~ long as it does not violate the U.S. Constitution, applicable laws o~ ~~~~~~~tional treaties.

~~~~sively from three sources: per(*arbitrios*). Although excise rsonal and corporate income rs of General Fund revenue. vhich has declined in imporgovernment activities. A comreveals that Puerto Rico's ratio average state but comparable to ribution, however, Puerto Rico corporate taxes, and flaws in the Rico's overall tax effort.

porate taxes is that the tax base idespread evasion, and the use orporations outside the reach 'isproportionate share of the tax i~ t in the tax net face potentially

Th ~~~~ ~e pervasive system of corporate ~~ doubtful effect in attracting foreign investm ~~st effective. Costs include reduced tax revenue, increase~ ~~ative costs, distorted investment decisions, and discrimination against firms that lack access to the special provisions.

Alm concludes by offering some suggestions for ways to improve Puerto Rico's tax system. He recommends eliminating most tax incentives and instead lowering the corporate taxation rate so that it is roughly in line with that of the United States. More broadly, he discusses ways to expand the tax base, including the introduction of a value added tax or a flat tax that would target consumption. A tax reform should also improve and simplify tax administration to reduce the amount of evasion and correct the inequities present in the current system. Above all, the author notes, the problems with the current tax system along with the overall fiscal imbalance make the need for reform paramount.

RITA MALDONADO-BEAR AND INGO WALTER study Puerto Rico's financial architecture. Drawing on a long literature, they begin from the premise that the

UTSA Library (Item Charged)

Patron Group: Undergraduate Student
Due Date: 4 to 2013 04 59 AM
Title: Economy of Puerto Rico : restoring growth / Susan M. Collins, Barry P. Bosworth, Miguel A. Soto-Class, editors.

Author:
Call Number: HC 154.5 E275 2006
Enumeration:
Chronology:
Copy: 1
Barcode: *1000000109245*

financial sector plays a special role in economic development. This role reflects the importance of financial intermediation in allocating savings to productive investments and ameliorating information asymmetries in the economy.

Maldonado-Bear and Walter present detailed summaries of each of the components of the financial sector. In 2004 total financial assets in Puerto Rico reached $218 billion. Private commercial banks (43 percent) and international banking entities (at 43 and 31 percent, respectively) account for the lion's share of the market, with insurance companies, two government banks, and a variety of other financial companies holding the remaining assets. Each of these is assessed using ten-year income statements and balance sheets to determine financial health and contribution to growth.

As in the United States, Puerto Rico's banking sector has declined in relative importance over time (albeit at a much slower rate), but the sector still accounts for about half of all financial assets and grew at 13 percent annually from December 1995 to June 2004. The banks are subject to regulation by the U.S. Federal Reserve System and the Federal Deposit Insurance Corporation, as well as by Puerto Rico banking authorities. Growth in private sector loans—which arguably contribute most directly to economic development—has lagged behind growth in the sector as a whole. Furthermore, the banks have emphasized debt, rather than deposits, to finance their growth. International banking entities have also been active in Puerto Rico, conducting transactions with nonresidents. Asset growth in these institutions averaged 15 percent annually over the decade, indicating the possibility that Puerto Rico could emerge as a global center of offshore banking.

Insurance companies, investment companies (mutual funds), mortgage companies, credit unions, finance companies, broker-dealers, small-loan companies, and a handful of venture capital firms constitute the remainder of Puerto Rico's private financial architecture. The high growth in assets of mutual funds and in assets managed by broker-dealers demonstrates the increasing importance of nonbank entities in managing private savings. Indeed, the $4 billion increase in assets managed by broker-dealers in 2004 alone appears at odds with the supposedly negative savings rate on the island.

Maldonado-Bear and Walter also discuss the crucial role played by the Government Development Bank (GDB). The GDB acts as fiscal agent for the government (including bond issues), financial adviser to the government and other public agencies, and lender to both the government and the private sector. It also has a number of official subsidiaries and affiliates, which are involved with various lending and investment projects.

While the GDB thus performs many crucial services, it has in recent years become weakened by the growing government budget deficits. The government has borrowed substantial sums from the GDB to cover its operating expenses. The recent downgrading of the commonwealth's bond status means the GDB's high exposure to government debt carries significant risk. In addition, government borrowing from the GDB crowds out private sector borrowers. Perhaps most troubling, the comparatively low interest rates offered by the GDB encourage government deficits beyond what many feel are prudent levels. These tensions have led to a succession of five GDB presidents during the six-year period 2000–05, a fact that leads Maldonado-Bear and Walter to propose seven-year terms as part of an effort to isolate the GDB from the political process.

The chapter concludes with a comparison of Puerto Rico's financial sector with those of the United States as a whole and the states of Hawaii and Florida in particular, along with a set of policy recommendations. These include changing the tax structure to induce banks to increase their share of commercial and industrial loans, strengthening the pension system, and enhancing the availability of financial statistics to facilitate effective oversight.

PUERTO RICO HAS A SMALL but extremely open economy. Thus its trade—both with the mainland and with rest of the world—is a central determinant of its economic performance. In chapter 9 of this volume, Robert Lawrence and Juan Lara examine Puerto Rico's trade experience and its implications for external adjustment, employment, and growth. They also present policy recommendations to strengthen Puerto Rico's future trade performance. Given that the island cannot conduct an independent trade policy, this discussion concentrates on industrial policy and the strengths and weaknesses of alternative approaches.

In the first section of their chapter, the authors suggest that concerns about maintaining external balance should not be a constraint to domestic growth, largely because Puerto Rican exports are estimated to be highly responsive to growth in mainland GDP. Indeed, the analysis suggests that import growth would not exceed export growth, even if GDP in Puerto Rico grew 60 percent more rapidly than on the mainland. With slower growth relative to the mainland in recent years, Puerto Rico's merchandise trade surplus has increased. At the same time, this trade surplus in goods is more than offset by a deficit in services, reflecting large payments of profits earned by foreign corporations.

The authors also empirically explore the extent to which Puerto Rico's exports are vulnerable to U.S. trade liberalization. This is a potential concern because the United States is by far its largest trading partner, and reductions in tariff barriers—for example, to countries that sign free trade agreements—erode Puerto Rico's unique access to the U.S. market. They conclude that the commonwealth's exports to the mainland are not dependent on tariff preferences and are thus unlikely to be affected by further liberalization.

They note, however, that tax considerations provide international firms with incentives to overstate their Puerto Rican activities and that the export data may give inaccurate pictures of value added and of the employment implications of trade flows. To explore this concern, the authors adjust exports for foreign profits and examine employment growth directly. They conclude that these adjustments do not alter their main conclusions.

The analysis does highlight the overwhelming role U.S. tax policy has played in determining Puerto Rico's comparative advantage. The commonwealth has become increasingly specialized in high-technology products such as pharmaceuticals, which Puerto Rico sells in astounding volumes to both the United States and other developed economies. Whatever may have been the original reasons for locating in Puerto Rico, and even if the connections with the rest of the economy are not deep, these high-tech sectors have now established a firm footing in the commonwealth. Despite recent repeal of section 936 tax provisions, the growth of these sectors has accelerated. Particularly noteworthy has been the robust employment growth in the pharmaceuticals sector. There is also evidence of smaller but rapidly growing services exports that are more closely linked to Puerto Rican factor endowments.

The final section of the chapter focuses on policy. Since it is part of the U.S. monetary system and subject to the U.S. customs regime, Puerto Rico can have neither an independent exchange rate policy nor an independent trade policy. Therefore, industrial policy is one of the few policy instruments the commonwealth government has at its disposal. The chapter's empirical analysis suggests that Puerto Rican growth is not constrained by its external performance, so that the focus of its industrial policies should be on stimulating growth.

Lawrence and Lara argue that the challenge for industrial policies is to concentrate on cases in which reliance on private market activities is likely to be inadequate—so called market failures—but to do so in a precise fashion that avoids providing financial support for private sector activities that would be undertaken in any case. Policies that simply stimulate all types of a particular activity (foreign investment, exports, import substitution) or sectors (pharmaceuticals, electronics) are likely to be wasteful. Rather, the authors note, the focus should be on stimulating learning and innovation, providing coordination, and investing in infrastructure and public goods throughout the economy. Lawrence and Lara also conclude that a policy focused on import substitution would be unsuccessful. Instead, they favor policies that promote innovation, learning, and coordination throughout the economy.

Finally, the authors observe that recent Puerto Rican industrial policies have emphasized promotion of clusters—particularly in the high-tech sector and exports more generally. There are some examples in which policy does seem to be aimed at dealing with market failures and improving public infrastructure, but in other cases the approach remains undeveloped or lacks focus and is therefore likely to be wasteful. An approach that narrows the scope to dealing only with clear cases of market failure is likely to give better results.

IN THE FINAL CHAPTER, Barry Bosworth and Susan Collins present a set of policy recommendations for restoring growth in Puerto Rico. Drawing on the analysis and conclusions of the preceding chapters, they focus their attention on increasing employment, improving the quality of education, upgrading infrastructure, and fixing government finances.

Policies to raise the employment level focus on both the supply of and the demand for labor. Bosworth and Collins suggest that the achievement of parity with the employment rate on the mainland is a reachable goal. Because of reduced future population growth, reaching parity would require a pace of job creation roughly comparable to what Puerto Rico has achieved over the past twenty-five years and below that reached in fast-growing states and other parts of the world. On the supply side, Puerto Rico must reform many of its antipoverty programs to strengthen incentives to seek employment. An example of such a policy endorsed by a number of authors in this volume is the earned income tax credit, which provides a transfer payment that increases with a recipient's earnings up to a ceiling amount. On the demand side, the commonwealth government needs to promote the growth of employment in private business. In this regard, the government must reform and simplify the regulatory and licensing process to ease the burden on new businesses. Increasing research and development on the island and the linkages between the universities and the private sector should also help spur development. Finally, workforce development programs and a minimum wage better suited to Puerto Rico's income level would have positive effects on both labor supply and labor demand.

The chapter also suggests policies to improve the quality of education and physical infrastructure. Noting that efforts to increase accountability in the school system failed in the 1990s, the authors suggest that Puerto Rico should consider the example of cities such as Chicago, which undertook major educational reforms in recent years. For higher education, there is a need to promote the research activities of the university system and alter the financing structure. The current system provides a tuition subsidy to high-income families but little financial assistance to low-income students. In the area of physical infrastructure, Bosworth and Collins focus on measures to lower the cost of electricity and on the need to improve the quality of the transportation and water and sewer systems.

Given the rising public debt and the recent downgrading of Puerto Rican bonds, fiscal policy constitutes the area perhaps most in need of immediate reform. The corporate income tax, which currently combines a high marginal rate with numerous exemptions, should be lowered to a globally competitive rate that applies to all corporations. Puerto Rico should also consider implementing a value added tax as a means of simplifying the tax code and raising revenue. Finally, the property tax requires major reform as part of an effort to resolve the financial problems of municipal governments.

Taken together, the analyses presented in this volume provide a detailed assessment of the Puerto Rican economy at the outset of the twenty-first century. This is an economy with the exciting potential for sustained high growth that would close the income gap with the mainland. We hope that our work contributes to implementation of the requisite policy reforms and the consensus needed to sustain them. More generally, we hope that these studies help stimulate a renewed research focus on the Puerto Rican economic experience and its implications for future policy.

2

Economic Growth

BARRY P. BOSWORTH AND SUSAN M. COLLINS

Puerto Rico is an extraordinary case study for those interested in the process of economic growth and its determinants. In the decades immediately after World War II, the island enjoyed rapid growth, comparable to that achieved by the so-called Asian Tigers.[1] A large portion of the population escaped the extreme poverty that had been so common in the first half of the twentieth century, and significant gains were made in narrowing the income gap between Puerto Rico and the United States. After the early 1970s, however, growth in income per capita slowed substantially, and progress in narrowing the income gap stalled.

Figure 2-1 highlights two critical aspects of Puerto Rico's economic growth relative to the corresponding measures for the United States. Gross domestic product per worker, a measure of the productivity of the workforce, rose from just 30 percent of the U.S. average in 1950 to 75 percent in 1980—a remarkable achievement. Growth slackened in subsequent years, however, and Puerto Rico has made little further progress in catching up with the mainland.

Starynee Adams provided extensive research assistance. Deepak Lamba-Nieves was crucial in obtaining the appropriate data, and we are indebted to individuals at the Puerto Rico Planning Board and Juan A. Castañer for assistance in obtaining and understanding the statistical data. William Baumol, Rita Maldonado-Bear, Orlando Sotomayor, and José Villamil provided helpful comments on an earlier draft.

1. Baumol and Wolff (1996).

Figure 2-1. *GDP and GNI, Puerto Rico Relative to the United States, 1950–2004*
Index (United States = 1.0)

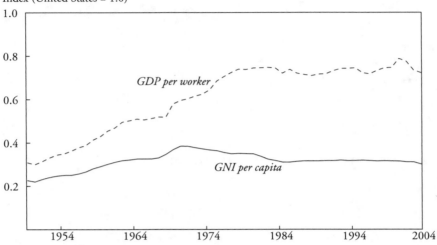

Source: Data from Puerto Rico Planning Board; authors' calculations, as explained in text.

Although GDP measures total production within Puerto Rico, it does not indicate how much of the income actually accrued to residents of the island. The second line in figure 2-1, gross national income (GNI) per capita, more accurately measures the average income of Puerto Ricans. This yields a dramatically different and much less favorable picture of the island's economic performance. Income per capita rose from a little more than 20 percent of the U.S. average in 1950 to roughly 40 percent by the early 1970s. But it has drifted back down to only about 30 percent in recent years.

A major objective of this chapter is to document the sources of the large difference between these two measures of economic performance and the reasons for the post-1975 slowing of growth. This effort addresses two unusual features of Puerto Rico's economy. First, large U.S. firms, originally attracted by the exemptions from U.S. corporate income tax on profits made in Puerto Rico, dominate the commonwealth's manufacturing sector. Therefore, much of the income reported as earned in Puerto Rico leaves the island and is rebated back to corporations on the mainland. In addition, American corporations appear to dramatically overstate value added in Puerto Rico, as a means of moving income earned on their patents outside of the U.S. corporate tax system.

Second, and equally important, Puerto Rico stands out for the extraordinarily low proportion of its population that is employed. Unemployment has been higher in Puerto Rico than on the mainland, and a large proportion of the island's population has emigrated to the United States. However, we argue that the most important factor is Puerto Rico's low labor force participation rate among both men and women and across a wide range of age groups. Possible explanations include limited job opportunities, an underreported underground economy, and weak incentives to seek employment. Understanding the causes of this low employment rate is central to developing a strategy for restoring growth.[2]

In the following section, we provide a brief overview of economic conditions in Puerto Rico. The second section is devoted to a more detailed analysis of the difference between per capita incomes in the United States and Puerto Rico. We look into sources of the divergence between GDP growth and GNI growth, highlighting factors that contribute to the low rate of overall employment. This leads us, in the next section, to an analysis of the extent to which section 936 provisions of the U.S. tax code may have distorted official production data and to the construction of adjusted output indicators. We then use growth accounting to examine the historical performance of the Puerto Rican economy in more detail, comparing it with that of the United States and selected other economies. The accounts enable us to focus on the contributions of increased physical capital per worker, increased educational attainment of the workforce, and improvements in economic efficiency. In the fourth section, we ask what lessons might be drawn from the experience of Ireland, an island economy with striking parallels to Puerto Rico, and one that has undergone a recent rejuvenation. The chapter concludes with a discussion of some future policy options that could be used to reinvigorate the Puerto Rican growth process.[3]

An Overview of Puerto Rico and Its Economy

The Commonwealth of Puerto Rico is roughly a thousand miles southeast of Miami. About the size of Ireland, its population of 3.86 million in 2004 implies a high population density, comparable to that of New Jersey, the most densely populated U.S. state. Ceded to the United States at the end of the Spanish-American War (1898), the territory became a commonwealth in 1952. Puerto Ricans were granted U.S. citizenship in 1917. They can migrate freely to and from the mainland, and roughly nine-tenths as many persons of Puerto Rican birth now live in the United States as on the island.

In some dimensions, Puerto Rico has converged steadily toward the United States. Average years of schooling rose from fewer than five in 1950 to 12.2 in 2000, compared with 13.8 in the United States. Fertility rates fell sharply from 5.2 births per woman in 1950 to just 1.9 in 2000, less than the current overall

2. Addressing the problem of low employment is the central theme of several chapters in this volume.

3. Our understanding of the Puerto Rican situation has been immeasurably aided by many prior studies. Among the most helpful are Dietz (2002, 2003), Estudios Técnicos (2003), Padín (2003), Pantojas-García (1999), Rivera-Batiz and Santiago (1996) and United Nations (2004).

rate for the United States (2.1).[4] Despite these changes, however, income levels continue to lag far behind. Fifty-eight percent of Puerto Rican children live in families whose income is below the poverty line, compared with 16 percent on the mainland.

However, living standards on the island continue to compare favorably with those elsewhere in the region. In terms of purchasing power parity, Puerto Rico's 2003 gross national income per capita is about 31 percent of the mainland level, compared with 29 percent for Argentina, 26 percent for Chile, 24 percent for Mexico, and 19 percent for Latin America overall.[5]

Puerto Rico benefits from strong institutions, a stable political and economic history, and access to U.S. financial markets. At the same time, its special status limits available policy tools. Puerto Rico uses the U.S. dollar and has no scope for an independent monetary or exchange rate policy. Its workers are subject to the U.S. minimum wage, though wages on the island average about only 60 percent of those on the mainland. Trade policies vis-à-vis other countries are determined by U.S. customs law, and the U.S. Interstate Commerce Act governs trade with the mainland. Because Puerto Ricans do not pay federal taxes on income earned on the island they cannot participate in the earned income tax credit or receive supplemental security income. However, they do contribute to Social Security and are eligible for other federal programs such as Temporary Assistance for Needy Families and Head Start. Federal tax policies have offered special treatment for companies doing business in Puerto Rico, in the form of section 936 of the U.S. tax code and its predecessors. Although section 936 provisions will have been phased out by 2006, they have had a major impact on the local economy.

As Puerto Rico is a commonwealth, its citizens elect their own governor, as well as local senators and members of their House. However, they do not vote in federal elections, and they elect a single, nonvoting delegate to the U.S. House of Representatives. Puerto Rico has its own constitution (approved by the U.S. Congress). Its legal system is based on Spanish civil code, with adaptations to U.S. law. The island maintains a unique cultural identity, with Spanish as its primary language.

Productivity and Income Levels

Figure 2-1 illustrates the apparently large and growing discrepancy between Puerto Rico's productivity, as measured by GDP per worker, and its living standards, as measured by GNI per capita. To follow Puerto Rico's progress in catching up to U.S. levels, both measures are reported relative to the United States.

4. The fertility rate for U.S. women of Puerto Rican descent is 2.6 percent.
5. Estimates for GNI per capita in Argentina, Chile, Mexico, the United States, and Latin America are from the World Bank database, September 2004 (www.worldbank.org/data/databytopic/GNIPC.pdf).

The gap in per capita income can also be related to underlying differences in the proportion of income that accrues to residents, productivity, labor utilization, and the age structure of the population. This is shown by the following equation:

$$(2\text{-}1) \qquad GNI\big/_{capita} = \left(GNI\big/_{GDP}\right) \times \left(GDP\big/_E\right) \times \left(E\big/_{P_{lf}}\right) \times \left(P_{lf}\big/_P\right),$$

where

$GNI\big/_{GDP}$ = the proportion of income from production that accrues to residents,

$GDP\big/_E$ = production per worker,

$E\big/_{P_{lf}}$ = the proportion of the population aged sixteen and over that is employed, and

$P_{lf}\big/_P$ = the proportion of the population aged sixteen and over.

These determinants of income per capita are reported in table 2-1.[6] The top two panels show measures for Puerto Rico and the United States, the third shows Puerto Rican measures as percentages of U.S. values. The extraordinary progress that Puerto Rico appears to have made in raising productivity is shown in the first column (bottom panel): GDP per worker increased from 31 percent of the U.S. average in 1950 to 74 percent by 1980. Since then, however, no further progress has been made in closing the productivity gap.

The second column of table 2-1 highlights demographics as a dimension on which the island has effectively caught up with the mainland. In 1950 Puerto Rico's population was relatively young. Only about half were aged sixteen and over, compared with more than two-thirds in the United States.[7] Thus a steady rise in the proportion of the population that was of labor force age contributed to a significant boost in Puerto Rico's per capita income. Today, at 76 percent, the proportion of the population aged sixteen and over is the almost identical to that in the United States.

The favorable effects of demographic change for the growth in income per capita, however, have been wiped out by a surprising and large decline in the proportion of the working-age population that is employed.[8] Between 1950 and

6. The income and product accounts of Puerto Rico are constructed on a base of 1954. We have rescaled the GDP and GNI data to prices of 2000, for expository purposes. Some of the statistical problems with the accounts are discussed in appendix 2C.

7. In 1950 the median age of the Puerto Rican population was only 18.2 years, compared with 30.4 years for the United States.

8. The offsetting changes in the demographic factor and the employment rate imply that employment in Puerto Rico and the United States has grown at nearly equal rates over the past fifty years. Thus the Puerto Rican economy has been able to create jobs, but not at a pace that matches the growth of the population of working age.

Table 2-1. *Gross National Income per Capita, Puerto Rico and the United States, Selected Years, 1950–2004*
Percent, except as indicated

Year	GDP per worker[a]	Demographic effect[b]	Employment/ population[c]	GNI/GDP	GNI per capita[a]
			Puerto Rico		
1950	9,037	54.0	48.8	107.1	2,551
1960	16,285	55.0	42.6	105.9	4,043
1970	27,866	58.8	43.0	97.3	6,866
1980	38,439	66.1	36.0	88.4	8,090
1990	42,701	70.8	38.9	76.7	9,004
2004	55,342	75.6	42.0	62.5	10,983
			United States		
1950	29,269	69.0	55.5	100.6	11,271
1960	37,905	64.9	56.1	98.2	13,882
1970	48,137	66.6	57.7	100.5	18,616
1980	52,164	73.5	59.6	101.5	23,119
1990	59,686	75.5	62.9	98.6	28,485
2004	76,622	76.0	62.3	96.2	36,442
			Puerto Rico/United States		
1950	30.9	78.4	87.9	106.5	22.6
1960	43.0	84.8	76.0	107.8	29.1
1970	57.9	88.4	74.6	96.8	36.9
1980	73.7	90.0	60.4	87.1	35.0
1990	71.5	93.7	61.8	77.7	31.6
2004	72.2	99.5	67.4	65.0	30.1

Source: Data from Puerto Rico Planning Board and U.S. Bureau of Economic Analysis; authors' calculations. Historical data on the population and employment, aged sixteen and over, were provided by Orlando Sotomayor.
a. In 2000 dollars.
b. Population aged sixteen and over as share of the total population.
c. For persons aged sixteen and over.

1980, the employment rate declined by 25 percent (from 49 to 36 percent)—at a time when it was rising in the United States. Although the situation has improved somewhat since 1980, Puerto Rico's employment rate is still only about two-thirds of that in the United States and is also far below that of any Organization for Economic Cooperation and Development member country, including Mexico. Unfortunately, we do not have comparable employment rates for most developing countries. Puerto Rico does have a high and variable unemployment rate (12 percent in 2004), but the secular decline in its employment rate may be more closely related to the marked deterioration in its labor force participation rate.

Finally, a large proportion of the income earned within Puerto Rico is transferred abroad, as reflected in the low ratio of GNI to GDP. In 1950 Puerto Rico had a net surplus on factor income transactions with the rest of the world, largely because of the wages of Puerto Ricans working for the U.S. government. However, in subsequent years, the net wage payment surplus has been overwhelmed by outflows of capital income paid on foreign direct investments in Puerto Rico. Net capital outflow grew substantially until the mid-1970s (15 percent of GDP in 1975 compared with 2 percent in 1950), largely reflecting a low rate of wealth accumulation within Puerto Rico.[9]

The passage of section 936 of the Tax Reform Act of 1976 introduced a new era of tax-induced economic transactions with Puerto Rico. The net outflow of capital income grew from 15 percent of GDP in 1975 to 36 percent of GDP in 2004. A change of this magnitude raises questions about the economic activities reported in Puerto Rican national accounts. Section 936 and its predecessor provisions had a major impact on the economic development strategy of Puerto Rico; but more important for the current context, they greatly distorted Puerto Rico's economic statistics—particularly the measure of GDP.

Two additional issues have been raised about Puerto Rican economic statistics. First, if the cost of living on the island were significantly different from that on the mainland, adjustments to the measure of income per capita would be required in order to make meaningful level comparisons. In fact, there have been extensive studies of relative living costs. As discussed further in appendix 2A, these studies show that overall, living costs in Puerto Rico are similar to those in the Washington, D.C., area. Therefore, all of our calculations are based on U.S. dollars.

A second issue is Puerto Rico's underground or informal economy. If it is large or growing rapidly, failure to capture such activity could bias official employment and output statistics downward. In appendix 2B, we consider a variety of approaches to measuring Puerto Rico's underground economy and its evolution in recent decades. Although there are weaknesses associated with each of the indicators we present and with those we cite from the literature, taken together they paint a consistent picture. None suggests that underground activity has grown significantly relative to official measures since the 1980s.

The Impact of Section 936 Corporations

The U.S. tax code has had a strong impact on Puerto Rican economic activity as well as on the measurement of this activity. U.S. corporate taxes are applied on the global operations of U.S. resident corporations. However, income of foreign subsidiaries is taxed only when it is repatriated to U.S. parent corporations. To eliminate double taxation, a credit is provided for taxes paid to foreign governments on

9. Data from Puerto Rico Planning Board; authors' calculations.

income from foreign sources, up to a ceiling of the U.S. tax liability. Operations in American possessions, however, are neither truly domestic nor foreign but occupy a middle position. Since 1921, income earned from operations in U.S. possessions has been exempt from U.S. taxation until it is repatriated, roughly matching the treatment of foreign source income. Beginning in 1947, Puerto Rico added to that incentive by exempting the income of qualifying U.S. corporations from its own corporate tax.[10]

The introduction of section 936 of the Tax Reform Act of 1976 greatly expanded the incentive. The change added a tax credit on repatriations that effectively excluded from federal tax liability all income of U.S. corporations operating in Puerto Rico. The exemption has also applied to the financial income received from reinvestment of retained earnings in Puerto Rico. Enacted to help Puerto Rico obtain employment-producing investments from the U.S. mainland, the section 936 provision distinguished Puerto Rico from foreign tax jurisdictions. In pursuit of tax benefits, various industries, epitomized by pharmaceuticals, transferred large portions of their manufacturing operations to Puerto Rico. However, the high cost to the U.S. Treasury and the lack of significant job creation led to the repeal of section 936, with a gradual phase-out over the 1995–2005 period. In the future, Puerto Rico will be treated as a foreign jurisdiction for tax purposes. Many corporations will convert to "controlled foreign corporations," deferring U.S. taxes until their income is repatriated. In this new context, Puerto Rico will have to compete directly with other low-tax locations, such as Ireland.

There is a long tradition of countries and states using tax measures to influence the location of economic activities. State and local governments in the United States, for example, frequently use tax incentives to attract enterprises. However, as Harry Grubert and Joel Slemrod observe, tax regimes may simply influence the jurisdictions in which incomes are reported without actually altering the location of the economic activity.[11] By means of intracorporate transfer pricing and various financial structures, income can be shifted between jurisdictions with differing tax rates. Income shifting can be largely carried out as a paper transaction, with little economic content in the sense of job- or resource-creating activities. This latter possibility is a particularly significant issue in Puerto Rico because of the extreme difference in effective tax rates between the island and the mainland United States.

Impact on Puerto Rico

Available data strongly suggest that there has been substantial income shifting by U.S. corporations operating in Puerto Rico under the provisions of section 936. Financial indicators for section 936 affiliates operating in U.S. possessions,

10. See the discussion in Dietz (2003, pp. 140–42). Joseph Pelzman (2002) provides an extensive and highly critical discussion of the application of U.S. tax law to Puerto Rico.
11. Grubert and Slemrod (1998).

Table 2-2. *Capital Income in Chemicals and Pharmaceuticals, Puerto Rico and the United States, 1997*

Ratio

Income indicator	Chemicals		Pharmaceuticals	
	United States	Puerto Rico	United States	Puerto Rico
Net income/total receipts	0.105	0.457	0.152	0.478
Net income/total assets	0.073	0.420	0.097	0.438
Net assets/stockholders' equity	0.155	0.478	0.254	1.118
Value added/employee compensation[a]	2.1	10.5	. . .	11.4

Source: Data from Contos and Legel (2000, tables 1, 12); Nutter (2003, tables 1, 2); Puerto Rico Planning Board (1996, tables 10, 13; 2003, tables 10, 13).

a. Based on average gross product data (from the income and product accounts), averaged over the period 1987–2004.

together with comparable calculations for the mainland, for the 1997 tax year are shown in table 2-2. We focus on the pharmaceutical industry within the chemicals group because these are readily identifiable in the Standard Industrial Classification index. Puerto Rico accounts for 99 percent of the tax credit for section 936 possessions. Sixty percent of this credit was within the chemicals group, and 57 percent was within pharmaceuticals.[12] The net return on stockholders' equity was 112 percent for pharmaceutical firms in Puerto Rico, compared with just 25 percent for pharmaceutical firms in the United States as a whole. For the broader category of chemicals, comparable values were 48 and 16 percent, respectively. The differences between Puerto Rico and the mainland are equally striking for returns on total assets and for net income as a percentage of total receipts. The last row of the table shows the ratio of capital income to employee compensation for the chemical industry, as reported in the Puerto Rican and U.S. income and product accounts. Over the period 1987–2001, this ratio averaged 10.5 in Puerto Rico compared with just 2.1 in the United States.[13] Differences in relative factor returns of this magnitude cannot credibly be attributed to differences in the underlying production processes.

The large value added figures reported for Puerto Rico also lead to high reported pharmaceutical exports and large reported trade surpluses. For example, chemical exports were $38 billion in 2004 (68 percent of total exports), compared with imports of only $19 billion (50 percent of total imports). As a

12. A 1993 report of the General Accounting Office (U.S. Congress [1993]) has estimated the 1989 subsidy to section 936 corporations at $2.6 billion (13 percent of Puerto Rico's GDP), or about $24,000 per employee.

13. The lower level of detail for pharmaceuticals is not available in the U.S. industry accounts. The full accounts are available at www.bea.doc.gov/ (August 2004).

result, the $19 billion surplus on trade in chemicals exceeds Puerto Rico's total trade balance of $14 billion. On the other hand, this is more than offset by a $28 billion outflow of capital income, resulting in a large current-account deficit. However, the unbelievable levels of value added relative to labor compensation suggest that much of this trade surplus is the result of distorted transfer prices. Mainland firms report a low value for raw materials shipped to Puerto Rico and a high value for final products exported from the island.[14] The difference between the two reflects the rent companies earn on research and development. In effect, their R&D expenses are recorded in the United States, where the tax rate is high, whereas the returns are recorded in Puerto Rico, where the tax rate is zero.

The section 936 provisions have also had an important impact on Puerto Rico's financial sector by exempting income from the reinvestment of retained earnings from U.S. taxation. Puerto Rico formerly imposed a 10 percent "tollgate" tax on dividends that were rebated to foreign stockholders. To encourage firms to reinvest locally, the rate was reduced for corporations that reinvested a certain portion of their earnings in Puerto Rico for a period of five or more years.[15] In the mid-1980s, section 936 deposits represented more than 40 percent of total bank deposits.[16]

Adjusted Output Measures

More important from the perspective of measuring growth, transfer pricing and income shifting by section 936 corporations have greatly distorted measurement of output and productivity growth in manufacturing. As shown in figure 2-2, the sharp decline in labor's share of value added after 1970 provides clear evidence of this distortion. Within manufacturing, the share fell from an average of 50 percent of gross product in 1950–70 to just 14 percent by 2004. The distortion has grown over time as the chemical industry, which accounts for the bulk of section 936 activity, has grown from 11 percent of manufacturing net income in 1970 to more than 60 percent in 2004. Outside of manufacturing, however, there is no evidence of any particular trend in factor shares. Thus we limit our adjustments to manufacturing.

We consider two alternative measures of gross product in manufacturing. The first, and more extreme, assumes that labor's share of total manufacturing

14. It is notable that the pricing of both raw materials and final products complies with U.S. tax law in that both can be justified by "arm's-length" or market prices. The key point is simply that the increase in value did not relate to any activity that took place in Puerto Rico but reflects instead the monopoly granted to the patent holder by the government.

15. The U.S. tax exemption for financial income from the reinvestment of earnings was removed in 1986, and Puerto Rico's tollgate tax was repealed in 1998. See Dietz (2003) and U.S. Congress (1997) for details.

16. Pantojas-García (1990, p. 164); Dietz (2003, p. 61).

Figure 2-2. *Labor Compensation as Share of Gross Product, Total Economy and Manufacturing, Puerto Rico, Fiscal Years 1950–2004*

Percent

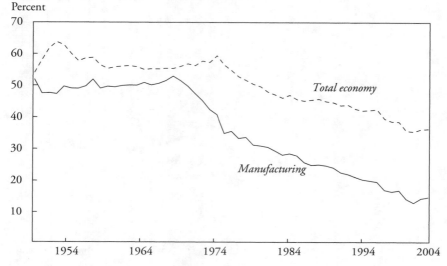

Source: Data from Puerto Rico Planning Board; authors' calculations, as explained in text.

gross product remains constant after 1970 at its 1969–70 average of 50 percent. Thus we assume that the entire rise in capital's share since 1970 is the result of increased income shifting by section 936 corporations. The second alternative limits the adjustment to a constant labor share (23 percent) within the chemical industry. This alternative recognizes that chemicals production is highly capital intensive (reflected in its relatively low labor share). However, it assumes no increase in the degree of capital intensity after 1970. It also allows the chemicals industry to grow as a share of total manufacturing. These assumptions are consistent with the developments reported for the chemical industry in the United States, where labor's share has been constant, at about 50 percent of gross product and about 65 percent for total manufacturing.

Computing our alternatives requires nominal measures of gross product and its distribution between employee compensation and property income since 1970. Unfortunately, these are available for the chemical industry only from 1982. We used estimates of net income (excluding depreciation) to extrapolate gross product back to 1970 and information from five-year economic censuses to make similar estimates of employee compensation.

The result is a dramatic downward adjustment of manufacturing output over the period 1970–2004. Relative to official data for 2004, our first measure cuts the estimates of manufacturing output and economy-wide GDP by 72 percent and 31 percent, respectively. Using the second measure, which limits the adjustment

Figure 2-3. *GDP per Worker, Using Alternative Measures of Manufacturing Output, Puerto Rico, 1950–2004*

Index (1950 = 1.0)

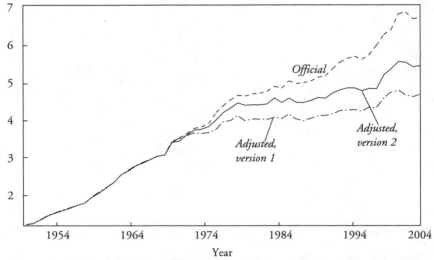

Year

Source: Data from Puerto Rico Planning Board; authors' calculations, as described in text. Version 1 is adjusted at level of total manufacturing. Version 2 is adjusted at level of the chemicals industry.

to the chemical industry, 2004 manufacturing output and economy-wide GDP are reduced by 45 percent and by 17 percent, respectively. This represents a 1.7 percent reduction in the annual growth of manufacturing and a 0.7 percent reduction in the annual growth of aggregate output and productivity. Figure 2-3 shows the implied paths of both versions of adjusted output per worker, as well as the published (official) data.

In terms of the Puerto Rico-U.S. comparisons shown in table 2-1, version 2 of the adjustment lowers the 2004 value of nominal GDP per worker in Puerto Rico from $56,000 to $46,000. Relative to the United States, Puerto Rico's 2004 GDP per worker is the same as in the mid-1970s, implying that no further catch-up with the mainland was achieved after 1970. However, it is important to note that there is an offsetting change in the ratio of GNI to GDP in table 2-1, so that the adjustment to the reported level of output does not alter the measure of GNI per capita. We are only arguing that much of what is recorded as production in Puerto Rico is a simple paper transaction in which income is transferred to Puerto Rico and then taken back out as dividend payments to mainland corporations. The magnitude of this output distortion may decline with the elimination of section 936 provisions. Nevertheless, the ability to defer income of controlled foreign corporations will continue to provide firms with a strong incentive to shift corporate income to Puerto Rico and other low-tax jurisdictions.

Analyses of growth focus on real output. In constructing alternative measures of real GDP, we are unable to adjust the GDP price deflator to account for the smaller role of the section 936 corporations because we do not have price deflators at the level of the pharmaceutical industry. The export price deflator probably provides the closest indicator of price trends in the pharmaceutical industry. As discussed more fully in appendix 2C, the export price deflator has risen about 25 percent more than the overall GDP deflator. This magnitude of price increase raises questions about the measurement of pharmaceutical prices. Furthermore, it suggests the possibility that official price deflators overestimate actual price changes, thereby offsetting some of the impact of income shifting on real GDP. Concerns about the measurement issues have led us to use both the official estimate of real GDP and our alternative (version 2) to construct the growth accounts in the following section.

Puerto Rico's Growth Performance

Unique characteristics of the Puerto Rican economy make its economic growth experience of particular interest. The island enjoys a number of features that are widely viewed as critical to sustaining growth. Contemporary literature on growth stresses the benefits of openness to the global economy. These include the strong competitive pressures and economies of scale that result from a larger market as well as enhanced opportunities to gain from the experiences and innovations of others. In this respect, Puerto Rico has long been among the most open of economies, with no significant restrictions on the free flows of people, goods, and financial capital between the island and mainland United States. Recent literature also emphasizes the significance of stable laws and institutional arrangements to protect property rights and promote entrepreneurial effort. The basic U.S. legal and regulatory framework has applied in Puerto Rico for most of the past century. In particular, investors are covered by U.S. intellectual property laws. A well-educated workforce constitutes a third critical ingredient for economic growth; and again, Puerto Rico stands out, with levels of educational attainment similar to those on the U.S. mainland.

At the same time, Puerto Rico's ability to conduct its own economic policy is severely constrained. As a dollarized economy, it has no independent monetary policy and must operate within the confines of an absolutely fixed exchange rate. Moreover, as part of the U.S. customs union, it must adhere to U.S. trade law. Finally, Puerto Rico is subject to U.S. minimum wage laws. This is a significant factor because the average wage in Puerto Rico is only about half that in the United States, making the minimum wage a far more relevant issue in employment decisions.

Growth Accounting

We use a simple growth accounting framework to examine Puerto Rican growth performance over the period 1950–2004.[17] The methodology (explained more fully in appendix 2D) decomposes growth in output (GDP) per worker into the separate contributions of increases in physical capital per worker, in education, and in a residual estimate of total factor productivity (TFP). Total factor productivity captures changes in the efficiency with which the factor inputs, capital and labor, are used, as well as underlying technological changes.

Table 2-3 summarizes the resulting growth accounts for the total economy over the entire period, and figure 2-4 illustrates output and capital per worker and TFP in graphic form for particular subperiods. The top panel of table 2-3 presents the results of our analysis based on the published measure of GDP; the bottom panel uses our alternative measure that adjusts for income shifting within the chemicals sector. As shown in the first column, real GDP grew at an average annual rate of 4.9 percent over the full period and peaked at a growth rate of 7.9 percent in the 1960s. However, growth slowed substantially in later decades. The pattern of growth in output per worker is similar to that for output alone, although the 1980s stand out as a particularly bad decade. In the last three columns, growth in output per worker is partitioned among the contributions of physical capital per worker, education (human capital) per worker, and the TFP residual.

The analysis suggests that Puerto Rico's growth experience can be divided into two broad periods. From 1950 to 1975, labor productivity increased rapidly, averaging about 5 percent annually. Improvements in physical capital per worker accounted for roughly half of this improvement. Improvements in the educational attainment of the workforce added another 0.7 percent a year. According to official data, the remaining, 1.7 percent a year can be traced to improvements in TFP.

However, productivity growth slowed sharply after the mid-1970s, weakening dramatically in the 1980s and improving only modestly in the most recent decade. What happened? Much of the story is in the failure of capital accumulation to maintain the prior rate of capital deepening (increasing capital per worker). During 1950–75, Puerto Rico resembled the East Asian economies, with capital per worker catching up with that on the mainland. After 1975, the slowing of capital deepening, from 2.7 to 0.4 percent a year, accounts for two-thirds of the falloff in labor productivity growth. There have also been slowdowns in the contributions of human capital and TFP, but these decelerations were much less dramatic. In contrast, we note that employment growth actually accelerated after 1975, offsetting part of the impact of the slowdown in productivity growth on GDP growth.

---

17. José Alameda and Alfredo Gonzalez (2001) also construct a set of growth accounts for Puerto Rico but use a different methodology (regression) to measure the contribution of the factor inputs.

Table 2-3. *Sources of Growth, Puerto Rico, Selected Years, 1950–2004*
Percent

Period	Output (per year)	Employment (per year)	Output per worker (per year)	Physical capital per worker	Human capital	Total factor productivity
				Contribution by component		
			Official output			
1950–2004	4.9	1.4	3.4	1.5	0.6	1.3
1950–60	5.4	−0.6	6.1	3.0	0.6	2.3
1960–70	7.9	2.3	5.5	2.5	0.8	2.2
1970–80	4.3	1.0	3.3	1.4	0.8	1.1
1980–90	3.6	2.5	1.1	−0.4	0.5	1.0
1990–2004	3.7	1.7	2.0	1.1	0.4	0.5
1950–75	6.0	0.7	5.2	2.7	0.7	1.7
1975–2004	3.9	1.9	2.0	0.4	0.5	1.0
			Adjusted output, version 2[a]			
1950–2004	4.5	1.4	3.0	1.5	0.6	0.9
1950–60	5.4	−0.6	6.1	3.0	0.6	2.3
1960–70	7.9	2.3	5.5	2.5	0.8	2.2
1970–80	3.7	1.0	2.7	1.4	0.8	0.5
1980–90	3.0	2.5	0.5	−0.4	0.5	0.4
1990–2004	2.9	1.7	1.3	1.1	0.4	−0.2
1950–75	5.9	0.7	5.1	2.7	0.7	1.6
1975–2004	3.2	1.9	1.3	0.4	0.5	0.4

Source: Authors' calculations as described in text and appendix 2C.
a. Adjusted at the level of the chemicals industry.

The weakness of capital accumulation is especially evident in the late 1970s and 1980s. As shown in figure 2-5, the total investment rate plunged from 27.8 percent of GDP in 1972 to 15.5 percent in 1977 and then drifted down to a low of 9.5 percent in 1983. Although there was a small falloff in public construction and a significant drop in housing, most of the decline was in private business investment. Despite some recovery in the private component after 1985, investment has never returned to the rates achieved in the 1960s. At 15 percent of GDP, the current rate is sufficient to support a long-term GDP growth of only about 2.5 percent a year.[18]

18. The computation is based on the assumption that the capital stock, currently twice that of GDP, would need to grow at the same rate of output. The capital stock is constructed with a 5 percent rate of annual depreciation. Thus a gross rate of investment of 15 percent translates into a net investment rate of 5 percent of GDP, or 2.5 percent of the capital stock.

Figure 2-4. *Growth in Output per Worker and Its Components, Puerto Rico,*
1950–2004[a]

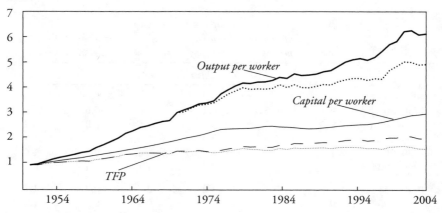

Index

Source: Authors' calculations as described in text and in appendix 2C.
a. For output per worker and total factor productivity, the solid lines are based on official data, and the
dotted lines on adjusted data.

The lower panel of table 2-3 shows how these results are affected by our
adjustment of GDP to reflect activities of section 936 corporations. In version 2,
which indexed nominal output in the chemicals industry to the growth in labor
compensation, our adjustment reduces the annual growth of overall GDP per
worker during 1975–2004 from 2.0 percent to 1.3 percent. Since the adjustment does not alter the contributions of physical or human capital, all of the
change falls through to lowering the residual growth in TFP. The result is an
improvement in TFP of just 0.4 percent a year, compared with 1.0 percent using
the official data. The deterioration in growth performance is particularly marked
in the 1980s, with the increase in labor productivity slowing from 2.7 percent
to 0.5 percent. Labor productivity growth picks up a bit after 1990, owing to a
larger contribution of capital deepening, but the change in TFP turns negative.
The adjustment greatly strengthens the pattern of steadily deteriorating productivity performance after 1975 that was already evident in the official data. It also
suggests that the problem extends beyond a weakening of capital formation to
include a large deceleration of the growth in TFP.

Sector Productivity

The national accounts of Puerto Rico do not normally include measures of real
output at the industry level. However, we were able to use unpublished price
indexes to compute output measures for the agricultural, goods-producing, and
service-producing industries for 1954 and annually since 1977. As shown in
table 2-4, these sectoral data highlight four interrelated issues.

Figure 2-5. *Investment Rate, Puerto Rico, 1950–2004*
Percent of GDP

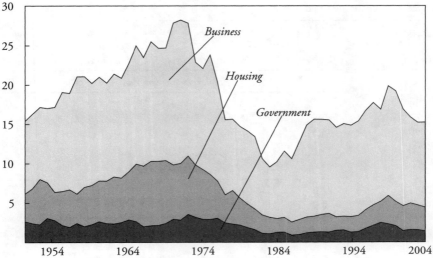

Source: Data from Puerto Rico Planning Board, tables 2 and 8; authors' calculations.

First, the shift out of agriculture over the past half century has been dramatic. The distributions of nominal GDP and employment among the three sectors are shown in the top panel. In 1954 agriculture accounted for a third of total employment and 17 percent of output. By 1977, it represented only 6 percent of employment and 3 percent of output; and by 2004, its share of output had fallen to less than 1 percent.

Second, adjusting output for the overstatement of income arising from activities of section 936 corporations substantially influences the implied picture of sectoral development on the island. The data in the top portion of table 2-4, based on published national accounts data, show the shift out of agriculture as fully offset by growth in industrial output (primarily manufacturing). However, as discussed earlier, that growth is undoubtedly inflated by income shifting. Our simple adjustment for the overstatement of income in the chemicals industry reduces industry's share of nominal output in 2004 from 49 percent, shown in the table, to 35 percent.[19] The adjusted data would suggest a growing role for the production of both industrial goods and services. In contrast, the employment

19. Dietz (2003, table 3.3) suggests an alternative adjustment in which he assumes all of the difference in aggregate GNI versus GDP can be attributed to manufacturing, and he calculates a net contribution of the manufacturing sector to Puerto Rican income. That calculation goes beyond our objective of obtaining a more meaningful measure of output in manufacturing.

Table 2-4. *Output and Productivity, by Major Sector, Puerto Rico, Selected Years, 1954–2004*

Percent, except as indicated

Period	Agriculture	Goods production	Services	Goods production, adjusted[a]	Total economy, adjusted[a]
		Employment distribution			
1954	31.9	23.9	44.2	...	...
1977	5.8	25.5	68.7	...	...
1990	3.7	23.3	73.0	...	...
2004	2.1	18.1	79.8	...	...
		National output distribution[b]			
1954	17.0	27.6	55.4	...	...
1977	2.9	39.2	58.0	...	...
1990	1.5	45.0	53.5	...	...
2004	0.5	49.4	50.2	...	...
		Labor productivity (thousands of 2000 dollars)[b]			
1954	2.0	12.3	10.5	12.3	11.6
1977	8.3	60.5	24.5	53.2	36.5
1990	12.2	84.5	29.1	62.4	42.6
2004	15.1	129.3	38.1	74.2	56.6
		Annual rate of change in labor productivity[b]			
1954–77	6.3	7.2	3.8	6.6	5.1
1977–2004	2.3	2.9	1.6	1.2	1.6
1977–90	3.0	2.6	1.3	1.2	1.2
1990–2004	1.6	3.1	2.0	1.3	2.1

Source: Authors' calculations as described in text.

a. Goods output adjusted after 1970 for the overstatement of property income in chemicals industry, version 2 in text.

b. Service sector output is defined to exclude owner-occupied housing.

data suggest a declining role for both agriculture and industrial production, with an increasingly dominant role for services production.

The third issue is labor productivity in Puerto Rico, both across sectors and relative to the mainland. The distortions induced by the section 936 corporations are also evident here, in the middle panel of table 2-4. The official data imply that labor productivity in Puerto Rican goods-producing industries in 2004 was about 40 percent higher than on the mainland.[20] Adjusting for the chemical

20. The 2004 value of $129,300 per worker shown in table 2-4 is equivalent to an estimate of $88,000 for the comparable industry group on the mainland.

industry alone reduces measured productivity by 43 percent, to roughly 20 percent below the mainland level. Even with the adjustment, the gap between labor productivity in the industrial and services-producing sectors remains surprisingly large. Although comparable data for the mainland yield nearly equal estimates of labor productivity in industry and services, our estimates suggest that for Puerto Rico, labor productivity in industry is twice that for services.

Finally, though the post-1975 slowdown in productivity growth noted earlier is evident in all three sectors, it is particularly pronounced in the industrial sector. This is shown in the bottom panel of table 2-4. Because worker productivity was much greater in industry and services, the large shift of employment out of agriculture added about 0.8 percent to the annual growth of labor productivity in 1954–77. However, the much smaller employment shift after 1977 has only added 0.4 percent to annual growth since then.

International Comparisons

We can obtain some context for Puerto Rico's growth experience by contrasting it with experiences elsewhere. Table 2-5 provides a comparable set of growth accounts for the United States and a range of other countries over the period 1960–2000.[21] The accounts for Puerto Rico are shown using both the published and the adjusted output measures. First, it is clear that Puerto Rico did achieve considerable convergence with the United States, given its growth in output per worker well above that of the mainland. However, it is also clear that nearly all of that convergence occurred before 1980. The adjusted output version suggests that Puerto Rico actually lost ground after 1980. Furthermore, Puerto Rico's catch-up can be traced primarily to a more rapid rate of physical capital accumulation and to substantial progress in narrowing the educational attainment gap. The island has performed less well in catching up to the mainland level of total factor productivity.

Table 2-5 also shows that Puerto Rico has performed well relative to an average of eighty-four other countries that make up about 95 percent of world GDP. However, using the adjusted output measure, its average growth in output per worker falls short after 1980. The most distinguishing feature is an unusually large contribution of improvements in educational attainment. Puerto Rico's growth performance looks particularly favorable in comparison with growth in Latin America. This is primarily because Puerto Rico avoided the financial (exchange rate) crises that periodically disrupted growth elsewhere in the region. Thus official measures of Puerto Rico's TFP growth stay positive after 1980,

---

21. The data are drawn from Bosworth and Collins (2003) and are available at www.brook .edu/es/research/projects/develop/develop.htm (June 2005). The estimates differ slightly from those given in table 2-1 because we have used estimates of labor force rather than employment to conform to the general lack of employment data for developing countries.

Table 2-5. *Sources of Growth, Selected Regions, Selected Years, 1960–2000*
Percent

			Contribution by component		
Location	Output	Output per worker	Physical capital per worker	Education	Factor productivity
Puerto Rico (published)					
1960–2000	5.0	3.1	1.1	0.6	1.3
1960–80	6.3	4.2	1.9	0.8	1.5
1980–2000	3.9	2.0	0.4	0.4	1.2
Puerto Rico (adjusted)					
1960–2000	4.5	2.6	1.1	0.6	1.2
1960–80	5.8	3.8	1.9	0.8	1.0
1980–2000	3.2	1.4	0.4	0.4	1.3
United States					
1960–2000	3.4	1.6	0.4	0.3	0.9
1960–80	3.6	1.5	0.1	0.6	0.8
1980–2000	3.3	1.8	0.6	0.1	1.1
World[a]					
1960–2000	4.0	2.3	1.0	0.3	0.9
1960–80	4.6	2.7	1.2	0.4	1.1
1980–2000	3.5	1.9	0.8	0.3	0.8
Latin America[b]					
1960–2000	4.0	1.1	0.6	0.4	0.2
1960–80	5.9	2.8	1.0	0.3	1.4
1980–2000	2.3	−0.4	0.1	0.4	−0.9
East Asia[c]					
1960–2000	6.7	3.9	2.3	0.5	1.0
1960–80	7.3	4.1	2.3	0.5	1.2
1980–2000	6.6	3.9	2.4	0.5	0.9
Mexico					
1960–2000	4.7	1.3	0.6	0.5	0.2
1960–80	6.9	3.1	1.1	0.4	1.6
1980–2000	2.7	−0.4	0.2	0.5	−1.1
Ireland					
1960–2000	4.9	4.0	1.3	0.3	2.3
1960–80	4.6	3.9	1.7	0.3	1.8
1980–2000	5.5	4.1	0.9	0.3	2.9

Source: Data from Bosworth and Collins (2003) and as described in text and appendix 2C; authors' calculations.
a. Eighty-four countries.
b. Twenty-three countries.
c. Excluding China; seven countries.

despite the general growth slowdown. On the other hand, after 1980, Puerto Rico was unable to keep up with the newly industrializing economies of East Asia, which achieved gains in educational attainment nearly as strong as Puerto Rico's but also maintained rapid physical capital accumulation.

Puerto Rico's growth is often compared to the growth experiences of Mexico and Ireland. Mexico is of interest as a nearby Latin American country, sometimes seen as a competitor in view of its expanding economic ties to the United States and its considerably lower labor costs. Despite some recovery in recent years, Mexico still suffers in comparison, both because of its disastrous 1980s economic experience and because of its 1994–95 financial crisis. Ireland is a small island economy of nearly identical population that has performed extraordinarily well in the past decade. Ireland's growth has resulted mainly from strong improvements in employment and TFP, in contrast to the emphasis on capital accumulation in East Asia. That focus has been particularly evident since 1990. As a highly successful island economy that overcame a prior period of slow growth, Ireland may offer some guidance for Puerto Rico. We return to this comparison later in this chapter, following a more detailed discussion of the role of factor inputs—employment, as well as physical and human capital—in Puerto Rico's growth.

Labor Inputs

In this section, we provide an overview of trends in the quantity (employment rate) and quality (education) of the workforce. The low Puerto Rican employment-to-population rate, shown in table 2-1, is a major contributor to the depressed levels of family incomes on the island. If Puerto Ricans were employed at the same rate as on the mainland (with unchanged income per worker), per capita incomes would be raised by 50 percent. However, we also find that the Puerto Rican workforce has levels of educational attainment well above those of other countries with comparable incomes.

Employment. Figure 2-6 and table 2-6 provide some basic information on employment trends. In 1950 Puerto Rico's labor force participation rate was roughly equivalent to that of the United States (58 and 60 percent respectively). However, the two rates diverged in subsequent decades. The U.S. rate rose largely because of an increase in female participation sufficient to offset a gradual decline in the male rate. Puerto Rico experienced a smaller increase in the female participation rate and a sharper decline in the male rate. At 58.3 percent in 2004, the labor force participation rate for men was 15 percentage points below the mainland rate, and the corresponding gap in rates for women was 22 points.

The fall in the male participation rate that began during the 1950s and 1960s increased during the 1970s (figure 2-6). The pre-1975 economic boom translated into surprisingly little job growth. In part, this can be traced to large emigration in that period, in some years leading to a decline in the male working-age population.

Figure 2-6. *Labor Force Participation Rates, by Gender, 1950–2004*

Percent

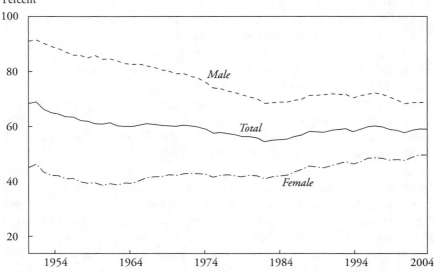

Source: Data from Puerto Rico Department of Labor and Human Resources (www.net-empleopr.
org/interempleo/index_interempleo.jsp [July 2005]); U.S. Department of Labor (www.bls.gov [July
2005]). Historical data, adjusted to conform to the population aged sixteen and over, were provided by
Orlando Sotomayor.

Those who emigrated may have been more likely to be in the labor force than
those who stayed behind.[22] There was also a large decline in participation rates
for young males (sixteen to twenty-four years of age) relative to the mainland. In
recent decades, the participation rate has actually seen a marginal increase.
However, relative to the mainland, participation rates in Puerto Rico are lower
today across all age and gender groups.

Attempts to explain the low labor force participation on the island often
focus on two developments: the dramatic increase in U.S. social welfare transfers to Puerto Rico that occurred during the mid-1970s and the U.S. minimum
wage phase-in from 1977 to 1981. The first factor is identified as reducing work
incentives, and the second with limiting employment opportunities. However,
some of the causes of a low participation rate seem to be more fundamental and
long-standing.

Several studies have questioned the quality of Puerto Rico's labor force survey.
Arguing that it does not accurately capture changes in the labor market, a number of these studies have relied instead on data from the decennial censuses.[23] In

22. Rivera-Batiz and Santiago (1996, chap. 3).
23. Rivera-Batiz and Santiago (1996, app. 1).

Table 2-6. *Labor Force Participation and Unemployment, Puerto Rico, Selected Years, 1950–2004*
Percent, except as indicated

Calendar year	Populationᵃ	Labor forceᵃ	Participation rate			Unemployment rate		
			Total	Male	Female	Total	Male	Female
			Puerto Rico (Labor force survey)					
1950	1,189	689	57.9	84.8	31.4	14.8	15.2	11.6
1960	1,286	629	48.9	77.1	23.4	11.8	12.4	9.3
1970	1,607	771	48.0	70.7	28.0	10.8	11.1	10.0
1980	2,116	916	43.3	60.6	27.8	17.0	19.5	12.2
1990	2,495	1,132	45.4	61.6	31.3	14.2	16.2	10.7
2000	2,806	1,294	46.1	59.2	35.0	10.1	11.9	7.6
2004	2,938	1,371	46.7	58.3	37.1	12.0	12.8	10.9
			United States (Labor force survey)					
1950	. . .	. . .	59.9	86.4	33.9	5.3	5.1	5.7
1960	. . .	. . .	59.4	83.3	37.7	5.5	5.4	5.9
1970	. . .	. . .	60.4	79.7	43.3	4.9	4.4	5.9
1980	. . .	. . .	63.8	77.4	51.5	7.1	6.9	7.4
1990	. . .	. . .	66.5	76.4	57.5	5.6	5.7	5.5
2000	. . .	. . .	67.1	74.8	59.9	4.0	3.9	4.1
2004	. . .	. . .	66.0	73.4	59.2	5.5	5.7	5.4
			Puerto Rico (census), fourteen years of age and over					
1950	1,301	597	45.9	70.7	21.2	5.3	5.4	5.1
1960	1,406	594	42.2	65.7	20.0	5.7	5.5	6.4
1970	1,788	684	38.2	54.7	22.9	5.6	4.9	7.1
			Puerto Rico (census), sixteen years of age and over					
1970	1,655	680	41.1	59.0	24.5	5.5	4.8	7.1
1980	2,106	866	41.1	54.6	29.1	14.9	14.2	16.1
1990	2,495	1,179	47.3	58.5	37.1	20.2	18.9	22.2
2000	2,847	1,162	40.8	48.8	33.7	19.0	17.5	21.0

Source: Puerto Rico Department of Labor and Human Resources (www.net-empleopr.org/interempleo/index_interempleo.jsp). Historical data, adjusted to conform to the population aged sixteen and over, were provided by Orlando Sotomayor. U.S. Department of Labor (www.bls.gov/).

the bottom panel of table 2-6, we provide comparable labor force measures from censuses. In all years except 1990, the census reports an even lower rate of labor force participation than the household survey. However, the basic trend since 1950 is similar to that in the survey, with a large decline in the male rate before 1970. There are obvious problems with the 2000 census, however, which shows a plunge in participation rates for both men and women. Neither the household nor the establishment employment surveys indicate such a development. Before 2000, the census also implied a much larger rise in the female participation rate.

As a final, additional check on the data, we compared the estimate of non-agricultural employment from the payroll records of the Current Employment Statistics survey. We would expect some differences, both because this survey excludes the self-employed and because it includes duplicate records for those holding multiple jobs. Since 1979, employment in the household survey has consistently exceeded that of the establishment report by about 10 percent. This could reflect growth in self-employment or a discrepancy between the surveys. However, there is closer agreement between the two surveys in terms of trends in labor market development than between either of the surveys and the census.

Puerto Rico has long had a high rate of unemployment. This accounts for much of the difference in the employment-to-population ratios of the United States and Puerto Rico in the early years. The reasons for such a persistently high rate, however, remain unclear. Writing in the mid-1980s, James Dietz noted that unemployment spells in Puerto Rico tended to be relatively short, with substantially lower rates of unemployment among females than males. Interestingly, this pattern has emerged on the mainland relatively recently.[24] Alida Castillo-Freeman and Richard Freeman have argued that the minimum wage has had a major effect on the employment rate—mainly because the minimum was so much higher relative to the average wage in Puerto Rico than in the United States.[25] However, their analysis emphasizes the years after 1970, when the U.S. minimum wage was extended to Puerto Rico. The minimum wage was not particularly high in the 1950s and 1960s, when the participation rate was already low and declining.[26] Again, it is interesting to note that the census indicates quite a different pattern of change in the unemployment rate (table 2-6). According to these data, unemployment was initially low but in 1990 and 2000 rose far above the rate implied by household survey data. This magnitude of deterioration seems improbable, giving us further reason to favor the employment data from the surveys over census data.[27]

We are left with a substantial puzzle: why is Puerto Rico's labor force participation rate so depressed? Other chapters in this volume focus on this issue (in particular, chapters 3 and 4). However, in the present context, labor force participation emerges as a critical part of any effort to raise Puerto Rican living standards.

24. Dietz (1986, pp. 273–81).

25. Castillo-Freeman and Freeman (1992).

26. Alan Krueger (1995) goes further in casting doubt on the robustness of the connection between the minimum wage and unemployment after 1970.

27. The determination of employment status in the census is based on the answers to two simple questions about having been employed in the prior week and having looked for work in the prior month. The household survey asks a more extensive set of questions.

Educational Attainment. Considerable caution must be used in associating increased levels of educational attainment with improvements in labor quality. Just as on the mainland, there has been extensive criticism of what some observers believe is a deteriorating educational system in Puerto Rico.[28] However, increased educational attainment appears to yield marginal income gains in Puerto Rico, roughly equivalent to those observed on the mainland.

Table 2-7 shows the distribution by levels of educational attainment for persons of working age during the period 1950–2000. Over the half century, the average level of education rose from five years to twelve years of schooling. The proportion of the working-age population with a high school diploma soared from 7 percent in 1950 to 63 percent in 2000. However, the pattern is somewhat bimodal: both the proportion of Puerto Ricans who dropped out before entering high school and the proportion with some college are relatively high. It is also notable that the educational attainment of females has exceeded that of males since the 1980 census. In 2000 half of Puerto Rican men aged twenty-five to thirty-four had reached their maximum educational attainment by graduating from high school, while 60 percent of women in this age range would go on to higher education. In addition, as of 2000, 4.5 percent of women had received graduate or professional degrees, compared with 3.3 percent of men.[29]

We use the Public Use Microdata Samples (PUMS) to make more detailed comparisons between Puerto Rico and the United States.[30] Results for 1970 and 2000 are shown in table 2-8. It is evident that Puerto Rico has largely caught up with the United States. In the 2000 census, average years of schooling in Puerto Rico was 12.2, compared with 13.8 in the United States. In fact, if we limit the comparison to employed persons aged twenty-five to thirty-four, any difference has essentially vanished—14.4 versus 14.5 years. It is surprising to note that Puerto Rican island residents are much more likely to have a college degree than are persons of Puerto Rican descent who live on the mainland. Recent emigrants to the United States are more likely to have at least some high school, but less likely to have a college degree, than are residents of Puerto Rico.[31]

In computing the growth accounts discussed earlier in this chapter, we assigned a 7 percent rate of return to each additional year of education. There is extensive international evidence of a strong relationship between income and educational attainment at the microeconomic level, although the correlation is weaker at the

28. That issue is explored more fully in chapter 5 in this volume.

29. Data from U.S. Census, Public Use Microdata Samples of Puerto Rico, 1970–2000.

30. These data sets are available from the U.S. Census Bureau for 1970, 1980, 1990, and 2000. The data for years of education had to be adjusted to harmonize the definitions among the various censuses. The data for the United States were obtained from the University of Minnesota's Integrated Public Use Microdata Surveys program, which allows downloads of multiple censuses in one file, with variable definitions already harmonized across time.

31. Recent emigrants are identified in the census as having emigrated in the past five years.

Table 2-7. *Educational Attainment, Puerto Rico, 1950–2000*
Percent of population

	Aged fourteen to sixty-four			Aged sixteen to sixty-four			
Highest level completed	1950	1960	1970	1970	1980	1990	2000
No schooling	21.9	12.7	7.2	6.7	3.3	2.2	2.6
Some elementary school (four years)	32.9	27.3	17.4	19.0	11.7	7.3	3.0
Some middle school (six years)	29.3	31.4	28.5	24.7	20.0	14.2	11.6
Some high school (ten years)	8.5	13.4	18.5	18.4	20.5	21.3	20.0
High school diploma (twelve years)	4.1	8.3	16.6	18.1	23.8	23.1	24.0
Some college or associate (fourteen years)	1.8	4.2	7.0	7.8	12.3	18.9	23.9
Bachelor's degree and higher (sixteen years)	1.4	2.7	4.8	5.3	8.5	13.2	14.8
Average years of schooling	4.7	6.2	8.0	9.1	10.6	11.8	12.2

Source: U.S. Census publications, 1950–70, various years; Public Use Microdata Samples (PUMS) of Puerto Rico, 1970–2000.

aggregate level of cross-national comparisons.[32] The PUMS data enable us to explore the return to an additional year of education in Puerto Rico. Focusing on individuals with wage income, we estimated regressions relating the log of earnings to a set of key determinants, including years of schooling, age, and gender.

Table 2-9 summarizes the regression results. Separate estimates are reported for each of the four censuses and for three distinct groups of individuals: Puerto Ricans on the island, all U.S. residents of the United States, and U.S. residents who identified themselves as being of Puerto Rican descent. Two findings from the results are of particular relevance to this discussion. First, the coefficient on years of schooling is actually slightly larger for Puerto Rican residents (2 percentage points) than for the United States as a whole and is much larger than for U.S. residents of Puerto Rican descent. Second, the male-female earnings differential is significantly smaller in Puerto Rico than in the United States, although the size of the differential has been declining on the mainland. We also explored the implications of coding educational attainment as a set of categorical variables,

32. See, for example, Bils and Klenow (2000), Psacharopoulos (1994), and the discussion in Bosworth and Collins (2003). A return of 7 percent is near the lower bound of the range of findings from that literature. However, the issue remains controversial because of the possibility that the correlation between education and income is the result of a sorting of individuals by native ability, as argued by Michael Spence (1973).

Table 2-8. *Educational Attainment, Puerto Rico and the United States,*
1970–2000[a]

Percent of population, except as indicated

Highest level completed	Puerto Rico		United States		Puerto Rican descent	
	1970	2000	1970	2000	1970	2000
No schooling	6.7	2.6	0.8	1.1	3.9	2.6
Some elementary school (K–4)	19.0	3.0	2.2	0.5	11.6	1.6
Some middle school (5–8)	24.7	11.6	14.8	3.5	28.4	7.4
Some high school	18.4	20.0	24.8	15.7	28.9	26.3
High school diploma	18.1	24.0	34.3	26.9	20.9	26.2
Some college or associate	7.8	23.9	13.1	29.6	4.2	25.5
Bachelor's	3.4	11.8	5.9	14.9	1.2	7.1
Five to seven years of postsecondary[b]	1.9	2.6	4.1	6.9	0.8	3.1
Doctoral degree[c]	. . .	0.3	. . .	0.8	. . .	0.2
Average years of schooling	9.1	12.2	12.2	13.8	9.5	12.5

Source: U.S. Census, PUMS files for 1970, 1980, 1990, and 2000.
a. Persons aged sixteen to sixty-four.
b. In 1970, five or more years.
c. Counted only in 2000.

but this yielded no significant improvement over the simple relationship with years of schooling. Our results are supportive of the argument, made by William Baumol and Edward Wolff, that the improved education of the workforce has been a primary source of Puerto Rico's economic growth.[33]

Wage Rates. Until the mid-1970s, Puerto Rico was able to generate rapid wage increases relative to the mainland while sustaining similar rates of employment growth. In recent years, however, though the island economy has continued to generate jobs at about the same rate as the United States, it has failed to achieve any further progress in convergence of wage rates. In fact, as shown in figure 2-7, relative wages have eroded significantly. This lack of convergence at the aggregate level contrasts with the earlier findings of strong overall gains in educational attainment and, in cross-sectional data, of a strong association between educational attainment and earnings. However, it is consistent with our finding of a pronounced slowing of labor productivity growth.

Table 2-10 provides information about the current industry composition of employment and wage rates in Puerto Rico and the United States. The distribution of employment across industries is surprisingly similar. With average wage

33. Baumol and Wolff (1996).

Table 2-9. *Regression of Income and Educational Attainment, Puerto Rico and the United States, 1970–2000*[a]

Dependent variable is log of wage income

Independent variable	All Puerto Rican residents				U.S. residents of Puerto Rican descent				All U.S. residents			
	1970	1980	1990	2000	1970	1980	1990	2000	1970	1980	1990	2000
Age	0.09	0.16	0.17	0.15	0.17	0.19	0.19	0.17	0.19	0.18	0.21	0.20
	(18.1)	(59.6)	(68.0)	(67.9)	(22.9)	(30.3)	(34.9)	(38.0)	(370.9)	(380.5)	(454.3)	(476.0)
Age$^2 \times 10^{-3}$	−1.03	−1.72	−1.80	−1.57	−1.91	−2.11	−2.07	−1.87	−2.01	−1.99	−2.27	−2.17
	(15.4)	(49.8)	(55.6)	(55.5)	(19.7)	(24.9)	(28.6)	(30.8)	(309.3)	(319.6)	(386.5)	(405.6)
Categorical variable for female	−0.32	−0.26	−0.31	−0.37	−0.56	−0.49	−0.43	−0.39	−0.88	−0.75	−0.58	−0.50
	(14.9)	−(26.0)	−(33.8)	(46.4)	(19.2)	(20.1)	(20.7)	(22.8)	(402.1)	(378.2)	(320.7)	(354.6)
Years of education	0.10	0.10	0.12	0.12	0.04	0.06	0.08	0.09	0.08	0.08	0.10	0.10
	(42.7)	(85.1)	(92.5)	(92.9)	(9.1)	(15.5)	(24.7)	(31.7)	(233.6)	(231.2)	(301.0)	(354.6)
Constant	4.92	3.90	3.68	4.56	4.83	4.56	4.67	5.09	3.71	4.48	4.13	4.54
	(51.7)	(77.9)	(77.7)	(108.9)	(35.7)	(40.2)	(46.5)	(61.1)	(382.1)	(503.1)	(476.7)	(564.0)
Summary statistic												
Adj. R^2	0.28	0.27	0.27	0.28	0.23	0.25	0.26	0.28	0.37	0.33	0.34	0.34
Standard error	0.79	0.91	1.00	0.92	0.92	1.00	1.05	1.01	0.97	1.00	0.99	0.95
N	6,384	36,826	49,347	56,117	4,367	6,784	9,071	13,028	819,063	1,040,000	1,190,000	1,340,000

Source: The data are drawn from the Public Use Microdata Samples (PUMS) for the decennial censuses of the United States and Puerto Rico. The sample is restricted to individuals aged sixteen and over with positive wage income in the prior year.

a. Numbers in parentheses are *t* statistics.

Figure 2-7. *Employment and Wage Growth, Puerto Rico Relative to the United States, 1950–2004*
Index (United States, 1950 = 1.0)

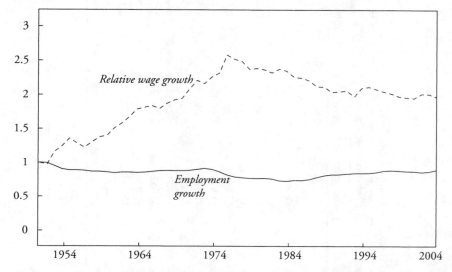

Source: Data from U.S. Department of Labor, Bureau of Labor Statistics, *Quarterly Census of Employment and Wages,* 1950–2004. Indexes of employment and wages for Puerto Rico are divided by corresponding indexes for the United States.

rates only about half those in the United States, we would have expected Puerto Rico to have a larger manufacturing sector. The low share of manufacturing employment is further evidence of the disappointing results from an industrial development strategy that used tax incentives to attract manufacturing firms from the mainland. Puerto Rico's average wage, equal to 54 percent of the mainland average, is very much in line with our adjusted estimate of Puerto Rican labor productivity, 58 percent of the U.S. level. The table also shows that the overall variance of wages across industry groups is nearly identical to that in the United States.[34]

The table uncovers some striking differences in wage structure across the two economies, however. Puerto Rican wages are relatively high in manufacturing (62 percent), retail trade (63 percent), and the leisure and hospitality industry (75 percent). The high relative wage in retail may largely reflect the notoriously low wages in U.S. retailing; but the result for tourism-related industries is striking. The low relative wage in business and professional services may reflect differences in the island's occupational structure relative to the mainland.

34. The ratio of the standard deviation to the mean is 0.34 and 0.36 in Puerto Rico and the United States, respectively.

Table 2-10. *Distribution of Employment and Relative Rates of Pay, Puerto Rico and the United States, 2003*[a]

Industry (NAICS classification)	Employment distribution (percent)		Annual wage rates (dollars)		Annual wage, PR/U.S. (percent)
	United States	Puerto Rico	United States	Puerto Rico	
Private industry	100.0	100.0	37,508	20,318	54.2
Goods producing	21.3	27.3	43,154	23,319	54.0
Natural resources and mining	1.5	1.8	33,729	9,192	27.3
Construction	6.2	9.3	39,509	17,347	43.9
Manufacturing	13.5	16.2	45,916	28,292	61.6
Service producing	78.7	72.7	35,981	19,192	53.3
Wholesale trade	5.2	4.4	50,835	29,878	58.8
Retail trade	13.9	18.0	23,804	15,064	63.3
Transportation and utilities	4.2	2.3	41,411	24,288	58.7
Information	3.0	3.0	58,002	32,310	55.7
Financial activities	7.3	6.3	57,143	28,352	49.6
Professional and business services	14.8	13.9	45,052	20,283	45.0
Education and health services	14.7	12.6	35,071	17,616	50.2
Leisure and hospitality	11.4	9.4	16,138	12,158	75.3
Other services, except public administration	4.0	2.6	24,348	14,848	61.0
Unclassified	0.2	0.2	35,787	21,681	60.6

Source: Data from U.S. Department of Labor, Bureau of Labor Statistics, *Quarterly Census of Employment and Wages*, 2003.

a. Data are limited to the private sector because not all U.S. government workers are included in the unemployment insurance program.

Capital Accumulation

As noted earlier in this chapter, a slowdown in capital accumulation accounts for a significant portion of the decline in Puerto Rico's growth after 1975. The collapse of investment during the 1970s, and the only partial recovery more recently, are evident in figure 2-5. The associated behavior of domestic saving and Puerto Rico's infrastructure are additional dimensions of these developments.

In addition to an unusually low rate of labor force participation, Puerto Rico's economic development has been characterized by an extremely modest rate of domestic saving. The balance of saving and investment for the period 1950–2004 is shown in table 2-11. These data should be interpreted with caution because it is difficult to estimate the amount of unreported income that may flow back and forth between Puerto Rico and the mainland. However, in the Puerto Rican national accounts, net household saving has been negative in each year since 1957. Although in recent decades investment has fallen off relative to GDP, it remains relatively high as a share of national income. Over the past quarter century, investment has been financed by a combination of capital inflows from the mainland and revenue from depreciation accounts. According to the national accounts, private saving has withered away. Even the relatively high level of corporate saving was undoubtedly influenced by the strong incentives for section 936 corporations to reinvest retained earnings in Puerto Rico.

Puerto Rico's apparent lack of private saving is quite unprecedented, but it is important to recognize that recorded statistics may overstate the problem. In principle, it should be relatively easy to construct reliable estimates of domestic investment and public sector saving. However, if foreign transfer payments to residents of Puerto Rico were underreported, a correction would raise household income and saving while reducing the reported size of the current-account deficit. Thus there is a possibility that household saving is understated and foreign saving (the current-account deficit) is overstated. This concern is reinforced by the suspension of published information on foreign direct investment in the early 1980s and the inclusion in the balance of payments of a large residual inflow of unknown transactions.

We examined several alternative indicators that might be expected to be correlated with private saving. The Puerto Rico Planning Board compiles estimates of financial assets of the household sector. These totaled $39 billion in 2004, or 0.83 times personal income. If truly a measure of total financial assets, this is very low. In comparison, a flow-of-funds estimate of U.S. financial wealth is roughly four times disposable income. However, the estimate for Puerto Rico includes no credit market assets and only a few nondeposit assets. Limiting the comparison to deposit-type accounts yields a ratio to disposable income of about 0.7 in both instances. Alternatively, we can compare household capital income. In 2004 net capital income was 13 percent of personal income in Puerto Rico versus 23 percent for the United States. Both of these calculations are more reflective

Table 2-11. *Gross Saving and Investment as Share of GNI, by Sector and Decade,*
1950–2004
Percent

Sector	1950–59	1960–69	1970–79	1980–89	1990–99	2000–04
Gross national saving	11.5	12.8	7.5	5.7	9.2	16.0
Net national saving[a]	5.7	5.3	−0.6	−2.6	−0.7	5.1
Private saving[b]	1.8	0.8	−3.6	−8.7	−5.7	2.3
Household saving	−0.6	−2.6	−5.3	−11.0	−7.5	−3.4
Corporate saving[b]	2.4	3.4	1.8	2.4	1.8	5.7
Government saving	3.9	4.5	3.0	6.1	4.9	2.9
Capital depreciation	5.8	7.5	8.0	8.3	9.9	10.9
Gross domestic investment	19.0	26.8	26.6	18.1	25.3	26.3
Private fixed investment[b]	14.7	21.0	21.2	14.9	21.1	22.8
Housing	3.2	5.9	5.3	2.3	3.0	4.5
Inventory accumulation	1.7	2.9	1.6	1.1	1.3	0.7
Government investment	2.6	2.9	3.7	2.1	2.9	2.8
Current account	−7.5	−14.0	−19.1	−12.4	−16.1	−10.3

Source: Data from Puerto Rico Planning Board; authors' calculations.
a. Net saving excludes capital consumption allowances (depreciation).
b. Activities of public enterprises are included with corporate saving and private fixed investment.

of differences in wealth than differences in saving. Still, they suggest a Puerto
Rican wealth-to-income ratio that is lower than in the United States but not so
low as to be consistent with a long-term pattern of negative household saving.

Is a low rate of national saving a constraint on growth in Puerto Rico? With the
end of the section 936 tax provision, there might be doubts that the island can
continue to rely so heavily on the foreign direct investment of U.S. corporations—
particularly if it wishes to diversify its economy away from reliance on those corporations. However, Puerto Rico's access to the U.S. financial market equals
that of any U.S. corporation. Thus if the commonwealth develops the financial
infrastructure to initiate and service loans to local business, access to capital
need not emerge as a serious constraint. At the same time, it would be preferable
for Puerto Rican incomes if future investment were financed domestically, since
a larger portion of the benefits of growth would remain within Puerto Rico.

How well developed is Puerto Rico's physical infrastructure? Following César
Calderón and Luis Servén, we focus on three areas: transportation, energy, and
telecommunications.[35] Some relevant indicators for Puerto Rico and selected
comparators are shown in table 2-12. We look first at roads as a measure of
transportation infrastructure. In terms of the length of its road network relative
to its surface land area, Puerto Rico has extensive road coverage—even com-

35. Calderón and Servén (2004).

Table 2-12. *Infrastructure and Communications Indicators, Puerto Rico and Selected Regions, 2002*
Units as indicated

Country	Roads[a]		Electric power		Telephones[b]		Internet		
								Secure servers	
	Per square kilometer	Per capita	Installed capacity[c]	Losses[d]	Main line	Mobile	Users[e]	Number	Coverage[f]
Puerto Rico	2,669	6,006	1,230	11	346	316	175	116	0.17
United States	662	21,918	3,206	6	621	543	551	198,098	1.24
Ireland	1,368	23,934	1,284	8	491	880	317	1,245	0.98
Korea	879	1,812	1,180	6	538	701	610	894	0.03
Chile	105	4,975	656	6	221	511	272	274	0.06
Mexico	168	3,231	449	15	158	291	118	634	0.05
Latin America and the Caribbean	n.a.	n.a.	n.a.	16	170	246	106	n.a.	n.a.
High-income countries	n.a.	n.a.	n.a.	6	560	708	377	n.a.	n.a.

Source: Carlos Marquez, "Is PREPA Prepared to Take Puerto Rico into the 21st Century?" *Puerto Rico Herald*, July 14, 2005 (www.puertorico-herald.org/issues2/2005/vol09n28/CBPrepaPrepared.shtml [August 2005]); World Bank (2005, tables 1.1, 5.9, 5/10, 5/11); Puerto Rico Planning Board, *International Energy Annual, 2003* (www.eia.doe.gov/pub/international/iealf/table64.xls [January 2005]).

a. Kilometers.
b. Per 1,000 people.
c. Megawatts per capita.
d. Percent of output.
e. Per 1,000 people.
f. Per 1,000 Internet users.

pared with countries with similarly high population densities, such as South Korea. Coverage per capita is less extensive than in the United States and Ireland. However, a comparison of road quality indicators for the island and the U.S. mainland does suggest reasons for concern. In particular, Puerto Rico suffers from higher traffic congestion than all U.S. states except for New Jersey, Maryland, and the District of Columbia. It also ranks poorly in terms of surface smoothness—well below estimates for the U.S. overall and below all the states except New Jersey, Connecticut, and the District of Columbia.[36]

Although considerably lower than the U.S. measure, installed electrical capacity per capita on the island in 2003 was just below that for Ireland and well above capacities in Chile and Mexico.[37] However, the island has been subject to transmission and distribution losses (11 percent of output in 2002) that are large by both mainland and international standards. This most likely reflects both the quality of the electrical generation and transmission system and activity in the informal economy. Furthermore, data for 2003 suggest that operations of the Puerto Rico Electric Power Authority, the island's sole provider of electric energy, are considerably less efficient than operations of its mainland counterparts.[38] Electricity is also very expensive on the island. Carlos Marquez reports average charges to industrial users of 11.60 cents per kilowatt hour in Puerto Rico versus 4.9 cents per kilowatt hour in the United States for the second half of 2004. Average electricity costs were higher on the island than for any state except Hawaii.[39] However, Sergio Marxuach finds that Puerto Rico charged more for electricity than seven of eight other island economies in 2001.[40] Overall, these indicators are consistent with aging facilities that operate at low levels of productivity.

36. Indicators of traffic congestion and pavement roughness are taken from U.S. Department of Transportation (2005, tables HM-62, HM-63). Unfortunately, similar indicators were not available for the comparator countries.

37. See Marxuach (2005) and Carlos Marquez, "Is PREPA Prepared to Take Puerto Rico into the 21st Century?" *Puerto Rico Herald,* July 14, 2005 (www.puertorico-herald.org/issues2/2005/vol09n28/CBPrepaPrepared.shtml [January 2005]), for more detailed recent assessments of Puerto Rico's electricity sector.

38. Marxuach (2005, p. 25, table 14) compares Puerto Rico with the U.S. median for nine indicators of efficiency in 2003, including customers per nongeneration employee and expenses per kilowatt hour sold. Marxuach shows energy loss figures of 12 percent for Puerto Rico compared with a median of just 4 percent for the U.S. states. He notes that many mainland producers use equipment and technology of similar vintage to that used on the island. Furthermore, Puerto Rico differs from many mainland producers in not having to transmit the energy over thousands of miles. Thus, he argues, metering and billing losses as well as electricity theft are the most plausible explanations for the high energy loss ratio.

39. Marquez, "Is PREPA Prepared to Take Puerto Rico into the 21st Century?" *Puerto Rico Herald,* July 14, 2005.

40. Marxuach (2005, table 13, p. 24) shows Jamaica with higher electricity prices than Puerto Rico to both industrial and residential users in the fourth quarter of 2001. Taiwan, the Dominican Republic, Haiti, Ireland, New Zealand, Trinidad and Tobago, and the United Kingdom all charged less.

Telephone mainlines per capita provide an indicator of telecommunications development. As shown in table 2-12, Puerto Rico lags behind other high-income countries on this measure, at only 56 percent of the U.S. level compared with 79 and 87 percent for Ireland and Korea, respectively. Interestingly, Puerto Rico's phone coverage compared favorably with Ireland's and Korea's during the 1970s and 1980s, all three steadily increasing relative to the U.S. mainland. Catch-up stalled on the island more recently while continuing in Ireland and Korea.

Puerto Rico is particularly far behind in its adoption of the new communications and information technologies. Mobile phone usage is lower than in some developing economies, such as Chile. Adjusting for population size, Puerto Rico has less than 65 percent as many Internet users as Chile and less than a third the number on the mainland. There are also relatively few secure servers on the island: in absolute terms, only half as many as Chile; and while Ireland has roughly one secure server for every thousand Internet users, the comparable figure for Puerto Rico is one for every six thousand users. These indicators do not suggest an untapped prowess in information technology, ripe for a sectoral takeoff.

Concerns about Puerto Rico's infrastructure are not new. Many studies have been undertaken focusing on different aspects and advancing numerous suggestions for improvement.[41] Some steps to address problems are under way, for example, in the electricity sector. Taken together, however, available indicators suggest a physical infrastructure that is falling behind, particularly in dimensions such as information and communications, and that could constrain Puerto Rico's prospects for increased growth.

Lessons from Ireland

Ireland offers an appealing exemplar for Puerto Rico's future growth. The two island economies share many common features. Both are small open economies with populations of roughly 4 million. Both are integral parts of much larger markets (Puerto Rico with the United States, Ireland with the European Union). Both have strong economic institutions and well-educated populations. Both have also made extensive use of tax incentives as a means of attracting multinational corporations. Ireland also had a history of disappointing growth, failing to converge toward income levels prevalent in the rest of Europe. Like Puerto Ricans, the Irish have responded to hard times by emigrating. During the 1980s, the Irish economy deteriorated sharply, and unemployment surged to more than 15 percent. However, the country did succeed in taming inflation, which had reached 20 percent in 1981. As recently as 1988, the *Economist* magazine concluded that Ireland was an economic failure, the basket case of Europe.[42]

41. For example, see Puerto Rico Planning Board (2004).
42. "Republic of Ireland: Survey," *Economist,* January 16, 1988, pp. 3–26.

Over the past decade, however, Ireland has been transformed. Economic growth (GDP) averaged 8.5 percent annually in the ten years leading up to 2004, and employment expanded by 50 percent. In 2001 Ireland ranked as the world's ninth highest country in terms of gross national income per capita, at $27,500 (based on purchasing power parity prices), surpassing the United Kingdom. Knowing what caused the turnaround in Ireland might provide a roadmap for reform in Puerto Rico.

Unfortunately, establishing convincing explanations for the Irish turnaround has proved difficult. Studies to date have been more successful at ruling out hypotheses than in identifying the key drivers. This may not be surprising in light of recent empirical research that finds the timing of growth accelerations to be highly unpredictable.[43] Nonetheless, a closer look at Ireland's experience suggests approaches that may be relevant for Puerto Rico.

Increased investment by foreign firms is high on the list of hypotheses that have been advanced to explain Irish growth. Because of Ireland's role as a tax haven for American multinational corporations, however, Irish economic statistics suffer from some of the same problems that were noted earlier for Puerto Rico. The tax advantage from investing in Puerto Rico under section 936 is larger than that from investing in Ireland, because the U.S. tax on earnings in the latter is only deferred. However, Ireland has long been aggressive in soliciting foreign direct investment, offering an extremely low tax on export earnings and other subsidies. Thus Ireland is another country in which GDP exceeds GNI because of the outflow of repatriated profits, albeit the magnitude there is smaller than in Puerto Rico. Some researchers have taken the GDP statistics at face value, attributing Ireland's growth to the role of the multinationals. In contrast, Patrick Honohan and Brendan Walsh adjust the Irish GDP for the overstatement of the output of the multinational corporations, with a consequent reduction in the rate of growth of GDP and productivity of 2 percent annually from 1995 to 1999.[44] After this adjustment, foreign firms still represent a major portion of the Irish economy, but expansion of neither their activities nor their employment can be identified as a driving element of Irish growth. These firms were there when Ireland was failing and there when it boomed.

Under pressure from the European Union, Ireland now offers a standard tax of 12.5 percent for all corporate payers.[45] However, it continues to pursue foreign firms actively, often in the same industries (pharmaceuticals and electronics) that have been drawn to Puerto Rico. Moreover, the 1995–2005 phase-out of section 936 in Puerto Rico may have helped Ireland by reducing the appeal

43. See Hausmann, Pritchett, and Rodrik (2004).
44. Honohan and Walsh (2002); their method of adjustment differs from ours for Puerto Rico in that they adjust the Irish output per worker to European Union norms.
45. Burnham (2003, p. 550).

of a primary competitor. James Burnham points to a 1982 report on Ireland's Industrial Development Authority, criticizing its policies as being overly generous toward the multinationals and providing the wrong incentives: The Irish authority favored capital-intensive firms, failed to penalize those that did not meet their employment projections, and did little to promote outsourcing to local firms.[46] The same report could have been written for Puerto Rico. Ireland's promotion programs were subsequently redesigned to place greater emphasis on a broader range of competitiveness factors.

Several studies have stressed Ireland's position as an English-speaking gateway to the European continent. Yet it is interesting to note that the expansion of trade has largely been in growth of exports to the United States—a finding consistent with the argument that Ireland has been a tax haven for U.S. firms.[47] Furthermore, the tradable goods sector represents a declining share of overall employment, a fact hard to reconcile with the notion of export-led growth.

Researchers have placed considerable emphasis on changes that improved the competitiveness of Irish labor.[48] Specifically, the government reached a social accord with the unions. There was also a small devaluation of the Irish pound in 1979, when Ireland joined the European exchange rate mechanism. The result, it can be argued, was lower costs, higher profits, and, in a highly open economy, large gains in output and employment.

Honohan and Walsh ultimately conclude that Ireland's growth resurgence can be traced to a coalescing of several factors.[49] The underlying fundamentals of a well-educated workforce and strong economic institutions should have provided the basis for high living standards, they argue, and the turnaround was initiated by a series of catalytic factors, such as devaluations of the Irish pound in 1986 and 1993, fiscal restructuring, and European structural funds. Employment growth was spread throughout all major economic sectors but was particularly marked in services. The Irish government has sought to promote the growth of an international financial services center in Dublin, placing considerable emphasis on modernizing the city's telecommunications sector. Ireland has also been successful in expanding its tourism industry, which has recently been growing at about 8 percent a year.[50]

One of the most striking aspects of the Irish experience is that the post-1992 growth is reflected in a sharp acceleration of employment gains rather than increases in total factor productivity.[51] Ireland has long shown a high rate of TFP

46. Burnham (2003).
47. Bosworth (2002, pp. 71–72).
48. Blanchard (2002).
49. Honohan and Walsh (2002).
50. See National Competitiveness Council of Ireland (2004) for further details on efforts to improve Ireland's competitive position.
51. Bosworth (2002); Slevin (2002).

growth, traceable in part to a movement out of agriculture and the overstatement of the output of foreign firms. There appears to be no significant acceleration of TFP growth after 1992: the contribution of capital per worker actually declined, and all of the pickup in output growth can be traced to increased employment. That, in turn, was made possible by a large net immigration that reversed the historical outflow.

What can we learn from a review of Ireland's experience that might be of value to Puerto Rico? First, the Irish experience provides further warning of the dangers of excessive reliance on tax considerations as a primary motivation for economic activity because of the distortions they can introduce. Second, the large expansion of employment and the sectoral breadth of those gains were important parts of Irish growth. Ireland has actually reduced the role of capital-intensive activities and achieved rapid growth in a wide range of service industries. Puerto Rico cannot engineer an exchange rate depreciation, and it has not been plagued with inflationary wage pressures; like Ireland, however, it is a very open economy, and an improvement in the competitiveness of its workers has the same potential for large gains in output and employment. For Puerto Rico, the initiating force would have to be gains in labor productivity (increased capital per worker) rather than devaluation.

Since the early 1990s, the evolution of the Irish economy has been very much in line with its comparative advantages, namely, its well-educated workforce, open economy, and integrated role in Europe. The result has been a surprisingly diversified growth experience. Puerto Rico would also be well served by emphasizing similar areas of comparative advantage and undertaking related measures to improve its competitiveness.

Summary and Policy Implications

The focus of this chapter has been the level and growth of production and income in Puerto Rico. Why did economic performance stall after the impressive performance of the 1950s and 1960s? What are the main characteristics of the current economy, and what challenges must it overcome to achieve sustained growth? Pulling together data from a variety of sources, including the national accounts, household and establishment surveys, and the decennial censuses, enables us to fill in some key pieces of this multidimensional puzzle and to highlight others that are the focus of subsequent chapters. To those who have studied Puerto Rico, many of the issues we address will be well known, and many of our conclusions will seem familiar. Indeed, a major objective and contribution of our work is an attempt to document and quantify frequently made claims. Our analysis also uncovers features that we believe warrant additional attention. In this final section, we highlight four sets of findings from our analysis. We then briefly advance some policy implications, which are discussed more fully in the last chapter of this volume.

It is clear that official statistics substantially overstate production of goods and services on the island. The problem arises from the behavior of U.S. corporations in response to provisions of the U.S. tax code. We have documented this in a number of ways, such as the implausibly low and declining labor share in manufacturing (especially in chemicals). We use the growing discrepancies vis-à-vis the United States to construct estimates that "adjust" GDP for this distortion. Our preferred indicator cuts Puerto Rican GDP by about 20 percent in 2004 and output growth by 0.7 percent a year since 1975. The adjustment explains much of the growing gap between Puerto Rico's measured production and national income and indicates just how sluggish economic performance has been in recent decades. Furthermore, the distortion has implications beyond its effects on measured output, labor productivity, and factor compensation. It also severely affects Puerto Rico's trade statistics, which show large exports of chemicals offset by even larger outflows of capital income. These and other reported measures are easily misleading and must be interpreted with considerable care.

Our examination of the relationship between productivity (GDP per worker) and living standards (income per capita) highlights the reasons why Puerto Rico's income per capita has fallen from 37 percent of that in the United States in 1970 to only 31 percent in 2003. This decline has occurred in spite of a striking demographic shift, owing to falling fertility rates and increased life expectancy, such that the share of the population of working age has converged with that of the mainland. In particular, we find that labor productivity in Puerto Rico (adjusted GDP per worker) failed to achieve any further catch-up with the mainland after 1970, contrary to some official claims that manufacturing productivity on the island exceeds U.S. norms. Furthermore, Puerto Rican employment relative to its working-age population continued to decline over this period, to just two-thirds of the U.S. level. We argue that a surprisingly low rate of labor force participation is the prime source of the low employment, though high (and variable) unemployment is an exacerbating factor. Much of the decline in labor force participation occurred before the dramatic rise in U.S. social transfers and the phase-in of the minimum wage, suggesting that these factors have interacted with other, long-standing issues. Both the low rate of labor force participation and the low labor productivity emerge as major themes of our analysis.

We undertake a growth accounting analysis that decomposes growth in Puerto Rico's output per worker into the contributions from increased physical and human capital per worker and a residual measure of total factor productivity. Our analysis clearly distinguishes two distinct periods in Puerto Rico's economic performance. In the early period (roughly 1950–75), the island sustained growth rates of nearly 5 percent a year in output per worker, comparable to rates achieved in the rapid growth phases for Ireland and East Asia and well above the Latin American average. With more than double the growth rate on the mainland, this was a period of significant catch-up for Puerto Rico, characterized by both capital deepening and increased efficiency of factor usage. In contrast, since 1975 Puerto Rico has fallen behind. Again based on the adjusted data, we estimate that Puerto Rican growth in output per worker dropped off to just over 1 percent a year, below that of the mainland.

The growth accounts uncover two reasons for Puerto Rico's slow growth in labor productivity. First, capital accumulation did not keep pace with increases in employment. Investment fell sharply as a share of output during the 1970s and 1980s, such that capital per worker actually declined in the 1980s. Although investment rates have recovered somewhat, they are insufficient to support long-term growth at the rates achieved in the earlier period. Our analysis draws attention to the striking lack of private saving in Puerto Rico. However, to the extent that some transfers to Puerto Rican residents are unrecorded, official measures may understate private saving and overstate foreign saving (the current-account deficit). It is also doubtful that the low rate of internal saving is a major constraint on growth, given Puerto Rico's access to mainland financial markets. However, as we also note, indicators of the island's infrastructure, particularly in telecommunications and information, do suggest potential growth constraints.

In contrast, Puerto Rico stands out for relatively high contributions of increased human capital to growth, owing to continued gains in educational attainment. Indeed, in terms of average years of schooling, the island has caught up with the mainland and compares favorably with countries such as Ireland. Our estimates also find that returns to education are similar to those achieved on the mainland. It is important to note that our measures of the contributions of capital accumulation and education do not depend on the measure used for GDP.

The second reason is a sharp and persistent slowing of growth in Puerto Rico's total factor productivity. Constructed as a residual, this component does depend on the measure of GDP. Using adjusted GDP, we find that TFP growth dropped after 1970, turning negative in the 1990s. This pattern suggests a secular deterioration, more worrisome than the typical Latin American experience, in which the 1980s emerged as a lost decade followed by varying degrees of recovery more recently.

Thus our analysis points to two major policy priorities for raising Puerto Rican growth rates and living standards. One is to increase the proportion of the population that is employed; indeed, were Puerto Ricans employed at the same rates as on the mainland, per capita incomes would increase by 50 percent. Presumably, this will require a combination of labor supply initiatives that increase incentives for work (for example, conversion of transfer programs to the equivalent of earned income tax credits) and labor demand responses that promote private sector job growth. The second priority is to raise labor productivity. Here, our analysis has identified capital deepening as a central issue, highlighting a need to raise private investment.

Finally, U.S. tax policy has done a tremendous disservice to Puerto Rico, encouraging U.S. corporations to convert the island into a major tax haven. One might have expected that free access to an undercapitalized nearby region, with a relatively well-educated labor force and strong, stable domestic institutions, would have provided fertile ground for large U.S. corporations to invest in a range of productive activities, thereby expanding employment opportunities and increasing linkages to local business.[52] This could have helped to address both of the central concerns just noted. Instead, tax incentives, particularly those related to section 936, have led to investments with little or no employment or local linkages. This experience suggests the potential benefits of exploring approaches that expand these linkages, ensuring that more of the gains are shared.

APPENDIX 2A

The Cost of Living and Purchasing Power Parity Adjustments

At various times, commentators have raised questions about the cost of living in Puerto Rico, suggesting that it may be inappropriate to compare the dollar magnitude of incomes in Puerto Rico with those on the mainland without making some adjustment for differences in living cost. Although Puerto Rico uses the dollar in all transactions, it is possible that its average cost of goods and services is higher or lower than on the mainland. Factors that might contribute to a living cost differential are the considerable geographic distance from the United States and the requirement to use high-cost American shipping, in keeping with the mandates of the Jones Act.

The issue has received considerable official interest because of lawsuits between the United States government and its employees in offshore areas. The United States pays cost-of-living adjustments to workers in several nonforeign areas, including Puerto Rico. As part of that program, the Office of Personnel Management conducts periodic surveys of the cost of a wide range of items in these areas. The structure of those surveys has been refined after review by a technical team of outside economists with expertise in price measurement issues.[53]

Most of the conflict between the government and its employees involves nonprice issues, such as private schooling and the transportation costs of home visits for employees who are not going to be permanent residents. However, the surveys do provide a useful data set for evaluating cost-of-living differences. Recent survey results are reported in table 2A-1. The base comparison is to living costs in the Washington, D.C., area. The 2002 survey uses a revised methodology that is the result of a detailed review by a technical advisory committee. In addition, as part of a court settlement, the base survey is increased by

52. Hanson (2001).

53. See U.S. Office of Personnel Management, "Special Research Relating to the Nonforeign Area Cost-of-Living Allowance (COLA) Program," July 2000 (www.opm.gov/oca/cola/html/Rsrch&ap.pdf).

Table 2A-1. *Cost of Living, Puerto Rico, 1996–1998 and 2002*
Index (Washington, D.C. = 100)

Item	1996	1997	1998	Average, 1996–98	2002
Goods and services	100.8	106.5	109.3	105.5	
Food at home	102.2	104.9	116.4	107.8	101.8
Clothing	90.5	103.9	104.2	99.5	112.8
Housing (own)	65.0	73.0	78.2	72.1	80.4
Housing (rent)	112.8	117.1	99.0	109.6	
Transportation	129.5	124.4	130.9	128.3	107.5
Miscellaneous	93.2	97.0	96.1	95.4	
Total cost index	102.0	105.4	105.9	104.5	103.6

Source: U.S. Office of Personnel Management (2000b, 2004).

7 percentage points for immeasurable differences in the cost of living. Thus although the final index in 2002 is 103.6, the actual survey found living costs to be lower in Puerto Rico (96.6 percent) than in the Washington, D.C., area.

It is difficult to make precise comparisons of living costs between two areas because of differences in consumption patterns; but we would interpret the evidence from the surveys as suggesting that the overall costs of consumption in Puerto Rico and the District of Columbia are quite similar. The two extreme values shown in the table are a relatively low cost of homeownership in Puerto Rico and a relatively high cost of transportation. Before 2002, the government survey used a concept of housing costs last used in the U.S. consumer price index in 1982. It focused on the out-of-pocket costs of owning a house rather than the costs associated with consumption of housing services. The index value is lower for Puerto Rico than for the D.C. area because of lower home prices and real estate taxes. The 2002 survey results, on the other hand, are based on a rental equivalency approach. The high cost of transportation before 2002 reflected higher costs of air travel to continental U.S. destinations from Puerto Rico than from Washington, D.C. The 2002 survey also found that medical care costs were substantially lower in Puerto Rico. Thus these survey data do not suggest sufficiently large average living cost differences to necessitate adjusting the Puerto Rican data.

APPENDIX 2B

Puerto Rico's Underground Economy

The underground or informal economy surfaces frequently in discussions about Puerto Rico's labor market. It offers one possible explanation for the low rate of labor force participation, since individuals working in underground activities may not report their work effort and would not be captured in establishment-based employment surveys. Furthermore, a large and growing underground economy would suggest that official measures understate true production, raising an additional reason for concern about the accuracy of output statistics (albeit in the opposite direction from the section 936 distortions). This appendix summarizes our attempts to explore the importance of Puerto Rico's underground economy. Our primary interest is in activity that has not been included in the official output and employment statistics. However, it is important to note that the *underground* or *informal* economy (the terms are used interchangeably here) has been defined in many ways, including to refer to illegal activities or activity involving tax avoidance, some of which are captured in the national accounts.

Many approaches have been used to estimate the size and evolution of underground economies.[54] The most comprehensive involve detailed surveys consistent with national accounts concepts.[55] No such effort has been undertaken in Puerto Rico. Smaller surveys, even if undertaken for different objectives, can provide insights into informal activities in a selected community. However, because such studies often focus on communities in which informal activities are expected to be pervasive, they do not provide a representative picture for the overall economy. We discuss one such survey below. A second approach focuses on discrepancies between alternate data sources. Thus we refer to a measure of tax avoidance constructed by the Puerto Rican Treasury. We also consider differences in the employment patterns suggested by the series available for Puerto Rico. However, a weakness of all of such indicators is that the discrepancies may reflect many things other than underground activities, including measurement error.

Finally, a number of researchers have used one or more observable indicators to estimate trends in the underground economy. This approach relies on assumptions (typically quite strong ones) linking the indicators to underground activity. An estimate based on growth of electricity demand in Puerto Rico is one such indicator discussed below. There are major weaknesses associated with each of the available approaches. When used alone, we find each of our indicators inconclusive. However, that they paint a similar picture gives us some degree of confidence in drawing conclusions.

First, we consider findings from ethnographic research on a poor inner-city neighborhood in San Juan.[56] Although the primary objective of the work is to understand the magnitude of and reasons for the 1990 census undercount, the study also explores the role of informal work. The research provides quite detailed information, but it is not representative, as it is based on a small number of

54. Friedrich Schneider and Dominik Enste (2000) provide a recent review of the empirical literature on informal economies, including a more detailed discussion of the alternative approaches to estimating size.

55. For example, see OECD (2002).

56. Duany (1996).

households (114) and a single time period (April–June 1990). One would expect residents in this type of community to be disproportionately connected with the underground economy, owing to the community's relatively low income and education level as well as to the concentration of undocumented immigrants, mostly from the Dominican Republic. Indeed, the study concludes that many of the adults on-site do engage in off-the-books work such as cleaning houses, gardening, making repairs, and peddling food. Many of the men are self-employed in construction or repair services.

These activities are important supplements to other income. However, the reported statistics focus on primary household income sources that show more limited evidence of underground activity in the sense we are using the term. Unregistered businesses are cited as the primary source of income for only 8 percent of the households. It is unclear how much of the "temporary, occasional, and seasonal labor" category includes work done off the books. This category provided the primary income for 13 percent of households. The corresponding figures are 38 percent for regular employment, 24 percent for retirement or disability pensions, and just 5 percent for public assistance.[57]

Second, the Puerto Rican Treasury constructs an indicator based on the gap between income declared for tax purposes (Internal Revenue Service) and a comparable definition of income from national accounts data (Planning Board).[58] Although this indicator reflects output that is captured in measured GDP, it may be relevant for our purposes to the extent that tax avoidance is correlated with underground activity. As shown in figure 2B-1, Treasury calculations find that the gap was initially quite large but has shrunk steadily—to about one quarter of the income constructed from national accounts data by 1990, and 15 percent by 2001. For comparison, over the period 1959– 2002 the gap averaged about 11 percent of total income for the United States, with no long-run trends.

We look next at the available employment data. Establishment data are expected to undercount workers because the surveys exclude self-employed workers and unregistered businesses.[59] Household surveys should capture both, unless respondents lie. For this source, concerns focus on the representativeness of the sample. Census data should be the most comprehensive. However, as discussed earlier, questions have arisen about the extent of census undercount in 1990,

---

57. Eight percent of the individuals surveyed listed off-the-books employment as their primary source of income, and 1 percent listed illegal activities. The study does find both significant census error and a high rate of undercount. Only 97 of the 107 housing units enumerated by the 1990 census were counted correctly; 84 of the 97 were occupied. Furthermore, the census was found to have missed 50 units (of which 30 were occupied) and 73 (27 percent) of the individuals found residing on site.

58. Data were provided by the Puerto Rican Treasury, December 2004. They use the same methodology as that used by the U.S. Bureau of Economic Analysis; see Ledbetter (2004).

59. The establishment count of workers may be inflated by the inclusion of some holding more than one job.

Figure 2B-1. *Informal Economy as Share of Adjusted GDP, Revenue Gap Approach, 1980–2001*

Percent

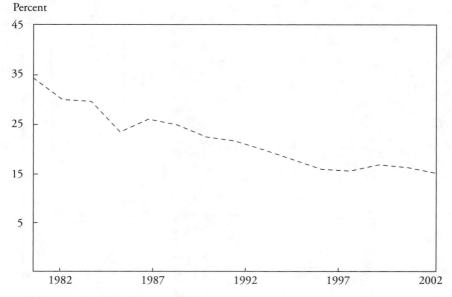

Source: Data from Puerto Rico Treasury.

and problems with the 2000 census appear to be considerably more severe.[60] We focus on the years 1970, 1980, 1990, and 2000, for which all three data sources are available. Employment is consistently greatest in the household survey data. The difference between the household and establishment survey is roughly 9 percent of workers in 1970. Over the next decade, employment grew more slowly according to household survey data than in establishment data, suggesting that informal employment (including self-employment) shrank to less than 4 percent of the total in 1980. However, this pattern has since reversed, suggesting that informal employment returned to about 9 percent in 1990 and to 10 percent in 2000.

Finally, we apply the electricity consumption approach. The simplest formulation assumes a unitary elasticity of electricity consumption with respect to the growth of the "overall" economy, defined as measured GDP plus the underground economy. Our preferred estimates use adjusted GDP, version 2, but we also construct estimates of the underground economy based on official measures of GDP. Then, given an estimated (assumed) size of the underground economy at some initial date and time series data on both electricity consumption and GDP, constructing estimates for the evolution of the underground activity is

60. Household survey data show roughly 3 percent more employment than census data in 1980 and 1990 but nearly 20 percent more in 2000.

Figure 2B-2. *Informal Economy as Share of Official and Adjusted GDP,*
Electricity Consumption Approach, Puerto Rico, 1980–2002[a]
Percent

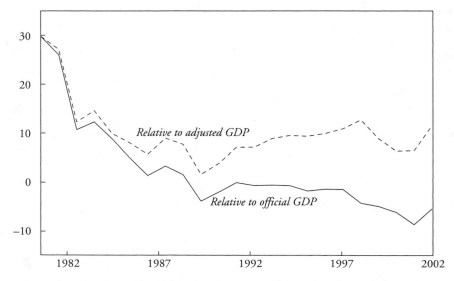

Source: Data from Puerto Rico Planning Board, *International Energy Annual,* 2003; (www.eia.doe.gov/
pub/international/iealf/table64.xls [January 2005]); authors' calculations.
   a. The informal economy was assumed to be 30 percent of GDP in 1980.

straightforward.[61] This method suggests that in the United States the underground economy represents about 10 percent of official output and finds large
and growing underground economies for many economies, including Ireland
and Mexico.

Annual data on Puerto Rican electricity consumption are available for 1980
to 2002. Strikingly, electricity consumption grew by just 0.7 percent a year during 1980–90, compared with a 3.0 percent increase for adjusted GDP, which is
already reduced from the official estimate. Comparable figures for 1990–2001
are 3.7 percent versus 3.1 percent. Thus the electricity consumption approach
implies that Puerto Rico's underground economy shrank sharply during the
1980s, recovering somewhat in the past decade. Suppose that the underground
economy had been 30 percent of adjusted GDP in 1980. As shown in figure
2B-2, our estimates suggest that it would have dwindled to less than 5 percent
of adjusted GDP by 1990, before growing to nearly 12 percent by 2002. Lower

61. Although supported by evidence from developed economies, a constant unitary elasticity is
clearly a strong assumption. This method is particularly problematic where there have been major
price changes (such as from deregulation) or technological innovations, and applications to transition economies have received considerable criticism.

guesstimates of the 1980 size of Puerto Rico's underground relative to its official economy would, of course, result in even smaller estimates of its 2002 size.

Estudios Técnicos has recently concluded a careful look at Puerto Rico's informal economy.[62] Their publication summarizes nine different studies undertaken since 1984 that use one or more of these methodologies. It also presents the results from its own two analyses. One of these uses the electricity consumption method and is similar to that discussed here. The other estimates the size of Puerto Rico's informal economy from differences between self-employment indicators on the island and those on the mainland. A larger share of Puerto Rican than U.S. workers report that they are self-employed, and this gap has grown over the past decade—largely owing, however, to declining U.S. self-employment shares. Thus it is unclear how closely the gap reflects activity in Puerto Rico's informal economy. Estudios Técnicos's work shows that, although the informal economy may have grown in nominal terms, it does not appear to have grown relative to Puerto Rico's formal economy.

Clearly, Puerto Rico has a vibrant informal sector, in which many of its residents participate. However, none of the evidence we have found points to an underground economy that either is unusually large or has grown rapidly since 1980.

APPENDIX 2C

Measurement Issues in the Macroeconomy

Our analysis of Puerto Rico's economic growth relies heavily on the island's income and product accounts. Yet questions have been raised about several issues in the measurement of nominal and real output. This appendix provides some added detail.

Intellectual Property

In the main text, we report on adjustments we made to reduce what appears to be an overstatement of value added in industries that are strongly affected by section 936. Owing to lack of data, we relied on a relatively simple adjustment to the nominal data. However, the role of pharmaceuticals in Puerto Rico actually raises a broader issue of how intellectual property and the income derived from it should be handled in a system of industry accounts. The basic problem is not that the value of pharmaceutical shipments is overstated in Puerto Rico but that no charge was made by the parent U.S. corporation for the use of its intellectual property (patent). Thus value added is overstated in Puerto Rico because purchased intermediate inputs (licensing and royalties) are understated. This distortion is reflected in the aggregate income accounts as an excessive estimate of

62. Estudios Técnicos (2004).

value added in the pharmaceutical industry and in the product accounts as an underreporting of imports. As noted in the text, a similar issue of income shifting also arises for Ireland.

At the same time, both revenues and value added in the U.S. pharmaceutical industry accounts will be underestimated. Although the costs of research and development are accurately recorded, much of the income from those activities is reported in the rest-of-world sector instead of in the domestic pharmaceuticals industry. As a result, U.S. GDP is understated by the failure to accurately record the export of intellectual property—or, alternatively, the receipt of licensing and royalty income by the parent company. Production relationships are misstated because revenues are not associated with the correct value-creating activity. (Although excluded from U.S. GDP, the income is captured in the concept of GNI, which includes the foreign income of U.S. corporations.) The absence of intellectual property revenues also distorts the balance of payments by implying an artificially high return on the foreign direct investment of U.S. firms.[63] Furthermore, it raises obvious concerns for the administration of the income tax system. This is an issue of growing importance, as intellectual property plays an expanding role in industries such as pharmaceuticals, computers, software, and business services.

The erroneous geographical attribution of the income from intellectual capital, however, is an integral feature of a U.S. tax system that tries to maintain a global reach while granting deferrals for income from foreign sources. For many corporations interested in expanding their global markets, deferral is nearly as good as an exemption. Because there is no market for most forms of intellectual property, any transfer price that is established will inevitably reflect a substantial degree of arbitrariness; and firms should be expected to attempt to transfer intellectual property income to low-tax jurisdictions.[64] Lacking other sources of information, the U.S. and Puerto Rican statistical systems rely on the corporate accounting records, which embed all the tax-induced distortions.

Price Deflators

The biases introduced into the measure of manufacturing output may be mitigated in the estimation of real output by overestimating the increase in the price of pharmaceutical products. We do not have direct estimates of the price deflator for the pharmaceutical industry or even for total manufacturing. However, we can observe that exports, which are dominated by pharmaceuticals, consistently

63. Income shifting of the return on intellectual property appears to be a major factor behind the oft-noted phenomenon that U.S. firms earn a much higher rate of return on their foreign investments than foreign firms earn in the United States.

64. The Internal Revenue Service attempts to apply several methods of valuation for intellectual property that parallel those for tangible goods; lacking a comparable price, they all have serious problems.

have the higher rate of price increase among the major expenditure categories.[65] Thus much of the growth in the nominal value of pharmaceutical exports does not translate into increases in real GDP.

Moreover, the measurement of price change is a critical and often overlooked aspect of the measurement of real output and gains in standards of living. In this regard, Puerto Rico's statistics are often criticized because the basic structure for the consumer price index dates back to 1954. Puerto Rico participates with the U.S. Department of Labor in the collection of some employment statistics and with the U.S. Census Bureau in its economic and population censuses. However, it constructs its own consumer price index. Whereas the methodology of the U.S. index has changed substantially over the years because of concerns about potential biases, the Puerto Rican index has changed little. Some of the questions about changes over time in the composition of the market basket are mitigated in the income and product accounts because items are converted to real values at relatively disaggregated levels.

The extent of the accumulated distortion in the Puerto Rican index is illustrated in figure 2C-1, which compares the index with the consumer price deflator in the expenditure accounts. After showing similar rates of increase up to the mid-1980s, the Puerto Rican consumer price index begins to report rates of price inflation far above those of the product accounts. Over the period 1993–2003, for example, the index reported an average rate of price inflation of 5 percent, nearly three times the 1.8 percent rate of increase for the expenditure price deflator.

Also surprising is the large variation in rates of price change across expenditure categories and the magnitude of difference relative to the mainland. The first two columns in table 2C-1 report average annual rates of nominal price change for components of GDP in Puerto Rico's expenditure accounts for the period 1975–2003 and for a shorter interval, 1990–2003. The last two columns report the price changes relative to those for the same expenditure categories in the U.S. national accounts. Thus if prices rose at the same rate in Puerto Rico and the United States, the relative rate of price change would be zero.[66]

As shown at the top of the table, overall prices have consistently increased more rapidly in Puerto Rico than on the mainland, but much of the divergence is the result of differences in the composition of gross product. We have already mentioned the rapid rate of price increase for Puerto Rican exports, but that is partially offset by large increases in import prices. Capital goods prices rise more

65. In 2001 pharmaceuticals accounted for two-thirds of merchandise exports. The behavior of the export price is particularly puzzling given that the U.S. import price index for pharmaceuticals rose at an annual rate of 0.7 percent over the period 1990–2003 compared with the Puerto Rico average of 4.2 percent.

66. It is important to note that the United States uses chained price indexes rather than the Laspeyres indexes (with a base of 1954) of the Puerto Rican accounts, and that may explain some of the difference. However, without large changes in relative prices, we would expect the overall bias to be relatively small.

Figure 2C-1. *Consumer Price Index and Personal Consumption Deflator, Puerto Rico, 1954–2003*

Index (1954 = 100)

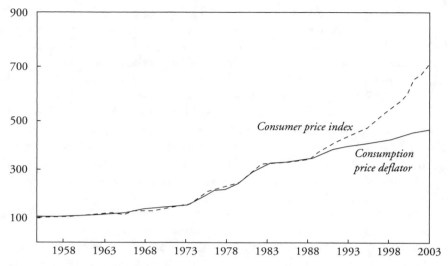

Source: Income and product accounts of Puerto Rico; Puerto Rico Planning Board.

rapidly in Puerto Rico, but that could be the result of a different treatment for the prices of high-technology products and Puerto Rico's exclusion of computer software from the capital goods category. If capital equipment is imported, a different price index would have no implications for GDP. It is more difficult to understand the low rate of price increase for government consumption before 1990, since it is dominated by employment costs, and the standard assumption is that the productivity of government workers is held constant. After 1990, the rate of price increase matches that of the mainland, which is consistent with an assumption that government workers received matching wage increases.

The largest puzzles are in the area of personal consumption expenditures, as shown in the lower part of the table. What accounts for the explosive rate of food price increase over the 1990–2003 period? How could apparel prices in Puerto Rico rise at an annual rate 1 percent below that of the mainland for twenty-eight years? Some categories match closely (housing and transportation), and the differences in home operation may reflect the differing role of energy costs. Although they seem very large, many of these differences are offset by other factors. If we were to apply the mainland price indexes to the twelve components of personal consumption, the annual rate of growth in real consumption expenditures would be reduced by 0.4 percent over the 1975–2003 period, and it would be raised by 0.1 percent in the 1990–2003 interval. Still, the magni-

Table 2C-1. *Annual Change in Price Index, Puerto Rico, 1975–2003*
Percent

Category	Nominal prices		Relative to the United States	
	1975–2003	1990–2003	1975–2003	1990–2003
Gross product	4.4	3.8	0.6	1.7
Gross domestic product	4.1	3.2	0.4	1.2
Personal consumption expenditures	3.1	1.8	−0.8	−0.3
Government consumption expenditures	2.6	3.0	−1.8	0.0
Gross domestic investment	3.5	1.8	0.8	0.8
Exports	4.9	4.2	3.0	4.1
Imports	3.5	2.6	1.3	2.9
Personal consumption expenditures	3.1	1.8	−0.8	−0.3
Food, alcohol, and tobacco	4.8	5.8	0.8	3.2
Clothing and accessories	0.1	−2.3	−1.0	−1.5
Personal care	2.7	2.1	−1.0	0.4
Housing	4.7	3.1	−0.2	0.1
Household operation	1.9	0.1	−1.2	−0.9
Medical services	5.1	3.7	−0.7	0.2
Personal business	2.9	1.0	−1.6	−1.5
Transportation	3.6	2.2	−0.1	0.3
Recreation	2.1	0.1	0.6	0.8
Education	4.1	3.1	−1.4	−1.2
Religious and welfare activities	4.4	5.0	0.0	1.8
Foreign travel and other	5.5	4.8	n.a.	n.a.

Source: Data from income and product accounts of Puerto Rico and the United States; authors' calculations.

tude of difference in the price indexes is far in excess of that observed in the consumer price indexes for U.S. cities and regions. In those comparisons, the regional indexes tend to fluctuate about the U.S. average rather than showing the sustained divergence of the Puerto Rican indexes. The differences are even more pronounced for other major components of GDP, but the large dissimilarities in composition make the exercise less useful.

The statistical resources of Puerto Rico are certainly far beyond those of a comparable U.S. state or region, and the data make it possible to analyze the island's economic performance at a level of detail that is not possible for any subjurisdiction of the United States. However, it also appears that there are growing problems with both the income and product accounts and the price statistics. There is a need to expand the coordination of the activities of U.S. and Puerto Rican statistical bureaus to address these issues.

APPENDIX 2D

Growth Accounts

In our discussion of the impact of section 936 of the U.S. tax code, we use growth accounting to examine Puerto Rico's growth experience over the period 1950 to 2003. As explained in earlier work, we use this methodology to construct consistent accounts for a sample of eighty-four countries during the period 1960–2000.[67] Drawing from this previous work enables us to put Puerto Rico's experience in context and to compare its growth with the experiences of a variety of other countries. Readers are referred to the earlier paper for additional details about the methodology and its usage.

Growth accounting is a useful framework for studying an individual country or a group of countries. This supply-side approach provides a means of decomposing observed output growth into the contributions from changes in factor inputs and a residual, total factor productivity, which measures a combination of changes in the efficiency with which those factors are used and changes in technology.[68]

Although growth accounts provide an informative benchmark, their limitations must be borne in mind.[69] First, growth accounting shows only the *proximate* sources of growth; it is not intended to determine the *underlying* causes of growth. Consider a country with rapid increases in both accumulation of capital per worker and factor productivity. The decomposition provides no information about whether the productivity growth caused the capital accumulation (for example, by increasing the expected returns to investment) or the capital accumulation made additional innovations possible—or some combination.

Second, we stress that total factor productivity is measured as a residual. This residual will reflect, in addition to changes in economic efficiency, a range of other determinants of growth not accounted for by the measured increases in factor inputs. Thus changes in total factor productivity should not be taken as a proxy for technological innovation.[70] Finally, some express concern that the decomposition is sensitive to measurement of inputs and outputs and to the underlying assumptions about the production process. Thus we pay considerable attention to measurement issues in constructing the data set.

67. See Bosworth and Collins (2003). Country coverage was determined by data availability, and the main exclusions are the transition economies and countries with populations of fewer than 1 million. The eighty-four included countries represented 95 percent of global GDP.

68. Growth accounting has been used in a wide variety of contexts. For example, growth accounts (often based on industry-level decompositions) are central to the ongoing debate over recent productivity growth in the United States and Europe and also to the role of computers and other information technology goods.

69. These limitations are noted briefly here and discussed further in Bosworth and Collins (2003).

70. See Hulten (2001) for a detailed discussion of growth accounting and the total factor productivity residual.

A country's output in any given year depends on its factor inputs—labor and (human and physical) capital—and on the efficiency with which factors are used in production Thus the key pieces to the procedure are a growth accounting equation for constructing the decomposition, parameter assumptions, and data on output and factor inputs.

Define Y as gross domestic product (GDP), K as the physical capital stock, and A as the level of technology. L is labor inputs (measured as "bodies of employed workers"), which we assume is "augmented" by H, an index of the average level of labor quality. We also assume that a country's output can be expressed as a function of these inputs, using the specific functional form in the following equation:[71]

$$Y = AK^{\alpha}(HL)^{(1-\alpha)}.$$

We report our results in a form that decomposes growth in output per worker into the contributions from the growth of physical capita per worker, the growth of education per worker, and the growth in total factor productivity, as shown below. (Lower-case letters denote a variable's average annual growth rate.)

$$y/1 = \alpha(k/1) + (1-\alpha)h + a.$$

Given an estimate for α and measures of Y, L, K, and H, it is straightforward to solve for A (or a) and construct the decomposition. As for our eighty-four-country study, this decomposition assumes a capital share, $\alpha = 0.35$. An analysis that used the actual income shares in each period would allow for the consideration of a much wider range of underlying production functions. However, few countries are able to allocate the incomes of the self-employed between capital and labor, and in the case of Puerto Rico there are additional problems with the recorded capital incomes, as discussed in the main text.[72]

The main data series for Puerto Rico were obtained from the Puerto Rico Planning Board. Again, Y is real GDP, and L is employment. The capital stock measure is constructed from investment data using the perpetual inventory method, with a depreciation rate of 0.05. Finally, to construct H, we assume that human capital is directly related to average years of schooling (S) and that there is a 7 percent return to each additional year of schooling:

$$H = (1.07)^{s}$$

Average years of schooling for those aged sixteen and older in Puerto Rico were obtained from the decennial census and interpolated to create an annual series.

71. This equation assumes constant returns to scale.
72. See Bosworth and Collins (2003) for further discussion and references in the cross-country context.

William J. Baumol

There can be no question about the quality of the study by Barry Bosworth and Susan Collins. It is an exemplary survey of the current state of economic affairs in Puerto Rico. I can find little or nothing to criticize or claim to correct. But I can attempt to add some comments on the issue that they have, quite legitimately, chosen not to address. Whereas Bosworth and Collins focus on the island's more immediate problems, I direct my attention here to what I consider even more urgent, the steps that must be taken today to ensure a prosperous island in the more distant future.

During the quarter century immediately following World War II, Puerto Rico had an enviable growth record. Few recognize that it was then among the world's growth leaders—alongside better-publicized cases such as Taiwan and Korea. Moreover, there is evidence that much of this achievement was the product of effort by Puerto Ricans themselves, through Operation Bootstrap in the 1950s. Support from the United States helped, but it was responsible for only a limited portion of the expansion of the economy's output and the striking improvement in its living standards that put Puerto Rico well ahead of the rest of Latin America and the Caribbean. More recently, however, growth in per capita output has slowed almost everywhere, and Puerto Rico's has slowed more than most. Puerto Rico's per capita GNP in 1970 was 46 percent of U.S. levels. By 2000 the ratio had fallen to 33 percent, whereas Singapore and Ireland had reached 80 and 76 percent, respectively. For all its warts and blemishes, clearly pointed out by Bosworth and Collins, the demise of section 936 and its incentive for U.S. industry to locate in the island gives good reason for concern about the future.

The short run presents dangers of its own, but so far the construction boom, with 8 percent annual growth from 1993 to 2004, has helped to maintain the vigor of the economy. Other steps can be taken to stimulate productivity and growth in the near future—strong measures to stimulate tourism and fiscal inducements for manufacturing activity are the usual suspects—and for a while they may have the desired effects.

However, I argue that over the longer term these activities are the way to disaster. The route toward prosperity in the future is not through hotels and restaurants, activities that thrive on a low-wage labor force. Nor is manufactur-

This paper would not have been possible without the very valuable comments, additions, and data provided by Heidie Calero, the president of the consulting firm H. Calero Consulting Group Inc. in Puerto Rico. Most of the historical data are taken from this firm's excellent publication, *Puerto Rico Economic Pulse*. My special thanks go to her for her support and enthusiasm in sharing her vision of the future Puerto Rico with the readers of this article and with me.

ing the answer: because of rapidly rising manufacturing productivity, throughout the industrial world, manufacturing accounts for an ever smaller share of every economy's employment. Puerto Rico is no exception, with manufacturing jobs representing only 11 percent of total employment in fiscal year 2004. Rather, the future, which in some places is already here, is to be found in the products of brain power—research, new knowledge, innovation, and their dissemination. This is a promising path for Puerto Rico for at least three reasons: first, because it is where successful economies are increasingly finding their payoffs; second, because the products of knowledge have low transportation costs—a major advantage for an island economy at some remove from prospective customer economies; third, because Puerto Rico, virtually alone among the islands of the Caribbean, already has a head start in this direction—far more than is generally recognized—though there is still a long way to go. It is no surprise that the governor of Puerto Rico has recently announced Operation Brainpower as the new strategy for economic development.

The Puerto Rican Income Achievement

The central background fact for this analysis is the relatively high level of income that Puerto Rico has already achieved, with a per capita personal income of $12,031 in fiscal year 2004. Although it is still well behind the U.S. mainland, the island is far ahead of many others. Puerto Rican income is one of the highest in Latin America. This is also true of the commonwealth's performance relative to those of the Caribbean island economies, many of which have per capita incomes averaging only about one-fourth of Puerto Rico's. The exceptions are Barbados and Trinidad and Tobago, which were only slightly below Puerto Rico, and the Bahamas, the only nearby place with a per capita income higher than Puerto Rico's.

High incomes and high wages, of course, are the main objectives of growth policy, and the last thing the island should wish for is a retreat from this achievement. Yet there is the other side of the matter: high wages are a serious impediment to an economy's competitiveness unless that economy can provide sufficiently offsetting benefits to customers. And that is the central point of this comment.

The Tourism Trap

Without question, tourism is a valuable economic activity. Puerto Rico, with its gorgeous landscapes, beautiful beaches, and superb climate, cannot avoid attracting tourists; this activity will surely contribute jobs and add to GDP and may do so for decades to come. But tourism's jobs are predominantly unskilled. Chambermaids, dishwashers, waiters, and bellhops, the mainstay of tourism, require little special education or special skills. Puerto Rico shares the seas with other islands, which also have beautiful beaches, where wages are far lower. Room rates in Santo Domingo, for example, are a fraction of those in Puerto Rico, in hotels of comparable elegance and amenities. Puerto Rico can compete by means of its cultural facilities, ranging from museums to theaters in different parts of the island, the relative absence of the ugliness of extreme poverty, and a number of other advantages. Ultimately, however, to compete with less affluent islands it will have to offer vacationers prices in the same range as those available in other attractive tropical locations.

The bottom line is that while tourism can help Puerto Rico's economy and offers other advantages, reliance on it as a mainstay of the economy will produce results the opposite of those at which the island is, and should be, aiming. If tourism becomes a primary source of GDP (in fiscal year 2004 it accounted for close to 6 percent), what will follow is market pressure for reduction, not increase, in wages. This, surely, is not the long-term direction for the achievement of prosperity.

Manufacturing

Manufacturing has already brought great benefits to the island's economy. It accounted for 43 percent of GDP in fiscal year 2004. The clothing and pharmaceutical and scientific instrument producers who were attracted by section 936 and associated rules have surely contributed employment opportunities and higher wages. That is good reason for current fears that, in the absence of these incentives, such industry will leave the island or that no new manufacturing will locate there. These dangers are a particular threat to experienced, skilled workers for whom few comparable opportunities exist outside this sector. Pharmaceuticals have continued to grow and invest in Puerto Rico because they have found comparable tax benefits to operate as controlled foreign corporations under the U.S. tax code. More growth in this and other manufacturing segments would surely be desirable.

The problem is that manufacturing employment is not growing in the industrial world. Rather, it is shrinking almost everywhere. Why are manufacturing jobs evaporating? The answer is that innovation has led to a revolution in manufacturing productivity. Fewer and fewer labor hours are required to produce a car, a computer, or a watch. Just as U.S. agricultural employment fell from more than 90 percent of the labor force two centuries ago to less than 3 percent today—despite rising farm outputs—manufacturing is already a declining source of jobs and will almost certainly continue to be so in the future. It is a source of hope and possible strength for Puerto Rico in the short term. In the long term, the island will have to look elsewhere.

Knowledge Industries and Longer-Term Prosperity

In the United States, the future that Puerto Rico may want to seek is already well on its way. Estimates are that more than 60 percent of the U.S. labor force is employed in information activities. Computing, engineering research, teaching, and a host of other such activities are the backbone of its prosperity. Silicon Valley is a much envied prototype, and the United Kingdom, Germany, Japan, and others are attempting to follow its example. According to the *Economist,* as of 1999 only Israel was close to succeeding, though Ireland is obviously also doing well in this direction.[1] This fourth industrial revolution sells one type of output— the product of brain power. If the products are good enough, they make it possible for an economy to have high wages and yet remain fully competitive.

But what does all this have to do with Puerto Rico? The answer is that in some respects the island already has a running start. Notably, according to World Bank data, it is ahead of every economy except the United States in terms of the share of the college-age population that is attending institutions of higher education. A higher percentage of its young people attend college than in Germany, France, the United Kingdom, Canada, or any other leading economy. This by itself, however, is not enough. Standards of research and teaching will have to be upgraded to match those of the world's education leaders. The faculties, too, will need further training and rewards that provide incentives for research and the acquisition of research skills. One or two decades may be required to carry out this task effectively. It will not be easy, it will not be cheap, and it will not be quick. It will not be enough to throw money at the problem. Careful planning will be required to design a program demonstrably capable of reaching the goal. Its accomplishment will require acceptance of powerful and demanding incentives that, at least at first, probably will not be politically popular. And the required planning must begin now if the capacity to attain a place at the forefront of world information activity is to be reached in Puerto Rico before the malaise evident in manufacturing becomes too great a handicap and prevents provision of the resources necessary for the island to compete effectively in this latest industrial revolution.

What Is Now Lacking in the Island?

Although the government of Puerto Rico has granted tax incentives for research and development, these are not enough. Some pharmaceutical companies have begun to conduct clinical trials, but this activity is still in its infancy. Both faculty and students at university levels lack incentives to conduct research. Far from the

1. "Silicon Envy" (1999).

arrangements in U.S. universities, research funds in the island's educational institutions are scarce, and salary incentives for faculty members with special research accomplishments are lacking, as are student performance incentives. For the technological corridors in the island to take off, it will be necessary to reinforce the quality of education at all levels, beginning with better teaching of English and other languages as well as science and math. High standards of performance will have to be enforced unflinchingly, and the requisite facilities provided.

Infrastructure and its services also urgently require improvement. Water, electricity, telecommunications, roads, ports, all are characterized by poor performance on the part of local government. Another urgent problem is the island's love affair with consumption: Puerto Ricans spent 98 percent of their disposable income in 2004 on durables, nondurables, and services. Poor saving and investment performance hampers future growth.

But the greatest challenge the island faces now and in the near term is vision. Where does the island want to be in twenty years? That decision will determine the necessary strategies. Puerto Rico is currently bogged down in internal politics arising from unceasing conflict between the two main political parties. The 2004 election gave control of the executive branch to one party and the legislative branch to the other. The result has been gridlock, with planning for the long-run future one of the main victims. These governmental problems have not been overlooked outside the island. In May 2005, Moody's credit rating agencies downgraded Puerto Rico's central government bonds from Baa1– to Baa2–, and Standard and Poor's lowered its from A– to BBB–. Although these securities are still of investment grade, in the coming months these agencies will once again evaluate the liquidity of the central government to determine whether yet another credit downgrade is in order for Puerto Rico.

This is not an unprecedented problem. Puerto Rico faced a similar situation in 1975, and tough decisions based on a vision for the future were adopted to correct the mess. The island is once again in the middle of a severe fiscal problem, with public debt taking center stage. Solutions to this immediate problem range from a much needed tax reform to curtailment of government expenditures by its various agencies. Education, health, and safety are, fortunately, three areas not slated for reductions. These arenas, together with vital physical infrastructure, require substantial reinforcement if Puerto Rico is to compete successfully worldwide.

Puerto Rico has recognized the importance of the digital revolution. Its public school system has tried to catch up, seeking to provide every child with access to a computer and all that goes with it. But computers are just instruments. Trained teachers are needed to revamp the educational system, and incentives for quality of performance by both teachers and students, currently lacking, must be introduced.

To deal with these matters, elected officials will need to demonstrate the courage to prepare adequately for the more distant economic future. No doubt, over the next decades the island will have to make tough decisions to ensure its continuing prosperity and competitiveness.

COMMENT
José J. Villamil

Barry Bosworth and Susan Collins's chapter is a good macroeconomic overview of Puerto Rico's recent economic history. By quantifying what many local economists have perceived to be the shortcoming of the "tax-driven model," it makes a major contribution toward an understanding of the Puerto Rican experience.

It is probably difficult to understand, in 2005, that in many ways the original attributes of the island's development process were not quite what they subsequently have been made out to be. In many ways, Puerto Rico benefited from a post–World War II context in which the United States was the dominating economy to a much greater extent than now, in which an ideological battle between the capitalist West and the socialist East was a central concern, and in which the modernization paradigm prevailed. Puerto Rico presented a unique example of the success that could be achieved by following the precepts of the West's view of development.

That Puerto Rico was a democracy strengthened its role as a model for the developing world. After the Cuban Revolution, this role became even more important. In many ways, then, Puerto Rico's main export was as a development ideology. This explains the substantial literature presenting the Puerto Rican experience in almost mythical terms and studies by well-known economists such as Werner Baer, Kenneth Boulding, Richard Meier, and W. Arthur Lewis. The *Annals of the American Academy of Political and Social Science* devoted its January 1953 issue, titled "Puerto Rico: A Study in Democratic Development," to a celebration of the Puerto Rican experience from a number of different perspectives.

Puerto Rico's second major export in the first two decades after World War II was its people—another theme that has been analyzed extensively. In effect, one can speak of emigration as a development policy. For years the fiction that migration was a spontaneous process persisted, but it is now abundantly clear that it was, in fact, a well delineated policy. Its contribution to the initial success of Puerto Rico's economic development efforts cannot be underestimated.

Although the Bosworth and Collins chapter deals primarily with more recent experience, and particularly with the impacts of section 936 as a distorting influence on the measurement of economic progress, it is useful to place the initial thrust of the development process in a historical context. Much of what transpired in the 1970s was a result of the experiences in the initial quarter century after World War II. The perception of success, the playing down of out-migration, and the misconception concerning the island's possibilities led Puerto Rico inexorably to the adoption of an even more intensively tax-driven approach. When, in the early and middle 1970s, the island faced its first major economic crisis as a result of a serious financial crunch and the oil embargo situation, the response was section 936. Puerto Rico believed in the myth that had been created concerning its success and became its captive.

Where perhaps the Bosworth and Collins chapter makes its major contribution is in its analyses of the overstatement of Puerto Rico's growth and its careful dissection of the impacts of section 936. It is now more apparent than ever that, rather than being a beacon of development for the rest of the world, Puerto Rico's experience reflects the failure of the export platform, tax-driven approach. As it turns out, the island is not significantly ahead of countries such as Chile, Argentina, and Mexico in terms of purchasing power parity, according to data presented in the chapter. Given the recent growth rates in these countries, we may see them surpass Puerto Rico in the near future.

Although some in Puerto Rico may take offense at its conclusions, the chapter is a welcome addition to the literature and a powerful stimulus to what is obvious: a major restructuring of Puerto Rico's economic policies is required. In view of these conclusions, the endogenous growth model becomes an attractive alternative.

The authors suggest the need to deal with the appropriate theoretical framework for analyzing the Puerto Rican economy. Economists, both local and foreign, have consistently dealt with the island as if it were a national economy. Conceptually, a wrong set of constructs and measurements are being applied, ones suitable for a national economy but not necessarily for a regional or subnational economy. This has happened for two reasons: First, the island does have national accounts, which makes it unique in comparison with other regions in the United States (although not in comparison with countries such as Spain, in which the autonomous regions produce GDP estimates and have balance-of-payments accounts). Second, most economists are trained in the tools that characterize national economic analysis. There are, in fact, fairly few regional economists. This leads to wrong policy prescriptions and approaches and also to wrong analysis.

Although in the past I have been guilty of benchmarking Puerto Rico with Singapore and Ireland, it would probably be more useful to compare the island with other regions: not Mexico, but the frontier states; not Ireland, but possibly Northern Ireland. There are, of course, important lessons to be learned from these two countries, as well as others, such as Finland and Denmark. I do not mean to imply otherwise, but I do feel that we need to improve the conceptual framework within which to study Puerto Rico.

The chapter presents three recommendations: increase the proportion of the population that is employed, increase labor productivity, and expand internal linkages. I have no quarrel with their desirability. In fact, I have been insistent on the need to focus on productivity, rather than job creation, for many years. Politicians, however, see things differently. As far back as 1992, the Puerto Rico Planning Board published a report that called for increasing internal linkages as the most effective way of stimulating growth, but movement in this direction has been almost nonexistent.

If we look at the present context it is clear that no significant movement can take place in these three directions without a major institutional transformation in the island. Puerto Rico has an obsolete institutional framework in terms of legislation, government regulations, and, of course, government organization and procedures. Many of the agencies dealing with economic policy were created in the 1940s and the 1950s and are still characterized by a culture firmly anchored in the model that Bosworth and Collins have so effectively sent back to the drawing board. Examples of the obsolescence of the institutional framework must include the Puerto Rico Industrial Development Company (at long last undergoing a much needed major restructuring), the Puerto Rico Planning Board (which is essentially the same entity it was fifty years ago), the Telecommunications Regulatory Board (which, curiously, does not include in its scope wireless communications), and a large number of laws and regulations designed for an economy that is being quickly superseded by a very different one.

A quick look at the composition of personal income in Puerto Rico suggests that there is something structurally wrong. According to a 2004 estimate, mentioned in the Bosworth-Collins chapter, the unreported economy represents around 23.3 percent of the reported economy, excluding income derived from the drug trade, which probably adds another 10 percentage points to the figure, using conservative estimates of the drug economy. Contrary to Bosworth and Collins's assertion that the informal economy has not grown, the increasing importance of the drug economy would lead to a different conclusion, but this is not a central issue in the chapter. Another 22 percent of personal income has its source in federal transfers to individuals, and the government payroll (including municipalities) constitutes another 18 percent. These sources can be categorized as nonproductive, and income derived from them goes directly to consumption. This explains in part the high consumption levels in comparison with reported income.

The welfare of these three groups—those who receive their personal income from the underground economy, from government transfers, and from the government payroll—depends not at all on improvements in productivity. This fact mitigates pressure to deal with the issue and, in fact, possibly generates obstacles to measures aimed at improving productivity (for example, reducing government employment). The high levels of consumption do not depend on the capacity to generate income from improving productivity in economic activities but rather on federal social policies, collective bargaining in the government sector, and, of course, trends in the drug trade.

This particular structure of the Puerto Rican economy probably explains the low labor force participation rate that is one of the concerns mentioned in the chapter. I, however, have some doubt as to whether the low rate is a cause rather than an effect of Puerto Rico's low growth rates and structural dependency on both the informal economy and federal government transfers.

The Bosworth and Collins chapter illustrates the need for a new synthesis in understanding development processes, one that integrates the macroeconomic approach, which characterizes the Bosworth-Collins paper, with a renewed emphasis on institutional economics. Although a reading of recent economic development literature suggests that there is movement in this direction, much remains to be done. Douglass North, Ronald Coase, and Oliver Williamson, among others, have laid the groundwork for this much-needed synthesis.

Any economic development process requires the presence of three groups of what, for lack of a better word, I would call "instruments": institutions, technology, and resources. How these are organized and to what purposes they are put essentially determine how development takes place. In the present global context, flexibility, innovation capacity, productivity, and pluralism are also requirements for development. Transformation must aim at ensuring that each of the three groups of instruments is used to achieve these four conditions.

In the case of Puerto Rico, over the last few decades the contrary has taken place. The policymaking process, because of the way it operates and its inclusion within the U.S. system, has generated a socioeconomic system that is inflexible, has lost its capacity to innovate, has forgone productivity as a policy objective (and thereby remains consumption driven), and has failed to provide for a satisfactory social system, allowing social inequality, high crime rates, and little socioeconomic mobility.

This implies that Puerto Rico's institutional framework must be addressed with a sense of urgency. Policymakers need to seriously rethink many of the commonwealth's laws, the structure of its government, its economic culture, and many of its characteristic processes and structures.

Bosworth and Collins's chapter conclusion that Puerto Rico's GNP has been significantly overstated and that growth has been overestimated by 0.7 percent a year since 1975 is enough to warrant a serious analysis of the future of the island's economy. Federal transfers, the underground economy, and a huge government establishment have created buffers that prevent a collapse. This fact, combined with the distortions caused by section 936, have lulled the commonwealth into complacency and, what's worse, smugness. Unless major transformations occur, beyond those Bosworth and Collins recommend, Puerto Rico's economy is headed for serious problems.

References

Alameda Lozada, José I., and Alfredo Gonzalez Martínez. 2001. "Cambio tecnológico, productividad, a crecimiento económico en Puerto Rico." *Ensayos and Monografías* 106. Unidad de Investigaciones Económicas (April). Mimeo.

Baumol, William, and Edward N. Wolff. 1996. "Catching Up in the Postwar Period: Puerto Rico as the Fifth Tiger." *World Development* 24, no. 5: 869–85.

Bils, Mark, and Peter J. Klenow. 2000. "Does Schooling Cause Growth?" *American Economic Review* 90, no. 5: 1160–83.

Blanchard, Olivier. 2002. "Comment on Honohan and Walsh, 'Catching Up with the Leaders: The Irish Hare.' " *Brookings Papers on Economic Activity,* no. 1: 55–66.

Bosworth, Barry. 2002. "Comment on Honohan and Walsh, 'Catching Up With the Leaders: The Irish Hare,' " *Brookings Papers on Economic Activity,* no. 1: 66–72.

Bosworth, Barry, and Susan M. Collins. 2003. "The Empirics of Growth: An Update." *Brookings Papers on Economic Activity,* no. 2: 113–79.

Burnham, James B. 2003. "Why Ireland Boomed." *Independent Review* 7, no. 4: 537–56.

Calderón, César, and Luis Servén. 2004. "The Effects of Infrastructure Development on Growth and Income Distribution." World Bank. Mimeo.

Castillo-Freeman, Alida, and Richard Freeman. 1992. "When the Minimum Wage Really Bites: The Effect of the U.S.-Level Minimum on Puerto Rico." In *Immigration and the Work Force,* edited by George Borjas and Richard Freeman, pp. 177–212. University of Chicago Press.

Contos, George, and Ellen Legel. 2000. "Corporation Income Tax Returns, 1997." *Statistics of Income Bulletin* (Summer): 101–21 (www.irs.gov/taxstats/article/0,,id=96388,00.html [August 2004]).

Dietz, James. 1986. *Economic History of Puerto Rico: Institutional Change and Capitalist Development.* Princeton University Press.

———. 2002. "Puerto Rico: The Three-Legged Economy." *Integration and Trade* 5, no. 15: 247–73.

———. 2003. *Puerto Rico: Negotiating Development and Change.* Boulder: Lynne Rienner.

Duany, Jorge. 1996. "Counting the Uncountable: Undocumented Immigrants and Informal Workers in Puerto Rico." *Latino Studies Journal* 7, no. 2: 69–107.

Estudios Técnicos. 2003. "The Study of Economic Development in Puerto Rico: Summaries of Major Contributions." Mimeo.

———. 2004. *La economía informal en Puerto Rico: Primero, segundo, y tercer informe.* Report prepared by Estudios Técnicos for the Department of Labor and Human Resources. San Juan (October).

Grubert, Harry, and Joel Slemrod. 1998. "The Effect of Taxes on Investment and Income Shifting to Puerto Rico." *Review of Economics and Statistics* 80, no. 3: 365–73.

Hanson, Gordon. 2001. "Should Countries Promote Foreign Direct Investment?" G-24 Discussion Paper 9. United Nations Conference on Trade and Development, and Center for International Development, Harvard University (February).

Hausmann, Ricardo, Lant Pritchett, and Dani Rodrik. 2004. "Growth Accelerations." Harvard University (October). Mimeo.

Honohan, Patrick, and Brendan Walsh. 2002. "Catching Up with the Leaders: The Irish Hare." *Brookings Papers on Economic Activity* no. 1: 1–57.

Hulten, Charles R. 2001. "Total Factor Productivity: A Short Biography." In *New Developments in Productivity Analysis: Studies in Income and Wealth,* edited by Charles Hulten, Edward R. Dean, and Michael Harper, 63:1–54. University of Chicago Press.

Krueger, Alan. 1995. "The Effect of the Minimum Wage When It Really Bites: A Reexamination of the Evidence from Puerto Rico." *Research in Labor Economics,* edited by Solomon W. Polachek, 14:1–22. Greenwich, Conn.: JAI Press.

Ledbetter, Mark. 2004. "Comparison of BEA Estimates of Personal Income and IRS Estimates of Adjusted Gross Income." *Survey of Current Business* 84, no. 11: 9–14.

Marxuach, Sergio M. 2005. "Restructuring the Puerto Rico Electricity Sector." White Paper 3. San Juan: Center for the New Economy (August 11).

National Competitiveness Council of Ireland. 2004. *Annual Competitiveness Report, 2004,* October (www.forfas.ie/ncc/reports/ncc_annual_04/).

Nutter, Sarah E. 2003. "U.S. Possessions Corporation Returns, 1997 and 1999." *Statistics of Income Bulletin* (Summer): 155–76 (www.irs.gov/pub/irs-soi/99posart.pdf [August 2004]).

Organization for Economic Cooperation and Development (OECD). 2002. *Measuring the Non-Observed Economy: A Handbook.* Paris.

Padín, José A. 2003. "Puerto Rico in the Post War: Liberalized Development Banking and the Fall of the 'Fifth Tiger.'" *World Development* 31, no. 2: 281–301.

Pantojas-García, Emilio. 1990. *Development Strategies as Ideology: Puerto Rico's Export-Led Industrialization Experience.* Boulder: Lynne Rienner.

———. 1999. "Los estudios económicos sobre Puerto Rico: Una evaluación critica." In *El futuro económico de Puerto Rico,* edited by Francisco Martinez, pp. 11–26. San Juan: Editorial de la Universidad de Puerto Rico.

Pelzman, Joseph. 2002. "Imported Capital Dependency as an Economic Development Strategy: The Failure of Distortionary Tax Policies in Puerto Rico." Discussion Paper 03-01. Center for Economic Research. George Washington University, Department of Economics.

Psacharopoulos, George. 1994. "Returns to Investment in Education: A Global Update." *World Development* 22, no. 9: 1325–43.

Puerto Rico Planning Board. 1996. *Income and Product (Ingreso y producto).* San Juan: Commonwealth of Puerto Rico, Office of the Governor.

———. 2003. *Income and Product (Ingreso y producto).* San Juan: Commonwealth of Puerto Rico, Office of the Governor.

———. 1950–2004. *Comprehensive Economic Development Strategy: Annual Reports.* San Juan: Commonwealth of Puerto Rico, Office of the Governor.

Rivera-Batiz, Francisco, and Carlos Santiago. 1996. *Island Paradox: Puerto Rico in the 1990s.* New York: Russell Sage Foundation.

Schneider, Friedrich, and Dominik Enste. 2000. "Shadow Economies: Size, Causes, and Consequences." *Journal of Economic Literature* 38, no. 1: 77–114.

"Silicon Envy." 1999. *Economist* 350, no. 8107: 25–26.

Slevin, Geraldine. 2002. "Is There a New Economy in Ireland?" Technical paper 3/RT/2. Dublin: Central Bank of Ireland.

Spence, A. Michael. 1973. "Job Market Signaling." *Quarterly Journal of Economics* 87, no. 3: 355–74.

United Nations Economic Commission for Latin America and the Caribbean (ECLAC). 2004. "Globalización y desarrollo: Desafíos de Puerto Rico frente al siglo XXI." Draft (December).

U.S. Congress. 1993. *Tax Policy: Puerto Rico and the Section 936 Tax Credit.* Report to the chairman of the Senate Committee on Finance. GAO/GGD-93-109. U.S. General Accounting Office.

———. 1997. *Tax Policy: Puerto Rican Economic Trends.* Report to the chairman of the Senate Committee on Finance. GAO/GGD-97-101. U.S. General Accounting Office.

U.S. Department of Transportation, Federal Highway Administration. 2005. *Highway Statistics 2003.* Springfield, Va.: U.S. Department of Commerce.

U.S. Office of Personnel Management. 2000a. "Report on 1998 Surveys Used to Determine Cost-of-Living Allowances in Nonforeign Areas." *Federal Register* 65, no. 137: 44103–172.
———. 2000b. "Special Research Relating to the Nonforeign Area Cost-of-Living Allowance (COLA) Program." July (www.opm.gov/oca/cola/html/Rsrch&ap.pdf).
———. 2004. "2002 Nonforeign Area Cost-of-Living Allowance Survey Report: Caribbean and Washington, D.C., Areas." *Federal Register* 69, no. 26: 6023–53.
World Bank. 2005. *World Bank Indicators.* Washington.

3

Labor Supply and Public Transfers

GARY BURTLESS AND ORLANDO SOTOMAYOR

Residents of Puerto Rico work substantially less than residents on the U.S. mainland. What is more, the gap between Puerto Rican and U.S. employment rates has widened over the past half century. Working-age men and women in Puerto Rico are less likely to be employed or looking for work than their counterparts in the United States, but only a small part of the difference is directly explained by Puerto Rico's higher level of unemployment. Most is the result of sharply lower labor force participation rates, and the gap in participation is evident across nearly all segments of the population.

Labor economists trying to account for the difference in employment levels in Puerto Rico and on the mainland can point to four main factors: differences in work opportunities, or employer demand; differences in worker skill endowment, which, in turn, produce disparities in gross wages; differences in the structure of taxes and social welfare benefits, which can affect the net return to work; and differences in preferences. Other chapters in this volume examine the first two sets of factors. Here, we treat the last two. Our chapter focuses, in particular, on the influence of government transfer payments on work incentives in Puerto Rico.

Because Puerto Rico is the recipient of substantial net transfers from the mainland government, taxpayers on the island do not have to pay for all the government benefits received by island residents. Low-income Puerto Ricans enjoy

We are grateful to Dan Theisen for excellent research assistance.

relatively generous income supplements and retirement benefits without imposing heavy tax burdens on highly compensated workers. The transfers received by
less affluent citizens depress the incentive for them to work or to migrate to the
mainland to find better jobs or wages. Because the commonwealth does not
have to pay for all these transfers, benefits are almost certainly more generous
than would be the case if their full cost fell on island taxpayers. As a result, relatively generous redistribution on behalf of Puerto Rico's poor, aged, and disabled
populations reduces employment rates below where they would be if all transfers in the island were financed with taxes imposed on Puerto Rico residents.

In the next section we describe trends in Puerto Rican labor force behavior and
compare them with trends in the United States. We also outline some of the main
developments in transfer program design and generosity and show how they have
influenced labor supply incentives. The following section focuses on five programs that influence the incentives facing working-age people—food stamps,
unemployment insurance, Social Security retirement and disability benefits,
government-provided health insurance, and Temporary Assistance for Needy
Families. We describe the potential effects of each program's benefit structure,
and we try to explain labor supply trends by reference to changes in the work
incentives offered by these programs. To provide an individual-level perspective,
the third section presents a series of budget lines that illustrate the opportunities
faced by hypothetical households when deciding whether to work and how much
time to devote to employment. An empirical section analyzes income and program participation data from the 1970–2000 decennial census files. This evidence
shows the breadth of possible effects of income transfer programs on Puerto
Rico's working-age population. Income transfer benefits are commonly received
even by men and women whose earnings place them near the middle of the
Puerto Rican earnings distribution. It is much rarer in the United States for
middle-income, working-age adults to receive public transfers. The final section
considers a policy reform that encourages work among middle- and lower-income
Puerto Ricans while preserving some of the redistribution that is essential to
maintaining living standards in the island.

Trends in Puerto Rican Labor Supply

Puerto Rico is considerably poorer than the mainland United States. As of the
2000 census, almost half of Puerto Ricans lived in poverty, compared with only
about an eighth of residents in the United States. A principal explanation for
Puerto Rico's relative poverty is the low employment rate of its adult population.[1] Among Puerto Ricans who are at least sixteen years old, the ratio of
employment to population was 40.6 percent in 2002, more than one-third

1. Sotomayor (2004).

below the equivalent employment rate on the mainland. A small part of this difference is explained by Puerto Rico's higher unemployment rate. Slightly less than 6 percent of Puerto Ricans aged sixteen and older were looking for work but unable to find a job in 2002, compared with about 4 percent of the U.S. mainland population.[2] The remaining difference between Puerto Rico and the mainland is the result of sharply lower participation rates in the island.

Participation

The difference between the island and the mainland has increased over time. The top panel in figure 3-1 shows the labor force participation rate and employment-to-population ratio in Puerto Rico measured as proportions of comparable rates on the U.S. mainland. In 2002, for example, the island's employment-to-population ratio (or employment rate) was 65 percent of the comparable ratio on the mainland. Before 1975, the ratio of Puerto Rican to U.S. employment rates was greater than 65 percent, and in the immediate postwar period it was between 85 percent and 90 percent. As the panel illustrates, the pattern closely follows that of the labor force participation rate, indicating that most of the long-term variation in Puerto Rico's employment-to-population ratio can be traced to that trend. Only a comparatively small part of the variation derives from changes in the relative unemployment rates of the two areas. In fact, the impact of the unemployment rate difference on the employment gap between Puerto Rico and the mainland has generally fallen over time.

The top chart in figure 3-1 suggests there were four distinct phases in the trend toward lower relative employment and participation rates in the island: a steep decline in the 1950s; comparative stability from the end of the 1950s to the beginning of the 1970s; a further steep fall between the early 1970s and 1982; and a modest recovery after the mid-1980s. The lower panel of figure 3-1, which shows the trend in relative participation rates separately for men and women, sheds some light on the long-term trends. Instead of reflecting the participation rate of the entire population over the age of fifteen, the chart focuses on adults who are most likely to be in the labor force, namely, men and women aged twenty to sixty-four years old. In addition, the panel eliminates the effects of differences in the Puerto Rico and U.S. age structures by calculating both the Puerto Rican and U.S. participation rates using the population age structure for

---

2. The percentage of the adult population without a job and seeking work is not the same as the unemployment rate. The unemployment rate is defined as the percentage of the active labor force that is jobless and actively seeking work. Since the labor force is smaller than the adult population, the unemployment rate is higher than the percentages mentioned in the text. The average Puerto Rican unemployment rate in 2002 was 12.2 percent, and the average U.S. unemployment rate was 5.8 percent. Because the labor force participation rate in Puerto Rico was far below the equivalent rate in the United States, the percentages of the adult populations that were unemployed in the two areas were much closer.

Figure 3-1. *Relative Labor Force Participation and Employment Rates in Puerto Rico Compared with the United States, 1947–2004*

Employment and labor force participation[a]

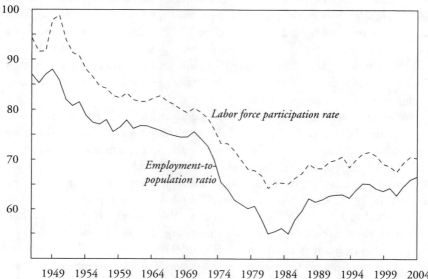

Index (United States = 100)

Labor force participation rate

Employment-to-population ratio

Labor force participation adjusted for age, by sex, 1948–2001[b]

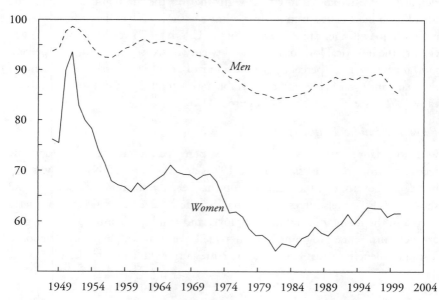

Men

Women

Source: Authors' estimates using Puerto Rico labor market survey data and U.S. Bureau of Labor Statistics tabulations for the mainland.

a. Employment and labor force participation for persons aged sixteen and older.

b. Labor force participation adjusted for age, by sex, for persons aged twenty to sixty-four, 1948–2004.

Puerto Rico.[3] That is, we formed an estimate of what the U.S. participation rate would have been had the U.S. age structure in each year been the same as the age structure in Puerto Rico. The panel presents the Puerto Rican participation rate relative to this adjusted U.S. participation rate. The calculations show that the steep decline in the island's relative participation rate during the 1950s was mainly driven by a decline in participation among Puerto Rican women. Whereas female participation in the early 1950s rose modestly on the mainland, it fell precipitously in Puerto Rico.

Both panels show a steep acceleration of decline in the island's relative participation rate after about 1973. Part of the acceleration was a result of the severe recession that began in 1974. Puerto Rico's unemployment rate jumped more than 8 percentage points between 1973 and 1977, reaching a peak rate of about 20 percent. In contrast, the peak annual unemployment rate on the mainland, attained in 1975, was 8.5 percent; by 1977 the U.S. unemployment rate had already declined to about 7 percent. Many jobless workers who would have looked for jobs in the U.S. market were probably too discouraged to keep looking for a job in the depressed Puerto Rican labor market. The worst was not over in Puerto Rico, as the second oil shock and a severe recession in the early 1980s sent unemployment to a record 23.4 percent, contributing to a further decline in the relative participation rate. Note, however, that Puerto Rico's participation rate remained low relative to that on the mainland even after the island's job market began to recover in the 1980s. In 2001 a labor force participation ratio equivalent to 85 percent of the U.S. rate (74 versus 87 percent) was close to the historical low for males aged twenty to sixty-four, and the 62 percent ratio for women (45 percent participation in Puerto Rico versus 72 percent on the mainland) was below any comparable ratio attained in the 1950s, 1960s, or early 1970s (see bottom panel of figure 3-1).

Receipt of Public Transfers

One explanation for the persistence of low participation rates after the economy recovered from the recessions of the 1970s and the early 1980s was the sharp increase in government transfer payments that began in the mid-1970s. Figure 3-2 shows trends in the sources of personal income received by residents of Puerto Rico and the mainland. Because employer and employee contributions to government insurance programs have increased over time to pay for higher social insurance benefits, gross labor income represents a gradually smaller percentage

---

3. We have reliable estimates of the Puerto Rico population age structure only for the decennial census years. We have interpolated estimates for the other years under the assumption that the population age structure changed linearly between the census years. Although this assumption is unlikely to be exactly true, it probably has little effect on the measured relative difference between the U.S. and Puerto Rican participation rates.

Figure 3-2. *Sources of Personal Income, Puerto Rico and the United States, 1950–2004*[a]

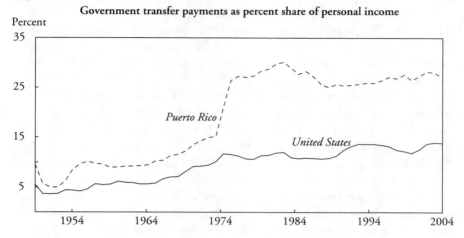

Government transfer payments as percent share of personal income

Percent

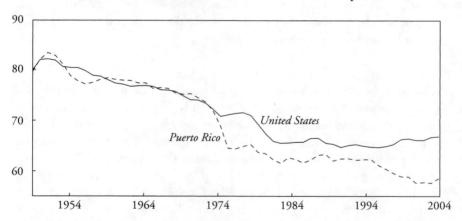

Labor income net of social insurance contributions as a share of personal income

Source: Authors' tabulations of U.S. and Puerto Rican national income and product accounts data.

a. U.S. data are for calendar years; Puerto Rican data are for fiscal years, which begin six months earlier than the corresponding calendar year.

of estimated personal income. The top panel in the figure shows the share of government transfer benefits—Social Security, Medicare, unemployment insurance, and so on—in personal income. Since the mid-1950s, government transfers have been significantly more important in Puerto Rico than on the mainland. In the prerecession year of 1973, government transfers represented 14.9 percent of Puerto Rican personal income and just 9.4 percent of the personal income of Americans on the mainland.

The Puerto Rico–U.S. gap increased dramatically in 1975 with the introduction of food stamp benefits in Puerto Rico. Food stamp coupons provided almost 5.5 percent of Puerto Rican personal income in 1975 and 7.5 percent of personal income by 1980. In contrast, food stamp benefits have never provided more than 0.5 percent of the personal income received by people on the mainland. Nearly all of the cost of food stamp benefits in Puerto Rico is borne by the U.S. Treasury and very little of it by Puerto Rican taxpayers. While the island's food stamp program has been overhauled to reduce costs, other transfer benefits have grown in importance, approximately offsetting the effect of lower food stamp outlays. Since 1990, government transfer benefits have provided 25 to 28 percent of Puerto Ricans' incomes, about twice the equivalent percentage on the mainland.

The bottom panel in figure 3-2 compares labor earnings as a share of personal income in the island and mainland. Labor income includes gross wages and salaries, fringe benefits, and the net incomes of unincorporated businesses less employee, employer, and proprietor contributions for social insurance. Not surprisingly, the importance of labor income shrank as the size of government transfers increased. Until 1974, the trend in Puerto Rico's labor income share was almost indistinguishable from that on the mainland. After 1974, the trends diverged sharply. By 2002, labor earnings provided a significantly smaller income share in Puerto Rico than on the mainland.

Age

As noted earlier, the gap between Puerto Rican and U.S. participation rates is wider for women than for men. In addition, it is proportionately larger among people under the age of twenty-five and over the age of forty-four than it is for people aged twenty-five to forty-four (see figure 3-3). The participation rate among twenty-five- to thirty-four-year-old Puerto Rican males is 93 percent of the rate among U.S. men in the same age group, but the participation rate of fifty-five- to sixty-four-year-old Puerto Rican men is just 71 percent of the U.S. rate for men in the same age group. For Puerto Rican men in every age group, the relative participation rate has fallen since 1973 (compare the top panels in figures 3-3 and 3-4). The falloff in relative participation was largest among men under twenty-five and men over forty-four. Participation rates among Puerto Rican men forty-five and older fell from rates that were close to or above the corresponding rates on the mainland. By 2000, participation rates at these ages were considerably lower in Puerto Rico than on the mainland.

Participation rates among women have increased both in Puerto Rico and on the mainland, but they have increased more in the United States, especially among younger and middle-aged women (see bottom panels in figures 3-3 and 3-4). At older ages the relative differences in participation rates have declined moderately, but the absolute differences have widened. The gap in participation between women in Puerto Rico and on the mainland has narrowed since the mid-

Figure 3-3. *Relative Labor Force Participation Rates, Puerto Rico and the United States, by Age and Sex, 2000*

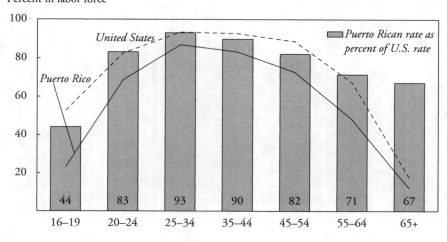

Men

Percent in labor force

Puerto Rican rate as percent of U.S. rate

United States

Puerto Rico

| 44 | 83 | 93 | 90 | 82 | 71 | 67 |

| 16–19 | 20–24 | 25–34 | 35–44 | 45–54 | 55–64 | 65+ |

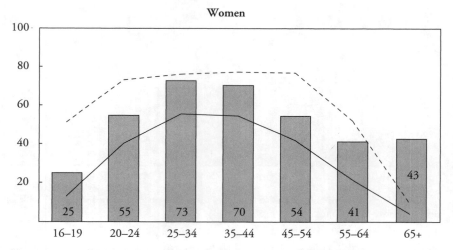

Women

| 25 | 55 | 73 | 70 | 54 | 41 | 43 |

| 16–19 | 20–24 | 25–34 | 35–44 | 45–54 | 55–64 | 65+ |

Source: Authors' estimates based on U.S. Bureau of Labor Statistics tabulations and Puerto Rico labor force survey.

1980s, but in 2000 the overall participation rates of Puerto Rican women aged twenty to sixty-four were still more than one-third lower than corresponding rates in the United States (see the bottom panel of figure 3-1).

In seeking explanations for the differences in Puerto Rican and U.S. participation patterns, then, it makes sense to focus on factors that can account for low participation early and late in workers' careers and incentives that affect women more than men. All the groups with low relative participation rates in Puerto Rico

Figure 3-4. *Relative Labor Force Participation Rates, Puerto Rico and the United States, by Age and Sex, 1973*

Men

Percent in labor force

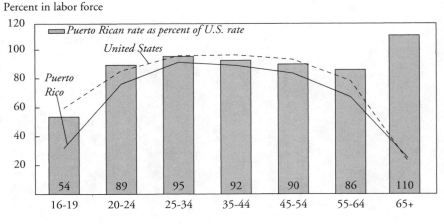

	54	89	95	92	90	86	110
	16-19	20-24	25-34	35-44	45-54	55-64	65+

Women

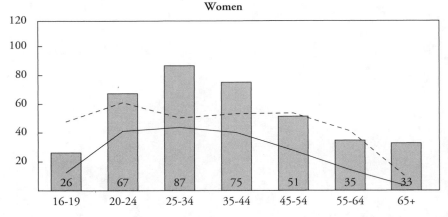

	26	67	87	75	51	35	33
	16-19	20-24	25-34	35-44	45-54	55-64	65+

Source: Authors' estimates based on U.S. Bureau of Labor Statistics tabulations and Puerto Rico labor force survey.

earn comparatively meager wages, both in Puerto Rico and the United States. People just entering the workforce or nearing the end of their careers typically earn lower wages than do workers with considerable job experience who are near middle age, and women typically earn less than men. Although a variety of explanations might account for relatively low participation rates among Puerto Ricans who have low potential earnings, the generosity of public transfers seems one plausible explanation. The steep drop in relative participation rates that took place after the mid-1970s occurred at about the same time as a major expansion of means-tested transfers available to working-age families. The expansion was far from trivial. The percentage of personal income derived from government transfers doubled from 1974 to 1983, climbing to 30 percent of Puerto Ricans' incomes. By 1980, more than half of Puerto Rico's residents received food stamps, a benefit that had been unknown in the island just six years earlier. Although government transfers and participation in means-tested programs also increased in the United States, the rise was more gradual and involved a much smaller percentage of the population.

Wages

Workers' willingness to seek and hold jobs is influenced not only by the availability and generosity of public transfers but also by the wages offered by employers. Compared with wages on the U.S. mainland, Puerto Rican wages rose relatively rapidly through the early 1970s and then stagnated or declined. Two main sources of information about the wages paid in Puerto Rico are available. The first is data on earnings subject to taxes under the unemployment insurance (UI) system, and the second is earnings reports from employers and self-employed workers who make contributions to Social Security and Medicare.

Figure 3-5 displays information on relative wages in Puerto Rico from both these sources. The top panel shows average weekly earnings received by Puerto Rican workers in private companies subject to the unemployment insurance tax; these earnings are measured relative to weekly earnings received by a comparable group of workers on the mainland. Three groups of mainland workers are used as bases for comparison. The largest, best-paid group consists of all workers on the mainland in private companies covered by the unemployment insurance system. From 1961 to 1977, Puerto Ricans' average earnings increased from 45 percent to 63 percent of this benchmark wage. Thereafter, Puerto Rican wages relative to the U.S. mainland average wage declined. By 2003, the Puerto Rican wage was less than 55 percent of the average mainland wage. The top panel also includes two other wage comparison benchmarks, one reflecting the average wage earned by UI-covered workers in Mississippi, and the other, average weekly earnings of workers in Alabama. Mississippi is the poorest state in the United States, and Alabama is among the five poorest. Wages in these two states are well below the U.S. average. The comparisons with Mississippi and Alabama follow the same basic pattern as the comparison with the U.S. average wage: Puerto Rican wages rose from 1961 to the early 1970s and then stagnated or declined.

A broadly similar trend is revealed when average earnings are measured using administrative data compiled by the Social Security Administration (see the lower panel in figure 3-5). These earnings records are assembled for purposes of administering payroll taxes and calculating Old-Age, Survivors, and Disability Insurance (OASDI) benefit payments. Using a sample of its records, the Social Security Administration calculates average taxes collected and benefits paid in states and localities covered by the Social Security program. Because only a sample of records is used, the state-level estimates have less statistical precision than the estimates

Figure 3-5. *Relative Earnings, Puerto Rico and Selected U.S. States, 1958–2003*
Average weekly earnings in UI-covered employment, Puerto Rico, 1961–2003
Index (United States = 100)

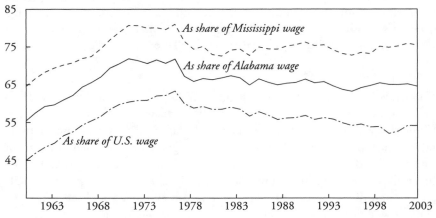

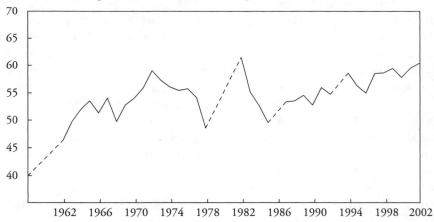

Average annual OASDI-taxed earnings, Puerto Rico, 1958–2002

Source: Authors' tabulations of U.S. Department of Labor, Employment, and Training Administration
financial data on unemployment compensation (top panel) and Social Security Administration, *Annual
Statistical Supplement,* 1962–2004 (workforcesecurity.doleta.gov/unemploy/hb394.asp [Jan. 15, 2005]).
Breaks in the data series, owing to breaks in the administrative data, are indicated by broken lines in the
bottom panel.

based on UI earnings records. On the other hand, the Social Security records
cover a broader range of employment, including self-employment, and they combine workers' earnings from all jobs held in a year. In contrast, UI-covered earnings reflect a worker's wages from a single private employer and exclude earnings
from self-employment. The Social Security earnings records show a trend toward
substantially higher relative wages in Puerto Rico from 1958 to 1972 followed by

Figure 3-6. *Educational Attainment of Adult Population, Puerto Rico and the United States, 1940–2000*[a]

Average years of schooling

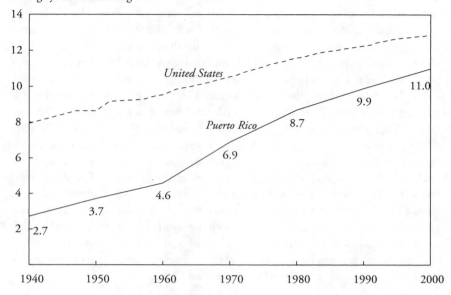

Source: Authors' estimates based on U.S. Census Bureau data. For United States: www.census.gov/ population/socdemo/education/tabA-1.pdf; for Puerto Rico, see Ladd and Rivera-Batiz, chapter 5, figure 5-1, in this volume.

a. Persons aged twenty-five and older.

an erratic but overall stagnant trend between the early 1970s and the early 1990s. Relative Puerto Rican wages have improved since the early 1990s, but they remain 40 percent lower than the average wage earned on the mainland.

The anemic progress of wages in Puerto Rico compared with the United States is something of a surprise. Educational attainment among Puerto Ricans continues to climb rapidly in relation to levels in the United States (see figure 3-6). In 1960 the average schooling of Puerto Rican adults was 4.9 years (52 percent) below the average level in the United States. By 2000 the gap had fallen by more than half to just 1.9 years, a shortfall equal to 15 percent of the average schooling level on the mainland. Puerto Rico's average educational attainment in 2000 was approximately the same as the average schooling level on the mainland in 1973, but the 2000 Puerto Rican real wage was about one-third lower than the U.S. wage in 1973.[4]

4. The average weekly UI-covered Puerto Rican wage in 2000 was $355.34, compared with an average 1973 wage on the mainland of $550.07. Both wage estimates are measured in constant 2000 dollars using the CPI-U-X1 price deflator.

One reason that Puerto Rican wages have grown slowly is that Puerto Ricans accumulate job experience more slowly than their counterparts in the United States. By the time they reach the age of twenty-five, Puerto Rican men have accumulated almost two fewer years of labor market experience than U.S. men of the same age, and twenty-five-year-old Puerto Rican women have accumulated three fewer years of job market experience than their U.S. counterparts. By the age of forty-five, the deficits in job experience rise to 3.5 years and 7.5 years, respectively, for Puerto Rican men and women.[5] The gap in experience almost certainly carries a penalty in terms of reduced hourly wages. Both education and job experience contribute to worker skills and hence to employers' willingness to pay higher wages. Although the average educational attainment of Puerto Rican workers has continued to improve relative to schooling attainment on the mainland, Puerto Ricans' average job market experience at successive ages has declined relative to that of mainland residents of the same age. The sharp break in Puerto Rican wage gains documented in figure 3-5 cannot be attributed to the deficit in job experience implied by figures 3-3 and 3-4, however. The cumulative deficit in labor market experience, like the steady rise in educational qualifications, should have a slow and cumulative effect on average wages. Nonetheless, the experience gap can help account for the failure of Puerto Rican wages gradually to converge with wage levels in the United States.

Summary of Trends in Labor Supply

The 1970s and the early 1980s witnessed large declines in relative labor force participation rates that were largest among Puerto Rican younger women and older men. Although participation rates rose in the context of declining unemployment during the ensuing decades, they remained low relative to levels evident during the 1950s and the 1960s and relative to current levels in the United States. Two factors stand out as partial explanations. After a period of catch-up during the 1950s and 1960s, wage levels in Puerto Rico stagnated relative to those in the United States as a whole and relative to those of the lowest-income states. At the same time, the share of transfers as a percentage of personal income almost doubled between 1973 and 2003.

Transfer Programs

Five forms of government transfer payments can affect work incentives: food stamps, unemployment insurance, Social Security (OASDI), government-provided health insurance, and Temporary Assistance for Needy Families. The conventional theory of labor supply as it applies to the analysis of government transfers

5. The deficits in job market experience are calculated using participation figures shown in figure 3-3. We also assume the participation rate differences shown in figure 3-3 persist from age sixteen up through age forty-five.

is a straightforward application of utility maximization. Labor economists usually assume that workers regard post-tax, post-transfer income as a "good" and hours spent in paid employment as a "bad." Workers' utility is increased by toiling fewer hours, holding spendable income constant, or receiving additional after-tax income, holding hours of work constant. Workers can earn a market-determined wage, which determines the price at which they can trade off leisure for additional spendable income.

A government transfer program typically introduces a distortion into workers' choice of optimal labor supply. It drives a wedge between the output workers produce and the income they derive from an additional hour of work. In addition, by providing a source of nonlabor income that supplements or replaces earned income, the transfer benefit reduces the necessity of work. Economists generally agree that a program that increases the marginal tax on labor income increases economic distortion and welfare loss. They also agree that programs offering more generous income support to people who do not work tend to reduce employment and hours of work more than programs providing less generous support. They do not agree, however, on the exact size of the effect of one extra dollar of income support on workers' willingness to work. The size of the effect will be determined by the precise details of the income supplement package and the composition of the target population that receives benefits. Transfers targeted on populations that do not work, such as the severely handicapped or very elderly, do not have much effect on average work effort.

In many cases, economists can predict the direction of the effect, though not its precise magnitude, when a new transfer program is introduced or an old one is modified. Consider, for example, a worker who receives a hike in post-tax, post-transfer income as a result of a new income supplementation program targeted on the needy. A typical transfer program provides income supplementation on a sliding scale depending on the worker's earnings. Workers who earn additional wages receive smaller transfer payments, and workers who earn more than a ceiling or break-even amount are denied benefits altogether. The effect of this kind of supplementation is straightforward. By increasing the worker's unearned income, the supplement reduces the necessity of work through an income effect. Some workers may reduce their weekly work effort, and a few may stop work altogether. In addition, because the supplementation scheme increases the marginal tax on earnings, it reduces the net return to work and may depress effort through a substitution effect. Because both the income and substitution effects operate in the same direction, workers who initially receive benefits under the new program should, on average, be expected to reduce their labor supply compared with their average effort in the absence of the program.

The example just described is hardly typical. Only rarely can governments introduce a generous new benefit without figuring out how to pay for it. When transfer benefits are financed under a pay-as-you-go rule, some taxpayers must

Figure 3-7. *Government Transfers as Share of Total Personal Income, Puerto Rico, 1950–2004*[a]

Percent

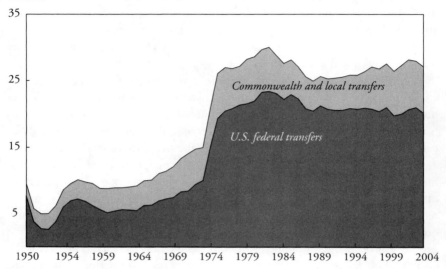

Source: Authors' tabulations of Puerto Rico national income and product accounts data.
a. Puerto Rico fiscal years.

face higher taxes to pay for more generous transfer benefits. If the tax hike takes the form of higher income tax rates or a higher payroll tax rate on earnings, then some taxpayers will see their marginal tax rates increase and their after-tax incomes fall, and the consequent reduction in the net reward to work may depress the labor supply. However, by lowering some workers' net incomes the tax hike will also induce greater work effort through an income effect. In this case, the income and substitution effects operate in opposite directions, so the net effect of the change on taxpayers' work effort is hard to predict. Although the introduction of a generous new benefit unambiguously induces lower work effort among workers initially entitled to receive extra benefits, the tax increase needed to pay for the new benefits has an ambiguous impact on the work behavior of taxpayers. Thus the overall impact of the new tax and transfer schedule is ambiguous.[6]

Puerto Rico represents an exception to the general rule that requires governments to pay for new benefits they wish to provide to transfer recipients. Most of the cost of new transfers offered in Puerto Rico in the mid-1970s was borne by taxpayers on the mainland. Figure 3-7 shows the proportion of Puerto Rican personal income that is derived from commonwealth and municipal transfers, on the one hand, and from U.S. federal government transfers, on the other.

6. See Betson and Greenberg (1986) for an illustration and explanation of the ambiguity.

Clearly, an overwhelming proportion of transfer benefits, especially after 1975, derived from federal programs.

Of course, this classification does not provide a clear basis for determining whether transfer benefits were financed by federal or Puerto Rican taxpayers. Medicare and OASDI, which are federal government programs, provide benefits that are financed out of payroll taxes. Although residents of Puerto Rico are mostly exempt from paying federal income taxes, they are required to make the same payroll contributions for Social Security and Medicare as mainland workers insured under those programs. Even in this case, however, workers in Puerto Rico do not have to pay for the full cost of the benefits they receive. A large fraction of Medicare benefits is financed with a contribution from the U.S. Treasury, that is, from taxes levied in the United States. Payroll taxes and premiums do not cover the full cost of Medicare, and a substantial subsidy from the federal government is needed to keep the program solvent. In addition, the redistributive tilt in the Social Security benefit formula means that workers in Puerto Rico can expect to receive pensions that are generous compared with their contributions. In 2002 Puerto Rican residents paid only 0.45 percent of all OASDI taxes, but they received 1 percent of all OASDI benefits.

Food Stamps

The most important new transfer introduced in the 1970s was food stamps. The cost of all food stamp benefit payments, as well as much of the program's administration, is borne by U.S. taxpayers. Puerto Rican taxpayers bear a small part of the direct cost of the program. The benefit formula for food stamps clearly discourages work by increasing recipients' unearned income and raising the marginal tax on their earned income. Food stamps were introduced in Puerto Rico in 1975, several years after the program was implemented on a nationwide basis in the United States. The program as originally implemented was designed to increase the food-purchasing ability of needy families. To achieve this goal, the program provided a monthly allotment of coupons, redeemable in many stores, that could be exchanged only for food. Families were expected to devote 30 percent of their spendable income to the cost of food. If the cost of a minimally adequate diet was more than 30 percent of the family's monthly income, food stamps were provided to make up the deficiency. A family without any countable income was given a large enough allotment of coupons to cover the full cost of a minimally adequate diet. As the family's countable income rose one dollar, its food stamp allotment fell by thirty cents.

After the food stamp program was introduced in Puerto Rico, both enrollment and benefit payments expanded rapidly (see figure 3-8). By 1980, about 60 percent of Puerto Rico's population was collecting benefits, and the program provided 7.5 percent of Puerto Rican personal income. Both the participation rate and the fraction of personal income derived from food stamps on the main-

Figure 3-8. *Participation and Benefit Payments under Food Stamp and Nutritional Assistance Programs, Puerto Rico and the United States, 1970–2003*

Participants as share of resident population[a]

Percent

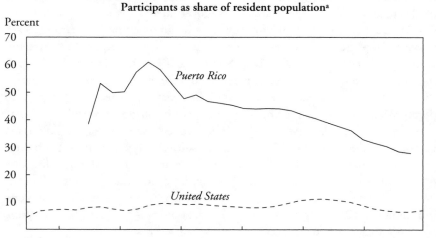

Benefits as share of personal income[b]

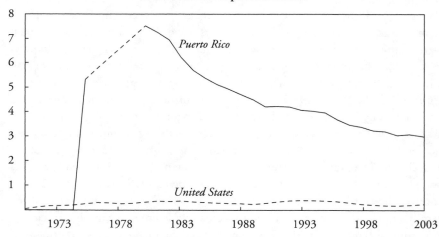

Source: Authors' tabulations of data from U.S. Department of Agriculture, Food and Nutrition Service; U.S. Census Bureau's International Data Base estimates of the midyear population; and national income and products data for Puerto Rico and the United States. Breaks in the data series, owing to breaks in the administrative data, are indicated by broken lines.

a. U.S. fiscal years. Food stamps were not available in Puerto Rico until 1975.

b. Calendar years in United States; Puerto Rican fiscal years in Puerto Rico.

land have been much lower. In the late 1970s and early 1980s the participation rate was five to six times higher in the island than on the mainland. It was also far higher than rates in the poorest American states. In 1981 the food stamp program in Puerto Rico accounted for 8 percent of all participation in the program and 8 percent of benefit outlays.[7]

In 1982 the federal government eliminated the standard food stamp program in Puerto Rico and replaced it with a nutrition block grant payable to the commonwealth government. The purpose of this move was to control the cost of nutrition assistance in Puerto Rico. The initial level of the block grant was about 10 percent less than federal government spending on food stamps in the immediately preceding year. Moreover, the federal government capped the block grant at a fixed nominal level before allowing the grant to grow with inflation after 1986. To maintain a food assistance program under a smaller budget, the commonwealth government established a replacement program known as the Nutritional Assistance Program (NAP) (Programa de Asistencia Nutricional [PAN]). The program provides assistance payments under a less generous formula and tighter eligibility restrictions than the food stamp program on the mainland. In addition, the commonwealth government replaced coupon allotments with cash payments, so NAP benefits, unlike food stamp coupons, can be used to buy items other than food. Since 2000 NAP benefits are delivered through an electronic benefit transfer (EBT) system that works like a debit card. Seventy-five percent of benefits must be spent on food and the remainder can be cashed out at ATM machines. While the restriction generated some controversy when enacted, it is irrelevant for most participants. A family that has a food budget larger than the NAP allotment can simply use benefits to buy food and use the cash freed by the program to buy anything else. In fact, Robert Moffitt finds little change in Puerto Rican food consumption patterns when food stamps were converted into cash in 1982. He attributed this finding to the fact that few families received benefits that were larger than their food expenditures.[8] In spite of reduced payments and tighter eligibility restrictions, participation in Puerto Rico's revamped NAP program has continued to be much higher than food stamp participation on the mainland (see the top panel of figure 3-8). In addition, NAP benefits still represent a much bigger share of personal income in Puerto Rico than do food stamps on the mainland (bottom panel of figure 3-8). Nonetheless, the budget cap implicit in the federal block grant has gradually reduced both participation in nutrition assistance programs and the contribution to personal income of NAP payments.

The theoretical effect of the NAP benefit schedule on desired work effort can be illustrated by reference to a standard diagram that depicts the trade-off between

7. See Fox, Hamilton, and Lin (2004, p. 286).
8. See Moffitt (1989).

Figure 3-9. *Work–Net Income Trade-off under Puerto Rico's Nutritional Assistance Program*

Monthly income[a]

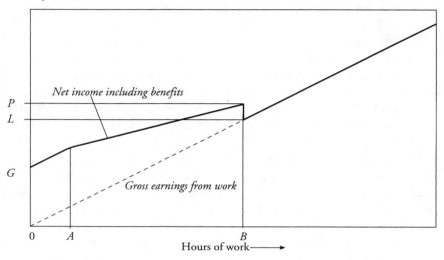

a. The sum of earnings plus the value of nutritional assistance benefits.

hours of work (on the horizontal axis) and net income from wages and assistance benefits (on the vertical axis). The diagram, displayed in figure 3-9, shows both the gross earnings a worker could obtain in the absence of assistance payments and the net income he or she receives when collecting a NAP benefit. Workers without any countable income receive only the basic NAP allotment, designated G on the vertical axis. Workers with low work hours also receive the basic assistance payment until their earnings exceed the basic exempt amount. In the figure, this exempt amount is reached when the worker is employed for A hours a month. At that point, further increases in the worker's hours result in a reduction in assistance benefits at a marginal rate t, which reduces the worker's net wage from W to $W(1-t)$. When the worker's monthly wages exceed an eligibility ceiling amount, L, the worker's family loses eligibility for benefits and the monthly assistance allotment is reduced to zero. In the diagram, this occurs when the worker's monthly hours are equal to B. A worker who is employed for slightly less than B hours receives the assistance payment defined by the difference between P and L on the vertical axis. A worker who is employed more than B hours receives nothing.

Obviously, workers who are initially employed less than B hours a month before implementation of the assistance program receive gains in net income as a result of the program's introduction. All who apply for benefits will have higher unearned incomes and may work less as a result of a negative income effect. In addition, people who initially work more than A hours but less than B hours will also see their net wage reduced and will experience a negative substitution effect. Workers who are initially employed slightly more than B hours a month will not initially qualify for assistance benefits but may reduce their hours to meet the income eligibility test so they can receive benefits. Thus the introduction of the assistance program offers unambiguous incentives for many low-income workers to reduce their labor supply.

Wages in Puerto Rico are quite low compared with the wage scale in the United States; therefore a much bigger percentage of the working-age population is eligible for nutrition assistance benefits (or would be eligible if workers modestly reduced their hours of work). Because the percentage of the Puerto Rican population affected by the adverse work incentives in the NAP is much larger than the percentage of Americans affected by food stamp–induced disincentives, it seems likely that the negative effects on the Puerto Rican labor supply will also be larger. The relative trends in U.S. and Puerto Rican labor force participation seem to reflect the historical pattern of benefit generosity in Puerto Rico's nutrition assistance programs. The steep decline in island participation rates after 1974 occurred at the same time as a dramatic expansion in the availability of nutrition assistance for island residents in the bottom half of the income distribution. Compared with labor force participation rates on the mainland, participation rates in Puerto Rico stabilized after the early 1980s and began a gradual recovery but remained low relative to their levels in the early 1970s (see figure 3-1). The availability of much more generous nutrition assistance today compared with the early 1970s helps explain this pattern.

Eileen Segarra has investigated some of the effects of the 1982–85 reform in Puerto Rico's nutrition assistance programs.[9] Segarra focuses on married-couple families containing a working-age husband. Although her estimates suggest the benefit cutbacks had little effect on the labor supply of men, the eligibility restrictions may have perversely reduced the work effort of wives in the affected families: some secondary earners reduced their earnings to remain eligible for nutrition assistance benefits. In spite of Segarra's surprising statistical result, it is hard to believe that the benefit reductions after 1982, on balance, reduced labor supply among workers with low potential earnings. The time series trend in benefit generosity and take-up clearly suggests that food stamps produced big increases in family net income between 1975 and 1982, when Puerto Rican labor supply fell sharply, while benefit cuts reduced participation and assistance payments after 1982, when relative labor force participation rates on Puerto Rico began to recover. Although other factors also influenced labor supply over this period, possibly offsetting or reinforcing the effects of food stamp liberalization and benefit cuts, it is suggestive that so much of the decline in relative participation rates on

9. Segarra (1999).

Puerto Rico was concentrated among groups with low potential earnings—precisely the groups most likely to qualify for nutrition assistance.

The block grant nature of Puerto Rico's nutrition program provides flexibility that the commonwealth has used to design a wage subsidy program to encourage work among some NAP participants. Able-bodied adults must sign up for the PAN y Trabajo program, which provides job training and guarantees full NAP benefits for a period of five months when an eligible NAP recipient is hired by an employer participating in the program. Receipt of nutrition assistance benefits is contingent on searching for or securing employment. Thus workers who voluntarily leave jobs obtained under the program can lose their NAP benefits. Businesses receive an hourly wage subsidy equivalent to one-half the legal minimum wage for a period of up to two years after hiring a PAN y Trabajo enrollee. Since it was established in 1988, the program has undergone modification regarding rules and geographic and sectoral scope, which have resulted in a gradual increase in the number of participants. Nonetheless, in 2002 only about 6 percent of all families receiving NAP benefits participated in the PAN y Trabajo program.

Unemployment Insurance

Unemployment compensation is a joint federal-state program that insures experienced workers against the risk of earnings loss following an involuntary layoff. The program in Puerto Rico is designed and administered in a way that will be familiar to people who are knowledgeable about unemployment compensation on the mainland. Both the benefit schedule and the payroll tax schedule are determined by the commonwealth legislature under broad federal guidelines. The commonwealth tax authorities collect a payroll tax from employers that is scaled to individual workers' earnings (up to an annual taxable limit). The payroll tax rate depends on the employer's recent layoff behavior. Employers who frequently lay off workers entitled to benefits face higher payroll tax rates than employers with few layoffs. Unemployment benefits are paid to eligible unemployed workers under a schedule that links weekly benefit amounts to wages earned by workers in a base period. The rules of the program also limit the potential duration of benefits. Workers who exhaust their benefits can receive benefit extensions when the unemployment rate is high and the Puerto Rican or federal government operates an extended UI benefit program.

Compared with unemployment benefits available on the mainland, the benefit replacement rate in Puerto Rico is relatively low and declining (see the top panel of figure 3-10). Since 1960, the average weekly benefit on the mainland as a fraction of the average earnings of workers covered by unemployment insurance has averaged between 34 and 37 percent of the average weekly wage. In the twenty years after 1968, Puerto Rico offered a similar though slightly lower replacement rate, but since 1989 weekly benefits have been scaled back. Since 2001 the Puerto Rican UI system has offered benefits that replace about 26 percent of

Figure 3-10. *Unemployment Insurance Compensation Payments, Puerto Rico and the United States, 1961–2003*

Average weekly UI benefit as share of average weekly wage in UI-covered employment

Percent

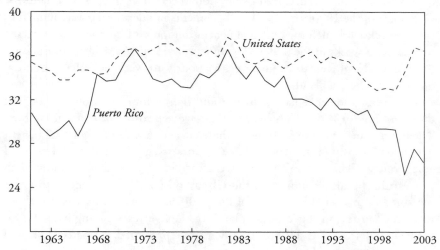

UI benefits paid as share of total earnings in UI-covered employment

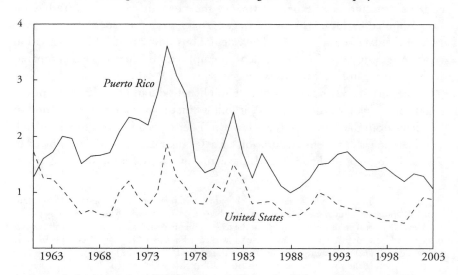

Source: Authors' tabulations of U.S. Department of Labor, Employment and Training Administration financial data on unemployment compensation.

the average weekly wage in UI-covered employment, substantially less than the replacement rate in the fifty states. The regular UI benefits provided in Puerto Rico also have a shorter potential duration than benefits available on the mainland. Most states offer regular benefits to fully insured workers for up to twenty-six weeks; the average potential benefit duration for workers who actually qualify for benefits has averaged twenty-four weeks over the past four decades. Over most of the 1970s and 1980s, UI payments in Puerto Rico were limited to twenty weeks, although the potential benefit duration was temporarily increased to twenty-six weeks in the mid-1990s. In recent years potential benefit duration has averaged eighteen to twenty weeks, about four weeks less than potential duration on the mainland.

In spite of a lower replacement rate and tighter limits on potential benefit duration, Puerto Rico incurs heavier-than-average costs to finance its system. The lower panel of figure 3-10 shows the average total cost of regular UI benefit payments, measured as a percentage of total wages earned in UI-covered employment. (The denominator reflects employers' total wage bills rather than just earnings that are subject to the UI payroll tax.) When benefit costs are measured in this way, the burden of Puerto Rican UI payments averages about twice the burden on the U.S. mainland. In the five years ending in 2002, for example, Puerto Rico's UI benefit payments represented 1.3 percent of total wages in jobs covered by UI. On the mainland, the comparable cost of compensation payments was 0.6 percent of wages. In the long run, both Puerto Rico and the fifty states can expect to finance their benefit payments with payroll taxes imposed on local UI-covered wages. There is no cross-state subsidy of the cost of regular UI payments.[10] The calculations imply that UI compensation represents roughly twice the burden on employers in Puerto Rico compared with that on mainland employers.

Since both weekly benefit payments and benefit duration are less generous in Puerto Rico than on the mainland, it follows that layoffs are more common or exit rates from the benefit rolls are lower in Puerto Rico than on the mainland. Even though the potential duration of a UI claim is substantially lower in Puerto Rico than on the mainland, the actual average duration of UI receipt is

---

10. A federal unemployment tax covers the administrative costs of the state and commonwealth UI programs, but it does not cover regular benefit payments, which are financed by payroll taxes levied on local employers. In addition, the federal unemployment tax also covers half the cost of extended UI benefits, which are available to workers who exhaust regular UI benefits in states where the local unemployment rate rises above a trigger level. Finally, the federal government pays for 100 percent of the cost of special supplemental UI benefits, which may be offered when nationwide unemployment is particularly high. The federal government does extend loans to states with deficits in their UI trust funds, but these loans are not subsidized. The discussion in the text focuses on compensation benefits provided under the regular UI system. Except during severe recessions, that system is the source for an overwhelming share of the UI benefits paid to unemployed workers, both in Puerto Rico and on the mainland.

higher in Puerto Rico. In 2000, for example, the average benefit duration of UI claims in Puerto Rico was 18.4 weeks. This is only slightly less than the upper limit on potential benefit duration, 20 weeks. By implication, a high percentage of Puerto Rico's UI claimants either exhausts or comes close to exhausting eligibility. On the mainland, the average benefit duration in 2000 was 13.7 weeks, substantially less than the 23.8 weeks of potential benefits that on average were available to a laid-off worker. These estimates suggest that the unemployment spell actually experienced by a typical laid-off worker was considerably longer in Puerto Rico than on the mainland.[11] This pattern has been repeated in virtually all years since the mid-1970s.

Insured unemployed workers take longer to find new jobs in Puerto Rico than they do on the mainland, though UI replacement rates are lower and potential benefit duration is shorter in Puerto Rico than on the mainland. This pattern suggests that Puerto Rico's unemployed are looking for work in a poor labor market rather enrolled than in a UI system that is providing overgenerous benefits. Other elements of the island's transfer system are more likely to be responsible for the low employment rate among Puerto Rican adults.

Social Security

Social Security is mainly targeted on the aged and disabled, populations that might be expected to work little if pensions were curtailed or eliminated. However, a growing body of evidence suggests that generous benefits have contributed to lower labor force participation rates among the near elderly and among workers with moderate to severe health problems. Social Security's disability insurance (DI) program has attracted growing attention because of its suspected role in reducing labor participation, especially among workers who have below-average schooling and wages.[12] Social Security's old-age insurance benefits may have similar effects on nondisabled workers nearing the early entitlement age (sixty-two).

Disability insurance benefits are likely to have larger effects on the working-age population, however, especially in the case of workers who are under the age of sixty. To become eligible for DI, workers must pass a medical screening for disability and have accumulated a minimum number of earnings credits as a result of employment in Social Security–covered jobs. In addition, some of the earnings credits must have been accumulated in the years immediately before the application for DI benefits is filed. Applicants must be disabled and jobless

11. Technically, the figures imply only that the average *compensated* spell of unemployment was longer in Puerto Rico than on the mainland. If those who exhausted their benefits experienced much longer spells of unemployment after benefit exhaustion on the mainland compared with Puerto Rico, it is conceivable that average spell length was longer on the mainland. However, this seems unlikely.

12. See Autor and Duggan (2003) and Bound and others (2004).

for a minimum of five months before DI benefits can begin. About half of all applicants for DI are ultimately accepted into the program, although many successful applicants are accepted only after appealing an initial denial of their application.

The attraction of the program for workers who earn low wages is no mystery. Because the Social Security benefit formula is quite redistributive, workers with low lifetime wages can anticipate receiving monthly benefit payments that replace a high percentage of their past earnings. Figure 3-11 shows the schedule of DI and full old-age benefits in relation to a worker's average earnings in previous covered employment.[13] The top panel shows the annual pension amount (on the vertical axis) mapped against the worker's average annual earnings (on the horizontal axis). The basic benefit formula provides 90 percent earnings replacement up through the first earnings bend point (about $6,000 a year in the 1999 formula). It provides 32 percent marginal earnings replacement between the first and second bend points and 15 percent marginal earnings replacement on earnings above the second bend point. The lower panel shows the earnings replacement rates that are implied by the benefit formula. For workers with previous annual earnings below about $6,000, the replacement rate is 90 percent. For workers with average U.S. earnings (about $30,000 a year) the replacement rate is about 43 percent; and for workers earning wages near the maximum taxed amount, the replacement rate is about 30 percent.

The vertical broken lines in the top and bottom panels indicate 1999 earnings amounts reported by respondents in the 2000 decennial census. Four vertical lines are shown in each chart. The two lines on the right indicate the average annual earnings reported by men on the U.S. mainland who were in the second and third quarters, respectively, of the male earnings distribution. The line on the far right, for example, shows the average reported earnings of men with earnings above the median earnings amount but below the 75th percentile amount. Average earnings in this population were slightly above $40,000. The vertical broken line immediately to the left shows average earnings among men earning less than the median amount but more than the 25th percentile amount. The two broken lines on the left show average earnings for the same two populations in Puerto Rico. Note that Puerto Rican annual wages are substantially lower than those on the mainland. On average, Puerto Rican earners in the second quarter of the male earnings distribution earned $10,750 in 1999, whereas male earners

---

13. Workers become eligible for a full old-age pension when they attain the normal retirement age, currently between sixty-five and sixty-six, depending on a worker's year of birth. Workers can claim an old-age pension as early as age sixty-two. Early claimants receive permanently reduced pensions, for which the early-retirement penalty is scaled according the number of months between the age of benefit claim and the person's normal retirement age. For workers enrolled in the DI program, benefits are converted to an old-age pension when they attain the normal retirement age. However, the monthly benefit amount is essentially unchanged.

Figure 3-11. *Social Security Benefit Entitlements in Relation to Preretirement Earnings, 1999*

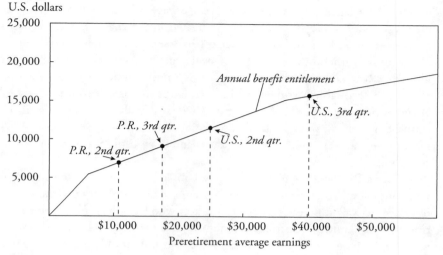

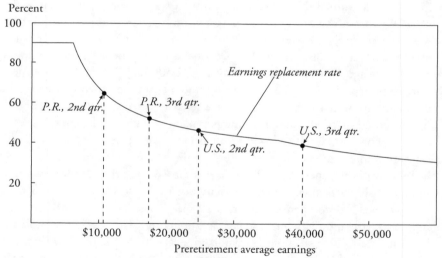

Preretirement average earnings

Source: Authors' calculations using U.S. Social Security Administration, *Annual Statistical Supplement*, 2003, and own tabulations of earnings reported in the 2000 decennial census.

in the same part of the mainland distribution earned $24,750. This implies, of course, that Puerto Rican workers will qualify for a much more generous level of income replacement when they retire. The replacement rate in this earnings class will be 65 percent in Puerto Rico versus 46 percent on the mainland. If workers experience a drop in earnings compared with their previous career wage, the relevant income replacement rate is even higher.

The replacement rates shown in the bottom panel of figure 3-11 reflect the ratio of potential benefits to average career wages. Workers with potential earnings that have fallen below their career average wage will obtain income replacement rates even more attractive than indicated in the chart. The DI benefits actually received by residents of Puerto Rico seem quite high relative to the average wage earned in the island. In recent years, the average disabled worker in Puerto Rico has received a DI check that is 85 percent of the average pension received by a disabled worker on the mainland. In comparison, the average Social Security–covered wage in Puerto Rico is only about 58 percent of the equivalent wage on the mainland. This comparison strongly suggests that DI replacement rates are much higher in the island than in the Social Security area as a whole.

If Puerto Rico and the mainland of the United States are considered as separate countries, the two nations have retirement and disability programs that offer distinctively different benefits to workers who have the same relative position in their country's earnings distributions. A male worker earning a wage near the midpoint of the Puerto Rican wage distribution earned about $14,000 in 1999. If he earned this amount as a constant wage throughout his career, his OASDI pension would replace 57 percent of his career average earnings. If he were to marry a spouse who had earned little throughout her career, his replacement rate would be 86 percent. A U.S. resident male in the same position in the mainland wage distribution earned about $32,500 in 1999. His OASDI pension would replace just 43 percent of that amount. Since married women on the mainland are much more likely to have lengthy careers, it is less likely that newly retired married women on the mainland will collect dependent spouse benefits. For workers with a lower earnings rank, the replacement-rate comparison would show an even larger advantage to the worker in Puerto Rico.

In view of the generosity of DI pensions for workers who earn low wages, it should not be surprising that the disability rate in Puerto Rico is well above the U.S. average. The top panel in figure 3-12 shows the trend in DI participation in Puerto Rico and the United States.[14] Although DI participation was initially lower in Puerto Rico than on the mainland, by 1970 the Puerto Rican rate significantly exceeded the rate in the fifty states and the District of Columbia. In 1980 Puerto Rico's disability take-up rate was about two and one-half times the disability rate in the United States. Program reforms in the early 1980s cut the rolls and discouraged DI applications, but eligibility standards were again relaxed after the mid-1980s. The trend toward higher DI application rates and

14. More precisely, the estimated DI participation rate for the United States represents the total number of DI workers, excluding the disabled in Puerto Rico, divided by the twenty- to sixty-four-year-old resident population of the United States. A very small number of DI recipients do not live either in Puerto Rico or the United States, but for purposes of this calculation these workers are assumed to be U.S. residents.

Figure 3-12. *Receipt of Social Security Benefits by the Nonaged Population, Selected Areas, 1961–2002*[a]

Percent of nonaged population

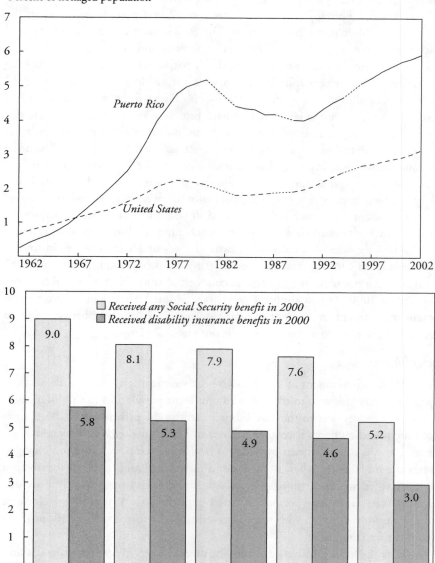

Source: Authors' tabulations of Social Security Administration, *Annual Statistical Supplement,* various issues, and U.S. Census Bureau population data.

a. The nonaged population is defined here as twenty- to sixty-four-year-olds. Breaks in the Puerto Rico and U.S. data series, owing to breaks in administrative data, are indicated by breaks in the lines in the top panel.

participation resumed by 1990, both in Puerto Rico and on the mainland.[15] By 2002, both the Puerto Rican and mainland disability rates exceeded their previous peaks. In 2002 receipt of DI benefits in Puerto Rico was almost twice the level on the mainland. The difference may account for 2 to 3 percentage points of the lower labor force participation rate in Puerto Rico compared with the United States and a greater part of the difference in participation rates at older ages.

To evaluate the extent to which high DI participation rates in Puerto Rico are related to low wages and high unemployment, the lower panel in figure 3-12 compares disability rates in Puerto Rico with rates in three states that have low wages and high levels of labor market hardship. Two sets of calculations are displayed in the chart. The first shows the fraction of the working-age population (twenty- to sixty-four-year-olds) who received a Social Security check and the second shows disability rates. Puerto Rico has a higher disability rate than low-income states on the U.S. mainland, although the margin of difference is not large. A bigger surprise is the high proportion of twenty- to sixty-four-year-old island residents who received some kind of benefit under Social Security. In addition to the disabled, working-age beneficiaries include surviving spouses, dependent spouses of the disabled, early retirees under the old-age insurance component of OASDI, and spouses of retired workers. About 9 percent of the working-age population in Puerto Rico received some kind of Social Security benefit in 2000. This is almost 4 percentage points higher than the fraction of mainland residents receiving benefits. However, the difference between Puerto Rico and the three low-income states is not especially large.

Health Insurance

In 1993 the government of Puerto Rico began a transition from its role as single provider of health care to the medically indigent population to that of a single insurer, with services to the insured provided by the private sector. Under the old regime, the Puerto Rico Department of Health owned and operated a system that was the dominant provider of health services. The situation changed after the mid-1960s, when Medicare was established and began to insure aged and disabled workers, thereby increasing the demand for privately provided medical care. Two large sectors coexisted until the early 1990s, when reform of the commonwealth's health system paved the way to the privatization of the public infrastructure.[16]

Under the health insurance system introduced in 1993, the state's role is limited to the negotiation of private insurance contracts, quality assurance, and the

---

15. Bound and Waidmann (2002).

16. The public sector program was financed by state and municipal government funds (80 percent), Medicaid (10 percent), Medicare (4 percent), and insurance and private payments (6 percent). The private sector received 40 percent of its funds through Medicare, 46 percent from private health insurance, and 14 percent from direct payments (Marín 1999).

facilitation of enrollment. Services are provided by health maintenance organizations catering to three main groups. The first consists of people eligible for Medicaid, namely, the low-income population of aged, blind, or disabled individuals, pregnant women, and children. Low income is defined by poverty thresholds set by Puerto Rico's Department of Health. The thresholds are currently about half those in effect on the mainland. A second covered population consists of some people who are ineligible for Medicaid because they are not in a covered category or because their incomes are too high. Families in this group can have incomes up to two times the Puerto Rican poverty line. Finally, any member of the police, regardless of income, can opt to receive health insurance under the state scheme.

In 2004 the commonwealth's insurance program covered 41 percent of the island's population. Eighty percent of the insured were Medicaid participants. Seventy-three percent of the cost of the $1.3 billion program was borne by the commonwealth government, 15 percent by federal Medicaid matching funds, and the remainder by municipal governments.[17] In principle, the federal government matches every dollar of commonwealth expenditures on Medicaid, but there is a low cap on federal contributions to the Puerto Rican program. The result is that the commonwealth pays most of the program's cost (hence the lower poverty thresholds, which have not been revised since 1992). Health insurance expenditures represent about a fifth of the commonwealth's government tax revenues.

Taxes levied to finance the program have an indeterminate effect on the supply of labor for reasons described earlier. However, the transfer benefits provided by the program unambiguously increase the demand for leisure through an income effect. The provision of free health services to program participants certainly increases their net income beyond what it might be in a no-insurance world. Unlike the payments provided under the Nutritional Assistance Program, health insurance benefits are not gradually reduced as household income increases. Hence there are no income and substitution effects related to a lower implicit wage. The net and gross wages received by insured workers are identical until the income threshold is reached, at which point insurance benefits are lost entirely. Figure 3-13 illustrates the trade-off between hours of work and net income under the Puerto Rican health insurance program. The line $0ABCD$ represents the budget constraint of a medically indigent individual under the old system, under which the government provided free health services until his or her income reached the poverty line at X hours of work. Under the new program (budget constraint $0AEFD$), insurance protection is extended to individuals with

17. "Presupuesto recomendado 2004–2005: Agencia de Seguros de Salud de Puerto Rico," February 2004 (www.presupuesto.gobierno.pr/PresupuestosAnteriores/af2005/Tomo_II/segurosSalud.htm), and personal communication with the Medicaid office in San Juan, Puerto Rico.

Figure 3-13. *Work–Net Income Trade-off under Puerto Rico's Health Insurance Program*

Monthly income[a]

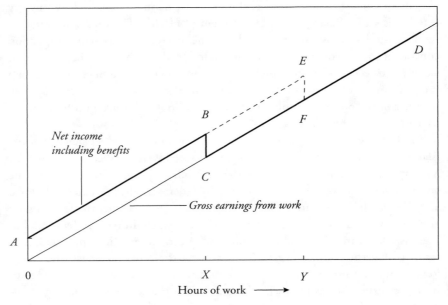

Hours of work ⟶

a. The sum of earnings plus the value of health insurance coverage.

incomes equivalent to two times the poverty line reached at *Y* hours of work, thus increasing the likelihood of a reduction in the work hours of those with incomes above the poverty line. Individuals who did not qualify for health services under the old system have an even greater increase in nonlabor income, going from budget constraint 0*D* to 0*AEFD*. Moreover, to the extent that the new system provides a higher quantity or quality of services, incentives to work are reduced across the entire hours range by shifting upward the nonlabor income portion of the budget constraint.

Temporary Assistance for Needy Families

Temporary Assistance for Needy Families (TANF) is a relatively small transfer program in Puerto Rico that operates along the lines of similar programs on the U.S. mainland. The target population consists of children who lack financial support from one or both parents owing to the parent's death, disability, or prolonged absence. Families or individuals who pass asset and income tests receive cash assistance payments based on an income-to-needs formula that is set at the state or commonwealth level. Accordingly, basic benefit levels vary widely across states, with 2004 maximum monthly benefits for a family of three ranging from

$164 in Alabama and $216 in Puerto Rico up to $679 in California and $923 in Alaska. In theory, the TANF program depresses labor supply through income and substitution effects that are essentially the same as those characteristic of the NAP. A family without any countable income receives the maximum benefit allotted by the state. As countable income rises, TANF benefits are reduced, although rarely on a dollar-for-dollar basis. Once a family's income exceeds the TANF income limit, benefits to the family are eliminated entirely.

The program was established in 1996 to replace the old Aid to Families with Dependent Children (AFDC) program. The goal of the legislation creating TANF was to end long-term dependency by encouraging aid recipients to become self-sufficient. This was to be accomplished through both financial incentives to recipients and time limits on the duration of potential benefits. To accomplish these goals, many states tinkered with benefit formulas. The enabling legislation gave them great flexibility for experimentation. Some states allowed inflation to erode the real value of basic benefits, and others reduced nominal benefits in the hope of increasing work effort through an income effect. Many states also experimented with income disregards, permitting recipients to earn some wages that are not immediately taken into account in the calculation of aid payments. Similarly, benefit reduction rates, the percentages by which benefits are reduced as the countable income of a family unit rises, were reduced from levels that had approached 100 percent in the AFDC program. Puerto Rico did not change the benefit reduction rates it imposed on aid recipients. Along with many states on the mainland, it did limit TANF payments to just sixty months. (Under AFDC, benefits could be collected as long as the youngest child in an indigent family was under the age of eighteen.)

Partly as a result of these program changes, U.S. welfare rolls fell dramatically after the early 1990s. Perhaps even more surprising, given the tough labor market in Puerto Rico, TANF participation in the commonwealth fell from 151,000 in 1996 to 54,000 in 2002, a decline of 64 percent. This decline was somewhat larger than the average decline observed in the fifty U.S. states. Only a small percentage of TANF cases were closed as a result of the sixty-month benefit limitation. The dramatic fall in Puerto Rico's welfare caseload also occurred in the absence of any work incentives under the earned income tax credit (EITC) program, since the EITC is not available in Puerto Rico. There is considerable evidence that the increased generosity of the EITC after 1993 played an important role in reducing welfare caseloads and increasing single mothers' employment rates on the U.S. mainland.[18]

A decline in the TANF caseload does not necessarily mean that work effort or income increased after AFDC was abolished, but research in the United States shows that the caseload decline occurred at the same time that labor force

18. Meyer and Rosenbaum (2000); Burtless (2002); Grogger (2003).

participation among less-skilled women rose and poverty rates among unskilled single-mother families fell.[19] Unfortunately, Puerto Rico's data are not good enough to tell us whether the same conclusions are valid for single mothers in the commonwealth. Of central interest to this study is the program's effect on employment and labor force participation rates. Most able-bodied adults who receive benefits under TANF are required to be employed or to participate in a work activity. In Puerto Rico only 6.6 percent of the adults to whom this work requirement applied actually participated in work activities in 2002. The comparable participation rate on the U.S. mainland was 33.4 percent and ranged from a low of 8.3 percent in Maryland to a high of 84.9 percent in Kansas. The low workforce participation rates in Puerto Rico's TANF program indicate that the program has been less successful than most in pushing aid recipients into jobs or job preparation. On the other hand, Puerto Rico has been more successful than most states in reducing the number of adults and households collecting benefits under TANF. If some of the adults leaving cash assistance programs found jobs, the reforms may have contributed to a small increase in parental employment rates.

Summary of Transfer Programs

Figure 3-14 shows the combined contributions of the three main cash benefit programs to personal incomes in Puerto Rico and the United States. In combination, the NAP program, unemployment insurance, and Social Security now provide about half of total government transfer benefits received by Puerto Rico's residents. The top panel shows the contribution of Social Security benefits to Puerto Rican and U.S. incomes. Because of differences in the national income and product accounts data for the two areas, the data refer to fiscal years in Puerto Rico and to calendar years in the United States. Social Security benefits provided a steadily rising proportion of personal income to U.S. residents through the early 1980s. Since that time, Social Security's contribution has leveled off. The Social Security share in personal income rose much faster and to a higher level in Puerto Rico. As in the United States, the peak contribution of the program was attained in the early 1980s, but the program continues to provide a much higher fraction of Puerto Ricans' income—10 percent, compared with just 5 percent on the mainland.

The combined contribution of nutrition assistance, unemployment insurance, and Social Security benefits to personal income is shown in the bottom panel of figure 3-14. In total these programs accounted for about 6 percent of U.S. and 14 percent of Puerto Rican personal income in 2002. The biggest increase in the U.S.–Puerto Rico difference occurred between 1974 and the early 1980s, when employment and labor force participation rates fell sharply in

19. Blank (2002); Burtless (2002).

Figure 3-14. *Selected Government Transfers as Percent of Personal Income, Puerto Rico and the United States, 1962–2002*[a]

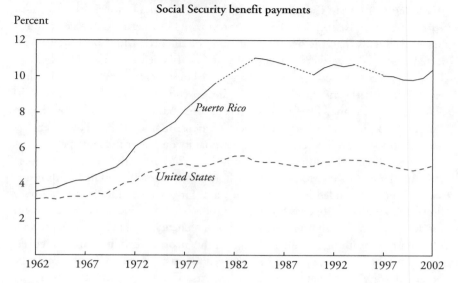

Social Security benefit payments

Percent

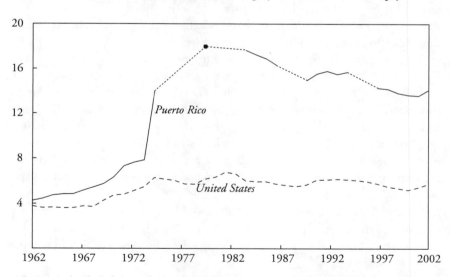

Nutrition assistance, social security, and unemployment insurance benefit payments

Source: Authors' tabulations of program data from the U.S. Social Security Administration, Food and Nutrition Service, U.S. Department of Agriculture, and Employment and Training Administration, U.S. Department of Labor, and national income and product accounts data from the Bureau of Economic Analysis and Puerto Rico. The Social Security Administration did not publish data for Puerto Rico in 1980–83, 1988–89, and 1994–96.

a. Data for Puerto Rico refer to Puerto Rican fiscal year; data for the United States refer to calendar year. Breaks in the Puerto Rico data series, owing to breaks in administrative data, are indicated by broken lines.

Puerto Rico relative to the United States. Both nutrition assistance and Social Security benefits include large explicit or implicit subsidies from U.S. taxpayers to residents of Puerto Rico. Food stamp and NAP benefits are entirely financed with federal funds, and Social Security recipients in Puerto Rico receive much bigger payments than the benefits that could be financed with OASDI taxes collected from island workers. Given that regular UI benefits are not subsidized by U.S. taxpayers, it is perhaps unsurprising that Puerto Rico's weekly payment levels and permitted benefit duration seem meager compared with UI benefits available on the mainland. Even so, the average contribution of UI compensation to Puerto Rico personal income has been 0.9 percent since 1975. These benefits accounted for just 0.5 percent of U.S. personal income over the same period.

Publicly financed health insurance provides an in-kind benefit that is an important supplement to Puerto Rican households' cash incomes. Public health insurance has been expanded in a number of ways. First, services that in the past were limited to access to public health clinics and hospitals now include reimbursement for doctor visits, prescription drugs, and hospital, dental, and mental care. Second, the commonwealth's government increased the income eligibility limits for coverage under the insurance program. This resulted in an increase in the size of the potential population that qualifies for benefits. Third, program take-up among the eligible population may have increased because health care rationing and quality are less important issues in private than in public facilities. Therefore, not only are more individuals receiving benefits, but their value has increased since the reforms of the early 1990s were undertaken.

Each program discussed here may have important work-discouraging effects. Even if the effect per dollar spent were no greater in Puerto Rico than in the United States, the effects would still be relatively more important in Puerto Rico because spending is higher in relation to the amount of income island residents can expect to earn in the labor market. There are also reasons to think the proportional effects of the programs are larger in Puerto Rico because so many more of the island's working-age residents are eligible for and receiving benefits. In contrast, a much smaller percentage of working-age people on the mainland are potentially eligible for food stamp benefits. Although in principle the same fraction of U.S. and Puerto Rican adults should be eligible for Social Security disability payments, those payments will be relatively more attractive to a larger percentage of Puerto Rico's workforce because benefit levels are high in relation to Puerto Rican wages.

The Labor Supply Decision

The labor supply decision boils down to an individual's choice of how to divide available time between work and other activities. The potential worker faces the problem of selecting the combination of hours of work and nonwork time that maximizes utility. The solution to this problem depends on individual preferences—the taste for work, on the one hand, and for the goods and services that can be obtained through work, on the other—and on available combinations of work hours and net income, or budget constraints. Potential workers' preferences are notoriously difficult to measure, but their budget constraints can be measured with some precision. To understand the influence of taxes and transfers on potential workers' labor supply decisions, it is useful to compare the budget constraints facing representative workers.

Table 3-1 presents the monthly budget line faced by a hypothetical household composed of two children and a single mother earning an hourly wage equal to Puerto Rico's legal minimum wage ($5.15 an hour in 2003). The estimates reflect tax rates and program rules in effect in 2003. The income figures are given for workweeks of various lengths; gross monthly wages are based on 4.3 workweeks a month. After the deduction of payroll and commonwealth taxes that would be paid out of the worker's gross wages, the gross monthly wage of $893 earned by a single mother of two who works a forty-hour week at minimum wage, for example, would be reduced to a net wage of $790. If the mother resided on the mainland instead of in Puerto Rico, she would also be entitled to receive a refundable tax credit under the EITC, which would more than offset her payroll and income tax liability. Under a proposed EITC for Puerto Rico suggested by María Enchautegui, the Puerto Rican mother's after-credit income would also be higher than her gross earnings.[20]

Both in Puerto Rico and on the U.S. mainland, single mothers with low incomes may qualify for TANF, nutrition assistance, a section 8 housing subsidy, and public medical insurance. Table 3-1 shows the corresponding amounts of public aid as a function of monthly gross earnings, using program rules and payment schedules for 2003. A single mother who has no earned income and qualifies for all the transfers would receive the monthly equivalent of $1,276 in cash and services. If she were to work part-time (twenty hours a week), her net income would *fall* by $15 a month. Working a forty-hour week would bring a slightly higher net income than not working at all, but the gain would be only $37 a month. The single mother would face very high implicit marginal tax rates as she increased her weekly hours of work. For example, when going from fifteen to twenty hours she would earn an additional $111 in gross earnings, on which she would pay $8 in payroll taxes and no additional commonwealth taxes. At the same time, she would lose $80 in section 8, NAP, and TANF benefits. The improvement in her family's net household income would be only $23, implying that she faces a 79 percent implicit tax rate on her extra earnings. The final column shows the average tax rate faced by a single mother at each level of working hours. Note that the average tax rate is always near or above 100 percent.

20. Enchautegui (2003).

Table 3-1. *Relation of Work Effort and Monthly Net Income, Household of Two Children and a Single Mother Working for the Minimum Wage, 2003*[a]

Dollars, except as indicated

Work week (hours)	Gross earnings	FICA taxes	Income taxes	Health plan	TANF	NAP	Section 8	Total income[b]	Marginal tax rate (%)	Average tax rate (%)
0	0	0	0	276	216	268	516	1,276	0	0
5	112	−9	0	276	161	268	483	1,291	87	87
10	223	−17	0	276	87	252	449	1,270	119	103
15	335	−26	0	276	12	225	416	1,238	129	111
20	446	−34	0	276	0	191	382	1,261	79	103
25	558	−43	−5	276	0	0	349	1,135	213	125
30	670	−51	−13	276	0	0	315	1,197	45	112
35	781	−60	−24	276	0	0	282	1,255	48	103
40	893	−68	−35	276	0	0	248	1,313	48	96

Source: Authors' tabulations of data from Puerto Rico public health insurance, TANF, NAP, and section 8 benefit schedules and applicable payroll and commonwealth tax schedules.

a. It is assumed that individuals live in San Juan, where the fair market value of rent for two-bedroom housing, according to the U.S. Department of Housing and Urban Development, is $516. Families get the maximum TANF benefit but no housing allowance. The price of health insurance is set at cost for a three-person family residing in San Juan. Monetary figures are all in monthly equivalences, and all tax and transfer schedules are those in effect in 2003.

b. Earnings, cash transfers, and the monetary value of in-kind transfers.

One consequence of the 1996 welfare reform is that most single mothers can count on TANF benefits for a maximum of five years over their lifetimes. Moreover, for most adults, receipt of Puerto Rico's NAP benefit is conditioned on looking for work. Thus the trade-off between work and net income shown in table 3-1 represents a short-term trade-off. In the long run, some transfer benefits would be withheld from mothers who failed to find work or refused to look for work.

Suppose the labor market improved and an unskilled worker could earn higher wages. How would the choices faced by a single mother change? Table 3-2 considers the situation of a single mother with two children whose wages doubled, reaching $10.30 an hour. If the woman accepted a full-time job (forty hours a week) at this wage, her combined net earnings and transfer income would provide a monthly income of $1,524. This is $248 above her income while remaining outside the workforce, implying that the average tax on labor earnings is 86 percent. The results in tables 3-1 and 3-2 show why many low-wage and even high-wage single mothers may choose not to join the workforce. However, single-mother families represent only about 10 percent of Puerto Rican households. Mothers in married-couple families are much more numerous than single mothers, so their labor force status is more important in explaining low participation rates of Puerto Rican women.

Table 3-3 presents tabulations of the trade-off between work and net income facing a mother whose husband works full-time hours at Puerto Rico's minimum wage. The couple is assumed to support two children under the age of eighteen. We assume that if the mother enters the workforce she can also earn the minimum wage ($5.15 an hour). The final column in table 3-3 presents the implicit average tax rates her household would face as her weekly work effort increased from five to forty hours. Note that the average tax on her earnings never falls below 86 percent, and at half-time and full-time weekly hours her average tax would actually exceed 100 percent. In some income ranges the implicit marginal tax rate is far higher than 100 percent. For example, as her weekly work effort increased from fifteen to twenty hours, her family would see a loss in total income of $190—from $1,737 to $1,547—as a result of the loss of section 8 housing subsidies. Similarly, an increase from thirty to thirty-five work hours a week would produce a loss of $368 in health insurance subsidies. The wife's work disincentives are considerably smaller if her husband earns a higher wage. In the case of a husband who earned twice the minimum wage, for example, the family would not be entitled to means-tested transfers, and the wife would face a marginal tax rate of only 18 to 23 percent. All of these calculations ignore the child care costs that would quite likely be incurred when the wife entered the workforce. If these were taken into account, the implicit tax on the mother's earnings would, of course, be much higher.

A trade-off between equity and efficiency is almost always present in the design of social protection policies. Income support programs such as TANF

Table 3-2. *Relation of Work Effort and Monthly Net Income, Household of Two Children and a Single Mother Working for Twice the Minimum Wage, 2003*[a]

Dollars, except as indicated

Work week (hours)	Gross earnings	FICA taxes	Income taxes	Health plan	TANF	NAP	Section 8	Total income[b]	Marginal tax rate (%)	Average tax rate (%)
0	0	0	0	276	216	268	516	1,276	0	0
5	223	−17	0	276	87	252	449	1,270	103	103
10	446	−34	0	276	0	191	382	1,261	104	103
15	670	−51	−13	276	0	0	315	1,197	129	112
20	893	−68	−35	276	0	0	248	1,313	48	96
25	1,116	−85	−57	276	0	0	181	1,430	48	86
30	1,339	−102	−80	276	0	0	0	1,433	99	88
35	1,562	−120	−102	0	0	0	0	1,341	141	96
40	1,785	−137	−124	0	0	0	0	1,524	18	86

Source: Authors' tabulations of data from Puerto Rico public health insurance, TANF, NAP, and section 8 benefit schedules and applicable payroll and commonwealth tax schedules.

a. It is assumed that individuals live in San Juan, where the fair market value of rent for two-bedroom housing, according to the U.S. Department of Housing and Urban Development, is $516. Families get the maximum TANF benefit but no housing allowance. The price of health insurance is set at cost for a three-person family residing in San Juan. Monetary figures are all in monthly equivalences, and all tax and transfer schedules are those in effect in 2003.

b. Earnings, cash transfers, and the monetary value of in-kind transfers.

Table 3-3. *Relation of Work Effort and Monthly Net Income, Household of Two Children, a Male Working Full-Time for the Minimum Wage, and a Female Working for the Minimum Wage, 2003*[a]

Dollars, except as indicated

Work week (hours)	Gross earnings	FICA taxes	Income taxes	Health plan	TANF	NAP	Section 8	Total income[b]	Marginal tax rate (%)	Average tax rate (%)
0	893	−68	−13	368	0	0	382	1,562	0	0
5	1,004	−77	−24	368	0	0	349	1,620	48	94
10	1,116	−85	−35	368	0	0	315	1,679	48	90
15	1,227	−94	−46	368	0	0	282	1,737	48	86
20	1,339	−102	−57	368	0	0	0	1,547	270	101
25	1,451	−111	−68	368	0	0	0	1,639	18	95
30	1,562	−120	−80	368	0	0	0	1,731	18	89
35	1,674	−128	−91	0	0	0	0	1,455	347	106
40	1,785	−137	−102	0	0	0	0	1,547	18	101

Source: Authors' tabulations of data from Puerto Rico public health insurance, TANF, NAP, and section 8 benefit schedules and applicable payroll and commonwealth tax schedules.

a. It is assumed that individuals live in San Juan, where the fair market value of rent for three-bedroom housing, according to the U.S. Department of Housing and Urban Development, is $650. The price of health insurance is set at cost for a four-person family residing in San Juan. Monetary figures are all in monthly equivalences, and all tax and transfer schedules are those in effect in 2003.

b. Earnings, cash transfers, and the monetary value of in-kind transfers.

and nutrition assistance provide essential consumption support that reduces inequality and protects living standards of families with the lowest incomes. These social goals must be weighed against their efficiency costs—in particular, their effects on incentives to work among able-bodied but indigent adults. Needs-based health coverage offers essential health protection for the medically needy, but the link between benefit entitlement and family income introduces a powerful disincentive for low-skilled workers to work lengthy hours.

Micro Evidence

The evidence on average employment behavior over time and on trends in aggregate transfers is consistent with evidence from the decennial census files indicating that a rising fraction of working-age Puerto Ricans received government transfers during the 1970s and 1980s. Moreover, transfer benefits became a much more important component of income over that period, even among working-age Puerto Ricans in the middle ranks of the earnings distribution. The decennial census files are the only consistent and widely available source of information about the detailed sources of income of individual Puerto Rican households. For households on the mainland there are many alternative sources of information containing Census Bureau microdata on income and work behavior, and some of these, including the Current Population Survey and the Survey of Income and Program Participation, offer more accurate information on labor force behavior. However, the decennial census appears to provide reasonably reliable information on major sources of household income, including wages, self-employment earnings, and Social Security benefits.

We have used this information to classify working-age adults into five equal-sized groups based on their reported earnings in four census files, those derived from the 1970, 1980, 1990, and 2000 censuses. The income reports submitted by respondents cover incomes received in 1969, 1979, 1989, and 1999, respectively. Fortunately, all four years occurred at similar points in the business cycle, near the end of a lengthy economic expansion. We separately ranked men and women in Puerto Rico and on the U.S. mainland based on their labor earnings in a particular calendar year. The analysis is restricted to people aged twenty to sixty-four, including respondents with self-reported disabilities.

Because many working-age people have no earned income, there are many men and women with a tied earnings rank at the bottom of the distribution. When dividing the population into fifths, these ties do not represent a problem unless more than one-fifth of the population has no earned income. Among twenty- to sixty-four-year-old males on the U.S. mainland, the percentage of nonearners never rises above 13 percent. Among men of the same age in Puerto Rico, however, the percentage without earnings never falls below 23 percent, so it is necessary to assign nonearners at random to the bottom two-fifths of the

Table 3-4. *Share of Working-Age Adults with No Earned Income,*
Puerto Rico and the United States, by Sex and Year, 1969–99[a]
Percent

	Men		Women	
Year	Puerto Rico	United States	Puerto Rico	United States
1969	23	7	67	44
1979	36	10	67	35
1989	33	11	59	26
1999	35	13	56	24

Source: Authors' tabulations of data from 1970, 1980, 1990, and 2000 PUMS.
a. Persons aged twenty to sixty-four.

earnings distribution. A much larger percentage of women reports no earnings, although the percentage has fallen over time (see table 3-4). Only one-third of Puerto Rican women reported labor earnings in 1969 and 1979, so the two-thirds of women without earnings were randomly assigned to the bottom three-fifths of the female earnings distribution.

After assigning respondents to one of five earnings categories, we analyzed the sources of family income of people within each category. Table 3-5 shows the results of these tabulations for men in Puerto Rico and the United States. The first two columns show the percentage of men in the two areas who reported that someone in their family collected Social Security benefits. Although this type of income was more commonly reported in Puerto Rico than on the mainland, the difference between the two areas was modest in 1969, when 5 percent of all working-age Puerto Rican men reported Social Security income versus 4 percent of all men living on the mainland (see the bottom panel in table 3-5.) Men in the bottom fifth of the earnings distribution in that year reported a nearly identical likelihood of receiving Social Security benefits in both areas. After 1969, receipt of Social Security benefits became more common among Puerto Rican men, especially in the second fifth of the distribution. In 1979 and later years, about 20 percent of Puerto Rican men in that income category received a Social Security check, versus only 3 percent on the mainland.

Statistics on the receipt of public assistance benefits are displayed in the middle two columns of table 3-5. In the decennial census the Census Bureau asks respondents to report only cash public assistance benefits. The responses therefore show means-tested public benefits, including Aid to Families with Dependent Children and cash assistance to the aged and disabled, but they exclude food coupons that are redeemable only for groceries. Consequently, the value of food stamps is not included for the United States in 1969–99 or for Puerto Rico in 1979, but Puerto Rico's NAP benefit is included in assistance benefits in 1989 and 1999.

Table 3-5. *Percentage of Working-Age Men Receiving Transfer Benefits, Puerto Rico and the United States, by Position in Male Earnings Distribution, 1969–99*[a]

Position in male earnings distribution and year	Social Security		Public assistance[b]		Social Security and public assistance as share of total income[c]	
	Puerto Rico	United States	Puerto Rico	United States	Puerto Rico	United States
Bottom fifth						
1969	16	15	10	7	23	10
1979	25	21	13	10	51	19
1989	23	18	27	11	46	16
1999	27	18	21	12	43	13
Second fifth						
1969	7	3	7	2	8	1
1979	22	3	14	3	45	1
1989	17	3	29	2	40	1
1999	21	3	20	3	32	1
Third fifth						
1969	3	2	2	1	1	0
1979	4	2	11	1	7	0
1989	3	2	25	1	9	0
1999	5	2	11	2	4	0
Fourth fifth						
1969	2	1	1	1	1	0
1979	2	2	6	1	2	0
1989	2	2	9	1	2	0
1999	5	2	11	2	4	0
Top fifth						
1969	1	1	0	0	0	0
1979	2	2	1	1	0	0
1989	2	2	2	0	0	0
1999	4	2	2	1	1	0
All men						
1969	5	4	3	2	2	1
1979	9	5	8	3	7	1
1989	8	4	15	3	7	1
1999	10	4	10	3	5	1

Source: Authors' tabulations of data from 1970, 1980, 1990, and 2000 PUMS.

a. In each year, men aged twenty to sixty-four are ranked by their labor earnings and divided into fifths. The tabulations include zero-earners, who are randomly assigned to the lowest ranks in the distribution.

b. Public assistance is defined in the decennial census as cash benefits. It includes the NAP program in Puerto Rico in 1989 and 1999, but excludes the food stamp program in 1979 and in 1969–99 in the United States. See discussion in text.

c. The sum of labor earnings, Social Security benefits, and public assistance.

This definitional problem makes the trend statistics difficult to interpret. It is probably safest to compare Puerto Rico's results for 1969 (before the introduction of food stamps in Puerto Rico), 1989, and 1999 while treating the results for 1979 with caution. As should be obvious from the data presented in figure 3-8, a large proportion of Puerto Rican transfer recipients are ignored if nutrition assistance benefits are excluded from the definition of public assistance. In other respects, however, the time pattern of public assistance reports is consistent with the aggregate evidence.

Participation in Puerto Rican means-tested programs increased enormously between 1969 and 1989 and then declined moderately in the 1990s. The comparison with public assistance trends in the United States is particularly interesting. A far higher proportion of Puerto Ricans in the second and third fifths of the earnings distribution reported having received means-tested benefits. Although this was also true in 1969, the growth in Puerto Rican participation in means-tested programs after 1979 is striking—especially given that the rise in participation between 1969 and 1979 does not include the growth in participation in the food stamp program.

The comparison of Puerto Rican and U.S. receipt rates in 1989 and 1999 is not exact, because the U.S. estimates do not include food stamp beneficiaries whereas the Puerto Rican statistics include participants in the NAP. We do not believe the inclusion of food stamp participation in the U.S. statistics would make much difference to the U.S. totals, however. First, the overwhelming majority of U.S. food stamp recipients also receive other public assistance or Social Security benefits, so only a small number of participants would be added to the U.S. totals if the Census Bureau asked about food stamps.[21] Second, food stamp receipt is highly concentrated in the lowest ranks of the U.S. income distribution. In 1999 almost 90 percent of U.S. food stamp beneficiaries had incomes below the official poverty line, and less than 1 percent had incomes greater than 130 percent of the poverty line.[22] Only 11.8 percent of Americans had incomes below the official poverty line in 1999. It follows that few male earners in the second fifth of the male earnings distribution received food stamps. In contrast, 29 percent of men in the second fifth of Puerto Rico's earnings distribution received public assistance benefits in 1989, as did 25 percent in the middle fifth of the distribution. Puerto Rican participation in public assistance declined from 1989 to 1999, but receipt of assistance benefits was still much more common than it was among men in the same position in the U.S. earnings distribution.

The last two columns in table 3-5 show the proportion of income in each fifth that is derived from Social Security and public assistance benefits. By *total income* we mean all labor income earned by the man and his spouse plus the

21. See Long (1988, esp. p. 30).
22. Rosso and Fowler (2000, p. 14).

income they received from Social Security and public assistance. In each of the bottom three earnings categories, government transfers were a much more important source of family income in Puerto Rico than in the United States. Moreover, the importance of Social Security and assistance income increased sharply among these groups after 1969. In the second-lowest earnings category, government transfer benefits accounted for 45 percent of Puerto Rican family income in 1979, 40 percent in 1989, and 32 percent in 1999. In contrast, in each of those years U.S. men in the second fifth derived only 1 percent of their family income from Social Security or public assistance, and men in the top three income groups essentially none. These tabulations suggest that the work-discouraging effects of government benefits affect a far larger proportion of the working-age men in Puerto Rico than on the mainland.

In table 3-6 we report statistics on the receipt of transfer benefits among working-age women. Many women do not earn any income, so their low earnings rank is assigned to them at random. If 40 percent or more women are not in the workforce, the participation rates and income sources of the women in the bottom two earnings categories will be the same. Many women who do not earn wages are married to husbands who do. A large percentage of such wives enjoy a comfortable standard of living because their husbands earn good wages. This implies that the earnings rank of many wives will not be highly correlated with the income position of their families. Nonetheless, the comparative statistics on women's participation in government transfer programs are suggestive. As is the case for men, women's receipt of Social Security benefits and public assistance is much more common in Puerto Rico than in the United States, and this is true in every earnings category. Women's participation in transfer programs has also risen much faster in Puerto Rico than on the mainland. Between 1969 and 1999, participation in Social Security increased from 8 percent to 13 percent of the working-age female population, and participation in means-tested cash public assistance increased from 4 percent to 14 percent. Participation rates on the mainland changed little over the same three-decade span. This comparison implies that government transfers have more important practical effects on Puerto Rican than on U.S. labor supply, because transfers are received by or potentially available to a far higher proportion of the working-age population.

Synthesis

There is little evidence of a long-term and *continuous* decline in Puerto Rican participation rates for the entire span of years from 1950 to the present. As table 3-7 illustrates, the decline in male participation rates that took place during the 1950s was concentrated among the youngest and the oldest males, groups that also experienced declining labor force participation on the U.S. mainland. The declines in these two age groups occurred as a result of expanded educational opportunities

Table 3-6. *Percentage of Working-Age Women Receiving Transfer Benefits, Puerto Rico and the United States, by Position in Female Earnings Distribution, 1969–99*[a]

Position in female earnings distribution and year	Social Security		Public assistance[b]		Social Security and public assistance as share of total income[c]	
	Puerto Rico	United States	Puerto Rico	United States	Puerto Rico	United States
Bottom fifth						
1969	12	13	6	7	4	3
1979	20	19	15	13	13	6
1989	19	18	36	16	17	6
1999	23	16	26	14	13	5
Second fifth						
1969	13	7	7	6	4	2
1979	21	8	15	10	14	3
1989	19	6	36	10	17	2
1999	24	5	26	8	14	2
Third fifth						
1969	12	51	7	5	4	2
1979	21	5	14	4	14	1
1989	19	3	35	3	17	1
1999	19	3	23	3	12	1
Fourth fifth						
1969	9	3	4	2	3	0
1979	12	3	9	2	6	1
1989	6	2	14	1	4	0
1999	7	2	6	1	2	0
Top fifth						
1969	3	2	0	1	0	0
1979	4	2	2	1	1	0
1989	4	2	1	1	1	0
1999	6	2	1	1	1	0
All women						
1969	8	5	4	3	2	1
1979	13	6	9	5	7	2
1989	11	5	20	5	8	1
1999	13	5	14	5	6	1

Source: Authors' tabulations of data from 1970, 1980, 1990, and 2000 PUMS.

a. In each year, women between twenty and sixty-four years old are ranked by their labor earnings and divided into fifths. The tabulations include zero-earners, who are randomly assigned to the lowest ranks in the distribution.

b. Public assistance is defined in the decennial census as cash benefits. It includes the NAP program in Puerto Rico in 1989 and 1999, but excludes the food stamp program in 1979 and in 1969–99 in the United States. See discussion in text.

c. The sum of labor earnings, Social Security benefits, and public assistance.

Table 3-7. *Labor Force Participation Rates, Puerto Rico and the United States, by Gender and Age, 1950–2001*
Percent

Gender and year	16–19	20–24	25–34	35–44	45–54	55–64	65+
			Puerto Rican males				
1950	60.1	89.3	89.0	96.1	95.3	87.0	57.7
1960	42.3	81.3	91.5	93.0	91.2	84.1	37.6
1967	37.7	81.4	93.5	92.4	89.6	78.4	32.4
1973	32.0	76.1	91.1	88.9	83.4	67.1	24.9
1982	19.6	65.9	84.9	84.2	75.8	50.0	11.5
1990	21.8	68.1	86.8	85.9	78.8	52.7	13.4
2001	21.1	67.5	85.5	82.3	72.4	47.2	10.6
			U.S. mainland males				
1950	63.2	87.9	96.0	97.6	95.8	86.9	45.8
1960	56.1	88.1	97.5	97.7	95.7	86.8	33.1
1967	55.6	84.4	97.2	97.3	95.2	84.4	27.1
1973	59.7	85.2	95.7	96.2	93.0	78.2	22.7
1982	56.7	84.9	94.7	95.3	91.2	70.2	17.8
1990	55.7	84.4	94.1	94.3	90.7	67.8	16.3
2001	50.2	81.6	92.7	92.5	88.5	68.3	17.7
			Puerto Rican females				
1950	32.2	39.0	37.3	36.9	26.2	15.4	6.3
1960	14.2	35.3	32.3	28.1	21.5	14.2	4.3
1967	14.7	40.1	39.0	36.0	25.7	14.3	3.5
1973	12.5	41.1	43.7	40.0	27.6	14.2	2.9
1982	6.7	31.4	43.3	41.3	30.7	13.7	1.7
1990	9.8	34.5	47.4	48.0	39.4	17.1	2.6
2001	11.8	38.5	55.5	54.2	43.9	19.8	3.4
			U.S. mainland females				
1950	41.0	46.0	34.0	39.1	37.9	27.0	9.7
1960	39.3	46.1	36.0	43.4	49.9	37.2	10.8
1967	41.6	53.3	41.9	48.1	51.8	42.4	9.6
1973	47.8	61.1	50.4	53.3	53.7	41.1	8.9
1982	51.4	69.8	68.0	68.0	61.6	41.8	7.9
1990	51.6	71.3	73.5	76.4	71.2	45.2	8.6
2001	49.0	72.7	75.5	77.1	76.4	53.2	9.6

Source: Authors' tabulations of data from Puerto Rico Department of Labor, Bureau of Labor Statistics, *Time Series on Employment and Unemployment, 1947–2001;* U.S. Department of Labor, Bureau of Labor Statistics, labor market survey data, selected years.

for younger men and improved retirement incomes for older men. Even among women, the steep decline in participation that occurred during the 1950s was to a large extent related to the near disappearance of the home needlework industry.[23]

Relative Puerto Rican participation rates fell precipitously during the 1970s, among both men and women. The oil embargoes hit Puerto Rico hard, and unemployment rose from 11.6 percent in 1973 to 19.9 percent in 1977. Unemployment declined modestly to 17.1 percent during the recovery from that recession only to soar to 23.4 percent as a result of a second oil shock and the worldwide recession of the early 1980s. Puerto Rican wages converged to U.S. levels for two decades up through the mid-1970s but then stagnated and gradually lost ground to those prevailing on the mainland. In view of the decline in relative wages in Puerto Rico, the drop in labor force participation rates is not surprising.

A number of factors suggest that improved public transfers after the mid-1970s may have played a role equal to or even more important than declining pretax wages in the trend toward lower relative participation. First, the fall in participation in Puerto Rico was concentrated among specific age groups. Facing youth unemployment rates that reached 33 percent in 1977 and 60 percent in 1982, young males became discouraged, and some decided to attend college. Men in the middle-age and older groups seemed to withdraw en masse from the labor force. Participation among forty-five- to fifty-four-year-olds fell from 83.4 in 1973 to 75.8 percent in 1982, reflecting a much larger decline than that which occurred in the United States (93 to 91.2 percent). More dramatic was the decline among fifty-five- to sixty-four-year-olds, whose participation rate fell from 67.1 to 50 percent. Social Security replacement rates rose during the decade, the program rolls grew sharply, and OASDI benefits became an important source of income, even for families near the middle of the earnings distribution.

After the early 1970s, unfavorable economic conditions pushed some older workers toward retirement, while improved old-age and disability benefits pulled many others into inactivity. The departure of older Puerto Rican men from the labor force began almost a decade before the recession of the early 1970s, however, which suggests that the liberalization of public pension benefits was influencing participation rates even before the deep recessions of the 1970s and early 1980s. From 1967 to 1973 participation among men aged forty-five to fifty-four fell by 6.2 percentage points, while that of men aged fifty-five to sixty-four fell 11.3 points. Social Security disability rolls were already increasing during the decade of the 1960s (see figure 3-12). Disability insurance participation as a percentage of the population aged twenty to sixty-four increased 1.4 percentage points in the ten years that followed 1973, but it rose 2.5 points during the ten

23. Reynolds and Gregory (1965).

years before 1973. The introduction of food stamps significantly improved the living standards of Puerto Rican families without breadwinners as well as families with breadwinners earning low weekly wages. The food stamp policy innovation cannot be interpreted as a response to Puerto Rico's economic crisis, however, because the decision to extend the program to the commonwealth preceded the recession of the early 1970s.[24] For some family breadwinners, access to food stamp benefits may have tipped the balance toward retirement and withdrawal from the labor force. For secondary earners, the availability of generous nutrition assistance may have deterred entry into the labor force.

Even after the major expansion of public transfers in the 1970s, transfers continued to play an important role. The Puerto Rican unemployment rate gradually declined from 23.4 percent in 1983 to 14.2 percent in 1990 and to 11.4 percent in 2001, but the male participation rate failed to recover fully. The male labor force participation rate in 2001 was 11 percentage points below the rate prevailing in 1973. Relative to the U.S. rate, male participation in Puerto Rico remained at a level close to the minimum reached during the severe recession in the early 1980s. Female participation in the island represented only 62 percent of the level on the U.S. mainland, a ratio that was lower than it had been at any point from 1950 to 1973. Although the relative participation rate among Puerto Rican women increased in the 1980s and 1990s, it did not come close to equivalent rates in the United States or most other developed countries.

Puerto Rican participation rates have certainly been influenced by a number of factors in addition to public transfers. The relative decline in participation and the currently depressed rate may reflect the increasing size of the informal sector rather than high levels of economic inactivity. However, we have found little evidence that the informal sector is growing faster in Puerto Rico than on the mainland. Migration could also play an important role in accounting for low participation. Lloyd Reynolds and Peter Gregory believe that when out-migration reached its peak in the 1950s, it lowered labor force participation rates in the island because emigrants were drawn overwhelmingly from groups with high participation.[25] When emigration declined in later decades, its effects diminished.

Finally, there is the issue of the Puerto Rican minimum wage. Although the effects of a high minimum wage on the participation rate are ambiguous, its theoretical impact on the employment rate is straightforward. If the minimum wage is above the lowest wage that would be negotiated in the absence of regulation, it will reduce the number of jobs offered by employers and eliminate some low-productivity positions. Although Reynolds and Gregory credit the rise in local minimum wages with boosting productivity in the island during the 1950s

24. See Weisskoff (1985, p. 162).
25. Reynolds and Gregory (1965).

and 1960s, they also suggest that it curtailed the economy's capacity to generate jobs. Under pressure from American trade unions and with the support of a local government that favored equality with the mainland in social, legal, and economic matters, the federal minimum wage was gradually phased in in Puerto Rico between 1977 and 1983, notwithstanding the high and rising unemployment rate during the period. Alida Castillo and Richard Freeman conclude that the extension of the U.S. minimum wage to Puerto Rico had a sizable negative effect on employment.[26] Alan Krueger, while not disputing the basic finding, concludes that it rests on fragile evidence.[27] The Puerto Rican minimum wage, like that on the mainland, has risen much more slowly than average wages and productivity since the early 1980s, suggesting that the negative effect on employment has probably declined over the past two decades.

Summary and a Policy Recommendation

A large part of the income difference between Puerto Rico and the United States can be traced to employment rate differences between the two regions. Although participation rates did not differ much in the early 1950s, by the early twenty-first century the difference was large. In 2001 less than half of Puerto Rican adults were working or looking for paid employment. In the same year, two-thirds of adults on the mainland were labor force participants. Barry Bosworth and Susan Collins, in chapter 2 in this volume, estimate that a rise in the Commonwealth's employment-to-population ratio to the current U.S. rate would boost per capita gross domestic product in the island by 50 percent.

Labor economists have assembled a wide range of empirical evidence showing that public transfers can depress work effort. Benefit programs that lift the incomes of working-age people who are poor or unemployed can discourage employment and reduce recipients' earnings in the short run. Equally important, they can slow the accumulation of work experience and skill in the long run. The rapid expansion of government transfers in the 1970s and early 1980s produced these effects in Puerto Rico. The benefit cuts and eligibility restrictions enacted after 1982 offset some of the adverse effects of earlier benefit expansions in the food stamp program.

We base these inferences on the following kinds of evidence. First, labor force participation and employment rates in Puerto Rico relative to the United States fell immediately after the expansion in government transfer programs in the mid-1970s. Second, participation and employment rates remained depressed long after the economy recovered from the severe recessions of the 1970s and 1980s. Third, the biggest shortfalls in Puerto Rican participation rates are observed

26. Castillo and Freeman (1991).
27. Krueger (1994).

among workers with low or moderate expected earnings—the young, the old, and women. These are groups for whom we would expect the impact of transfers to be particularly noticeable, because workers with below-average earnings are the ones most likely to be eligible for benefits. In addition, the structure of many benefit formulas provides better income replacement to low-wage than to high-wage workers. Although other factors, including a minimum-wage hike and severe recessions after 1973, can help explain some of these developments, it seems clear that changes in the generosity of transfer benefits played a crucial role.

If voters want to reform social protection programs in such a way as to encourage rather than discourage work, they must consider alternative benefit schedules and eligibility conditions for assistance. It is not inevitable that public transfers will reduce workers' incentive to work or to earn high wages. Some transfer programs have features that encourage the unemployed to enter the workforce or induce active workers to remain employed. For example, retirement programs can be designed to encourage workers to remain in their jobs. Retirement benefits can be structured so they grow faster for workers who have contributed to the plan for a minimum period, say, twenty-five years. Although this kind of design might encourage older workers to retire once they become eligible for a benefit at the pensionable age, it can encourage younger workers to stay employed long enough to qualify for a generous pension.

One feature of programs that encourage work is that they target benefits on people who are employed or on workers who work long hours. An example of such a program is the earned income tax credit in the United States. The EITC supplements wage earnings of low-income breadwinners by providing them with refundable income tax credits. The program was established in the 1970s to offset Social Security payroll taxes and to encourage job holding among poor breadwinners with child dependents. Unlike most transfers, which shrink as a recipient's earnings grow, the credit rises, at least up to a limit. At low earnings levels the program provides a tax credit of $0.34 or $0.40—depending on whether the worker has one or more than one dependent child—for each extra dollar earned by the breadwinner. Parents who have no wages are not eligible to receive the credit, so the credit provides a big incentive for unemployed parents to find work.

The maximum credit is now about $4,300 a year for families with two or more children. This maximum is achieved when annual earnings reach about $10,800. (The annual earnings of a full-time worker who is paid the U.S. minimum wage are slightly more than $10,000.) When a family's annual earnings rise above a moderate threshold (roughly $13,500), the credit begins a gradual phase-out and is eliminated altogether when family income reaches about $35,000 a year.[28]

28. The exact income limit depends on the number of children and the marital status of the parents. The amount mentioned in the text was approximately the income limit for a married-couple family with two or more dependent children.

Liberalized in 1986, 1990, and 1993, the EITC now transfers substantially more money to low-income U.S. families than the cash assistance program for indigent children or the food stamp program.

The EITC is a type of transfer known as an earnings subsidy. Although benefits are targeted on families earning low or moderate incomes, they are denied to the very neediest families—namely, those without any earned income. Most transfers encourage behavior on the part of recipients that offsets part of the intended redistributive effect of the transfer. A typical assistance program, such as Puerto Rico's NAP, discourages work among recipients for reasons described earlier. An earnings subsidy raises recipients' net incomes, much like any other transfer program. But for many low-wage workers, it also raises rather than reduces the reward for work by increasing the recipient's net wage.

If an earnings subsidy is to be redistributive, however, it must be targeted in some way to the low-income population. Otherwise, highly paid workers would receive much bigger subsidies than the poor. As noted earlier, the peak EITC credit on the U.S. mainland is earned at incomes of about $10,800, and thus it provides an inducement to work extra hours only for those who are unemployed or have very low earnings. In Puerto Rico, that population includes a substantial percentage of working-age adults. Americans whose earned wages are above $10,800 are made better off by the credit, but their reward for working longer hours is left unchanged or actually reduced.

For breadwinners earning more than about $13,500 a year, the EITC constitutes an unambiguous work disincentive, no different in effect from traditional social assistance. In the earnings range between $13,500 and $35,000, breadwinners' net incomes are higher than they would be without the credit. Moreover, the phase-out of the credit raises the marginal tax rate on earnings by 16 or 21 percentage points, yielding a marginal tax rate that is more than double the marginal federal income tax rate faced by low-income Americans who do not receive the EITC.

Most labor economists who have studied the EITC conclude that it has contributed to a sizable increase in job holding among unmarried mothers.[29] Some potential breadwinners who would not otherwise be employed have been encouraged to take jobs as a result of the credit. By increasing the net income a family receives when the breadwinner goes to work, the earnings subsidy can tip the balance in favor of work and against continued collection of unemployment or social assistance benefits. From the point of view of public perceptions, at least in the United States, this is a powerful argument in favor of the program. Of course, the work-encouraging effect of the program may be partly offset by the program's work disincentive effects among families earning between $10,800 and $35,000 a year. In the United States there are more breadwinners

29. For example, Meyer and Rosenbaum (2000).

in this income range, where work effort is discouraged, than there are breadwinners earning less than $10,800, who are encouraged to begin working or to work longer hours. On balance, however, economists who have studied the EITC think the program's positive work incentive effects on the unemployed and underemployed have outweighed the adverse incentive effects on single parents and married couples with earnings in the phase-out range.

A compelling argument in favor of plans like the EITC is that they raise the employment rates and net incomes of participating families without causing a sizable reduction in their own self-support. In comparison with other methods of reducing the tax burdens or raising the transfer benefits of the working poor, the EITC offers a strong inducement to work, has positive effects on the earned incomes of people who earn the lowest wages, and has a relatively small work disincentive effect on people in the phase-out range of the benefit schedule.

From a taxpayer's perspective, however, an earnings supplement in Puerto Rico would represent a costly new commitment to redistribution in behalf of the poor. The reform may boost employment rates among indigent parents, and it might eventually produce greater self-sufficiency among the disadvantaged. But for the foreseeable future, taxpayers must assume a costly new burden to encourage and reward employment among people with low incomes. To limit the financial burden of the program, Enchautegui has proposed a targeted earnings subsidy for Puerto Rico that would provide a maximum annual benefit of $1,500 to families with household incomes between $10,000 and $12,000. The subsidy would be progressively reduced to $586 when income reached $15,000 and eliminated altogether after that point.[30]

To reduce program costs and encourage bigger increases in workers' weekly earnings, a Puerto Rican wage supplement program could require that participating workers hold jobs that meet minimum hours conditions. For example, a family could be required to have at least one breadwinner who works no less than thirty hours a week if a wage supplement is to be paid. This kind of benefit condition has proved effective in experimental wage subsidy programs, such as the Canadian Self-Sufficiency Project, which was designed to encourage single parents to move from social assistance into work.[31] By restricting supplements to breadwinners who worked nearly full-time hours, the Canadian program eliminated payments to many workers who earned low weekly wages because they worked relatively few hours. This meant that larger subsidy payments could be provided to workers who dramatically increased their labor market earnings.

Even without increasing its combined budget for income transfers and earnings supplement payments, Puerto Rico could implement a fairly generous earnings subsidy program targeted on low-wage breadwinners. Revenue sources

---

30. Enchautegui (2003).
31. Michalopoulos and others (2000).

could include NAP block grant funds in excess of benefits payable, with savings resulting from a time limit on NAP benefits to the working-age population and from a reorientation of funds previously devoted to the underused PAN y Trabajo program.[32] Alternatively, tax deductions available to higher-income families could be reduced in order to pay for an earnings subsidy program. For example, deductions on interest paid on first and second home mortgages totaled $1.7 billion in 2003, according to tabulations provided to the authors by the Puerto Rico Treasury Department. Whatever the source of funds, it is essential that redistribution in behalf of Puerto Rico's poor and disabled population be restructured to encourage rather than discourage paid employment.

32. As this book went to press, the PAN y Trabajo program was discontinued as a result of a number of program deficiencies detailed in U.S. Department of Agriculture (2005).

Eileen V. Segarra Alméstica

Gary Burtless and Orlando Sotomayor offer a clear explanation of the disincentive effects that means-tested welfare programs are expected to have on labor supply. They also present convincing evidence of why those effects are expected to be stronger in Puerto Rico than in the United States, owing to the commonwealth's lower income levels and tighter labor market conditions.

Nevertheless, their analysis is missing important pieces of the explanation for Puerto Rico's low employment rates. First, the chapter does not give enough attention to more recent changes. Although welfare programs have become less attractive, labor supply has continued to decline, suggesting that such transfer programs can be, at most, only part of the story. The study focuses too much attention on welfare programs and not enough on the possible labor supply effects of Social Security payments; these effects need to be studied further. Second, there is a serious identification problem arising from the simultaneity of changes in transfer payments and changes in unemployment conditions; these factors may have interacted in affecting the labor supplies of Puerto Rican men and women. Finally, there are concerns regarding the comparability of the U.S. and the Puerto Rican labor market data.

Accounting for Recent Changes in Transfer Programs

Burtless and Sotomayor examine in detail the changes that occurred during the 1970s with regard to welfare programs and labor market conditions in Puerto Rico. Contrary to the 1970s, however, which saw expansions of federal transfer payments to the island, the decades that followed were characterized by new restrictions on welfare programs.

As the authors explain, the substitution of the food stamp program by the Nutritional Assistance Program increased eligibility restrictions and reduced benefits. Furthermore, the lack of continuous cost-of-living adjustments has eroded the value of NAP benefits. More recently, a new rule has been put in place restricting 75 percent of NAP benefits to food purchase.

The welfare reform of 1996 imposed further requirements on Temporary Assistance for Needy Families recipients that were intended to promote the integration of welfare recipients into the labor force and made the assistance program less attractive. Overall, welfare programs have become less attractive and participation has declined. To fully understand the effect of transfer payments on labor supply, these changes should be studied further.

The effect of Social Security payments on the labor supply of the working-age population also requires more study. As the authors note, by 2003 NAP benefits as a percentage of personal income had decreased to approximately 3 percent, whereas Social Security payments accounted for 10 percent of personal income. Between 1970 and 2000, the proportion of the population between the ages of twenty-one and sixty-one that reported receiving Social Security income doubled from 4 to 8 percent.[1] Further research should concentrate on this population of Social Security recipients, its labor supply behavior, and its characteristics.

The Identification Problem

Burtless and Sotomayor's failure to measure the size of the effect that transfer payments have on labor supply in Puerto Rico arises from two fundamental limitations. First, adequate data for Puerto Rico are lacking because no detailed income survey is conducted on an annual basis. Second, an identification problem arises from the fact that major changes in transfer payments and unemployment conditions happened simultaneously.

Three mayor changes occurred during the 1970s: the increased participation in the Social Security disability program, the increase in unemployment owing to the recession, and the introduction of food stamps in Puerto Rico. All these changes can be expected to have reduced labor force participation. In 1975, when the food stamp program was introduced in Puerto Rico, the unemployment rate stood at 18 percent; the rapid expansion of the program should therefore not come as a surprise. If the program had been introduced in more favorable economic times, the effect on labor force participation might have been much smaller. The coincidence of these three changes may have affected labor force participation patterns drastically, causing a permanent reduction in labor force attachment.

Comparability of U.S. and Puerto Rican Labor Market Data

Because Burtless and Sotomayor measure participation and employment rates in Puerto Rico relative to U.S. rates, the comparability of the labor market data for Puerto Rico and for the United States requires some attention. At first glance, one can think of two reasons why the data pertaining to the two countries may not be comparable.

First, the ongoing discussion in Puerto Rico about the informal sector suggests that informal labor markets may be more prevalent in Puerto Rico than in the United States. This implies that the official labor market data in Puerto Rico

---

1. The percentages were obtained from tabulations of the PUMS data for Puerto Rico. This population group corresponds to the adults who do not yet qualify for early retirement.

underestimate participation rates. There have been few studies that attempt to measure the size of the informal sector in Puerto Rico. The 1997 *Economic Report to the Governor* summarizes some of the studies conducted between 1984 and 1996.[2] Two of these studies evaluate the effect of the informal sector on the unemployment rate. Their results imply that, owing to informal labor market participation, the unemployment rate is overestimated by 40 to 50 percent. A second group of studies mentioned in the report examines tax evasion as a proxy to measure the size of the legal component of the informal economy. These studies find that about 25 percent of taxable income is not reported. One of these studies was conducted in 1984 by the firm Booz-Allen & Hamilton at the request of the Internal Revenue Department of Puerto Rico. A 1987 report by the department cites Booz-Allen & Hamilton's findings. It observes that in relative terms the informal sector in Puerto Rico is twice as large as that in the United States. The general findings of these studies are similar to those presented by Wilfredo Camacho and Wilfredo Toledo in their study of tax evasion.[3]

The existence of an informal labor market brings new elements to the analysis of welfare payments and labor supply, which, in the case of Puerto Rico, should be acknowledged, though it is difficult to measure its effect. In theory, whether the existence of welfare programs with high implicit tax rates increases or decreases the labor supply in the informal economy is not clear. There are two competing effects. On the one hand, the income effect of the cash transfer may increase the reservation wage and therefore decrease participation in the informal sector. On the other hand, the high implicit tax rate tied to formal sector employment may increase the relative attractiveness of the informal sector and, therefore, increase labor supply within it. Using data from Quebec City, Thomas Lemieux, Bernard Fortin, and Pierre Fréchette find that taxes redirect labor activities from the formal to the informal sector; and although this effect is small for the average worker, the effects can be substantially bigger for welfare recipients.[4] It is therefore relevant to study not only the size of the informal sector but also any significant changes that may have occurred in the characteristics of its workers.

Second, cultural differences might also engender a lack of comparability. For example, Burtless and Sotomayor show that women's labor force participation in Puerto Rico has fallen relative to the United States, even though in absolute terms it increased. However, trends in female labor force participation in Puerto Rico should not be expected to follow the patterns observed in the United States. Cultural differences regarding household composition and the distribution of tasks within the household may result in different patterns of participa-

2. Puerto Rico Planning Board (1997).
3. Camacho and Toledo (1996).
4. Lemieux and others (1994).

Figure 3-15. *Women's Labor Force Participation, Puerto Rico and the United States, by Age Group, 2000*
Percent

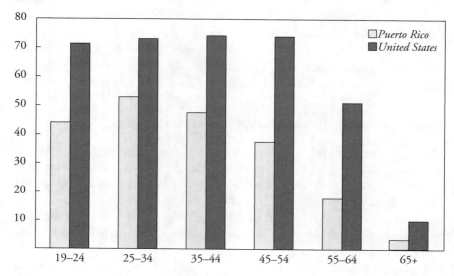

Source: Data from Ruggles and others (2004); U.S. Bureau of the Census, *2000 Census of Population and Housing, Public Use Microdata Sample, 5 Percent Sample* (ftp2.census.gov/census_2000/datasets/PUMS/FivePercent/PuertoRico [August 2003]).

tion. María Enchautegui presents evidence of the importance of women's household work in Puerto Rico. She cites a special report from Puerto Rico's Department of Labor and Human Resources indicating that for 77 percent of the women who are out of the labor force, household responsibility is the main reason not to look for employment.[5]

When women's employment status, as reported in the Census Bureau's 2000 Public Use Microdata Set (PUMS), is analyzed by age group, an interesting result is found. Figure 3-15 shows the women's labor force participation rates by age group for the United States and Puerto Rico. Women twenty-five to fifty-four years old, who are considered to be in their prime working years, are divided into three age groups: twenty-five to thirty-four, thirty-five to forty-four, and forty-five to fifty-four. In the United States, labor force participation rates for these three groups are similar to one another (between 73 and 74 percent). In Puerto Rico, for the same three age groups, the labor force participation rate decreases with age. This indicates significant cultural or socioeconomic differences between the two countries.

5. Enchautegui (2004, p. 45).

A plausible explanation may be differences in the timing or intensity of social changes promoting women's labor force participation in Puerto Rico, such that older women in the island were not strongly influenced by them. An alternative explanation may be that Puerto Rican women in these age groups may have different household responsibilities, including taking care of an older relative or a related child. The 2000 PUMS data indicate that whereas 9 percent of households in the United States include a relative other than the spouse, daughters, and sons, the corresponding percentage in Puerto Rico is 15 percent.

Evaluation of the Labor Market Evidence Presented

One argument presented by Burtless and Sotomayor is that the employment-to-population ratio for Puerto Rico relative to the United States decreased as food stamps were introduced and experienced a small recovery after the program was replaced by the more restrictive NAP. Nevertheless, figure 3-1 suggests alternative interpretations that should be discussed. First, this decline in the ratio began after 1965, coincident with the liberalization of the eligibility rules for the Social Security disability program.[6]

Figure 3-16 presents the unemployment rate for Puerto Rico from 1960 to 2004 and the relative employment-to-population ratio (the employment rate) presented by Burtless and Sotomayor. Over these years, the relative employment rate followed a pattern inverse to the unemployment rate in Puerto Rico. The employment rate declined sharply from 1973 to 1977 as the unemployment rate increased. Starting in 1979, the unemployment rate saw a short and small improvement. During this time the relative employment rate remained fairly constant until the beginning of the 1980s, when it started to fall again as the unemployment rate began to climb. The relative rate improved again after 1985 as the unemployment rate decreased. Therefore the labor market restrictions do seem to play a dominant role in the labor force participation trends. If Puerto Rico's relative employment rate is compared with its relative unemployment rate (relative, that is, to the United States), the conclusions would be the same. The relative unemployment rate followed a similar pattern to the unemployment rate presented in figure 3-16 until 1993, although it was a bit more volatile. After 1993, the relative unemployment rate continued to increase.

The authors also argue that the groups most affected have been the young, the elderly, and women, all of whom tend to have lower earnings capacity. Undoubtedly, the increases in Social Security benefits paid during the 1970s would affect the labor supply of the elderly. Nevertheless, if one wants to study

6. In 1965 the definition of a qualifying disability was changed from an impairment of long, continuous, and indefinite duration to an impairment expected to last for a continuous period of not less than twelve months. See Social Security Online, "Compilation of the Social Security Laws: Disability Determination" (www.ssa.gov/OP_Home/ssact/title02/0221.htm [October 2005]).

Figure 3-16. *Puerto Rico's Unemployment Rate and the Relative Employment-to-Population Ratio, 1960–2004*
Percent

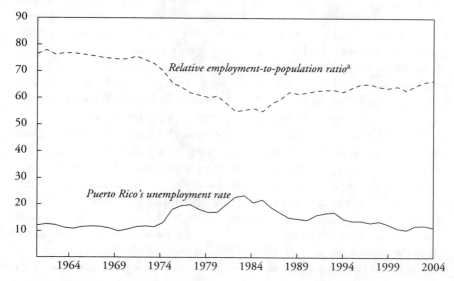

Source: Data from U.S. Bureau of Labor Statistics and Puerto Rico Department of Labor and Human Resources, Historical Series of Employment and Unemployment.
a. Puerto Rican rate as percent of U.S. rate.

the labor supply trends of groups with low earnings capacity, one should look at groups with low levels of education. This is especially true when one examines the effect of means-tested transfer programs. According to Census Bureau data, median education for welfare recipients fluctuated from second grade in 1970 to ninth grade in 2000. Only 35 percent of recipients in 2000 had a high school diploma. Therefore it seems natural to focus on the population with less than twelve years of education when one studies the effect of welfare programs on labor supply, keeping in mind that this group also confronts more detrimental labor market conditions during a recession.

Puerto Rico's unemployment rate for workers with less than twelve years of education climbed to 26 percent in 1977 and to 31 percent in 1983. It decreased substantially between 1985 and 1990 and then began to increase slightly. Since 1993 the unemployment rate for this group has been falling. Still, the rate in 2000 was 4 percentage points higher than the 1970 rate. One possible group that could be used for comparison is the population with only a high school education.[7] The relative labor market conditions for the less educated

7. This population includes those who achieved a high school diploma and did not continue further studies.

could be measured by calculating the ratio between the unemployment rates for dropouts and for high school graduates. This ratio increased during the 1970s, which implies that the less educated were harder hit by the recession of that decade. As for net changes through the decades, the ratio increased from 124 percent in 1970 to 144 percent in 1990, showing a relative worsening of labor market conditions for the less educated during that period.

A preliminary way to examine the changes in labor market behavior of these groups is to estimate the employment-to-population ratios. Owing to the lack of intercensus estimates of the island's population by education group, the employment-to-population ratios are measured using PUMS data.[8]

Table 3-8 compares the employment-to-population ratio for working-age adults with less than high school education with the ratios for two alternative comparison groups.[9] The first group comprises Puerto Rican adults aged twenty-four to sixty-four with a high school diploma. The disadvantage of this comparison is that even though both groups are affected by increases in unemployment, the less educated tend to suffer a bigger impact.[10] For this reason, it is difficult to separate the effect of the recession from the effect of increased transfer payments during the 1970s. The second comparison group consists of U.S. adults in the same age group with less than a high school education. This group was not affected by the introduction of food stamps and should suffer a similar relative impact from the recession. Nevertheless, as explained earlier, the employment data from the two countries may not be strictly comparable.

Table 3-8 also presents the ratios of the measure for Puerto Rico's less educated group relative to each of the comparison groups. The top panel includes both sexes, while the lower panels give the corresponding measures for males and females. For males, as well as for both sexes combined, the employment-to-population ratio of the less educated in Puerto Rico decreased moderately during the 1970s compared with the corresponding ratio for those with a high school degree and then recovered slightly during the 1980s. When compared with their U.S. counterparts, Puerto Rico's less educated adults experienced a substantial decrease in their employment-to-population ratios during the 1970s and the 1990s. For women, the results are somewhat different. When compared with females with a high school diploma, the less educated women increased their relative employment between the 1970s and the 1990s, while compared

8. From 1982 on, the employment-to-population ratios by education group could also be estimated using data from the Household Survey conducted by the Department of Labor and Human Resources of Puerto Rico. However, those microdata are not available for previous years.

9. Owing to changes in the variables definitions through the years, in this table, for comparability purposes, anyone with twelve years of education is assumed to have received a high school diploma.

10. In 1970 and 1980 most working-age adults receiving Social Security payments had less than a high school education. Therefore the increase in Social Security payments should also have a bigger effect on the less educated.

Table 3-8. *Employment-to-Population Ratio among Working-Age Adults,*
Puerto Rico and the United States, by Education Group, Selected Years,
1970–2000[a]

Percent

Group	1970	1980	1990	2000
Both sexes				
Puerto Rico, less than high school	39.8	31.2	30.2	22.2
Puerto Rico, high school	64.1	54.5	51.0	36.7
United States, less than high school	61.7	56.7	54.5	50.7
Puerto Rico, less than high school:				
Puerto Rico, high school	62.1	57.2	59.3	60.6
Puerto Rico, less than high school:				
United States, less than high school	64.5	55.0	55.4	43.8
Males				
Puerto Rico, less than high school	66.1	49.4	45.8	33.5
Puerto Rico, high school	81.0	71.0	66.2	48.8
United States, less than high school	84.2	73.5	67.7	61.5
Puerto Rico, less than high school:				
Puerto Rico, high school	81.6	69.6	69.2	68.5
Puerto Rico, less than high school:				
United States, less than high school	78.5	67.2	67.7	54.4
Females				
Puerto Rico, less than high school	17.3	15.3	16.0	10.9
Puerto Rico, high school	45.7	39.6	36.4	24.9
United States, less than high school	40.2	41.2	41.4	39.1
Puerto Rico, less than high school:				
Puerto Rico, high school	37.7	38.5	43.9	43.7
Puerto Rico less than high school:				
United States, less than high school	43.0	37.0	38.5	27.8

Source: Authors' tabulations of data from Ruggles and others (2004); 1970, 1980, 1990, and 2000 IPUMS data for the United States; 1970, 1980, 1990, and 2000 PUMS data for Puerto Rico.

a. Persons aged twenty-four to sixty-four.

with their U.S. counterparts their relative participation decreased during those same decades. Various hypotheses can be drawn from these data. Still, owing to the data limitations, the results should be interpreted with caution. The data tend to indicate that the increase in transfer payments during the 1970s may have contributed to the decrease in men's labor force participation since the employment-to-population ratio of less educated males decreased relative to both comparison groups, although the possibility that the decrease may result from the recession's having a stronger impact on the less educated group cannot be ruled out.

For females, the relative increase in the employment-to-population ratio of the less educated compared with high school graduates indicates that increases in welfare payment are unlikely to be the major cause of the stagnation in female labor force participation. Moreover, reductions in welfare participation, which occurred during the 1980s and the 1990s, did not cause a substantial increase in the relative employment-to-population ratio of the less educated. This suggests the presence of an asymmetric effect such that increases in welfare transfers decrease labor force participation but reductions in the programs do not have a significant effect on labor force attachment. This asymmetry could be explained by the high unemployment rates for less educated workers. Once out of the labor forces, the labor market may not be able to reabsorb those workers.

The sharp decrease in the relative employment-to-population ratio of less educated females relative to their U.S. counterparts could indicate that the welfare reform of 1996 did not have the same positive effect in Puerto Rico that it is thought to have had in the United States. This is true despite a caseload reduction in Puerto Rican Temporary Assistance for Needy Families rolls of 47 percent between 1993 and 2000.[11]

Evaluation of the Microdata Evidence Presented

Using PUMS data, Burtless and Sotomayor divide males and females by quintiles according to their earnings. They then estimate the percentage of males and females living in households that received Social Security or welfare income in each quintile and compare the percentages for Puerto Rico and the United States.

The microdata evidence strengthens the argument that transfer payments play a more important role in Puerto Rico than in the United States. Nevertheless, they do not contribute to the measurement of the actual size of the effect. In addition, there are three major limitations to this analysis that should be discussed.

First, it is not clear what is to be gained from this comparison. It should be expected that Puerto Rico, with substantially lower income levels, will have higher percentages for each quintile than the United States. Second, such comparisons should try to control for different aspects of family composition. For example, if Puerto Ricans are more likely to have their elderly parents living with them, then one would expect to see a higher percentage of working-aged adults living in households that receive Social Security payments. Finally, the analysis for females is inadequate since a large proportion of Puerto Rican working-age women are assigned randomly to the quintiles and the rest are assigned according to their earnings rather than by household earnings.

11. The figures were obtained from U.S. Department of Health and Human Services Administration for Children and Families and *Tabla de Casos Programa TANF Categoría C,* provided by the TANF Program Office, Puerto Rico Socio-Economic Development Administration. For more details, see Segarra (2000).

Concluding Remarks

A relative decrease in work effort preceded the introduction of food stamps and continued for three years after the reduction in food stamp benefits. On the other hand, fluctuations in the unemployment rate matched well the timing of fluctuations in the relative employment rate. Nevertheless, to simply look at historical trends is not enough to establish the relative importance of changes in labor markets versus those in transfer payments. The convergence of increases in the unemployment rate and transfer payments may have caused prolonged changes in labor behavior, either by taking a sector of Puerto Rico's adult population out of the labor force or by driving them to participate in informal labor markets.

When policies to increase labor force attachment in Puerto Rico are designed, the possible asymmetric effect of changes in welfare programs should be taken into consideration. If the labor market is incapable of absorbing more workers with low levels of education, then restrictions to welfare programs may have a small effect on labor supply. Although the idea of establishing an earned income tax credit in Puerto Rico is a step in the right direction, it should not be assumed that the effect of such a program in Puerto Rico will be the same as the one observed in the United States. The problem of incorporating the nonworking poor into the labor market requires a complete set of integral policies that should emphasize the role of education and the elimination of barriers to work.

COMMENT
Katherine Terrell

The chapter by Gary Burtless and Orlando Sotomayor is an impressive analysis that argues that the low labor force participation rates in Puerto Rico, relative to the United States, from 1970 to 2004 are principally explained by government transfers to Puerto Ricans. The authors provide a great deal of information, including macro evidence on trends in labor force participation rates and public transfers and micro evidence on the work disincentive effects of five transfer programs: food stamps, unemployment insurance, the Social Security disability program (Old-Age, Survivors, and Disability Insurance), government-provided health insurance, and Temporary Assistance for Needy Families. My comments focus on two aspects of the chapter: the comparison of Puerto Rico with the United States and the weight given to transfers over other explanations. I begin with a brief summary of their line of argumentation.

The evidence shows that Puerto Rico's labor force participation rates relative to those of the United States fell from 1950 to 1985 and rose from 1985 to 2004 (figure 3-1, top panel). The authors note that the steepest decline in participation rates—from 1971 to 1983—corresponds to the steepest increase in government transfers as a share of personal income, from 1974 to 1983 (figure 3-2). The ratio of transfers to income in Puerto Rico fell substantially from 1983 until 1989, when some programs were downsized, but since then it has remained stable at about 25–28 percent. The authors are alarmed at how high this share continues to be, especially given that in the same period the U.S. ratio was only about 11 percent. Hence in addition to trying to show that the increase in transfers in the mid-1970s and early 1980s drove the decline in labor force participation rates during that period, they also argue that the relatively low participation rates in 1990–2003 were brought about by the relatively high remaining transfers.

The authors' deconstruction of the trend in relative labor force participation rates by gender indicates that women's relative rates are driving the overall trend.[12] Comparing the ratios of participation rates in Puerto Rico with those in the United States, they demonstrate that the gap is much larger for women than for men (figure 3-1), and they note that the rates of the oldest (above fifty-five and older) and youngest (sixteen to nineteen) age groups in Puerto Rico are especially low (for both men and women) (figure 3-3). The authors use these figures to argue that women, the young, and the elderly are the most likely to receive means-tested public transfers because they tend to be the lowest paid.

The authors proceed to link the evolution of transfer payments in five programs to these labor force participation rate trends. They conclude that two of the programs—unemployment insurance and Temporary Assistance for Needy Families—are of little importance in explaining the low labor force participation rates and high level of transfers. Unemployment insurance benefits in Puerto Rico have been low relative to the United States (34–37 percent replacement rates in 1968–89 and 26 percent thereafter), and the authors therefore believe that the longer duration of unemployment must be a function of poor labor market conditions. Temporary Assistance for Needy Families, established in 1996, is a relatively small transfer program in Puerto Rico and is not likely to have had much of an impact, as not many adults and households collect benefits under this scheme.

Of the remaining three programs, only one was important in driving the participation rate trend and the high level of transfers in the past. Burtless and Sotomayor attribute to the food stamp program the steep decline in labor force participation rates from the mid-1970s to the early 1980s. At the program's peak in 1980, about 60 percent of Puerto Rico's population was using food

---

12. However, this relative pattern seems to derive from the behavior of women's labor force participation rates in the United States. The rates for Puerto Rican males and females reported in figures 3-3 and 3-4 and table 3-7 indicate that men's rates declined more than women's, bottoming out in 1980, whereas women's rates have been rising since 1960.

stamps (in contrast to 10 percent of the U.S. population), and this benefit accounted for about 7.5 percent of their personal income (compared with about 0.3 percent in the United States). Since 1980, however, when the Nutritional Assistance Program replaced food stamps with a less generous formula and tighter eligibility rules, the gap between the Puerto Rican and U.S. shares receiving nutrition assistance fell, from 50 percent in 1980 to 20 percent in 2003. Hence the Nutritional Assistance Program should not be seen as an important source of the problem of high transfers and low labor force participation rates in the 1990s, although it might explain some of the lower labor force participation rates among some low-income households.

The two programs that loom large today are Social Security's disability insurance and the new government-provided health insurance. The authors focus a great deal of attention on Social Security benefits, noting that the replacement rates are high—90 percent, for example, for individuals with annual incomes of up to $6,000. Puerto Rican men in the second quarter of the earnings distribution receive a more generous level of income replacement when they retire (65 percent) than do men on the mainland in the same part of the distribution (who receive 46 percent). The disability insurance benefits received by island residents are also relatively high—85 percent of the average pension received by a disabled worker on the mainland, though the average wage of island residents is only 58 percent of the equivalent mainland worker's. The authors therefore conclude that the disability insurance benefit levels explain why the disability rate in Puerto Rico is so much higher than in the U.S. mainland and why so many more Puerto Ricans—9 percent of the twenty- to sixty-four-year-old population—receives some kind of Social Security benefit compared with about 5 percent on the mainland (figure 3-12). Finally, Burtless and Sotomayor argue that the commonwealth's health insurance system, introduced in 1993, which provides free health services for individuals with incomes up to two times the poverty line, increases the likelihood of a reduction in work hours. Health insurance expenditures represent about one fifth of Puerto Rico's tax revenues.

However, because its average income is relatively high, the United States may not be the appropriate benchmark in evaluating Puerto Rico. The comparison is understandable: policymakers on both the island and the mainland would like the two economies to be harmonized and hence are concerned about gaps between them. But the average Puerto Rican today continues to be much poorer than the average person on the mainland. As figure 3-5 clearly shows, since 1985 the average weekly earnings of Puerto Ricans in the formal sector (covered by unemployment insurance) have been about 55 percent of average earnings on the mainland and about 75 percent of average earnings of the poorest U.S. state, Mississippi. In the one case where the authors compare Puerto Rico's welfare statistics to Mississippi (figure 3-12), the differences are not so great. For example, 9.0 percent of Puerto Ricans aged twenty to sixty-four received Social Security benefits in 2000 compared with 8.1 percent in Mississippi and 5.2 percent in the United States as a whole. Hence the difference in the levels of transfers can be explained, in part, by the relative levels of poverty in Puerto Rico and the United States, and the appropriate benchmark is not the United States as a whole but rather the poorest area of the United States. In future research, it will be valuable to carry out a head-on comparison over time between Puerto Rico and poor states, such as Mississippi.

To what extent are the Puerto Rican labor force participation rates explained by transfers as distinct from other factors? This is a key question, since Burtless and Sotomayor argue that transfers are important, which implies, in turn, that changes in the welfare programs that reduce the work disincentive effects would have a big impact on participation rates. In my view the transfers carry a smaller weight than the authors give them. As shown in figure 3-1, the fall in labor force participation began in the 1950s; yet until 1974 the level of transfers in Puerto Rico was very close to that in the United States. Hence other factors (which the authors also discuss) must explain the fall during the early period. More important, the authors put a great deal of stock in the rise in transfers (especially food stamps) from the mid-1970s to the early 1980s as the cause of the fall in labor force participation rates. However, this does not seem to be the likely story, given that Puerto Rican participation rates fell sharply in 1971, some years before transfers began to rise steeply in 1974. Although the authors acknowledge the fall in labor demand from the two oil shocks, they do not concede that the order of events and causality could be reversed: that is, that the fall in employment and labor force participation rates might have been a cause, rather than an effect, of the rise in transfers. Moreover, since the U.S. economy was also experiencing higher unemployment at this time, it is likely that fewer Puerto Ricans migrated to the United States and that some migrants who could not find work on the mainland may have returned to Puerto Rico, putting further pressure on the welfare budget.

What explains the slow growth in labor force participation since 1985? Why has the employment rate in Puerto Rico remained at 65 percent of the mainland's employment rate for the past decade? The work disincentive effects of the Social Security disability program probably help explain the lower rates of older workers. However, what explains the relatively low participation of women and the young in the labor force? In seeking to answer these questions, I would turn to the demand side of the labor market and ask, why has job creation, especially among the less-skilled low-wage earners, been so low (as pointed out by Steven J. Davis and Luis A. Rivera-Batiz in chapter 6 of this volume)? As Barry Bosworth and Susan Collins note in chapter 2, private investment has been growing since 1985, but it has not yet reached levels of the 1960s. Moreover, it seems that some of this investment, generated by section 936 of the 1976 Tax Reform Act, did not lead to much job creation. Perhaps the low level of investment and job creation has been the result of wages that are high relative to productivity. Burtless and Sotomayor have pointed out that the Puerto Rican wage as a share of the U.S. wage has fallen from about 64 percent in 1977 to only 55 percent in 2003 (figure 3-5). The question is whether this explains enough. Could government transfer programs be raising the reservation wage of the low-wage groups? It might be argued that reducing the generosity of transfers would help wages adjust downward. However, given Puerto Rico's relationship with the United States, the question arises, how much of a decrease in transfers would be required to create a downward wage adjustment? Since the United States provides an alternative (high-wage) labor market for Puerto Ricans, part of the adjustment would undoubtedly be increased migration to the United States. Moreover, remittances from Puerto Ricans working in the United States also help to keep the reservation wage in Puerto Rico high.

In this context, I am struck by the similarity of the relationship between Puerto Rico and the United States to that between East and West Germany. Both East Germany and Puerto Rico started with low labor productivity relative to their neighbors. With unification, the East Germans received, virtually overnight, an enormous increase in their wages and large transfers from West Germany. Similarly, with the increase in Puerto Rico's minimum wage to U.S. levels from 1977 to 1983 and the large increase in transfers over part of this period, Puerto Rico also received a boost to its wages. Hence in both cases, wages in the poor economy rose dramatically and seemingly faster than productivity. Until the two wealthier economies equilibrate in terms of their unit labor cost, there will tend to be high unemployment in the neighboring poorer economies.

If the Puerto Rican story is about wages that are too high relative to productivity, and if wages cannot be adjusted downward, then it seems that the way to increase employment and labor force participation rates in the long run is to increase the productivity of workers. This means increasing the levels and quality of education still more (the subject of chapter 5) and stimulating more private investment by improving the business environment (the topic of chapter 6).

In the end, I cannot disagree with the authors' policy recommendation that Puerto Rico consider restructuring its welfare benefits to include features of the earned income tax credit available to low-income workers in the United States. However, I wonder about the extent to which the tax credit would increase Puerto Rico's labor force participation, if, as I suspect, the problem has more to do with depressed demand for labor than with depressed supply of labor. Overall, the authors have produced an impressive analysis of an important issue. Their chapter increases our understanding of five important transfer programs, and in the final analysis their policy recommendations are appropriate for Puerto Rico.

References

Autor, David, and Mark G. Duggan. 2003. "The Rise in the Disability Rolls and the Decline in Unemployment." *Quarterly Journal of Economics* 118, no. 1: 157–205.

Betson, David M., and David H. Greenberg. 1986. "Labor Supply and Tax Rates: Comment." *American Economic Review* 76, no. 3: 551–56.

Blank, Rebecca. 2002. "Evaluating Welfare Reform in the United States." *Journal of Economic Literature* 40, no. 4: 1105–66.

Bound, John, and Timothy Waidmann. 2002. "Accounting for Recent Declines in Employment Rates among Working-Aged Men and Women with Disabilities." *Journal of Human Resources* 37, no. 2: 231–50.

Bound, John, and others. 2004. "The Welfare Implications of Increasing Disability Insurance Benefit Generosity." *Journal of Public Economics* 88, no. 12: 2487–2514.

Burtless, Gary. 2002. "Can Supply-Side Policies Reduce Unemployment? Lessons from North America." *Australian Economic Review* 35, no. 1: 3–28.

Camacho, Wilfredo, and Wilfredo Toledo. 1996. "Evasión contributiva y economía informal en Puerto Rico." In *Reforma contributiva en Puerto Rico 1994: Estudio Técnico,* edited by Ramón J. Cao and Suphan Andic, pp. 247–78. San Juan: Editorial de la Universidad de Puerto Rico.

Castillo, Alida, and Richard Freeman. 1991. "Minimum Wages in Puerto Rico: Textbook Case of a Wage Floor?" Working Paper 3759. Cambridge, Mass.: National Bureau of Economic Research.

Enchautegui, María E. 2003. *Reaping the Benefits of Work: A Tax Credit for Low-Income Working Families in Puerto Rico.* San Juan: Center for the New Economy.

———. 2004. "Integrando a las trabajadoras de hogar en la política pública de Puerto Rico." In *Amarres en el trabajo de las mujeres: Hogar y empleo, Dos investigaciones de María E. Enchautegui,* pp. 25–74. San Juan: Oficina de la Procuradora de las Mujeres.

Fox, Mary Kay, William Hamilton, and Biing-Hwan Lin. 2004. *Effects of Food Assistance and Nutrition Programs on Nutrition and Health.* Vol. 3, *Literature Review.* Food Assistance and Nutrition Research Report 19-3. U.S. Department of Agriculture, Economic Research Service.

Grogger, Jeffrey. 2003. "The Effects of Time Limits, the EITC, and Other Policy Changes on Welfare Use, Work, and Income among Female-Headed Families." *Review of Economics and Statistics* 85, no. 2: 394–408.

Internal Revenue Department of Puerto Rico. 1987. "Informe del secretario de hacienda sobre reforma contributiva." San Juan (August).

Krueger, Alan. 1994. "The Effect of the Minimum Wage When It Really Bites: A Reexamination of the Evidence from Puerto Rico." Working Paper 4757. Cambridge, Mass.: National Bureau of Economic Research.

Lemieux, Thomas, Bernard Fortin, and Pierre Fréchette. 1994. "The Effect of Taxes on Labor Supply in the Underground Economy." *American Economic Review* 84, no. 1: 231–54.

Long, Sharon K. 1988. *Multiple Program Participation among Food Stamp Recipients.* MPP Project 7665-120. Report prepared for the Food and Nutrition Service, U.S. Department of Agriculture. Washington: Mathematica Policy Research.

Marín, Heriberto. 1999. "Apuntes hacia una política racional para la promoción de la salud pública en Puerto Rico." In *El futuro económico de Puerto Rico,* edited by Francisco Martínez, pp. 255–84. San Juan: University of Puerto Rico Press.

Meyer, Bruce D., and Dan T. Rosenbaum. 2000. "Making Single Mothers Work: Recent Tax and Welfare Policy and Its Effects." *National Tax Journal* 53, no. 4: 1027–62.

Michalopoulos, Charles, and others. 2000. *The Self-Sufficiency Project at 36 Months: Effects of a Financial Work Incentive on Employment and Income.* Ottawa: Social Research and Demonstration Corporation.

Moffitt, Robert A. 1989. "Estimating the Value of an In-Kind Transfer: The Case of Food Stamps." *Econometrica* 57, no. 2: 385–409.

Puerto Rico Planning Board. 1997. "Algunas consideraciones sobre la economía subterránea en Puerto Rico." In *Economic Report to the Governor.* San Juan.

Reynolds, Lloyd, and Peter Gregory. 1965. *Wages, Productivity, and Industrialization in Puerto Rico.* Homewood, Ill.: Irwin.

Rosso, Randy, and Lisa Fowler. 2000. *Characteristics of Food Stamp Households: Fiscal Year 1999.* FSP-00-CHAR. Report prepared for the Food and Nutrition Service, U.S. Department of Agriculture. Washington: Mathematica Policy Research.

Ruggles, Steven, and others. 2004. *Integrated Public Use Microdata Series: Version 3.0.* Machine-readable database. Minneapolis: Minnesota Population Center (www.ipums.org).

Segarra Alméstica, Eileen. 1999. "The Effect of Income Eligibility Restrictions on Labor Supply: The Case of the Nutritional Assistance Program in Puerto Rico." UIE Working Paper 97. Río Piedras: University of Puerto Rico, School of the Social Sciences.

———. 2000. "Expectativas de éxito para la reforma de bienestar social y el mercado laboral en Puerto Rico." *Ensayos y Monografías* 102. Río Piedras: Universidad de Puerto Rico, Unidad de Investigaciones Económicas (June).

Sotomayor, Orlando. 2004. "Development and Income Distribution: The Case of Puerto Rico." *World Development* 32, no. 8: 1395–1406.

U.S. Department of Agriculture. 2005. *Food and Nutrition Service Special Wages Incentive Program in Puerto Rico.* Report Number 27099-60-AT. Atlanta: Office of Inspector General—Southeast Region, U.S. Department of Agriculture.

Weisskoff, Richard. 1985. *Factories and Food Stamps: The Puerto Rican Model of Development.* Johns Hopkins University Press.

4

Why Don't More Puerto Rican Men Work? The Rich Uncle (Sam) Hypothesis

MARÍA E. ENCHAUTEGUI AND RICHARD B. FREEMAN

One of the biggest economic problems facing Puerto Rico is the low employment rate of its adult population. In 2000 only 31 percent of the overall population was employed, giving the island the lowest employment-to-population ratio in the Americas and the Caribbean, if not in the world. By way of comparison, in the same year 44 percent of the population in the Dominican Republic, 40 percent of the Mexican population, and 50 percent of the U.S. population was employed. The low employment rate compromises the island's development by diverting resources away from investment and into public assistance and services to the poor.

Low participation of women in the workforce contributes to the overall low employment rate, but it is the low employment rate for men that drives Puerto Rico's overall rate off the map compared with other countries. Moreover, the male participation rate has been falling, even during the growth period in the latter half of the 1990s, while the female participation has been increasing.

In laying out the dimensions of the male employment problem in Puerto Rico, we use data from both the census and labor force surveys, which give somewhat different figures on the Puerto Rican participation rate. Despite differences between them, however, both data sets indicate that the employment rate among men on the island is exceptionally low and declining. A number of factors could explain the low employment of Puerto Rican men, such as the rising divergence between the island's gross domestic product and its gross national product; the industrial distribution of output and employment; Social Security disability insurance and related welfare payments; migration to the United States; opportunities for work in the informal economy; and relatively high wages in low-skill occupations. Our discussion is organized around a new hypothesis, which we call the "rich uncle (Sam) hypothesis." A rich uncle provides resources to poorer relatives for consumption, reducing their production requirements. The rich uncle reduces incentives for relatives to supply labor and lowers the demand for their services as well. We argue that the connection of the relatively poor economy of Puerto Rico to the advanced and rich economy of the United States has created conditions that generate low employment.

In support of this hypothesis, we present data that show an increasing divergence between gross income (GNP) and GDP on the island, which has distorted the relationship between GDP and employment, owing to potential federal tax benefits to companies operating in Puerto Rico; transfers accruing to Puerto Rican families, funded mainly by the U.S. federal government, which account for about 22 percent of personal income; open borders to the United States, which give unemployed individuals incentive to migrate to the United States and potentially create a lower bound for wages on the island; a wage structure in which low-paying jobs have relatively higher earnings than in low-income U.S. states, possibly related to the federally imposed minimum wage, free mobility of labor between the United States and Puerto Rico, and high reservation wages determined by the amount of transfers available in the event of failure to find work; and employment in the informal sector, which is unmeasured in official statistics. The rich uncle contributes to the sizable informal sector by enabling workers who earn means-tested government transfers to supplement those earnings with "unreported" income and by reducing labor supply pressures for lower wages in the formal sector.[1]

From the vantage of this hypothesis, Puerto Rico's seemingly unique experience is comparable to that of other economies connected to rich uncles, such as East Germany after unification with West Germany or southern Italy with northern Italy, that have also experienced high unemployment while attached to a much richer economy.[2] The rich-uncle analysis also links Puerto Rican economic

1. Our rich-uncle analysis has links to Carlos Santiago's (1992) study of Puerto Rico employment. Antonio Spilimbergo (1999) has developed a general equilibrium model in which workers from a rich country finance a transfer to the unemployed in a poor country to limit migration, but this does not fit the Puerto Rican case.

2. The German experience is particularly insightful for analyzing how linking a poorer economy to a wealthier economy can adversely affect employment in the former. This is because the timing of the rich-uncle linkage can be dated fairly precisely. Before unification, East Germany had essentially full employment. Following monetary union with the West in June 1990 and adoption of West German wage levels and social benefits, the employment rate for East Germans aged eighteen to fifty-four fell from 89 percent to 73 percent in six years, and unemployment rose to as high as 20 percent (Hunt 2004). Firms made different capital investments in the East from those they had made before unification. West German firms dominated the East's economy, with few locating headquarters in the East, so that profits were "repatriated" to the West.

Figure 4-1. *Labor Force Participation Rate, Men and Women, Selected Countries, 2000–03*

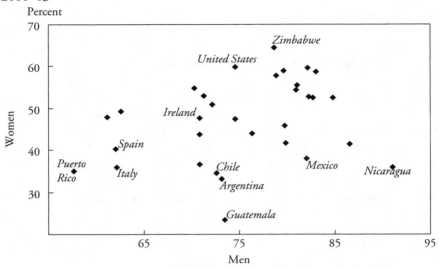

Source: Data from International Labor Organization, online statistics (lasborsta.ilo.org [May 2005]).

problems to those faced by low-income indigenous groups in wealthier societies, such as Native Americans in the United States, Maori in New Zealand, and Aborigines in Australia. All of these groups also receive great social support from the wealthier society, live in particular geographic areas, and have employment problems. The details vary, but in each case attachment to the wealthier "uncle" produces economic problems—including low employment, high dependency on social benefits, migration from the poorer area to wealthier areas, and potentially higher reservation wages than are consistent with full employment for the lower-income group—that resemble the employment problems in Puerto Rico.

The Male Labor Participation and Employment Problem

Figure 4-1 displays the labor participation rates of men and women of working age in Puerto Rico, the United States, nineteen Latin American and Caribbean countries, and eleven other countries from around the world. The horizontal axis gives male participation rates, while the vertical axis gives female rates. Each point represents a country. Puerto Rico, with a male participation rate of 57.7 percent, is the lowest among the countries, and its female participation rate of 35.0,

Figure 4-2. *Labor Force Participation Rate, Men and Women, Puerto Rico and the United States, 1971–2003*

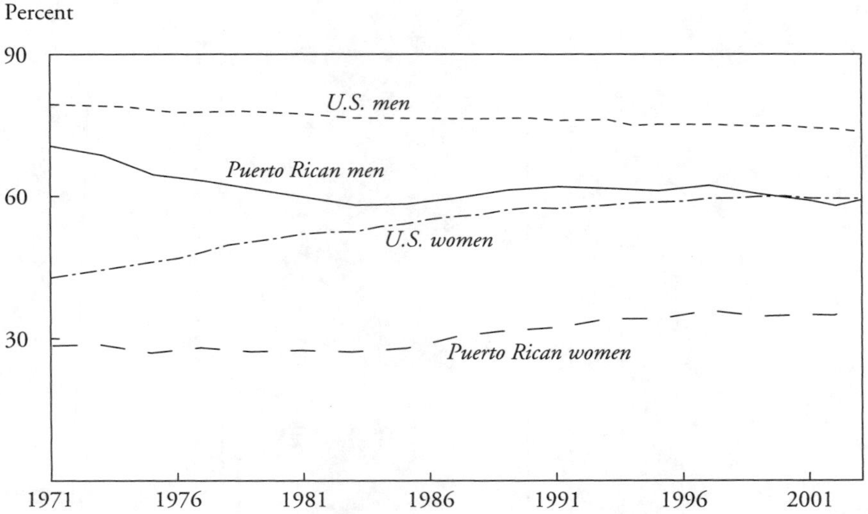

Percent

Source: Estado Libre Asociado de Puerto Rico (2002) and U.S. Bureau of Labor Statistics (www.bls.gov/webapps/legacy/cpsatab1.htm [May 2006]).

though also low, is comparable to that in some other countries, such as Italy, Chile, Nicaragua, and Argentina.

Over time, moreover, the participation rate of men in Puerto Rico has fallen while female participation has increased. Even in the boom of the late 1990s, when the Puerto Rican economy was growing and the rate of unemployment falling, male labor force participation dropped by 3 percentage points. Figure 4-2 displays the labor force participation rates for men and women aged sixteen and over in Puerto Rico from 1971 to 2003, using labor force household survey data, and also gives comparable rates for men and women in the United States. Over this period, the male participation rate in Puerto Rico fell by 11.5 percentage points, from 70.8 to 59.3, with most of the decline occurring between 1971 and the early 1980s. The U.S. male participation rate also fell over the thirty-two year period, but by 5.7 percentage points, from 79.4 to 73.7—only half as much as in Puerto Rico. During the same period, the labor participation rate of Puerto Rican women rose by 9.0 percentage points, while that of U.S. females increased by 13.4 percentage points. In sum, the U.S.–Puerto Rico gap in labor force participation increased twice as much for men (67 percent) as for women (33 percent). By 2003, the participation rate for U.S. females stood close to that for Puerto Rican males.

Data on participation by age group given in table 4-1 show that participation fell more among older men than among younger men in Puerto Rico. Between

Table 4-1. *Labor Force Participation, Men, Puerto Rico and the United States, by Age Group, 1970–2003*[a]
Percent

Year	Puerto Rico					United States				
	All	25–34	35–44	45–54	55–64	All	25–34	35–44	45–54	55–64
1970	70.8	91.7	90.3	85.7	73.8	79.4	95.7	96.4	94.2	82.5
1975	64.6	88.7	86.2	79.6	61.0	78.2	95.2	95.6	92.1	75.7
1980	60.7	86.8	85.2	75.8	50.6	77.7	95.1	95.2	91.3	72.4
1985	58.4	85.9	84.5	77.5	50.	76.5	94.7	95.1	91.0	68.1
1990	61.6	86.8	85.9	78.8	52.7	76.6	94.1	94.4	90.6	67.3
1995	61.2	86.6	85.2	76.1	53.8	75.3	93.25	92.4	89.0	65.6
1999	60.5	87.4	84.5	74.6	49.5	74.9	93.3	92.8	89.0	67.9
2000	59.2	n.a.	n.a.	n.a.	n.a.	75.0	93.7	92.6	88.7	67.1
2003	59.3	n.a.	n.a.	n.a.	n.a.	73.7	92.0	91.9	87.9	68.5
Change, 1971 to 1999	−10.3	−4.3	−5.8	−11.1	−24.3	−4.5	−2.4	−3.6	−5.2	−14.6

Source: Data from Estado Libre Asociado de Puerto Rico (2002); and U.S. Bureau of Labor Statistics (data.bls.gov/PDQ/outside.jsp?survey=ce [February 2005]).
a. Persons aged sixteen to sixty-four.

Table 4-2. *Labor Force Participation and Employment Rates, Men,*
by Education Level, Puerto Rico and the United States, 2000[a]
Percent

Education	Puerto Rico	United States	United States/Puerto Rico
Labor force participation rate			
Less than high school graduate	41	58	17
High school graduate	59	79	20
Some college	64	84	20
Bachelor's or more	76	91	15
All educational levels	59	81	22
Employment rate			
Less than high school graduate	29	53	24
High school graduate	47	75	28
Some college	55	79	24
Bachelor's or more	72	89	16
All educational levels	46	76	30

Source: Data from Ruggles and others (2004); and 5% Public Use Microdata Sample, U.S. Census
Bureau, 2000 Census of Population for Puerto Rico; authors' tabulation.

a. Persons eighteen to sixty-four years of age.

1970 and 1999, participation fell by 4.3 points for men aged twenty-five to thirty-
four, by 5.8 points among men aged thirty-five to forty-four, by 11.1 points
among men aged forty-five to fifty-four, and by a huge 24.3 points among men
aged fifty-five to sixty-four. The decline of male participation in the United States
was also larger at older age groups, but for all groups the declines were considerably less than in Puerto Rico: 2.4 points for men aged twenty-five to thirty-four,
3.6 points for men aged thirty-five to forty-four, 5.2 points for men aged forty-
five to fifty-four, and 14.6 points among men aged fifty-five to sixty-four.

To see how male participation and employment varies by education in Puerto
Rico, we examined data from the Census of Population for Puerto Rico. The census shows a lower rate of male employment in 2000 than does the household survey for the same year, for reasons that statisticians have not resolved. The census
has the virtue of large sample sizes, allowing for analysis of the rates for detailed
groups, and is the natural comparison for data from the U.S. Census of Population. We use both the household survey and the census data sets to make sure that
any conclusions we reach are not dependent on the particular source of data.

Table 4-2 records participation and employment rates by education for Puerto
Rican men from the 2000 Puerto Rican census and for comparison, participation rates for U.S. men from the 2000 U.S. census. At all education levels, the
labor force participation rate of men in Puerto Rico lies below that of men in
the United States. The magnitude of the difference is lowest among men with a
bachelor's degree or higher education (15 points) and is largest among those
with a high school education but without a bachelor's degree (20 points). The

Table 4-3. *Labor Force Participation Rate, Men and Women, Puerto Rico, by Synthetic Age Cohorts, 1970, 1980, 1990*
Percent

Year cohort was 25–34	25–34 (1)	35–44 (2)	45–54 (3)	55–64 (4)	Change (3)–(1)	Change (4)–(3)
Men						
1970	91.7	85.2	78.8	48.1	−12.9	−30.7
1980	86.8	85.9	72.2	...	−14.6	...
1990	86.8	83.2	...	...	...	...
Women						
1970	40.5	39.8	39.4	21.4	−1.1	−18.0
1980	45.5	48.0	41.8	...	−3.7	...
1990	47.4	54.4	...	...	...	...

Source: Data from Estado Libre Asociado de Puerto Rico (2002).

employment-to-population ratio shows a similar but more pronounced set of differences, owing to Puerto Rico's higher rate of unemployment. The employment gap is highest among high school graduates and lowest among those with a bachelor's degree. Given the sizable increase in educational attainment among Puerto Rican men since World War II, the pattern of participation and employment rising with education should have increased male labor force activity. Instead, participation and employment both fell. This shows the unreliability of using analyses based on cross-section patterns of labor participation to investigate patterns of change.

Another way of examining the low participation of Puerto Rican men in the workforce is to follow the labor force behavior of a given cohort as it ages over time. Since we do not have longitudinal data that follow the same person over time, we use synthetic cohort data that compare the behavior of increasingly older age groups over time—that is, for example, we use the participation of persons aged thirty-five to forty-four in 1980, forty-five to fifty-four in 1990, and fifty-five to sixty-four in 2000 to simulate the participation of the twenty-five- to thirty-five-year-old 1970 cohort at ten-year intervals.

The top panel of table 4-3 records the trajectory of labor force participation by Puerto Rican men in these synthetic age cohorts; the bottom panel gives the trajectory for Puerto Rican women. The first column records the participation of persons aged twenty-five to thirty-four in the appropriate year, the second column gives the participation of persons in the same cohort ten years later, at age thirty-five to forty-four, the third the participation of persons in the same cohort twenty years later, at age forty-five to fifty-four, and the fourth the participation of the cohort in 2000, when it reached fifty-five to sixty-four years of age.

The labor force attachment of the male group aged twenty-five to thirty-four in 1970 fell by 12.9 percentage points as they aged twenty years from 1970 to

Table 4-4. *Work Status, Men, Puerto Rico and the United States, 2000*
Percent

Category	Puerto Rico	United States
Annual weeks worked among those employed		
50–52	60.9	70.3
48–49	11.3	4.8
27–47	12.5	12.6
Less than 27	15.3	12.3
Weekly hours usually worked among those employed		
35 or more hours	82.6	86.0
15–34	12.2	11.0
1–14	5.2	3.0
Work status over past five years among those out of the workforce		
Worked	35.0	68.0
Did not work	65.0	32.0

Source: Data from Ruggles and others (2004); and 5% Public Use Microdata Sample, U.S. Census Bureau, 2000 Census of Population for Puerto Rico; authors' tabulation.

1990 and then another 30.7 points in the next decade. The 1980 cohort also shows a sharp drop in participation when it enters the forty-five to fifty-four age group. By contrast, the data for women show modest drops in participation for each cohort as it ages, with no major decline in participation as the cohorts enter the forty-five- to fifty-four-year age bracket. Finally, the youngest female cohort shows a rise in participation of 7.0 points between 1990 and 2000 (54.4–47.4). This contrasts with a decline in participation of 3.6 points for men in the same cohort from 1990 to 2000.

A low annual participation or employment rate could reflect low levels of weeks worked by most of the population, or it could reflect a sharp division between persons who work full-year and persons who work little if at all. Table 4-4 gives the share of Puerto Rican and U.S. employed men by weeks and hours worked in 1999, as reported in the 2000 Census of Population for the island and for the United States, and the proportion of nonworking men who worked in the past five years. The data on weeks worked show that relatively fewer men worked fifty to fifty-two weeks over the year in Puerto Rico than in the United States; the greatest proportional difference occurred among those reporting working forty-eight to forty-nine weeks a year. The difference is modest[3]—and

3. Since a two-week difference in weeks worked over the year would be associated with almost a 4-point difference in employment in a given period (2 weeks / 52 weeks = .038), the difference in weeks worked is associated with some of the difference in employment rates.

Figure 4-3. *Principal Activity for Those out of the Labor Force, by Gender, Puerto Rico, 1972–2002*

Percent

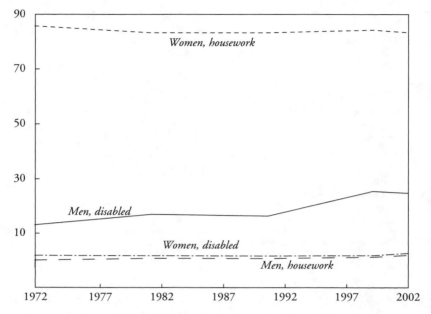

Source: Data from Estado Libre Asociado de Puerto Rico (2002).

possibly spurious, owing to differences in how some workers deal with vacation time in reporting weeks worked. Additional tabulations of weeks worked in Puerto Rico for earlier censuses show little change over time. The hours data in the table also show only a modest difference between the proportion of Puerto Rican and U.S. men working thirty-five hours or more a week.

The big difference in table 4-4 is in the proportion of nonworking men who had worked in the previous five years—just 35 percent of Puerto Rican men out of the labor force compared with 68 percent of nonworking men in the United States. This is not the result of any huge difference in the age distribution of Puerto Rican and U.S. men but rather reflects the relatively permanent detachment of a large number of Puerto Rican men from the workforce—another measure of the employment problem for men on the island.

Figure 4-3 shows the principal activities of Puerto Rican men and women who are out of the labor force, based on the limited data on nonwork activities provided in the Puerto Rican labor force household surveys for 1970 through 2002. The two principal nonwork activities are household work and reporting oneself as disabled. A sizable and rising proportion of men report themselves as out of the labor force and disabled. The proportion of men reporting themselves as disabled jumped from 16.4 percent in 1990 to 25.6 percent in 2000. By contrast, most women out of the labor force were engaged in household work; and less than 3 percent reported themselves as disabled.

In sum, diverse measures of labor force activity from the census and household surveys show that Puerto Rican men had an exceptionally low involvement in the labor market at the turn of the twenty-first century—the result of a downward trend in participation in the 1970s that produced a permanent detachment of many men from the workforce and a rising proportion who reported themselves disabled in the 1990s. Why don't more Puerto Rican men work?

The Distorted Relationship between Aggregate Demand and Employment

Since the implementation of section 936 of the U.S. tax code in the late 1970s, a divergence has grown between gross national production, which measures national income, and gross domestic production. The ratio of GNP to GDP in Puerto Rico fell from 0.93 in 1970 to 0.74 in 1985 to 0.67 in 1997, which means that GDP grew much more rapidly than did GNP. By contrast, the ratio of GNP to GDP in the United States and most other countries shows little or no trend over this period.[4] The reasons are twofold. First, GDP includes profits of foreign companies, particularly in the highly productive manufacturing sector, which then leave the island economy. Second, Puerto Rico's tax structure creates incentives for companies to shift profits to Puerto Rico by underreporting imported inputs such as R&D and thereby overstating value added (see chapter 2 in this volume). As a consequence, Puerto Rico seems to have generated a type of growth based on production of highly productive manufacturing firms that does not translate into large gains in employment.

To the extent that GDP does not accurately measure production on the island, employment should be more closely related to the slower-growing GNP than to the faster-growing GDP. To assess this possibility, we regressed the natural logarithm (ln) of employment separately on the natural logarithms for real GNP and real GDP (allowing for first-order serial correlation) and also regressed the first difference of the natural logarithm of employment on the first difference of natural logarithms of GNP and of GDP. In addition, we also regressed the first difference in the absolute change in employment on the first difference in the absolute change in GDP. As our counterfactual or norm for assessing the coefficients, we estimated the same regressions for the United States over the same period.

Table 4-5 summarizes the results of these regressions. For Puerto Rico, ln GNP has a higher estimated impact on ln employment than does ln GDP in all

4. Data downloaded from University of Pennsylvania, *Penn World Tables* (pwt.econ.upenn.edu/php_site/pwt_index.php [January 2005]).

Table 4-5. *Effects of Output on Employment, United States and Puerto Rico,*
1970–2003[a]

Coefficient	Functional form of regression equation		
	ln form	*Change in ln*	*Change in level*
Puerto Rico			
GNP	0.72	0.78	0.140
	(0.09)	(0.21)	(0.043)
GDP	0.49	0.67	0.045
	(0.05)	(0.16)	(0.025)
United States			
GNP	0.54	0.53	0.008
	(0.03)	(0.07)	(0.001)
GDP	0.54	0.54	0.008
	(0.03)	(0.07)	(0.001)

Source: Data from Estado Libre Asociado de Puerto Rico (various years); U.S. Department of Commerce, Bureau of Economic Analysis, National Economic Accounts (www.bea.gov/bea/dn/nipaweb/SelectTable.asp?Popular=Y [March 2005]).

a. All equations are corrected for serial correlation. Ln is natural logarithm. The form of ln is regression of ln employment on ln output. Change in ln is a regression of change in ln employment on change in ln output. Change level form is regression of change in employment on change in output, measured in thousands of constant dollars. Standard errors are in parentheses.

specifications. By contrast, there is no such difference in regression coefficients of ln employment on ln GDP and ln GNP in the United States. The ln forms indicate that the impact of GNP on employment is modestly larger for Puerto Rico than for the United States, presumably reflecting the lower productivity on the island, though the absolute form shows a higher impact of changes in output on changes in employment in the GNP analysis, but a lower impact in the GDP analysis, for Puerto Rico than for the United States.

These estimates and the slower growth of GNP per capita than GDP per capita suggest that aggregate economic growth in Puerto Rico has been less favorable to employment than first appears to be the case, because it took the form of GDP growth that is not part of GNP. The divergence between GNP and GDP is largely the result of section 936 companies' operating in Puerto Rico. The tax benefit given by the federal government to Puerto Rico to attract foreign capital has produced a highly capital-intensive and nominally highly productive manufacturing sector, in which the extra GDP has a smaller impact on employment than would be the case if manufacturing firms made a different set of investments, ones not distorted by the tax breaks.

Table 4-6 shows the extent to which the pattern of GDP and employment in Puerto Rico may have been distorted by the close relation to the United States and the tax incentives given for investing in capital-intensive activities. In 2003

Table 4-6. *Distribution of GDP and Employment, by Industry, Puerto Rico, 2003*
Percent

Industry	GDP	Employment
Manufacturing	42.1	11
Finance, insurance, and real estate	17.1	4
Trade	11.6	21
Services	9.9	28
Government	9.6	21
Transportation and other public utilities	6.9	5
Construction and mining	2.4	7
Agriculture	0.3	2

Source: Data from Universidad de Puerto Rico, Unidad de Investigaciones Económicas database (uprrp.edu/uie/ [August 2005]).

manufacturing accounted for 42.1 percent of Puerto Rican GDP, whereas just 11 percent of Puerto Rican employment was in manufacturing. The ratio of the share of output to the share of employment in manufacturing was nearly 4 to 1— compared with a ratio of about 1.1 to 1.0 in the United States.[5]

Firms operating in Puerto Rico invest in capital-intensive manufacturing and declare large profits from those activities. Within manufacturing, one-quarter of Puerto Rican employment is in the highly capital-intensive chemicals sector, whereas just 6 percent of U.S. manufacturing employment is in chemicals.[6]

Transfer Programs

In 2003 island residents received $14.3 billion in transfers, according to the *Economic Report to the Governor* of Puerto Rico; most of these transfers came from the U.S. federal government. By contrast, residents paid out $4.4 billion in taxes, largely as employee contributions to Social Security and Medicare.[7] The $9.9 billion net transfer represented 22 percent of personal income and 26 percent of net income on the island. This has to be one of the largest proportionate

5. U.S. Council of Economic Advisers, *Economic Report of the President,* November 2005 (www.gpoaccess.gov/eop/download.html).

6. U.S. Bureau of Labor Statistics, "Industry Wages by Occupation," May 2003 (www.bls.gov/oes/2003/may/naics3_325000.htm#b00-0000 [January 2005]); U.S. Bureau of Labor Statistics, "The Employment Situation," May 2003 (ftp://ftp.bls.gov/pub/news.release/History/empsit.06062003.news [January 2005]); U.S. Bureau of Labor Statistics, "Estado Libre Asociado 2003" (www.bls.gov/oes/oes_dl.htm#2003.m [January 2005]).

7. These numbers are from Estado Libre Asociado de Puerto Rico (2003). They differ from those reported by the U.S. Social Security Administration (2004), which reports $10.4 billion in transfers and $2.9 billion paid out by residents, giving a net transfer of $7.5 billion.

transfer payments from one economy to another, with potentially significant impacts on labor supply.

Disability Insurance

The major federally funded transfer program in Puerto Rico is Old-Age, Survivors, and Disability Insurance (OASDI). A larger proportion of OASDI spending in Puerto Rico consists of disability payments than in the United States. Administrative data from the Social Security Administration show that 19 percent of Puerto Rican Social Security beneficiaries were on disability payments, in comparison with 12 percent of U.S. Social Security beneficiaries.[8]

Census data also provide information about disability. In 2000, among the Puerto Rican male population aged eighteen to sixty-four, 17 percent reported having an employment disability, defined as a disability "that affects their ability to work at a job or business," compared with 13 percent in the United States (see table 4-7).[9] Among those reporting a work disability, Puerto Rican men are much less likely to be employed than men in the United States. Thirty-eight percent of Puerto Rican men with a work disability were working in 2000. By contrast, 63 percent of U.S. men with some work disability were working. The employment ratio in Puerto Rico relative to the employment ratio in the United States among those with a work disability (0.60 [38/63]) is slightly lower than the ratio of the overall male employment rate in Puerto Rico to the male employment rate in the United States (0.62 [47/67]). Among men without a high school diploma, the differences between Puerto Rico and the United States are even larger: among these men who report a work disability, only 26 percent in Puerto Rico are employed, while 52 percent in the United States are employed.

Using census data, we can infer receipt of Social Security disability insurance among working-age men from whether or not they receive Social Security benefits. Almost one in every ten adult men in Puerto Rico under the age of sixty-five received Social Security income in 1999. The comparable figure for the United States is one in every twenty. Social Security income is quite common among men aged forty-six to sixty-four, of whom 22 percent receive this type of income. Among men aged eighteen to sixty-four, a much larger proportion of Puerto Ricans receive benefits from Social Security disability insurance than U.S. men—9.8 percent versus 4.4 percent. The absolute difference in the rates reporting receipt of Social Security disability benefits is larger for older than for younger workers and larger for less educated workers, while the relative difference varies in a less clear pattern.

Across time, however, the census data show a small decrease in the rate of receipt in Puerto Rico and a small increase in the United States. The implication is that while differences between Puerto Rico and the United States in

8. On the mainland, West Virginia is the outlier, with 17 percent.
9. Mississippi had the next highest percentage, with employment disability at 14.4 percent.

Table 4-7. *Work Disability and Receipt of Social Security Income, Men, Puerto Rico and the United States, Selected Years*
Percent

Category	Puerto Rico	United States	Puerto Rico/ United States
Men with work disability, 2000	17	13	1.3
Employed, total	38	63	0.63
Employed, less than twelve years of education	26	52	0.50
Employed, twelve years or more of education	47	68	0.69
Men receiving Social Security disability, 1999	9.8	4.4	2.2
Aged 18–30	2.1	1.1	1.9
Aged 31–45	5.7	2.1	2.7
Aged 46–64	21.7	9.8	2.2
Without a high school diploma	15.3	7.4	2.1
With at least a high school diploma	6.6	3.7	1.8
Men receiving Social Security, 1979	9.2	4.9	1.9

Source: Data from Ruggles and others (2004); 5% Public Use Microdata Sample, U.S. Census Bureau, 1980 Census of Population for Puerto Rico; and 5% Public Use Microdata Sample, U.S. Census Bureau, 2000 Census of Population for Puerto Rico; authors' tabulation.

receipt of disability insurance contribute to differences in employment rates, they cannot account for trends or differences in trends between Puerto Rico and the United States. On the other hand, the Puerto Rican labor force survey, which allows for a self-reported "disabled" category in labor force status, shows a steady rise in the proportion of men reporting that they are disabled, reaching 25 percent in 2000, as shown in figure 4-3.

Finally, administrative data also show that the ratio of disabled workers to the overall workforce is higher in Puerto Rico than in the United States. In Puerto Rico 131,340 persons claimed disability insurance in 2002, according to administrative data, among 1.157 million employees, giving a ratio of disabled workers to employees of 0.11 and ratio of disability insurance recipients to the working-age population of 0.06. By contrast, the comparable ratios for United States are .04 and .03, respectively.[10]

The potential for disability insurance to discourage work in Puerto Rico is enormous, considering the low earnings of Puerto Rican workers and the high levels of unemployment. In 2002 support for disabled workers in Puerto Rico was $713 per month—80 percent of the $891 monthly support for disabled workers in the United States. This compares with retirement benefits and wages that are about 66 percent of those in the United States. Given monthly earnings of male

10. The United States had 5.4 million workers with disability insurance in a workforce of 137 million persons.

workers in Puerto Rico of $1,032 as reported by the Department of Labor, the ratio of disability income to wages is 69 percent. By contrast, the ratio of disability income to wages in the United States, where monthly earnings of workers are on the order of $1,600, is about 56 percent. Hence availability of disability income creates stronger incentives not to work in Puerto Rico than in the United States. David Autor and Mark Duggan find that receipt of disability insurance affected male labor force behavior in the United States, and it is likely to have done the same in Puerto Rico.[11] High unemployment levels may also be pushing Puerto Rican men into claiming disability insurance, since this same study also finds that disability insurance participation is responsive to aggregate demand shocks.[12] In sum, these figures suggest that Social Security disability insurance may be encouraging Puerto Rican men, particularly those with low levels of education, to drop from the labor force.

Nutritional Assistance Program

Another component of federal transfers to Puerto Rico is the Nutritional Assistance Program (NAP), the most widespread government assistance program on the island. This program was initially created as a food stamp program but was cashed out in 1985. In 2000 the government instituted an Electronic Benefit Transfer system, wherein 75 percent of the benefits must be used at certified establishments that have electronic systems hooked up to the Department of the Family NAP account, and only 25 percent can be cashed out at ATMs. The Puerto Rican NAP has high implicit tax rates and covers a huge proportion of the workforce, in contrast to the low implicit marginal tax rates of the U.S. food stamp program and its limited coverage. In Puerto Rico, NAP supplies assistance to far more families than Temporary Assistance to Needy Families. The Department of the Family reports about half a million "units" on NAP. While NAP units are not exactly families as measured by the census, approximately 1 million families were counted in the 2000 census, which suggests that on the order of half of the families in Puerto Rico receive government assistance. A family of four with no income may receive about $300 a month on NAP.

Although single mothers are the most likely demographic group to be on assistance because they are generally poorer, NAP covers married couples as well. We have not estimated the effect of this program on the low labor participation rate of Puerto Rican men, but the sheer volume of participation in the program suggests the presence of negative labor supply effects on men. Taken together, the Social Security disability program and the NAP program combined could have large effects on male employment behavior. However, there

---

11. Autor and Duggan (2003). There remain debates over the magnitude of the effect and over how men who said they were disabled might have behaved absent disability insurance (Bound and Waidmann 1992; Haveman, DeJong, and Wolfe 1991).

12. Autor and Duggan (2003).

are no data rich enough to sort out these effects. The only source of household data collected regularly in Puerto Rico is the labor force survey, which does not ask questions on annual income and or its sources. Decennial census data are also limited in the information they contain, making these issues difficult to address rigorously. Still, we can draw some inferences about the potential effect of nonwork income on labor supply from data on the work patterns of married couples. If we assume that any couple in which neither the husband nor wife works must be deriving income from some other source, of which transfer payments (particularly from the NAP program) are a likely part, the proportion of families that are without work gives some notion of the proportion of husbands for whom nonwork income reduces the pressure to obtain a job.

To determine the work patterns of married couples, we matched wife and husband records for persons aged eighteen to sixty-four from the 2000 Census of Population for Puerto Rico census and tabulated the employment status of both spouses within four work arrangements: husband and wife both jobless; husband employed, wife jobless; husband jobless, wife employed; and both husband and wife employed. In 36.1 percent of the cases, both the wife and husband were without work. This is the largest of the four groups, giving Puerto Rico an extraordinarily high proportion of "jobless families."[13] In 30.8 percent of the cases, the husband worked and the wife did not; in 7.9 percent of the couples, the wife was working and the husband was not. In just 25.2 percent of the cases were both spouses working.[14]

Given the data at hand, it is not possible to estimate how many of the husbands in the "jobless families" were not working because their families could obtain income from transfers; however, the huge proportion of couples falling into that category suggests that the effects of transfers on male employment could be quite large. The families with no earners are making money in some fashion. With about half the families receiving NAP support and many men obtaining disability insurance, we would expect that many of the near 40 percent of jobless families are recipients of either or both of these forms of income, depressing their incentive to work, at least in the formal sector.

Migration

Puerto Ricans are U.S. citizens with the right to a U.S. passport and the freedom to travel and reside on the mainland at their discretion. For more than half a century, tens of thousands of Puerto Ricans have migrated to the United States each

13. Gregg and Wadsworth (2001).

14. Analyzing this pattern further, we estimated a logit model in which the dependent variable took the value of 1 if the husband was employed and 0 otherwise, with the education and age of the husband and whether or not the wife was employed as right-hand-side variables. The regression shows that a husband with a nonemployed wife had a 63 percent lower likelihood of employment than a husband with an employed wife.

year, many of whom return to the island. The legal right to move back and forth
between the mainland and Puerto Rico distinguishes Puerto Ricans from persons
in other developing economies with close ties to the United States, such as Mexico or the Dominican Republic. It leads to a potentially different pattern of
migration, with some workers going back and forth within relatively short periods of time.[15] As table 4-8 indicates, 37 percent of men aged eighteen to sixty-
four who had been born in Puerto Rico were living on the mainland in 2000.

Migration can affect the Puerto Rican employment-to-population and labor
participation ratios in three ways. First, if unemployed persons leave the island
to seek work in the United States, the employment rate will rise because both
the number of unemployed persons and the number of resident persons of
working age will be reduced. Thus migration can serve as a way to export the
unemployed. In fact, time series data show a positive correlation between the
rate of unemployment and net migration.[16] But when unemployed persons
leave the island, their movement lowers the labor force participation rate,
because it reduces the number of persons in the labor force by proportionately
more than it reduces the working-age population.[17]

Second, migration could reduce the labor participation rate through selective
migration if persons with strong attachment to the labor market migrate to the
United States. The migration of those who want to work but do not have jobs
would lower the number of persons in the labor force proportionately more than
it would lower the population. Consistent with this, one study has found that the
labor force participation rates of recent migrants and prior migrants to the
United States are higher than those of persons who remain on the island, even
within the same age and education groups.[18]

Third, migration can affect employment and participation indirectly by raising the reservation wages of persons on the island. Since migration gives Puerto
Ricans access to higher-wage U.S. jobs, some persons might set their reservation
wages on the basis of what they could get working in the United States, producing a lower bound on wages that could be too high to accommodate excess
labor. This could reduce the labor force participation rate if persons with high

15. Ricardo Godoy and colleagues report that 13.5 percent of persons in Puerto Rico in 1990
had lived on the mainland at various times in the preceding decade. Ricardo Godoy and others,
"English Proficiency and Quality of Life among Puerto Ricans: Does It Matter?" Sustainable International Development Program, Heller Graduate School, Brandeis University, November 2001
(www.heller.brandeis.edu/sid/downloads/englishpro.pdf).

16. Pol (2004a).

17. A numeric example demonstrates this. Assume ten people of working age, of whom five are
in the labor force, two are unemployed, and the remaining three are working. The migration of
one unemployed worker reduces the working-age population to nine persons and the labor force to
four persons. The labor participation rate falls from 50 percent (5/10) to 44 percent (4/9), while
the employment rate rises from 30 percent (3/10) to 33 percent (3/9).

18. Enchautegui (2005).

Table 4-8. *Emigration and Employment Rates, Puerto Rican Men, Puerto Rico and the United States, by Education, 2000*[a]

Percent

Category	Educational attainment				
	To eleven years	Twelve years	Thirteen to fifteen years	Sixteen or more years	All
Emigration rate	45	37	26	27	37
Employed in Puerto Rico	32	48	54	72	46
Employed in the United States	43	61	70	84	55
Simulated employed in Puerto Rico[b]	37	53	58	75	49
Difference					
Employed in the United States – employed in Puerto Rico	11	13	16	12	9
Puerto Ricans employed in Puerto Rico, simulated – actual	5	5	4	3	3

Source: Data from Ruggles and others (2004); and 5% Public Use Microdata Sample, U.S. Census Bureau, 2000 Census of Population for Puerto Rico; authors' tabulation.

a. Persons eighteen to sixty-four years of age.

b. The simulation assumes that all migrants return to Puerto Rico and are employed at the same rate as in the United States.

reservation wages dropped out of the workforce. For migration to help explain the low rate of employment, the second and third factors must dominate. But even if migration is only an outlet for the unemployed, it will contribute to the low participation rate.

We use census data on the employment of Puerto Rican–born men residing in Puerto Rico and those residing as migrants in the United States to assess the maximum contribution that selective migration could make to the low employment rate in Puerto Rico. We make the strong assumption that migrants to the United States have higher rates of employment than comparable persons in Puerto Rico solely because they have positively selected themselves according to their desire or ability to get a job and that if migrants returned to Puerto Rico, they would obtain work at the same rate as in the United States. By attributing all of the difference in employment rates to selective migration, we obtain the maximum possible contribution that selective migration could make to the low level of employment on the island.

Table 4-8 shows the result of our calculation for men aged sixteen to sixty-four. It gives the proportion of Puerto Rican–born men living in the United States, for all men and for men by education group; the employment rates for Puerto Rican–born men living in Puerto Rico and on the mainland; the difference between the two rates; and the results of a simulation we performed. The proportion living in the United States was much higher for persons with less education than for those with more education—a pattern of migration that has long characterized the island. Moreover, 46 percent of those living in Puerto Rico were employed, as compared with 55 percent of those who migrated to the United States—a 9-point differential. Within educational groups, the difference in employment rates is even greater.

Our simulation estimates what the male employment rate on the island would be if all migrants returned to Puerto Rico and were employed at the same employment rate as on the mainland. If the 37 percent living in the United States moved back to Puerto Rico and were employed at the 55 percent rate of employment they experienced in the United States, the rate would rise to 49 percent—a 3-point increase over the 46 percent rate for island residents. Within the four education groups, the increase in the rate of employment under this simulation ranges from 3 to 5 percentage points. This suggests that selective migration is a modest factor in the low employment rate on the island. If migration is a major contributor to the low employment rate, it must also be placing a lower bound on the structure of wages.

The Structure of Wages

From the perspective of labor demand analysis, low employment suggests an imbalance in the level and pattern of wages. Are wages too high relative to the level of economic development of Puerto Rico? Is the structure of wages by skill inconsistent with the supply of skills? If so, the wage structure could be part of the island's employment problem.

Table 4-9 compares earnings in Puerto Rico, the United States, and Mississippi, the state with the lowest per capita income. The upper panel of the table records data on earnings in Puerto Rico from establishment surveys for 2003. In manufacturing, the hourly pay and labor costs (which include fringe benefits) for production workers is about two-thirds of the hourly pay and labor costs in the United States. Puerto Rican production workers in manufacturing receive between 81 and 85 percent of the hourly pay and labor costs of Mississippi's production workers in manufacturing. Since living expenses are comparable between the island and the mainland, these figures are indicative of differences in real earnings.[19]

The data for the hourly earnings of all workers show a bigger gap. Puerto Ricans earn 59 percent of the earnings of workers on the mainland and 74 to 79 percent the earnings of workers in Mississippi, depending on whether earnings are given as medians or means. The larger gap in earnings among all workers reflects manufacturing's disproportionate share of GDP in Puerto Rico, as

---

19. Bosworth and Collins (chapter 2 in this volume) show that Puerto Rico's cost of living is similar to that of the District of Columbia.

Table 4-9. *Wages and Labor Costs in Puerto Rico, the United States, and Mississippi, Selected Years*
Dollars, except as indicated

Category	Puerto Rico	United States	Mississippi	Puerto Rico/ United States (percent)	Puerto Rico/ Mississippi (percent)
Establishment data, 2003					
Production workers in manufacturing					
Hourly earnings	9.87	15.18	12.12	.65	.81
Hourly labor costs	13.91	20.93	16.45	.66	.85
All workers					
Mean hourly wage, May 2003	10.41	17.56	13.13	.59	.79
Median hourly wage, May 2003	7.92	13.65	10.73	.59	.74
Census household data, by gender and years of schooling, 2000					
Annual earnings, male					
All	20,200	39,142	31,199	.52	.65
4 or more years of college	37,151	66,842	54,304	.56	.68
1–3 years of college	19,127	35,612	30,142	.54	.63
12 years of schooling	15,888	30,316	27,821	.52	.57
Less than 12 years of schooling	12,639	19,415	19,825	.65	.54
Annual earnings, female					
All	15,499	24,074	18,966	.64	.82
4 or more years of college	22,231	37,902	30,161	.59	.74
1–3 years of college	12,994	22,278	18,174	.55	.71
12 years of schooling	10,922	19,013	16,102	.57	.66
Less than 12 years of schooling	9,580	12,513	12,278	.77	.78

Source: Data from Commonwealth of Puerto Rico (www.pridco.com/english/operational_advantages/4.2opr_adv_wages_salary.html [August 2005]); U.S. Bureau of Labor Statistics (www.bls.gov/oes/2003/may/oessrcst.htm [August 2005]); Ruggles and others (2004); and 5% Public Use Microdata Sample, U.S. Census Bureau, 2000 Census of Population for Puerto Rico; authors' tabulation.

shown in table 4-6: the manufacturing sector diverges more from the rest of the economy in Puerto Rico than it does in the United States, consistent with the huge productivity difference on the island between manufacturing and the rest of the economy.

Using data from the 2000 U.S. Census of Population and the 2000 Census of Population for Puerto Rico, the lower panel of table 4-9 gives annual earnings by gender and years of schooling. The annual earnings of men in Puerto Rico were 52 percent of male annual earnings in the United States in 2000. This ratio is lower than the hourly pay ratio because workers in Puerto Rico work fewer weeks and fewer hours than those on the mainland. Male workers in Puerto

Rico earned 65 percent as much as workers in Mississippi. Women's annual earnings in Puerto Rico were closer to those of women in the United States. For all women, average annual earnings in Puerto Rico were 64 percent of those in the United States and 82 percent of those in Mississippi. The data by education show that island earnings relative to U.S. earnings for both men and women were highest among the most and the least educated. Compared with earnings in Mississippi, the relative earnings of men on the island were highest for the most educated; for women, they were highest for the least educated.

The normal pattern in earnings differences among countries with different levels of income is that earnings in a lower-income economy are closer to earnings in a higher-income economy among the most educated or skilled. The reason is that lower-income economies have fewer highly skilled workers than advanced economies and thus pay relatively high wages in the top occupations.[20] However, in three of the four comparisons in table 4-9, the highest relative earnings were for less educated workers.

To see whether the pattern of relatively high earnings among low-paid workers holds across occupations, we compare earnings by occupation in Puerto Rico and in Mississippi, our low-income mainland comparison area, using data from the Occupational Employment Survey (OES) conducted by the Bureau of Labor Statistics.[21] This survey obtains earnings and employment data at the three-digit occupation level for detailed geographic areas of the United States and outlying areas. Since the data come from establishment records, they offer a more accurate measure of rates of pay than self-reported earnings in the decennial census. The OES contains data on the relative earnings of persons in Puerto Rico in 538 detailed occupations from the May 2003 survey and in 643 detailed occupations from the comparison state, Mississippi. Do these data show high relative pay for Puerto Ricans with limited skills?[22]

Table 4-10 summarizes the OES data for a selection of high-wage, middle-wage, and low-wage occupations. Earnings in Puerto Rico were higher than in Mississippi in the selected occupations at the top of the earnings distribution, markedly lower for the occupations in the middle of the distribution, and comparable for occupations with low earnings. The wages for maids and housekeeping cleaners were higher in Puerto Rico than in Mississippi, possibly reflecting the island's comparative advantage in tourism and the consequent demand for these workers.

20. Freeman and Oostendorp (2002).

21. The Occupational Employment Survey (www.bls.gov/oes/current/oessrcst.htm [January 2005]) samples approximately four hundred thousand establishments each year and, over a three-year period, contacts approximately 1.2 million establishments. It provides wage and employment estimates for detailed geographic areas, including Puerto Rico and its main metropolitan areas.

22. U.S.A. Data Engine, "U.S. Wages and Salaries" (www.ctdataengine.com/uswages/index0008.html [January 2005]).

Table 4-10. *Yearly Earnings, Selected Occupations, by Wage Level, Puerto Rico and Mississippi, 2003*
Dollars, except as indicated

Occupation and wage level	Puerto Rico	Mississippi	Puerto Rico/ Mississippi (ratio)
All workers	21,650	27,310	0.79
High wage			
Chief executive	113,500	101,540	1.12
Marketing manager	68,860	63,570	1.08
Optometrist	53,580	95,970	0.59
Lawyer	53,850	73,310	0.73
Mechanical engineer	50,450	55,800	0.9
Middle wage			
Loan officer	34,250	42,070	0.81
Accountant, auditor	30,700	43,190	0.71
Firefighter	17,630	27,350	0.64
Child, family, and school social worker	22,690	29,090	0.78
Registered nurse	22,300	43,990	0.51
Low wage			
Maid, housekeeping cleaner	14,420	14,280	1.04
Security guard	13,520	16,910	0.8
Laborer	16,300	18,730	0.87
Cook, fast food	12,630	13,390	0.94
Bus driver, school	13,360	15,910	0.84

Source: Data from U.S. Bureau of Labor Statistics, Occupational Employment Survey, May 2003 (www.bls.gov/oes/oes_dl.htm#2003_m [August 2005]).

To see if the pattern of relatively high wages at both the top and bottom of the earnings distribution holds over the entire spectrum of occupations, we performed two additional calculations. First, we ranked earnings in all of the occupations reported for both Puerto Rico and Mississippi. We divided the distribution of earnings by decile and calculated the average earnings for occupations in each decile of the distribution for each area. For example, for occupations in the lowest 10 percent of earnings in Puerto Rico, we averaged the earnings in that decile, for occupations in the second decile, we averaged the earnings in that decile, and so forth. We made the same calculations for the occupations in Mississippi, ranked by the Mississippi distribution. This contrast uses the data on all occupations in both areas and places occupations in its area-specific distribution. Dividing the average earnings in each decile in Puerto Rico by the average earnings in each decile in Mississippi, we estimated the pattern of earnings differences from low-wage to high-wage occupations. These calculations are shown in figure 4-4 in the line labeled "All occupations." The ratio of wages among occupations by decile fits a U-shaped curve: the Puerto Rico-to-Mississippi wage

Figure 4-4. *Earnings Ratio, Puerto Rico to Mississippi, by Decile for Occupations,*
May 2003

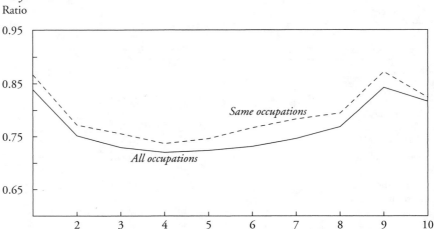

Source: Data from U.S. Bureau of Labor Statistics, Occuptional Employment Survey (www.bls.gov/
oes/2003/May oessrcst.htm [February 2005]).

ratio is high for low-wage occupations, falls for middle-wage occupations, and
then rises for high-wage occupations.

We also examined the distribution of earnings in the 513 occupations that
were the same in both locations. This eliminates occupations found in only one
of the two localities. The correlation coefficient between the wages by occupation
in this case was .82, indicating some difference in the ranking of occupations by
wages in the two areas. We computed the mean wage of the occupations in each
decile for Puerto Rico and Mississippi taken separately and took the ratio of
those wages as our measure of the pattern of earnings differences from low-wage
to high-wage occupations. Again, the U-shaped curve shows that the ratio of
Puerto Rico to Mississippi is high for low-wage occupations, falls for middle
wage occupations, and then rises for high-wage occupations.

As a final check on this pattern, we categorized the 513 occupations for
which we had earnings in both localities by the average of their ranking in the
Puerto Rican and Mississippi earnings distributions,[23] computed the decile in
which each occupation fell by the average rank, and regressed the natural logarithm of the ratio of earnings in Puerto Rico to that in Mississippi on each of
ten dummy variables for the decile in which the occupation fit. Table 4-11 gives

23. That is, if an occupation was ranked sixth in Puerto Rico and fourteenth in Mississippi, we
gave it an average rank of ten.

Table 4-11. *Coefficient for Regression of ln of Earnings in Puerto Rico Relative to ln of Earnings in Mississippi, by Decile*

Decile[a]	Coefficient[b]
1	−.15
2	−.26
3	−.29
4	−.26
5	−.30
6	−.31
7	−.22
8	−.21
9	−.17
10	−.15
$R^2 = 0.55$	

Source: Data from U.S. Bureau of Labor Statistics, Occupational Employment Survey, May 2003 (www.bls.gov/oes/oes_dl.htm#2003_m [August 2005]).

a. The regressions summarize the data for the 513 occupations that overlap. The natural logarithm of the ratio of Puerto Rico to Mississippi equals the ratio of the ln of earnings in Puerto Rico to the ln of earnings in Mississippi. The decile location of an occupation is determined by the occupation's fit on the basis of its average rank. Standard error for all deciles is .03.

b. Decile 1 is the lowest.

our regression results, in which the same pattern emerges. Puerto Rican wages were 0.15 ln point below wages in Mississippi for occupations in the lowest decile, fell to 0.31 ln point below Mississippi wages in the sixth decile, and then rose to 0.15 ln point below wages in Mississippi in the highest decile.

Given Puerto Rico's relatively high wages at the bottom of the earnings distribution and high joblessness, the natural question to ask is why the high joblessness in Puerto Rico has not driven wages down at the bottom of the wage distribution to create more jobs. Our rich-uncle hypothesis directs attention to three possible answers.

On the demand side, it is possible that Puerto Rico's adoption of U.S.-level minimum wages limited downward wage adjustments.[24] Since 1977, employers in Puerto Rico covered by the federal Fair Labor Standards Act have been subject to the federal minimum; those not covered by the act must pay at least 70 percent of the federal minimum wage or the applicable mandatory decree rate set by the Department of Labor, whichever is higher. Since Puerto Rico has lower productivity and lower average wages than the United States, this means that the minimum wage affects a larger proportion of the workforce in Puerto Rico than in the United States. However, Puerto Rican minimum wage law allows

24. Castillo-Freeman and Freeman (1992).

the secretary of labor and human resources to authorize a lower rate to any employer who can show that implementation of the 70 percent rate would substantially curtail employment in that business. Debate over the impact of the minimum wage law on the island's employment has focused on the period when the island adopted the federal minimum.[25] As the federal minimum rate was constant at $5.15 an hour from 1997 through 2004, it would bound annual earnings of full-time workers on the island at about $10,700 a year. This level is below the earnings for low-wage occupations shown in table 4-10, however, and indeed falls below the mean earnings in the lowest decile of the Puerto Rican earnings distribution, $13,399 for the sample of 538 occupations. The minimum wage may affect the lower part of the wage distribution, but given this large gap we suspect that other factors are more important.

A second possible reason for the relatively high level of Puerto Rican wages in occupations that usually pay low wages is that income transfers have created a reservation wage considerably higher than the minimum and higher than full employment wage rates. Our survey of men in communities along the Martín Peña channel in San Juan asked them for their reservation wage. The reservation wage of the nonemployed men was $7.00 an hour. Virtually no one said he would take a job for less than that wage. Seven dollars an hour would produce a lower bound on earnings around $14,500, consistent with earnings at the bottom of the occupational wage structure and considerably higher than the minimum wage.

The third possible reason for a high reservation wage on the island is that potential migration to the United States creates a floor for wages above the minimum. Given an annualized cost of mobility to the mainland of C and mainland earnings of W, annual earnings on the island could be bounded by $W - C$, with workers migrating when unemployment develops at that wage. Arguably, if migrants returned to Puerto Rico, they would increase the labor supply and drive down the wage, which would raise employment. However, this would not necessarily raise the rate of employment, which would change depending on how much wages fell and the elasticity of demand to labor. The rich-uncle impact of migration on the wage structure reverses the Harris-Todaro migration mechanism, according to which people from rural areas migrate to urban areas with institutionally determined wages until urban unemployment equates the expected earnings in the two areas. In our model, the potential of migration to the higher-wage mainland sets a lower bound on wages in Puerto Rico, which depresses employment there. What makes the lower employment tolerable is the existence of diverse social benefits for persons on the island, paid by the mainland; the option to migrate to the United States to earn higher wages; and the potential to make money outside the formal sector.

25. Krueger (1995).

The Role of the Informal Economy

There is a widespread belief that many jobless Puerto Rican men work in the informal sector, and that standard labor force surveys fail to measure this type of employment. Employment in the informal sector grew in many Latin American countries in the 1980s and 1990s—part and parcel of poor economic growth and the deindustrialization of Latin American economies, which has made informalization of work a major issue in understanding the economic circumstances of workers in those economies. In Puerto Rico, the informal labor market provides job opportunities for men who cannot find work in the formal labor market while allowing them to receive government benefits like NAP and disability insurance, both of which are work-tested or means-tested, that they could lose if they took formal sector jobs. The low measured employment of Puerto Rican men could be a measurement problem owing to the failure of official statistics to capture work in this sector.

For the informal sector to explain the low level of labor participation in Puerto Rico, it must constitute a large share of the economy. Some studies estimate that it accounts for more than 23 percent of Puerto Rican GDP.[26] For the informal sector to explain the declining participation and employment population rate in Puerto Rico, however, it would have to have grown since the 1970s; on this, the evidence is not as clear.

Standard labor force data provide indirect evidence on the possible size and development of informal sector work. One natural indicator of the informal sector is the proportion of workers who are self-employed. Since 1980 the proportion self-employed reported by the Department of Labor in Puerto Rico has fluctuated between 11 and 12 percent, about 5 points above the 6–7 percent self-employed in the United States. Since the self-employed are counted as workers, these figures do not measure nonparticipants in the labor force who work in the informal sector. Still, if many workers work in the informal sector, one would expect some to report that they are self-employed, so that a high level of self-employment is consistent with a large number working in the informal sector. The constancy of the self-employment rate in Puerto Rico suggests that the proportion of men in the informal economy has not grown over the past twenty years.

Another indicator of the potential level and growth of the informal sector is the proportion of men who are out of the labor force, not disabled, not going to school, and not doing household work. These men may be idle, but they could just as readily be informal sector workers, since they have no other reported income activity and have no reported physical or other impediments to work. Figure 4-5 shows that the proportion of men in this category declined from 1970 to 2000. Based on self-employment rates and the proportion of nonwork-

26. Pol (2004b); Estudios Técnicos (2004).

Figure 4-5. *Men out of the Labor Force, Percentage in No Productive Activity,*
Puerto Rico, 1970–2000

Percent

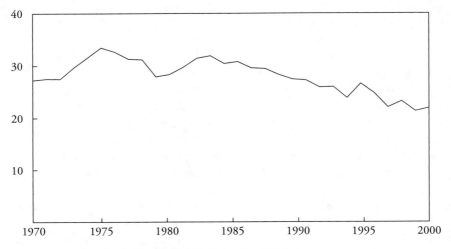

Source: Data from Estado Libre Asociado de Puerto Rico (2002).

ing men who are idle, the informal sector does not appear to have grown significantly since 1980, although it still may be a significant constant in the Puerto
Rican labor market structure and a sector that needs close examination.

Despite the fact that the informal sector is commonly perceived as a contributor to the low participation rate of Puerto Rican men, there has been no direct
study of workers involved in the sector. To fill this gap, we undertook a pilot survey in summer 2004 to find out what men in communities with potentially low
employment were doing. The Department of Transportation and Public Works
was undertaking a massive infrastructure project related to the cleaning of the water
route of the Martín Peña channel in the capital city of San Juan and had commis-
sioned a census of the eight communities along the channel. This census provided
us with a sampling frame from which to draw participants for the survey. We randomly selected men in households from three of these communities, Marina, Bella
Vista Hato Rey, and Bella Vista Santurce, that were in the middle of the income
distribution for the eight communities. We drew samples from households containing men aged eighteen to sixty-four and not attending school. We interviewed
133 men. While our sample has some drawbacks for analyzing the informal sec-

27. One drawback is that employment opportunities in the metropolitan area of San Juan tend
to be better than elsewhere on the island, which would lead to an underestimate of islandwide
informal work. Another drawback is that the area has a sizable number of foreign-born men,
mainly Dominican, whose behavior may differ from that of men born in Puerto Rico.

tor,[27] it offers new insight into informal sector work on the island and illustrates how workers in the informal sector report that work on the household survey.

The first question asked on our survey was the same question the Department of Labor and Human Resources in Puerto Rico uses in its monthly survey: "Can you tell me what were you doing last week?"[28] The possible answers were working, looking for work, with employment but not at work, domestic chores, going to school, disabled, retired, and other. These responses are problematic for describing workers with contingent informal labor market arrangements. Men in sporadic employment or in contingent employment of short duration may not see themselves as working and may not report that activity. To capture these types of work activities, we also showed men a flash card that asked, "Which of the following best describes your employment situation?" with answers such as occasional or casual worker without a fixed job, occasional worker, contract worker, worker on call, worker in daily contract, worker through the duration of project, and handyman. These are the types of nontraditional employment situations associated with the informal labor market and those most likely to be missed in standard surveys. We classified men who answered yes to any of these employment situations as nontraditional workers.

Table 4-12 summarizes the responses to the standard Department of Labor question and to our question about informal sector work, categorized by the number of people whose responses put them into particular categories and the proportion of men with specified characteristics who fit into those groups. The top panel shows work activity as reported on the household survey: 94 men (71 percent of the sample) reported that they worked, 11 (10.5 percent) of those in the labor force reported that they were seeking work, for a total of 105 (79 percent of the sample) reported being in the labor force. The bottom panel gives the results from our nontraditional work question. The question identified 29 workers in nontraditional employment situations—22 percent of the sample. Most of these men reported activities in construction, the most common category being *chivero* (taking occasional jobs on construction or other related tasks and working for the duration of the project).[29] The household survey question would have classified 15 of those workers (11 percent of the sample) as not working, which implies that the household survey would have missed the work activity of approximately half of those in informal sector work. Five men who reported that they were doing nontraditional work had responded that they were neither employed nor looking for work on the household survey—4 percent of the

28. The U.S. Current Population Survey and Census of Population ask, "Did this person do any work for pay last week?" This question is more specific, since any work, no matter how small, for which pay was received is expected to be reported, though people may still interpret it to refer to formal jobs.

29. The amount of work reported varied from six to thirty hours weekly. Men in these activities reported incomes of $550 a month.

Table 4-12. *Labor Force Activity according to Pilot Survey and Household Survey, Men, Selected Puerto Rican Communities, 2004*

Units as indicated

Activity	Number	Share of sample (percent)
N for pilot survey	133	100.0
According to household survey question		
Working, traditional work	94	71.0
Not working but looking for work (unemployed)	11	8.0
Working or unemployed (in labor force)	105	79.0
According to pilot survey question		
Reporting nontraditional work	29	22.0
Reporting nontraditional work but reported not working on household survey question	15	11.0
Reporting nontraditional work but reported neither working nor looking for work on household survey question	5	4.0
All working, including the fifteen nontraditional workers who reported they were not working on household survey	109	82.0
Reporting participating in the labor force, including nontraditional employed	110	83.0

Source: Data from Encuesta de Empleo y Uso del Tiempo–El Caño.

sample. Counting the 15 men engaged in some kind of informal work but who had reported being unemployed on the household survey, we obtain an estimated employment in the sample of 109 (82 percent). Adding those 15 men in informal work to the number counted in the labor force (the first two lines of table 4-12) gives a total in the labor force, including nontraditional workers, of 110—or 83 percent of the sample.

If these magnitudes are reasonably accurate, how much of low male employment and participation might be the result of informal sector work? Our survey has one problem in answering this question: the reported employment level in the pilot survey was higher than on the household survey and on the Census of Population for Puerto Rico, which makes it hard to generalize magnitudes. Still, the estimated proportion working in our sample increased from 71 percent under the traditional question to 82 percent under the wider definition of working—an 11-point or 15 percent increase.[30] If we assume that this 15 percent greater employment holds in comparisons with the lower reported rate of

30. The 71 percent rate of employment implicit in responses to the Department of Labor question exceeds the 55 percent labor participation rate for Puerto Ricans found in the household survey.

employment in the household and census data, our calculations suggest that a better counting of informal workers would increase the employment rate for working-age men not attending school from 48 percent (on the household survey) to 55 percent.

But this adjustment would not produce as large an effect on the labor participation rate found in both the census and household survey. The reason is that most of the men in nontraditional employment situations reported themselves as looking for work on the household survey question. Only 5 of the 29 men working in nontraditional employment in our survey reported on the household survey that they were neither working nor looking for work. These men constitute just 4 percent of the total sample, and their inclusion would raise the labor force participation rate by 5 percent, to 83 percent. If this increase is applied to the overall working-age male population not attending school, it would raise the labor force participation rate among Puerto Rican men from 58 percent in the household survey to 61 percent.

In sum, our pilot survey suggests that the official Department of Labor question understates employment considerably but understates labor force participation only modestly. Since, as noted, our survey covered a group of men that had a relatively high rate of employment and participation even by Department of Labor standards, it is possible that the understatement, particularly of labor force participation, may be larger in a more representative sample. If our results are valid, informal sector work helps explain a significant part of the low employment rate of Puerto Rican men but can explain only 3 or so percentage points of their low participation rate.

Conclusion and Implications

Our analysis shows that a variety of factors contributed to the low employment rate of Puerto Rican men: the pattern of economic growth, with GNP increasing much less rapidly than GDP, and GDP heavily weighted to capital-intensive manufacturing; the emigration of men with potentially high attachment to the workforce to the United States; the attractiveness of disability insurance and NAP transfers funded in large part by the federal government; relatively high wages in otherwise low-wage occupations; and opportunity to work in the informal sector. The common thread behind all these separate factors is what we have termed the rich-uncle hypothesis: Puerto Rico's unique relationship with the United States has produced an economic environment that discourages work on both the supply and demand sides of the market. The rich-uncle hypothesis suggests that the close tie between the island and the mainland has been a double-edged sword, offering Puerto Ricans many of the benefits of living in a highly advanced economy but also contributing to the employment problem. As anyone with rich relatives knows, having a rich uncle is a mixed blessing.

The analysis points to the difficulties facing Puerto Rico in solving the employment problem of its male population. Factors that affect employment, such as the level of benefits of Social Security and eligibility into this program, the minimum wage, federal tax incentives, the amount of transfers to the poor, and border control, are regulated not by Puerto Rico but by the federal government. Puerto Rico needs to work with the U.S. government to redesign these programs, which help reduce poverty on the island, to be more work friendly. Government transfers to the poor need to reward work effort in various ways. The Nutritional Assistance Program could adopt work incentives and time limits similar to those mandated by the U.S. welfare reform enacted in 1996, the Personal Responsibility and Work Opportunity Reconciliation Act. Currently able-bodied participants are required to show that they are looking for work (if not in school). However, there are no time limits on how long a person can be looking for work nor on an individual's participation in the program. Puerto Rico could seek ways to make support of low-income persons more compatible with employment—for instance, through an earned income tax credit for workers or tax credits to firms that create jobs. Although section 936 federal tax benefits have ended, Puerto Rico should seek ways to encourage the high-technology industries engendered by the program to expand employment in the future and to shift some of their purchases of intermediate services and goods to the island. For instance, pharmaceutical companies could set up distribution centers and costumer service centers in Puerto Rico and use Puerto Rican agencies for some of their marketing campaigns.

Nongovernmental organizations could try to combine their services to the low-income population with efforts to increase employment. Work activities common to the informal labor market such as construction and reparation work could be organized through cooperatives of community workers or through community organizations, bringing these workers out of the shadows of informality. Since much of the low participation of men occurs among older men, a shift in compensation toward deferred benefits such as pensions or health insurance might reduce the rate of withdrawal from the workforce. The goal should be to link benefits to work rather than to nonwork, to induce adult men who are out of the workforce or in informal work into regular jobs, and to raise Puerto Rico from its current position at the bottom of country or area tables of male employment and labor force participation rates.

Belinda I. Reyes

I commend the Center for the New Economy and Brookings for this ambitious project, but especially I commend María Enchautegui and Richard Freeman for the effort to examine this complex issue. The low employment rate among its people is one of the biggest problems confronting the Puerto Rican economy. As the authors note, in 2000 only 31 percent of the Puerto Rican population was employed. This has serious consequences for the economic prospects of the island and points to a dependency ratio that is difficult to sustain.

Exploring the reasons for the low employment and labor force participation rates among Puerto Rican men, Enchautegui and Freeman look at five potential explanations:

—distortions generated by section 936 of the federal tax code

—transfer programs, such as disability insurance and the Nutritional Assistant Program (NAP)

—migration and selectivity

—the structure of the labor market and the extension of the federal minimum wage to the island

—growth in the informal economy

They argue that the distortion of the section 936 provisions on the patterns of growth and the opportunity to work in the informal sector are critical factors in explaining low and declining rates in the official statistics of employment in the island. They also find that wages in Puerto Rico relative to those on the U.S. mainland have a U-shaped distribution, indicating that there is less difference between the island and the mainland at the lowest and highest wage deciles and that there may be high reservations wages at the bottom of the wage distribution. This distribution could respond to the availability of federal minimum wages in the island, income transfers, or the potential for U.S. employment through migration. Enchautegui and Freeman argue that although the adoption of the federal minimum wage in the island could have an impact on this distribution, other factors are more critical. They hypothesize that income transfers to the island and the potential for migration to the United States created a floor for wages above the minimum and led to an increase in the reservation wage for Puerto Rican workers, thereby decreasing employment at the bottom of the wage distribution.

These are intuitive explanations, consistent with the economic literature, and they result from a careful examination of the limited data available. The authors even conducted a pilot survey in a community in San Juan to gather additional information on reservation wages and nontraditional employment. Although one cannot generalize from this small survey in a community with higher employment and participation rates than the rest of the island, it is still suggestive of the impact of the informal economy in the labor market.

Enchautegui and Freeman argue that the common thread among these factors is the relationship between Puerto Rico and the United States. On the one hand, the social services and employment opportunities on the mainland lower labor supply by increasing the reservation wage. On the other hand, tax incentives to encourage companies to locate in the island decrease the demand for labor. They call this the "rich-uncle hypothesis" and argue that similar relationships can be found between East and West Germany, southern and northern Italy, and between indigenous groups and the wealthier societies within which they reside. This is made worse by incentives that have concentrated growth in industries that do not create sustainable development but instead create more dependency.

While the chapter is careful in its analysis, some of the policy recommendations are not supported by the evidence. The recommendations emphasize reductions in welfare programs or the linking of programs to employment, but they do not show conclusive evidence that transfer programs have had a strong impact on participation and employment in the island. The findings are mainly descriptive, and there is no clear connection presented between participation or employment trends and transfer payments. Although transfer payments must play a role in the decline in participation and employment, the decline in participation began in the 1950s and 1960s, whereas the dramatic increase in U.S. social welfare transfers to Puerto Rico did not take place until the mid-1970s.[1] Other factors may be more critical, and they predate increases in transfer payments. The authors discuss the potential impact of migration on the reservation wage. Migration flows to the United States accelerated in the 1950s and 1960s at the same time that participation rates in the island began to flatten. It seems more plausible, therefore, to attribute the decline in employment to migration than to increased social services. Without a formal model, however, it is impossible to know whether emigration caused the decline in employment rates or whether instead both trends reflect the presence of an underlying third factor.

Also clear from the chapter's findings is that labor demand is a serious problem. The Puerto Rican economy needs to create more jobs. The authors' analysis of the island's GNP and GDP points to a need to restructure incentives so as to attract more local investment and more labor-intensive production. But their survey also suggests a large unexplored underground economy, which is missed by most survey data. Although males in their survey were 1.5 times more likely to work than males in the rest of the economy (71 versus 46 percent employed), employment rates increase to 82 percent if informal employment is included—

---

1. See chapter 2 in this volume.

almost twice the average in the island and a rate above that in the United States).[2] But also, in this survey, 10 percent of the workers who had indicated on the traditional household survey that they were working were employed in informal employment.[3] Thus formal employment in the locality was only 64 percent, while another 18 percent of respondents were engaged in informal employment. Although these findings cannot be generalized, they suggest a large underground economy. The authors note that some of this employment could be formalized through cooperative arrangements or other mechanisms. These are critical and difficult problems that need to be addressed if the Puerto Rican economy is to improve living standards.

Two other findings of the study deserve closer attention and further analysis: the high proportion of the disabled adults in the Puerto Rican population and the role of migration on employment and wages. Figure 4-3 shows that in 2000, 25.6 percent of males out of the labor force were reported as disabled. Table 4-7 also shows high disability rates. Seventeen percent of all Puerto Rican males aged eighteen to sixty-four were on work disability, and a higher proportion was out of the labor force in the island than in the United States. Disability rates were especially high for males between forty-six and sixty-four years of age. The authors argue that this high rate is a result of a benefits package that discourages work. But what if, instead, disability is truly higher on the island than on the mainland? Many of the males in the forty-six- to sixty-four-year-old cohort could be veterans of the Vietnam War. Almost forty-eight thousand Puerto Ricans participated in that war, a significant number given that the island population in 1970 was only 2.7 million. Moreover, other studies have found high alcoholism, drug addiction, AIDS, and other social ills in the island, which could also translate to high rates of disability. Social conditions in the island may be creating a high rate of disability that has nothing to do with the benefit level and could have serious consequences on the Puerto Rican economy.

Enchautegui and Freeman point out that migration to the United States can reduce reservation wages in the island because workers can move to the United States to find employment at a low cost. However, migration is still an expensive and risky endeavor, even for Puerto Ricans. In addition to moving costs, people have to leave family members behind and learn to live with different language and cultural traditions. For Puerto Ricans with contacts in the United States or prior migration experience, however, employment in the United States can be a real alternative for employment in the island. Some may be engaging in

2. The average for the United States was 76 percent. See table 4-1.

3. Table 4-12 shows that of the 133 men in the pilot survey, 29 reported that they worked in nontraditional employment. Of these 29, 15 had responded on the formal household survey that they were not working, and 5 had said they were neither working nor looking for work. I speculate that the remaining 9 answered that they were working even though they were employed in nontraditional jobs.

cyclical migration and commuting between employment in the United States and leisure and consumption in the island. As the target income hypothesis suggests, some migrants may choose to work in one location and consume in another.[4] In the Mexican experience, migrants live in the United States for a number of months or years and work to remit money home for consumption or investment. Some of them return to Mexico and stay permanently in the home community. Others stay only temporarily and continue to migrate to the United States for employment. This could also be happening among Puerto Ricans, which would explain some of the island's low employment rates. How prevalent the patterns of sojourner migration are in the island is uncertain, but some scholars have suggested significant cyclical migration among Puerto Rican migrants.[5]

Although the analysis in this chapter is comprehensive, some issues are not addressed. For one, the authors ignore the role of government. Government is a major employer in the island. In chapter 7 of this volume, James Alm observes that the consolidated budget outlays as a percentage of GNP exceeded 50 percent through most of the period of analysis—a time in which the government employed more than one in five workers in the island. What might be the impact of that on the labor market, wages, private sector employment, and reservation wages? Furthermore, the share of workers employed by the government began to decline in the early 1980s. Recent privatizations also reduced government outlays. How is that related to the decrease in labor force participation and employment?

The role of unions is also ignored in the chapter. The labor movement in the island is very strong. What does that mean for employment, remuneration, and policy formation? What is the role of unions in the Puerto Rican economy? Many government workers are unionized. Do union settlements with the government affect private sector employment and wages?

Finally, the authors stress the importance of the underground economy as an explanation for employment and participation. But Puerto Rico also has a large proportion of undocumented immigrants. Puerto Rico not only is a major sending country of immigrants, but it also receives a large number of illegal immigrants from the Caribbean. What is the consequence of large undocumented immigrant flows to the Puerto Rican labor market and its economy?

---

4. Hill (1987).
5. For a review of the literature, see Godoy, Jenkins, and Patel (2003).

References

Autor, David H., and Mark G. Duggan. 2003. "The Rise in Disability Rolls and the Decline in Unemployment." *Quarterly Journal of Economics* 118, no. 1: 157–205.

Bound, John, and Timothy Waidmann. 1992. "Disability Transfers, Self-Reported Health, and the Labor Force Attachment of Older Men: Evidence from the Historical Record." *Quarterly Journal of Economics* 107, no. 4: 1393–1419.

Castillo-Freeman, Alida, and Richard B. Freeman. 1992. "When the Minimum Wage Really Bites: The Effect of the U.S.-Level Minimum on Puerto Rico." In *Immigration and the Work Force,* edited by George Borjas and Richard B. Freeman, pp. 177–212. University of Chicago Press.

Enchautegui, María E. 2005. "Selectivity Patterns in Puerto Rican Migration." Paper prepared for the annual meetings of the Population Association of America. Philadelphia, March 31–April 2.

Estado Libre Asociado de Puerto Rico. 2002. *Serie histórica de empleo y desempleo: Años naturales, 1970–2001.* San Juan: Departamento del Trabajo y Recursos Humanos, Negociado de Estadísticas.

———. 2003. *Informe económico a la gobernadora.* San Juan: Oficina de la Gobernadora, Junta de Planificación.

———. Various years. *Informe económico a la gobernadora.* San Juan: Oficina de la Gobernadora, Junta de Planificación.

Estudios Técnicos. 2004. *La economía informal en Puerto Rico: Primer, segundo, y tercer informe.* Report prepared for the Puerto Rico Department of Labor and Human Resources. San Juan (October).

Freeman, Richard B., and Remco Oostendorp. 2002. "Wages around the World: Pay across Occupations and Countries." In *Inequality around the World,* edited by Richard B. Freeman, pp. 5–37. London: Palgrave.

Godoy, Ricardo, Glenn P. Jenkins, and Karishma Patel. 2003. "Puerto Rican Migration: An Assessment of Quantitative Studies." *Centro Journal* 15, no. 2: 206–31.

Gregg, Paul, and Jonathan Wadsworth. 2001. "Everything You Ever Wanted to Know about Measuring Worklessness and Polarization at the Household Level but Were Afraid to Ask." *Oxford Bulletin of Economics and Statistics* 63: 777–806.

Haveman, Robert, Philip DeJong, and Barbara Wolfe. 1991. "Disability Transfers and the Work Decisions of Older Men." *Quarterly Journal of Economics* 106, no. 3: 939–49.

Hill, John K. 1987. "Immigrant Decisions Concerning Duration of Stay and Migratory Frequency." *Journal of Development Economics* 25, no. 1: 221–34.

Hunt, Jennifer. 2004. "Convergence and Determinants of Non-Employment Durations in Eastern and Western Germany." *Journal of Population Economics* 17, no. 2: 249–66.

Krueger, Alan. 1995. "The Effect of the Minimum Wage When It Really Bites: A Reexamination of the Evidence from Puerto Rico." In *Research in Labor Economics,* edited by Solomon Polachek, 14:1–22. Greenwich, Conn.: JAI Press.

Pol, Julio Cesar. 2004a. "Determinantes económicos de la migración entre Puerto Rico y Estados Unidos." *Ensayos y Monografías* 119. San Juan: Universidad de Puerto Rico, Unidad de Investigaciones Económicas.

———. 2004b. "Estimaciones de la economía subterránea: El caso de Puerto Rico." *Ensayos y Monografías* 117. San Juan: Universidad de Puerto Rico, Unidad de Investigaciones Económicas.

Ruggles, Steven, and others. 2004. *Integrated Public Use Microdata Series: Version 3.* Minneapolis: Minnesota Population Center (www.ipums.org).

Santiago, Carlos. 1992. *Labor in the Puerto Rican Economy.* Westport, Conn.: Praeger.

Spilimbergo, Antonio. 1999. "Labor Market Integration, Unemployment, and Transfers." *Review of International Economics* 7, no. 4: 641–50.

U.S. Social Security Administration. 2004. *Statistical Abstract.*

5

Education and Economic Development

HELEN F. LADD AND FRANCISCO L. RIVERA-BATIZ

Puerto Rico has one of the strongest recent records of educational development in the world. With the exception of the Republic of Korea, the rise in
the educational attainment of Puerto Rico's labor force between 1960 and 2000 is
unmatched by any other country. During this forty-year period, the average
schooling of Puerto Rican workers doubled, from 6.2 years to 12.2 years.

Despite this remarkable accomplishment, Puerto Rico's education system
today stands at a crossroads. The consensus among policymakers, the education establishment itself, and the population in general is that the public education system on the island is currently in crisis. Although substantial reforms
intended to improve the system have been implemented over the past fifteen
years, the reforms have failed to meet their objectives. Not only have they not
improved the system, they may have weakened it. Thus it is not surprising that
the newly elected governor of Puerto Rico, the Honorable Anibal Acevedo
Vilá, has made improvement of the island's schools one of the three top priorities of his administration.

The authors are grateful for the comments and suggestions of Alan Krueger, Carlos Santiago,
Barry Bosworth, Susan Collins, and Carlos E. Chardón as well as the assistance of Idrani Acevedo
Hilario, Luis Bermúdez, María Colón de Marxuach, Aida Díaz de Rodriguez, Néstor Figueroa,
Antonio Magriñá, Manuel Maldonado Rivera, William Ortiz Ramirez, Pablo Rivera Ortiz, José A.
Santana González, and Migdalia Wiscovich Colberg.

The problems with the education system are cause for concern for Puerto Rico's prospects for economic growth. The average growth rate of per capita income on the island has already slowed down compared with its high values in the golden era of the 1950s and 1960s. From an average annual growth rate in per worker output of 4.8 percent in the period from 1950 to 1980, Puerto Rico's growth slowed down sharply to an average of 0.8 percent in 1980–2003 and could fall even further. An accounting of Puerto Rican economic growth suggests that the rise of schooling has been increasingly essential to its economic expansion, accounting for close to half of the increase in output per worker between 1975 and 2000.[1] Recent research also indicates that a drop in the quality of education can have a significantly negative impact on sustained economic growth.[2] Failure to reverse the education slump currently faced by Puerto Rico could severely constrain any prospects for the return of high growth to the island.

What has been Puerto Rico's experience with educational development? What are the main education challenges facing Puerto Rico at the present time? How do these challenges affect the island's prospects for economic growth? This chapter provides a comprehensive answer to these questions.

Expansion of the Education System

With the emergence in 1941 of the newly created Popular Democratic Party and its subsequent political success, economic and social development in Puerto Rico began to take off. With a program emphasizing development and social justice, the new policymakers implemented an array of reforms during the period of the island's dramatic economic growth.[3]

One of the priority areas was education. Starting in the mid-1940s, the government committed itself to raising the educational attainment of Puerto Rico's population. To this end, between 1944 and 1962 public spending on education quadrupled in real terms, resulting in a massive expansion of schools, teacher hiring, and purchase of books, materials, and equipment. The expansion of investments in education at both the school and university level has continued unabated until the present time.

Primary and Secondary Education

Table 5-1 reports trends in public and private school enrollments for selected years. Following the path of public school enrollments, which accounted for more than 95 percent of all students in the 1940s, total enrollments grew rapidly for several decades and then peaked in the early 1980s. The more than doubling

1. See chapter 2 in this volume.
2. Hanushek and Kimko (2000).
3. For details of Puerto Rico's economic history during this time, see Dietz (1986) and Rivera-Batiz and Santiago (1996).

Table 5-1. *School Enrollment, Puerto Rico, Selected Years, 1950–2003*[a]

School year	Public	Private	Total	Private as share of total (percent)
1940	286,098	12,374	298,472	4.1
1950	416,206	25,552	441,758	6.1
1960	573,440	63,300	636,740	9.9
1970	686,770	89,106	775,870	11.5
1980	712,880	98,500	811,380	12.1
1990	644,734	145,800	790,534	18.7
2000	607,626	163,946	771,572	21.2
2003	565,763	185,745	751,508	24.7

Source: Data from Rivera-Batiz (1993); Commonwealth of Puerto Rico (1994, 1996a, 1998, 2000, 2004a).

a. Fall enrollment in public and private primary and secondary schools and public prekindergarten and kindergarten programs.

of the number of elementary and secondary school students from 1940 to 1970 is partly attributable to the growth in the school-age population. Contributing even more was the significant rise in the proportion of children who attended school. Among children of elementary school age (seven to thirteen), the net enrollment rate climbed from 66.8 percent in 1940 to 91.2 percent in 1970. For children of secondary school age (fourteen to nineteen), the net school enrollment rate of 24.5 percent prevailing in 1940 rose sharply to 72.7 percent by 1970.[4] Thus by the late 1960s most children of elementary school age, and, remarkably, two out of three children of secondary school age, were attending school.

After reaching its peak of 712,880 students in 1980, enrollment in public schools declined by 20.6 percent to 565,763 students in 2003. Total enrollment, which includes the increasing number of students in private schools, decreased by somewhat less, about 7.4 percent, during this period. This decrease in total enrollment reflects a decline in fertility as well as an out-migration of the island's population, both of which have led to a contraction of the school-age population. It does not reflect a drop in enrollment rates. Census Bureau data indicate that as of 2000, the net enrollment rate of children in the elementary school age range had risen to 98.9 percent and in secondary education to 91.3 percent. By 2003 a quarter of all elementary and secondary school students were in private schools.

The school system in Puerto Rico is divided into four levels: preschool, which includes prekindergarten and kindergarten; elementary school, which covers first to sixth grade; intermediate school (*escuela intermedia*), encompassing the seventh to ninth grades; and high school (*escuela superior*), which covers the tenth to

4. Vázquez-Calzada (1988, pp. 370–71).

Table 5-2. *Enrollment in Institutions of Higher Education, Puerto Rico, Selected Years, 1949–2002*

School year	Total	Public sector[a]	Private sector	Private as share of public (percent)
1949–50	12,497	11,348	1,149	9.2
1959–60	24,532	18,223	6,309	25.7
1970–71	63,073	42,516	20,557	32.5
1980–81	131,184	54,127	77,057	58.7
1990–91	154,055	55,691	98,374	63.9
1999–2000	175,453	73,653	101,800	58.0
2000–01	185,015	74,018	110,997	60.0
2001–02	190,776	73,838	116,938	61.3
2002–03	199,842	74,506	125,336	62.7

Source: Data from Commonwealth of Puerto Rico, Council on Higher Education (2004).

a. Enrollment in the University of Puerto Rico system and in specialized higher education institutions (Colegio Universitario de Justicia Criminal, Colegio Tecnológico de San Juan, Conservatorio de Música, Escuela de Artes Plásticas, and the Institutos Tecnológicos in Manatí, Guayama, Ponce, and San Juan).

twelfth grades. Of the 565,763 students in the public school system in 2003–04, 40,673 were enrolled in prekindergarten and kindergarten, 272,719 in elementary schools, 137,773 in intermediate schools, and 114,598 in high schools.

Higher Education

A similar expansion occurred at the tertiary level, as documented in table 5-2. From 12,500 students in 1949–50, total enrollment rose to almost 200,000 in 2002–03. As with primary and secondary education, the initial expansion of tertiary education was primarily in the public sector. The University of Puerto Rico—the island's main public institution of higher education—was created in 1903 on its Río Piedras campus, which is now the largest (with an enrollment of 21,666 students in 2002–03). Over time, new campuses were created in Mayagüez, Aguadilla, Arecibo, Bayamón, Carolina, Cayey, Humacao, Utuado, and Ponce. In addition, the University of Puerto Rico system includes a Medical Sciences campus.

Fewer than twenty thousand students were enrolled at the University of Puerto Rico in 1960, when only three campuses were operating; by 2002–03, the university system had expanded to close to seventy thousand students. In addition to the University of Puerto Rico system, the higher education public sector is in charge of a set of smaller, career or vocationally oriented institutions, including the Colegio Universitario de Justicia Criminal, Colegio Tecnológico de San Juan, Conservatorio de Música, Escuela de Artes Plásticas, and the Institutos Tecnológicos in Manatí, Guayama, Ponce, and San Juan.

Expanding even more rapidly, enrollment in the private institutions overtook enrollment in the public sector in the mid-1970s and now accounts for 62.7 percent of all students in tertiary education. The largest private university is the Interamerican University, which had eleven campuses scattered over the island and 43,269 students enrolled in 2002–3, followed by the three campuses of the Ana G. Mendez University System (Metropolitan University, University of the East, and University of Turabo), with a total of 27,227 students.

Educational Attainment

The sharp rise in enrollment rates at various levels of education in Puerto Rico since the late 1940s has led to a remarkable increase in educational attainment among its adult population. From an average level of schooling in 1940 of 2.7 years, by 2000 Puerto Rico's population twenty-five years of age or older had achieved an average of 11.0 years of schooling (see figure 5-1).

Correspondingly, Puerto Rico's gains in educational attainment have sharply increased the human capital of its workforce. Between 1960 and 2000, the average schooling of the island's labor force fifteen years of age and older rose by 6.0 years, far exceeding the worldwide average expansion of 3.2 years and exceeding the gains in all countries other than the Republic of Korea.[5] The 12.2 years of average schooling of Puerto Rico's labor force in 2000 was about the same as that of the United States (with an average of 12.1 years for its labor force fifteen years or older), beyond that of the most-educated Latin American nations, such as Chile (8.5 years), Argentina (8.5 years), Peru (7.8 years), or Uruguay (7.7 years), and matching or exceeding that of many high-income countries, such as France (8.9 years), Denmark (10.6 years), Great Britain (11.0), Finland (10.5), and Ireland (9.5).

The dramatic increase in enrollment in—and graduation from—colleges and universities has been associated with a sharp increase in the proportion of Puerto Rico's population that has attained a college degree or more. Table 5-3 reports the educational level attained by persons twenty-five years of age or older every ten years since 1960. In 1960 the proportion with a college degree or more was 3.5 percent. By 2000 that proportion had risen to 18.2 percent. When the adults who had attended some college are added to those who received a degree, the 2000 proportion doubles.

These data place Puerto Rico in the upper tier of nations ranked by their proportion of college-educated adults. As of 2000, the United States topped the list, with 28 percent of adults aged twenty-five to sixty-four having been awarded a college degree. Puerto Rico's 20.2 percent put it below Norway and the Netherlands but above or tied with all other Organization for Economic Cooperation

---

5. By this measure, Puerto Rico increased its schooling from 6.2 to 12.2 years during the period 1960–2000. The Republic of Korea's gain of 6.4 years started from a slightly lower base of 4.7 years. Jordan also had a gain of 6.0 years but started from an even lower base of 2.4 years. Bosworth and Collins (2003).

Figure 5-1. *Educational Attainment of Adult Population, Puerto Rico, Selected Years, 1940–2000*[a]

Years of schooling

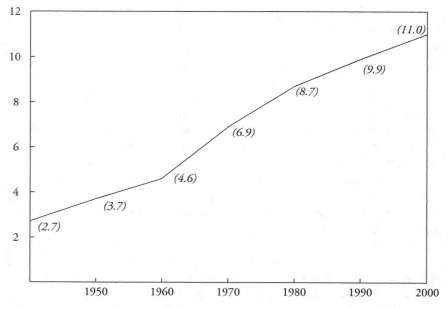

Source: U.S. Census of Population for Puerto Rico, various years.
a. Persons aged twenty-five and older.

and Development member nations and well above developing countries with equivalent levels of per capita income. Of interest as well is that our analysis of 2000 Census Bureau data shows the proportion of college graduates in Puerto Rico also exceeded the proportion of Puerto Ricans in the United States with a college degree, which was 13.4 percent for the population aged twenty-five to sixty-four.

School Retention and High School Graduation Rates

Despite these rapid gains in average educational attainment, many policymakers in Puerto Rico believe that the school dropout rate remains excessively high and constitutes a serious problem, perhaps the most serious problem in the island's education system.[6] Children and youth aged twenty-one or younger are required by law to attend school until they complete high school, but those laws do not guarantee that students remain in school, and many in fact do not complete

6. See, for example, Commonwealth of Puerto Rico, Department of Education (2003c, p.1).

Table 5-3. *Educational Status of the Adult Population, Puerto Rico,*
Selected Years, 1960–2000[a]

Percent

Highest level of education attained	1960	1970	1980	1990	2000
Less than high school	85.0	72.9	59.5	50.4	40.2
High school graduate	7.5	15.0	21.3	21.0	22.2
Some college	4.0	6.0	8.9	14.3	19.4
College or more	3.5	6.1	10.3	14.3	18.2

Source: Data from Rivera-Batiz and Santiago (1996); U.S. Department of Commerce (2003).
a. Persons aged twenty-five and older.

high school. The question here is whether the dropout picture is as dismal as many perceive it to be.

The simplest measure of school dropouts is the event dropout rate, which is calculated as the percentage of students who left school between the beginning of one school year and the beginning of the next. The cumulative dropout rate is the sum of the event dropout rates over several years. In Puerto Rico, the cumulative dropout rate for public high schools (for grades nine through twelve) was 34.4 percent in 2002–03, down from 39.4 percent in 1991–92. The cumulative dropout rate for all levels in public schools (grades one through twelve) was 40.1 percent in 2003–04, down from 56.5 percent in 1991.[7]

These estimated dropout rates are relatively high and, if valid, would constitute a serious problem for Puerto Rico, although it is worth noting that they are currently declining. However, this indicator is flawed in that it does not account for the many students who leave the public school system for reasons other than dropping out.[8] Some of them may migrate with their families out of Puerto Rico, enrolling in schools on the U.S. mainland or in other countries. Census data indicate that between 1990 and 2000 as many as 103,078 children aged six to eighteen, constituting about 12 percent of the population in that age group residing on the island in 1990, migrated from Puerto Rico to the U.S. mainland. Other students may leave the public school system to enroll in a private school. The share of private school students has now risen to about 25 percent. Finally, some students who leave the school system participate in the General Educational Development (GED) program, which is widely offered in Puerto Rico. Many young people aged seventeen, eighteen, and nineteen take and pass the GED, thereby earning

7. Commonwealth of Puerto Rico, Department of Education (2003c, p. 11). By following student cohorts over time and calculating the cumulative dropout rate on this basis, Neil Allison and Arthur McEwan (2003) calculate that the proportion of students entering public middle schools who did not complete high school was 35.1 percent in 2000, down from 44.6 percent in 1994.
8. See NCES (2004a).

high school equivalency certificates. Whatever one may think about the relative skills indicated by—and the relative value of—a high school diploma versus a GED certificate, both provide equivalent credentials and allow students to pursue higher levels of education. Therefore, it seems inappropriate to consider GED graduates as part of the population that has dropped out of school.

An alternative measure, the status dropout rate, is not subject to the deficiencies of event dropout rates. This approach measures the dropout rate as the percentage of young persons (aged eighteen to twenty-four in our case) who are older than the typical high school completion age but who are not enrolled in high school and never received a high school credential (diploma or GED certificate). This indicator measures more closely the proportion of school dropouts in the population, that is, those youth living in Puerto Rico who dropped out of school at some time in the past and never received their high school credential.[9]

Table 5-4 shows the distribution of school enrollment of Puerto Ricans aged eighteen to twenty-four and their U.S. mainland counterparts in the year 2000; estimated dropout rates are presented in the third row of the table. Overall, 55.1 percent of the relevant Puerto Rican population was not enrolled in school. This figure can be disaggregated into the 33.8 percent who had already completed high school and the 21.3 percent who had not received a high school credential. The latter constitute high school dropouts, since they are young people past the high school completion age who were not enrolled in school and had not received a high school diploma or equivalency. This estimate is substantially lower than the 40 percent rate obtained through the use of cumulative event dropout rates from the public school system. Thus the flaws in the event dropout rate in the Puerto Rican context lead to a significant overestimate of the true dropout rate.

The true dropout rate in Puerto Rico is quite comparable to that for blacks in the United States and is far lower than that for U.S. Latinos, as shown in the second through fifth columns of table 5-4. To be sure, it is significantly higher than that for the United States as a whole (21.3 versus 16.2 percent), but that differential is consistent with the far lower average income of Puerto Ricans. Thus we conclude that though Puerto Rico does indeed have a dropout problem, the problem is not as serious as some policymakers believe.

A related issue is school delay, defined as the proportion of students who fail to be promoted from one grade to the next. One can estimate the magnitude of accumulated school delay by calculating the proportion of students aged eighteen

9. Although preferable to cumulative event dropout rates, this method is not without problems. As Allison and McEwan (2003, p. 4) observe, "Surveys tend to under-represent lower income, jailed, and other populations. Respondents also tend to over-state their educational attainment and avoid admitting to dropping out of school." At the same time, there is no reason to conclude that individual responses to surveys in Puerto Rico are less reliable than those in the United States, providing a stronger basis for data that are comparable with the mainland.

Table 5-4. *School Enrollment of Persons Aged Eighteen to Twenty-Four,*
Puerto Rico and the United States, 2000
Percent

Status	Puerto Rico	United States			
		Total	White	Black	Latino
Not enrolled in school	55.1	55.4	52.0	58.4	69.0
Completed high school[a]	33.8	39.2	42.0	38.4	32.4
Did not complete high school (estimate of dropout rate)	21.3	16.2	10.0	20.0	36.6
Enrolled in school	44.9	44.6	48.0	41.6	31.0
Enrolled in high school or less (estimate of school delay)	10.5	10.7	9.9	13.7	11.2
Enrolled in college	34.4	33.9	38.1	27.9	19.8

Source: Data from U.S. Department of Commerce (2003); authors' tabulations.
a. Includes GED certificate.

to twenty-four who are still enrolled in high school or a lower grade, as reported in the next to last line of table 5-4. Those proportions are about the same in Puerto Rico (10.5 percent) and the United States (10.7). However, school delay among black and Latino youth in the United States is higher than the Puerto Rico average. In 2000 close to 14 percent of African American youth aged eighteen to twenty-four was still enrolled in high school or a lower grade. Among Latinos in the United States, the proportion was 11.2 percent.

Despite the slightly higher high school dropout rate on the island, the data in the final row of table 5-4 show that the percentage of youth aged eighteen to twenty-four enrolled in higher education is about the same in Puerto Rico and the United States (34.4 versus 33.9). Since the United States has one of the highest tertiary education enrollment rates in the world, this constitutes a remarkable achievement for Puerto Rico.

This discussion confirms that in terms of years of schooling, the island stands as one of the great educational miracles of the past fifty years. From a dismal situation in the 1940s, by 2000 Puerto Rico had rates of school attainment that were comparable to those of the top countries in the world. Furthermore, Puerto Rico's ability to keep students in the system, especially as they move from secondary to higher education, matches that of the United States, one of the world's leading countries with respect to higher education.

School Quality and Student Achievement

Although Puerto Rico's progress in educational attainment is beyond dispute, less clear is what has been happening to the quality of education, especially during the past fifteen years. Rapid expansion of education need not bring with it higher quality. In Latin America, countries such as Chile, Brazil, and Mexico, where educational attainment levels have risen quickly, continue to rank among the worst performers in international assessments of student achievement such as the Trends in International Mathematics and Science Study (TIMSS) and the Program for International Student Achievement (PISA).[10] Yet in other countries the quality of education has been sustained at high levels at the same time that the quantity has expanded. Such is the case with the East Asian tigers, including Singapore, Korea, and Taiwan.

Student Achievement: Current Levels

Evaluating student achievement in Puerto Rico's school system is made difficult by the absence of any systematic student testing in schools until the mid-1990s. Even then, the implementation of schoolwide testing occurred only gradually, and the tests cannot be compared over time since they were changed from year to year in a haphazard way. Only in response to the requirements of the federal No Child Left Behind legislation, enacted in January 2002, did Puerto Rico establish a more reliable testing battery, designed and managed by the Educational Testing Service in Princeton, New Jersey. The tests, called Puerto Rican Tests of Academic Achievement (Pruebas Puertorriqueñas de Aprovechamiento Académico), were first administered in April 2003 to all public school students in the third, sixth, eighth, and eleventh grades. In April 2004 the fourth, fifth, and seventh grades were added. Given that one out of four students is now in private schools, even these new tests provide an incomplete picture of overall student achievement in Puerto Rico.

Table 5-5 presents the overall results of the Puerto Rican achievement tests for the years 2002–03 and 2003–04. Following the No Child Left Behind guidelines, the test scores are converted into three levels: basic, proficient, and advanced. Students who score at the basic level are considered not to be proficient in the subject matter. In Puerto Rico, tests have been administered in three subject areas: mathematics, Spanish (reading), and English (as a second language). The table includes test scores for students tested in grades three, six, eight, and eleven.

Assuming that the test makers have defined proficiency in a reasonable way, the results in table 5-5 present a sobering picture of the overall student achievement in Puerto Rico's public school system. In all three subjects and for both years, more than half of the students scored at the basic level, indicating that less than half were proficient in the indicated subject areas. With only two years of data, it is difficult to say much about trends. Nonetheless, the increase from 51.8 percent scoring at the basic level in Spanish in 2002–03 to 58.0 percent in the following year is worth noting. Both because the levels measure the performance of differ-

10. OECD (2004); Gonzalez and others (2004).

Table 5-5. *Public School Student Performance on the Puerto Rican Achievement Test, 2002–04*[a]

Percent

	Students at basic (below proficient) level	
Subject	*2002–03*	*2003–04*
Math	54.3	54.8
Spanish	51.8	58.0
English as a second language	50.0	50.3

Source: Data from Commonwealth of Puerto Rico, Department of Education (2003a, 2004b).
a. All students tested in grades 3, 6, 8, and 11.

ent groups of students and because of random variation from one year to another, one must be careful not to make too much of the change. At the same time, the apparent decline in student performance in Spanish is fully consistent with longer-term trends indicated by scores on the Puerto Rican equivalent of the Scholastic Assessment Test (SAT) (discussed below) and also with curriculum reforms enacted during the 1990s that put more focus on the teaching of English in an effort to promote a more bilingual society.

Of course, the proportion of students performing below a standard of proficiency is closely related to the chosen standard. The higher is the standard, the lower will be the proportion of students who meet it. Given that under No Child Left Behind each state sets its own standards, it is not appropriate to compare the results in Puerto Rico with those of other states. The only comparable measures across states emerge from the nationwide National Assessment of Educational Progress (NAEP), in which Puerto Rico does not participate. Given that most, if not all, states have adopted proficiency benchmarks well below (and sometimes substantially below) the NAEP standards, it is reasonable to suspect that this is true of Puerto Rico as well. Thus it is likely that had performance been measured against the U.S. NAEP standards, the performance of public school students in Puerto Rico would have appeared even less satisfactory.

Students also appear to do less well on the Puerto Rican Tests of Academic Achievement as they progress through school. In both Spanish and math, the percentage of students performing at the basic level—that is, below proficiency—is greater in the higher grades than in the lower grades. This pattern is particularly pronounced in math. As shown in table 5-6, the percentage of students performing at the basic level in math rises steeply from about 40 percent in third grade to 65 percent in eleventh grade. This pattern contrasts with the reverse pattern emerging from NAEP scores in the United States, where students at higher grade levels show proficiency equal to or greater than those in lower grades.[11]

11. See NAEP (2000, 2004).

Table 5-6. *Public School Student Performance in Math Achievement, 2002–04*
Percent

	Students at basic (below proficient) level	
Grade	2002–03	2003–04
Overall	54.3	54.8
Third	41	39
Sixth	49	48
Eighth	65	65
Eleventh	65	67

Source: Data from Commonwealth of Puerto Rico, Department of Education (2003b, 2005).

That two-thirds of public school students in the eleventh grade failed to display basic proficiency in math skills attests to a major educational concern for Puerto Rico, particularly as the island seeks to compete with other countries in attracting industries such as pharmaceuticals, biotechnology, electronics, and finance that rely heavily on highly educated technical workers.

Trends in Puerto Rican College Board Scores

The only Puerto Rican student achievement data available over time are for high school seniors who take the battery of tests included in the University Assessment and Admissions Program (Programa de Evaluación y Admisión Universitaria). This Puerto Rican equivalent of the SAT is specially designed and administered by the College Board's Puerto Rico and Latin America Office for high school students applying to colleges and universities in Puerto Rico. The battery includes the Academic Aptitude Test (Prueba de Aptitud Académica), with verbal and quantitative components, and Achievement Tests (Pruebas de Aprovechamiento Académico) in English, Spanish, and mathematics.

Data of this type need to be interpreted with caution. First, the rising enrollment rates documented earlier suggest that student populations previously not represented in the educational system have increasingly gained access to primary and secondary schools. The resulting change in the composition of students, particularly in public schools, can alter student outcomes, even when school quality remains the same. Thus declining test scores may reflect the changing characteristics of students rather than a decline in the quality of schooling.

Second, the increasing share of students who attend private schools compounds this issue. One must be particularly careful in interpreting the separate test score trends for students in the two education sectors. To the extent that the more able students have been shifting to private schools, the average test scores for public school students might well decline even in the absence of a decline in the quality of the public schools. In addition, the average scores for students in

Table 5-7. *Puerto Rico College Board Test Scores, Selected Years, 1994–2003*[a]

Test	1984–86			1994–96			2002–03		
	All	Public	Private	All	Public	Private	All	Public	Private
Aptitude									
Verbal	471	457	552	468	453	520	463	444	526
Quantitative	484	466	587	489	470	550	489	466	549
Achievement									
Spanish	476	463	552	471	456	520	449	434	497
Mathematics	483	464	595	490	471	556	441	460	546
English	434	418	533	447	425	522	440	416	535

Source: Data from College Board (1991, 2005); averages calculated by the authors.

a. Data for 1984–86 cover only October test scores; for other periods, the data include June and August test scores. "Public" refers to test takers in public schools; "private" to those in private schools. "All" also includes students who cannot be easily classified.

private schools might also fall as these schools absorb new students who perform at lower levels than the average for private schools.

With these interpretative warnings in mind, data on test scores for the University Assessment and Admissions test are presented on table 5-7, where we report average scores for all students and average scores disaggregated by type of school. Because scores jump around from year to year, we have simplified the table by averaging multiple years of results for each entry.

Based on the averages for all students, the trends that emerge for the early period display differences by the subject tested. Between the mid-1980s and the mid-1990s, test scores in quantitative reasoning, mathematics achievement, and English achievement all rose, while test scores on the verbal component of the aptitude test and on Spanish achievement fell. From the mid-1990s to the 2000–03 period, however, the patterns are clear: average test scores in all subjects either remained constant (quantitative reasoning) or fell. Most notable was the forty-nine-point drop in math achievement and the twenty-two-point drop in Spanish achievement. The decline in Spanish achievement might well be attributable to language policies and, in particular, an effort during the 1990s to raise the level of English proficiency.[12] At the same time, however, the drop in English achievement from the mid-1990s to the later period suggests that that effort was not successful. Although the declining test scores could potentially reflect changes in the tests over time or in the methods used to scale the test scores, a recent study examining these issues concludes that this is not the case.[13]

12. Marco (2004b).
13. Marco (2004a, p. 5); see also Marco (2004b).

The pattern of change in test scores since the 1980s also differs for private and public schools. For private school students, scores have dropped continuously since the mid-1980s, with the exception of English achievement test scores, which declined between the mid-1980s and mid-1990s but have since recovered, and verbal aptitude scores, which declined substantially in the 1980s and by 2003 had risen only slightly. For public school students, the patterns are also clear: although test scores mostly rose between the mid-1980s and the mid-1990s, the trend abruptly turned around after the mid-1990s, when average test scores fell in all subjects.

One potential contributing factor that applies particularly to the decline in the scores of private school students is the increasing number of students who are opting out of the University Assessment and Admissions Program in favor of the U.S. version of the SAT so that they can attend mainland universities. Our analysis of Census Bureau data indicates that in 1980 there were 5,064 persons enrolled in U.S. universities who had been born in Puerto Rico and who had been living in Puerto Rico in 1975. By 2000, the comparable figure had grown to 8,744. This growth would contribute to the decline in test scores to the extent that such students had indeed opted out of the Puerto Rican test and were among the more academically talented students. Nonetheless, it would not help explain the declining test scores for public school students unless such students came from the public system. More relevant, but not the whole explanation, for that trend is the movement of students between the public and private schools.

A Bifurcated System

Emerging clearly from the data in table 5-7 are striking differences in average test scores of private and public school students. These differences illustrate the bifurcation of the education system, and they do not bode well for the long-term health of the island's public school system. On one side is the public school system that historically served more than 90 percent of all Puerto Rican students but now increasingly serves the lower-performing students of poor and lower-middle-class families. On the other is the private system that has tradition-ally catered to the higher-performing children of wealthy and upper-middle-class families.

About 25 percent of all Puerto Rican school children are now in private schools, more than double the current rate in the United States and also more than double the 1980 rate for Puerto Rico. The socioeconomic divide between public and private schools is dramatic, as shown in table 5-8. Data from the 2000 census show that the average income of Puerto Rican households with stu-dents in public schools is only about a third that of households with students in private schools. Consistent with that difference, the poverty rate among house-holds with public school students, at 66.8 percent, is almost three times that of households with private school students (23.0 percent).

Table 5-8. *Economic Profile of Public and Private School Students, Puerto Rico, 2000*
Units as indicated

Group	Average household income per capita (dollars)	Poverty rate (percent)
Puerto Rico, overall	8,066	48.7
Households with public school students	4,170	66.8
Households with private school students	11,960	23.0

Source: Data from U.S. Department of Commerce (2003); authors' tabulations.

That private schools are increasingly the schools of choice for those who can afford them is evident from the rising share of students enrolled in them. As a result, the private school sector has grown from a relatively small one offering elite education to a small portion of the wealthy population to a much larger and more diverse system. In 1960–61 there were 63,300 students in 133 private schools in Puerto Rico; 54 percent of these schools were Catholic schools, 21 percent were non-Catholic religious (mostly Protestant), and 25 percent were nonsectarian.[14] By 1990–91, 145,800 students were enrolled in 875 private schools; and in 2003–04, an estimated 185,745 students attended 987 private schools, 77,000 of whom (slightly more than 40 percent) were in Catholic schools.[15]

Why has the private sector grown at the expense of the public school system? Despite considerable diversity in both the private and public school systems, private schools are generally perceived to offer on average a richer academic environment (especially in the teaching of English), with fewer discipline problems and greater safety, differences that have been found as well between private and public schools in the United States and other countries.[16] Such differences seem to be particularly significant in Puerto Rico. For instance, the newspaper *El Nuevo Día* reports that a group of school teachers and other professionals interviewed informally "all agree that a major factor why parents send children to private schools is that the latter offer a curriculum that is more demanding than that offered in public schools. . . . Security is another essential factor in an environment where violence and crime permeates all levels of society."[17]

Private schools generate their revenues from tuition and fees as well as from private sources and the federal government. Although Puerto Rico's constitution prohibits the use of state and local public funds for schools other than public schools, private schools do receive U.S. government federal funds, which they apply for through the commonwealth's Department of Education.

14. Lopez Yustos (1992, p. 169).
15. Commonwealth of Puerto Rico, General Council of Education (2004).
16. See Coleman, Hofer, and Kilgore (1982).
17. Yadira Valdivia, "Attractiveness of Private Schools," *El Nuevo Dia,* August 13, 1991, p. 19.

Although they continue to offer education to the middle- and higher-income classes of Puerto Rico, the private schools have become increasingly heterogeneous, with the academic standards of some of the new ones falling far below those of the more established elite private schools. To operate a private school, a license must be obtained from the General Council of Education. Although these licenses must be periodically renewed, the renewal process does not require a significant academic review. The council accredits schools, but only at the request of the institution. Many private schools are accredited by U.S.-based accreditation organizations or have their own accountability systems. However, there is currently no mechanism for public monitoring of the quality of private schools.

Both the greater heterogeneity of private school students and the growth of institutions with lower-quality offerings help explain the falling test scores in the private school system. Thus it is no coincidence that the expansion of the private sector coincides with the declining average College Board test scores of students in private schools over the past twenty years and particularly from the mid-1980s through the mid-1990s, as shown in table 5-7.

The consequences of private sector growth for the public school system are also potentially profound, especially to the extent that the students who leave the public school system are the more able. As such students leave, it becomes increasingly difficult for the public system to keep its test scores from falling and thereby to convince families that the public system is not deteriorating, leading to another round of departures; and so the cycle continues.

Disparities within the Public School System

Even within the public school system wide differences in achievement exist between students in wealthier neighborhoods and those in lower-income communities. For instance, in the 2003–04 school year, the average score of students taking the College Board's University Assessment and Admissions Program quantitative test at the Antilles Public High School in Guaynabo, a wealthy suburb of San Juan, was 555, which exceeds the average among private high schools. In contrast, the average score in the Maria Teresa Piñero School, serving low-income students in the municipality of Toa Baja, was 397, and in the Lola Rodriguez de Tió School, in a low-income community in Carolina, 401.

Income-related disparities in educational outcomes are also visible in other indicators, such as school dropout rates. In some poor communities, high dropout rates lead to a significant emptying of schools in the higher grades. Table 5-9 illustrates this exodus for a set of high schools in low-income neighborhoods in various parts of the island. Overall, in 2002–03, fall enrollment in the twelfth grade was 73.6 percent of the fall enrollment in the tenth grade. In the specific schools shown in the table, however, twelfth-grade enrollment was substantially lower: only about 50 percent of tenth-grade enrollment in three of the schools and as low as 24 percent in one school. Although some of this emptying of schools

Table 5-9. *Public High School Enrollment, Puerto Rico, Selected Schools,*
2002–03 School Year

School	Grade			Twelfth grade as share of tenth grade (percent)
	Tenth	Eleventh	Twelfth	
Overall, Puerto Rico	44,922	38,353	33,062	73.6
San Juan, ID 62422	164	139	98	60.0
Trujillo Alto, ID 69047	378	227	206	54.5
Utuado, ID 16220	189	124	92	48.7
Ponce, ID 52514	703	537	342	48.6
San Juan, ID 61440	228	118	99	43.4
Mayagüez, ID 42168	313	123	76	24.2

Source: Data from NCES (2004b).

could reflect the movement from public schools into other schools within and outside Puerto Rico, most of it appears to be the result of students' dropping out of the system.

The higher dropout rates for students from low-income families are more explicitly illustrated in table 5-10. The third row of the table shows that the dropout rate—defined as the share of the eighteen- to twenty-four-year-old population who are not in school and did not complete high school—was 35.3 percent for youth in low-income households in contrast to only 8.7 percent for students in households at the top of the income distribution.

In addition, the table shows that 12.9 percent of the youth aged eighteen to twenty-four residing in low-income households were still enrolled in high school, a school delay rate more than 50 percent higher than the 8.0 percent delay rate among the richest third of the households. Although school delay is not as negative an indicator as dropping out of school, the grade retention and repetition that it reflects are often associated with poor academic performance. Furthermore, evidence suggests that forcing a student to repeat a grade is not likely to lead to any significant improvement in academic achievement and typically increases the probability that he or she will drop out of school.[18]

If the dropout and school delay rates for youth residing in households at the low end of the income ladder are combined, 48.2 percent of persons aged eighteen to twenty-four were still in high school or had dropped out of school altogether. That almost half of the youth residing in the poorest households in Puerto Rico were experiencing severe school difficulties suggests a cycle of poverty and poor schooling that would need to be broken for the island to increase in any significant way the income and education of its most disadvantaged populations.

18. Hauser (2004); Alexander, Entwisle and Kabbani (2001); Holmes (1989).

Table 5-10. *School Enrollment of Persons Aged Eighteen to Twenty-Four,*
by Household Income, Puerto Rico, 2000[a]

Percent

Status	Overall	Low income	High income
Not enrolled in school	55.1	61.5	47.3
Completed high school[b]	33.8	26.2	38.6
Did not complete high school (estimate of dropout rate)	21.3	35.3	8.7
Enrolled in school	44.9	38.5	52.7
Enrolled in high school or less (estimate of school delay)	10.5	12.9	8.0
Enrolled in college or more	34.4	25.6	44.7

Source: Data from U.S. Department of Commerce (2003); authors' tabulations.

a. Low- and high-income households are defined here as those in the bottom 30 percent and the top 30 percent, respectively, of the income distribution.

b. Includes GED equivalency.

The lack of progress in overall student achievement, the movement of students out of the public system, and the education system's apparent failure to meet the needs of the bulk of Puerto Rico's poor population are all cause for concern. They are not, however, the result of inattention or lack of concern on the part of education policymakers within Puerto Rico.

Policy Initiatives Related to Schools: 1990 to the Present

During most of Puerto Rico's history, and especially since 1898, when it became a territory of the United States, the public elementary and secondary school system on the island was a highly centralized, state-controlled enterprise. Reforms in the 1960s introduced seven educational regions but only as a means of providing more structure to the governance system, not to decentralize it. No major changes in the system were undertaken until serious reform discussions began in the late 1980s.[19] The effort to reform and improve the system during the 1990s included both the attempt to decentralize the system and the investment of significant new resources.

School Governance

After an intensive process of study and discussion, a major overhaul of Puerto Rico's school system was passed by the Puerto Rican legislature, and signed into law by the governor, in 1990. The Organic Law of the Department of Education (Law 68, passed on August 28, 1990) starts by noting the significant changes

19. See Osuna (1923), Rodriguez Bou (1947), Gómez Tejera and Cruz López (1970), and Lopez Yustos (1992) for historical accounts of Puerto Rico's educational system.

occurring globally that affect education, acknowledging the general level of dissatisfaction with the Puerto Rican school system, and stating the need to implement a package of comprehensive school reform. The introduction ends with the following statement: "With this law we state our commitment to bring high-quality educational opportunities on an equal basis to all Puerto Ricans."[20]

The 1990 Organic Law made some significant changes in the governance of the school system. Before that point, the Department of Education of Puerto Rico, which operates a unified school district in charge of K–12 education for the whole island, tightly controlled all areas of public schools, from the curriculum and instruction to teacher selection and textbooks. Its administrative structure was organized on the basis of a few regions, each of which encompassed large parts of the island. No formal mechanism existed for the active participation of teachers, parents, and school directors in the operation of schools or the design of curriculum and instruction. The Organic Law was intended to decentralize the system and increase participation by adding an administrative layer of local school districts (each headed by a superintendent) that would aid in the administration of the system and in distributing the curriculum and instructional services offered by the regions to schools; and creating more participation of stakeholders through the introduction of school-based councils that would foster the input of parents, teachers, students, and community members into the curriculum of the school and its interactions with the community.

Despite the rhetoric of decentralization, the Organic Law had little effect on the distribution of authority because virtually all administrative decisions remained in the hands of the Department of Education. But the law was quickly extended in 1993, when an ambitious new legislative initiative further decentralized the school system. The first step in this process occurred with the passage of the Community Schools Development Act (Law 18) in June 1993, which turned over major decisionmaking powers to the schools. The building block of the new school-based management reforms was the creation of autonomous community schools (*escuelas de la comunidad*) governed by school councils in collaboration with school directors. The school-based management team was to take responsibility not only for school curriculum but also a variety of management, fiscal, and instructional affairs, from the selection and payment of contractors for repair and maintenance services to the design of new instructional methods and activities. The Community Schools Development Act was implemented quickly, and over the course of a few years in the mid-1990s, all elementary and secondary schools were converted into community schools.

After the system of community schools was fully in place, the government replaced the Organic Law of 1990 with the law that currently governs the public education system in Puerto Rico, the 1999 Organic Law of the Department of

20. Commonwealth of Puerto Rico (1990, p. 2).

Education (Law 149). This law formally placed community schools at the center of the system, providing them, in principle, with even broader autonomy in controlling their instructional, curricular, fiscal, and managerial affairs, including the hiring of teachers and management of their budgets. At the same time, the law reassigned functions and powers to the system of ten regions and eighty-four school districts, giving districts the function of managing academic affairs and regions the function of managing administrative affairs. The Central Office of the Department of Education retained its decisionmaking power over schools, meaning that the more than fifteen hundred school directors respond directly to the secretary of education, and the Central Office continues to monitor and approve a myriad of school-based decisions.

In addition to these major governance reforms, a number of other legislative actions have been introduced over the past fifteen years, including an attempt to establish a voucher system that would have permitted public school students to use public funds to attend private schools. This effort was derailed by a ruling from Puerto Rico's Supreme Court that such a program would represent an unconstitutional use of public funds for the support of religious institutions. Other reforms include changes to the teacher certification requirements and teacher salary structures in 2002, as well as reforms related to the unionization of teachers and other public employees in the school system.

Financing Primary and Secondary Education

In addition to these changes, during the 1990s Puerto Rico significantly increased its public spending on elementary and secondary education. Included in public spending are both operating or current fund expenditures and capital expenses or general improvements. The latter, which are used for school construction, major repairs, and remodeling, generally constitute a small fraction of the overall budget and are highly volatile. As a result, we focus here on operating expenses, which include categories such as the salaries of teachers, books and materials for schools, and administrative expenses.

Table 5-11 shows the changes in real operating public expenditures per student in elementary and secondary education between the 1970–71 and 2002–03 fiscal years (adjusted for inflation using the Puerto Rico Consumer Price Index). As can be seen, expenditures rose in the 1970s and remained essentially unchanged until the 1990s. Between 1990–91 and 2001–02, total spending for public education increased by more than 50 percent in constant dollars, despite declining enrollment. By 2002–03, spending had increased another 14 percent. As a result, by 2003, spending per student had risen to $4,145, about double its level in 1990 and more than triple its level in 1970.

Despite this sharp spending increase in the 1990s, in 2001–02 Puerto Rico's spending per student was only about half the U.S. average, only a third that in wealthy high-spending states such as New Jersey, New York, and Connecticut,

Table 5-11. *Public Spending on Elementary and Secondary Education,*
Puerto Rico, Selected Years, 1970–2003[a]

Dollars, except as indicated

Fiscal year	Spending (millions of dollars)	Number of students	Spending per student
1970–71	945,457	686,770	1,377
1980–81	1,454,991	712,880	2,041
1990–91	1,414,572	644,734	2,194
1994–95	1,909,456	619,655	3,081
2001–02	2,176,361	604,177	3,602
2002–03	2,482,733	598,933	4,145

Source: Data from Commonwealth of Puerto Rico, Department of Education (1973, 1983, 1993, 1996, 2004a).

a. Operating expenditures, in constant 2003 dollars.

and significantly less than in Utah and Mississippi, the lowest-spending U.S. states (table 5-12). Nevertheless, Puerto Rico's expenditures on primary and secondary education per student relative to personal income (33.2 percent in 2001–02) greatly exceeded the average in the United States (25.4 percent) and in each of the states listed in the table.

One reason for the growth in spending during the 1990s was the rise in island income. Reflecting the rebound of economic growth in the United States, Puerto Rico's GNP per capita grew at an average annual rate of 1.7 percent in real terms between 1990–91 and 2002–03. But there is more to the story than income growth. While income per capita grew at the rate of 1.7 percent a year, public expenditure per student rose at an annual rate of 5.3 percent. As a result, education spending per student as a percentage of GNP per capita rose from 22 percent in 1990–91 to close to 34 percent by 2002–03.

Not all of this spending was financed by taxes collected in Puerto Rico. As a territory of the United States, Puerto Rico receives federal aid for education, primarily in the form of Title I funds for disadvantaged students and Title VI grants for educational improvement. Combined, these two sets of programs accounted for close to 60 percent of the more than $700 million in federal appropriations for the 2000–01 fiscal year. The combination of a high poverty rate among its children and low spending per student means that federal aid accounts for a far larger share of education spending in Puerto Rico than in any U.S. state. Such aid accounted for 31.4 percent of all operating expenditures in 1990–91 and 32.6 percent in 2002–03. These shares contrast with an average share of about 7 to 8 percent in the United States as a whole, 13 to 14 percent in Mississippi, and 8 to 9 percent in Tennessee.[21]

21. NCES (2003).

Table 5-12. *Public Spending on Elementary and Secondary Education, Relative to Personal Income, Puerto Rico and Selected U.S. States, 2001–02*
Dollars, except as indicated

Region	Spending per student	Per capita personal income, 2001	Spending as share of per capita personal income (percent)
Puerto Rico	3,563	10,733	33.2
United States	7,734	30,413	25.4
High-spending states			
Washington, D.C.	12,102	40,539	29.9
New Jersey	11,793	38,625	30.5
New York	11,218	35,878	31.3
Connecticut	10,577	42,377	25.0
Massachusetts	10,232	38,864	26.3
Low-spending states			
Utah	4,910	24,639	19.9
Mississippi	5,354	21,653	24.7
Tennessee	5,959	26,808	22.2
Arizona	5,964	25,878	23.1
Idaho	6,011	24,506	24.5

Source: Data from NCES (2004c); U.S. Department of Commerce (2004); Commonwealth of Puerto Rico (2004b).

Even after adjusting for this federal aid, it appears that by world standards Puerto Rico is making an unusually large effort in public education. Based on the standard measure of education effort—spending (from own sources) per student divided by GNP per capita—figure 5-2 shows that Puerto Rico's share of 25 percent exceeds the average share of 22 percent for Organization for Economic Cooperation and Development member nations, the U.S. share of 22 percent, and also the far lower shares in Mexico (16 percent), Ireland (15 percent), and Argentina (16 percent).[22]

Another way to measure Puerto Rico's effort in financing public education is to look at its expenditures on education as a share of its general fund budget. This share has hovered around 20 percent for many years. In fiscal year 2002–03, for instance, the primary and secondary education expenditure charged to the general education fund of Puerto Rico's government was equal to $1,580,573,000, whereas the government's total general fund was $7,842,700,000, so that edu-

22. The share for Puerto Rico includes only public spending (financed by state and local sources), while the shares for other countries include both private and public spending; see UNESCO (2003) and OECD (2003).

Figure 5-2. *Public Spending on K-12 Education per Student as Share of GNP per Capita, Selected Countries*

Percent

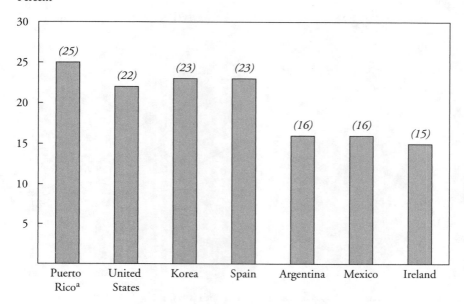

Source: OECD (2003); Commonwealth of Puerto Rico (2004a).
a. Excludes U.S. (federal) government spending on education.

cation expenditures were 20.1 percent of all government expenditures.[23] This share far exceeds that in most other countries. In 2000, for example, elementary and secondary education spending as a proportion of total government expenditures was 14.4 percent in the Republic of Korea, 10.3 percent in Denmark, 7.1 percent in Ireland, 9.2 percent in Spain, 15.2 percent in Chile, 10.9 percent in Argentina, and 9.4 percent in Uruguay.[24]

The greater investments made by Puerto Rico in the area of public education in the 1990s partly financed the hiring of teachers. Figure 5-3 shows the sharp drop in the student-to-teacher ratio in Puerto Rico since the 1950s. In the 1952–53 school year, 9,251 teachers were serving 458,000 students in the regular program of the public school system, a ratio of 49.5 pupils per teacher. By 1980–81, the number of students had risen to 712,880, but the teaching labor force had increased by 32,292, achieving a ratio of 22.1 students per teacher. From 1980–81 to 2003–04, the rising number of teachers was combined with a

23. Commonwealth of Puerto Rico (2004a); for details on the behavior of education expenditures over time, see Rivera-Batiz (1995a).
24. UNESCO (2003).

Figure 5-3. *Student-to-Teacher Ratio, Puerto Rico, Selected Years, 1952–2003*[a]
Percent

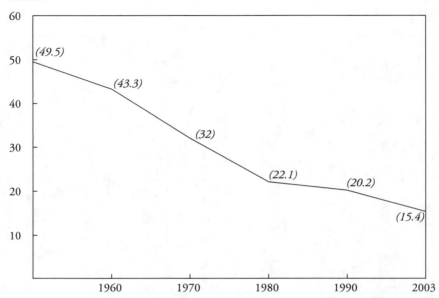

Source: Rivera-Batiz (1993); Commonwealth of Puerto Rico (1994, 1996a, 1998, 2000, 2004a).
a. Students and teachers in regular programs of instruction.

drop in the public student population, leading to a drop in the student-to-teacher ratio to 15.4 in 2003–04—lower than the U.S ratio of about 16.1 pupils per teacher in 2002–03.[25]

Teacher salaries in Puerto Rico are about half those in the mainland United States. For the 2002–03 school year, the average annual salary of teachers in Puerto Rico was $22,164, compared with $45,771 in the United States.[26] Even states with the lowest salaries, such as South Dakota ($32,414), Oklahoma ($32,277), North Dakota ($33,869) and Mississippi ($35,135), have substantially higher salaries than Puerto Rico.[27] The average starting salary of a teacher in Puerto Rico with a bachelor's degree was $18,000 in 2002–03, the equivalent of a base salary of $1,500 a month. By comparison, the average starting salary in the United States was $29,564, or $2,464 a month.

Teacher salaries in Puerto Rico are lower today in real terms than they were in the late 1960s. From 1968–69 to 1992–93, the base monthly salary for those with

25. NCES (2003, p. 18).
26. American Federation of Teachers (2004, table 1).
27. The salary differences between Puerto Rico and these states would be greater if the differences in the cost of living among them were taken into account. See Nelson, Drown, and Gould (2001, p. 13).

a bachelor's degree (adjusted for inflation and measured in 2003 dollars) declined from $1,768 to $1,408. Since that time, it has slightly increased to $1,500. One of the main stated objectives of the teacher union is to raise this base salary.

Historically, and up to the late 1990s, teachers in Puerto Rico were organized through labor organizations that acted to improve the working conditions of teachers but did not negotiate directly with the government. The three main teacher organizations in Puerto Rico are the Puerto Rican Teachers Association (Asociación de Maestros de Puerto Rico), the Federation of Teachers of Puerto Rico (Federación de Maestros de Puerto Rico), and Puerto Rican Educators in Action (Educadores Puertorriqueños en Acción). In 1998 the Labor Relations Law of Public Service Employees in Puerto Rico (Law 45) officially sanctioned the syndication of public sector employees, allowing them to negotiate collective bargaining agreements with the government. Because the law specified that only one organization could represent the employees of any specific group of government workers, in 1999 teachers selected the Federation of Teachers as their collective bargaining organization, and since that time the federation has been in charge of negotiating with the Department of Education.

The Failure of School Reform

Given the trends and patterns in achievement levels documented earlier, it is clear that the combination of governance reforms and significant additional spending on education has not yielded the desired results. Instead of rising, achievement levels have failed to increase and may have actually deteriorated. Families have shown their lack of confidence in the public system by increasingly opting for private schools. Instead of promoting more equity in the sense of high quality education for all, the system continues to fail students from the poorest households. Their glossy promotion by government authorities notwithstanding, the governance reforms have failed to introduce fundamental change in teaching and learning and may, in fact, have made things worse.

The problems with the reform effort were many and are not hard to identify. One is that a good number of the reforms implemented after the first Organic Law was passed in 1990 were imposed from above by the Department of Education. They were quickly passed as laws before a consensus had been created among stakeholders. They were then implemented without much preamble, in the form of orders from the Department of Education. This process created widespread distrust and resistance as well as an unenthusiastic response to the reforms from those most central to their dictates: teachers, students and their parents, and school directors. This problem is not unique to Puerto Rico. Governments in various other countries have forced decentralization programs upon schools in an authoritarian way.[28]

28. See, for instance, the case study of decentralization reforms in Colombia in Hanson (1995).

The politicized environment in which most public institutions operate on the island complicated the situation. As a political party comes into power, not only do policies change, but also most aspects of government decisionmaking—from personnel and procurement to the official languages used in the public sector—become colored by party loyalty. Policies are often designed and implemented with the goal of seeking political gain, not necessarily because they are the most appropriate. In the area of education, politically motivated policies are often used to manipulate broad areas in the school system, from curriculum and language policy to testing and assessment.

The environment among teachers epitomizes the problem. Each of the three teacher organizations in Puerto Rico has a core membership that is affiliated with one of the three main political parties. Even after the Federation of Teachers became the sole bargaining agent for the teachers, the other two organizations remained in existence and have been publicly critical of the federation's actions and initiatives. The competing organizations have also questioned the legitimacy of the federation and have even gone to court to try to void its authority as their members' representative.

A second problem with the governance reforms is that they were introduced too abruptly. As a result, much of the school system was unprepared for the massive administrative shifts associated with decentralization. A recent qualitative study of the impact of the reforms on the effectiveness of school directors observes that the decentralization program failed to generate a more efficient system in part because school directors were unprepared for the new tasks they were asked to do:

> An example is the management of school budgets, for which directors have no assistance. In the conversations I have had over the last year with over 200 school directors, I have not found a single one that has received adequate support to handle the new management functions. Furthermore, many directors indicate that they have had to reduce their academic management duties in order to deal with the financial management of the schools. One of the tasks they can no longer fulfill is the supervision of the teachers and their instructional activities, to ensure that the quality of schooling is increasing.[29]

Although new institutional structures were created on paper to foster increased school autonomy and participation, a third limitation of the reforms is that these structures—to a greater or lesser extent—did not succeed in doing so. A case study of the implementation of the reforms in one school during the late 1990s concludes that "in the dimension of participation, this research . . . failed to identify any significant changes relative to the situation before the reforms

---

29. Castillo Ortiz (2002, p. 3).

were implemented."[30] The school had created a school council, as required under the Community Schools Development Act (Law 18), but the council never met. Furthermore, the author of this study observed no change in the way parents, teachers, and students worked together nor in the way the school was involved with the community.

These failures have been systematic throughout the school system. An exhaustive study carried out in 2002 and 2003 by the management consultants McKinsey & Company led the Department of Education itself to conclude that despite the reforms, the administrative system remained highly centralized. The island's fifteen hundred schools still report directly to the secretary of education but are also subject to several layers of authority that embody different and often conflicting approaches.[31] The McKinsey study finds that the department continues to have "highly-centralized processes that block the effective implementation of school autonomy."[32] It also concludes that the reforms have made the administrative process more confusing, with "a lack of clarity of roles and functions, leading to gaps and duplication of effort," and have created a "bureaucratic structure" that has "insufficient lines of communication throughout the school system."[33] A 2000 survey of school directors finds that an "excessive administrative burden" and a "lack of parental involvement and assistance in schools" were two of the three main problems they faced (teacher absenteeism, discussed later in this chapter, being the third).[34]

A fourth problem is that the substantial increase in resources flowing into the school system in the 1990s had an unhealthy side effect. As often happens when government institutions receive large sums of money over short periods of time, corruption turned out to be a problem. From 2001 to 2004, the Department of Education was the subject of extensive local and federal investigations regarding the diversion of education funds for personal or political gain in the period 1993 to 2000. Indeed, the former secretary of education, Victor Fajardo, who was at the helm of the Department of Education in the middle and late 1990s, is currently in jail, having been charged with and convicted of a variety of law violations associated with the use of department funds. Many of his aides and other staff have also been investigated, and some convicted, as well. In response to the irregularities, the federal Department of Education froze hundreds of millions of dollars in funding for Puerto Rican schools during the 2002 through 2004 fiscal years.[35]

30. Martí-Vazquez (2000, p. 238–39). See also Quintero (2006, p. 5).
31. Commonwealth of Puerto Rico, Department of Education (2004c, p. 6).
32. Commonwealth of Puerto Rico, Department of Education (2003).
33. Commonwealth of Puerto Rico, Department of Education (2004c, p. 6).
34. Castillo Ortiz and Marrero (2003, p. 1).
35. Camile Roldán Soto, "Up to Date the Department of Education with the Federal Government," *El Nuevo Día,* June 16, 2004, p. 10.

Table 5-13. *Administrative Density in Schools, Puerto Rico and the United States, Selected Years, 1988–2001*
Percent

	Puerto Rico		United States
Characteristic	1988–89	2003–04	2000–01
Nonclassroom staff per 100 classroom staff	86.7	88.5	59.2
Administrative staff per 100 classroom staff	33.5	28.0	13.6
Administrative staff per 1,000 students	16.4	18.2	8.5

Source: Data from Commonwealth of Puerto Rico (1992, 2004a); NCES (2003).

That the school governance legislation over the past fifteen years has yet to generate a simpler and more decentralized system is clear from the continuing bureaucracy within the Department of Education. The total staff of the department increased from 61,611 in 1988–89 to 69,906 in 2003–04, and the department remains by far the largest agency within the government of Puerto Rico. In 2003–04 there were 219,835 government employees, and the Department of Education accounted for 31.8 percent, or almost one out of every three.

Table 5-13 presents some indicators of the bureaucratic and administrative density of the Puerto Rican Department of Education. The staff of the regular program of the Department of Education can be divided into classroom staff (teachers and teaching aides) and nonclassroom staff (all other employees). Among the latter, the administrative staff (which includes management as well as office workers) can also be identified. From 1988–89 to 2003–04, the number of employees in nonclassroom staff per 100 employees in classroom staff rose from 86.7 to 88.5. Although the administrative staff per 100 employees in classroom staff declined from 33.5 to 28.0 over the period, this decline reflects the large increase in classroom teachers rather than any absolute decline in bureaucratic bloat. If administrators are measured relative to students, the story changes: that indicator rises from 16.4 in 1988–89 to 18.2 in 2003–04.

These figures are exceedingly high compared with those in the United States in 2000–01, the nearest year for which there are comparable data. The number of nonclassroom employees per 100 employees in classroom staff was 59.2 in the United States, substantially lower than the 88.5 in Puerto Rico in 2003–04. The number of administrative staff per 100 employees in nonclassroom staff was 13.6 in the United States, less than half the equivalent figure on the island in both 1988–89 and 2003–04. The number of administrative employees per 1,000 students was 8.5 in the United States, again about half the equivalent figure for Puerto Rico. Even when one makes the comparison to a state such as New York, which includes New York City and is not known for its bureaucratic leanness, Puerto Rico does not look good. For instance, though the number of nonclassroom staff per 100 classroom employees was 68.1 in New York in 2000–01, which exceeds the U.S. average of 59.2, it still falls far short of the indicator for Puerto Rico. Thus Puerto Rico appears to have ended up with the worst of both worlds: a poorly implemented effort at decentralization that disrupted the functioning of schools and an increasingly bloated centralized bureaucracy.

The last failure of the governance reforms, and perhaps the most important, is their insufficient attention to accountability throughout the school system. In line with the McKinsey & Company study, the Department of Education concluded in 2004 that "there is no accountability in any part of the school system."[36] The student assessment component of the reforms has become operational only in the past two years, with the outsourcing of the testing to an independent, external agency (the Educational Testing Service, headquartered in Princeton, New Jersey) and only in response to the pressures originated by the federal No Child Left Behind legislation.

Beyond assessment, accountability at the school level continues to be a problem. Absenteeism among both students and teachers is rampant. A recent study documents that among both groups, the average level of absenteeism is equivalent to five weeks of class during the academic year.[37] With respect to students, the problem could be reduced by tougher enforcement of truancy laws at the school level. The absenteeism of teachers is more complicated and deserves additional research. To the extent that high absenteeism reflects poor working conditions in the schools, such as student violence, the situation might improve if teachers in Puerto Rico had greater assistance in the form of teacher aides. Such aides are virtually absent, accounting for only 0.3 percent of all school system staff on the island in 2001–02, in contrast to their 11.4 percent share in the United States. Regardless of the cause of the absenteeism, however, there is little doubt that it is harmful to students. This is especially true in Puerto Rico, where schools often do not provide substitute teachers; if teachers are absent, students are typically sent home.

Given the many serious problems with how the school governance reforms were implemented, it is probably safe to conclude that they contributed to the decline in student achievement within the public schools during the 1990s both directly, by the disruption they generated, and indirectly, by inducing some students to shift to private schools. In addition, as noted earlier, some specific aspects of the reform effort may be directly implicated in the declining test scores—for example, the marked emphasis on English instruction may be to some degree responsible for the decline in Spanish scores.

Policy Issues in Higher Education

Higher education raises its own set of policy issues. These include the level and composition of funding for the public university system, concerns about its

36. Commonwealth of Puerto Rico, Department of Education (2004c, p. 6).
37. Castillo Ortiz and Marrero (2003, p. 28).

Figure 5-4. *Public Spending on Higher Education per Student, Puerto Rico, Selected Years, 1975–2003*[a]
Constant dollars (2003)

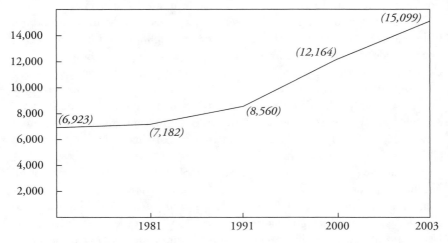

Source: NCES (2004a; 2003, p. 379, table 337).
a. Data for University of Puerto Rico system only.

productivity, and questions about potentially adverse distributional consequences of government funding of a system that serves the wealthier students on the island.

Funding and Spending

With the rapid growth in enrollment in the island's public university system noted earlier, one might suspect public spending to have lagged behind. In fact, that has not been the case. As shown in figure 5-4, public spending, expressed in constant 2003 dollars, has risen quickly in the University of Puerto Rico system. Despite rising enrollments, the University of Puerto Rico managed over recent years to more than double its real expenditures per student, from $7,182 in 1980–81 to $15,099 in 2002–03. This spectacular growth has brought public spending on higher education in Puerto Rico close to the U.S. average. In 1980–81 public spending per student in Puerto Rico was about 75 percent of that in the United States; by 2000–01 it had risen to about 95 percent of the U.S. average.

That Puerto Rico's per capita income is so much lower than that of the United States means that the island is spending a far higher percentage of its income on education. Our calculations for 2001–02 show that public spending per student in Puerto Rico expressed as a percentage of per capita gross national product, at 133.8 percent, was triple that of the United States (41.0 percent), triple the average in Latin American and Caribbean countries (44.9 percent), and more than double that of upper-income countries (66.5 percent).[38]

The comparatively high ratio of public spending on higher education per student in Puerto Rico does not extend to the private sector. In 2000–01, private colleges and universities in Puerto Rico spent, on average, $4,507 per student, less than a third of that spent in the public institutions. This pattern contrasts with that in the United States, where in the same year private colleges and universities spent an average of $25,245 per student, far exceeding the $14,494 spent by public universities. These differences translate into significant differences in the numbers of students per faculty member across the two sectors. In 1999–2000, the ratio of 14.9 students per faculty member in the island's four-year public universities was about two-thirds the ratio of 23.7 in the less well funded private universities. The patterns are reversed for U.S. universities, where four-year public institutions had an average of 14.6 students per faculty member (about the same as in Puerto Rico), while the much better funded private universities were able to reduce their ratios to 12.4 students per faculty member.[39]

Although Puerto Rico spends almost as much per student in its public universities as does the United States, it pays its professors less. Table 5-14 shows the average pay differentials between full-time instructional faculty in four-year degree-granting institutions in Puerto Rico and the United States. This pay differential widens with the seniority of the faculty: assistant professors in Puerto Rico's public sector earn 73.2 percent the salary of their counterparts in the United States, whereas for full professors the rate is only 60.7 percent. These differences are not readily attributed to differences in qualifications. At the University of Puerto Rico at Río Piedras, for instance, close to 70 percent of full-time faculty holds a doctorate, while the equivalent average for research universities in the United States is 72.7 percent.[40]

Student Outcomes and Quality

Only a small proportion of students in four-year higher education institutions in Puerto Rico graduates in four years. At the University of Puerto Rico at Río Piedras, for example, only 12.5 percent of undergraduate students complete their degrees within four years of entering the institution, and about 50 percent of undergraduates take six years.[41] These extended times to graduation are not atypical among urban institutions serving populations of part-time students, many of whom work and go to school at the same time. For instance, the six-year

38. NCES (2003); World Bank (2004).
39. NCES (2003). These data are for full-time equivalent students per full-time equivalent faculty.
40. For Puerto Rico, see University of Puerto Rico at Río Piedras (2005); for the United States, see NCES (2003).
41. University of Puerto Rico at Río Piedras (2005).

Table 5-14. *Average Salary of Full-Time Instructional Faculty at Public Universities, Puerto Rico and the United States, 1999–2000*
Dollars

Rank	Puerto Rico	United States
Assistant professor	35,612	48,671
Associate professor	41,270	57,984
Full professor	49,960	82,344

Source: Data from NCES (2003, p. 292).

graduation rate is 48.6 percent at George Mason University, 44 percent at San Diego State University, and 37.8 percent at the University of Nevada at Las Vegas. By the standards of most comprehensive research universities, including public universities, these graduation rates are quite low.

About 61 percent of those graduating from Puerto Rican institutions of higher education in 2000–01 were granted bachelor's degrees, approximately 24 percent associate degrees, and the remaining 15 percent graduate-level or professional degrees.[42] In the United States, the share of graduate and professional degrees is significantly higher, equal to 25 percent of all those receiving degrees in the country in 2000–01. The shortfall in Puerto Rico is not in professional degrees but rather at the master's and doctoral levels, where Puerto Rican universities lag in their program offerings and enrollments.[43]

Compared with their United States counterparts, students who graduate in four years from Puerto Rican institutions tend to be focused on science, technology, and business. Of the students who graduated in four years and received their degrees in Puerto Rico in 2000–01, 55.2 percent were enrolled in the computer science, engineering, natural science, and business fields, while the equivalent proportion for U.S. students was only 37.8 percent. These data suggest that many university students are responding to signals provided by the labor market on the island. Indeed, the growing pharmaceutical, biotechnology, electronics, transportation, finance, and banking sectors all have increased the demand for the technical and professional workers that Puerto Rican universities are churning out in high numbers.

This synergy between the most dynamic sectors of the Puerto Rican economy and the island's universities has been intensifying in recent years, as typified by linkages between the pharmaceutical industry and the universities. At the University of Puerto Rico at Río Piedras, external research and development funding of study in the natural sciences tripled during the past five years, rising to $18.9 million in 2004–05 and accounting for two-thirds of the external fund-

42. NCES (2003).
43. NCES (2003).

ing received by the institution.[44] Three major biotechnology research centers at the University of Puerto Rico have been funded by the National Institutes of Health and the National Science Foundation: the Neuroscience Center for the Molecular Study of Development and Behavior, the Center for the Study of Protein Structure, Performance, and Dynamics, and the Center for the Development of a Biomedical Research Information and Collaboration Network. Several pharmaceutical companies with operations in Puerto Rico have expressed interest in participating in the research activities of the centers, including SmithKline, Pfizer, and Bristol-Myers Squibb. According to Dr. Manuel Gomez, the University of Puerto Rico's vice president for research and academic affairs at the time these projects were funded, "We identified a niche in the scientific academic R&D that could be used to produce technology transfer, generate new patents, and develop human resources for the growing biotechnology industry."[45]

Determining how productively higher education funding in Puerto Rico is being used is difficult, given the almost complete absence of data on student achievement for college seniors or recent college graduates. The only data available come from the College Board's Teacher Certification Exam. This exam, a requirement for teachers in the public school system, was first offered in 1989 and is taken primarily by recent graduates. The proportion of test takers who pass the exam exhibited virtually no trend in the period from 1989 to 2003. For example, the proportion of students who passed the Test of Fundamental Concepts and Communication Skills component (by scoring above 89 in a scale that ranges from 40 to 160) ranged between 72 percent and 80 percent over that period, with no upward or downward trend observed. Note, though, that the number of students taking the exam rose, from 2,350 in 1989 to 5,116 in 2003.

Furthermore, it is difficult, if not impossible, to compare the quality of higher education institutions in Puerto Rico and in the United States. The rankings provided by institutions such as the National Research Council and popular publications such as *U.S. News & World Report* do not typically include Puerto Rican colleges and universities. The few surveys that have ranked Puerto Rican institutions focus mostly on graduate-level or professional education. In these surveys, the island universities—both public and private—are usually at the bottom of the list of American universities examined.

In the absence of any systematic evidence on the extent to which public higher education institutions in Puerto Rico—whose expenditures per student are broadly equal with those in the United States—produce learning and achievement among its graduates comparable with those of the American institutions, the most one can do is raise questions and point to the need for additional research on the productivity of the system as measured by the relationship

44. University of Puerto Rico at Río Piedras (2005).
45. Martinez (2002), p. 1.

between academic outcomes and spending. A further question is the extent to which any evidence of low productivity reflects the problems affecting the elementary and secondary education system—which are then sequentially transmitted to higher education institutions in the form of underprepared students—or whether any shortfall is mostly the result of internal deficiencies of the public universities. These issues should be a matter for future research.

Distributional Concerns

The United States and Puerto Rico differ quite significantly in the way they finance expenditures for public higher education (see table 5-15). One striking difference is in the portion of spending accounted for by tuition and fees: 18.1 percent in the United States in contrast to only 7.3 percent in Puerto Rico. These differences reflect major differences in annual revenue from tuition and fees. In the United States, the average annual tuition and fees for four-year institutions was $3,746 in 2001–02; the equivalent range that year for the University of Puerto Rico was $790 to $1,245.

Close to 70 percent of funding for the University of Puerto Rico system comes from the commonwealth government. The commonwealth supplies funds to the university by using a formula based on the University Act of 1966, which granted the University of Puerto Rico system a fixed percentage of central government revenues.

The second major source of funds for Puerto Rican public higher education is the federal government. These funds include federal appropriations, grants, and contracts, which amounted to 15.8 percent of all university revenues in 2000–01. In addition, the federal government indirectly funds a significant portion of the 7.3 percent of revenues generated through tuition. This funding comes in the form of student aid, available through Title IV of the federal Higher Education Act, the largest source of which is the Pell grant program. Because much of this financial aid is awarded on the basis of need, and because the average income of Puerto Rican families is relatively low, a large share of Puerto Rican students enrolled in higher education institutions is eligible for a Pell grant. Overall, Puerto Rico received more than $600 million in higher education financial assistance from the U.S. government in 2003–04. Only six states received a greater volume of funds: California, Florida, New York, Pennsylvania, Texas, and Virginia.

In fiscal year 2002–03, the maximum Pell grant was $4,050. Estimates are that as many as 50 percent of the students in the University of Puerto Rico system receive Pell grants.[46] Evidence suggests that students enrolled in private colleges and universities on the island rely even more heavily on Pell grants to fund

46. José A. Delgado, "Possible Reductions in the Pell Grants," *El Nuevo Día,* January 14, 2004, p. 18.

Table 5-15. *Sources of Financing of Public Higher Education, Puerto Rico and the United States, 2000–2001*
Percent, except as indicated

Source	Puerto Rico	United States
Current fund revenue (dollars)	1,000,293,000	176,645,215,000
Tuition and fees	7.3	18.1
Federal appropriations, grants, and contracts	15.8	11.2
State appropriations	68.9	35.6
Other revenues (local appropriations, endowment income, revenue from hospital services, and auxiliary enterprises)	8.0	35.1

Source: Data from NCES (2004a).

their studies. In 2003–04, for example, as many as 86 percent of students at the Interamerican University and 85 percent of those in the Ana G. Mendez University System received Pell grants.[47]

This higher reliance on Pell grants in the private sector implies that, unlike elementary and secondary education, the public universities cater to the wealthier components of Puerto Rican society. Indeed, both the University of Puerto Rico at Río Piedras and the University of Puerto Rico at Mayagüez, which would be considered among the elite universities in Puerto Rico, tend to enroll a larger proportion of students who attended private high schools, most of whom come from families with incomes above the Puerto Rican average. Although these institutions seek diverse populations, their relatively high admissions standards generally favor students from higher socioeconomic backgrounds. For instance, the 2004–05 freshman class at the University of Puerto Rico in Río Piedras had an average combined score of 1,166 on the Academic Aptitude part of the Puerto Rico College Board test, compared with an average of 945 for the overall population taking the test battery.

The distributional implications of this pattern are perverse given that tuition and fees are lower at public than at private universities. In 2003–04, tuition and fees at the University of Puerto Rico at Río Piedras were equal to $920, compared with $3,703 at Interamerican University, the largest private university, and $2,848 at the private Metropolitan University. These relative costs imply that the large subsidies to the public sector, which allow it to keep its tuition low, represent subsidies to the students from high-income families who attend the elite public higher education institutions. Thus the generous funding of the public institutions ends up redistributing income in favor of rich families and worsens the already highly skewed income distribution on the island. The perverse distri-

47. José A. Delgado, "Possible Reductions in the Pell Grants," *El Nuevo Día*, January 14, 2004, p. 18.

butional effect associated with the funding of public universities is not unique to Puerto Rico. It was identified as an issue in the late 1960s in the United States and more recently has received attention in the rest of the world.[48]

Low Male Enrollment

One final concern about higher education in Puerto Rico is that women far out-number men in the island's institutions of higher education, in both the public and private sectors. In 2002–03 men constituted just 39 percent of the student body. Although this figure is somewhat lower than the 44 percent in the United States, it is consistent with the pattern evident in many other countries, where men often forgo higher education to enter the labor market.

The consequence of the growing gap in college enrollment between men and women is that in Puerto Rico women currently have higher educational attain-ment than men. In 2000 the proportion of women twenty-five years of age or older who had some schooling beyond high school was 40.1 percent. For men, the corresponding figure was only 34.7 percent. One possible reason for the dif-ferentially high enrollment of women in college is the relatively high economic return to university education in Puerto Rico, particularly for women.

Education, Labor Market Returns, and Economic Growth

Viewed as an investment in human capital, education is intended to make persons more productive and thereby to raise the wages they can command in the labor market. Cross-sectional models from many different countries and time periods consistently confirm that more education, as traditionally measured by years of schooling, is associated with higher earnings.[49] Some studies have also found a significant effect of educational quality on labor market outcomes.[50] Somewhat less clear in the literature are the returns to education in the form of national economic growth. Various theoretical models in the economics literature posit a strong relationship between education and growth, though both the theorists and the empiricists disagree about whether it is the growth of human capital, as measured by changes in spending on education or changes in educational attainment, or the stock of human capital, as measured, for example, by the level of educational attainment of the population—that matters for growth.

Labor Market Returns to Education

In Puerto Rico, as elsewhere, the correlation between education levels and labor market outcomes is strong. This relationship is shown separately for men and women in table 5-16, with attention both to the probability of being unemployed

48. Hansen and Weisbrod (1969); Task Force on Higher Education and Society (2002).
49. See Psacharopoulos (1994), Card (1999), and Patrinos and Psacharopoulos (2004).
50. Card and Krueger (1992, 1996).

Table 5-16. *Education and Labor Market Outcomes, Puerto Rico, by Sex, 1999–2000*[a]

Education level	Unemployment rate (percent)		Annual wages (dollars)	
	Male	Female	Male	Female
Overall	13.5	17.1	25,320	19,826
Less than high school	22.4	37.0	15,382	13,551
High school diploma or equivalent	15.0	23.2	17,526	14,313
Some college	10.3	17.5	23,058	16,904
College degree	4.8	6.3	37,264	22,950
More than college	2.4	3.6	61,367	34,029

Source: Data from U.S. Department of Commerce (2003); authors' tabulations.

a. Data are for persons sixteen years of age or older in the labor force. Unemployment rate is for 2000; wages are 1999 annual earnings of full-time, year-round workers.

and to annual wages. Women at all levels of education fare less well in the labor market then men in that they have higher rates of unemployment and lower annual salaries. For both men and women, higher levels of education are associated with lower rates of unemployment—and hence greater probabilities of being employed—but the relationship is particularly striking for women. In 2000 a woman with a college degree had more than a 93 percent chance of being employed, in contrast to the far lower probability of about 77 percent for a woman with only a high school diploma (or its equivalent) and only 63 percent for one without a high school degree. With respect to wage differentials, the relative differences are reversed, with men exhibiting larger expected gains than women in annual earnings, both absolutely and relatively, from higher levels of education.

These patterns may help explain the higher enrollment of Puerto Rican women in colleges and universities. For women, a college education greatly increases the likelihood of finding employment. Moreover, though the wage gains associated with a college degree are smaller for women than for men, without a college degree a woman's earning prospects are bleak. Indeed, table 5-16 indicates that women need to acquire more education than men to achieve earnings comparable to those of men. For instance, women with a college degree earn on average close to $23,000, an amount that is almost 70 percent higher than average earnings of women without a high school diploma but still somewhat less than the average earnings of men with some college.

Women's need to acquire substantially higher levels of education to attain a certain salary level provides a strong incentive for them to invest in greater levels of human capital and helps explain the overwhelming female presence in institutions of higher education in Puerto Rico. The lower salaries received by women also were found in analyses in which we controlled for age, experience, hours of

Table 5-17. *Return to Education and Experience, Puerto Rico, Selected Years, 1970–2000*[a]

Variable	Estimated coefficients			
	1970	*1980*	*1990*	*2000*
Constant	−0.7038	−0.0371	0.1905	0.6853
	(−16.2)	(−1.9)	(25.0)	(41.0)
Education	0.0848	0.0806	0.0850	0.0852
	(31.6)	(68.3)	(72.1)	(79.4)
Experience	0.0236	0.0230	0.0266	0.0215
	(10.2)	(24.0)	(29.5)	(27.4)
Experience squared	−0.0003	−0.0002	−0.0003	−0.0002
	(−7.3)	(−13.0)	(−29.4)	(−11.8)
Summary statistic				
R^2 (adj.)	0.18	0.14	0.13	0.16
N	5,116	29,997	40,021	40,067
Sample mean	0.405	1.200	1.580	2.120

Source: Data from U.S. Department of Commerce (1974, 1983, 1994, 2003); authors' tabulations.
a. Standard deviations in parentheses. The dependent variable here is the natural log of hourly wages.

work, marital status, and other variables. One suspects that occupational segregation and pay discrimination may be significant forces operating in Puerto Rican labor markets.

Statistical models are commonly used to estimate so-called Mincerian returns to an additional year of education. These rates of return emerge from regression models in which the logarithm of hourly wages of persons in the labor market is estimated as a function of years of schooling and years of work experience. For our estimates, we use as the dependent variable the logarithm of the hourly wage of persons in the labor market aged sixteen or older (with positive wages). The explanatory variables are years of schooling, years of experience (calculated as age minus years of schooling minus six), and experience squared.

Table 5-17 presents our regression results using Census Bureau data for 1970, 1980, 1990, and 2000. The rate of return to an additional year of education in Puerto Rico declined from 8.48 percent in 1970 to 8.06 in 1980 before rising to 8.52 in 2000. Thus the return in the most recent year was essentially the same as it was in 1970.

This flat trend for Puerto Rico contrasts sharply with the rising rate of return to education in the United States over the same period.[51] Table 5-18 also pre-

51. See, for example, the survey by Katz and Autor (1999) and Murphy and Welch (2001). Similar patterns have emerged for a variety of other high-income as well as many developing countries; see for instance, Pavcnik (2003).

Table 5-18. *Return to Education, Puerto Rico and the United States, Selected Years, 1970–2000*[a]

Location	1970	1980	1990	2000
Puerto Rico	0.0848	0.0806	0.0850	0.0852
U.S. mainland	0.0729	0.0726	0.0866	0.0933
Puerto Ricans on U.S. mainland	n.a.	0.0562	0.0681	0.0804
Born in Puerto Rico	n.a.	0.0504	0.0592	0.0727
Born on U.S. mainland	n.a.	0.0662	0.0811	0.0900

Source: Data from U.S. Department of Commerce (1974, 1983, 1994, 2003); authors' tabulations.
a. Mincerian rate of return to education per year of schooling.

sents the Mincerian rates of return for the mainland United States. In contrast to Puerto Rico, the rate of return to education in the United States rises steeply, from 7.3 percent in 1970 to 8.7 percent in 1990 and 9.3 percent in 2000. Thus although rates of return to education on the island exceeded those on the U.S. mainland in 1970, the opposite was true in 2000.

The rising rates of return to schooling in the United States over the past two decades apply as well to Puerto Ricans living on the mainland. Nonetheless, rates of return to education for Puerto Ricans on the mainland are lower than those for the overall population in the United States. As table 5-18 shows, this wedge is particularly significant for Puerto Ricans born on the island who migrated to the mainland. This shortfall in the rewards to schooling for out-migrants may be connected to a wide array of factors, including, for example, the possibility that rewards are lower for Spanish speakers and the possibility that employers underestimate the skills of Puerto Rican migrants.[52]

The behavior of the Mincerian returns to education in Puerto Rico and the United States is similar to that of other measures connected to the returns to education. Table 5-19 compares the trends in the wage premium of college graduates relative to high school graduates with the comparable premium in the United States. In Puerto Rico, the ratio declined from 1.73 in 1970 to 1.47 in 1990 and then rose to 1.61 in 2000, leaving it still far below the 1970 level. In contrast, the wage premium for college graduates in the United States fell from 1970 to 1980 but then recovered and increased. The 2000 premium of 1.60 was far above its 1970 level.

Changes on both the supply and demand side account for the trends in the return to a college degree in Puerto Rico and for the differences between Puerto Rico and the United States. On the supply side, the key factor is the large increase in the number of college graduates on the island over the thirty-year period, which has exerted substantial downward pressure on the relative wages

52. Katz and Stark (1987).

Table 5-19. *Wage Premium of College Graduates Relative to High School Graduates, Puerto Rico and the United States, Selected Years, 1970–2000*
Percent

Year	Puerto Rico	United States
1970	1.73	1.46
1980	1.48	1.35
1990	1.47	1.55
2000	1.61	1.60

Source: Data from U.S. Department of Commerce (1974, 1983, 1994, 2003); Murphy and Welch (2001).

of college-educated workers in Puerto Rico.[53] By contrast, one of the reasons for the rising rate of return to education in the United States from 1980 to 2000 has been the slowdown in the rate of increase of schooling of the American population since 1950.[54]

On the demand side, the public sector is the largest single employer of college graduates in Puerto Rico. Forty-two percent of all employed workers on the island with more than a college degree (master's, doctorate, professional degrees) and 38 percent of all workers with a college degree were working for the government in 2000. Within the government sector alone, the wage premium for those with a college degree or more relative to those with only a high school diploma fell continuously throughout the thirty-year period. The ratio was equal to 1.95 in 1970, 1.63 in 1980, 1.54 in 1990, and 1.44 in 2000.

The wage premium for private sector employees also exhibited an overall downward trend from 1970 to 1990, dropping from 2.08 to 1.77. During the 1990s, however, it rose back to 1.97. This sharp increase in the wage premium for college-educated workers in the private sector presumably reflects the economic boom of that period. Census Bureau data show that from 1990 to 2000, the unemployment rate among men decreased from 19 percent to 13 percent and among women from 22 percent to 17 percent. This spike in the demand for private sector labor appears to have increased the demand for educated workers,

53. This effect could have been less significant if the substantial out-migration from the island since the 1950s had been associated with a brain drain. But various studies on this issue indicate that there has not been an overrepresentation of college graduates in the migrant outflows. See Ortiz (1986), Rivera-Batiz (1989), and Rivera-Batiz and Santiago (1996). Our analysis of Census Bureau data indicates that even in the 1990s, holding other things constant, the average schooling of out-migrants was slightly lower than that of the Puerto Rican population. For instance, in 1990 Puerto Ricans on the island aged twenty-five to thirty-four had 12.0 years of schooling. But those in this age cohort who out-migrated to the mainland between 1990 and 2000 had average schooling of 11.7 years. María Enchautegui (2005) has observed that the incentives to out-migration from Puerto Rico favor less skilled workers.

54. Katz (2004, p. 271).

resulting in the partial reversal of the declining returns to education in the 1990s. Whether there are also influences of technological change, industrial shifts in employment, or the impact of globalization on Puerto Rican labor markets is a matter for future research.

Education and Economic Growth

The impact of education on economic growth can occur through two mechanisms. First, education enters directly into production as an input. Workers with more education have greater knowledge and skills that contribute to the production process. Human capital, like physical capital, contributes to output growth as it is accumulated over time. Second, education influences total factor productivity growth or, more specifically, technological change. The endogenous growth models built by Robert Lucas and Paul Romer, for instance, identify human capital as a key determinant of technological change.[55] One expects that greater levels of human capital—and the attached knowledge and information base that comes with it—are a precondition for the innovation process to get started. As a result, some studies have postulated that the rate of technological change between two periods is dependent on the level of human capital existing in the initial period.[56] There might also be other, indirect mechanisms through which human capital can influence total factor productivity growth. For instance, higher levels of education are generally associated with improved public sector governance, and governance has been shown to be strongly connected to total factor productivity growth.[57]

In chapter 2 in this volume, Barry Bosworth and Susan Collins provide a growth-accounting methodology and decompose the sources of economic growth in Puerto Rico between 1950 and 2003. They find that in the 1950–75 period, Puerto Rico's accelerated annual growth in output per worker of 4.7 percent was explained mostly by increased physical capital per worker (55.3 percent) and somewhat by total factor productivity growth (29.8 percent). Human capital accumulation had a significant but smaller role, accounting for 14.9 percent of the growth. In the period 1975–2003, as both physical capital accumulation and total factor productivity growth slowed down, human capital became the dominant engine of growth in Puerto Rico. During this time, human capital accumulation accounted for 41.6 percent of the island's 1.2 percent annual growth in output per worker, exceeding the role of both increased physical capital per worker (33.3 percent) and total factor productivity growth (25.1 percent).

Bosworth and Collins examine the impact of increased education only through its role as a factor input in production. But both in theory and in empirical work,

55. Lucas (1993); Romer (1990).
56. See Krueger and Lindahl (2001) and Barro and Sala-i-Martin (2004).
57. Hall and Jones (1999); Rivera-Batiz (2002).

higher levels of education have been found to have an impact on total factor productivity growth. In the case of Puerto Rico, the relatively low levels of schooling back in the 1940s and 1950s would perhaps suggest a relatively minor effect of education on total factor productivity growth during those years. But by the 1960s and later, the accelerated increase in educational attainment on the island is likely to have had a positive impact on rates of innovation and total factor productivity growth.

In terms of Puerto Rico's prospects for growth, one can assume that the island's remarkable boom in educational attainment cannot be sustained for much longer and will slow down in the future. As a result, the contribution of human capital to Puerto Rican growth must come predominantly through its effects on total factor productivity growth. In this regard, quality of education becomes essential. Some recent evidence suggests that quality of schooling is indeed highly associated with total factor productivity growth.[58] For instance, in a cross-country study examining the relationship between scores in international student achievement tests and growth in income per capita, Eric Hanushek concludes that "a difference in test performance of one standard deviation was related to a one percent difference in the annual growth rate of per-capita Gross Domestic Product."[59]

It is precisely in this area that Puerto Rico's educational system is confronting serious challenges. As noted earlier, the available evidence from College Board test scores and elsewhere is that both the public and private school systems may be gradually deteriorating in quality. Unless policymakers deal seriously with raising the quality of schooling, or at least preventing further deterioration, the prospects for the contribution of education to growth are not good.

Improving quality is also crucial for other reasons. Given the large share of resources devoted to education, the island simply cannot afford to use them unproductively. Unproductive uses of those resources means taxes that are higher than necessary, which could, in turn, distort labor supply decisions and have an adverse effect on growth.

What Next? Policies for Education and Economic Development

Both in terms of gains in the educational attainment of its population and financial investments in education relative to the wealth of the island, Puerto Rico has an impressive record. The changes in educational attainment have undoubtedly made a significant contribution to Puerto Rico's recent economic development. Nonetheless, the island faces serious challenges at the present time.

Our analysis documents the presence of large disparities in educational outcomes, both between the public and private sectors and between public schools

58. Hanushek and Kimko (2000).
59. Hanushek (2002, p. 13).

in high- and low-income areas. Although the overall high school dropout rate on the island is close to 20 percent, rather than the much higher rates typically cited, the dropout rate in some poor neighborhoods is 50 percent or higher. The continuing presence of large numbers of students living in poverty with access only to low-quality schooling and experiencing high dropout rates not only is harmful to those students individually but also gives rise to social trauma and violence that spill over into all of Puerto Rican society.

Nor have the substantial waves of reform in the school system since 1990 done much to reduce inequities in the school system or to generate higher levels of student achievement. Because of a lack of accountability for performance throughout the system, smaller class sizes and more financial investments have not improved the quality of public schools enough to keep middle-class families within the public school system. Indeed, by disrupting the normal functioning of the public school system, the politicized reform process may well have contributed to the exodus of the more able students to the private sector, thereby increasing the challenges faced by the public school system and providing ongoing incentives for additional outflow.

The failure of the past fifteen years of reform poses a serious challenge for the island. The system is now facing the worst of both worlds: a large and politicized bureaucracy at the center and a failed program of decentralization of authority to the school level, with little or no accountability at either level. Any policy remedies for the island must be designed to reduce inequalities, raise overall student achievement and school quality, and make the public system more productive. Designing such policy remedies is difficult in any context. Any careful attempt to do so would require a much more detailed understanding, not only of the education system itself but also of the broader political and economic environment in which it operates, than we can contribute here. At the same time, we can bring to bear some of the international experience that may be relevant to the policy discussion. This experience relates most specifically to school-based management, accountability, instructional quality, and nonschool challenges.

School-Based Management

Decentralizing authority to the school level is not a policy idea unique to Puerto Rico. Many countries around the world, including England, Australia, New Zealand, and Chile, engaged in similar reforms at about the same time. Moreover, the World Bank has widely promoted school autonomy as a key reform for school effectiveness for many years: "If effective use is to be made of instructional inputs, institutions must be autonomous. . . . Fully autonomous educational institutions have authority to allocate their resources (not necessarily raise them), and they are able to create an educational environment adapted to local conditions inside and outside school."[60]

60. World Bank (1995), p. 126.

Nonetheless, evidence from various countries suggests that the World Bank may have been overly optimistic about the benefits of school autonomy. New Zealand is a particularly interesting example because of the magnitude of its change.[61] In contrast to Puerto Rico, New Zealand took great care in implementing its 1989 program of shifting operating authority away from its highly centralized national department of education to parent-dominated boards of trustees at the school level. In addition, the establishment of an independent review office provided an external mechanism for holding schools accountable both for national education goals and for school-specific goals articulated in school charters. On the positive side, most New Zealanders valued the new flexibility for schools, and ten years after the reforms it was difficult to find anyone who wanted to return to the centralized, bureaucratic system of the past. At the same time, despite the country's attention to implementation and the presence of the accountability system, emerging quite clearly from New Zealand's experience is the realization that the benefits of self-governance were far greater for the schools serving advantaged students than for those serving large proportions of poor students. School-based management not only failed to help the latter group of schools, in many situations it harmed them, largely because they lost various support systems to which they had had access under the previous system.

Further evidence that shifting authority to the school level is not a panacea emerges from the city of Chicago. In 1988 the parent-dominated councils of 550 local schools were given significant new authority to hire and fire school principals, to set school priorities, and to spend discretionary funds. Studies show that the effects of this program were mixed, at best. Although some schools performed better, some remained unchanged, and others' performance declined.[62] About half the schools apparently did not even take advantage of the new freedom to change their schools.[63] Similarly, other studies of school-based management in the United States and elsewhere show essentially no evidence of statistically significant increases in achievement, although some find evidence of higher student attendance.[64]

The lessons for Puerto Rico are mixed. Given its past efforts to decentralize authority to the school level, additional efforts to make the system work better are probably warranted. Island policymakers should be under no illusion, however, that decentralization of authority to schools will, by itself, generate higher achievement. Nor will it reduce educational disparities across schools. At the same time, to the extent that it brings more parents into the schools and gives the local community, rather than the far-off bureaucracy in Hato Rey, some control, it could in some instances lead to better-managed schools, particularly

61. Fiske and Ladd (2000).
62. Bryk and others (1998).
63. Sebring and others (1996).
64. Ladd and Hansen (1999, p. 186).

in those communities in which families are most likely to consider opting out of the public school system in favor of private schools. A crucial element to making the system work, however, is the provision of support services to those schools that need them and the recognition that some schools may need alternative forms of governance arrangements.

Accountability

Missing from Puerto Rico's efforts to decentralize authority to the school level was any formal system of accountability. Supporters of the concept of decentralizing authority to the school level often suggest that accountability administered from the top down is not needed once authority is turned over to school communities, on the ground that the communities themselves have strong incentives to hold teachers and schools accountable. Yet that argument does not withstand close scrutiny. One reason has to do with the distinction between the private interest and the public interest in education. Parents themselves clearly have a direct private interest in the quality of their own children's education. In addition, however, the public has a large stake, as is evident from the fact that schooling is deemed so important to children's life chances that attendance is compulsory and schools are publicly funded. With that public funding comes the responsibility to make sure that the public interest is being served. A second reason relates to the differential capacities of local school communities to monitor the activities of their schools and to hold schools accountable for the quality of education provided. For these reasons, countries such as New Zealand and England included as central components of their decentralization efforts school inspection systems, to ensure that the schools were meeting national standards, and, in the case of England, national tests that provide publicly available information on the performance of the students in each school.

Like the U.S. states, Puerto Rico is now subject to the test-based accountability provisions of the federal No Child Left Behind Act of 2001 (NCLB). This law requires that states, including Puerto Rico, test all students annually in grades three through eight. As noted earlier, student testing has already begun in several grades and is expected to be extended to all grades by 2010. In addition, NCLB requires all states to assess schools based on whether they have made "adequate yearly progress" toward the 2014 goal of having all students achieving at proficient levels as determined by each state. Districts, in this case the Puerto Rico Department of Education, must provide supplemental services to students in schools that do not meet their average yearly progress goals for two years in a row, and after three years of failure, students in such schools are allowed to transfer to other public schools, at the discretion of the parents.

Certain parts of this legislation should be helpful to Puerto Rico. The greater assessment and accountability measures associated with NCLB are likely to have a positive effect on the system, given the lack of any reliable accountability and student assessment tools in the past. The system has already introduced more-reliable test batteries, and it can build further on this effort by participating in the NAEP, the U.S.-wide testing benchmark. Doing so would allow the student achievement of Puerto Rican students to be compared with that of other children in the United States. Puerto Rico might also be well advised to become part of international assessment efforts, such as Trends in International Mathematics and Science Study (TIMMS) and the Program for International Student Assessment (PISA), which would allow its educational system to be compared with that of other countries.

In some ways, the NCLB-mandated reforms fit well with the island's past efforts to promote school autonomy. In particular, they provide greater incentives for schools to become agents of change. In fact, the NCLB may prove to be a catalytic influence on Puerto Rico's school system by forcing the centralized authorities to implement more effectively the school autonomy measures that were previously passed on paper but in reality have not yet been carried out across most of the system.

At the same time, NCLB could have some undesirable side effects. Unless the proficiency standards for Puerto Rico are set so low as to be meaningless, it is likely that large numbers of schools, particularly those serving the most disadvantaged students, will fail to meet their requirement of adequate yearly progress. Because the goal of 100 percent proficiency applies to all schools, the schools currently serving high proportions of low-performing students are required to make the greatest gains each year to meet the goal. Based on reasonable proficiency standards in the U.S. context, the required gains are likely to be far higher than any gains that have historically been attained.[65] A high rate of failure, in turn, will introduce a new element of mobility into the Puerto Rican system, as students in failing public schools are permitted to transfer to other, more successful public schools, and it also could well further discredit the public school system, leading to a greater movement of students to the private sector. Although some students will undoubtedly benefit from the new options available to them, the overall effect could well be to exacerbate further the problems faced by many schools serving concentrations of disadvantaged students.

School-based accountability systems need not lead to these unintended consequences. The challenge for Puerto Rico will be to do as much as it can to avoid the negative effects of the federal legislation while seizing the opportunity to develop a more reasonable and constructive accountability system. Central to that approach will be attention to value added measures of accountability—that is, measures that are based on gains in performance rather than on proficiency levels—so that schools are not viewed as failures simply because they serve large proportions of students who initially perform poorly. In addition, such an

65. Linn (2005).

accountability system, if it is to raise achievement, must include additional support and assistance for schools determined to be underperforming. North Carolina's relatively sophisticated school-based accountability system provides insight into the elements needed for an effective system.[66]

Chicago also has an accountability system that appears to have raised student achievement, albeit not by as much as simple comparisons of test scores over time might suggest.[67] The North Carolina system initially focused on holding schools accountable. In contrast, the Chicago accountability system, which was introduced in 1996 after the district's early efforts to decentralize authority to the school level failed to raise overall achievement, concentrated not only on schools but also on students. In particular, it required all students to pass high-stakes tests in grades three, six, and eight before they would be promoted to the next grade. Over the course of five years, 147 Chicago elementary schools were placed on probation, with the threat that they could be closed down and reconstituted if they did not improve.

The new high-stakes initiatives were accompanied by three specific efforts to improve student learning.[68] These included expanded instructional time in the form of mandatory summer school for students who failed the test in the spring and longer school days for all students, big investments in a highly scripted curriculum, and the provision of an external partner to provide additional services and professional development for teachers in the schools on probation. The reforms were implemented by a new leadership team under the direct control of the mayor and with strong powers, including the ability to limit the authority of the teachers' union, and additional funding to improve the system's physical plant and raise teacher salaries. One lesson for Puerto Rico from the Chicago experience is that within the context of a highly politicized education system, it takes strong leadership to impose an effective accountability system. A second, crucial, lesson is that an effective accountability system requires much more than the imposition of high-stakes testing and identification of low-performing schools.

Improving Instruction

Indeed, evidence from around the world indicates that changes in governance, including both the decentralization of authority to the school level and accountability systems administered from the top down, are unlikely to have much effect on student achievement in the absence of fundamental efforts to improve the quality of instruction in the classroom. The New Zealand experience illustrates that most clearly. Although schools serving disproportionate shares of disadvantaged students had not only significant autonomy to make their own decisions but also strong incentives to improve school quality so as to minimize the out-

66. Ladd (2004).
67. Bryk (2003); Jacob (2003).
68. Bryk (2003, p. 244).

flow of students to other schools, there was little they could do to remedy the situation. Part of the problem was the difficulty in attracting high-quality teachers; another part was limited knowledge about what works best for students from economically disadvantaged and immigrant families.[69] At first, New Zealand policymakers attributed the failures of such schools to poor leadership, but over time they have increasingly recognized the need to provide additional support to such schools that is more directly related to instructional needs.

Evidence from the United States increasingly highlights the importance to learning of high-quality teachers, and other studies provide support for the importance of teacher preparation and certification.[70] For Puerto Rico, ensuring that all students have access to good teachers would require higher standards for entry and graduation from teacher education programs;[71] improved programs of professional development; the fostering of a professional ethos among teachers that would, among other things, reduce rates of absenteeism among teachers; and new strategies for attracting high-quality teachers to the most impoverished schools.

Families, Communities, and Schools

Despite the significance of schools and school systems in determining student outcomes, a substantial literature in educational research suggests that socioeconomic background is often paramount.[72] Although the school system cannot be expected to cure all of society's ills, there are things that can be done through the education system to counter some of the adverse effects of poverty. Compared with children from more advantaged families, those from poor families typically come to school less ready to learn, tend to lose more knowledge during the summer months, and have more difficulty making the transition from school to work. In each of these areas, Puerto Rico could undoubtedly do more than it is now doing. For example, following the literature on the benefits derived from preschool and summer school programs,[73] the island could invest more heavily in preschool programs and summer school programs for low-income students. In addition, the Department of Education could do more than it has to date to implement school-to-work programs and to involve the private and service sectors in such programs.[74]

The neighborhoods in which children and youth live can also have a significant impact on their learning. The most proximate force connected to the inequities in education documented in earlier sections of this chapter is residen-

69. Fiske and Ladd (2000), chapter 9.
70. Hanushek, Kain, and Rivkin (1998); Sanders and Rivers (1996); Ferguson and Ladd (1996); Darling-Hammond and Post (2000); Ladd and Hansen (1999, pp. 168–79).
71. See Rivera-Batiz (1995b).
72. Coleman and others (1966); Hanushek (1997); most recently and cogently, Rothstein (2004).
73. See the review by Krueger (2004, pp. 24–33).
74. See Rivera-Batiz (2003).

tial segregation on the basis of income. The concentration of low-income families in *barriadas* (neighborhoods), *residenciales* (public housing projects), and slums in various parts of the island also leads to public schools with high concentrations of children from low-income families. These schools, as we have seen, tend to have lower average student achievement rates and higher dropout and school delay rates.

The lack of social capital, the economic dislocation, and the violent environment permeating some low-income communities can severely affect learning by disrupting the learning process as well as by diminishing educational expectations.[75] Similarly, a few peers—both in the local school and outside the school—can have significant negative impacts on the student achievement of many other students.[76] Tackling this problem will require the close monitoring of children by parents and communities. Substantial social and economic policies intended to benefit low-income families have been implemented over the years in Puerto Rico. Yet there has been no significant effort to integrate schools into the operations of these programs. Both geographically and institutionally, the two sets of programs rarely overlap. Such integration could potentially strengthen the bonds between schools and communities to beneficial effect.

Higher Education

Expenditures on public higher education per student in Puerto Rico are broadly equal to those in the United States. One suspects, however, that except in some specific areas they do not produce learning and achievement among its graduates comparable to those of the average American institution. The potentially low productivity of the system as measured by the relationship between academic outcomes and spending deserves further investigation. The extension of higher education opportunities over the past four and a half decades has made a significant contribution to Puerto Rico's economic growth, but increases in the quantity of education are subject to diminishing returns. A refocus on quality enhancements, in both public and private sectors, must be achieved if the tertiary education sector is to continue contributing to—instead of hindering—the island's growth prospects. Recently, some universities have been increasing their levels of research and development in the fields of science and technology, with the goal of promoting synergies with the substantial pharmaceutical, biotechnology, electronics, and other industries on the island. These efforts should continue, as they could contribute to Puerto Rico's prospects for growth.

The large subsidies that the public tertiary sector receives allow it to keep tuition and fees low, but they tend to disproportionately benefit the high-income families that send their children to the elite public colleges and universities.

75. Grogger (1997).
76. Hoxby (2000).

Thus public funding of public institutions ends up redistributing income in favor of rich families and worsens the distribution of income on the island. To reverse this perverse regime, a combination of policies should be implemented that encourage higher tuition and fees for those families that can afford them and provide scholarships for students who cannot. Implementing such reforms will be politically difficult, as is evident from the recent student general strike at the University of Puerto Rico in response to the administration's decision to raise tuition charges. To be successful, future efforts to raise tuition will need to be combined with additional financial aid.

Puerto Rico has joined the club of nations in the world with the highest proportion of college graduates in its population. But women far outnumber men in Puerto Rican colleges and universities. Although there are good economic reasons for women to invest more heavily in higher education than men, the sharply declining proportion of men attending tertiary education institutions should be a matter of concern. In the long term, the prospects of creating an underclass of Puerto Rican men whose lack of higher education prevents entry into mainstream labor markets may have profound social implications.

Conclusion

Puerto Rico can look back with pride at its miracle years in the area of educational development. However, today it stands at a crossroads. The high rate of growth in educational attainment can be expected to slow down considerably in the next few years. As this happens, the nation's prospects for growth from increases in the quantity of education are bound to decline sharply, and the island will have to rely on improvements in the quality of education. Enhancing quality is far more difficult than increasing quantity, however. Despite sharply rising funding for both K–12 and postsecondary education in recent years, quality has not improved. Moreover, almost fifteen years of governance reforms have not produced much in the way of positive results from the school system, and in the absence of other reforms additional governance reforms, particularly in the area of accountability, are likely to have, at best, small impacts. Instead, the focus must be on improving the academic environment and the quality of curriculum and instruction at the level of the classroom, in both K–12 and higher education. Unless the commonwealth makes a concerted effort on this front, the contributions of education to future economic growth are likely to be severely limited.

Alan B. Krueger

Helen Ladd and Francisco Rivera-Batiz have produced a chapter on the economic aspects of education in Puerto Rico that is as thorough as possible. It is well written and touches on all the right issues. I learned a lot from reading it. It also raises a lot of questions in my mind—as a good paper should. Indeed, the chapter provides a nice road map for future research projects.

As many of the other authors in this volume have noted, since 1960 Puerto Rico has seen one of the greatest expansions in educational attainment in the history of humankind. Average years of schooling for people aged twenty-five and older were 4.6 years in 1960, 6.9 years in 1970, 8.7 years in 1980, 9.9 years in 1990, and 11.0 years in 2000 (figure 5-1). Since the measure represents a stock, not a flow, this is a remarkable achievement. Moreover, given the low employment rates in Puerto Rico, especially among those with a low level of education, the social rate of return to education is likely to exceed the private return because an increase in education raises an individual's earnings capacity as well as the likelihood that he or she works. The increase in educational attainment—along with the museums that Will Baumol mentions in his comment on chapter 2—should be an important sales point for Puerto Rico's economic development.

Of course, the issue of the quality of education is also paramount, and improvement in school quality is most likely a key factor for future economic growth. Here I would counsel some caution about recent trends. There is a long history of claiming that education is failing and getting worse, regardless of the actual record. Consider the following sampling of evaluations of the state of public education on the mainland: In 1958 the historian Arthur Bestor opined, "Our standard for high school graduation has slipped badly. Fifty years ago a high-school diploma meant something. . . . We have simply misled our students and misled the nation by handing out high-school diplomas to those who we well know had none of the intellectual qualifications that a high-school diploma is supposed to represent—and does represent in other countries. It is this dilution of standards which has put us in our present serious plight." This view would have horrified the editors of the *New York Sun,* who in 1902 warned readers that school had become "a vaudeville show. The child must be kept amused and learns what he pleases." Going back even further, in 1845 Massachusetts's secretary of public education, Horace Mann, complained that students were not learning higher-order thinking skills, only memorizing "words of the textbook, without having . . . to think about the meaning of what they have learned."[1]

---

1. The quotations in this paragraph are drawn from Rothstein (1998), which contains the original sources.

If all these criticisms were correct, it is hard to imagine how the United States became and has remained a superpower. If nothing else, the frequent complaints about education in the past—when it was exclusive and reserved for the elite—should lead to some skepticism toward contemporary pronouncements of deteriorating educational quality. Perhaps opinion leaders have an idealized view of the past, when they were students.

Ladd and Rivera-Batiz conclude that the education system on the island is badly malfunctioning and that the quality of schooling has declined. They may be right, but I am not persuaded by the evidence that is available. In view of the paucity of such evidence, and the long history of false pronouncements about the demise of education, I recommend reserving judgment.

Evaluating changes in the quality of education in Puerto Rico is exceedingly difficult for three reasons. First, with a vast increase in school enrollment, the composition of the student body has changed. If, as appears to be the case, the expansion in education occurred mainly among students from disadvantaged backgrounds, then the average achievement of students might have fallen as average years of schooling rose. But this does not necessarily mean that the average *quality* of schooling for students who historically would have gone to school has fallen; the average observed quality might have fallen because weaker students were added to the enrollment pool.

An analogy may be instructive. Think about the effect of adding an expansion team to major league baseball—say, the Tampa Bay Devil Rays. The Devil Rays (with a 27-56 win-loss record as of this writing) were staffed with below-average players, as they had turned to the expansion draft, minor leagues, and other sources to fill their roster. With the addition of the below-average team, the average quality of major league baseball players fell. Yet no one would say that the quality of baseball training had gotten worse or that players were exerting less effort. Similarly, one should be cautious about concluding that the quality of schools in Puerto Rico declined at a time when enrollment was drastically expanding to include students from less-advantaged families.

Second, the dramatic flight to private schools documented by the authors suffers from a similar problem. The portion of Puerto Rican school children attending a private elementary or high school increased from 12 percent in 1980 to almost 25 percent in 2003 (table 5-1). This is a remarkable increase. In the United States, by contrast, the portion of students attending private school has stayed relatively stable, at around 10 percent, for decades. If private schools siphoned off the higher-achieving students from the public schools, then, again, the composition of the students in public schools would have changed, making it appear that the quality of education had fallen when in fact only the composition of raw materials that the schools are supplied to work with has changed.

Third, because of a dearth of time-series data on student performance on the island, the evidence on which Ladd and Rivera-Batiz must base their conclusions on school quality is necessarily sketchy. Basically, they have data on high school dropouts (rates that are not excessively high, though they are sometimes misinterpreted as being so), on achievement test scores in 2002–03 and 2003–04 (in grades 3, 6, 8, and 11), and scores from the College Board's Puerto Rican equivalent of the Scholastic Assessment Test since the mid-1980s.

Overall Puerto Rican College Board scores are essentially flat: from 1984–86 to 2002–03, verbal scores fell from 471 to 463, while quantitative scores rose from 484 to 489. But these scores are impossible to interpret because the percentage of students taking the exam surely increased. If more marginal students were added to the test-taking population, there is potentially a serious selection bias problem. Given the rapid rise in enrollment, maybe staying even is a sign of progress. (The trend in the achievement test scores is marred by a similar bias.)

I do agree with the authors that proficiency rates are low on the island's new standardized test. But how one interprets that fact depends entirely on how the test is scaled. In an influential article in *Education Week,* Ronald Skinner shows that state proficiency levels are almost arbitrary.[2] Mississippi and Colorado both claim that 87 percent of their fourth-graders are proficient in reading, based on their state tests in 2003. Yet only 18 percent of fourth-graders in Mississippi and 37 percent of those in Colorado scored at the level of proficiency on the 2003 NAEP exam. In light of this finding, how does one interpret Ladd and Rivera-Batiz's report of 58 percent reading proficiency (in Spanish) among Puerto Rican students in 2003–04? The test was designed by the Educational Testing Service—which also administers the NAEP—so perhaps that is a high level of proficiency. How the test aligns with other assessments, and where the line is drawn for proficiency, is a matter worth investigating.

The shortage of data on student performance is a stinging indictment of the Puerto Rican educational bureaucracy. I have a constructive suggestion, though. If Puerto Rico were to give the International Adult Literacy Survey, the data could be used to perform an analysis like that reported in figure 5-5. The data presented in this figure are "back-casted," in that people from different birth cohorts were given the literacy test at the same time, and mean scores were assigned based on their birth cohort. Although people's skills can obviously deteriorate or improve as they age, such effects should be more or less constant across countries.[3] It is clear from the figure that the United Kingdom and the United States saw rising scores and then appear to have peaked in the late 1940s, whereas Sweden (perhaps because of its efficient public sector) saw continued improvement. It would be instructive to add Puerto Rico to this type of graph.

---

2. Skinner (2005).

3. Because psychologists find that there is not much deterioration in mental capacity before the early sixties, the aging effects may not be important anyway. Moreover, longitudinal data could be used to adjust for aging effects, if this is a major concern.

Figure 5-5. *Adult Literacy, Selected Countries, Five-Year Moving Average, by Year of Birth, 1929–67*[a]

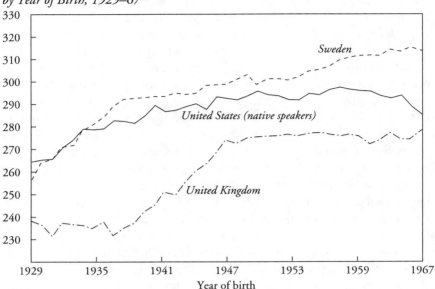

Year of birth

Source: Data from International Adult Literacy Survey, 1994 and 1996; authors' calculations.

a. Data are average scores on the prose component of the International Adult Literacy Survey. The scale is from 0 to 500.

Absent better data on cognitive tests, I would have a preference for looking at the monetary return to schooling. Here, the authors turn up little cause for alarm. The rate of return to schooling on the island was rock steady. (This contrasts with the Collins and Bosworth table 2-9, which shows a small rise in the payoff to schooling on the island, but the implication is the same.) This finding strikes me as remarkable for a couple of reasons. First, if the quality of education falls, one would expect the payoff to education to fall as well. Second, Puerto Rico witnessed an extremely fast rise in educational attainment, so the supply of skilled labor rose quickly; this supply shift would be expected to reduce wages for skilled workers. Yet the payoff to better-educated workers did not fall.[4] It is possible that an increase in relative demand for skilled workers occurring at the same time caused the relative price of skilled labor to remain constant. (That the return to education did not rise in Puerto Rico is consistent with the island's

4. By way of a reference point, note that only the Palestinians come close to Puerto Rico in terms of the rapid expansion of education in the 1980s (Angrist 1995), and the Palestinians saw a sharp decline in the payoff to education. Puerto Rico can be thankful that it avoided other problems experienced by the Palestinians.

having a less than fully open labor market with the mainland, which saw a dramatic rise in the return to education in the 1980s.) Another possibility is that the mainland's relatively generous safety net has provided a floor that prevented wages of the less educated from falling, as they did on the mainland.

Third, in table 5-17 the authors report the return to a year of schooling for Puerto Ricans living on the mainland, both for those born in Puerto Rico and for those born on the mainland. The return is lower for the Puerto Rican migrants, which is not unusual for migrants—but the percentage gap was no larger in 2000 than it was in 1980, and in fact it is a little smaller, 24 percent versus 19 percent.[5] (Of course, this is difficult to interpret if there was a change in selective migration.) To probe these results further, the authors could compare the payoff to education for Puerto Ricans educated on the island and for those educated on the mainland, when they are observed in the same local labor markets on the mainland—similar to what David Card and I did in our 1992 paper for the *Journal of Political Economy*.[6]

Although not dispositive, neither of these facts suggests that the quality of education on the island has deteriorated or strayed far from that on the mainland. Hence I would counsel caution in interpreting trends in the quality of education in Puerto Rico.

What is it that the authors are seeking to measure? Are they interested in how Puerto Rico's students would have performed absent the increase in educational attainment that occurred as compared with their actual performance, given the increase in educational attainment? Are they interested in Puerto Rico's performance relative to the rest of Latin America? Are they interested in Puerto Rico's performance compared with the mainland? It is not always clear which counterfactual the authors have, or should have, in mind.

These concerns notwithstanding, I agree with the authors that the next phase of Puerto Rico's educational policy will be much more difficult. I like to distinguish between the intensive and the extensive margins. The extensive margin is more years of education. The intensive margin refers to human capital attainment at a given number of years of education; that is, school quality. Because the extensive margin is approaching the college level, I would suspect that it is much harder to increase now than it has been in the past; this has been the mainland's experience since the extensive margin reached the college level in the 1970s. The situation may be better in Puerto Rico because college tuition costs are lower, owing to the prevalence of Pell grants, but I suspect that average years of education in Puerto Rico will increase more gradually in the future. As for the intensive mar-

5. One caveat to this conclusion, however, is that Puerto Rico has a particularly low employment rate, so one needs to be concerned that the estimated return to education does not represent the return for the whole population.

6. Card and Krueger (1992).

gin, most countries have found that raising the quality of human capital for a given year of schooling is much harder than raising educational attainment.

The authors' policy recommendations strike me as eminently sensible. I would suggest that they go somewhat further, however. For example, more could be done on teachers' incentives. Adam Smith wrote, "In modern times, the diligence of public teachers is more or less corrupted by the circumstances, which render them more or less independent of their success and reputation in their particular professions."[7] Ladd and Rivera-Batiz claim that Puerto Rican teachers average five weeks of absence, and apparently substitute teachers are not used to fill the void. If so, then students in Puerto Rico attend 14 percent fewer days of school (25/180) than students on the mainland—which might account for the lower payoff to a year of education on the island than on the mainland.

I am also not persuaded that more teacher aides would help in Puerto Rico. The U.S. experience has been that teacher aides are not particular effective.[8] If aides are used as substitute teachers, however, they may be able to bring about some improvement.

I conclude by highlighting some of the questions that, based on my reading of the chapter, should be a priority for future research:

—To what extent can the rapid rise in income in Puerto Rico over the past half century explain the rapid rise in educational spending? That is, can an Engle curve predict the increase in spending on education in Puerto Rico? One way to approach this question would be to use historical time-series evidence on the relationship between educational spending and income on the mainland to predict the growth in educational spending in Puerto Rico, based on Puerto Rico's income growth.

—Why has private school enrollment increased so much in Puerto Rico? Is this phenomenon an income effect? Is it a result of religious affiliation? Is it because the quality of public school instruction has declined? Is it because parents are seeking a different peer group for their children from that which is available in public schools?

—Why is the college graduation rate of Puerto Ricans on the island higher than that of Puerto Ricans on the mainland? What does this say about the quality of education on the island? What does this say about the nature of education and expectations on the mainland? How do second-generation Puerto Ricans fare on the mainland insofar as college education is concerned?

—Now that No Child Left Behind requires regular assessment, what are the trends in student achievement on the island? Will the standards used for assessment remain constant over time? Will standards and increased accountability improve Puerto Rican public schools?

7. Smith (1937, p. 733).
8. Krueger (1999).

COMMENT
Carlos E. Santiago

Helen Ladd and Francisco Rivera-Batiz take up possibly the most important issue facing the future of the Puerto Rican economy today—the contribution of education to economic development. The transition to a knowledge-based economy should be Puerto Rico's highest priority, given its basic character as an export-oriented open economy with limited natural resources. The chapter provides an excellent overview of topics relating education and economic development in Puerto Rico, and it does so from a sobering perspective.

Clearly, the conclusion that the dramatic gains made in schooling and educational attainment over the past forty years have not translated into a labor force that is prepared for today's economy deserves considerable discussion. The conversion of universal education to a highly trained labor force capable of meeting the needs of the emerging knowledge-based economy will continue to be a challenge for the island.

Why should educational quality matter more than widespread educational attainment in the Puerto Rican context? It is clear that the economy itself is requiring a more highly skilled labor force. Those individuals with basic capabilities in the sciences, mathematics, engineering, and technology are increasingly highly valued. This has become a real challenge for Puerto Rico, which in many respects has focused on universal educational attainment at all levels.

The expansion of private education in Puerto Rico, from K–12 to college and beyond, is a significant phenomenon. The growth of private education relative to public education recalls some of the debates going on in the United States, particularly in many urban centers. However, the issues of school choice and school vouchers have not made much headway in Puerto Rico. A long tradition of religion-based educational institutions and the expansion of other private institutions in Puerto Rico suggests that the private-public dichotomy does not play out in the same way as it does in the United States.

Another significant topic raised by Ladd and Rivera-Batiz is the intrahousehold changes in educational attainment by gender. The changes at the household level beg for additional analysis. The dramatic increase of women in higher education institutions has important implications for explaining changes in labor force participation, male-female expected wage differentials, and reliance on transfer payments, as well. Divorce rates in Puerto Rico, which have matched those of the United States since the early 1970s and are among the highest in Latin American and the Caribbean, are another possible factor in the gender imbalance in higher education.

Another question raised is whether public policy matters in educational reform in Puerto Rico. In particular, have the educational reforms of the 1990s been able to halt the decline in student quality? The authors argue that they have not, but it may be a bit too soon to tell. We have a sense of what it takes to enhance student quality, more generally—small classes, appropriate physical plant and infrastructure, neighborhood and parental involvement, decentralization, well-trained teachers, good administration, and accountability. Unfortunately, almost all these elements have to be in place if there is to be a real turnaround in educational quality. Again, these are issues that are hotly debated and contested in many parts of the United States, and some of those discussions should be applicable and instructive to the Puerto Rican context.

The authors also explore the issue of higher education financing in Puerto Rico. The Puerto Rican experience runs contrary to what has been happening at universities in the United States, particularly public universities over the past twenty years. That the Puerto Rican public higher education system—the University of Puerto Rico—is constitutionally mandated to receive a fixed percentage of island budget expenditures is a formula that, on the surface, many university administrators would love to have. In the United States, both tuition and fees have been rising and are now outpacing the growth of tax revenue support for public higher education.

The chapter suggests that general purpose revenues from the Puerto Rican government cover approximately 70 percent of operating expenses in public higher education. This figure contrasts sharply with the trend of public higher education financing in the United States, which continues to decline. For example, the share of operating expenses covered by tax support is between 20 and 25 percent for the University of Wisconsin and the State University of New York systems and less than 10 percent for the University of Colorado system; and institutions in Virginia, such as the University of Virginia, Virginia Tech, and William and Mary, are now lobbying hard with their legislature to try to achieve charter university status. The declines in funding for public higher education in the United States can be attributed to a number of factors, one of the most important being that mandated health care expenditures are crowding out spending on public higher education in state budgets.

A great deal of change is occurring in the landscape of public higher education financing in the United States, and some of those trends do not appear to be taking place on the island. This is not to suggest that public higher education is adequately funded in Puerto Rico; but certainly the transition to increased private funding that many U.S. public universities are experiencing does not seem to be taking place on the island.

The relevant question is this: Are universities in Puerto Rico serving as catalysts for economic development and growth? If not, why not? Research universities are increasingly stimulating economic development as they generate new technologies, drive innovation, and commercialize their research. Technology transfer programs and incubator sites have become mainstays of research universities in the current economic environment. More than ever before, institutions of higher education need to be stimulating entrepreneurship as well as training individuals in science, technology, engineering, and mathematics. These are now functions that are increasingly expected in light of the changing needs of the high-tech economy. Puerto Rico simply cannot afford to bypass this stage if it wants to compete effectively at the national and international level. We know that, within the U.S. context, the areas that are growing at the most rapid pace are those that are in some proximity to one or more major research universities that are fueling growth in today's economy.

Another area that needs greater attention is an assessment of the quality of the teaching corps on the island. This issue is not directly addressed in the chapter, but the need to professionalize the teaching corps at the K–12 level is receiving increasing attention in broader circles. This is clearly an expensive undertaking, but it is crucial to enhancement of teacher quality. The need to merge pedagogy and content is essential; the former needs to be addressed by schools of education, while the latter must emanate from schools of arts and sciences.

In reviewing the island experience with education and economic development, it is important to acknowledge and integrate into the analysis the growing numbers of Puerto Ricans who reside in the continental United States. The frequency of migration between the island and the mainland is considerable. Moreover, recent Current Population Survey data suggest that the size of the Puerto Rican population on the U.S. mainland is surpassing that of the island population. In and of itself, that may not be an important feature in the analysis, but the reality is that the Puerto Rican population is, to some extent, a commuter population traveling back and forth from island to mainland with increasing frequency. During the early stages of Puerto Rican industrialization, massive numbers of people moved from rural to urban areas and then migrated off the island. In just one decade, from 1950 to 1960, 25 percent of the labor force and more than 25 percent of the population left the island.[9] This fact certainly makes the Puerto Rican experience unique.

In evaluating the role of education in Puerto Rican economic development it is also important to take into account the relative stagnancy of the economy since the mid-1970s. To better understand the impact of education on the economy, one needs to move beyond a narrow focus on education and instead explore larger economic conditions. Some of the structural changes occurring in the mid-1970s in Puerto Rico culminated in long-term sluggish growth. The theme of significant positive change and yet substantial challenges runs through most of the chapters in this volume. Dramatic oil price increases in the early 1970s disrupted the island's petrochemical industry as oil tankers circumvented the island on their way to U.S. refineries. At the same time, major public policy

9. Rivera-Batiz and Santiago (1996, pp. 44–45).

shifts occurred on the island, including parity between commonwealth and federal minimum wages and the advent of significant expansion of transfer payments. In the mid-1970s New York City, which at the time was the primary mainland destination for Puerto Rican out-migrants, was in bankruptcy. This had a devastating effect on the Puerto Rican population in the United States: income levels plummeted, and Puerto Ricans moved from the United States to the island in large numbers. New York City's default has not been repeated, but among its deleterious effects was the claim that Puerto Ricans in the United States were not following the path of economic success as had other immigrant groups. This led some authors to claim that Puerto Ricans in the United States constituted a segment of the urban underclass.

This reality has changed dramatically over the past twenty years, and increasing educational attainment among Puerto Ricans in the United States has been the most important factor in rising incomes. Data from the 1990 and 2000 censuses show that growth in household per capita income among Puerto Ricans in the United States has surpassed that of the population at large. Educational attainment has been the key to this phenomenon, particularly increases in the numbers of Puerto Ricans holding two-year associate degrees.

Another comparative perspective can be taken from the experience of Ireland. Puerto Rico's push for economic development during the 1950s was of particular interest to the Irish. As an island economy, Ireland looked at Puerto Rico's promotion of foreign direct investment as a strategy that would lead to higher incomes and lower unemployment. Ireland also embarked on a development path that focused on foreign investment and export growth and was led by a development agency similar to that in Puerto Rico.

In the past twenty-five years, Ireland has joined the ranks of the highest-income countries in Europe, while the Puerto Rican economy remains sluggish, at best. The lesson for Puerto Rico lies in the massive investments that the Irish made in their educational system, particularly in higher education. Their focus on training in science, mathematics, and engineering has paid off dramatically, and the correlation between the growth in expenditures on education and the growth in GDP is remarkable.

Between 1995 and 2001, university spending in Ireland (from public and private sources) grew by 70 percent, the largest growth rate in Europe and one that far outpaced the U.S. rate (21 percent). Ireland's GDP rose 69.7 percent over that same period, again surpassing the rest of Europe and the United States (22.3 percent).[10] Ireland has been able to make a successful transition to the knowledge economy and now stands as a leader in crucial areas such as software development. It may be time for Puerto Rico to look at the recent Irish experi-

10. John Schmid, "Stealing Some Roar from the Celtic Tiger," *Milwaukee Journal Sentinel,* August 18, 2005 (www.jsonline.com/bym/news/aug05/349423.asp).

ence, just as the Irish once replicated the early strategies of Puerto Rico to grow their economy.

Finally, one of the underlying themes through this chapter, as well as some of the other contributions to this volume, is the notion that Puerto Rico's development experience has deviated from the norm and that the island currently stands at a crossroads in terms of immediate directions for the economy. Ladd and Rivera-Batiz convey a sense of urgency in addressing some of the issues discussed—a message that should be heeded.

References

Alexander, Karl L., Doris R. Entwisle, and Nader S. Kabbani. 2001. "The Dropout Process in Life Cycle Perspective: Early Risk Factors at Home and School." *Teachers College Record* 103, no. 5: 760–822.

Allison, Neil, and Arthur McEwan. 2003. "Students Dropping Out of Puerto Rico Public Schools: Measuring the Problem and Examining the Implications." Working Paper. Boston: University of Massachusetts.

American Federation of Teachers. 2004. *Annual Survey of Teacher Salaries: 2002–2003.* Washington.

Angrist, Joshua. 1995. "The Economic Returns to Schooling in the West Bank and Gaza Strip." *American Economic Review* 85, no. 5: 1065–87.

Barro, Robert J., and Xavier Sala-i-Martin. 2004. *Economic Growth.* 2nd ed. MIT Press.

Bosworth, Barry, and Susan Collins. 2003. "Growth Accounts Database." Excel file. Brookings.

Bryk, Anthony S. 2003. "No Child Left Behind: Chicago Style." In *No Child Left Behind? The Politics and Practice of School Accountability,* edited by Paul E. Peterson and Martin R. West, pp. 242–68. Brookings.

Bryk, Anthony S., and others. 1998. *Academic Productivity of Chicago Public Elementary Schools.* Chicago: Consortium on Chicago Schools Research.

Card, David. 1999. "The Causal Effect of Education on Earnings." In *Handbook of Labor Economics,* edited by Orley Ashenfelter and David Card, 3A:1801–63. Amsterdam: North Holland.

Card, David, and Alan Krueger. 1992. "Does School Quality Matter? Returns to Education and the Characteristics of Public Schools in the United States." *Journal of Political Economy* 100, no. 1: 1–40.

———. 1996. "Labor Market Effects of School Quality: Theory and Evidence." In *Does Money Matter? The Effect of School Resources on Student Achievement and Adult Success,* edited by Gary Burtless, pp. 97–140. Brookings.

Castillo Ortiz, Alicia. 2002. "Critical Analysis of Models, Approaches, and Strategies of School Supervision." *Cuadernos de Investigación en la Educación,* no. 17: 1–6.

Castillo Ortiz, Alicia, and Glory Marrero. 2003. "Study of Absenteeism among Teachers and Students in the Public Schools of Puerto Rico." San Juan: University of Puerto Rico, Graduate School of Education.

Coleman, James S., and others. 1966. *Equality of Educational Opportunity.* U.S. Government Printing Office.

Coleman, James S., Thomas Hoffer, and Sally Kilgore. 1982. *High School Achievement: Private and Public Schools Compared.* New York: Basic Books.

College Board. 1991. "Profile of the Students Tested by the University Assessment and Admissions Program (PEAU)." San Juan: College Board Office of Puerto Rico and Latin American Activities. Mimeograph.

———. 2005. "Profile of the Students Tested by the University Assessment and Admissions Program (PEAU)." San Juan: College Board Office of Puerto Rico and Latin American Activities. Mimeograph.

Commonwealth of Puerto Rico. 1975. *Economic Report to the Governor.* San Juan: Planning Board of Puerto Rico.

———. 1985. *Economic Report to the Governor.* San Juan: Planning Board of Puerto Rico.

———. 1990. *Organic Law of the Department of Education of Puerto Rico (Law Number 68).* San Juan.

———. 1992. *Budget of the Commonwealth of Puerto Rico.* San Juan: Office of Management and Budget of Puerto Rico.

———. 1994. *Budget of the Commonwealth of Puerto Rico*. San Juan: Office of Management and Budget of Puerto Rico.

———. 1996a. *Budget of the Commonwealth of Puerto Rico*. San Juan: Office of Management and Budget of Puerto Rico.

———. 1996b. *Economic Report to the Governor*. San Juan: Planning Board of Puerto Rico.

———. 1998. *Budget of the Commonwealth of Puerto Rico*. San Juan: Office of Management and Budget of Puerto Rico.

———. 2000. *Budget of the Commonwealth of Puerto Rico*. San Juan: Office of Management and Budget of Puerto Rico.

———. 2004a. *Budget of the Commonwealth of Puerto Rico*. San Juan: Office of Management and Budget of Puerto Rico.

———. 2004b. *Economic Report to the Governor*. San Juan: Planning Board of Puerto Rico.

Commonwealth of Puerto Rico, Council on Higher Education. 2004. "Higher Education Enrollment: Historical Statistics." San Juan (October).

Commonwealth of Puerto Rico, Department of Education. 1973. *Analysis of Budget Proposal*. San Juan.

———. 1983. *Analysis of Budget Proposal*. San Juan.

———. 1993. *Analysis of Budget Proposal*. San Juan.

———. 1996. *Analysis of Budget Proposal*. San Juan.

———. 2003a. "Puerto Rico State Report Card 2002–2003." San Juan: Commonwealth of Puerto Rico (September).

———. 2003b. "Report on Student Achievement of the Commonwealth's Public Schools." San Juan: Commonwealth of Puerto Rico (September).

———. 2003c. "Rethinking Our Department of Education: Transition Report." San Juan.

———. 2004a. *Analysis of Budget Proposal*. San Juan.

———. 2004b. "Preliminary Summary Statistics, Annual Yearly Progress." San Juan: Commonwealth of Puerto Rico (October).

———. 2004c. "Rethinking Our Department of Education: Proposed Model." San Juan.

———. 2005. "Summary of Statistics of Annual Yearly Progress." San Juan (January).

Commonwealth of Puerto Rico, General Council of Education. 2004. "School Enrollment in Puerto Rico, 2003–2004." San Juan: Department of Education.

Darling-Hammond, Linda, and Laura Post. 2000. "Inequality in Teaching and Schooling: Supporting High-Quality Teaching and Leadership in Low-Income Schools." In *A Notion at Risk: Preserving Public Education as an Engine for Social Mobility*, edited by Richard Kahlenberg, pp. 127–67. New York: The Century Foundation Press.

Dietz, James L. 1986. *Economic History of Puerto Rico: Institutional Change and Capitalist Development*. Princeton University Press.

Enchautegui, María E. 2005. "Selectivity Patterns in Puerto Rican Migration." Paper presented to the annual meetings of the Population Association of America. Philadelphia: March 31–April 2.

Ferguson, Ronald, and Helen F. Ladd. 1996. "How and Why Money Matters: An Analysis of Alabama Schools." In *Holding Schools Accountable: Performance-Based Reform in Education*, edited by Helen F. Ladd, pp. 265–98. Brookings.

Fiske, Edward B., and Helen F. Ladd. 2000. *When Schools Compete: A Cautionary Tale*. Brookings.

Gómez Tejera, Carmen, and David Cruz López. 1970. *The Puerto Rican School*. Sharon, Conn.: Troutman.

Gonzalez, Patrick, and others. 2004. *Highlights from the Trends in International Mathematics and Science Study (TIMSS)*. U.S. Department of Education.

Grogger, Jeff. 1997. "Local Violence and Educational Attainment." *Journal of Human Resources* 32, no. 4: 659–82.

Hall, Robert E., and Charles I. Jones. 1999. "Why Do Some Countries Produce So Much More Output per Worker than Others?" *Quarterly Journal of Economics* 114, no. 1: 83–116.

Hansen, W. Lee, and Burton Weisbrod. 1969. "The Distribution of Costs and Direct Benefits of Public Higher Education: The Case of California." *Journal of Human Resources* 4, no. 2: 176–91.

Hanson, Mark. 1995. "Democratization and Decentralization in Colombian Education." *Comparative Education Review* 34, no. 1: 101–19.

Hanushek, Eric A. 1997. "Assessing the Effects of School Resources on Student Performance: An Update." *Educational Evaluation and Policy Analysis* 19, no. 2: 141–64.

———. 2002. "The Seeds of Growth: The Long-Run Importance of School Quality." *Education Next* 2, no. 3: 10–17.

Hanushek, Eric A., John Kain, and Stephen Rivkin. 1998. "Teachers, Schools, and Academic Achievement." Working Paper 6691. Cambridge, Mass.: National Bureau of Economic Research.

Hanushek, Eric A., and Dennis A. Kimko. 2000. "Schooling, Labor-Force Quality, and the Growth of Nations." *American Economic Review* 90, no. 5: 1184–1208.

Hauser, Robert M. 2004. "Progress in Schooling." In *Social Inequality,* edited by Kathryn M. Neckerman, pp. 271–335. New York: Russell Sage Foundation.

Holmes, C. Thomas. 1989. "Grade Level Retention Effects: A Meta-Analysis of Research Studies." In *Flunking Grades: Research and Policies on Retention,* edited by Lorrie Shephard and Mary Smith, pp. 16–33. London: Falmer Press.

Hoxby, Caroline. 2000. "Peer Effects in the Classroom: Learning from Race and Gender Variation." Working Paper 7867. Cambridge, Mass.: National Bureau of Economic Research.

Jacob, Brian A. 2003. "A Closer Look at Achievement Gains under High-Stakes Testing in Chicago." In *No Child Left Behind? The Politics and Practice of School Accountability,* edited by Paul E. Peterson and Martin R. West, pp. 269–91. Brookings.

Katz, Eliakim, and Oded Stark. 1987. "International Migration under Asymmetric Information." *Economic Journal* 97, no. 3: 718–26.

Katz, Lawrence F. 2004. "Comments on Inequality in America." In *Inequality in America: What Role for Human Capital Policies?* edited by Benjamin Friedman, pp. 269–79. MIT Press.

Katz, Lawrence F., and David H. Autor. 1999. "Changes in the Wage Structure and Earnings Inequality." In *Handbook of Labor Economics,* edited by Orley Ashenfelter and David Card, 3A:1463–1555. Amsterdam: North Holland.

Krueger, Alan. 1999. "Experimental Estimates of Education Production Functions." *Quarterly Journal of Economics* 114, no. 2: 497–532.

———. 2004. "Inequality in America: Too Much of a Good Thing." In *Inequality in America: What Role for Human Capital Policies?* edited by Benjamin Friedman, pp. 1–75. MIT Press.

Krueger, Alan B., and Mikael Lindahl. 2001. "Education for Growth: Why and for Whom?" *Journal of Economic Literature* 39, no. 4: 1101–36.

Ladd, Helen F. 2004. "Policy Brief on Accountability." In *Education Finance and Organizational Structure in New York State Schools: Symposium Proceedings,* edited by David H. Monk and James Wyckoff, pp. 151–76. Albany, N.Y.: Education Finance Research Consortium.

Ladd, Helen F., and Janet Hansen, eds. 1999. *Making Money Matter: Financing America's Schools.* Washington: National Academy Press

Linn, Robert. 2006 (forthcoming). "Scientific Evidence in Educational Policy and Practice: Implications for Adequate Yearly Progress." In *Measurement and Research in the Accountability Era,* edited by Carol Ann Dwyer, pp. 28–52. Mahwah, N.J.: Lawrence Erlbaum.

Lopez Yustos, Alfonso. 1992. *A Documentary History of Education in Puerto Rico.* San Juan: Publicaciones Puertorriqueñas.

Lucas, Robert E. 1993. "Making a Miracle." *Econometrica* 61, no. 2: 251–72.

Marco, Gary L. 2004a. "Future Research Related to the Score Declines in Puerto Rico College Admissions Test Scores." Research report. San Juan: College Board, Office of Puerto Rico and Latin America.

———. 2004b. "Test and Item Statistics and Their Relationship to Puerto Rico Admissions Test Scores." Research report. San Juan: College Board, Office of Puerto Rico and Latin America.

Martí-Vazquez, Lillian. 2000. "The Impact of Decentralization and School-Based Management in Puerto Rico: A Case Study." Ph.D. dissertation, Teachers College, Columbia University.

Martínez, Marialba. 2002. "UPR Invests $26.3 Million in Three Biotechnology Centers: Research Aimed to Benefit Puerto Rico's Pharmaceutical Industry." *Caribbean Business,* March 21, p. 1.

Murphy, Kevin, and Finis Welch. 2001. "Wage Differentials in the 1990s: Is the Glass Half-Full or Half-Empty?" In *The Causes and Consequences of Increasing Inequality,* edited by Finis Welch, pp. 341–64. University of Chicago Press.

National Assessment of Educational Progress (NAEP). 2000. *Trends in Academic Progress: Three Decades of Student Performance.* U.S. Department of Education.

———. 2004. *The Nation's Report Card: Mathematics 2003.* U.S. Department of Education, Institute of Education Sciences.

National Center for Education Statistics (NCES). 2003. *Digest of Education Statistics 2002.* U.S. Department of Education.

———. 2004a. *Digest of Education Statistics 2003.* U.S. Department of Education (October).

———. 2004b. *National Public School Database, School Year 2002–2003.* U.S. Department of Education.

———. 2004c. *Revenues and Expenditures for Public Elementary and Secondary Education, School Year 2001–2002.* U.S. Department of Education (June).

Nelson, F. Howard, Rachel Drown, and Jewell C. Gould. 2001. *Survey and Analysis of Teacher Salary Trends 2000.* Washington: American Federation of Teachers.

Organization for Economic Cooperation and Development (OECD). 2003. *Financing Education: Investments and Returns, An Analysis of World Education Indicators.* Paris: UNESCO Institute for Statistics.

———. 2004. *Learning for Tomorrow's World: First Results from PISA 2003.* Paris.

Ortíz, Vilma. 1986. "Changes in the Characteristics of Puerto Rican Migrants from 1955 to 1980." *International Migration Review* 20, no. 3: 612–28.

Osuna, Juan José. 1923. *Education in Porto Rico.* Teachers College Press.

Patrinos, Harry, and George Psacharopoulos. 2004. "Returns to Investment in Education: A Further Update." *Education Economics* 12, no. 2: 111–34.

Pavcnik, Nina. 2003. "What Explains Skill Upgrading in Less Developed Countries?" *Journal of Development Economics* 71, no. 2: 311–28.

Psacharopoulos, George. 1994. "Returns to Investment in Education: A Global Update." *World Development* 22, no. 9: 1325–43.

Quintero, Ana Helvia. 2006. *Many Reforms, Few Changes.* San Juan: Publicaciones Puertorriqueñas Editores.

Rivera-Batiz, Francisco L. 1989. "The Characteristics of Recent Puerto Rican Migrants." *Migration World* 17, no. 2: 7–13.

———. 1993. *Study of the Budget of the Department of Education of Puerto Rico.* San Juan: General Council of Education.

———. 1995a. *Financing Public Education in Puerto Rico.* San Juan: General Council of Education.

———, ed. 1995b. *Shifting Gears: Teacher Preparation and Education Reform in Puerto Rico.* San Juan: General Council of Education.

———. 2002. "Democracy, Governance, and Economic Growth: Theory and Evidence." *Review of Development Economics* 6, no. 2: 225–47.

———. 2003. "The Impact of School-to-Work Programs on Minority Youth." In *The School-to-Work Movement: Origins and Destinations,* edited by William J. Stull and Nicholas M. Sanders, pp. 169–88. Westport, Conn.: Praeger.

Rivera-Batiz, Francisco L., and Carlos E. Santiago. 1996. *Island Paradox: Puerto Rico in the 1990s.* New York: Russell Sage Foundation.

Rodríguez Bou, Ismael. 1947. *Education Problems in Puerto Rico.* San Juan: University of Puerto Rico.

Romer, Paul M. 1990. "Endogenous Technological Change." *Journal of Political Economy* 98, no. 5, pt. 2: S71–S102.

Rothstein, Richard. 1998. *The Way We Were? The Myths and Realities of America's Student Achievement.* New York: The Century Foundation–Twentieth Century Fund Report.

———. 2004. *Class and Schools: Using Social, Economic, and Educational Reform to Close the Black-White Achievement Gap.* Washington: Economic Policy Institute.

Sanders, William L., and June C. Rivers. 1996. "Cumulative and Residual Effects of Teachers on Future Student Academic Achievement." Value-Added Research and Assessment Center, University of Tennessee, Knoxville.

Sebring, Penny B., and others. 1996. *Charting Reform in Chicago: The Students Speak.* Chicago: Consortium on Chicago Schools Research.

Skinner, Ronald A. 2005. "State of the States." *Education Week* 24, no. 17: 77–80.

Smith, Adam. 1937. *An Inquiry into the Nature and Causes of the Wealth of Nations.* New York: Random House, Modern Library edition. (Orig. published 1776.)

Task Force on Higher Education and Society. 2002. *Higher Education in Developing Countries: Peril and Promise.* Washington: World Bank.

United Nations Educational, Scientific, and Cultural Organization (UNESCO). 2003. *Global Education Digest.* Montreal: UNESCO Institute for Statistics.

U.S. Department of Commerce. 1974. *1970 U.S. Census of Population and Housing, Public Use Microdata Samples for Puerto Rico.* U.S. Bureau of the Census.

———. 1983. *1980 U.S. Census of Population and Housing, 5% Public Use Microdata Samples.* U.S. Bureau of the Census.

———. 1994. *1990 U.S. Census of Population and Housing, 5% Public Use Microdata Samples.* U.S. Bureau of the Census.

———. 2003. *2000 U.S. Census of Population and Housing, 5% Public Use Microdata Samples.* U.S. Bureau of the Census.

———. 2004. *Statistical Abstract of the United States.* U.S. Government Printing Office.

University of Puerto Rico at Río Piedras. 2005. *Self-Study Report to the Middle States Commission on Higher Education.*

Vázquez-Calzada, José L. 1988. *La población de Puerto Rico y su trayectoría histórica.* Río Piedras: Raga.

World Bank. 1995. *Priorities and Strategies for Education.* Washington.

———. 2004. *World Development Indicators.* Washington.

6

The Climate for Business Development and Employment Growth

STEVEN J. DAVIS AND LUIS A. RIVERA-BATIZ

The employment rate among Puerto Rican residents is stunningly low, and it has been so for decades. Household census data for 1980, 1990, and 2000 yield employment rates in the neighborhood of 40 percent for persons sixteen to sixty-five years of age. Comparable data for the United States yield employment rates in the range of 65–70 percent. The Organization for Economic Cooperation and Development reports an average employment rate of 66 percent for member countries in 2000; Turkey, at 49 percent, is the only OECD member with an employment rate below 54 percent.[1] These comparisons underscore the puzzle presented by Puerto Rico's persistently low employment rate.

I and the other participants of this project were deeply saddened by the untimely death of my coauthor, Luis Rivera-Batiz, during the final stages of this volume's production.

We thank Marinés Aponte, David Audretsch, Barry Bosworth, Susan Collins, colleagues at the University of Chicago, and participants in the Center for the New Economy–Brookings conference for many helpful comments. We also greatly appreciate the many persons who cooperated in interviews, often lengthy, about the Puerto Rican business climate. Barry Bosworth and Orlando Sotomayor kindly supplied data, Sophie Castro-Davis and Christopher Pope provided research assistance, Juan Castañer clarified aspects of the methodology in Estudios Técnicos (2004), and Ricardo Solá supplied figure 6-4.

1. OECD (2004, statistical appendix, table B). The statistics for Puerto Rico and the United States reflect our tabulations of household census data. It is worth remarking that the OECD figure for the 2000 U.S. employment rate is 5 percentage points higher than our census-based figure, implying that the two data sources are not fully compatible. There are also concerns about the accuracy of the Puerto Rican household census data. However, there is little doubt regarding the central point that Puerto Rico has a remarkably low rate of employment.

This chapter investigates the employment record in Puerto Rico and its climate for business development. Our goals are

—to shed new light on the reasons for Puerto Rico's low employment rate by taking a close look at its employment structure,

—to highlight some longer-term consequences of Puerto Rico's business climate and chronically weak employment performance, and

—to identify government policies and institutional arrangements that impede employment growth and business development.

In terms of our third goal, we pay close attention to the permitting process whereby the government oversees and regulates construction and real estate development projects, the commercial use of equipment and facilities, and the periodic renewal of various business licenses. Several factors contribute to Puerto Rico's poor employment performance, but there are good reasons to suspect that the permitting process is one important obstacle to business development and employment growth. Anecdotal evidence suggests that the permitting process is excessively slow and costly, fraught with uncertainty, subject to capricious outcomes, susceptible to corruption, and prone to manipulation by business rivals, politicians, and special interest groups. Problems and inefficiencies in the permitting process raise the costs of creating new business establishments, undercutting the drive for employment growth. Sizable fixed costs in learning how to navigate the system fall more heavily on smaller and younger businesses and on would-be entrepreneurs who lack political connections. For these reasons, the permitting process is also likely to repress the emergence of a productive entrepreneurial culture—or drive it into the underground sector.

The permitting process is one aspect of an obtrusive and often counterproductive role for government in Puerto Rico's economy. There are many others. Section 936 provisions in the U.S. tax code distorted Puerto Rico's industry structure at great cost to the U.S. Treasury with modest benefits for Puerto Rican residents.[2] Puerto Rico's own tax code is replete with provisions that benefit special business interests at the expense of the general welfare. Various "buy local" laws and tax provisions lessen competitive pressures on local business interests by disfavoring foreign producers. Regulatory entry barriers abound. The Jones Act raises the cost of international trade by requiring the use of American vessels for goods shipped by water between U.S. and Puerto Rican ports. Puerto Rican employers are subject to U.S. minimum wage requirements, even though the average Puerto Rican wage is roughly half the average U.S. wage. Government transfer payments account for more than a quarter of Puerto Rican household incomes in recent decades (chapter 3, this volume). And the Puerto Rican government has traditionally accounted for a large share of employment and production activity on the island, much larger than in the United States.

2. Pelzman (2002); Hunter (2003); chapter 2 in this volume.

A truly striking feature of Puerto Rico's economy is the underdeveloped state of its private sector. Private sector employment rates in Puerto Rico are less than half the U.S. rates in recent decades. Even fewer Puerto Rican residents have firsthand experience, as owners or employees, in "free enterprise" organizations: private businesses that operate in the formal economy without large government subsidies, special tax breaks and regulatory advantages, or heavy-handed oversight by government bureaucracies.

These observations about Puerto Rico's economy point to some key challenges and concerns. First, chronically low employment rates imply that Puerto Rican residents are short on work experience, opportunities for learning on the job, and marketable skills.[3] Second, the management skills and business savvy required for a thriving entrepreneurial class are likely to be in especially short supply. Relatively few Puerto Ricans work in the private sector, and business persons have learned to focus their creative energies on how to curry favor with government officials and circumvent bureaucratic obstacles to commercial success rather than on how to develop and execute business models that can withstand the rigors of competition in an unfettered marketplace. Even if reform creates an institutional framework that is advantageous for productive entrepreneurial activity and long-term growth, it will be difficult to rapidly upgrade business skills and reorient a rent-seeking business culture. Third, most Puerto Ricans have a strong financial stake in maintaining certain aspects of an expansive public sector—as salaried government employees, as recipients of transfer payments and public sector pensions, or as beneficiaries of government contract awards, subsidies, tax breaks, and special regulatory advantages. This web of vested interests in a highly socialized economy presents a formidable barrier to effective economic reform.

A Comparative Perspective on Employment in Puerto Rico

There is an enormous gap of 20–30 percentage points between employment rates in Puerto Rico and the United States in recent decades (table 6-1, figure 6-1).[4] Puerto Rico's employment situation was much stronger at the midpoint of the twentieth century, with an employment shortfall relative to the United States of

3. The importance of work experience and on-the-job training for skill formation and earnings growth are recurring themes in modern labor economics. See Mincer (1962) and Becker (1993, chap. 2) for seminal contributions.

4. Barry Bosworth and Susan Collins, in chapter 2 of this volume, raise questions about the reliability of the Puerto Rican household census, especially the 2000 census. Based on comparisons to the labor force survey and payroll records, Bosworth and Collins conclude that the 2000 census seriously understates the participation rate (and presumably the employment rate). Their table 2-6 shows that the participation rate in the 2000 census is about 6 percentage points below the rate in the labor force survey. The accuracy of the Puerto Rican labor force survey has also been called into question (see Rivera-Batiz and Santiago [1996]). In any event, all sources show a huge U.S.–Puerto Rican gap in employment rates. We rely heavily on the household census for our study because several of our empirical exercises require large samples of individual workers.

Table 6-1. *Employment Rate, Puerto Rico and the United States, by Schooling, 1980, 1990, 2000*[a]

Percent

Schooling and year	Overall economy		Private sector		Free enterprise		Public sector	
	United States	Puerto Rico	United States	Puerto Rico	United States	Puerto Rico	United States	Puerto Rico
All levels								
1980	65.2	38.5	53.0	25.3	46.9	21.8	12.2	13.2
1990	70.0	42.3	58.4	29.1	51.1	24.9	11.6	13.2
2000	68.8	37.5	58.2	28.2	51.0	24.0	10.6	9.3
More than fourteen years								
1980	78.8	66.1	56.8	33.8	49.6	28.7	21.9	32.3
1990	84.5	70.6	64.0	39.6	55.4	33.3	20.5	31.0
2000	82.5	61.6	63.9	40.7	56.8	35.9	18.6	20.9
More than sixteen years								
1980	83.4	76.8	55.5	34.1	47.9	27.5	27.9	42.6
1990	85.5	75.2	62.7	39.8	53.6	32.6	22.8	35.4
2000	83.3	65.5	63.1	41.3	55.7	35.5	20.2	24.2

Source: Data from household census for 1980, 1990, and 2000; authors' calculations.

a. The data are for persons aged sixteen to sixty-five. The public sector includes all employees of federal and subfederal governments. The private sector encompasses the rest of the economy. The free enterprise segment of the private sector excludes nongovernmental employees in public utilities and sanitary services, primary and secondary education, colleges and universities, construction and several small industries for which public sector employment exceeds 35 percent of industry employment in Puerto Rico. For 1990 these industries are museums, galleries, and zoos; business, trade, and vocational schools; bus service and urban transit; research, development, and testing; social services; forestry; libraries. For 1980 the excluded industries are nearly identical. For 2000 the set is slightly narrower. Unpaid family workers are not counted among the employed.

less than 7 percentage points. U.S. employment rates drifted upward over the next five decades, but they fell sharply in Puerto Rico—by 7 percentage points in the 1950s and by another 10 percentage points from 1973 to 1982—before recovering some lost ground. The U.S.–Puerto Rican employment gap widened greatly for both sexes after the early 1950s, from 5 to 25 percentage points among women and from 10 to 20 percentage points among men.

These data indicate that, since 1975, Puerto Rican residents have been accumulating work experience at only 55–65 percent of the rate in the United States. This huge experience deficit is a negative legacy of Puerto Rico's chronically weak employment performance, and it cannot be erased overnight.[5] It will depress the earnings potential of Puerto Ricans for years to come. By the same

5. A careful effort to quantify the experience deficit among Puerto Rican residents would account for work experience accumulated on the mainland by return migrants and any U.S.–Puerto Rican difference in average hours worked by employed persons. We address the latter issue shortly.

Figure 6-1. *Employment Rate among Workers Sixteen Years and Older, Puerto Rico and the United States, 1947–2001*

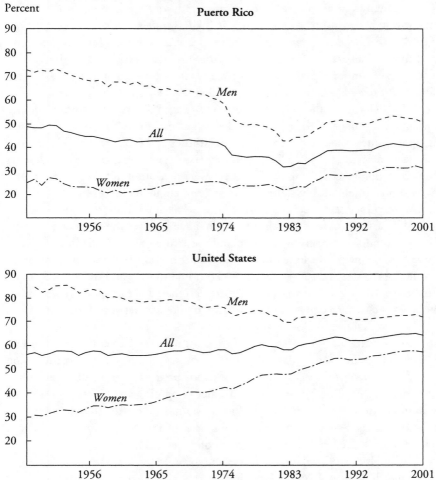

Source: Data supplied by Orlando Sotomayor and derived from Puerto Rico Department of Labor, Bureau of Statistics (1978, 2003).

token, strong and sustained increases in the employment-to-population ratio are essential for long-term development of Puerto Rico's human capital.

Private, Public, and Free Enterprise Employment Rates

The U.S.–Puerto Rican gap in private sector employment rates is even more extreme than the gap for overall employment. According to census data, only 28 percent of Puerto Rican adults worked in the private sector in 2000, less than half the 58 percent figure for the mainland. A similar pattern prevails in 1980 and 1990. These private sector employment figures overstate firsthand exposure to employment in the unfettered free enterprise segment of the formal economy. Indeed, many Puerto Ricans with private sector jobs work in industries with a major role for government employment (like hospitals and schools), industries that owe their Puerto Rican operations to special tax subsidies (pharmaceuticals), and industries that face costly bureaucratic obstacles to business activity (construction). Similar remarks apply to many private sector jobs in the United States, but the government's role is typically more extensive on the island.

Table 6-1 reports the percentage of Puerto Rican adults who work in the free enterprise segment of the economy, defined as private sector employment less nongovernmental employment in public utilities and sanitary services, primary and secondary education, colleges and universities, and several smaller industries for which public sector employment exceeds 35 percent of industry employment. We do not systematically subtract nongovernmental employees in all industries for which public sector employment exceeds a specified threshold, although that would be a reasonable approach. A separate issue involves the manner of achieving consistency between Puerto Rico and the United States in defining the free enterprise segment. We opted for a uniform list of industries that are designated as outside the free enterprise segment in both Puerto Rico and the United States. An alternative approach would allow the designated list of industries to differ between the two, recognizing industry-level differences between Puerto Rico and the United States in public sector employment shares and the extent of government involvement. We exclude construction from the free enterprise segment because of the major role played by the government bureaucracy in construction and development projects. We do not exclude pharmaceuticals or other industries that receive large government subsidies or special tax breaks, although the Puerto Rican operations of such industries do not reflect unfettered free enterprise outcomes. Based on our classification, less than one-quarter of Puerto Rican adults work in the free enterprise segment of the economy.[6]

Low levels of work experience in free enterprise activity are potentially important for at least three reasons. First, jobs in the free enterprise segment probably require somewhat different skills and work habits than jobs in the public and regulated sectors. This view resonates with evidence that experience-related human capital is imperfectly portable across industries and evidence that many displaced workers suffer large, persistent earnings losses.[7] Thus the skills and earnings potential acquired through work experience in the public and regulated sectors may not easily transfer to jobs in the free enterprise segment.

6. Excluding pharmaceuticals, the proportion of Puerto Rican adults working in the free enterprise segment of the economy was 21.0 percent in 1980, 23.7 percent in 1990, and 22.9 percent in 2000.

7. On portability, see Neal (1995) and Parent (2000). On displaced workers, see, for example, Jacobson, LaLonde, and Sullivan (1993).

Second, private sector work experience is a more powerful incubator of entrepreneurial skills and ambitions than jobs in the public and regulated sectors. This proposition finds support in research on the propensity to become a business owner and the determinants of business success. Studies consistently find that self-employment and business ownership rates are much higher among children of business owners.[8] According to U.S. data, half of all business owners had a self-employed family member before starting a business; moreover "the business human capital acquired from prior work experience in a family member's business appears to be very important for business success."[9] This study finds that less than 2 percent of small U.S. businesses are inherited, consistent with the view that business experience rather than business transfer explains the strong intergenerational link in business ownership propensities.

Third, the nature of work experience—one's own and that of friends and family—probably plays an important role in shaping attitudes toward business regulation, taxation, public sector employment, and income redistribution. In countries with higher social welfare spending, for example, there is a greater belief in the propositions that "poverty is society's fault" and "luck determines income."[10] And in countries with a history of socialized production there is stronger support for the view that "it is the responsibility of the government to reduce income differences."[11] These cross-country patterns suggest that limited work experience in free enterprise activity leads to limited political support for economic reforms that would aggressively promote private business activity and employment.

Despite Puerto Rico's huge shortfall in overall employment rates, the percentage of adults who work in the public sector was actually larger on the island than on the mainland in 1980 and 1990. For example, 13.2 percent of adult Puerto Ricans worked in the public sector in 1990, compared with 11.6 percent of U.S. adults (table 6-1). The situation reversed over the next decade as public sector employment rates in Puerto Rico fell sharply to 9.3 percent of the adult population in 2000. Part, perhaps a large part, of the decline in Puerto Rico's public sector employment rates reflects the privatization of state-owned enterprises.[12] The partial privatization of telecommunications in the 1990s faced strong labor union resistance and included a long strike and widespread sabotage. It would be useful to know how wages and employment fared in privatized

8. See Dunn and Holtz-Eakin (2000); Hout and Rosen (2000); Fairlie and Robb (2003).

9. Fairlie and Robb (2003, abstract). "Family member" means a spouse, parent or guardian, sibling, or other immediate family member.

10. Alesina and Glaeser (2004, chap. 7).

11. Corneo and Gruener (2002, table 1).

12. We have been unable to obtain the data required to quantify the role of privatizations in the decline of public sector employment. However, we have been informed that privatized enterprises routinely hired former government employees, often as a requirement to secure government contracts.

Puerto Rican firms before and after privatization. It would also be useful to know whether Puerto Ricans who lost public sector jobs during the 1990s experienced particular difficulties in finding new jobs in the private sector. We are unaware of direct evidence on these issues.

The public sector continues to absorb a bigger percentage of more educated persons on the island, and a much bigger percentage of more educated workers. Consider college-educated persons (at least sixteen years of education) in 2000. In Puerto Rico, 24.2 percent worked in the public sector, 41.3 percent worked in the private sector, and the rest were not employed. In the United States, 20.2 percent worked in the public sector, and 63.1 percent worked in the private sector. Put differently, the public sector absorbs 37 percent of college-educated workers in Puerto Rico compared with 24 percent in the United States. The share of college-educated persons working in Puerto Rico's public sector was even larger, indeed much larger, in 1980 and 1990 than in 2000, and the share working in the private sector was smaller in 1980 and 1990 than in 2000. The upshot is that college-educated persons with private sector work experience are much more abundant in the United States than in Puerto Rico. If higher education produces forms of human capital that are useful for entrepreneurial endeavors in the private sector, then Puerto Rico faces another type of large human capital deficit compared with the United States—larger than a simple comparison of schooling levels would suggest. We attach numbers to this point below.

Employment Rates by Educational Attainment

Puerto Rico's employment shortfall is most acute for less educated persons. Tables 6-2 and 6-3 describe the situation for men and women, respectively, based on household census data for 1980, 1990, and 2000. The tables show that U.S. employment rates exceed Puerto Rican rates in every schooling category except for college-educated women in 1980. For both men and women there is a clear pattern of bigger gaps in the employment rate at lower levels of schooling.

Less educated persons are also relatively abundant on the island. Hence, in an accounting sense, one can attribute a sizable portion of the U.S.–Puerto Rican employment gap to schooling level, but the data weigh heavily against such an explanation. U.S.–Puerto Rican gaps in the employment rate are remarkably large *within* schooling groups. In the 2000 census every schooling group shows a double-digit gap in the employment rate. For Puerto Ricans with a high school diploma or a General Educational Development certificate, which was the median schooling level among Puerto Rican adults in 2000, the employment rate was 47 percent for men and 25 percent for women. The corresponding U.S. figures are 75 percent for men and 62 percent for women.

Moreover, schooling level cannot account for the time-series behavior of Puerto Rican employment. According to census data, Puerto Rico's employment rate fell by 4.8 percentage points between 1990 and 2000—from an

Table 6-2. *Employment of Working-Age Men, Puerto Rico and the United States, by Schooling, 1980, 1990, 2000*[a]

Year and schooling	As share of population (percent)		Share employed (percent)		Annual hours worked			
					Per person		Per employed	
	Puerto Rico	United States	Puerto Rico	United States	Puerto Rico	United States	Puerto Rico	United States
1980								
All	100.0	100.0	51.2	77.2	920	1,643	1,666	1,895
To four years	14.8	2.2	34.1	56.1	579	1,128	1,435	1,779
Five to eight years	20.8	9.2	42.8	64.2	746	1,375	1,529	1,860
Secondary	21.3	19.8	38.6	60.6	650	1,151	1,510	1,547
High school diploma or GED	23.5	33.6	63.3	82.4	1,155	1,802	1,744	1,974
Postsecondary	11.0	17.8	62.6	81.1	1,147	1,737	1,757	1,881
College degree	5.0	8.8	83.8	91.3	1,622	1,991	1,938	2,081
Advanced degree	3.7	8.5	85.7	92.0	1,713	2,019	2,008	2,115
1990								
All	100.0	100.0	52.7	77.3	1,027	1,675	1,713	1,934
To four years	9.8	1.9	31.3	56.4	581	1,103	1,487	1,729
Five to eight years	15.2	4.8	39.9	58.4	732	1,228	1,502	1,780
Secondary	22.5	17.7	38.6	57.2	713	1,094	1,524	1,518
High school diploma or GED	23.8	27.8	61.9	80.4	1,196	1,762	1,733	1,980
Postsecondary	16.9	26.9	62.7	81.9	1,244	1,790	1,784	1,944
College degree	8.5	13.4	79.1	90.0	1,674	2,018	1,989	2,124
Advanced degree	3.3	7.5	85.8	92.1	1,867	2,129	2,084	2,228
2000								
All	100.0	100.0	44.8	74.0	1,024	1,680	1,720	1,991
To four years	5.8	1.8	22.1	50.4	472	1,169	1,453	1,765
Five to eight years	12.2	4.0	29.2	54.6	625	1,247	1,469	1,822
Secondary	21.6	16.7	29.1	51.7	611	1,043	1,480	1,546
High school diploma or GED	24.7	26.9	47.3	74.5	1,107	1,713	1,706	2,013
Postsecondary	21.9	27.8	55.2	79.2	1,277	1,798	1,770	2,003
College degree	9.9	14.6	69.5	88.2	1,653	2,052	1,957	2,185
Advanced degree	4.0	8.2	77.2	89.2	1,823	2,129	2,064	2,263

Source: Data from household census for 1980, 1990, and 2000; authors' calculations.

a. The data are for persons aged sixteen to sixty-five. Employed refers to the percentage of persons with a job in the reference week. Annual hours worked refer to the previous calendar year and are calculated as the product of weeks worked times usual hours of work per week. The differences across census years in the coding of educational attainment are modest for the schooling categories reported.

Table 6-3. *Employment of Working-Age Women, Puerto Rico and the United States, by Schooling, 1980, 1990, 2000*[a]

Year and schooling	As share of population (percent)		Share employed (percent)		Annual hours worked			
					Per person		Per employed	
	Puerto Rico	United States	Puerto Rico	United States	Puerto Rico	United States	Puerto Rico	United States
1980								
All	100.0	100.0	27.1	53.7	461	914	1,556	1,428
To four years	15.9	1.8	8.8	29.6	142	495	1,412	1,412
Five to eight years	19.5	8.1	14.4	34.0	236	592	1,406	1,432
Secondary	19.4	20.3	14.9	39.6	234	598	1,299	1,175
High school diploma or GED	23.7	40.2	35.9	56.8	636	1,004	1,617	1,498
Postsecondary	13.2	17.7	43.5	62.1	743	1,062	1,598	1,419
College degree	6.2	7.3	68.6	68.4	1,153	1,143	1,674	1,491
Advanced degree	2.1	4.7	71.8	77.4	1,272	1,318	1,737	1,562
1990								
All	100.0	100.0	32.7	62.8	600	1,129	1,597	1,553
To four years	9.7	1.6	9.8	33.0	170	585	1,381	1,472
Five to eight years	13.5	4.0	15.1	34.5	263	624	1,406	1,444
Secondary	19.9	16.9	16.1	42.0	279	662	1,307	1,213
High school diploma or GED	22.2	31.2	34.1	62.4	621	1,137	1,565	1,583
Postsecondary	20.3	28.9	43.1	71.0	779	1,290	1,568	1,569
College degree	11.6	12.2	69.3	77.5	1,319	1,421	1,793	1,673
Advanced degree	2.8	5.2	77.4	83.8	1,543	1,578	1,857	1,771
2000								
All	100.0	100.0	30.7	63.7	643	1,213	1,563	1,639
To four years	5.0	1.5	8.4	31.7	160	631	1,332	1,480
Five to eight years	10.2	3.2	10.1	33.5	191	656	1,274	1,474
Secondary	17.8	14.7	11.1	41.2	214	662	1,169	1,216
High school diploma or GED	22.3	27.0	25.2	61.6	517	1,194	1,463	1,656
Postsecondary	25.4	31.3	38.7	70.6	808	1,344	1,531	1,643
College degree	15.3	15.1	59.7	76.5	1,292	1,489	1,740	1,774
Advanced degree	4.0	7.2	67.7	81.2	1,454	1,630	1,811	1,866

Source: Data from household census for 1980, 1990, and 2000; authors' calculations.

a. The data are for persons aged sixteen to sixty-five. Employed refers to the percentage of persons with a job in the reference week. Annual hours worked refer to the previous calendar year and are calculated as the product of weeks worked times usual hours of work per week. The differences across census years in the coding of educational attainment are modest for the schooling categories reported.

Table 6-4. *College-Educated Workers in the Private Sector and the Free Enterprise Segment as Share of Working-Age Persons, Puerto Rico and the United States, 1980, 1990, 2000*[a]

Percent

Year	Private sector employment			Free enterprise segment employment		
	Puerto Rico	United States	United States/ Puerto Rico	Puerto Rico	United States	United States/ Puerto Rico
1980	2.9	8.1	2.8	2.3	7.0	3.0
1990	5.2	10.1	1.9	4.3	8.7	2.0
2000	6.9	14.2	2.1	5.9	12.6	2.1

Source: Data from household census for 1980, 1990, and 2000; authors' calculations.

a. The data are for persons aged sixteen to sixty-five. The private sector encompasses all workers except employees of federal and subfederal governments. The free enterprise segment of the private sector excludes nongovernmental employees in public utilities and sanitary services, primary and secondary education, colleges and universities, construction and several small industries for which public sector employment exceeds 35 percent of industry employment in Puerto Rico. For 1990 these industries are museums, galleries, and zoos; business, trade, and vocational schools; bus service and urban transit; research, development, and testing; social services; forestry; libraries. For 1980 the excluded industries are nearly identical. For 2000 the set is slightly narrower. Unpaid family workers are not counted among the employed.

already low base. It fell by 3.6 percentage points relative to the United States over the same period. These absolute and relative declines in Puerto Rico's employment rate coincide with rising schooling levels among Puerto Rican adults and a sharp narrowing of the schooling gap vis-à-vis the United States. The labor force survey (figure 6-1) presents a more favorable picture of Puerto Rico's employment performance in the 1990s, but even these more favorable data suggest that dramatic gains in schooling are associated with very modest increases in the rate of employment.

The enormous U.S.–Puerto Rican work experience gap holds in terms of hours worked as well as employment rates. For employed men, U.S. work time exceeds Puerto Rican work time by 220 to 270 hours a year. This sizable gap in hours per employed worker amplifies the work experience gap calculated from employment rates. For employed women, annual work hours are somewhat greater for Puerto Rico in 1980 but somewhat less in 2000. On net, the hours-worked data reinforce and strengthen the view that Puerto Rican residents have accumulated a huge shortfall in work experience relative to U.S. residents.

Table 6-4 combines data on the population schooling distribution and employment rates by schooling levels to calculate the percentage of adults who are college educated and working in the private sector. Relative to the population, college-educated persons working in the private sector are nearly three times more abundant on the mainland than on the island in 1980 and roughly twice as abundant in 1990 and 2000. A similar pattern holds with respect to

Table 6-5. *Public Sector Employment as Share of Total Employment, Puerto Rico and the United States, 1980, 1990, 2000* [a]

Percent

Year	Government employment as share of paid employment				Puerto Rico's industry-level shares for government employment evaluated at U.S. industry mix	Puerto Rico's industry mix evaluated at U.S. shares for government employment
	U.S. mainland		Puerto Rico			
	Total	Subfederal	Total	Subfederal		
1980	17.3	13.2	33.9	30.1	24.2	26.7
1990	16.6	11.7	31.4	27.6	22.6	25.9
2000	15.4	11.8	24.9	21.6	19.3	21.5

Source: Data from household census for 1980, 1990, and 2000; authors' calculations.

a. There were 232 census industry codes in 1980, 243 in 1990, and 264 in 2000.

college-educated persons working in the free enterprise segment of the economy. Recall from our earlier discussion that we designate the same set of industries as making up the free enterprise segment in Puerto Rico and the United States, even though the government role at the industry level looms larger in Puerto Rico. For this reason, we think table 6-4 understates the relative scarcity of college-educated Puerto Ricans engaged in free enterprise work.

The Structure of Public Sector Employment

Table 6-5 provides a closer look at public sector employment in Puerto Rico and provides additional comparisons to the United States. In 1980 the percentage of workers with government jobs was nearly twice as large in Puerto Rico. The public sector share of Puerto Rican employment fell from 34 percent in 1980 to 31 percent in 1990 and to 25 percent in 2000. Nevertheless, the public sector continues to account for a much bigger fraction of overall employment on the island. The entire gap, and then some, between Puerto Rican and U.S. public sector shares reflects bigger employment shares at the subfederal government level. In fact, the discrepancy arises almost entirely at the state and commonwealth levels of government. The share of total employment accounted for by local governments is similar on the island and the mainland.

Does Puerto Rico's high public employment share reflect an industry mix that leans toward goods and services that, even in the United States, tend to be supplied by the public sector? (This is called an industry-mix effect.) Or does Puerto Rico's high public employment share reflect a bigger government role within narrowly defined industries? (This is called a within-industry effect.) To address these questions, we express the public sector share of employment in Puerto Rico and the United States as

(6-1) $\quad PUB^{PR} = \sum_i S_i^{PR} PUB_i^{PR} \text{ and } PUB^{US} = \sum_i S_i^{US} PUB_i^{US}$,

where S_i is the share of employment in industry i and PUB_i is the public sector share of employment for industry i. Next, evaluate Puerto Rico's industry-level government employment shares at the U.S. industry distribution of employment:

(6-2) $\quad PUB^{PR}(\text{U.S. Industry Distribution}) = \sum_i S_i^{US} PUB_i^{PR}$.

Also, evaluate the U.S. industry-level government employment shares at the Puerto Rican industry distribution of employment:

(6-3) $\quad PUB^{PR}(\text{U.S. Government Shares}) = \sum_i S_i^{PR} PUB_i^{US}$.

By calculating equations 2 and 3, we can quantify the contribution of the industry-mix effect and the within-industry effect to the U.S.–Puerto Rican difference in the public sector share of overall employment. We carry out these calculations using detailed census classifications into 232 to 264 distinct industries, depending on year.

The results of calculating equations 2 and 3 appear in the two right-hand columns of table 6-5. The basic story is similar for each census year: the industry-mix effect accounts for about 60 percent of the U.S.–Puerto Rican difference in public sector employment shares, and the within-industry effect accounts for about 40 percent.[13] Recall that the U.S.–Puerto Rican gap in the public sector share of overall employment has been shrinking. Hence we infer that Puerto Rico's economy has been evolving toward a less government-intensive industry mix relative to a contemporaneous U.S. benchmark, and that at the same time the average U.S.–Puerto Rican gap in public sector employment shares within industries has also been shrinking.

Table 6-6 illustrates the latter point with specific examples. As of 1980 Puerto Rico's public sector share of employment was much larger in several sizable industries, involving a broad range of production activities. After 1980 the public sector share of employment in these industries shrank on the island and in the United States. The declines in within-industry public sector shares are bigger in absolute percentage terms for Puerto Rico. However, the 2000 census data show that government employment continues to play a relatively large role on the island in a broad range of industries that includes electric light and power, sugar and confec-

13. The decomposition into between and within effects is not exact, but the cross-product terms are small in these data.

Table 6-6. *Public Sector Employment as Share of Total Employment, Puerto Rico and United States, Selected Industries, 1980, 1990, 2000*
Percent

Industry[a]	Puerto Rico			United States		
	1980	1990	2000	1980	1990	2000
Electric light and power	93	79	83	15	13	13
Telephone	62	65	...	1	1	...
Wired and other telecom carriers	...	...	0	...	...	0
Sugar and confectionery manufacturing	55	32	16	1	1	0
Residential care without nursing	83	46	32	30	19	12
Nursing facilities	70	39	33	17	10	8
Child day care	66	55	55	19	8	7
Job training, vocational rehabilitation	80	62	...	38	24	...
Vocational rehabilitation	...	...	80	...	...	19
Hospitals	68	53	32	28	21	15
Museums, galleries, and zoos	63	48	79	37	26	34
Sanitary services	88	86	...	68	52	...
Waste management and remediation	...	...	48	...	...	19
Construction	20	13	6	9	7	5

Source: Data from household census for 1980, 1990, and 2000; authors' calculations.

a. There were 232 census industry codes in 1980, 243 in 1990, and 264 in 2000. Some industries listed here are not fully comparable over time because of changes in census industry classifications.

tionary manufacturing, residential care, nursing facilities, child day care, job training, hospitals, museums and zoos, and sanitary services. According to these data, there remains considerable room for shifting employment and production activity from the state sector to the private sector in many Puerto Rican industries.

The Industry Structure of Employment

Among the fifty states there is a close relationship between average years of schooling in the adult population and the schooling intensity of the industry mix. In particular, the employment mix tilts toward industries that rely more heavily on highly educated workers in states with more educated populations. Figure 6-2 depicts this strong, perhaps unsurprising, relationship using household census data. We calculate the state-level measure of schooling intensity in two steps. In the first step, we compute the schooling intensity of each census industry as the mean years of completed schooling among all U.S. workers in the industry, weighting each worker in proportion to hours worked. In the second step, we compute a schooling intensity index for the state (or commonwealth) as the employment-weighted mean of the industry-level schooling intensity values. By construction, an industry has the same schooling intensity in all states and in Puerto Rico. So the index quantifies the extent to which the employment distribution tilts toward schooling-intensive industries.

Figure 6-2. *Schooling Intensity of State's Industry Mix Plotted against Mean Schooling Years of Its Adult Population, 1980, 1990, 2000*[a]

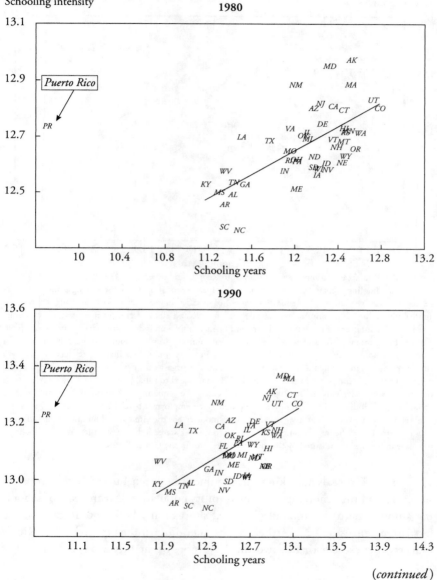

(*continued*)

Figure 6-2. (*continued*)

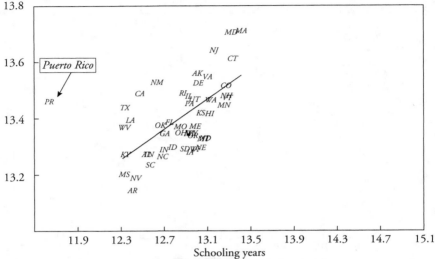

2000

Source: Authors' calculations based on data from Ruggles and others (2004).

a. Mean schooling years is calculated as the simple mean years of completed schooling among residents sixteen to sixty-five years old. For education codes not specified in terms of years of schooling, we assigned approximate values. For example, "associate degree" in 1990 and 2000 became fourteen years of schooling. The schooling intensity of the states' industry employment mix is an index constructed in two steps. First, the schooling intensity of each census industry was computed as the hours-weighted mean years of completed schooling among all U.S. workers in the industry. Industry affiliation reflects the worker's current primary job, defined as the one that generates the largest earnings. The hours-worked measure pertains to the reference week in the 1980 and 1990 census and to usual hours worked each week during the previous calendar year in the 2000 census. Second, the schooling intensity index for the state or commonwealth industry distribution was computed as the employment-weighted mean of the industry-level schooling intensity values. By construction, an industry has the same schooling intensity in all states and in Puerto Rico. The index quantifies the extent to which a state's industry mix tilts toward schooling-intensive industries, as measured by the industry workforce in the United States.

Figure 6-2 reveals a striking misalignment between Puerto Rico's industry structure and the schooling attainment of its population. Mean years of schooling among Puerto Rican adults fall well short of any U.S. state in each of the last three censuses.[14] Nevertheless, the schooling intensity of Puerto Rico's industry mix exceeds that of two-thirds or more of the fifty states.[15] In terms of

14. Helen Ladd and Francisco Rivera-Batiz (chapter 5 of this volume) provide a detailed comparison of U.S. and Puerto Rican schooling levels.

15. Robert Lawrence and Juan Lara (chapter 9 of this volume) provide complementary evidence that the factor content of Puerto Rican exports is out of line with its factor endowment mix. Using industry-level measures of factor intensity, they find that Puerto Rican exports are much more capital intensive than U.S. exports but are similar in terms of research and development and labor skill intensity, where compensation level proxies for skill.

schooling intensity, Puerto Rico's industry mix ranks thirteenth of fifty-one in 1980 (comparable to Virginia, Minnesota, Delaware, and Hawaii), tenth of fifty-one in 1990 (above Delaware and Vermont), and sixteenth of fifty-one in 2000 (tied with Utah and Washington). Thus the Puerto Rican economy has for decades failed to generate jobs that, in terms of educational requirements, fit the qualifications of the Puerto Rican population.[16]

This finding provides an important clue regarding Puerto Rico's anemic employment performance and its especially low employment rates among persons with lower schooling levels. In an important sense, the "missing jobs" in Puerto Rico are to be found largely in labor-intensive industries that rely heavily on less educated workers. Table 6-7 provides additional evidence on this point. Consider the industry group that provides eating, drinking, and lodging, which accounts for 5–6 percent of employment in the United States. Most workers in this industry group have relatively low schooling levels.[17] Puerto Rico's share of employment in this industry group is less than any of the fifty states in 1980 and 1990 and near the bottom of the distribution in 2000. The story is similar but less pronounced for entertainment and recreation services. To fully appreciate the glaring nature of Puerto Rico's employment shortfall in these industries, three facts should be kept in mind. First, table 6-7 considers employment shares, but as we have shown, Puerto Rico's employment rate is only 55–65 percent of the U.S. rate. Hence Puerto Rico's employment shortfall in these industries is much greater as a percentage of the working-age population. Second, Puerto Rico has a relative abundance of less educated persons to potentially fill jobs in these industries. Third, Puerto Rico is blessed with a tropical climate and interesting topography that could potentially attract many more visitors from the United States and elsewhere, visitors who would intensively demand the types of goods and services that these industries produce. In light of these last two points, the magnitude of Puerto Rico's employment shortfall in these industries is a powerful testament to the decades-long failure of industrial and employment policy on the island.

16. A small caveat to this conclusion is worth a mention. The same economic policies that distort Puerto Rico's industry structure may also alter the mix of production activities within industries, relative to the United States. In the case of pharmaceuticals, section 936 tax subsidies stimulated the sourcing of physical production to the island, while the more schooling-intensive research and development activities remained on the mainland. For two reasons, we do not see this issue as a big concern in the interpretation of figure 6-2. First, the scope for this type of outsourcing arises mainly in certain manufacturing industries. Second, section 936 subsidies are highly concentrated in a small number of capital-intensive industries that account for only a small share of employment. Pharmaceutical manufacturers, which received the bulk of section 936 subsidies, account for only 2–3 percent of Puerto Rican employment in recent decades.

17. Steven Davis and Magnus Henrekson (2005b, table A.2) report workers' mean schooling years for sixty-one industry groups based on data from the Current Population Surveys for 1984 through 1986. Eating and drinking establishments rank fifty-fourth of sixty-one industry groups on this measure of skill, and hotels and lodging rank forty-seventh.

Table 6-7. *Industry Employment as Share of Total Employment, Puerto Rico and the United States, Selected Industries, 1980, 1990, 2000*[a]

Percent

Industry and year	Puerto Rico	United States	Fifty-state range	State with highest percentage	Selected state and share
Construction					
1980	7.3	5.8	3.7–9.9	Wyoming	Hawaii (6.4)
1990	7.5	6.2	4.8–8.8	Nevada	Hawaii (7.0)
2000	8.4	6.8	5.2–9.4	Nevada	Hawaii (5.6)
Sugar and confectionery manufacturing					
1980	0.65	0.11	0–1.1	Hawaii	North Dakota (0.30)
1990	0.23	0.08	0–0.6	Hawaii	North Dakota (0.24)
2000	0.12	0.06	0–0.4	North Dakota	Hawaii (0.20)
Pharmaceuticals					
1980	2.0	0.2	0–1.3	New Jersey	Indiana (0.7)
1990	2.8	0.2	0–1.2	New Jersey	Indiana (0.7)
2000	3.0	0.3	0–1.5	New Jersey	Indiana (0.6)
All other manufacturing					
1980	17.5	22.1	5.2–31.9	Rhode Island	Hawaii (5.6)
1990	13.7	17.4	5.1–25.6	North Carolina	Hawaii (5.1)
2000	10.6	13.8	3.0–22.5	Indiana	Hawaii (3.0)
Utilities and sanitary services					
1980	2.3	1.4	0.9–2.5	Tennessee	Hawaii (1.0)
1990	2.0	1.3	0.8–2.4	Wyoming	Hawaii (0.9)
2000	1.8	1.2	0.9–2.2	West Virginia	Hawaii (1.1)
Eating, drinking, and lodging					
1980	3.6	5.3	3.7–19.5	Nevada	Hawaii (11.4)
1990	3.4	5.8	4.2–17.4	Nevada	Hawaii (12.6)
2000	5.5	6.1	4.5–14.1	Nevada	Hawaii (12.7)
Entertainment and recreation services					
1980	0.7	1.1	0.5–9.3	Nevada	Hawaii (1.5)
1990	1.0	1.4	0.6–9.0	Nevada	Hawaii (1.7)
2000	0.9	1.7	0.9–11.9	Nevada	Hawaii (2.3)
Elementary and secondary schooling					
1980	8.7	5.9	4.2–7.8	Alaska	Hawaii (4.5)
1990	7.7	5.5	3.8–8.2	Wyoming	Hawaii (4.3)
2000	7.2	6.0	4.2–7.9	Wyoming	Hawaii (5.8)
Public administration					
1980	12.5	5.2	3.5–14.2	Maryland	Hawaii (8.9)
1990	14.0	4.8	3.2–11.7	Maryland	Hawaii (7.5)
2000	10.7	4.8	3.3–10.8	Alaska	Hawaii (7.3)

Source: Data from household census for 1980, 1990, and 2000; authors' calculations.

a. Figures for the United States include the District of Columbia, but the fifty-state range does not. State-level employment figures reflect the location of the worker's residence, not the location of the job. Thus for example public administration accounts for a relatively high percentage of Maryland employment, because many Maryland residents commute to government jobs in the District of Columbia.

One might hope that Puerto Rico's rising schooling levels would eventually eliminate any employment shortfall created by the misalignment of its industry structure. However, figure 6-3 suggests that such a hope is largely in vain. We carry out the same type of exercise as before, except that we now relate the industry structure of employment to the schooling attainment of employed, rather than all, persons. For 1980 and 1990, figure 6-3 tells a similar story to that of figure 6-2. By 2000, however, the misalignment between the schooling intensity of Puerto Rico's industry structure and the schooling attainment of its workers had largely vanished. Puerto Rico remained an outlier in 2000 but no more so than Texas, California, and New Mexico. Yet, as we have seen, the U.S.–Puerto Rican gap in the employment-to-population ratio remained enormous in 2000. In other words, Puerto Rico achieved a reasonable alignment between its industry structure and the educational attainment of its workers by 2000—roughly in line with the relationship among the fifty states—but it did so by excluding the less educated from jobs.

One other fact, readily visible in figure 6-2, belies the hope that Puerto Rico can educate its way out of a huge jobs shortage for less educated persons. Between 1980 and 2000, the U.S.–Puerto Rican gap in average schooling attainment shrank by roughly two-thirds. Yet over the same twenty-year period, the Puerto Rican employment rate, according to the labor force survey, rose only slightly, from 61 percent to 64 percent of the U.S. rate, and according to the household census it fell relative to the U.S. rate. If more education were the key to addressing Puerto Rico's employment shortfall, the island would have a spectacular record of employment growth in recent decades.

The Size and Ownership Structure of Employment

Tables 6-8 and 6-9 report the distribution of employees by establishment size in four major industry groups for Puerto Rico and the United States. These statistics derive from the Economic Census of 1997, an establishment-level census of all tax-paying business units in covered sectors. In comparison to the United States, Puerto Rico's construction and manufacturing employees are considerably more concentrated at larger establishments. In contrast, the island's retail trade employees are dramatically less concentrated at larger establishments. Remarkably, only 36 percent of retail employees in Puerto Rico work at establishments with fifty or more paid employees, as compared with 76 percent in the United States. The two employee-size distributions are similar in wholesale trade, although Puerto Rico has smaller shares at the smallest and largest establishments. In short, there is no simple characterization of Puerto Rico's small business employment share, relative to the United States, that holds across major industry groups.

The Economic Census also provides limited information about the ownership structure of employment. As seen in tables 6-10 and 6-11, unincorporated

Figure 6-3. *Schooling Intensity of State's Industry Mix Plotted against Mean Schooling Years of Its Workers*[a]

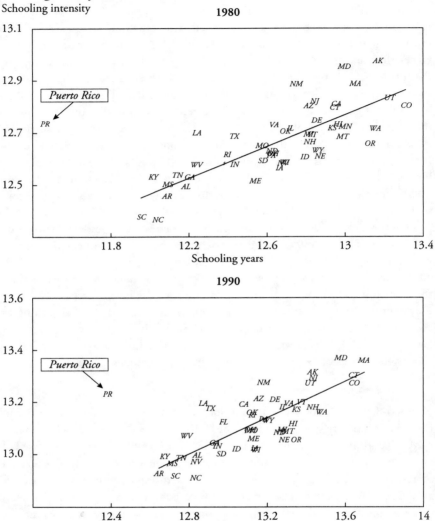

Schooling intensity

1980

1990

Schooling years

Figure 6-3. (*continued*)

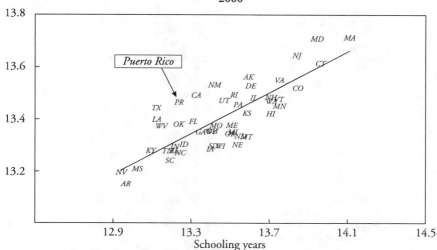

Source: Authors' calculations were based on data from Ruggles and others (2004).

a. Mean schooling years were calculated as the simple mean years of completed schooling among employed persons sixteen to sixty-five years old. In other respects, the calculations follow those used in figure 6-2. Note that the range of the horizontal axes is 2.0 years in figure 6-3 but 3.6 years in figure 6-2.

Table 6-8. *Distribution of Employees, by Establishment Size, Construction, and Manufacturing, Puerto Rico and the United States, 1997*[a]

Percent

Number of employees at establishment	Construction		Manufacturing	
	United States	Puerto Rico	United States	Puerto Rico
1–4	13.5	2.8	1.5	0.8
5–9	13.9	5.0	2.5	1.1
10–19	15.7	7.6	4.6	3.2
20–49	20.8	15.9	10.6	7.3
50–99	13.1	18.3	11.7	7.2
100–249	12.1	24.4	20.4	16.2
250–499	5.4	13.8	16.2	23.4
500 and more	5.4	12.3	32.5	40.7

Source: 1997 Economic Census of Puerto Rico and the Island Areas (www.census.gov/csd/ia/p_puerto97.htm); and 1997 Economic Census (www.census.gov/epcd/www/econ97.html). The most recent economic census of Puerto Rico is June 2005.

a. Size distribution statistics are for paid employees, and they exclude unpaid family workers and the proprietors and partners of unincorporated businesses. Size categories reflect the finest breakdowns available on a consistent basis in the Economic Census of 1997. The economic census does not report measures of economic activity by firm size for Puerto Rico.

Table 6-9. *Distribution of Employees, by Establishment Size, Retail and Wholesale Trade, Puerto Rico and the United States, 1997*[a]
Percent

Number of employees at establishment	Retail trade		Wholesale trade	
	United States	Puerto Rico	United States	Puerto Rico
1	0.3	1.8	1.2	0.7
2	0.7	2.6	1.7	1.3
3–4	2.1	6.2	4.2	3.3
5–6	2.6	5.5	4.4	7.5
7–9	3.6	7.3	5.9	6.4
10–14	4.2	9.0	8.5	8.8
15–19	2.6	6.7	6.7	6.6
20–49	7.6	24.5	22.4	23.8
50 and more	76.3	36.4	44.9	41.5

Source: 1997 Economic Census of Puerto Rico and the Island Areas (www.census.gov/csd/ia/ p_puerto97.htm); and 1997 Economic Census (www.census.gov/epcd/www/econ97.html). The most recent economic census of Puerto Rico is June 2005.

a. Size distribution statistics are for paid employees, and they exclude unpaid family workers and the proprietors and partners of unincorporated businesses. Size categories reflect the finest breakdowns available on a consistent basis in the Economic Census of 1997. The economic census does not report measures of economic activity by firm size for Puerto Rico.

Table 6-10. *Employment in Individual Proprietorships and Unincorporated Partnerships as Share of Total Employment, Construction and Manufacturing, Puerto Rico and the United States, 1997*
Percent

Form of ownership	Construction		Manufacturing	
	United States	Puerto Rico	United States	Puerto Rico
Individual proprietorships	9.6	8.4	1.7	1.4–1.7
Unincorporated partnerships	3.4	16.0	1.9	≤0.6

Source: 1997 Economic Census of Puerto Rico and the Island Areas (www.census.gov/csd/ia/ p_puerto97.htm); and 1997 Economic Census (www.census.gov/epcd/www/econ97.html). The most recent economic census of Puerto Rico is June 2005.

a. Statistics are for paid employees and exclude unpaid family workers and the proprietors and partners of unincorporated businesses. Certain figures for Puerto Rico are available only within a range.

partnerships account for very small shares of employees in manufacturing. They account for bigger shares, ranging from 5 percent to 24 percent, in construction, wholesale trade, and retail trade. Notably, the share of employees of unincorporated enterprises in these industry groups is roughly twice as big in Puerto Rico as in the United States. Retail trade again presents a sharp contrast: about 16 percent of employees work for individual proprietorships in Puerto Rico, compared with only 6 percent in the United States.

Table 6-11. *Employment in Individual Proprietorships and Unincorporated Partnerships as Share of Total Employment, Retail and Wholesale Trade, Puerto Rico and the United States, 1997*

Percent

	Retail trade		Wholesale trade	
Form of ownership	United States	Puerto Rico	United States	Puerto Rico
Individual proprietorships	6.2	15.6	2.8	7.8
Unincorporated partnerships	2.2	≤1.1	2.3	≤0.8

Source: 1997 Economic Census of Puerto Rico and the Island Areas (www.census.gov/csd/ia/p_puerto97.htm); and 1997 Economic Census (www.census.gov/epcd/www/econ97.html). The most recent economic census of Puerto Rico is June 2005.

a. Statistics are for paid employees, and they exclude unpaid family workers and the proprietors and partners of unincorporated businesses. Certain figures for Puerto Rico are available only within a range.

The retail trade figures for Puerto Rico are especially noteworthy in light of developments in the United States in recent decades. Wal-Mart, Target, Staples, Best Buy, Home Depot, and other national chains have propelled the introduction and diffusion of larger stores with greater product selection, lower prices, electronic credit card processing, bar code scanners, and advanced inventory management techniques.[18] In the process, they have transformed the U.S. retail sector, dramatically increasing productivity and displacing thousands of smaller and independent retail enterprises. Using microeconomic data from the U.S. Census of Retail Trade, Lucia Foster, John Haltiwanger, and C. J. Krizan document that retail establishments owned by large national chains have higher labor productivity than establishments owned by single-unit firms.[19] They also show that essentially all of the productivity growth in the U.S. retail sector between 1987 and 1997 reflects the displacement of less productive single-establishment retail firms by the entry of more productive, typically larger, establishments owned by national chains.

Wal-Mart, in particular, has been at the forefront of these developments and has attracted attention in several careful studies. The McKinsey Global Institute describes Wal-Mart's role in the transformation of the retail sector this way:

In general merchandise retailing, productivity growth accelerated after 1995 because Wal-Mart's success forced competitors to improve their operations. In 1987, Wal-Mart had just 9 percent market share, but was 40 percent more productive than its competitors. By the mid-1990s, its share had

18. For description and analysis of these developments in the U.S. retail trade sector, see Nakamura (1999); McKinsey Global Institute (2001); Sieling, Friedman, and Dumas (2001); Foster, Haltiwanger, and Krizan (2004); Hausman and Leibtag (2004); Basker (2005a, 2005b); and Holmes (2005).

19. Foster, Haltiwanger, and Krizan (2004).

grown to 27 percent while its productivity advantage widened to 48 percent. Competitors reacted by adopting many of Wal-Mart's innovations, including the large scale ("big box") format, economies of scale in warehouse logistics and purchasing, electronic data interchange (EDI), and wireless bar code scanning.[20]

Tables 6-10 and 6-11 imply that Puerto Rico's retail sector lags well behind the mainland in the type of creative destruction process documented by both Foster and others and the McKinsey Global Institute—to the detriment of its residents. Some of the most powerful consumer benefits of the U.S. retail transformation take the form of lower prices. Jerry Hausman and Ephraim Leibtag find that "Wal-Mart offers identical food items at an average price about 15%–25% lower than traditional supermarkets."[21] A complementary study by Emek Basker finds that the entry of a new Wal-Mart store leads to significantly lower prices at competitor stores in the same city.[22] Basker also provides evidence that the entry of a new Wal-Mart store leads to a modest net increase in countywide employment.[23]

Why has Puerto Rico lagged in the transformation of its retail sector? The permitting process for new construction and real estate development projects has slowed the transformation of the retail sector for reasons explained below. Municipal government oversight of retail store entry and location decisions has also played a role, as we discuss below.

Informal Sector Employment

The underground, shadow, or informal economy refers to output and incomes generated in market production activity that are not declared to the government, particularly the tax and regulatory authorities. Standard establishment-based measures of output and employment are unlikely to capture underground activity. In principle, household surveys capture employment in the underground economy, but respondents may be reluctant to provide information about employment in illegal or undeclared activities. This leaves open the possibility that official estimates of Puerto Rico's employment rate are so low because they miss a high rate of employment in the underground economy.

Estudios Técnicos provides a figure for informal sector employment in Puerto Rico that is 20.5 percent as large as the official labor force measure.[24] However, the figure is based on a methodology that attributes the U.S.–Puerto Rican gap in labor force participation rates to the U.S.–Puerto Rican gap in informal sector employment. So the 20.5 percent figure is essentially a restate-

20. McKinsey Global Institute (2001, p. 2).
21. Hausman and Leibtag (2004, p. 29).
22. Basker (2005b).
23. Basker (2005a).
24. Estudios Técnicos (2004).

ment of the participation (and employment) gap, and it cannot tell us how much of the measured employment gap reflects informal sector activity. Direct, survey-based evidence on informal sector employment for a random sample of Puerto Rican residents is absent. The lack of direct evidence leaves us unable to confidently adjust the U.S.–Puerto Rican employment gap for informal activity.

It is unlikely, however, that the informal sector accounts for the bulk of the U.S.–Puerto Rican employment gap, as measured by standard labor force surveys. Many persons who work off the books for a portion of their income also hold formal sector jobs, and they already show up in measured employment. Many other persons who work only in the informal sector are also counted as employed in household surveys. Hence any U.S.–Puerto Rican gap in the rate of missing employment is smaller in magnitude, probably much smaller, than the U.S.–Puerto Rican difference in informal sector employment rates. In addition, the available evidence suggests that underground activity in Puerto Rico has declined relative to gross domestic product in the past quarter century, moving closer to U.S. levels.[25]

Policy Influences on Business Development and Employment Growth

Compared with many middle-income countries, Puerto Rico enjoys strong institutions and favorable economic policies. By virtue of its association with the United States, Puerto Rico benefits from sound monetary policy, a stable financial environment, and open migration to and from the U.S. mainland. Puerto Rico's international trade regime is largely governed by U.S. trade policies and World Trade Organization (WTO) rules. As a result, tariffs on traded goods and services are relatively low and somewhat insulated from manipulation by political authorities on the island. Price controls are minimal, and there are no burdensome currency regulations or capital controls. Many aspects of the overall economic environment are shaped by U.S. laws.

Set against these favorable features of Puerto Rico's economic environment are several unfavorable ones. There are peculiarities and loopholes in the application of U.S. trade laws that raise effective trade barriers. Section 936 and other tax subsidies have distorted Puerto Rico's industrial structure. Minimum wage laws raise the cost of employing less skilled workers. An extensive role for government transfer payments undermines work incentives. An inefficient and

25. Bosworth and Collins (chapter 2, appendix B) report that the revenue gap between income in the national accounts and income declared for tax purposes diminished sharply after 1976 in Puerto Rico. This trend suggests that underground activity motivated by tax avoidance activity also declined. In recent years Puerto Rico's revenue gap as a percentage of GDP has declined to levels only a few percentage points above the U.S. level. A standard indicator based on electricity usage suggests that underground activity in Puerto Rico fell sharply relative to GDP in the 1980s and then partly recovered in the 1990s.

cumbersome regime for business licenses and permits impedes construction activity, new business development, and cost-effective operation of existing businesses. More generally, many government services are of poor quality, and there is a culture of dependence on the government as a source of employment and favors. In addition, the traditional prevalence of state-owned enterprises has probably softened competitive pressures and lowered productivity throughout much of the economy.

Table 6-12 shows business climate indicators compiled by the World Bank for Puerto Rico and other countries. According to these indicators, Puerto Rico compares favorably with the Latin American and Caribbean region in terms of the costs of starting a formal business, the regulation of employment, institutional support for credit markets, and the costs of closing an insolvent business. The business climate in Puerto Rico is roughly comparable to that of the average OECD country according to many of the indicators, and there is greater employment flexibility on the island. The most unfavorable aspects of Puerto Rico's business climate pertain to the cost and difficulty of enforcing commercial debt obligations.

The picture of Puerto Rico's business climate suggested by the World Bank data presented in table 6-12 is too rosy, in our view, because it fails to capture several factors that increase day-to-day operating costs, raise artificial barriers to entry and expansion, and cultivate a rent-seeking business culture. Unfortunately, these factors are difficult to quantify. Hence portions of our discussion here rely on descriptive and anecdotal evidence drawn from a variety of sources, including informal interviews with business persons and government officials.

Trade Protectionism

The U.S. Jones Act raises the cost of trade between Puerto Rico and the United States by requiring that American vessels be used for all goods shipped by sea between Puerto Rican and U.S. ports. The effect is equivalent to a tariff on Puerto Rican imports from the United States and on U.S. imports from Puerto Rico.

Puerto Rico has also established protectionist measures that are incompatible with WTO rules for international trade. For instance, Law 69 of 2002 levies a higher excise tax for high-volume producers than for low-volume producers. High-volume producers tend to be foreign, and low-volume producers tend to be local. The Supreme Court of Puerto Rico has ruled that Law 69 does not discriminate against foreign producers because it does not explicitly target foreign firms for higher tax rates.[26] In recent cases involving Japan, Korea, and Chile, however, the WTO has ruled that what matters is the outcome, not the precise manner in which local authorities structure a tax.[27]

---

26. U.S. federal courts did not assume jurisdiction in this matter, leaving it to Puerto Rican courts.
27. Rodríguez Santiago (2005).

Table 6-12. *World Bank Business Climate Indicators, Selected Countries, 2004*

Indicator	Puerto Rico	Chile	Latin America and Caribbean islands	OECD countries	Ireland	Singapore	United States
Starting a formal business							
Number of required procedures	7	9	11	6	4	7	5
Time to complete procedures (days)	7	27	70	25	24	8	5
Cost to complete procedures, excluding bribes (percent of annual income per capita)	7.0	10.0	62.8	8.0	10.3	1.2	0.6
Minimum capital to register business (percent of annual income per capita)	1.0	0.0	28.9	44.1	0.0	0.0	0.0
Hiring and firing workers[a]							
Difficulty of hiring index	22.0	17.0	44.4	26.2	28.0	0	0.0
Rigidity of hours index	20.0	20.0	53.3	50.0	40.0	0	0.0
Difficulty of firing index	20.0	20.0	34.3	26.8	20.0	0	10.0
Rigidity of employment index	21.0	19.0	44.0	34.4	29.0	0	3.0
Firing costs (weeks of wages)	0.0	51.0	70.8	40.4	52.0	4	8.0

(continued)

Table 6-12. (continued)

Indicator	Puerto Rico	Chile	Latin America and Caribbean islands	OECD countries	Ireland	Singapore	United States
Getting credit							
Cost to create and register collateral (percent of income per capita)	0.1	5.3	19.4	5.2	3.2	0.3	0.1
Legal rights index[b]	6.0	4.0	3.8	6.3	8.0	10.0	7.0
Credit information availability index[c]	5.0	6.0	4.7	5.0	5.0	4.0	6.0
Public credit registry coverage (borrowers per 1,000 adults)	0.0	290	85.7	76.2	0.0	0.0	0.0
Private credit bureau coverage (borrowers per 1,000 adults)	643	220	325.1	577.2	1,000	335	1,000
Enforcing a debt obligation							
Number of required procedures	43	28	35	19	16	23	17
Time to complete procedures (days)	270	305	462	229	217	69	250
Recovery cost (percent of debt)	21.0	10.4	23.3	10.8	21.1	9.0	7.5
Closing an insolvent business							
Time required (years)	3.8	5.6	3.7	1.7	0.4	0.8	3.0
Cost of insolvency process (percent of estate value)	8.0	18.0	15.8	6.8	8.0	1	8.0
Recovery rate (percent)	61.4	19.3	26.6	72.1	88.9	91.3	68.2

Source: World Bank (2005) (www.doingbusiness.org/Default.aspx [accessed on August 21, 2005]).
a. Indexes range from 0 to 100, with higher values indicating more rigid regulation.
b. Index ranges from 0 to 10, " with higher scores indicating that collateral and bankruptcy laws are better designed to expand access to credit."
c. Index ranges from 0 to 6, with higher values indicating greater availability.

Puerto Rico also has other "buy local" laws with a strong protectionist element. These laws support certain local enterprises, but they also distort purchase decisions, lessen competitive pressures, and lower government tax revenues. For example, Law 110 (August 2001) provides for a 25 percent credit on Puerto Rican corporate income taxes for the purchase of eligible products manufactured and sold in Puerto Rico. Law 169 (December 2001) contains similar provisions for manufactured goods that are purchased for export. A June 2005 executive order issued by the governor requires government agencies to earmark 15 percent of their purchase contracts for small and mid-sized local enterprises.

Tax Subsidies That Distort the Structure of Production and Employment

Tax incentives for industry have a long history in Puerto Rico. Section 936 of the U.S. tax code "largely exempted U.S. corporations from paying federal tax on income earned by their Puerto Rican subsidiaries. Puerto Rico has a parallel tax subsidy program effectively exempting 936 corporations from Puerto Rican income taxes as well."[28] At one time these tax subsidies were seen as useful tools for stimulating employment in labor-intensive industries and easing Puerto Rico's unemployment problems. In practice, section 936 tax subsidies proved most attractive to capital-intensive manufacturing industries that produce proprietary products with big price markups over marginal costs. Products of this type facilitate tax-minimizing transfer prices and profit shifting between jurisdictions with different effective tax rates.

According to a study by the U.S. General Accounting Office cited by Barry Bosworth and Susan Collins in chapter 2 of this volume, section 936 tax subsidies to U.S. corporations with Puerto Rican operations amounted to $2.6 billion in 1989, or 13 percent of Puerto Rico's GDP.[29] One view is that subsidies of this magnitude profoundly influenced Puerto Rico's economy and industrial structure. Another view is that section 936 subsidies mainly reflect paper transactions with little impact on the Puerto Rican economy but with a high cost to the U.S. Treasury. Both views contain an important element of truth. On the one hand, Bosworth and Collins make a convincing case that a large portion of section 936 subsidies reflects income shifting by U.S. corporations through distorted transfer

28. J. Thomas Hexner and Glenn Jenkins, "Puerto Rico: The Economic and Fiscal Dimensions," 1998, Citizens Educational Foundation (www.puertorico-herald.org/issues/vol2n03/hexner-jenkins.shtml [March 2005]). Section 936 was established by the U.S. Tax Reform Act of 1976, but precursors in the U.S. and Puerto Rican tax codes date back several decades. Section 936 tax credits were phased out in 2005, but U.S. firms can still defer U.S. corporate income tax on Puerto Rican earnings by converting their Puerto Rican operations into controlled foreign corporations. See Odishelidze and Laffer (2004, pp. 174–80) for a useful synopsis of the evolution of section 936 and related features of the U.S. and Puerto Rican tax codes. Joseph Pelzman (2002) provides a detailed and highly informative description.

29. U.S. General Accounting Office (1993).

prices and other means. On the other hand, it is widely acknowledged that phar-maceutical firms sourced much of their production activity in Puerto Rico to exploit section 936 subsidies. The employment statistics for pharmaceuticals in table 6-7 support this view. The share of employment accounted for by the phar-maceuticals industry in Puerto Rico is about ten times larger than in the United States as a whole and two or three times larger than in any single state.

If the goal is to stimulate employment, one would be hard pressed to devise a less effective, more costly tool than section 936 provisions or similar tax subsidies. Lawrence Hunter reports that, in 1993, 98.5 percent of section 936 tax credits for the Puerto Rican operations of U.S. corporations accrued to manufacturing and public utilities.[30] These are among the most capital-intensive sectors of the econ-omy. According to Bosworth and Collins, 60 percent of the subsidies accrued to the manufacture of chemicals and allied products such as medicines. Thomas Hexner and Glenn Jenkins refer to a 1992 General Accounting Office study find-ing that "drug companies with manufacturing operations in Puerto Rico received tax benefits worth $72,788 for each job paying an average of $26,471."[31]

Tax Subsidies, Entry Barriers, and Rent-Seeking Behavior

Section 936 tax subsidies merit special attention because of their enormous magnitude, historically, and their impact on the structure of employment and output. But they are only part of a larger story. The Puerto Rican tax code and regulatory system abound with provisions that cater to special business interests. Some provisions take the form of targeted tax breaks, others restrict business entry and expansion, and others involve licensing requirements and burden-some regulations that favor incumbents over potential rivals. In this climate, profitability and survival often hinge on obtaining and exploiting special tax breaks and regulatory advantages. The result is a complicated web of policy-induced financial incentives that help sustain a rent-seeking business culture and an overly intrusive role for the government.

As an illustration, table 6-13 presents a list of business incentives enacted into law in Puerto Rico from August 2001 to August 2002.[32] Various provi-sions aim to encourage the industrial, agricultural, and export sectors; the film industry; call center operations; stagnant municipalities; and the employment of high-skill workers and handicapped workers. These various provisions, which

30. Hunter (2003, fig. 4).
31. J. Thomas Hexner and Glenn Jenkins, "Puerto Rico: The Economic and Fiscal Dimen-sions," 1998, Citizens Educational Foundation (www.puertorico-herald.org/issues/vol2n03/hexner-jenkins.shtml [March 2005]).
32. The number of industrial incentives enacted into law during this year is unusually large, but the characteristics of the incentives described in table 6-13 are typical of other periods as well. See Cao Garcia (2004) for a historical account of federal and home-grown tax incentives in Puerto Rico, and chapter 7 of this volume for a comparative analysis of Puerto Rico's tax system.

Table 6-13. *Illustrative Business Incentives Enacted into Law from August 2001 to August 2002 by the Puerto Rican Government*

Law	Description
Law 109	Grants a 50 percent tax credit, under certain conditions, for the acquisition of a business in the process of closing operations in Puerto Rico.
Law 110	Raises the tax credit on the purchase of products manufactured in Puerto Rico by certain enterprises from 10 to 25 percent.
Law 112	Grants certain businesses the option of recognizing a deduction for spending on the purchase or construction of buildings, structures, and equipment and machinery.
Law 113	Grants double deductions for spending on employee training and on research and development.
Law 115	Liberalizes administrative restrictions on credit cooperatives to allow them to act as agents in selling mortgage loans and in launching new products.
Law 117	Creates the Credit and Guarantees Fund for Agricultural Loans (Fondo de Credito y Guarantias de Prestamos Agricolas). If a farmer cannot meet a loan obligation to a private bank, the farmer can request a grant from the fund to cover the debt. The fund is authorized to grant up to $100 million during a four-year period.
Law 121	Creates the Corporation for the Development of the Arts, Sciences, and Film Industry of Puerto Rico. The corporation offers incentives and administers the funds financing productions.
Law 141	Exempts associations of legal owners of vacation clubs from income taxes, promoting the time-share industry.
Law 143	Exempts fees earned by financial institutions for issuing guarantees or letters of credit to finance tourism development projects from income taxes.
Law 145	Provides tax incentives to innovative technology industries that establish operations in Puerto Rico and that generate high-skill scientific, technological, and managerial employment.
Law 169	Amends the 1994 Internal Revenue Code to grant eligible businesses a tax credit equal to 10 percent of the purchase value for products manufactured in Puerto Rico.
Law 174	Grants excise tax exemptions to enterprises for the purchase of machinery and equipment to fulfill environmental, security, and health requirements. This law also grants income tax credits on machinery and equipment acquired for businesses devoted to call centers established in Puerto Rico.
Law 163	Permits the Industrial Development Company (Compania de Fomento Industrial) to rent space at low cost to nonprofit organizations for the establishment of factories that employ handicapped workers.
Law 225	Reduces the income tax rate on call center operations to 4 percent or 2 percent, depending on geographic service area. It also grants full exemption from real estate taxes, municipal patents, and other municipal taxes during the first five years after the law takes effect.
Law 226	Grants full exemption from income taxes and partial exemption on municipal patents and other municipal taxes to certain businesses located in Vieques, Culebra, or any other municipality with similar economic or unemployment situations.

add to a large set of older incentive programs, exhibit several noteworthy characteristics. First, they typically benefit special business interests. Second, the form of the benefits—for example, credits and deductions on business taxes—makes it difficult to assess the magnitude of the subsidy and the likely drain on the government treasury. Third, the incentive provisions often enlarge the powers of the government bureaucracy, especially at the commonwealth level. Fourth, several of the industrial incentives erode the revenue base at the municipal level. Examples include exemptions from local property taxes and municipal patent requirements. Fifth, some provisions contain an element of trade protectionism, such as tax exemptions for the purchase of Puerto Rican manufactures. Finally, when taken as a whole, table 6-13 suggests that rent seeking is an important feature of the Puerto Rican business climate. Much effort and large expenditures are devoted to lobbying the legislature for special-interest provisions. The bills actually passed into law represent a small sample of the proposals that shuttle around the legislature.

Rent-seeking behavior extends beyond tax breaks and subsidized credit to a variety of entry barriers that protect incumbents and local business interests. Some of the most important barriers arise at the municipal government level. Businesses in Puerto Rico usually must obtain a patent from the local municipality to operate within its boundaries. The steps required for obtaining municipal patents look straightforward on the books, but in practice the process can be plagued with difficulties. A key problem is that a patent is granted only for a particular location, as determined by the municipal authority. Municipalities often grant patents only for slow business areas, effectively protecting incumbents in desirable locations.

Other entry barriers arise at the commonwealth level. A recent federal appeals court decision explains how entry barriers work for retail pharmacies in Puerto Rico.[33] Law 189 of July 29, 1979, requires a proposed new pharmacy establishment to obtain a Certificate of Need and Convenience from the secretary of the Puerto Rico Health Department. Certificates are routinely granted in the absence of local merchant opposition, but they are subjected to a costly and lengthy legal proceeding if any "affected party"—invariably a rival pharmacy—opposes the proposed pharmacy. In such cases, the certificate is often denied, as it was for several Walgreens outlets. Walgreens filed suit in federal court, claiming that Law 189 amounted to an unconstitutional infringement on interstate commerce, and in 2005 Walgreens prevailed at the appellate level. The Walgreens matter pertains to pharmacies only, and similar certification requirements remain in effect for other health care facilities.

More generally, licensing requirements restrict entry into many professions, services, and business activities. A wave of lobbying efforts has recently tried to

33. See U.S. Court of Appeals for the First Circuit (2005b).

establish new professional licensing requirements and compulsory dues for collegiate associations. One example is the legal requirements for producing a public performance, such as a theatrical production or a music concert. The current requirements under Law 182 are reasonably straightforward: a $20 license fee, a certificate of good conduct, evidence that tax payments are current, and the posting of a bond or insurance policy. Law 182 also provides for a $10,000 fine for anyone who produces an event without a license. But House Bill 1460, approved by the Puerto Rican House with bipartisan support on June 21, 2005, would raise entry barriers by requiring that a producer have five years of experience as a promoter, work at least one year with an established producer, and hold a specified college degree. In addition, the proposed law would create a Puerto Rico College of Public Performance Producers (Colegio de Productores de Espectáculos Públicos), which would have the power to license, regulate, sue, and investigate the actions of collegiate members. Similar legislation is currently under review in the Senate. Other recent examples of efforts to erect professional entry barriers include Senate Project 1842 for psychologists, a proposed college of journalists for newspersons, and House Project 3755 for economists. This last one is favored by the Puerto Rico Association of Economists, suggesting that economists are just as ready as anyone else to erect entry barriers in their own interests.

The similarity of these licensing requirements and collegiate organizations to medieval guilds is striking. These measures are sold as arrangements that ensure quality and protect local interests against foreign interests or large companies. Their clear economic effect, however, is to restrict competition and raise prices for consumers. Adam Smith developed this theme more than two centuries ago in his vigorous critique of mandatory apprenticeships and other restrictions on entry into cutlery, weaving, and other trades in eighteenth-century Britain.[34] More recently, Simeon Djankov and colleagues, examining data for start-up firms in eighty-five countries, report that countries with heavier entry regulation have more corruption and larger underground economies but not better quality of private or public goods.[35] The implication is that stronger entry regulation accentuates corruption and expands the underground economy without any compensating improvement in the quality of goods and services.

Taxes on Labor Income and Consumption

Taxes on labor income and consumption expenditures encourage households to leave the legal market in favor of untaxed activities—leisure, household production, and the underground economy. Substitution of the illegal market for the legal market is relatively easy for certain goods and services, such as meal preparation

---

34. See Smith (1976, bk. 1, chap. 10, pt. 2). For a modern analysis of the adverse price, output, and cost effects of artificial entry restrictions, see Carlton and Perloff (2000, pp. 74–76).
35. Djankov and others (2002).

and cleaning services; it is relatively difficult for others, such as automobile production and surgery. Hence high tax rates on labor and consumption discourage work in the legal market sector; in addition, these tax rates systematically alter the mix of market production. Tax-sensitive sectors include eating and drinking establishments, laundry and cleaning services, child care, consumer repair services, domestic household help, and most personal services. As suggested by these examples, tax-sensitive sectors tend to rely heavily on workers with lower schooling and lower wages. It follows that high tax rates on labor and consumption have disproportionately large negative effects on the demand for less skilled workers.

Steven Davis and Magnus Henrekson investigate these issues in a sample of rich countries and find that higher tax rates on labor and consumption lead to less activity in the legal market, a bigger underground economy, and an altered industry mix.[36] The estimated effects are quite large. Consider, for example, a between-country difference of 12.8 percentage point in the tax rate, a unit standard deviation in the cross section of their sample. Using data for the mid-1990s and their preferred specification, Davis and Henrekson find that a tax rate increase of this size leads to 122 fewer hours worked per adult per year in the legal market sector, a drop of 4.9 percentage points in the employment-to-population ratio, and a rise in the underground economy equal to 3.8 percent of GDP. It also lowers by 10–30 percent the economy-wide share of production and employment in tax-sensitive sectors such as eating, drinking, and lodging establishments. As Davis and Henrekson stress, these estimates reflect the direct effect of taxes on labor supply and labor demand plus the effects of tax-funded welfare and social insurance programs on labor supply incentives.

The impact of tax-funded transfer programs is of particular concern in Puerto Rico, because so many residents rely on government transfers as a major source of income. As analyzed in detail by Gary Burtless and Orlando Sotomayor (chapter 3 of this volume) and María Enchautegui and Richard Freeman (chapter 4 of this volume), these transfer programs often confront recipients with very high implicit tax rates if they move from welfare to work. On the U.S. mainland, earned income tax credits for working families mitigate the adverse labor supply incentives introduced by means-tested transfer programs. Puerto Rican residents are not eligible for earned income tax credits because they do not pay federal income taxes.

Minimum Wage Laws

The U.S. Federal Fair Labor Standards Act regulates minimum wages and working conditions for covered workers. It has applied to Puerto Rico since its inception in 1938, but for decades it allowed for less extensive coverage and

---

36. Davis and Henrekson (2005a). Many other studies also investigate the role of tax rates in cross-country differences in work activity and the size of the underground economy.

lower minimum wages in Puerto Rico. Starting in 1974, amendments to the act increased coverage in Puerto Rico and gradually brought the federal minimum for Puerto Rico into line with the U.S. minimum. Since 1983, Puerto Rican employers have faced essentially the same minimum wage requirements as U.S. employers.[37] The current federal minimum of $5.15 an hour for covered workers is about 30 percent of the average hourly wage in the United States and more than 60 percent of the average hourly wage in Puerto Rico.[38] The federal minimum has also been quite high historically relative to the average wage in Puerto Rico.

There is compelling evidence that minimum wage laws have profoundly affected the earnings distribution in Puerto Rico.[39] For example, half of all covered workers in 1979 were paid at the prevailing U.S. minimum of $2.90 an hour, and another 13 percent were paid within 10 cents of the U.S. minimum.[40] Furthermore, the increase in the federal minimum from $2.90 in 1979 to $3.35 in 1983 had a pronounced effect on earnings distribution.

The evidence regarding employment effects is much less clear. Based on an investigation of aggregate and industry-level data, Alida Castillo-Freeman and Richard Freeman conclude that the extension of the U.S. minimum wage to the island starting in 1974 caused "massive job losses" and greatly altered Puerto Rico's industry mix.[41] However, Alan Krueger revisits the same data and concludes that the evidence regarding employment effects is "fragile" and "surprisingly weak."[42] He shows that the estimated employment effects found by Castillo-Freeman and Freeman are sensitive to reasonable alternatives for the empirical specifications and estimation methods. In short, the existing literature has reached no clear conclusions about the employment effects of minimum wage requirements in Puerto Rico.

Previous studies are largely silent about the longer-term employment consequences of minimum wage requirements. This is a major drawback for the purposes of policy analysis, because the disemployment effects of minimum wage requirements are probably (much) larger in the longer term. It takes time to substitute away from low-skill labor in response to mandatory wage floors. These substitution responses can take the form of higher capital-to-labor ratios, greater reliance on relatively skilled workers, and the adoption of labor-saving technology. Even with fixed factor intensities and unchanging technologies, disemployment effects mount over time if minimum wage requirements operate

37. Castillo-Freeman and Freeman (1992).

38. Puerto Rico's average hourly wage is about $8.00. The U.S. Bureau of the Census (2005, table 620) reports an average hourly wage of $17.35 for the United States in 2002.

39. See Reynolds and Gregory (1965); Santiago (1989); Castillo-Freeman and Freeman (1992).

40. Castillo-Freeman and Freeman (1992).

41. Castillo-Freeman and Freeman (1992); Santiago (1989) reaches similar conclusions based on a different approach to the aggregate time series.

42. Krueger (1995).

on the entry margin for new employers and new job positions. Given the overwhelming evidence that minimum wage laws have pushed up the lower half of Puerto Rico's wage distribution, it is highly likely that they also slowed the entry of new employers and the creation of new jobs for less skilled workers. In this regard, the evidence presented in figure 6-2 is highly suggestive: Puerto Rico's missing jobs are concentrated in industries with relatively low schooling requirements. Employment in these industries is much more likely to be depressed by minimum wage requirements than employment in schooling-intensive industries.

Slow-working disemployment effects also arise through the impact of minimum wage requirements on the accumulation of work-related skills.[43] The skill accumulation effects work through two main channels. First, wage floors can reduce employment and hours directly, lowering work experience. Second, even when there is no direct effect on employment and hours, a binding wage minimum reduces the scope for learning and training on the job. For both reasons, workers then accumulate marketable skills more slowly. The result is a reduction in future earnings capacity and weaker attachment to the labor market.[44] Longerterm effects on labor market attachment are of particular concern when meanstested government transfer payments prop up reservation wages, as they do in Puerto Rico for a large fraction of the population. In summary, there are good reasons to think that the application of U.S.-level minimum wages has had a large negative impact on the rate of employment in Puerto Rico and on the accumulation of marketable skills among Puerto Rican residents.

Other Labor Market Regulations

Private business owners and public sector managers in Puerto Rico frequently complain about an inability to address worker abuse of labor market regulations. There are important abuses pertaining to vacation time, sick leave, and worker dismissal. For example, employee claims of work-related stress are routinely endorsed by medical authorities without serious examination. As another example, the law mandates twelve days of sick leave a year for employees. However, employees are required to submit a medical report only if absent from work for more than two consecutive days. Many workers abuse the system by claiming health-related absences two days at a time up to the maximum number of days a year. Health-related absences are not determined in advance, so business planning

43. See Hashimoto (1982) and Mincer (1984), among many others.
44. See Neumark and Nizalova (2004). Previous research provides little direct evidence on the longer-term effects of minimum wage requirements, but the work by Neumark and Nizalova is an exception. They present evidence that, for U.S. residents, exposure to higher minimum wage requirements at young ages leads to lower earnings and fewer work hours later in life. The estimated effects are sizable: one additional year of a teenager's exposure to an 11 percent increase in the minimum wage above the level of the federal minimum lowers that person's earnings in his or her twenties by 1.9 percent. Reduced hours account for about one-quarter of the earnings reduction.

and the performance of work groups suffer from unscheduled absences. These unscheduled absences raise labor costs and discourage employment growth.

Other problems arise in connection with dismissals and long-term leaves of absence. If an employee is granted a long-term leave for health-related reasons, the rules of the State Security Fund (Fondo de Seguro del Estado) require the employer to keep the employee's post open for a full year. During that time, the employer need not pay wages but must pay social benefits. The rules also specify that the employer cannot phone the employee or the State Security Fund to discuss the issue. As a result, it is difficult for the firm to plan and operate efficiently. Worker dismissal often ends in lawsuits, causing employers to refrain from legally justifiable dismissals owing to incompetence at work or a business slowdown. In turn, the difficulty and cost of dismissing workers make employers reluctant to hire.

The Effect of State-Owned Enterprises on the Competitive Environment

As documented above, the public sector accounts for a large but declining share of economic activity in Puerto Rico. This evidence raises two questions: Historically, how has a large public sector affected the competitive environment in Puerto Rico? And how is Puerto Rico's competitive environment likely to evolve in response to a declining role for the public sector? Definitive answers to these questions are beyond the scope of this chapter, but we can draw on recent research to suggest some tentative answers. In this regard, our main point is twofold: a large role for the public sector lessens competitive pressures, and a lessening of competitive pressures yields lower productivity.

A large public sector lessens competitive pressures in the economy for several reasons. First, state-owned enterprises operate with "softer" budget constraints than private enterprises in the sense that financial distress is more likely to result in taxpayer-funded bailouts for public enterprises. Second, the private sector can rely on the profit motive and high-powered incentives much more readily and effectively than can the public sector. Third, when public and private sector enterprises potentially compete in the same line of business, the state often restricts private sector entry or expansion opportunities in order to protect the public enterprise. The U.S. Postal Service, with its government-granted monopoly in the delivery of first-class mail, is a classic example.

Several recent studies provide evidence that greater competitive pressure leads to higher labor productivity. This research suggests that the beneficial productivity effects of competitive pressure work through a variety of channels that vary with circumstances. Jose Galdon-Sanchez, James Schmitz, and Arilton Teixeira offer some of the most compelling evidence that competitive pressure can provide the impetus for dramatic productivity gains.[45] An intensification of

---

45. Galdon-Sanchez and Schmitz (2002); Schmitz (2005); Schmitz and Teixeira (2004).

competitive pressure in the iron ore industry in the early 1980s led, within a few years, to a doubling of labor productivity at U.S. and Canadian mines.[46] Work-rule reforms that cut overstaffing requirements in collectively bargained labor contracts drove most of the productivity gains; the exit of low-productivity mines and the adoption of new technology played minor roles. In their study of the privatization of state-owned iron ore mines in Brazil in 1989, Schmitz and Teixeira find that, before privatization, about 60 percent of the industry was state owned.[47] In the first few years after privatization, labor productivity doubled at newly privatized mines and, even more remarkably, at previously private mines. These productivity gains were much larger than contemporaneous gains at iron ore mines in other countries. Several other studies produce evidence that an intensification of competitive pressure raises productivity by displacing less efficient producers, triggering the reallocation of factor inputs to higher value uses, and stimulating reform in work practices.[48]

These observations suggest that a large public sector has suppressed productivity levels in Puerto Rico for decades. By the same logic, they suggest that the rapid downsizing of Puerto Rico's public sector in the 1990s is a potentially important source of long-term productivity gains. This issue merits further attention by researchers and policymakers.

The Permitting Process as a Barrier to Business Development

Through the permitting process the government oversees and regulates construction and real estate development projects, the commercial use of equipment and facilities, and the periodic renewal of various business licenses. To the best of our knowledge, there is little systematic research on the permitting process in Puerto Rico and no comprehensive sources of information about the process and its consequences. Persons with in-depth knowledge of the permitting process are reluctant to speak for attribution, because the topic is politically sensitive and because public statements could jeopardize their commercial interests.

In light of these realities, we took the following two-pronged approach in our efforts to understand the functioning of the permitting process. First, we conducted informal interviews with more than one hundred persons who have expertise on or firsthand experience with the permitting process in Puerto Rico. Second, we sought to corroborate the claims and characterizations of interviewees by drawing on external public sources such as newspaper articles, judicial proceedings, and government laws and regulations. The result, we believe, is a first-pass description and analysis that delivers some insights into how the permitting process in Puerto Rico raises the cost of doing business, corrodes the business and

---

46. Schmitz (2005).
47. Schmitz and Teixeira (2004).
48. See Eslava and others (2004); Holmes and Schmitz (2001); Markiewicz, Rose, and Wolfram (2004); Sivadasan (2003); Syverson (2004).

regulatory climate, hampers economic development, and undermines the drive for employment growth. Our discussion focuses on the permitting process for construction and real estate development projects, but our interviews indicate that the problems we identify also plague the permitting process for the commercial use of equipment and facilities and the periodic renewal of business operating licenses.

We conducted face-to-face interviews with about ten contractors and construction engineers, fifteen real estate developers and their employees, ten business persons with experience as clients of construction contractors and real estate developers, five lenders and employees of financial institutions, twenty current and former government office holders, fifteen attorneys and permit specialists, and thirty others—among them small-business owners and their employees, entrepreneurs, and academics with knowledge of the permitting process. We did not select the interviewees randomly. Instead, we initially approached and interviewed several experts on the permitting process, and these experts referred us to other potential interviewees. As we proceeded, we also independently contacted other persons to clarify particular issues or seek out additional information. Interviews varied widely in depth and duration. The average interview lasted about thirty minutes, but many others lasted no more than ten minutes, and several interviews took a few hours. Follow-up interviews to clarify particular questions typically took place by phone and were usually brief.

Overview of the Permitting Process

The permitting process for construction and real estate development projects in Puerto Rico comprises four main elements:

—Consultation regarding the proposed project's location (*consulta de ubicación*), which requires approval by the Planning Board (Junta de Planificación), an arm of the governor's office. Zoning variances and proposed exceptions to standard construction requirements are also treated at this stage.

—The preparation and filing of environmental assessments and environmental impact statements. The latter are more detailed and extensive.

—Applications to the Regulations and Permits Administration (Administración de Reglamentos y Permisos, or ARPE) for permits pertaining to construction, renovation, and the placement of signs and advertisements. These permits are required by law for project development, the construction of new facilities, the refashioning of sites when starting new businesses, and for merely putting up signs.

—Applications for various use permits required to operate a completed or renovated facility. These use permits include health certificates and fire department endorsements.

This high-level overview suggests that the permitting process is reasonably straightforward, but the reality is far more complex and fraught with uncertainty, compliance costs, and delays. To help provide a sense of the complexity and uncertainty, figure 6-4 depicts the main elements of the permitting process.

Figure 6-4. *Permitting Process for Construction and Real Estate Development Projects, Puerto Rico*

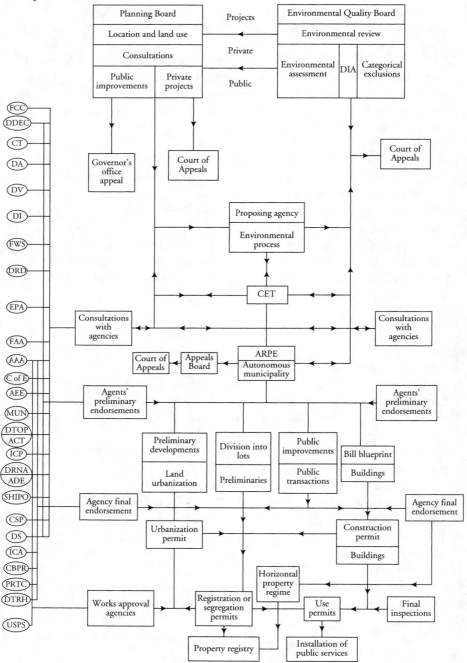

Figure 6-4. (*continued*)

Source: Based on Solá (2004, p. 16).

AAA: Autoridad de Acueductos y Alcantarillados (Aqueduct and Sewage Authority)
ACT: Autoridad de Carreteras y Transportación (Highways and Transportation Authority)
ADS: Autoridad de Desperdicios Sólidos (Solid Waste Authority)
AEE: Autoridad de Energía Eléctrica (Electric Power Authority)
ARPE: Administración de Reglamentos y Permisos (Regulations and Permits Administration)
C of E: Corps of Engineers
CBPR: Cuerpo de Bomberos de Puerto Rico (Fire Corps of Puerto Rico)
CET: Centro Expreso de Trámites (Express Center for Procedures)
CSP: Comisión de Servicio Público (Public Service Commission)
CT: Compañía de Turismo (Tourism Company)
DA: Department of Agriculture
DDEC: Departamento de Desarrollo Económico y Comercio (Department of Economic Development
    and Commerce)
DE: Departamento de Educación (Department of Education)
DIA: Declaración de Impacto Ambiental (Environmental Impact Statement)
DRD: Departamento de Recreación y Deportes (Department of Recreation and Sports)
DRNA: Departamento de Recursos Naturales y Ambientales (Department of Natural and Environmental
    Resources)
DS: Departamento de Salud (Health Department)
DTOP: Departamento de Transportación y Obras Públicas (Department of Transportation and Public
    Works)
DTRH: Departamento del Trabajo y Recursos Humanos (Department of Labor and Human Resources)
DV: Departamento de la Vivienda (Department of Housing)
EPA: Environmental Protection Agency
FAA: Federal Aviation Administration
FCC: Federal Communications Commission
FWS: U.S. Fish and Wildlife Service
ICP: Instituto de Cultura Puertorriqueña (Institute of Puerto Rican Culture)
JCA: Junta de Calidad Ambiental (Environmental Quality Board)
MUN: Municipality
PRTC: Puerto Rico Telephone Company
SHIPO: State Historic Preservation Office
USPS: United States Postal Service

The sheer number of government agencies with hands in the process provides some indication of the complexities and the potential for bottlenecks.

Ricardo Solá, an experienced construction engineer, describes the process as follows:

> There are at least thirty-four public agencies that intervene in the process, in at least . . . 119 procedures and twelve stages. . . . There are about sixty sets of regulations that regulate land development and construction, many of them, or the amendments to them, realized incoherently and without an integrated vision of the objectives of the regulation. . . . The budget assigned to pay needed technical and management personnel and to adequately equip regulatory agencies and the reviewing units of

the agencies providing endorsements is excessively low. It is therefore necessary to restructure the processes in all . . . agencies simultaneously. Without adequate funding these tasks cannot be realized.[49]

All industry participants interviewed for this study stressed that the permitting process has been a nightmare for a long time and remains so. Many interviewees remarked that construction and development projects must overcome a wide range of bureaucratic obstacles, which can delay or derail a project both in its initial stages and after construction has begun. In the case of environmental reviews, many interviewees remarked that bureaucratic inaction, legal ambiguities, and political uncertainties lead to overly long approval delays and uncertainties. Interviewees tend to agree with the statement that the permitting process requires more than incremental change. Instead, the predominant view is that effective reform requires a full scrapping of the existing system and a fresh set of rules and procedures.

Project Approval, Zoning and Construction Variances, and Environmental Review

Two government agencies oversee the regulation of construction and development projects: the Planning Board and ARPE. The Planning Board is responsible for guiding the island's overall economic, social, and physical development. It prepares the *Economic Report to the Governor* and elaborates the government's fiscal, social, and economic plans as well as its zoning and other regulations. The board was created in the early 1940s as the brainchild of Governor Rexford Guy Tugwell, who made it the main government arm to control and plan development of the island.

The Planning Board has an explicit consultation role in the permitting process when there are requests for variances (*variaciones*) from existing construction regulations and zoning requirements. Variances arise when some aspect of the project does not abide exactly by the existing regulations and requirements, which is the case for most substantial projects. Approval of variances requires consultations with the Planning Board as the first step in the permitting process. If a project does not involve any variances, the developer proceeds directly to ARPE, which oversees the operational process related to the granting of permits. The Permits and Regulations Administration was created in 1975 (Law 76, June 24, 1975) as a spin-off from the Planning Board, which formerly undertook the operational functions now performed by ARPE. These two agencies now enter at different stages in the permitting process and have distinct roles.

49. Solá (2004, p. 15).

If the Planning Board approves a project's location and all variances, ARPE takes over for the remainder of the process. It applies the regulations, laws, and ordinances that govern the use and development of land; the construction, use, and alteration of buildings and structures; and the installation of signs and announcements (*rótulos y anuncios*). However, if some unapproved variance is detected by ARPE, the developer proposing the project must return to the Planning Board for additional consultations and decisions.

According to interviewees, the Planning Board typically takes one to two years and even as many as four years for the approval of a major construction or development project. The next step, preliminary approval from ARPE, may take as little as one week for projects with no variances from existing regulations and zoning requirements, but major projects typically require another six to twelve months for approval by ARPE. As mentioned by several developers whom we interviewed, environmental disputes can further delay the start of development projects for many years. One example is the Serene Coast project in the Piñones area of Loíza, first proposed in 1995. The developer originally presented an environmental assessment but, in response to a judicial proceeding, it submitted a more detailed environmental impact statement in 1997. As of 2005 the project has yet to obtain Planning Board approval, reportedly because public agencies have not determined whether the project abides by the Environmental Public Policy Law of 1970. In July 2005 the Department of Natural and Environmental Resources requested modifications to the project on environmental grounds. Opposition to the Serene Coast project by environmental groups set against strong support for the project by the mayor of Loíza suggests that a stalemate will continue for some time.[50]

Centralization, Politicization, and Corruption in the Permitting Process

Key aspects of the permitting process—location consultation, zoning variances, ARPE permits, and environmental approvals—are centralized in the governor's office. This anomalous state of affairs traces back to the creation of the Planning Board. Governor Tugwell concentrated the power to grant location and use permits in his office as a planning tool. When the Environmental Quality Board was created in 1970 it was incorporated into the governor's office as well. When the operational part of the permitting process was separated from the Planning Board to form ARPE, it was also kept in the governor's office. Thus new business activity on the island that requires real estate development, new construction, or major renovations to existing structures must be approved by the governor's office—that is, by agencies operating under the direct supervision of

50. See *El Nuevo Día*, July 15, 2005, pp. 8–9; *El Nuevo Día*, July 16, 2005, p. 26.

the governor. (Exceptions for projects in autonomous municipalities are discussed below.)

Perhaps as a result, the regulation of project development and construction activities is highly politicized and susceptible to corruption. Experienced government workers, knowledgeable about the consultation and permitting process, are often transferred to other government offices after a change in administration and are replaced by less experienced employees affiliated with the winning political party. Corruption in the permitting process, and the harm it does to the business climate, came up repeatedly in our interviews. Consistent with comments by interviewees, corruption in the permitting process has also received attention in public forums. The president of the Retailers' United Center (Centro Unido de Detallistas) has stated that it is an "open secret" that in the agencies responsible for granting permits, such as ARPE, the Planning Board, and the Health Department, "money is passed under the table" to obtain the permits.[51] In recent years a number of government officials and employees have been convicted in federal court on corruption-related charges in connection with the permitting process. Examples include the deputy chief of staff to the governor in the first half of the 1990s and an executive assistant to the governor in the latter portion of the 1990s. Both officials accepted regular cash payments from contractors in return for access to government officials and expedited permitting. One official's services also included efforts to encourage other government officials to relax construction requirements.[52]

Information Costs in the Permitting Process

The procedure for obtaining construction permits and agency endorsements is complex and lacking in transparency. In addition, there is no readily accessible central source for the detailed information required to comply with the wide array of regulations. These features of the permitting process raise the information costs of compliance, increase uncertainty about approval, and add to the potential for unexpected delays and bottlenecks. The nature of the bureaucratic regime compounds informational costs and related problems by undermining the development of an experienced, apolitical workforce in key regulatory agencies.

Larger developers mitigate informational costs by employing permitting specialists. These in-house specialists are drawn from the ranks of former government workers at the Planning Board or ARPE, engineers who have acquired experience in the permitting process, and formerly independent permit specialists or facilitators (*gestores*). Developers also retain independent permit specialists

51. See Marian Díaz, "Ideas del sector privado al cogobierno," *El Nuevo Día,* January 5, 2005, p. 70.
52. See U.S. Court of Appeals for the First Circuit (2005a). The court's review of the facts is quite instructive about the business climate surrounding the permitting process and the role of corruption.

who handle the permitting maze for fees that vary according to the specific tasks performed. There is an active market for these independent permitting specialists and facilitators, often working in conjunction with law and accounting firms. Businesses that lack the scale to efficiently employ an in-house permit manager, and are unwilling to pay the fees commanded by independent permitting specialists, must fall back on their own efforts to comply with regulations and to navigate the permitting process. This approach typically involves a great deal of trial and error. Several interviewees mentioned the difficulties that confront entrepreneurs and employees who attempt to deal with the permitting process without specialized assistance.

Interviewees also pointed out that even permit specialists often make mistakes and present inadequate documentation to government agencies. Similarly, some interviewees mentioned that a lack of knowledge and professional responsibility on the part of some permitting specialists is a problem. Because many specialists obtain their initial work experience in only one of the many agencies involved in the permitting process, they are not always cognizant of the procedures and rules followed by other agencies.

Coordination Problems and Inefficient Implementation

Apart from high informational costs, the permitting process is also plagued by inefficient implementation on the part of government agencies and the problem of "too many cooks." Certain stages of the permitting process can require the endorsements of up to nineteen agencies. Each endorsing agency has the power to delay or halt the entire development project, and this is more likely to occur when the project faces opposition on political, commercial, or environmental grounds. Renewal of agency endorsements during an ongoing construction project can also be a problem. As a result, developers and contractors face substantial uncertainties. The common practice of requiring administrative and public hearings regarding permitting issues increases the need to rely on attorneys to navigate the process.

Many interviewees described the government agencies involved in the permitting process as inefficient. This segment of the government bureaucracy is faulted for excessive complexities, a shortage of personnel and resources, and inadequate employee supervision. Communications with ARPE employees require excessive on-site visits for reasons as mundane as the fact that phone calls often go unanswered. One of us experienced the phone problem firsthand on many occasions. On one occasion, several efforts to contact ARPE by phone resulted in two calls that were answered and referrals to several extension numbers of engineers who evaluate projects. However, none of these extensions yielded a response, and the effort to acquire information ended unsuccessfully. Similar communication problems were mentioned by interviewees, who noted that it is often more efficient to obtain information in person at the agency rather than by phone or from agency web pages.

Autonomous Municipalities

The Autonomous Municipalities Law (Law 81, August 30, 1991) allows a municipality to bypass the Planning Board and ARPE for construction and development projects confined to its boundaries. To do so, the municipality must meet certain financial standards, be able to manage its own accounting system, have an approved territorial organization plan, and meet other conditions. The municipality can then take over a number of responsibilities from the central government, including management of the permitting process and enforcement of zoning regulations. Although the Autonomous Municipalities Law has been in effect for fourteen years as of this writing, only six municipalities achieved autonomous status as of June 2005, and only twenty-four of seventy-eight municipalities have an approved territorial organization plan. Fiscal limitations and human resource constraints apparently account for the inability or unwillingness of many municipalities to seek autonomous status.

The six autonomous municipalities are Bayamón, Caguas, Carolina, Cidra, Guaynabo, and Ponce. An informal performance ranking (emerging from interviews) suggests that the permitting process functions more smoothly under the autonomous municipalities. Among autonomous municipalities, Ponce is generally praised for efficiency and speediness and is reportedly the only municipality that has fully and efficiently implemented the permitting process. Bayamón and Guaynabo are also classed as efficient, followed by Caguas and Carolina. Interviewees had little experience with Cidra. At the bottom, generally described as far less efficient than the autonomous municipalities, is the central government (ARPE). Nevertheless, interviewees did not react positively to the idea of a decentralization of ARPE.

The experience thus far indicates that a few municipalities can manage the permitting process more efficiently than the central government. However, the approach provided by the Autonomous Municipalities Law offers at best a partial solution to problems in the permitting process. Fiscal problems at the municipal level have hampered the process of becoming autonomous, and only two municipalities, Cidra and Guaynabo, became autonomous between 1999 and 2005. Over time many public services have been transferred from the central government to the municipal level, but there has not been a corresponding increase in municipal financial resources. In fact, as we note above, certain tax incentives enacted into law have cut the flow of revenues to municipalities. In addition, as mentioned by several interviewees, many municipalities lack the scale, infrastructure, and human resources to efficiently oversee the permitting process.

Other Public Policy Responses

In addition to the Autonomous Municipalities Law, there have been several other government initiatives to streamline or otherwise improve the permitting process. The government's Express Center for Procedures (Centro Expreso de Trámite, CET) began operations in 2002. The CET follows an earlier one-stop procedure established in 1998 (Law 264, September 4, 1998). In principle, the CET offers concurrent project evaluations by nine agencies, including ARPE, and consideration of environmental issues. While the CET mechanism is helpful, it does not greatly simplify the permitting process, in large part because the CET lacks authority to grant permits. Instead, it functions as a messenger service to other agencies. The project's permit manager submits basic information about the project over the Internet and then visits the CET with required documents. The CET process reduces paperwork, but filing requirements remain burdensome. For instance, consider projects that require a location consultation with the Planning Board. By obtaining agency endorsements and comments through the CET, the permit manager need file only ten copies of certain documents instead of nineteen. Filing requirements are otherwise the same. Most important, the CET takes the regulations as given and cannot issue permits on its own authority.

In an effort to promote ethical conduct and control the operation of the agency, the government in 2000 created ARPE's Governmental Ethics Committee and Internal Auditing Office. Other efforts to streamline the permitting process include a recent reform of the Puerto Rico Environmental Public Policy Act. Before the reform, the Planning Board issued its own environmental evaluation of proposed construction and development projects, duplicating the efforts of other government agencies and increasing paperwork burdens, filing requirements, and government costs. In March 2005 the environmental assessment was delegated to other government agencies, eliminating the redundant assessment by the Planning Board. This reform streamlines the permitting process somewhat, but it merely eliminates one of the many bureaucratic steps concerning the Planning Board location and approval process sketched above.

Despite awareness that many elements of the permitting process are counterproductive, restrictive regulations continue to proliferate. For example, Law 270 (September 14, 2004) amends the Regulations and Permits Law to require a favorable report, through a certification issued by the Puerto Rico Tourism Company, before approving a construction permit for a hotel, *parador* (inn), or other project of tourist interest. This amendment, ostensibly designed to ensure the quality of tourist-oriented facilities, adds one more hurdle to an already burdensome permitting process.

Summary and Concluding Remarks

Puerto Rico has struggled with an employment shortfall of stunning dimensions. The employment rate among working-age persons stood at nearly 50 percent in the early 1950s, then declined over the rest of the decade and again after 1971 to reach levels below 35 percent in the early 1980s. In the past thirty years, Puerto Rican employment rates have ranged from 55 to 65 percent of U.S. rates. This enormous shortfall holds for men and women, cuts across all education groups, and is deeper for persons without a college degree—about four-fifths of Puerto Rico's working-age population.

To help shed light on the reasons for Puerto Rico's persistently low rate of employment, we investigated several aspects of its employment structure. In this regard, two results stand out. First, the employment shortfall is concentrated in the private sector, particularly the free enterprise segment comprising businesses that operate in the formal economy without large subsidies, special regulatory advantages, or heavy-handed oversight by government bureaucracies. Even by rather relaxed criteria, less than one-quarter of working-age Puerto Ricans hold a job in the free enterprise segment of the economy. By the same criteria, more than half of working-age persons in the United States hold free enterprise jobs. The strikingly underdeveloped state of the private sector supports the view that Puerto Rico suffers from an inhospitable business climate.

Second, Puerto Rico's industry structure has for decades been grossly mis-aligned with the human capital mix of its population. The average schooling level of working-age persons in Puerto Rico is, and remains, below that of any U.S. state. Yet in terms of the schooling intensity of its industry structure, Puerto Rico ranks among the top third of U.S. states. Put differently, the missing jobs in Puerto Rico are concentrated in labor-intensive industries that rely heavily on less-educated workers. For example, Puerto Rico's employment rate in the eating, drinking, and lodging sector is lower than the rate for any U.S. state in recent decades and less than one-third the rate in Hawaii. The persistent inability of the Puerto Rican economy to generate jobs that fit the human capital mix of its population testifies to a profound failure of industrial and employment policy.

The evidence does not support the view that more schooling can, by itself, resolve Puerto Rico's employment problems. Large gains in schooling attainment in recent decades have accompanied very modest employment gains. Relative to the United States, Puerto Rico's employment shortfall exceeds 10 percent of the population for college-educated persons and 20 percent or more for groups with less education. Thus, if and when Puerto Rico matches U.S. schooling levels, very large employment shortfalls will persist absent deep reforms.

No single policy or institutional deficiency fully accounts for Puerto Rico's huge employment shortfall, underdeveloped private sector, and misaligned indus-try structure. Indeed, the list of significant contributing factors is long and varied:

—Large government transfer payments undermine work incentives and con-tribute to a deficit of work experience and marketable skills.

—Minimum wage laws discourage the hiring of less skilled workers, suppress the growth of employment in industries and activities that rely heavily on less educated workers, and diminish opportunities to acquire experience and train-ing on the job.

—Historically, the large role for public sector employment and production in Puerto Rico has softened competitive pressures on the island and discouraged the emergence of a vibrant private sector.

—Section 936 of the U.S. tax code and other federal tax incentives have helped create an industry structure in Puerto Rico that is poorly aligned with the type of jobs needed by its population. At best, section 936 provides for a modest number of jobs in Puerto Rico at enormous cost to the U.S. Treasury.

—Puerto Rico's own tax code is replete with provisions that benefit special business interests at the expense of the general welfare. These tax code provisions both reflect and contribute to a business climate in which profitability and survival too often rest on the ability to obtain favors from the government, rather than the ability to innovate, raise productivity, and serve consumers.

—Puerto Rico's regulatory environment deters business entry, hampers job creation, and erodes competitive pressures in many ways. Occupational licensing requirements create artificial entry barriers, restricting the supply of services and raising prices to consumers. Government oversight of business entry and location decisions raises entry costs and affords commercial rivals the opportunity to block entry. "Buy local" laws insulate business interests from foreign competition and raise prices for consumers. Like many provisions of the tax code, these aspects of the regulatory environment serve special business interests at the expense of the general welfare. They reflect and promote a business culture focused on rent seeking.

—The permitting process—whereby the government oversees construction and real estate development projects, the commercial use of equipment and facilities, and the periodic renewal of various business licenses—suffers from several serious problems. These problems raise the costs of doing business, undercut the drive for employment growth, and retard economic development.

As part of our study, we interviewed more than one hundred persons who have expertise in or firsthand experience with the permitting process. The view that the permitting process is excessively slow and costly, fraught with uncertainty, subject to capricious outcomes, prone to corruption, and susceptible to manipulation by business rivals, politicians, and special interest groups is widely shared by interviewees. Independent evidence from public sources supports this view.

Efforts to reform the permitting process have met with limited success. A partial exception is the Autonomous Municipalities Law of 1991, which allows municipal governments to take over much of the permitting process from the governor's office, if the municipality meets several conditions. Many interviewees stated that the permitting process functions much more smoothly in a handful of autonomous municipalities. Fourteen years after the law's enactment, however, only six municipalities had achieved autonomous status. For reasons of insufficient scale, limited financial resources, and lack of personnel, it is doubtful whether the other seventy-two municipalities can efficiently manage the permitting process, at least in its current form.

Our study emphasizes employment outcomes, but the policies and institutional arrangements we consider also lower real incomes and living standards by undermining productivity. Transfer payments and minimum wage laws lower worker productivity by contributing to a deficit of work experience. Special interest tax subsidies distort market price signals that would otherwise guide capital and labor to their best uses, lowering productivity in the process. Inefficiencies in the permitting process raise the cost of doing business, lowering productivity directly. Regulatory entry barriers, "buy local" laws, and a large role for the public sector soften competitive pressures. In turn, softer competition weakens the pressure to innovate and provide value for customers. Artificial entry barriers and inefficiencies in the permitting process also retard the type of creative destruction process that transformed the U.S. retail sector in recent decades, bringing dramatic productivity gains for businesses and lower prices and wider product selections for consumers. Finally, institutional arrangements that foster rent-seeking behavior lower productivity because they encourage socially wasteful efforts to secure preferential treatment from government officials, rather than socially productive efforts to better serve customers, improve products, and expand markets.

COMMENT
Marinés Aponte

The chapter by Steven Davis and Luis Rivera-Batiz, on entrepreneurship, is developed in three principal parts after the introduction: a comparative perspective on employment in Puerto Rico relative to that in the United States, the policy influences on business development and employment growth, and the permitting process as a barrier to business development. According to the authors, the chapter's main objective is to investigate "the employment record in Puerto Rico and its climate for business development." Owing to space limitations, I limit my comments to some of its principal aspects.

General Comments

The employment rate analysis presented in the chapter follows a traditional approach within a macroeconomic perspective. The authors use household census data to calculate the percentage of jobs provided by the public sector relative to the percentage of jobs in the private sector in Puerto Rico and the United States. In my view, the analysis would have been more adequate if the comparison had been made with a country similar to Puerto Rico in terms of income.

The authors find that Puerto Rico's employment shortfall compared with that of the United States is concentrated in the private sector. According to their findings, less than one-quarter of working-age Puerto Ricans hold a job in the free enterprise segment of the economy. However, the definition of free enterprise used by the authors is cause for concern, because it results in an underestimated private sector employment rate.[1] The authors' general conclusion in this area is that "the strikingly underdeveloped state of the private sector supports the view that Puerto Rico suffers from an inhospitable business climate."

My principal concern with the chapter is related to its approach to the theme. The link between Puerto Rico's employment record and the country's business climate—a link the authors intend to establish—is not quite clear to me. The authors make no reference to a conceptual framework to support their analysis, neither explicitly nor through a review of the literature.

---

1. Free enterprise is defined as private sector employment less nongovernmental employees in public utilities and sanitary services, primary and secondary education, colleges and universities, and several smaller industries (museums, galleries, zoos, business, trade and vocational schools, bus service and urban transit, research, development and testing, social services, forestry, and libraries) for which public sector employment exceeds 35 percent of industry employment. Construction was also excluded.

From an entrepreneurial point of view, the generally applied analysis linking business climate and employment growth is based on the study of the country's determinants of new business creation, which influence the creation of new firms and new jobs. Several conceptual models are available at the microeconomic level from diverse disciplines, including economics, psychology, and sociology, in which occupational choice models have been developed for understanding the entrepreneurial decision.[2] At the macroeconomic level, the Global Entrepreneurship Monitor study has developed a model distinguishing nine determinants of entrepreneurial opportunity and entrepreneurial capacity, which in turn influence the creation of new business and therefore of new jobs.[3] These determinants are financial support, government policies, government programs, education and training, research and development, commercial and legal infrastructure, internal market openness, physical infrastructure, and cultural and social norms. Each of these is a necessary part of the business climate of a country and should be taken into consideration in a holistic analysis. The Davis and Rivera-Batiz chapter develops only two of the nine determinants: government policies (trade protectionism, tax subsidies, entry barriers, taxes on labor income and consumption, and minimum wage laws) and the permitting process. To the extent that the other determinants are left out of the investigation, the analysis is fragmented.

The subject of assistance to business start-ups has attracted a lot of interest from researchers in the entrepreneurship field who have assumed that the use of support mechanisms can have positive effects both on the number of firms and jobs created and on the improved survival rate of these firms.[4] This literature also assumes that providing assistance in creating new business has a positive impact on employment generation, economic growth, and innovation.[5] Puerto Rico has a complete spectrum of institutions providing economic support (loans, subsidies, risk capital) as well as noneconomic support (information and orientation, consulting, training, incubators support), which are not considered in the chapter. In fact, support institutions in Puerto Rico, as well as services and programs, are overdiversified; more efficient coordination of these would serve the island's economy well.[6]

Entrepreneurial activity has been measured using a variety of indicators: self-employment rates, business ownership rates, and new firm start-up rates, among others.[7] The employment rate (which is based on jobs in all firms already oper-

2. Sternberg and Wennekers (2005).

3. Acs and others (2004).

4. Cooper (1982); Vesper (1982); Birley (1986); Westhead (1990); Cromie (1991); Hawkins (1993); White and Reynolds (1996).

5. On employment generation, see Storey (1982, 1988, 1994); Birley (1987); Kirchoff and Phillips (1988, 1992); White and Reynolds (1996); on economic growth, see Kent (1982); Sexton (1986); Dubini (1989); Storey (1994); Wennekers and Thurik (1999); on innovation, see Drucker (1984, 1985); Pavitt, Robson, and Townsend (1987); Acs and Audretsch (1988).

6. Aponte, Urbano, and Veciana (2002).

7. Audretsch (2003).

ating in the economy) seems to be neither a good indicator of new business development and entrepreneurial activity nor an adequate indicator of the country's business climate. Therefore, even if the finding that less than one-quarter of working-age Puerto Ricans hold a job in the free enterprise segment of the economy were validated, it would not be sufficient evidence to conclude that Puerto Rico suffers from an inhospitable business climate.

Policy Influences on Business Development

I agree with the authors' view that business in Puerto Rico is highly regulated. As the chapter presents in a detailed way, abundant legislation oriented toward employee rights, minimum wage laws, required use of American vessels in maritime transportation, as well as antitrust statutes, laws that regulate specific types of businesses, and environmental controls translate into very high operating costs for business in the Puerto Rican market.

However, some of the opinions concerning public policy expressed in the chapter concern me. Certainly, government has a major impact on the business climate, for it is the mix of public services, taxation, and regulation that creates the context within which companies operate. Yet the term "favorable business climate" has become, in a dangerous way, almost synonymous with pressure to cut taxes, reduce services, and remove impediments, particularly employment and environmental regulations.[8] This view is evident in several arguments concerning labor market regulations and requirements for real estate development projects. I consider this viewpoint totally inadequate from the perspective of sustainable economic development, especially in the case of a country like Puerto Rico, with limited land.

One of the few tax laws that favor local enterprise—the tax credit for the purchase of products manufactured in Puerto Rico—is identified by the authors as a protectionist measure—and therefore a negative one. In my opinion, this tax credit is a good way to stimulate local business.[9] Indeed, one of the principal deficiencies of the tax incentive law in Puerto Rico is precisely that it does not direct the tax benefits for foreign enterprises toward the establishment of economic linkages with the local economy. When linkages between big foreign enterprises and the local economy are weak, domestic entrepreneurial activity is not stimulated.[10] On the other hand, national income in Puerto Rico is dependent to a large extent on foreign entrepreneurial activity, owing to an economic model in use since the 1940s. This model is based on creating fiscal incentives to attract foreign enterprises to Puerto Rico. In my perspective, and contrary to

8. Dabson, Rist, and Schweke (1996).

9. To take just a few examples, most of the advanced industrial countries—including the United States and Japan—built up their economies by wisely and selectively protecting some of their industries until they were strong enough to compete with foreign companies. Stiglitz (2002, p. 16).

10. Keating (1989); Florio (1996).

the authors' argument, this results in a difficult competition situation for smaller domestic enterprises, since they do not receive significant tax exemptions but are subject to the same operating costs imposed by regulations. The model therefore impairs the development of domestic entrepreneurial activity.

The Permitting Process

The multiple regulations and complex and inefficient permitting processes required to create new businesses have been extensively recognized as a major obstacle to new business development in Puerto Rico.[11] The chapter gives a detailed view of the complexities in this area, but the methodology used to arrive at its strong conclusions are, as the authors note, anecdotal interviews. The reader does not have access to the questions asked of the interviewees. Moreover, I consider that the sample is biased since, as the authors explain, they did not select the interviewees randomly but proceeded by references given by the first persons interviewed. Although the existence of the permitting problem has been documented, the anecdotal methodology used by the authors impairs the strength of the arguments presented.

The authors describe the World Bank's relatively positive ranking of the business climate in Puerto Rico as "too rosy." However, compared with the quantitative methodology and large sample used by the World Bank, the negative anecdotal opinions presented in the chapter appear fragile. Furthermore, the authors concentrate most of their attention on permitting in construction and project development, which because of their complexities and impact on the environment are more regulated and intricate than the permitting process for other types of business. The chapter's strongly negative conclusions about the business climate in Puerto Rico can therefore be seriously questioned. In addition, from my point of view, the chapter should have concluded with recommendations as to how to improve the climate for business development and employment growth in Puerto Rico.

COMMENT
David B. Audretsch

The chapter by Steven Davis and Luis Rivera-Batiz addresses perhaps the central public policy concern confronting Puerto Rico: the persistent and long-term low rate of employment. The employment gap between the United States and Puerto

11. Centro para el Desarrollo Económico (1995); Aponte (2002).

Rico is striking. The authors report, for example, that only slightly more than one-third of Puerto Rican residents were employed at any one time in 2000, while in a benchmark comparison just over two-thirds of U.S. residents were employed. As a result, economic growth in Puerto Rico has been tepid and unsatisfactory.

Rather than look for solutions to long-term stagnation of employment and growth in terms of traditional macroeconomic policy instruments, the authors turn to microeconomic solutions. In particular, they focus on the "business climate" and "government policies and institutional arrangements that impede employment growth and business development." The government policies and institutional arrangements address five issues. The first involves the permitting process, which is costly and slow and has served to deter the start-up of new businesses and the growth of existing enterprises. The second is trade protection in general, and the U.S. Jones Act in particular, which has served as a barrier to trade between Puerto Rico and the United States. The third involves section 936 of the U.S. tax code, which has created a "complicated web of policy-induced financial incentives that help to sustain a rent-seeking business culture and an overly intrusive role for the government." The fourth is the application of the U.S. federal Fair Labor Standards Act, which regulates minimum wages and working conditions in Puerto Rico. The fifth is an underdeveloped private sector.

Why should improving the business climate, or what some refer to as the entrepreneurial culture, matter for employment and economic growth? According to the policy tradition reflecting the Solow growth model, it should not. According to the Solow approach, it is investment in physical capital that matters.[12] The view of the economy characterized by this model frames the policy debate by focusing on economic growth. The main mechanism for inducing higher growth rates is almost universally viewed as investment in physical capital. While technical change is recognized as shifting the production function, in the Solow model it is considered to be exogenous and, therefore, beyond the reach of policy. Thus the policy debate during the postwar era, which may best be reflected by the Solow model, disputed not the mechanism—physical capital—but rather the instruments. A vigorous dispute emerged both in the economics literature and in the public policy community about which particular instruments are best suited to encouraging investments in physical capital.

If physical capital is at the heart of the Solow economy, knowledge capital replaced it in the Romer economy. While the policy goal of economic growth remains relatively unchanged, the Romer model reflects a new emphasis on a different policy mechanism, knowledge capital, involving very different policy instruments.[13] The new policy instruments corresponding to the knowledge-driven economy, suggested by the Romer model, generally involve inducing investments in knowledge capital. While knowledge capital seems more vague and less con-

12. Solow (1956).
13. Romer (1986).

ducive to measurement than physical capital, it clearly involves knowledge-augmenting investments in human capital and research and development. Such instruments are different from their counterparts in the Solow model. These instruments include, but are not limited to, education at all levels, public research support, and tax and subsidy incentives to encourage private research and development (R&D).

But what do new and small businesses have to do with R&D and knowledge? Small business would seem to be at least as alien in the Romer model as in the Solow model. Just as small business has a competitive disadvantage in a model in which capital investment and scale economies are decisive, it is also disadvantaged in a model in which investments in R&D are needed to generate new knowledge and innovation.

As Davis and Rivera-Batiz point out, in fact, it would seem that Puerto Rico has a relatively strong endowment of one of the factors that matter the most in models of endogenous growth: human capital.[14] Shifting to a policy focus on knowledge capital involving instruments to induce investments in knowledge capital has clearly been successful in generating economic growth in many regions. However, as the knowledge spillover theory of entrepreneurship suggests, investments in knowledge capital may be a necessary but not a sufficient condition for ensuring that such investments are actually commercialized and generate economic growth. The existence of a severe knowledge filter will impede the spillover and commercialization of investments in new knowledge, thereby choking off the potential for economic growth.

There are certainly many examples of cities and regions exhibiting vigorous investments in new knowledge that have, at least until now, not triggered economic growth. For example, Maryann Feldman and Pierre Desrochers carefully document how large and sustained investments in research and human capital at Johns Hopkins University have not spawned commercialization and growth.[15]

Perhaps it is at the country level where the failure of knowledge investments to generate economic growth is most striking. Consider the case of Sweden. Throughout the postwar era, Sweden has consistently ranked among the highest in the world in terms of investments in new knowledge. Whether measured in terms of private R&D, level of education, university research, or public research, Sweden has exhibited strong and sustained investment in knowledge. As recently as 2003 Sweden had the world's highest ratio of GDP invested in R&D. Yet even in the face of such investments in knowledge, the return in terms of employment creation and economic growth has been modest—and a disappointment to the Swedish public policy community. Similar examples of high investments in new knowledge but low performance in terms of economic growth can be found throughout Europe to such an extent that the European Union has invented a

14. Lucas (1993).
15. Feldman and Desrochers (2003, 2004).

name for the European failure to commercialize its investments in new knowledge: the "European paradox."

High investment in knowledge accompanied by low growth performance is not restricted to Europe. One Asian example is Japan, where, as in Sweden, investments in private R&D and human capital have ranked among the highest in the world. Still, Japan has been bogged down with low and stagnant growth for more than a decade. It would seem that Europe does not have a monopoly on the paradox.

As the traditional policy instruments targeting either physical capital or knowledge capital failed to generate sustainable economic growth, employment, and competitiveness in globally linked markets, policymakers began to look elsewhere. The political mandate presumed that entrepreneurship was to replace or at least augment physical capital. Regions sought a mechanism to improve the returns on investments made in knowledge, investments that were not being realized in terms of economic growth and employment where the investments were funded. New businesses and the growth of existing ones are important because they provide a mechanism for getting knowledge and ideas into the market that might otherwise remain uncommercialized.

Within the economics literature, the prevalent theoretical framework has been the general model of income choice, which is also referred to as the general model of entrepreneurial choice. The model of income or entrepreneurial choice dates back to 1921, but it was extended by scholars later in the century.[16] In its most basic rendition, the model suggests that individuals are confronted with a choice of earning their income either from wages earned through employment in an incumbent enterprise or from profits accrued by starting a new firm. The essence of the income choice is made by comparing the wage an individual expects to earn through employment, W^*, with the profits that are expected to accrue from a new-firm startup, π. Thus the probability of starting a new firm, $P(E)$, can be represented as

$$P(E) = f(\pi - W).$$

An important qualifier to the basic model of income choice implied by Davis and Rivera-Batiz is that public policy and institutions can erect barriers to entrepreneurship, β, resulting in impediments to the start-up and growth of new firms.

$$P(E) = (1/\beta)(\pi^* - W).$$

16. See Knight (1921). The model of income choice is extended by Kihlstrom and Laffont (1979) to incorporate aversion to risk; and by Lucas (1978) and Jovanovic (1994) to explain why firms of varying size exist. The model is also used as the basis for empirical studies on the decision to start a new firm: see Blau (1987); Evans and Leighton (1989a, 1989b, 1990); Evans and Jovanovic (1989); Blanchflower and Oswald (1990); Blanchflower and Meyer (1994). It has also been extended and updated by Holmes and Schmitz (1990).

As the authors demonstrate, an important role for public policy in Puerto Rico is to stimulate employment and economic growth through the reduction of barriers to entrepreneurship, β. This would induce greater business opportunities, lead to additional start-ups, and spur growth companies.

An additional area that could prove to be fruitful for spurring entrepreneurship and ultimately employment along with economic growth is the use of policy instruments, such as incubators, science parks, and technology transfer programs to actively spur the start-up of new firms with a high-growth potential. As Timothy Bresnahan and Alfonso Gambardella observe,

> Clusters of high-tech industry, such as Silicon Valley, have received a great deal of attention from scholars and in the public policy arena. National economic growth can be fueled by development of such clusters. In the United States the long boom of the 1980s and 1990s was largely driven by growth in the information technology industries in a few regional clusters. Innovation and entrepreneurship can be supported by a number of mechanisms operating within a cluster, such as easy access to capital, knowledge about technology and markets, and collaborators.[17]

Similarly, Scott Wallsten argues that "policy makers around the world are anxious to find tools that will help their regions emulate the success of Silicon Valley and create new centers of innovation and high technology."[18]

The success of Puerto Rico's efforts to generate high-technology entrepreneurial clusters remains to be seen. Davis and Rivera-Batiz are surely correct in their careful analysis, suggesting that economic development prospects are not optimistic as long as the imposing current barriers to entrepreneurship deter entrepreneurial activity and business development.

17. Bresnahan and Gambardella (2004, p. 1).
18. Wallsten (2004, p. 229).

References

Acs, Zoltan J., and David B. Audretsch. 1988. "Innovation in Large and Small Firms: An Empirical Analysis." *American Economic Review* 78, no. 4: 678–90.

Acs, Zoltan J., and others. 2004. "Global Entrepreneurship Monitor 2004 Executive Report." London: Babson College and London Business School, GEM Consortium.

Alesina, Alberto, and Edward L. Glaeser. 2004. *Fighting Poverty in the U.S. and Europe: A World of Difference.* Oxford University Press.

Aponte, Marinés. 2002. "Factores condicionantes de la creación de empresas en Puerto Rico: Un enfoque institucional." Bellaterra: Universitat Autónoma de Barcelona (April).

Aponte, Marinés, David Urbano, and José M. Veciana. 2002. "Institutions and Support Programmes for Entrepreneurship: A Two-Country Comparison." Paper presented to the International Council for Small Business, Puerto Rico, June 16–19.

Audretsch, David. 2003. "Entrepreneurship: A Survey of the Literature." Indiana University, Institute for Development Strategies.

Basker, Emek. 2005a. "Job Creation or Destruction? Labor-Market Effects of Wal-Mart Expansion." *Review of Economics and Statistics* 87, no. 1: 174–83.

———. 2005b. "Selling a Cheaper Mousetrap: Wal-Mart's Effect on Retail Prices." University of Missouri (March).

Becker, Gary S. 1993. *Human Capital: A Theoretical and Empirical Analysis with Special Reference to Education.* 3rd ed. University of Chicago Press.

Birley, Sue. 1986. "The Role of New Firms: Births, Deaths, and Job Generation." *Strategic Management Journal* 7, no. 6: 361–76.

———. 1987. "New Ventures and Employment Growth." *Journal of Business Venturing* 2, no. 2: 155–65.

Blanchflower, David, and Bruce Meyer. 1994. "A Longitudinal Analysis of Young Entrepreneurs in Australia and the United States." *Small Business Economics* 6, no. 1: 1–20.

Blanchflower, David, and Andrew Oswald. 1990. "What Makes an Entrepreneur?" Working Paper 3252. Cambridge, Mass.: National Bureau for Economic Research.

Blau, David. 1987. "A Time-Series Analysis of Self-Employment in the United States." *Journal of Political Economy* 95, no. 3: 445–67.

Bresnahan, Timothy, and Alfonso Gambardella. 2004. *Building High-Tech Clusters: Silicon Valley and Beyond.* Cambridge University Press.

Cao Garcia, Ramón J. 2004. *Impuestos en Puerto Rico: Treinta años de experiencias y estudios.* San Juan: Grupo Editorial Akron.

Carlton, Dennis W., and Jeffrey M. Perloff. 2000. *Modern Industrial Organization.* 3rd ed. Reading, Mass.: Addison-Wesley.

Castillo-Freeman, Alida, and Richard Freeman. 1992. "When the Minimum Wage Really Bites: The Effect of the U.S.-Level Minimum on Puerto Rico." In *Immigration and the Work Force,* edited by George Borjas and Richard Freeman, pp. 177–212. University of Chicago Press.

Centro para el Desarrollo Económico. 1995. "Los dueños de pequeñas y medianas empresas en Puerto Rico: Características y necesidades." Mayagüez: University of Puerto Rico (May).

Cooper, Arnold. 1982. "The Entrepreneurship Small Business Interface." In *Encyclopedia of Entrepreneurship,* edited by C. A. Kent, D. L. Sexton, and K. H. Vesper. Englewood Cliffs, N.J.: Prentice-Hall.

Corneo, Giacomo, and Hans Peter Gruener. 2002. "Individual Preferences for Political Redistribution." *Journal of Public Economics* 83, no. 1: 83–107.

Cromie, S. 1991. "The Problems Experienced by Young Firms." *International Small Business Journal* 9: 43–61.

Dabson, Brian, Carl Rist, and William Schweke. 1996. "Business Climate and the Role of Development Incentives." *The Region* 10, no. 2: 47–49.

Davis, Steven J., and Magnus Henrekson. 2005a. "Tax Effects on Work Activity, Industry Mix, and Shadow Economy Size: Evidence from Rich-Country Comparisons." In *Labour Supply and Incentives to Work in Europe,* edited by Ramon Gomez-Salvador and others, pp. 44–104. Cheltenham, U.K.: Edward Elgar.

———. 2005b. "Wage-Setting Institutions as Industrial Policy." *Labour Economics* 12, no. 3: 345–77.

Djankov, Simeon, and others. 2002. "The Regulation of Entry." *Quarterly Journal of Economics* 117, no. 1: 1–37.

Drucker, Peter. 1984. "Our Entrepreneurial Economy." *Harvard Business Review* (Jan.–Feb.): 59–64.

———. 1985. *Innovation and Entrepreneurship.* New York: Harper and Row.

Dubini, Paola. 1989. "The Influence of Motivations and Environment on Business Start-ups: Some Hints for Public Policies." *Journal of Business Venturing* 4, no. 1: 11–26.

Dunn, Thomas A., and Douglas J. Holtz-Eakin. 2000. "Financial Capital, Human Capital, and the Transition to Self-Employment: Evidence from Intergenerational Links." *Journal of Labor Economics* 18, no. 2: 282–305.

Eslava, Marcela, and others. 2004. "The Effect of Structural Reforms on Productivity and Profitability Enhancing Reallocation: Evidence from Colombia." *Journal of Development Economics* 75, no. 2: 333–71.

Estudios Técnicos. 2004. *La economía informal en Puerto Rico: Primer, segundo, y tercer informe.* Report prepared for the Puerto Rico Department of Labor and Human Resources.

Evans, David, and Boyan Jovanovic. 1989. "An Estimated Model of Entrepreneurial Choice under Liquidity Constraints." *Journal of Political Economy* 97, no. 4: 808–27.

Evans, David, and Linda Leighton. 1989a. "The Determinants of Changes in U.S. Self-Employment." *Small Business Economics* 1, no. 2: 11–120.

———. 1989b. "Some Empirical Aspects of Entrepreneurship." *American Economic Review* 79, no. 3: 519–35.

———. 1990. "Small Business Formation by Unemployed and Employed Workers." *Small Business Economics* 2, no. 4: 319–30.

Fairlie, Robert W., and Alicia Robb. 2003. "Families, Human Capital, and Small Business: Evidence from the Characteristics of Business Owners Survey." Discussion Paper 871. Yale University, Economic Growth Center.

Feldman, Maryann, and Pierre Desrochers. 2003. "Research Universities and Local Economic Development: Lessons from the History of the Johns Hopkins University." *Industry and Innovation* 10, no. 1: 5–24.

———. 2004. "Truth for Its Own Sake: Academic Culture and Technology Transfer at Johns Hopkins University." *Minerva* 42, no. 2: 105–26.

Foster, Lucia, John Haltiwanger, and C. J. Krizan. 2004. "Market Selection, Reallocation, and Restructuring in the U.S. Retail Trade Sector in the 1990s." Working Paper. U.S. Bureau of the Census.

Florio, Massimo. 1996. "Large Firms, Entrepreneurship, and Regional Development Policy: Growth Poles in the Mezzogiorno over 40 Years." *Entrepreneurship and Regional Development* 8, no. 3: 263–95.

Galdon-Sánchez, Jose E., and James A. Schmitz Jr. 2002. "Competitive Pressure and Labor Productivity: World Iron Ore Markets in the 1980s." *American Economic Review* 92, no. 4: 1222–35.

Hashimoto, Masanori. 1982. "Minimum Wage Effects on Training on the Job." *American Economic Review* 72, no. 5: 1070–87.

Hausman, Jerry, and Ephraim Leibtag. 2004. "CPI Bias from Supercenters: Does the BLS Know That Wal-Mart Exists?" Working Paper 10712. Cambridge, Mass.: National Bureau of Economic Research.

Hawkins, Del. 1993. "New Business Entrepreneurship in the Japanese Economy." *Journal of Business Venturing* 8, no. 2: 137–50.

Holmes, Thomas J. 2005. "The Diffusion of Wal-Mart and Economies of Density." Paper presented at the National Bureau of Economic Research Summer Institute, Cambridge, Mass. (July).

Holmes, Thomas, and James Schmitz Jr. 1990. "A Theory of Entrepreneurship and Its Application to the Study of Business Transfers." *Journal of Political Economy* 98, no. 2: 265–94.

———. 2001. "Competition at Work: Railroads vs. Monopoly in the U.S. Shipping Industry." *Federal Reserve Bank of Minneapolis Quarterly Review* 25, no. 2: 3–29.

Hout, Michael, and Harvey S. Rosen. 2000. "Self-Employment, Family Background, and Race." *Journal of Human Resources* 35, no. 4: 670–92.

Hunter, Lawrence A. 2003. *Leave No State or Territory Behind: Formulating a Pro-Growth Economic Strategy for Puerto Rico.* Policy Report 177. Institute for Policy Innovation, Lewisville, Tex. (August).

Jacobson, Louis, Robert J. LaLonde, and Daniel G. Sullivan. 1993. "Earnings Losses of Displaced Workers." *American Economic Review* 83, no. 4: 685–709.

Jovanovic, Boyan. 1994. "Entrepreneurial Choice When People Differ in Their Management and Labor Skills." *Small Business Economics* 6, no. 3: 185–92.

Keating, Michael. 1989. "Local Government and Economic Development in Western Europe." *Entrepreneurship and Regional Development,* no 1: 301–12.

Kent, Calvin. 1982. "Entrepreneurship in Economic Development." In *Encyclopedia of Entrepreneurship,* edited by C. A. Kent, D. L. Sexton, and K. H. Vesper. Englewood Cliffs, N.J.: Prentice-Hall.

Kihlstrom, Richard, and Jean-Jacques Laffont. 1979. "A General Equilibrium Entrepreneurial Theory of Firm Formation Based on Risk Aversion." *Journal of Political Economy* 87, no. 4: 719–48.

Kirchhoff, Bruce, and Bruce Phillips. 1988. "The Effect of Firm Formation and Growth on Job Creation in the United States." *Journal of Business Venturing* 3, no. 4: 261–72.

———. 1992. "Research Applications of the Small Business Data Base of the U.S. Small Business Administration." In *The State of the Art of Entrepreneurship,* edited by D. L. Sexton and J. D. Kasarda, pp. 243–67. Boston: PWS-Kent.

Knight, Frank. 1921. *Risk, Uncertainty, and Profit.* Boston: Houghton-Mifflin.

Krueger, Alan. 1995. "The Effect of the Minimum Wage When It Really Bites: A Reexamination of the Evidence from Puerto Rico." In *Research in Labor Economics,* edited by Solomon W. Polachek, 14: 1–22. Greenwich, Conn.: JAI Press.

Lucas, Robert. 1978. "On the Size Distribution of Business Firms." *Bell Journal of Economics* 9, no. 2: 508–23.

———. 1993. "Making a Miracle." *Econometrica* 61, no. 2: 251–72.

Markiewicz, Kira, Nancy Rose, and Catherine Wolfram. 2004. "Does Competition Reduce Costs? Assessing the Impact of Regulatory Restructuring on U.S. Electric Generation Efficiency." Working Paper 11001. Cambridge, Mass.: National Bureau of Economic Research.

McKinsey Global Institute. 2001. *U.S. Productivity Growth, 1995–2000.* Washington.

Mincer, Jacob. 1962. "On-the-Job Training: Costs, Returns, and Some Implications." *Journal of Political Economy* 70, no. 5, pt. 2: 50–79.

————. 1984. "The Economics of Wage Floors." *Research in Labor Economics* 6: 311–33. In *Research in Labor Economics,* edited by Solomon W. Polachek, 6: 311–33. Greenwich, Conn.: JAI Press.

Nakamura, Leonard. 1999. "The Measurement of Retail Output and the Retail Revolution." *Canadian Journal of Economics* 32, no. 2: 408–25.

Neal, Derek. 1995. "Industry-Specific Human Capital: Evidence from Displaced Workers." *Journal of Labor Economics* 13, no. 4: 653–77.

Neumark, David, and Olena Nizalova. 2004. "Minimum Wage Effects in the Longer Run." Working Paper 10656. Cambridge, Mass.: National Bureau of Economic Research.

Odishelidze, Alexander, and Arthur Laffer. 2004. *Pay to the Order of Puerto Rico: The Cost of Dependence to the American Taxpayer.* Fairfax, Va.: Allegiance Press.

Organization for Economic Cooperation and Development (OECD). 2004. *OECD Employment Outlook 2004, Statistical Annex.* Paris.

Parent, Daniel. 2000. "Industry-Specific Capital and the Wage Profile: Evidence from the National Longitudinal Survey of Youth and the Panel Study of Income Dynamics." *Journal of Labor Economics* 18, no. 2: 306–21.

Pavitt, Keith, Michael Robson, and Joe Townsend. 1987. "The Size Distribution of Innovating Firms in the UK: 1945–1983." *Journal of Industrial Economics* 35, no. 3: 297–316.

Pelzman, Joseph. 2002. "Imported Capital Dependency as an Economic Development Strategy: The Failure of Distortionary Tax Policies in Puerto Rico." Discussion Paper 03-01. George Washington University, Department of Economics, Center for Economic Research (December).

Puerto Rico Department of Labor, Bureau of Statistics. 1978. *Serie histórica de empleo, desempleo y grupo trabajador, 1947–1970.* San Juan.

————. 2003. *Serie histórica de empleo, desempleo, y grupo trabajador, 1970–2001.* 2003. San Juan.

Reynolds, Lloyd, and Peter Gregory. 1965. *Wages, Productivity, and Industrialization in Puerto Rico.* Homewood, Ill.: Richard Irwin.

Rivera-Batiz, Francisco L., and Carlos E. Santiago. 1996. *Island Paradox: Puerto Rico in the 1990s.* New York: Russell Sage Foundation.

Rodríguez Santiago, Elizabeth. 2005. "Los arbitrios sobre la cerveza y el ron en Puerto Rico y la obligación del trato nacional del GATT: Comparación con la jurisprudencia de la OMC sobre impuestos a las bebidas alcohólicas." Working Paper 1. Río Piedras: University of Puerto Rico, Center for Business Research and Academic Initiatives, Faculty of Business Administration (March).

Romer, Paul. 1986. "Increasing Returns and Long-Run Growth." *Journal of Political Economy* 94, no. 5: 1002–37.

Ruggles, Steven, and others. 2004. *Integrated Public Use Microdata Series: Version 3.0.* Machine-readable database. Minneapolis: Minnesota Population Center (www.ipums.org).

Santiago, Carlos. 1989. "The Dynamics of Minimum Wage Policy in Economic Development: A Multiple Time-Series Approach." *Economic Development and Cultural Change* 38, no. 1: 1–30.

Schmitz, James A., Jr. 2005. "What Determines Productivity? Lessons from the Dramatic Recovery of the U.S. and Canadian Iron Ore Industries Following Their Early 1980s Crisis." *Journal of Political Economy* 113, no. 3: 582–624.

Schmitz, James A., Jr., and Arilton Teixeira. 2004. *Privatization's Impact on Private Productivity: The Case of Brazilian Iron Ore.* Staff Report 337. Federal Reserve Bank of Minneapolis, Research Department.

Sexton, Donald. 1986. "Role of Entrepreneurship in Economic Development." In *Entrepreneurship, Intrapreneurship, and Venture Capital,* edited by R. D. Hisrich. Lanham, Md.: Lexington Books.

Sieling, Mark, Brian Friedman, and Mark Dumas. 2001. "Labor Productivity in the Retail Trade Industry, 1987–1999." *Monthly Labor Review* 124, no. 12: 3–14.

Sivadasan, Jagadeesh. 2003. "Barriers to Entry and Productivity: Micro-Evidence from Indian Manufacturing Sector Reforms." University of Chicago, Graduate School of Business.

Smith, Adam. 1976. *An Inquiry into the Nature and Causes of the Wealth of Nations,* edited by Edwin Cannan. University of Chicago Press.

Solá, Ricardo. 2004. "La necesidad de simplificar la compleja relación entre los procesos ambientales, de planificación, consultas, endosos, y permisos." *Columna* 2, no. 4: 14–17.

Solow, Robert. 1956. "A Contribution to Theory of Economic Growth." *Quarterly Journal of Economics* 70, no. 1: 65–94.

Sternberg, Rolf, and Sander Wennekers. 2005. "Determinants and Effects of New Business Creation Using Global Entrepreneurship Monitor Data." *Small Business Economics* 24, no. 3: 193–203.

Stiglitz, Joseph. 2002. *Globalization and Its Discontents.* New York: Norton.

Storey, David. 1982. "Impact on the Local Economy." In *Entrepreneurship and the New Firm,* edited by D. J. Storey. London: Croom Helm.

———. 1988. "The Role of Small and Medium-Sized Enterprises in European Job Creation: Key Issues for Policy and Research." In *Small and Medium Size Enterprises and Regional Development,* edited by M. Giaoutzi, P. Nijkamp, and D. J. Storey, pp. 140–60. London: Routledge.

———. 1994. "Employment." In *Understanding the Small Business Sector,* edited by D. J. Storey. London: Routledge.

Syverson, Chad. 2004. "Market Structure and Productivity: A Concrete Example." *Journal of Political Economy* 112, no. 6: 1181–222.

U.S. Bureau of the Census. 2005. *Statistical Abstract of the United States,* 12th ed. U.S. Government Printing Office.

U.S. Court of Appeals for the First Circuit. 2005a. *United States* v. *María de la Angeles Rivera-Rangel.* Appeal from the U.S. District Court for the District of Puerto Rico, Opinion 03-2544, February 8.

———. 2005b. *Walgreen Co., Walgreen of San Patricio, and Walgreen of Puerto Rico* v. *John V. Rullan, Secretary of the Puerto Rico Health Department.* Appeal from the U.S. District Court for the District of Puerto Rico, Opinion 03-2542, April 22.

U.S. General Accounting Office. 1993. *Tax Policy: Puerto Rico and the Section 936 Tax Credit.* GAO/GGD-93-109. Report to the Chairman, Committee on Finance, U.S. Senate (June).

Vesper, Karl. 1982. "Research on Education for Entrepreneurship." In *Encyclopedia of Entrepreneurship,* edited by C. A. Kent, D. L. Sexton, and K. H. Vesper. Englewood Cliffs, N.J.: Prentice-Hall.

Wallsten, Scott. 2004. "The Role of Government in Regional Technology Development: The Effects of Public Venture Capital and Science Parks." In *Building High-Tech Clusters: Silicon Valley and Beyond,* edited by Timothy Bresnahan and Alfonso Gambardella, pp. 229–79. Cambridge University Press.

Wennekers, Sander, and Roy Thurik. 1999. "Linking Entrepreneurship and Economic Growth." *Small Business Economics* 13: 27–55.

Westhead, Paul. 1990. "A Typology of New Manufacturing Firm Founders in Wales: Performance Measures and Public Policy Implications." *Journal of Business Venturing* 5, no. 2: 103–22.

White, Sammis, and Paul Reynolds. 1996. "Government Programs and High-Growth New Firms." Paper presented at *Frontiers of Entrepreneurship Research 1996* conference. Babson College.

World Bank. 2004. *Doing Business in 2005: Removing Obstacles to Growth.* Washington: Oxford University Press.

7

Assessing Puerto Rico's Fiscal Policies

JAMES ALM

The Puerto Rican fiscal system has undergone some major changes in recent years, changes that have been beneficial in a variety of dimensions. Nevertheless, the system is plagued by a number of problems. On the tax side, extensive tax evasion significantly reduces revenues and compromises the distributional objectives of the system. In part as a result of evasion, the tax base has shrunk over time, reducing revenues and leaving the more visible taxpayers (mainly wage earners) still in the tax net. The tax base has also been reduced by the extensive system of tax incentives available, incentives that are seldom tracked, quantified, and evaluated and whose intended effects on economic growth are uncertain. The incentives are only one of the features that contribute to an overly complicated system, complications that also illustrate the limitations of tax administration. The tax system was designed for times and circumstances that are long past, and it has evolved over time in a piecemeal, ad hoc manner with little apparent thought given to the ways in which the pieces of the system need to fit together.

I am indebted to Ramón Cao Garcia for the discussions that we have had on Puerto Rico's tax and expenditure policies and for his extensive contributions to my thinking about these issues, particularly the historical perspective and some of the tables and figures included here that have also appeared in some of his own work. Although initially a coauthor for this chapter, he was unable to participate during the later stages of the project.

I am grateful to Artidiantun Adji, Raul Ponce, Djatugbe Amendah, and Rhucha Samudra for able research assistance. I am also grateful to Fuat Andic, Barry Bosworth, Susan Collins, Ron Fisher, William Lockwood, Mike Soto, and others for helpful comments and discussions.

Even beyond the limitations of the tax system, there are other persistent and growing fiscal problems. Overall revenues have been insufficient to cover current expenditures, and fiscal deficits have been the usual outcome over most of the past two decades. Short- and long-term public debt has been growing at rates higher than gross national product (GNP) or gross domestic product (GDP). At the end of fiscal year 2003–04 the total accumulated deficit of the central government stood at roughly $13 billion on a net asset basis.[1] The government budget for fiscal year 2004–05 was enacted with a General Fund deficit forecast at $550 million; however, the actual deficit exceeded $1 billion.[2] The commonwealth government has increased its reliance on nonrecurring revenues to camouflage the magnitude of the deficit. New major infrastructure projects (for example, an urban train, a coliseum, a transshipping port) have been finished or will be completed in the near future, but no funds have been assigned to cover subsidies needed for their operations. Numerous government enterprises are largely operated as separate units but remain the financial responsibility of the government. The pension fund for public employees has unfunded liabilities amounting to more than $11 billion, and, if nothing is done, this actuarial deficit implies future payments out of tax revenues, with concomitant higher fiscal deficits in the future.

As a result of these and other factors, credit-rating agencies (Moody's and Standard and Poor's) have in recent years continually downgraded the credit classification of the central government's bond rating; indeed, in May 2005 they lowered their ratings to the bottom of the investment grade category, citing such factors as the use of nonrecurring revenues to finance the operating fund deficit and looming shortfalls in the pension fund. More broadly, the quality of public expenditures in such basic areas as education, public infrastructure, and security is so lacking that many individuals and businesses have resorted to using their own funds to ensure adequate services.

Consequently, there are important issues that must be addressed in the Puerto Rican fiscal system, issues that relate to the yield, neutrality, progressivity, and simplicity of the tax system and also to the provision of public services and the overall budget balance of the fiscal system. Many of these issues are not new and have been considered in previous studies of the Puerto Rican fiscal system.[3] This chapter discusses these issues with a focus on the tax side of the fiscal system. I briefly describe the overall budget balance of the Puerto Rico fiscal system and discuss the current Puerto Rican tax and expenditure systems. I compare Puerto Rican tax practice with international practices, examine the major taxes that are imposed in Puerto Rico, and identify the main problems with

1. Commonwealth of Puerto Rico, "Comprehensive Annual Financial Report, Fiscal Year Ending June 30, 2004" (www.hacienda.gobierno.pr), p. 21.
2. Moody's Investors Service (2005a).
3. Andic and Mann (1976); Hexner and Jenkins (1995).

these taxes. The final section presents some issues that need to be considered in any possible reforms, again focusing mainly on reform of the tax system.

Public Debt in Puerto Rico

Public debt complements taxes and federal transfers in financing government expenditures. When public debt is issued, the funds are available and used in the present, but the obligation to pay is levied in the future. In issuing public debt, the current generation therefore imposes a burden on future generations, and the opposite occurs when public investments are financed out of current fiscal income.

In the case of Puerto Rico, public debt is classified in four categories: general obligation bonds issued by the central government, bonds issued by state enterprises, bonds issued by municipal governments, and loans to the different government entities, usually emitted by the Government Development Bank for Puerto Rico. (In addition, the central government also regularly issues tax revenue anticipation notes to cover seasonal fluctuations in tax revenues that allow synchronization of available cash flows with expenditures; these notes are short term and are paid in the fiscal year in which they are issued, and so they are not considered part of the public debt.) The last category, loans to different government entities, is what is usually called "extraconstitutional debt." This form of debt is incurred either as interim financing for public investment until a bond issue is organized to be sold on the municipal bond market or as a way to cover operational deficits in the budgets of the central government, the municipalities, and the state enterprises.

Figure 7-1 shows the trends in public debt in Puerto Rico over the past fifteen years for the first three categories of public debt in Puerto Rico. State enterprises are the principal debtors in the public sector, and all three categories show upward trends. Figure 7-2 presents the annual growth rate of debt and GNP over roughly the same period. Public debt growth in Puerto Rico generally exceeds the rate of growth in the economy. This is particularly true in the case of municipalities, which were granted increased autonomy in determining their internal finances after the municipal reform of 1991. Over the fiscal years 1990 to 2004, GNP grew at an average annual rate of 6.4 percent, while total public debt grew at an annual rate of 7.4 percent. The public debt of state enterprises grew at an average yearly rate of 7.2 percent, debt issued by the central government by 7.3 percent, and municipal debt at an annual rate of 11.5 percent.

That public debt in Puerto Rico has been growing at a faster rate than GNP is quite worrisome and has contributed to the continued downgrading of the government's bond rating over time. Even so, other practices may be of more concern. As noted earlier, recent budgets have been characterized by large and growing deficits. In the year 2002 the central government issued $2 billion in long-term debt to refinance short-term loans previously issued by the Government Development Bank to finance past budget deficits. State enterprises regularly

Figure 7-1. *Public Debt in Puerto Rico, 1989–2004*
Millions of dollars

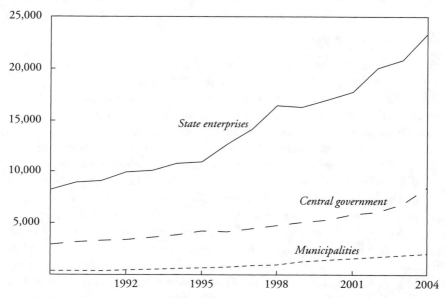

Source: Data from Puerto Rico Planning Board, *Economic Report to the Governor, Statistical Appendix,* various years.

Figure 7-2. *Annual Change in Public Debt and GNP, 1990–2004*
Percent

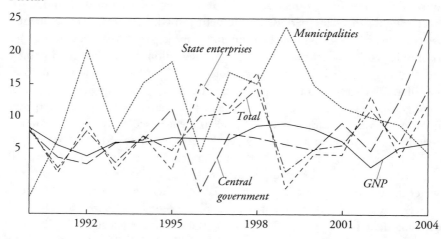

Source: Data from Puerto Rico Planning Board, *Economic Report to the Governor, Statistical Appendix,* various years.

capitalize maintenance expenditures and finance them through long-term public debt. So-called pork-barrel funds of legislators are used for social expenditures (for example, current outlays) but are financed out of public debt. There are major unfunded infrastructure projects that are the responsibility of the government. A sizable portion of the debt is regularly used to finance current expenditures rather than public investment; future generations receive no benefits from these current expenditures, but they will have the burden of paying the debt; moreover, as the debt grows, debt service payments grow concurrently, leaving a smaller proportion of future current revenues to finance discretionary expenses in the government budget. The pension fund for public employees has enormous—and growing—unfunded liabilities. According to government officials, over the past three years contributions have averaged only about one-half of the annual pension cost, and the unfunded liabilities of the pension system now amount to more than $11 billion. Overall, there is little doubt that the Puerto Rico government suffers from major structural imbalances in the budget situation.

Indeed, there is much evidence that the level of public debt in Puerto Rico is significantly higher than that of any of the U.S. states. According to Moody's, the ratio of net tax-supported central government debt in Puerto Rico in 2003 was more than twenty times the median of the fifty mainland states; state debt and combined state and local government debt as a percentage of personal income are also significantly higher in Puerto Rico than in the fifty states.[4] It should be noted that these types of comparisons are made more difficult by the fact that the functional scope of government in Puerto Rico is considerably different from that in the average mainland state. Some services that are provided by public corporations in Puerto Rico (whose debt is included in Puerto Rico's government debt calculations) are provided in the United States either by local governments, private firms, or the federal government, so that the debt associated with these services is not included in state calculations. Debt ratios of Puerto Rico may therefore be somewhat inflated because the island's government shoulders a larger responsibility for services that are provided by other sources in the states.

Even so, the evidence is largely consistent with a high—and growing—level of public debt relative to the U.S. states. It is this that has led to the recent downgrading of Puerto Rico's bond rating.

The Puerto Rican Tax System

The current tax system in Puerto Rico was structured at the beginning of the 1950s as a part of a broader attempt to industrialize and modernize the economy.[5]

---

4. Moody's Investors Service (2005b).
5. This section is based largely on the detailed analysis in Cao Garcia (2004).

The policies enacted at that time reflected the conventional wisdom on development strategies in the immediate postwar era, which assumed active participation of the state in providing incentives through tax payment exemptions, direct subsidies to firms promoted by the Administracion de Fomento Económico (the Puerto Rican Industrial Development Company), and an infrastructure designed for the modernization of the economy. Since then, the tax system has been reformed on several occasions, in 1975, 1987, and 1994. Nevertheless, the legacy of the 1950s remains strong.

In discussing the Puerto Rico tax system, it is important to keep in mind the island's unique, and possibly confusing, status as a commonwealth. Puerto Rico is a self-governing territory free from the interference of the U.S. Congress, at least with respect to its internal government and administration. However, its government is bound by U.S. international treaties and agreements and cannot negotiate, for example, trade treaties with other countries. Furthermore, its citizens are U.S. citizens even though they are not subject to federal income taxation, do not participate in U.S. general elections, and do not have voting representation in the U.S. Congress. Even so, the island is subject to the provisions of the U.S. Constitution, and its citizens are eligible for federal government transfer payments. As has been noted by Francisco Rivera-Batiz and Carlos Santiago, the island literally sits "between two worlds," the United States and Latin America.[6]

Fiscal Revenues

The government of Puerto Rico receives revenues from sources internal to the local economy and also from external sources. Table 7-1 shows the relative distribution of these funds by broad categories and the evolution of these categories over time.

There are three principal components of revenues from internal sources: the General Fund (*Fondo General*), composed mainly of tax revenues; earmarked or special funds (*fondos especiales*), which receive their resources from either some earmarked taxes, proceeds from general obligation bonds, or transfers from the General Fund; and revenues from public enterprises. It is through the General Fund that the executive, legislative, and judicial branches are financed. The special or earmarked funds are those devoted by law to a particular use and are derived from taxes, licenses, user fees, federal donations, legislative allocations, and contributions from persons and other sources. The purpose of the special funds is to ensure that specific areas receive revenues. For instance, the financing of highway and transportation construction (through the Puerto Rican Highway and Transportation Authority, or Autoridad de Carreteras y Transportación) comes from an *arbitrio* (excise tax) on gasoline, annual licenses for engine

6. Rivera-Batiz and Santiago (1996).

Table 7-1. *Fiscal Revenues, by Type, as Share of Total Revenues, Puerto Rico, Selected Fiscal Years, 1977–2002*

Percent

Revenue type	1977	1982	1987	1992	1997	2002
Internal sources	88.2	86.2	86.3	80.4	81.5	79.1
General fund	31.0	30.3	35.6	32.9	32.3	37.3
Special (earmarked) funds	2.7	3.0	3.8	4.0	4.0	4.4
Revenues of state enterprises	43.7	40.4	37.0	35.0	33.2	25.2
Other	10.8	12.4	10.0	8.6	12.1	12.2
Federal funds	11.8	13.8	13.7	19.6	18.5	20.9

Source: Computed from data provided by Estado Libre Asociado de Puerto Rico (Management and Budget Office), various years.

vehicles, the payment of tolls, and the first $120 million collected from the *arbitrio* on imported crude oil and derivatives. The Highway and Transportation Authority also receives federal transfers for the maintenance of the public transportation system.

These three sources accounted for 77.4 percent of total fiscal revenues in year 1977 and 66.9 percent in year 2002. (Percentage allocations are also devoted to the University of Puerto Rico, to subsidies to the municipalities, and to different transfers granted to firms, organizations, and persons.)

Table 7-1 reveals several trends in the evolution of fiscal revenues over the past twenty-five years. Although income from internal sources is the principal component of fiscal revenues, its relative importance has declined somewhat over time, while funds transferred from the federal government have increased in relative importance. The sole reason for the decline in the relative importance of income from internal sources is the declining trend in revenues from state enterprises. Privatization of the telephone company could explain part of the decline in the share of revenues from state enterprises between fiscal years 1997 and 2002, but it cannot explain trends in earlier years.

Table 7-2 shows the annual average growth rates for these fiscal funds, as well as for the GNP of Puerto Rico, for five-year periods from 1972 to 2002. General Fund revenues grew at a higher rate than GNP between 1972 and 1977, in large part because of a tax reform enacted in 1975 to deal with a fiscal crisis. The 1975 reform adopted a general excise tax of 5 percent (a broad-based indirect tax on imports and sales of local manufacturers) as well as a temporary surcharge in the personal income tax. The income tax surcharge was phased out by 1982, and the rate of growth of General Fund revenues became smaller than that of GNP. By 1987 the pattern was reversed, and the General Fund again grew at a higher rate than GNP; this occurred because the government adopted various temporary measures between 1985 and 1987 that generated nonrecurrent income, including tax amnesties and a one-time 20 percent tax on certificates of

Table 7-2. *Average Annual Growth Rate of Fiscal Revenue, Puerto Rico, by Type, Five-Year Fiscal Periods, 1972–2002*
Percent

Revenue type	1972–77	1977–82	1982–87	1987–92	1992–97	1997–2002
Internal sources						
General fund	10.4	8.6	8.0	6.1	6.1	6.2
Special (earmarked) funds	−5.2	11.7	9.3	9.1	6.4	5.2
Revenues of state enterprises	n.a.	7.4	2.8	6.5	5.4	−2.4
Other	n.a.	12.3	0.1	4.6	14.0	3.4
Federal funds	19.9	12.5	4.4	15.8	5.3	5.8
Gross national product	7.2	9.2	6.2	6.7	6.4	6.9

Source: Computed from data provided by Estado Libre Asociado de Puerto Rico (Management and Budget Office), various years.

deposit. After 1987 the yearly average growth rate of revenues to the General Fund has been consistently lower than GNP growth.

Special or earmarked funds show a different pattern. The negative figure in 1972–77 reflects the fiscal crisis of 1975, after which Puerto Rico was unable to sell general obligation debt on the municipal bond market for a number of years. Since the special Permanent Improvements Fund receives its resources from the proceeds of newly issued public debt for government investment, the fund was empty for various years, including 1977. By 1982 the municipal bonds market was open, and the Permanent Improvements Fund was again able to receive resources, resulting in an upward jump in the growth rate of earmarked funds.

Table 7-2 also indicates that the growth rate of special or earmarked funds was higher than that for GNP, at least from 1977 to 1992. This was a result of an increasing pattern of transfers of revenues from the General Fund to the special funds over the period; indeed, growth in the special funds is one of the factors contributing to the sluggish growth in General Fund revenues. No new transfers from the General Fund to the special funds have occurred over the past few years, which helps explain why the growth rate of these funds became lower than GNP growth by fiscal year 2002. In addition, from fiscal years 1997 to 2002 the growth rate for special or earmarked funds was even lower than that for the General Fund.

The third category of government income is revenues from state enterprises. In all periods, the growth rate of these revenues was smaller than GNP growth. Overall, this pattern reflects mainly financial problems in some of the state enterprises, where tariffs have been frozen or raised by only a fraction of increases registered in current expenditures.

The category "Other" refers to a myriad of financial transactions, including the sale of government property, transfers from previous fiscal years and from different accounts, proceeds from short-term loans, and the like. The growth rate in these transactions fluctuated widely over the period because these resources are not recurrent revenues but are mainly accounting and financial devices designed to balance expenditures with revenues.

Federal funds also show an unstable pattern, resulting from changes in federal policies. In the first years of the period, federal funds exhibited a high rate of growth, caused by the gradual extension to Puerto Rico of the food stamp program in 1976 and other War on Poverty programs and by President Richard Nixon's New Federalism. From 1982 to 1987 the growth rate fell, becoming smaller than the one for GNP, and between 1987 and 1992 it accelerated again before declining over the last decade of the period. There is little for Puerto Rico to do to modify the wide fluctuations in the growth rate of federal funds. Still, the behavior of federal funds in recent years has contributed to local fiscal problems.

Tax Revenues

The present structure of taxation in Puerto Rico acquired its basic form between 1941 and 1954. Since then there have been numerous piecemeal changes and three major tax reforms. Overall, the system shows a movement over time away from relative reliance on indirect taxation toward a focus on direct taxation.

The Puerto Rican tax structure consists of indirect and direct taxes, and, as noted, the collection of taxes constitutes the main source of revenue for the General Fund. The major tax sources in Puerto Rico are the personal income tax, the corporate income tax, and excise taxes; the government also obtains revenue from the property tax, the inheritance tax, and various other minor taxes. Direct taxes are derived mainly from taxes on the income of persons and firms. In 2002 direct taxes contributed more than three-fourths of the tax revenue of the General Fund. The *arbitrio* is the other important source of funds, constituting 22.8 percent of the tax revenue in the General Fund in 2002. There have also been taxes on inheritances and donations, but these revenues have always been quite small. The property tax is an unimportant source of revenue, largely because the tax base is greatly undervalued (currently set at the value that would have existed in 1958), even though the statutory tax rates (which vary marginally across municipalities) fluctuate around 8 percent.

The tax structure of Puerto Rico has changed considerably over time. Table 7-3 illustrates the evolution of the tax structure (in the General Fund) from 1950 to 2002. Perhaps the most important change during this time occurred with taxes on income. The combined share of personal income and corporate income taxes increased from less than one-third of General Fund tax revenues in 1950 to roughly three-quarters in 2002. The relative importance of all excise taxes fell from one-half to one-fifth of tax revenues; property tax has

Table 7-3. *Distribution of Tax Revenues as Share of General Fund, Puerto Rico, by Type, Selected Years, 1950–2002*
Percent

Tax type	1950	1960	1970	1975	1980	1985	1990	1995	2000	2002
Property	15.2	7.7	4.9	7.9	6.8	6.4	5.2	0.1	0	0
Personal income	15.9	21.0	31.9	37.7	35.4	35.8	34.3	35.6	37.9	39.3
Corporate income	14.7	14.9	16.9	17.7	20.8	25.7	28.9	35.5	38.7	36.6
Arbitrio	48.1	51.0	41.7	32.5	34.4	30.0	30.2	27.6	22.2	22.8
Inheritance	0.8	1.0	1.2	1.3	0.7	0.3	0	0	0	0

Source: Data from Puerto Rico Planning Board, *Statistical Year Book,* various years.

also declined significantly in importance as a share of revenue, and, as noted earlier, the inheritance tax has always been a minor source of revenues.

It is worth noting that tax revenue relative to gross domestic product increased from 12.1 percent in 1950 to 15.1 percent in 1990. At the beginning of the 1950s, owing to a tax restructuring, there was a significant increase in the collection of taxes as a percentage of GDP. The second half of the 1970s saw another increase, owing to the reform of 1975 (which introduced new taxes and increased the tax rates).

Individual Income Tax. Individual income is the most important source of tax revenues to the Puerto Rico government, accounting in 2002 for 39.3 percent of General Fund tax revenues. Individuals in Puerto Rico are not subject to the U.S. federal income tax. However, they are subject to the Puerto Rico individual income tax, whose structure closely resembles that of the U.S. income tax. Individuals in Puerto Rico are taxed on their worldwide, or global, income, including capital gains and other types of capital income. They are allowed several types of deductions (for example, for medical expenses, charitable contributions, professional expenses); they may instead elect a standard deduction. There are also personal allowances, and the tax return form for year 2003 listed fourteen tax credits taxpayers could claim (aside from the credit for taxes paid to other jurisdictions) that relate to investments in the ownership of various types of properties or enterprises. It is of some interest that tax credits can be bought and sold. Almost all revenues are collected by employer withholding. Individuals are also subject to the federal payroll tax, at the same rates as individuals in the United States.

The income tax system was reformed in 1954, at which time taxable income was broadly defined and the tax rate structure was made steeply progressive, with twenty-four brackets and marginal tax rates going from 12.60 percent to 82.95 percent at taxable income over $200,000. Over time, brackets have been redefined and marginal tax rates have been reduced, so that today there are only four brackets. Even so, the current marginal tax rate structure is steeply graduated, with rates starting at 7 percent (on the first $2,000 of taxable income for single individuals) and rising to 38 percent on income over $50,000. Currently, income from interest, dividends, and capital gains is taxed at rates that range from 0 percent to 17 percent; rents derived from various types of activities are exempted, and profits from agricultural activities have a 90 percent exemption. Exemptions and other tax preferences have also been enacted in a piecemeal, ad hoc manner over time, changing (and eroding) the tax base and transforming the tax into one mainly on earned income. In spite of the gradual erosion in the base of the personal income tax, the tax has become the principal revenue generator in the system, and its share grew from 15.9 percent of total tax revenues in 1950 to 39.3 percent in 2002.

Corporate Income Tax. The corporate income tax is another major revenue source for Puerto Rico, accounting for 36.6 percent of General Fund tax revenues in 2002. The normal tax rate that applies to regular corporations in Puerto Rico is 20 percent, to which various surtaxes are added that make the rates vary from 20 to 39 percent. As discussed later in this chapter, there are also other tax regimes that apply to different types of firms.

These tax rates are applied to a tax base that uses the worldwide income of Puerto Rico companies as the base of the corporate income tax. This tax base is defined as net accounting profits, which equals gross revenues less operating costs plus capital adjustments. Most Puerto Rican firms use a straight-line method of depreciation, although the 1994 tax reform introduced a more flexible, accelerated depreciation scheme. The Tax Incentives Act of 1998 allows for expensing (or immediate write-off of capital purchases) but only for certain firms (for example, manufacturing and exporting firms). In addition, inventories are generally stated at the lower of cost or market: if last-in first-out (LIFO) is used for book purposes, it can also be used for tax purposes.

The burden of corporate taxation is significantly affected by the presence of numerous fiscal incentives available to firms. The most widely known and studied is that given under section 936 of the U.S. Internal Revenue Code, now being phased out over the 1996–2006 period. The basic features of this incentive originated with the Revenue Act of 1921; the current (and expiring) version of this incentive dates from the Tax Reform Act of 1976. Under section 936 of the law, as enacted in 1976, any qualifying U.S. corporation could choose to receive a tax credit equal to the portion of its U.S. corporate income tax liability attributable to taxable income from activities outside the United States from the conduct of operations in a U.S. possession (for example, Puerto Rico) as well as from income generated by qualified investment in a U.S. possession. To qualify for this tax credit, a U.S. domestic corporation had to derive at least 80 percent of its gross income over a three-year period from sources in Puerto Rico and at least 75 percent of its gross income from active business income. Under the section 936 credit, then, income earned in Puerto Rico is effectively exempt from

U.S. corporate income taxation; that is, the section 936 credit is essentially a tax-sparing credit, which is given to a corporation regardless of its income tax liability in Puerto Rico.

The U.S. Congress has amended section 936 several times since 1976, in order to reduce perceived abuses in its use. As noted, it is now scheduled for elimination in 2006. However, several general incentives are available to most firms, and there are several other incentives targeted to specific sectors and industries (for example, for research and development, for targeted employment generation, for regional development, for export activities).

Like the personal income tax, the corporate income tax has experienced rate reductions and base erosion over the years. As only one example of these changes, more than fifteen separate tax changes were enacted in 2001, almost all of which reduced corporate tax liabilities. The trend of adopting new provisions has continued, which explains the decline in the share of this tax in the revenues of the General Fund in the past several years. For example, there was a reduction in the tax rate to 2 percent on firms that establish Puerto Rico regional headquarters to service other jurisdictions or countries (Law 225 of August 29, 2002); there have also been provisions that allow the secretary of the treasury to reduce the tax rate to be applied to royalties, rents, and franchise fees paid by firms owned by nonresidents and doing business in Puerto Rico (Law 289 of December 24, 2002), provide a tax exemption for value added activities located in the zone of the transshipping port in Ponce (Law 300 of December 25, 2002), and expand tax preferences for purchasing manufactures made in Puerto Rico (Law 367 of September 16, 2004, and Law 368 of September 21, 2004).

Corporations and partnerships are essentially ruled by three different tax regimes: one that applies to regular corporations and partnerships, another that applies to a myriad of so-called special cases, and one that applies to exempt corporations operating under the dispositions of the Tax Incentives Act of 1998 (or a previous law). This last category represents companies in the manufacturing and services sectors, whose production is sold at offshore markets. Consider each regime.

Regular corporations, or corporations and partnerships that are taxed under the regular rules, are mostly limited to the wholesale and retail trade and to some services (provided that the total number of stockholders is more than thirty-five), since almost all other industrial sectors are covered under special provisions. Currently, these firms pay a maximum tax rate of 39 percent on taxable net income. The tax rates are progressive, reaching the top rate at a net taxable income level of $275,000. Over time the rates have generally fallen.

Several groups of business enterprises are known as *special corporations* because they are subject to special tax rules that drastically reduce their tax liability. Among the special corporations and the applicable rules are the following:

—Companies that are not subject to the corporate income tax and instead pay a "withholding tax" of 33 percent on net profits, which is passed on to their stockholders or partners as a credit for their personal income tax. Stockholders or partners are allowed to deduct their share of losses incurred by these companies from their taxable income under the personal income tax. These companies include corporations of individuals that are organized under the appropriate section of the tax revenue code and have no more than thirty-five stockholders, limited partnership firms organized to do business in high-risk ventures such as construction, employee-owned special corporations, and real estate investment trusts.

—Most hospitals and educational institutions, which are organized as nonprofit corporations and are exempted from this tax.

—Hotels and other enterprises devoted to the tourist industry, which are taxed under the Tourism Incentives Laws. These laws provide a 90 percent tax exemption and tax credits for investments, as well as various subsidies.

—Agricultural businesses, including agro-industrial activities, which also enjoy a 90 percent tax exemption, tax credits, and numerous subsidies.

—Cooperatives, which enjoy a complete tax exemption.

—Business enterprises located in zones designated by the Special Laws for Rehabilitation and Development of selected regions.

—Foreign and domestic life insurance companies, which are subject to special accounting rules in computing taxable income, rules that allow them to reduce their tax liabilities.

—Enterprises located in areas of special development or in historic zones, which are subject to various tax preferences and subsidies.

—Branches of overseas corporations, which are subject to special tax rules.

—Financial institutions, where accounting rules allow them to reduce tax liabilities.

The end result of all these provisions is that the regular corporate income tax basically applies by exception, and a company pays its full liability only if it cannot find a preference or loophole.

Puerto Rico's industrialization strategy was designed in the late 1940s and focused on promoting external investment in export-oriented activities. This strategy was based largely on the practice of granting tax exemptions and subsidies to targeted *exempted corporations,* of which the most important was the section 936 credit. This tax exemption was a full one for many decades, but early in the 1980s it was changed to exempt 90 percent of taxable income. The companies were also exempted from 90 percent of the property tax and the same proportion of municipal taxes. However, they were subject to a tollgate tax on profits sent to headquarters; the tollgate tax had a statutory, or nominal, rate of 10 percent but an actual, effective rate that was individually negotiated with each company, with rates ranging from 0 to 10 percent. The particular tax treatment for each individual company was (and still is) spelled out in an exemption decree signed by government and company representatives that has the force of a contract among the parties. Provisions in an exemption decree cannot be changed by an act of law but only by an agreement among the parties to modify the decree.

Under the Tax Incentives Act of 1998, the rules were modified. The tollgate tax was repealed, and the tax rate was defined as variable, ranging from 2 to 7 percent depending upon the conditions of the firm. Provisions on tax rates have subsequently been modified further, allowing for a 0 tax rate at the discretion of the secretary of the treasury if it is considered that the exemption redounds to the general good of society. Many corporations renegotiated their exemption decrees after Congress decided to phase out the provisions of section 936. Furthermore, many exempt companies doing business in Puerto Rico converted to controlled foreign corporations (CFCs). Under this regime, the CFCs will not repatriate their profits to the United States but will send them elsewhere to finance multinational operations of the matrix company. These firms are not U.S. subsidiaries. As a result, the CFCs have to pay royalties for patents held by the matrix company, and these payments are subject in Puerto Rico to the withholding tax for nonresidents, which used to be 29 percent of gross payments but which under the Tax Incentives Act was reduced to 10 percent. In 2002 the secretary of the treasury was empowered to reduce the rate even further if he or she considered that action to be beneficial to Puerto Rico.

Property Tax. Property tax is paid on real estate, inventories, and other business movable property; individuals pay the tax only on real estate. The share of this tax in General Fund revenues declined from 15.2 percent in fiscal year 1950 to 5.2 percent in 1990 and disappeared thereafter.

This trend stems from the ways in which the tax base has been defined. The tax on real estate is levied on the assessed value of the property. The last assessment of property values took place in 1958, so that assessed value is the market price of the property in 1958 (or the one it would have had at that time, if the property was built at a later date). There is an exclusion of the first $15,000 of assessed value for homes inhabited by their owners. The statutory tax rate is about 8 percent, with some small variations among municipalities. Since the tax base does not change when market values change, revenue collections can be increased only through new construction or an increase in the tax rates. Overall, this situation severely limits the capacity of this tax to generate revenues.

Not all property values have increased at the same rate. In consequence, assessed value is a smaller proportion of market prices in zones of higher economic development, where there has been a larger appreciation in real estate market prices. This results in a proportionally heavier tax levy on properties in depressed areas, further limiting economic incentives and opportunities in these zones. The tax also becomes regressive with regard to property values, since the effective rate is larger for properties located in depressed areas.

Originally, revenues from the property were divided between three funds: the central government's debt redemption fund, the General Fund of the central government, and the treasury of the municipal government in which the property was located. In 1991 the laws regulating municipal governments were reformed. At that time, the General Fund's share of property tax collections was transferred to municipal governments, and an 8 percent ceiling was enacted for the tax rate. A special additional tax (*contribución especial adicional*) was allowed as a surcharge on the tax, in order to back the issuance of public debt for investment projects in the neighborhood of those subject to the additional tax. The 1991 law also allowed for properties to be assessed at market prices, but only if the seventy-eight mayors in the island reach an agreement, including an agreement on the process to be used to conduct any new assessment of property values. Those municipalities that show faster development rates, and so greater appreciation of property values, have little interest in a general assessment of property values.

Inventories and other business movable property are self-assessed by the taxpayer and levied at a rate of 6 percent. Mayors frequently complain that the prevailing honor system of self-assessment results in undervaluation, but there is no evidence on the extent of this practice.

Inheritance Tax. In principle, a tax on inheritances and donations can be designed to promote social equity and to avoid the concentration of property and monopoly power in markets.[7] However, in Puerto Rico (as in other countries) its role is much more limited. Indeed, its ability to generate revenues is quite modest, owing to the free mobility of persons and goods between Puerto Rico and the continental United States. This mobility puts downward pressure on the local tax; otherwise, persons with valuable net worth would have an incentive to emigrate or to transfer their assets to the United States as they approach their later years.

Indirect Taxes. Indirect taxes levied by the commonwealth government fall into three categories: a broad-based tax on imports and manufacturers' sales, called the 5 percent general excise tax; specific excise taxes; and a customs duty on coffee imports. As noted earlier, the fiscal importance of these taxes has been declining significantly over time, from collecting roughly one-half of total tax revenues in 1950 to just 22.8 percent in 2002.

The 5 percent general excise tax is not really an excise tax; instead, it is closer to a general sales tax levied on imports and manufacturers' sales of merchandise in Puerto Rico that are not taxed by any specific excise tax. Excluded from its base (besides merchandise taxed under the specific excise taxes) are the following categories of exempt goods:

—raw materials used by certified manufacturers

—machinery and equipment used in the actual production process of manufacturing firms

7. Meade (1972).

—forklifts purchased by manufacturers

—purchases by certified farmers

—purchases by nonprofit organizations

—basic necessities of consumption, such as food, drugs, children's clothes, soap and detergents, printed materials, religious merchandise, and the like.

The tax rate is 5 percent of the tax price of the good, with the definition of *tax price* varying for goods that are imported and those locally manufactured. If the good is imported, the tax price is the cost in Puerto Rico plus 20 percent, where *cost in Puerto Rico* is defined as the f.o.b. price plus 10 percent (to take into account insurance and freight); this provision means that the effective tax rate is 6.6 percent of the f.o.b. price. If the good is locally manufactured, the tax price is again cost in Puerto Rico plus 20 percent, but here cost is defined as 60 percent of the price charged by the manufacturer, so that the effective tax rate is now 3.6 percent of the manufacturer's price.

An important feature of this tax is that it is levied one time at the beginning of the distribution chain, thereby resulting in a cascading (or turnover) effect and implying that tax revenue is lower than the increase in consumers' expenditures resulting from the tax. The tax is also regressive with regard to income and distorts production patterns.[8]

The 5 percent general excise tax was introduced in 1975 as part of the tax reform adopted that year.[9] The Tax Reform Commission considered the adoption of a broad-based consumption tax and, in fact, recommended a value added tax (VAT).[10] However, because of the fiscal crisis at the time, it was decided that implementing a VAT would take too much time. The 5 percent general excise tax could be implemented in weeks, using the same organization that the Treasury Department used to administer excise taxes. At the time, this tax did not include durable consumption goods because they were already taxed with excises at a higher rate, averaging 20 percent. This feature was changed in 1987, when durable goods were incorporated in the 5 percent general excise tax, in an effort to impose uniformity in most indirect tax rates at the lower rate.[11]

This general excise tax was responsible for 30.6 percent of total indirect tax collections in fiscal year 2002 and for 7.3 percent of total tax revenues to the General Fund. Its revenues have declined in nominal terms since 2000. Because there have been no changes in the law with respect to this tax during the period, and because consumption of taxable goods has increased, the decline is consistent with an increase in tax evasion.

8. Friedlander (1967); Cao Garcia and Andic (1996).

9. Estado Libre Asociado de Puerto Rico (1975).

10. Organización de Estados Americanos (1974).

11. Agosto (1987).

Specific excise taxes are levied at various rates on a variety of items:
—motor vehicles
—alcoholic beverages
—cigarettes and other tobacco products
—petroleum and petroleum products
—gasoline
—aviation fuel
—occupancy of hotel rooms
—movies and other public shows
—horserace betting
—casino gambling
—sugar
—cement

There is also a 5 percent retail sales tax on watches and jewelry.

Many of these excises impose different levies on or grant exemptions to particular products or services, and in many instances, tax collections are earmarked for special funds. For example, most collections from the excise on petroleum products and all revenues from the excise on gasoline go to the Highway and Transportation Authority; revenues from gambling are distributed between an educational fund and a fund to promote tourism; the proceeds from the hotel occupancy tax go to a special fund to promote tourism.

In the early years of the twentieth century, the U.S. Congress authorized Puerto Rico to levy a *custom duty on coffee imports.* This was enacted as a measure to help finance the creation of a civil government in Puerto Rico after the military occupation in 1898. The tax remains on the books mainly as a historical curiosity, and Puerto Rico is the only jurisdiction in the United States that levies an import duty. Revenues from this tax are not significant, but the tax nevertheless plays an important protective role for coffee growers and processors by creating a barrier to shield them from external competitors.

U.S. customs duties and excise taxes, collected by the federal government on imports arriving from foreign countries to Puerto Rico, are refunded to the island, after deducting administration costs. Federal excise taxes on alcohol and tobacco products levied on the mainland on this merchandise manufactured in Puerto Rico are also refunded on a similar basis; currently, rum is the only product produced in Puerto Rico that is subject to a federal excise tax. Since the 1980s, the refunds of excises on alcohol and tobacco products have been subject to some scrutiny by Congress, and for some brief periods of time the refunds were established at a fraction of total collections.

Refunds from U.S. customs duties and from federal excise taxes on rum accounted for 4.6 percent of the commonwealth's General Fund net revenues in fiscal year 2004 and registered an average yearly growth rate from 1995 to 2004 of 5.7 percent. The first $86 million of this approximately $300 million annual revenue stream has been pledged to repay $1.47 billion in bonds issued by the Puerto Rico Infrastructure Financing Authority since 1988 (not included in central government debt discussed earlier), including a 2005 issue that provided a $317 million reimbursement to the central government to balance the budget. Besides the rebate adjustments, increases in underlying rum sales have allowed Congress to transfer a portion since 1999 to finance the Conservation Trust Fund of Puerto Rico endowment, a private not-for-profit entity.

Municipal Finances

Fiscal conditions are also clouded for municipal governments in Puerto Rico. Thirty-nine of the seventy-eight municipalities in Puerto Rico registered fiscal deficits in 2003.[12] Their fiscal situations worsened after the Municipal Reform Laws of 1991 because more tasks were transferred from the central government to the municipalities but adequate revenue instruments were not provided to finance increased responsibilities.[13]

The principal revenue sources for municipalities in 2002 were the property tax (32.9 percent of total revenue) and *patentes municipales* (23.4 percent of total revenue). The *patentes municipales* is a turnover tax and as such is widely seen as a poor tax along several dimensions: it is a regressive tax, and it suffers from tax pyramiding and tax cascading. It is, however, a productive tax, even at low rates (for example, 0.5 percent for all transactions, except financial institutions, which pay at a rate of 1 percent). In addition, local governments can charge an exaction tax, a one-time tax levied on new construction in the jurisdiction of the municipality as a sort of user cost (or impact fee) to cover the expected increase in fixed costs that the local government will incur for providing services to the new development. Municipal public debt is another source of revenues. Local governments also receive state and federal transfers, which account for most of all other municipal revenues (or 43.7 percent of total revenues).

The fiscal situation of the municipalities has been made worse by the practices of the central government. State law exempts most residences from the property tax, but the central government compensates the municipality for the tax loss only on residences bought before 1992. The tax incentive laws covering manufacturing also grant a tax exemption to qualified corporations, which can go up to 100 percent of the legal tax liability; however, the tax cost of these provisions is transferred to the municipalities in the cases of the property tax and the *patentes municipales*. Since 1998, municipalities have had to pay a percentage of their gross revenues to the central government to help finance the state health insurance plan for the poor. The Municipal Reform Laws of 1991 transferred tasks that had been the responsibility of the central government to the

12. Data provided by the Puerto Rico Office of the Comptroller, 2004.
13. Cao Garcia (1992).

Figure 7-3. *Central and Municipal Government Expenditures as Share of GNP, 1955–2004*
Percent

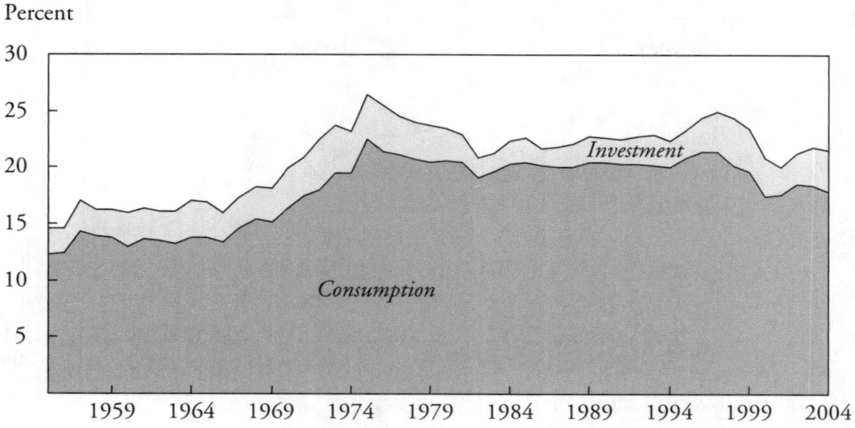

Source: Data from Puerto Rico Planning Board, *Economic Report to the Governor, Statistical Appendix*, various years.

municipalities but without compensating the municipalities for the increase in responsibilities and expenses.

In summary, the municipal governments face a difficult fiscal situation: revenues are inelastic, expenditures grow with population growth and inflation, and the responsibilities delegated by the central government have been increased without compensating funding. Under these circumstances, discretionary outlays are severely limited. At the present time, some mayors are pressing for enacting a municipal sales tax with a rate of 1 percent. The justice secretary has issued an opinion stating that such a tax is outside the legal powers of municipalities, thereby creating a controversy that will probably end in the courts.

Public Expenditures in Puerto Rico

Although the focus of this chapter is the Puerto Rico tax system, it is important also to discuss the major features of public expenditures in Puerto Rico. Figure 7-3 shows central and municipal government consumption and investment expenditures as a percentage of GNP for fiscal years 1955 to 2004. Public consumption expenditures exhibited an upward trend from 1955 to 1975, increasing from 12.2 percent of GNP in 1955 to 22.5 percent in 1975, while investment expenditures increased from 2.4 percent of GNP in 1955 to 3.9 percent in 1975. In 1975 came a fiscal crisis, which resulted in a shrinking in the relative size of the government and which lasted until 1982. After this came a period of sustained, albeit slow, growth in the relative share of government, a period that

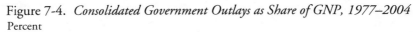

Figure 7-4. *Consolidated Government Outlays as Share of GNP, 1977–2004*
Percent

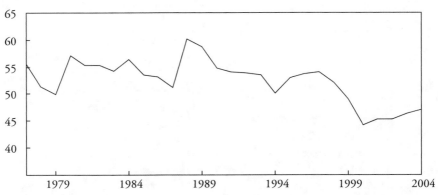

Source: Data from Puerto Rico Office of Management and Budget.

lasted until 1997, when combined central and municipal government expenditures (consumption and investment) were 25.0 percent of GNP. From the year 1997 to 2000 the relative size of government fell, and the last four years have shown oscillations, without any definite pattern.

The government today is relatively smaller than it was thirty years ago. Indeed, it should also be noted that central and municipal government outlays as a percentage of GNP tend to be lower in Puerto Rico than in most developed countries. The common notion that the government has grown too big in Puerto Rico cannot easily be justified by the actual relative size of government expenditures in economic activity.

To expand the analysis, consider the consolidated budget, or central and municipal government expenditures plus outlays of state enterprises. Figure 7-4 shows the consolidated budget as a percentage of GNP for fiscal years 1977 to 2004. Consolidated budget outlays as a percentage of GNP oscillated in the range of 50 to 57 percent between fiscal years 1977 and 1987. The consolidated budget had a sudden upward shock in 1988 and peaked at 61 percent of GNP in 1990, and until 1999 the percentage again varied from 50 to 55 percent. In fiscal year 1999 there was a sharp decline in the relative size of outlays because of the privatization of the telephone company, and in 2000 government outlays fell to their minimum value (44 percent) for the period under consideration. Since then, the share of government has shown a slight upward trend, reaching 47 percent in fiscal year 2004.

Even when state enterprises are included, the relative size of government is smaller today than thirty years ago. It therefore seems likely that any discontent with government in public opinion has to be about something other than the size of outlays. To further explore this issue, figure 7-5 presents central and

Figure 7-5. *Central and Municipal Government Employment in Puerto Rico, 1971–2004*
Thousands

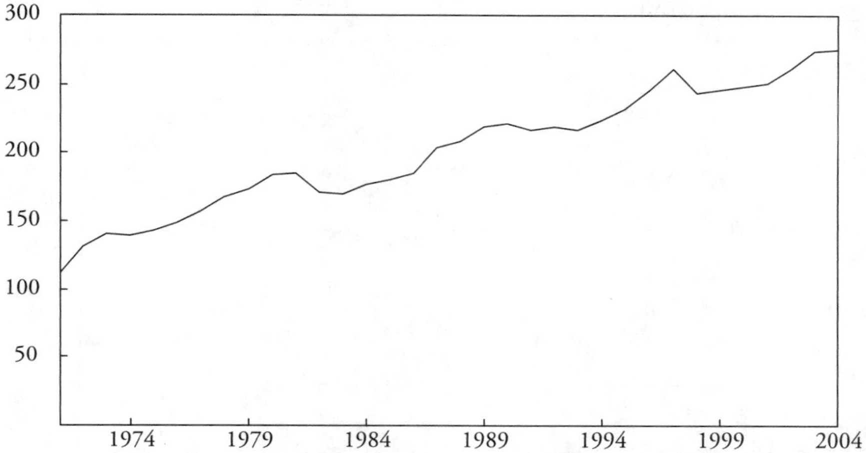

Source: Data from Puerto Rico Department of Labor and Human Resources, *Household Surveys*.

municipal government employment for fiscal years 1971 to 2004, which shows a clear upward trend in public sector employment over the period.

Finally, figure 7-6 compares central government employment as a percentage of total employment with government consumption expenditures as a share of GNP. Government consumption expenditures as a percentage of GNP grew until 1975 and then began a downward trend that continued until 1982. However, government employment as a share of total employment grew until 1980, creating an ample gap between the two measures that widened up to 1983. This gap shrank in size from 1984 to 1999 and then widened again, expanding the divergence up to 2004. The decline in the relative size of government consumption outlays, coupled with an increase in the share of government in total employment, suggests that working conditions in the public sector or the use of other inputs in public sector production (or both) may have deteriorated over time.

If workers' compensation declines and the availability of complementary inputs also diminishes, then there may well be a reduction in public sector productivity. If so, this could explain the apparent paradox in which public opinion complains about the "large" size of government at the same time that the actual (relative) size of government has in fact declined. The situation might well be that government does not provide an excessively large amount of services but that the services provided are increasingly unsatisfactory because of continuously declining productivity in the public sector.

Figure 7-6. *Central and Municipal Government Employment and Consumption as Share of Total Employment and GNP, Puerto Rico, Fiscal Years 1971–2004*
Percent

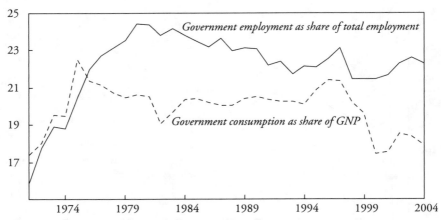

Source: Data from Puerto Rico Department of Labor and Human Resources, *Household Surveys*; Puerto Rico Planning Board, *Economic Report to the Governor, Statistical Appendix*, various years.

If productivity declines in the public sector, overall productivity in the economy may also decrease, being pulled down by what is going on in government. Moreover, if inputs provided by government are inadequate, then firms have to incur an additional resource cost to compensate for government failure in providing adequate services. Low government productivity therefore pulls down overall productivity in the economy. Also, and more important, if government-provided inputs are inadequate, the rest of the economy has to incur an additional resource cost. Such a situation increases production costs and diminishes productivity in the private sector.

Public sector inefficiencies also have adverse consequences for consumers. Many individuals find themselves substituting with private expenditures what the government is supposed to provide (through taxes already paid by these same individuals) but does not, at least with the quality and quantity demanded. This has been characterized as "spontaneous privatization" of government services, whereby many residents purchase from private suppliers what government had traditionally provided. This privatization trend is most obvious in the areas of private security, land transportation (where only 5 percent of Puerto Rican workers use mass transit to go to work), and water reserves (where an increasing proportion of homes are equipped with water cisterns).

Education provides another particularly good example. According to Helen Ladd and Francisco Rivera-Batiz (in chapter 5 of this volume), notwithstanding the sharp increase of schooling levels in the population over the past fifty years and various attempts to reform the public school system in recent years, the overall quality of education has declined, giving rise to social discontent with the school system and limiting the ability of education to contribute to economic growth.[14] One indicator of the failure of the public school system is student scores in the University Assessment and Admissions Program, the Puerto Rican equivalent of the College Board Scholastic Assessment Test. The mean scores for public school students on the verbal aptitude tests declined from 457 in the mid-1980s to 444 in the early part of the new century, while the quantitative aptitude mean scores remained roughly constant over the same period. The mean scores for the Spanish achievement tests also declined over this period, and the mean scores for the mathematics and English achievement tests were largely unchanged.[15]

The source of the problem does not appear to be a lack of government spending on public schools. According to A. T. Kearney Management Consultants, Puerto Rican public expenditures on education accounted for 8.2 percent of GNP in fiscal year 2000, a higher figure than in Organization for Economic Cooperation and Development (OECD) member countries like Canada (7.6 percent), the United States (5.7 percent), the United Kingdom and Italy (both 5.2 percent), France (4.8 percent), Germany (3.4 percent), and Japan (2.0 percent).[16] The issue seems rather to be the inability of the Puerto Rican government to deliver an adequate educational product. For example, A. T. Kearney has found that only 36 percent of payroll expenditures in public education in Puerto Rico is devoted to teachers' salaries, while the OECD average is 65 percent. This implies a misallocation of resources within the public school system.[17]

Discontent with public schools has given rise to an increasing demand for private education in Puerto Rico. At the beginning of the 1940 academic year, private schools accounted for only 4.1 percent of total school enrollment, but in 2003 this proportion rose to 24.7 percent[18] and total public and private enrollment nearly tripled in absolute numbers. Many taxpayers are paying twice for the same service: once when they pay their taxes and a second time when they pay tuition at a private school.

Table 7-4 shows a more detailed breakdown of government expenditures in the last decade or so. As discussed in more detail in the next section, the composition of government expenditures in Puerto Rico is comparable to that of the average state in the United States, although there is also a relatively higher percentage of spending on health and welfare in Puerto Rico than on the mainland, and a relatively lower percentage on education. For example, in 2002 average state and local expenditures on health, welfare, and education were 7, 14, and

14. See chapter 5 in this volume.
15. See chapter 5 in this volume.
16. A. T. Kearney (2003).
17. A. T. Kearney (2003).
18. See chapter 5 in this volume.

Table 7-4. *Distribution of Government Expenditures as Share of Total General Government Expenditures, Puerto Rico, by Type, Selected Fiscal Years, 1990–2004*

Percent, except as indicated

Expenditure type	1990	1992	1994	1996	1998	2000	2002	2004
General government	5.25	5.66	5.68	8.38	4.84	8.46	8.38	11.71
Public safety	8.94	9.41	13.30	11.74	12.41	13.00	10.86	11.63
Health	3.62	2.76	3.20	3.12	6.56	9.65	12.98	14.34
Public housing and welfare	25.67	21.13	25.39	21.57	19.02	20.86	17.84	18.04
Education	20.97	23.11	25.18	23.23	27.44	24.17	21.88	22.89
Economic development	8.75	6.35	3.93	1.12	1.86	3.35	4.17	5.73
Intergovernmental	4.06	4.84	3.07	3.88	0.56	3.70	3.05	3.48
Lottery	5.22	6.08	0	0	0	0	0	0
Capital outlays	8.21	10.90	9.15	15.91	15.15	8.27	3.32	3.83
Debt service	9.31	9.75	11.09	11.05	12.15	8.54	17.52	8.33
General government outlays[a] (millions of dollars)	6,807	7,567	6,975	9,071	10,423	11,283	13,031	14,445

Source: Puerto Rico Department of Treasury, *Comprehensive Annual Financial Reports* for 1990–2004.

a. After 2001, payments to component units were reported as expenditures by function as called for under Governmental Accounting Standards Board Statement No. 34. For comparison purposes, the expenditure totals reported here are adjusted to include inter-fund transfers for all years. The expenditure totals exclude repayment of debt principal.

29 percent, respectively, of total state and local expenditures of the average U.S. state; in Puerto Rico, the comparable percentages were 13, 18, and 22 percent.

Puerto Rico Tax Practice in the International Context

As noted earlier, any comparison of Puerto Rico with other countries is complicated by its status as a commonwealth within the United States. In many respects Puerto Rico is similar to a typical state in the United States, but it also has status as a somewhat more independent entity. Consequently, I compare Puerto Rico both to U.S. states and to countries, especially those in the Caribbean.

Puerto Rico Compared with the U.S. States

Tables 7-5 and appendix 7A-1 present various types of information about the tax structure of U.S. state and local governments; for completeness, tables 7-6 and appendix 7A-2 present similar information about the expenditure structure of U.S. state and local governments. There is a good deal of information in these tables. Notably, Puerto Rico generates considerably more revenue from its corporate income tax (as a percentage of total revenues) and considerably less from its collection of excise taxes than the average U.S. state and local government. (Recall from table 7-3 that the personal income, corporate income, and *arbitrios* taxes accounted for 39.3, 36.6, and 22.8 percent, respectively, of General Fund revenues in 2002.) Even so, taxes as a percentage of total income are significantly higher in Puerto Rico than in the typical U.S. state, although the per capita level of Puerto Rican taxes is somewhat lower than that of the average state and local government sector in the United States. As noted earlier, the composition of expenditures in Puerto Rico is roughly the same as in the average U.S. state, although Puerto Rico tends to spend more heavily on health and less heavily on education than the average mainland state.

Puerto Rico Compared with Selected Countries

Consider now the Puerto Rican system of taxation relative to other countries, especially smaller countries and those in the Caribbean. Puerto Rico raised roughly one-quarter of GDP in taxes in 2002. A natural question to ask is whether Puerto Rico has an "adequate" level of revenue mobilization. This is no easy question to answer. There is also the question of whether the competitiveness of the Puerto Rico economy is weakened by taxes that are too high relative to GDP or GNP (or by expenditures that are too low or quality too poor to provide adequate levels of public service).

When the level of taxation in Puerto Rico (as a percentage of GDP in 2001) is compared with that of a group of small Caribbean and Central American countries (that is, those with a population between 2 million and 4 million, including the

Table 7-5. *Distribution of State and Local Government Taxes Collected, United States, by Type, Selected Fiscal Years, 1980–2002*
Percent, except as indicated

Tax type	1980	1985	1990	1995	2000	2002
Individual income[a]	18.83	20.04	21.06	20.88	24.26	22.41
Corporate income[a]	5.96	5.48	4.70	4.75	4.13	3.11
Sales and gross receipts[a]	35.77	36.10	35.46	35.92	35.45	35.81
Property[a]	30.65	29.66	31.02	30.80	28.56	30.85
Motor vehicle[a]	2.56	2.34	2.28	2.04	1.88	1.87
Other[a]	6.23	6.38	5.48	5.61	5.70	5.95
Total taxes, as share of gross state product	8.01	8.29	8.64	8.93	8.89	8.63
Per capita (dollars)	981.28	1,466.85	2,005.42	2,478.18	3,089.19	3,140.48

Source: Data from United States Bureau of Census, State and Local Government Finances (www.census.gov/govs/www/estimate.html).
a. As share of total taxes collected.

Table 7-6. *Distribution of State and Local Expenditures, United States, by Type, Selected Years, 1980–2002*
Percent

Expenditure type	1980	1985	1990	1995	2000	2002
Public education[a]	30.69	29.29	29.53	28.07	29.86	29.04
Highways[a]	7.67	6.84	6.26	5.72	5.80	5.64
Welfare[a]	10.89	10.86	11.32	14.33	13.36	13.65
Health and hospitals[a]	7.41	7.54	7.65	7.86	7.29	7.15
Police and fire protection[a]	4.43	4.54	4.48	4.31	4.57	4.42
Administration[a]	4.71	4.39	4.59	4.45	4.67	4.53
Insurance trust[a]	6.63	6.72	6.49	7.96	7.17	8.29
Utility and liquor store[a]	8.34	9.09	7.97	6.99	6.58	6.98
Other[a]	19.22	20.73	21.71	20.31	20.70	19.65
Total expenditures						
As share of GDP	15.56	15.59	16.82	18.22	17.80	19.54
Per capita (dollars)	1,910.32	2,765.12	3,912.15	5,059.21	6,207.56	7,110.69

Source: Data from United States Bureau of Census, State and Local Government Finances (www.census.gov/govs/www/estimate.html).
a. As share of total expenditures.

Bahamas, Costa Rica, Jamaica, Nicaragua, Panama, and Trinidad and Tobago) for which data are available, I find that while taxes relative to GDP are somewhat lower for Puerto Rico (23.3 percent) than the median of other small countries (29.1 percent), Puerto Rican taxes are quite high relative to income (36.4 percent). I have also carried out a more traditional tax effort analysis. Using International Monetary Fund data, I compared the tax ratio (tax as a share of GDP) for 117 countries. These data show the average tax ratio in 2001 for this sample of countries to be 23.6 percent of GDP. Thus, relative to GDP, this simple comparison suggests that the level of taxation in Puerto Rico is about average. However, averages are misleading because of countries' differing capacity to tax.

I attempted to explain the variation among these countries using an ordinary least squares regression analysis and a set of explanatory variables that reflect country differences in taxable capacity.[19] These independent variables and the hypotheses about the ways in which they should affect tax revenue mobilization are as follows:

—The level of per capita GDP should be positively related to the tax ratio because higher GDP suggests a greater capacity to tax.

—The degree to which the economy is open to trade is a determinant of the tax ratio. The greater a country's propensity to trade with other countries, the easier it is to raise revenues because the (administrative) tax handles are in place; the government may also play a larger risk-reducing role in more open economies that are exposed to greater external risks. I measure openness as the sum of imports and exports divided by GDP.

—The size of the agricultural sector relative to GDP should dampen taxable capacity and be negatively related to the level of the tax ratio. Countries with a larger agricultural share have fewer good (administrative) tax handles, and the agricultural sector itself can be politically hard to tax.

—Countries with smaller populations should raise a greater share of GDP in revenues than countries with larger populations because there are fixed costs of government that are independent of country size.

—The rate of population growth is also related to the level of revenue mobilization. Faster-growing places tend to lag behind in the amount of revenue they raise per dollar of GDP, in part because of the lag in moving the increased population into the tax base.

I have estimated ordinary least squares regressions against various combinations of these explanatory variables, with all variables measured in logarithms. (Note that in the case of Puerto Rico this analysis might be more appropriately applied to taxes relative to GNP, given that GDP exceeds GNP by 64 percent and that GNP is a better measure of resources that are actually available for domestic use in Puerto Rico.)

The estimation results for the 1990s (not shown) indicate that the explanatory variables are statistically significant and have the expected signs. The tax ratio is significantly higher in countries where per capita GDP and openness are higher and where the agricultural share of GDP and the population growth rate are lower. The explanatory variables are able to explain between 47 and 64 percent of the variation, depending on the specification. These results can then be

19. Bahl (1971).

used to estimate an expected level of the tax ratio for Puerto Rico. For example, across the various specifications, I predict that Puerto Rico should raise, on average, 21 percent of GDP in taxes. The actual ratio of taxes to GDP in the 1990s was 23 percent. The ratio of the actual to the estimated is the "tax effort" coefficient. Puerto Rico's tax effort coefficient is 1.1, which can be interpreted as showing that Puerto Rico ranks slightly (10 percent) above the international average tax effort.

Based on this international comparison, I conclude that Puerto Rico is neither a high-tax nor a low-tax country but approximately an average-tax country. Some could point to this result as one of the competitive features of the Puerto Rican economy and argue that taxes should be held at their present level. Others may see this as evidence that there is at least some room for additional taxation.

There are important reservations to this conclusion. The results show that collections in Puerto Rico are roughly at (or slightly above) the international average. It may well be the case that liabilities are high and that Puerto Ricans who comply with the tax laws face tax burdens that are high by international standards; however, I cannot make such a comparison among the countries in the sample here because data are not available. Some have argued that the rate of revenue mobilization in Puerto Rico is even lower than that reported, because GDP is underreported owing to the existence of the underground or informal economy. However, I know of little systematic evidence that the understatement of GDP in Puerto Rico is any different from that in other developing countries,[20] and so I have made no adjustment for an understatement of GDP. In contrast, it can also be argued that revenue mobilization in Puerto Rico is actually much higher than the use of GDP in the denominator indicates. As noted earlier, GDP exceeds GNP by a substantial amount. If GNP is a better indicator of income available for domestic use, then it should be used to calculate tax effort.

Table 7-7 examines a different issue: whether Puerto Rico's tax structure (as opposed to the level of taxation) is similar to that of other countries. In table 7-7, using International Monetary Fund data for 2000, I divide taxes into four groups: income and payroll taxes, property taxes, indirect taxes, and taxes on international trade.[21] I report separately an "other" category that includes taxes that could not be allocated. Social Security taxes have been excluded from this computation. The contribution of each of these groups as a share of total tax collections is shown in table 7-7 for all countries for which I could find data. Mean values are reported in the last row of the table.

Table 7-7 suggests that for Puerto Rico the burden of income taxation (measured by income taxes as a percentage of total taxes, where income taxes include individual, corporate, and payroll taxes, where relevant) is the highest, and that

20. Schneider and Enste (2002).
21. International Monetary Fund (2003).

Table 7-7. *Tax Structure of Selected Countries as Share of Total Tax, by Tax Type, 2000*
Percent

Country	Income and payroll taxes	Property taxes	Indirect taxes	Taxes on international trade	Other taxes
Argentina	26.3	8.4	35.0	3.8	0.1
Bahrain	36.3	3.8	16.1	43.8	0.0
Belarus	27.1	3.2	62.3	4.9	0.0
Bhutan	53.4	0.4	42.6	3.6	0.0
Bolivia	10.9	10.5	65.1	6.2	0.1
Bulgaria	31.6	1.5	61.2	3.8	1.8
Canada	57.0	11.7	27.3	0.8	0.0
Chile	22.8	4.1	61.3	7.6	4.2
Congo, Democratic Republic of	12.6	0.0	23.8	24.7	38.8[a]
Congo, Republic of	11.3	0.0	64.5	22.9	1.4
Costa Rica	22.4	0.5	68.7	8.4	0.0
Côte d'Ivoire	29.1	1.7	23.3	45.4	0.5
Croatia	22.1	1.8	66.4	8.7	1.0
Czech Republic	40.1	2.4	53.9	3.1	0.4
Denmark	60.8	3.6	34.6	0.0	1.0
Dominican Republic	20.5	1.1	28.5	48.5	1.4
Estonia	39.2	2.2	58.4	0.2	0.0
Georgia	25.9	9.4	54.6	6.1	0.0
Hungary	36.1	2.6	55.6	4.0	1.7
India	37.3	0.1	37.3	25.1	0.2
Iran, Islamic Republic of	53.0	2.5	19.9	23.3	1.3
Israel	53.2	7.7	37.3	0.9	0.7
Jamaica	41.9	0.6	40.5	8.9	8.1
Kazakhstan	52.7	6.0	36.3	4.1	0.7
Latvia	36.9	4.9	56.6	1.6	0.0
Lithuania	40.5	2.7	55.3	1.5	0.0
Macao, China	8.9	6.5	82.1	0.0	2.5
Madagascar	15.7	1.0	29.1	53.5	0.6
Maldives	4.6	0.0	29.7	64.4	1.3
Mauritius	14.6	5.8	46.2	33.4	0.1
Mexico	32.6	1.7	59.6	3.9	0.7
Moldova	17.5	6.1	68.9	7.5	0.1
Mongolia	28.4	0.1	56.2	10.1	1.3
Myanmar	34.5	0.0	58.2	7.2	0.0
Nepal	22.4	3.4	41.6	32.6	0.0
Nicaragua	17.1	−0.2	73.6	9.4	0.0
Pakistan	28.1	1.2	44.7	16.0	10.1[b]
Paraguay	17.9	0.0	59.4	18.2	4.4
Peru	26.8	0.0	67.0	12.4	3.2
Poland	35.5	5.2	55.9	3.5	0.0
Puerto Rico	66.8	0	22.0	0	11.2

(continued on the following page)

Table 7-7. *(continued)*

Country	Income and payroll taxes	Property taxes	Indirect taxes	Taxes on international trade	Other taxes
Romania	34.5	2.7	54.8	6.2	1.1
Russian Federation	33.2	4.5	44.4	13.0	0.1
Seychelles	26.7	0.1	7.8	63.1	2.3
Singapore	50.2	6.5	31.2	2.5	9.6
Slovak Republic	35.9	2.8	54.3	7.0	0.0
Slovenia	36.3	2.5	57.6	3.6	0.0
South Africa	54.0	5.8	34.8	3.1	0.7
Switzerland	58.1	12.3	28.6	1.1	0.0
Tajikistan	16.0	5.6	63.8	12.6	0.0
Thailand	32.2	2.3	53.1	11.9	0.5
Tunisia	28.5	1.9	51.8	15.5	2.2
Turkey	37.4	4.0	52.1	1.7	4.7
Ukraine	42.3	0.0	52.4	5.3	0.0
United States	66.4	13.2	19.5	1.0	0.0
Uruguay	26.2	9.3	57.1	4.7	3.1
Venezuela, RB	42.5	5.5	39.7	11.4	0.9
Mean	32.6	3.6	47.5	13.4	2.0

Source: Data from International Monetary Fund (2003). Data exclude Social Security taxes.
a. Some direct taxes are classified as "other."
b. This includes surcharges on natural gas and petroleum.

of indirect taxes and taxes on international trade the lowest, among all the countries included in the sample. These tax structure differences suggest that income taxes, particularly individual income taxes, are used much more heavily in Puerto Rico than in most other countries, supporting the observation made by many that Puerto Rico heavily taxes labor. However, it should be noted that it would take a significant reduction in income taxes to bring Puerto Rico to a level of direct tax reliance similar to that observed elsewhere. The data also suggest that Puerto Rico taxes consumption much less heavily than most other countries. Even so, the relative reliance on combined income and indirect taxes in Puerto Rico is broadly similar to that of the United States.

Personal and Corporate Income Taxes

Puerto Rico generates roughly an average amount of revenues from the personal income tax, relative to selected other countries of roughly similar size. Nevertheless, the combined importance of individual and corporate income taxes in total taxes is considerably higher in Puerto Rico than in many other countries.

By comparing actual income tax revenue to estimated potential income tax revenue, I can again calculate indexes of tax effort for the countries in the sample. As in the previous analysis, the first step in calculating income tax effort is to identify variables that measure the capacity of a country to raise income tax revenue. Per capita GDP is an overall measure of capacity, and I expect that countries with higher per capita GDP will raise more income tax revenue. Population size is used as an independent variable to adjust for the size of a country, with the expectation that large countries are more prone to tax personal income. The openness of a country's economy (measured as imports plus exports divided by GDP) could be expected to identify countries with more sophisticated administrations and therefore an ability to support an individual income tax. I have estimated an ordinary least squares regression of the individual income tax as a percentage of GDP on a sample of thirty-five countries, where all variables were entered in log form and where I used averages of the income tax to GDP ratio for countries for the period 1990–2000. The signs of the coefficients (not shown) are as hypothesized, and all three independent variables are statistically significant.

I then used these regression results to estimate an expected or predicted level of individual income tax for Puerto Rico. For the 1990–2000 period, I predict that a country of Puerto Rico's income, population, and openness would raise 3.3 percent of its GDP in individual income tax revenue. In fact, Puerto Rico raises 5.2 percent, well above the predicted amount. Puerto Rico's tax effort index for the individual income tax (or the actual percentage of individual income tax revenue divided by the estimated percentage) is 1.58, among the largest in the sample. This analysis shows that Puerto Rico has a relatively large yield from the individual income tax. Although there are some issues with the tax (as discussed later), international comparisons suggest that there is not much room for increasing the effective tax rate for the individual income tax.

Corporate Income Tax in CARICOM Countries

It is instructive to examine the practice of corporate income taxation in the broader Caribbean community, especially in the Caribbean Community and Common Market (CARICOM), even though Puerto Rico is not a member. The group comprises fifteen member states (Antigua and Barbuda, Bahamas, Barbados, Belize, Dominica, Grenada, Guyana, Haiti, Jamaica, Montserrat, St. Kitts, St. Lucia, St. Vincent and the Grenadines, Suriname, and Trinidad and Tobago) and five associate members (Anguilla, Bermuda, British Virgin Islands, Cayman Islands, and Turks and Caicos). Its purpose is "to provide dynamic leadership and service, in partnership with Community Institutions and Groups, toward the attainment of a viable, internationally competitive and sustainable Community, with improved quality of life for all."[22]

---

22. Caribbean Community and Common Market, mission statement (www.caricom.org/jsp/secretariat/mission_statement.jsp?menu=secretariat).

There are some obvious similarities between the CARICOM countries: most are English speaking, they are all former colonies that have become independent in the past 100 years, and their economies are tourism driven. Even so, each nation has a different tax structure with different incentives for foreign investors. Additionally, there is clear evidence of tax competition in the region. Twelve of the countries have lower corporate income tax rates today than they had twenty years ago. The Bahamas has had no corporate income tax for the past twenty years; only Antigua and Barbuda has not lowered its corporate income tax rate. Clearly, the CARICOM countries compete with one another for foreign direct investment. Puerto Rico must therefore take into account the tax structures in neighboring countries to remain a competitive destination for investment, even though Puerto Rico itself is not a member of CARICOM and cannot negotiate trade treaties on its own.

As for the major features of the corporate income tax in CARICOM countries (for tax year 2004), the Bahamas has the lowest corporate income tax rate, at 0 percent; the next lowest rate is 25 percent in Belize. The highest rate is Guyana's 45 percent. The median rate is 35 percent (Antigua, Haiti, St. Kitts, and Trinidad and Tobago). The unweighted average rate is approximately 32 percent. At 39 percent, Puerto Rico's (maximum) corporate rate is higher than both the median and the average rate.

Tax Incentives

Tax incentives are widely used in almost all countries, usually in the form of special provisions that favor investment. According to Howard Zee, Janet Stotsky, and Eduardo Ley, 22 percent of the foreign affiliates of U.S. companies operating abroad in the 1990s received some form of tax concession, and nearly all countries offer tax concessions.[23] These concessions are designed to encourage two kinds of investments: those from investors in foreign countries and those from domestic investors.

The general principle regarding foreign investors is that capital imports should be encouraged as long as their contribution to the domestic economy (the "marginal product of capital") exceeds the cost to the economy. A small, open economy like Puerto Rico must compete with investment opportunities in other countries, so it must offer the foreign investor the going after-tax rate of return. In general, this means that the country should not tax capital imports, because doing so reduces the rate of return earned by foreign investors and thereby discourages capital imports. However, an important exception to this rule of thumb is the case in which the capital-exporting country taxes multinational companies on their worldwide income but allows a credit against home-country corporate income taxes on taxes paid in foreign countries. The

---

23. Zee, Stotsky, and Ley (2002).

failure by a capital-importing country (say, Puerto Rico) to impose its own corporate income tax on profits earned within Puerto Rico simply means that the capital-exporting home country of the enterprise (say, the United States) collects the taxes on income earned by the company in Puerto Rico. Failure to impose the tax therefore transfers taxes from the capital-importing country (Puerto Rico) to the treasury of the capital-exporting country (the United States).

This suggests that a small country should aim for tax rates that are close to—neither higher nor lower than—the tax rates of the countries from which capital imports can be expected. This result also follows when it is recognized, as it must be, that countries compete with one another for capital. If one country lowers its taxes on capital, then other countries may respond in kind. The result may be that no country is able to gain a tax advantage against its rivals, and all that occurs is that the countries in total lose tax revenues, either to the capital-exporting country or to the multinational enterprise.

There are several major types of incentives, most of which depend upon the existence of positive profits and most of which are targeted toward specific types of assets (for example, plant or machinery) or certain types of industries (for example, manufacturing) that the country wishes to encourage. These include investment tax credits and deductions, accelerated depreciation, tax holidays, investment grants, and miscellaneous investment incentives.

Under the first type, the enterprise is allowed a deduction or a credit that is a percentage of the purchase price of the investment good, over and above the depreciation provisions of the asset. These incentives bias a firm's investment choices in favor of shorter-lived assets: the tax credit is like a gift that is more valuable the more often it is used.

Under accelerated depreciation, the enterprise is allowed to write off the price of the capital good at a faster rate than the standard accounting practice (or the true economic depreciation) for the asset. This can be accomplished by shortening the tax life of the asset or by moving the write-offs toward the early years of the asset. Accelerated depreciation biases a firm's choices in favor of longer-lived capital goods: accelerated depreciation is like an interest-free loan that is more valuable on investments whose tax write-off is farther in the future.

Tax holidays allow the enterprise an exemption from taxation for a given number of years immediately following its establishment, typically five to ten years. This incentive is of value only to a firm that has profit income, which eliminates many enterprises that may not post yields in the early years. It may well be that a firm will dissolve after the holiday ends, selling its capital to a new firm that is then eligible for the tax holiday; it may also be that a firm will deliberately invest in shorter-lived assets so that it may exit quickly after the holiday ends; and it may be that a firm will use transfer-pricing methods to reallocate income between branches eligible for a tax holiday and branches that are not eligible.

Often an enterprise is given a direct cash grant that depends on the magnitude of its investment, independent of its level of profits. Another related type of incentive, effectively an investment grant, is one in which the enterprise is given a waiver or a rebate on the duties paid on imported factors of production, often on imported capital goods. Miscellaneous incentives include provisions such as reduced corporate income tax rates, reduced tax rates on some activities, exempt purchases, and the like.

In all cases, the exact magnitude of the benefit to the enterprise depends upon the specific features of the incentive: the period in which the incentive applies, the magnitude of the incentive, the tax rates in the corporate income tax (both in the country itself as well as in the home country of the enterprise, if relevant), the assets and sectors to which the incentive applies, the amount and time profile of the expected profits of the enterprise, and so on.

Evidence from Elisabeth Gugl and George Zodrow (based on a somewhat small sample of countries) suggests that the most popular type of investment incentive is the tax holiday.[24] This is followed by accelerated depreciation, investment tax credits, and import duty exemptions. Nearly all countries use several incentive schemes rather than a single one.

It is in fact possible to quantify the magnitude of these incentives, using a variety of fairly complicated formulas. However, application of these formulas by countries seems to be quite limited, and it appears that most countries do not undertake such analyses. When the formulas have been applied, the analysis has typically shown that tax holidays and investment tax credits lower the marginal effective tax rate more than other incentives and that the interaction between different incentive schemes is crucial in determining their overall impact.[25]

All CARICOM countries offer tax holidays, preferential duty and consumption tax rates, investment tax credits, accelerated depreciation, and relief from other business taxes in order to attract investment. Many of them also provide corporate income tax holidays for agriculture, capital-intensive industries, export companies, manufacturing, mining, and tourism.

Taxes on Consumption

Puerto Rico imposes a variety of *arbitrios,* or excise taxes. Even so, Puerto Rico, like the United States, is different from most other countries in its practice of consumption taxation because it does not impose a value added tax. Every country in the OECD now has a VAT, as do most countries in Latin America and many in the Caribbean. The average standard rate in the OECD countries is now almost 18 percent, compared with 14 percent in the Western Hemisphere countries, although rates in the latter area range from as low as 5 percent

24. Gugl and Zodrow (2005).
25. Gugl and Zodrow (2005).

in Panama to as high as 23 percent in Uruguay. In the Caribbean region, Haiti and the Dominican Republic led the way in introducing VATs in the 1980s, followed by Trinidad and Tobago in 1990, Jamaica in 1991, and Barbados in 1997. Rates in these five countries currently range from 10 to 15 percent, with an average standard rate of 13.4 percent. In most countries, VAT rates have gone up over time.

As with total taxes and also with personal income tax, it is possible to estimate potential revenues from indirect taxes and to compare actual revenues with estimated potential revenues to calculate indexes of indirect tax effort for the countries in the sample. These results (not shown) indicate that indirect tax effort in Puerto Rico is considerably lower than the average of the countries in the sample, at only 0.69, among the lowest in the sample here.

Evaluating the Puerto Rico Tax System

Tax systems are designed to achieve multiple objectives. Most obviously, they seek to raise the revenues necessary to finance government expenditures (sometimes termed "adequacy") and also to ensure that the growth in revenues is adequate to meet expenditure requirements ("elasticity"). Another purpose is to distribute the burden of taxation in a way that meets a society's notions of fairness; such "equity" is typically defined in terms of "ability to pay," such that those with equal ability should pay equal taxes ("horizontal equity") and those with greater ability should pay greater taxes ("vertical equity"). Taxes can also be used to influence the behavior of those who pay them; in choosing taxes, a common goal is to minimize the interference of taxes in the economic decisions of individuals and firms. Taxes should be simple, both to administer and to comply with, because a complicated tax system wastes the resources of tax administrators and taxpayers. Consider now the performance of the Puerto Rico tax system in achieving these objectives. While some successes have been achieved, I find significant problems with the system.

There Are Large Amounts of Tax Evasion

By all accounts, large amounts of income and consumption escape taxation in Puerto Rico. Firm evidence on tax evasion is obviously difficult to find. Wilfredo Toledo and Wilfredo Camacho estimate that evasion of the personal income tax amounted to 29.7 percent of actual income tax revenues in 1987 and 24.9 percent of tax revenues in 1992.[26] This represents a significant amount of tax evasion. Estimates of the size of the underground economy in Puerto Rico are also quite large.[27]

26. Toledo and Camacho (1997).
27. Schneider and Enste (2002).

After 1993, the Puerto Rico Treasury Department took a number of measures to control tax evasion, including annual estimations of its extent and a yearly workshop of Treasury employees and state and federal agencies on the topic of tax evasion control.[28] Available indicators show that these measures were effective. In the case of the personal income tax, Toledo and Camacho estimate a steady decline in the rate of evasion of the income tax, from 24.9 percent in 1992 to 16.0 percent in 1997.[29]

There Is a Narrow and Shrinking Tax Base

The goal of most tax reform is to broaden the tax base, thereby allowing marginal tax rates to be reduced. However, the tax base in Puerto Rico has been narrowed in at least two important ways. One is legal and takes the form of exemptions or preferential treatment (for example, tax expenditures). To my knowledge, there is no systematic listing of tax expenditures in the Puerto Rico tax system, which in itself is a problem. The second stems from administrative failures (especially enforcement problems) that allow the existence of enormous amounts of tax evasion.

One result of a small and falling tax base is that the government must emphasize collection of taxes from those "tax handles" that are more readily available. The more visible taxpayers (such as wage earners) end up bearing increasing amounts of the tax burden.

There Is Widespread Use of Tax Incentives

The use of tax incentives, especially in the corporate income tax, is widely acknowledged. Indeed, for the past fifty years Puerto Rican development policy has centered on the use of these incentives.

A common argument is that, without fiscal incentives, Puerto Rican firms simply cannot compete in the world economy, especially firms in the manufacturing and tourism sectors. For this reason, tourism receives many tax incentives under the current law. A counterargument is that incentives (and the resulting preferential tax treatments) have created a misallocation of investment that has led, in turn, to a loss in competitiveness. Moreover, there is little question that incentives are a significant fiscal drain on the budget, a cost that can be reflected in higher taxes on labor or in public investments that have been forgone (for example, education or infrastructure).

Still, many small countries believe that the incentives are necessary if they are to compete with rival countries, especially when the country has little in the way of market size or resource endowment to attract foreign investors. Put differently, the introduction of a tax incentive by one country leads to strategic

28. Cao Garcia (2004).
29. Toledo and Camacho (1997).

responses by other, rival countries. The introduction of tax incentives also stems from the power of large domestic firms that pressure the government to take measures that favor their enterprises. In both cases, the result is the same: the incentives have little impact on investment because other countries have similar incentives, but they have a large and negative impact on the tax collections of all countries and simply transfer revenues to large enterprises.

Even so, it is important to consider—and quantify—the benefits and costs of incentives. The possible benefits to a country that offers tax incentives may include increases in investment, gains from industrialization, the creation of jobs for persons who otherwise would be unemployed or employed at lower wages, the transfer of technology and training, and increases in revenues from taxes to which the incentives do not apply or from taxes payable after the initial reduction has ended. Few countries have actually undertaken a rigorous analysis of these benefits. Overall, there is little evidence that tax incentives are able to attract or to induce investment that would not have been undertaken anyway. The possible costs of the incentives include the loss of revenue, distortions in investment behavior leading to investments that are socially unproductive, administrative complications, political discord generated by favors to foreign-owned corporations, and discrimination against smaller firms that lack the resources or the influence to apply for incentives.

The actual evaluation of benefits and costs has seldom been done. In one study, the benefits were generally found to be positive but small, and smaller than their costs.[30] Another study examined Indonesia's elimination of all its investment incentives as part of a comprehensive tax reform in the mid-1980s.[31] The reasons for this were several. There was much evidence that few if any incentives had the desired effects; all they had accomplished was a massive loss in tax revenues. Furthermore, what investment had been attracted was not, on balance, beneficial to the Indonesian economy. The administrative problems associated with the tax incentives, especially for tax holidays, were also enormous. The presence of tax incentives for some groups of taxpayers required higher tax rates on other nonfavored taxpayers, and these taxpayers lobbied for their own special treatment. Finally, smaller firms did not generally receive tax incentives, and these firms had been an important source of job growth in Indonesia. On balance, these costs were deemed to be far in excess of the potential benefits. In particular, there was little evidence that the incentives were more important to potential investors than such factors as political stability, potential market size, economic growth, or infrastructure. The result in Indonesia was that the best policy for investment was deemed to be a reduced rate of taxation in the corporate income tax. Jamaica is currently considering

30. Thirsk (1991).
31. Gillis (1985).

the elimination of most of its incentives as part of a comprehensive tax reform there because of similar considerations.[32]

Indeed, there is now some evidence that the best way to encourage investment is simply to lower the tax rate on corporate income, not to offer targeted incentives. There is also increasing evidence that the main effect of tax incentives is on the transfer of income across jurisdictions (through such mechanisms as transfer pricing and financial policies) rather than on the location of real activity across jurisdictions.[33] Even the analysis of Puerto Rico tax incentives is somewhat clouded.[34] The main message of this research is that tax incentives can stimulate investment but that a country's overall economic characteristics are much more important for the success or the failure of industries than any package of tax incentives; even if tax incentives stimulate investment, they are not generally cost effective. Again, this is not to deny that tax incentives can affect the movement of capital, broadly defined. It is to question whether any such movement represents a transfer of real economic activity as opposed to simply a transfer of paper transactions that reduce a firm's tax liabilities without generating any genuine economic gain. It is also to question whether the benefit-cost ratio of any such incentive is greater than one. Overall, then, in the few instances in which detailed analyses have been performed, the benefits of incentives have been found to be outweighed by their costs.

All this suggests some general lessons related specifically to the corporate income tax and investment incentives:

—Avoid the use of tax incentives for investment. Incentives have little impact on investment and seem mainly to reduce tax revenues. Even where they do attract investment, the investment is not often socially productive.

—Resist the temptation to promote industrial or social policies through the tax system. Such attempts are likely to result in a proliferation of tax incentives to enterprises and in the preferential treatment of particular groups of taxpayers, which will lead to other groups' requesting them. Moreover, tax incentives are difficult to eliminate once they are in place.

—Keep enterprise tax rates in line with those of neighboring countries and with those of the capital-exporting countries: neither higher nor lower. Higher tax rates reduce the capital stock, and lower tax rates lead to strategic behavior by other countries, which simply reduces tax revenues in all countries. Recent experience shows that is difficult, if not impossible, to prevent the movement of capital either into or out of a country.

32. Rider (2004).

33. See Grubert and Slemrod (1998); Fisher (2002); Zee, Stotsky, and Ley (2002); Desai and Hines (2004); Hines (2004); Morisset and Pirnia (1999).

34. Marrero Velasquez (1989); Liard-Murient (2003).

However, if investment incentives are desired as part of an attempt to encourage investment and attract foreign investors, then appropriate policy suggests the following:

—Rationalize investment incentives—that is, adopt schemes that, while making all eligible projects more profitable, do not alter the relative ranking of those projects. A rational scheme does not lead an investor to chose project A over project B when, in the absence of the scheme, project B is more profitable than project A. A number of such incentives are now available, including reducing the tax rate on corporate income, extending a tax credit on net investment, and allowing full expensing. Tax holidays, in particular, should be discouraged.

—Define clearly the types of investment activities that will receive incentives, and then grant these incentives automatically, minimizing discretion and negotiation. The incentive should be linked closely to the type of activity that the government deems socially productive (for example, export activities, labor employment). Negotiation leads to delays, uncertainty, and corruption.

—Permit unrestricted entry of foreign investment.

—Do not favor foreign over domestic investors. To do so is unfair to national entrepreneurs, encourages questionable joint ventures, and discourages the development of a national entrepreneurial class.

—Permit unrestricted transfers of capital income abroad. Investors invest to earn a return, and they must be assured that they can take their profits home.

It should also be borne in mind that a number of nontax features affect investment, notably a stable political environment and the existence of private property guarantees.

There Are Significant Limitations in Tax Administration

A dominant theme in most assessments of the Puerto Rico tax system is the absence of effective tax administration. If taxes cannot be administered efficiently and equitably, then the goals of any tax reform will not be achieved. As Stanley Surrey has noted, "The concentration of tax policy on the choice of taxes may lead to insufficient consideration of the aspect of tax administration. In short, there may well be too much preoccupation with 'what to do' and too little attention to 'how to do it.' "[35] Put differently, tax administration should be placed at the center, not on the periphery, of tax reform efforts.[36]

One indicator of administrative efficiency is the extent of tax evasion. As discussed earlier in this chapter, tax evasion appears to be widespread in Puerto Rico and has a range of negative effects. Evasion reduces the revenue and the elasticity of the tax system. It necessarily undermines the horizontal and vertical

35. Surrey (1958).
36. Goode (1981); Bird (1989).

equity of the tax system, since equals are no longer taxed equally and the well-to-do are generally more successful in exploiting opportunities for evasion. The actual allocative effects of the tax system are likely to differ significantly from those implied by the statutes. In short, poor tax administration frustrates the achievement of virtually all goals of the tax system.

Other problems with tax administration in Puerto Rico stem from the tax structure: the tax base has been narrowed by preferences; the system is overly complex, especially in its use of tax incentives; and over time the rate and base structures have become more and more complex. The structural and administrative problems are clearly related. Complexity in the rate and base structure makes administration more difficult and also reduces the compliance rate.

The Tax System Is Excessively and Unnecessarily Complex

The limitations in tax administration in Puerto Rico are magnified by the overly complex tax system. Over time, the tax system has been adjusted variously to raise revenue, to respond to requests for more favorable tax treatment, to promote specific activities, to redistribute income, and to protect the poor. Each of these changes has most likely complicated the tax system. Complexity leads, in turn, to higher administrative costs, more arbitrariness in administration, and an increasing erosion of confidence in the fairness and effectiveness of the tax system. Taxpayers are not inclined to pay a tax that they do not understand, imposes high compliance costs, and is administered by a tax administration viewed as arbitrary and ineffective.

There are numerous elements that complicate the tax system. Sometimes complication is a by-product of well-intentioned adjustments to the tax structure (for example, the exemption of the purchases of items consumed by low-income individuals). The corporate income tax in Puerto Rico, like that in most countries, is particularly complicated.

There are areas where the system is especially complex. Clearly, this is true for tax incentives. It is also especially true for capital allowances. A great deal of effort goes into the calculation of capital depreciation amounts. Many countries have elected to avoid such complicated schemes by grouping assets into broad categories.

All taxes impose compliance costs on taxpayers and administrative costs on government. Taxpayer compliance costs include time spent keeping receipts, logging appropriate books, and filing tax returns. Administrative costs include assessment, audit, and collection. Some taxes are less expensive to administer and to comply with than other taxes. This is a result of such factors as the complexity of particular tax laws, taxpayers' familiarity with various taxes, the process by which taxes are collected, and the status of data collection, enforcement, and monitoring for the various taxes. For example, taxes that are subject to source withholding are less costly to administer than taxes that require individual filing.

It is difficult to quantify the costs of administration and compliance across countries. However, as noted earlier, some work has calculated these costs, using a variety of methods.[37] These studies demonstrate substantial variation in the compliance and administrative costs across taxes and countries. Income taxes appear to be especially high in terms of administrative costs per dollar of revenue collected; the more complicated the system, the higher the cost. Broader-based taxes may be less costly to administer, but administration of capital gains taxes is notoriously difficult.

There are no data on compliance and administrative costs in Puerto Rico, so I cannot directly compute these costs. However, I believe that it is likely that Puerto Rico's tax structure is a high-cost one. There is an inordinately high reliance on direct taxes and much less use of indirect taxes; the structure of the corporate income tax is complex; and there is extensive use of tax incentives. All these factors imply higher compliance and administrative costs than would be the case for a less complicated system or for one that relies more on indirect taxes.

There Are Horizontal and Vertical Inequities in Taxation

The practice of taxation in Puerto Rico introduces significant vertical and horizontal inequities into the system. One way to examine the vertical equity of the personal income tax is to determine how quickly an individual enters the income tax net. Many countries, Puerto Rico among them, exempt a portion of income from taxation; the relative amount varies widely. I have made estimates of the level of income at which a single individual enters the tax net in a sample of countries. This representative taxpayer in each country faces different thresholds for taxation, as shown in table 7-8. For example, in the British Virgin Islands and Guyana, individuals get into the tax net at relatively low levels of income. Within this limited sample, individuals in Puerto Rico get into the income tax net at relatively high levels of income. Note that this calculation examines only the individual income tax and does not include the payroll taxes.

Furthermore, if a tax system is fair, equally situated individuals and companies will face the same tax obligations. When this is not the case—when the tax system is horizontally inequitable—some individuals will bear a heavier burden than others who have roughly comparable means. This weakens confidence in the system and may encourage some taxpayers to look for avenues of nonpayment that will have negative consequences for revenues. It also may lead individuals and companies to make different economic choices in order to capture tax advantages, which will lead, in turn, to losses in economic efficiency.

---

37. Sandford, Godwin, and Hardwick (1989); Sandford (1995); Blumenthal and Slemrod (1992, 1996); Chattopadhyay and Das-Gupta (2002a, 2002b).

Table 7-8. *Individual Income Threshold for Personal Income Tax,*
Selected Countries, 2003
Units as indicated

Country	In local currency	As share of per capita income (percent)[a]
Antigua and Barbuda	0 East Caribbean dollars	0
Barbados	15,000 bars	94.0
British Virgin Islands	3,000 U.S. dollars	18.8
Costa Rica	1,316,000 colons	39.5
Dominican Republic	138,420 pesos	109.0
Guyana	216,000 Guyanese dollars	30.0
Jamaica	120,432 Jamaican dollars	82.7
Puerto Rico	10,000 U.S. dollars	88.9
United States	7,800 U.S. dollars	21.0

Source: Authors' calculations based on PricewaterhouseCoopers (2004).
a. Calculations based on per capita GDP figures for 2002.

Indeed, there are many sources of horizontal inequities in the Puerto Rican tax system, including the following:

—Individuals who work in the formal sector of the Puerto Rico economy are subject to employer withholding on their wage income, while those who are self-employed or who work in the informal sector are less likely to pay the personal income tax. The result can be very different tax burdens, even for individuals with the same "true" income.

—Some individuals receive nontaxable benefits from their employer, while others do not receive such benefits or receive them at a lower rate. Again, the result can be very different tax burdens for households with equal income.

—Consumers face different effective *arbitrios* tax rates, given the uneven pattern of exemptions on the excises.

—The corporate income tax discriminates among firms, largely because of the existence of tax preferences that are available to some firms and sectors and not to others.

—In addition to the formal provisions for tax relief, there is discretionary relief on a case-by-case basis.

The horizontal inequity that may be the most contentious in Puerto Rico is that between workers subject to income tax withholding and workers in the self-employed sector.

There are also possible sources of vertical inequity. Table 7-9 indicates the effective rates of taxation (as taxes paid divided by adjusted gross income) by income class for 1992 and 1997. Effective rates of taxation clearly increase with

Table 7-9. *Effective Rate of Taxation as Share of Adjusted Gross Income,*
Puerto Rico, 1992 and 1997
Percent

Income class (dollars)	1992	1997
10,000–20,000	5.10	4.69
20,000–30,000	8.29	6.91
30,000–40,000	11.09	9.00
40,000–50,000	13.86	11.17
50,000–75,000	17.55	14.92
75,000–100,000	21.79	19.02
100,000–150,000	25.26	22.92

Source: Data from Puerto Rico Department of Treasury.

Table 7-10. *Contribution to Personal Income Taxes Collected,*
by Income Quintile, Puerto Rico, 1986 and 1997
Percent

Income quintile	1986	1997
First (lowest)	2.75	2.17
Second	5.14	4.00
Third	9.20	7.89
Fourth	16.95	15.84
Fifth (top)	65.96	70.10

Source: Data from Puerto Rico Department of Treasury.

income. However, there has been a decline in the degree of progressivity from 1992 to 1997, and the degree of effective progressivity is considerably less than that implied by the statutory rate structure in the personal income tax. Table 7-10 gives similar information, showing the percentage contribution to total personal income tax revenues by income quintile in 1986 and 1997. Over the period there was a slight decrease in the share of personal income taxes paid by lower-income quintiles and an increase in the share paid by the top quintile. Table 7-11 shows the tax burden on different income groups in 2004, from the individual income tax and from all excise taxes.

I have also calculated the Gini coefficients for before-tax and after-tax income for 1986 and 1997. (A lower Gini coefficient indicates greater equality.) These Gini coefficients show somewhat conflicting trends. The before-tax Gini coefficient increased significantly from 1986 to 1997, from 0.3492 to 0.4126, indicating greater inequality in the distribution of before-tax income in 1997 than in 1986. The after-tax Gini coefficient was also larger in 1997 (0.3553) than in 1986 (0.3226). However, the capacity of taxes to reduce

Table 7-11. *Tax Burden as Share of Individual Income, Puerto Rico, 2004*
Percent

Modified adjusted gross income (dollars)	Individual income tax	All excise taxes	Combined tax burden
0 to less than 5,000	0.0	4.8	4.8
5,000 to less than 10,000	0.1	4.8	4.8
10,000 to less than 15,000	0.2	4.5	4.6
15,000 to less than 20,000	1.2	4.3	5.4
20,000 to less than 25,000	2.3	3.7	6.0
25,000 to less than 30,000	3.2	3.2	6.4
30,000 to less than 40,000	4.0	2.9	6.9
40,000 to less than 50,000	5.1	2.7	7.7
50,000 to less than 75,000	7.3	2.4	9.7
75,000 to less than 100,000	10.0	2.1	12.1
100,000 to less than 200,000	14.7	1.7	16.4
200,000 and over	20.2	0.4	20.6
Total	5.7	3.0	8.7

Source: Bearing Point (2004).

inequality was considerably greater in 1997 than in 1986, as reflected in the greater relative decline from before-tax to after-tax Gini coefficients in 1997 than in 1986.

There Are Likely to Be Large Efficiency Costs

A commonly accepted notion about "good" tax policy holds that the tax system should raise revenues with minimal interference in the decisions of consumers and firms. When a tax leads individuals and business to make decisions solely because of its existence, then the tax is said to impose an efficiency cost, or an "excess burden." The system of taxes in Puerto Rico is likely to introduce a wide range of distortions in individual and firm behavior.

The corporate income tax, for example, generates many distortions, perhaps more than any other tax in the system. Together with the extensive system of tax incentives, the corporate tax gives preferential treatment both to different types of investments and to different sectors, thereby leading firms to base their investment decisions mainly on tax considerations rather than on market forces. As discussed earlier, the use of tax incentives to increase investment and to generate growth is a questionable and unproven practice. The personal income tax also generates distortions: it discourages work effort, it reduces the return to savings, it encourages overuse of items that are tax deductible or that generate tax credits, and it encourages individuals to move to the informal sector. Unfortunately, there are no estimates of the overall efficiency cost of Puerto Rico taxes.

There Is an Apparent—and Largely Undocumented—Belief That Taxes Can Be Used to Generate Economic Growth

Closely related to the issue of tax incentives is the notion that the tax system can be used to encourage economic growth. A large literature attempts to demonstrate the possible linkage between taxation and economic growth. Much of this literature focuses on the experience of U.S. states and examines the possible connection between state tax policies and economic growth.[38] This literature is somewhat inconclusive, but recent work by James Alm and Janet Rogers examining the effects of measurement error and estimation technique demonstrates that there are some connections between policy variables and economic growth but also that these results are not robust. For example, in some regression results it is possible to show that higher state tax revenues are associated with lower growth rates; however, this connection is fairly weak and is not present in all regressions and in all time periods.[39]

Alm and Rogers also find weak evidence that the mix of taxes (for example, a heavier reliance on income taxes or on sales taxes) affects state economic growth; in particular, they find fairly consistent results that greater use of sales taxes is associated with higher economic growth. As for state expenditure policy, they find that higher welfare expenditures are correlated with lower economic growth, as expected, but that greater spending on education and highways tends to be negatively associated with state economic growth. In short, there is some connection between various policy variables and economic growth, but the connection is tenuous and is not robust across all time periods, estimation methods, or specifications. There is also a growing literature that uses the World Bank's *World Tables* to examine the determinants of country economic growth; as Ross Levine and David Renelt demonstrate, many of the results in this literature are also quite fragile.[40]

The Current System of Indirect Taxation Has Many Problems

There are many ways of taxing consumption. Perhaps the most familiar method, at least to U.S. taxpayers, is the retail sales tax, under which the tax base is final retail sales of goods and services. This tax is used by most state and local governments in the United States. Puerto Rico taxes consumption largely through a general tax (the 5 percent general excise tax) and a system of specific excise taxes.

Another common variant on a consumption tax is the value added tax, which has been widely used in Europe for nearly four decades and has been adopted by

---

38. Yu, Wallace, and Nardinelli (1991); Berry and Kaserman (1993); Mendoza, Milesi-Ferretti, and Asea (1997).

39. Alm and Rogers (2005).

40. Barro (2000); Levine and Renelt (1993).

numerous other countries around the world. Value added is the value that a firm adds during production to materials and services purchased from other firms. It equals the difference between a firm's gross receipts and the costs of all intermediate inputs (including the cost of capital goods but excluding wages) used to produce the product; it also equals the sum of wages, interest, rents, and profits of the firm. A tax on the value added of all businesses, therefore, has as its base the total value of all final products, thereby making a VAT equivalent to a national retail sales tax.

Indeed, at least 123 countries worldwide now have some form of VAT; to my knowledge, no tax has ever spread so quickly and so widely. Other than the United States, every country in the OECD now has a VAT, as do most countries in Latin America and many in the Caribbean. The average standard rate in the OECD countries is now almost 18 percent, compared with an average 14 percent in the Western Hemisphere countries, although rates in the latter area range from as low as 5 percent in Panama to as high as 23 percent in Uruguay. In the Caribbean region, Haiti and the Dominican Republic led the way in introducing VATs in the 1980s, followed by Trinidad and Tobago in 1990, Jamaica in 1991, and Barbados in 1997. In most countries, VAT rates have increased over time.

Both the retail sales tax and the value added tax are collected by and from businesses. A third, less common, variant is the personal consumption tax, which levies taxes entirely at the individual level. This tax is based on the identity that income equals consumption plus saving, so that consumption can be measured as income less saving. An individual's personal consumption could be measured by subtracting amounts saved in allowable assets from all amounts earned (including the returns on and withdrawals from saving). Because the tax is imposed at the individual level, various exemptions and deductions can be allowed, and a graduated tax rate structure can also be introduced. Both features make the tax more progressive.

A fourth variant on a consumption tax splits the collection of the tax between businesses and individuals. This variant, suggested by Robert Hall and Alvin Rabushka and introduced in the U.S. Congress as the "flat tax," was the centerpiece of the 1996 Steven Forbes presidential campaign.[41] Recall that the tax base for the value added tax is the difference between a firm's gross receipts and the costs of all intermediate inputs (including the cost of capital goods but excluding wages), and so the VAT base equals the sum of wages, interest, rents, and profits of the firm. Suppose that wages are taken out of the tax base at the business level, by allowing them as a business deduction, but are then taxed at the individual level. The total tax base on businesses and individuals would still be consumption, but the tax would now be collected both at the business and at the individual level. The "business tax" portion of the proposed flat tax is simi-

41. Hall and Rabushka (1995).

lar to a VAT, except that labor costs are allowed as a deduction, along with other input costs and capital costs. The "individual wage tax" in the proposal is imposed on wage income, at the same rate as the business tax; however, because this part of the tax is collected at the individual level, some progressivity can be introduced by the use of generous personal allowances or by progressive marginal tax rates. There are also additional variants on consumption-based taxes, such as a wage tax and a "hybrid tax."

There are at least two major advantages of any consumption tax. First, because a consumption tax removes investment and saving from the tax base, it will lower the cost of capital or raise the return on saving (or both). In either case, the likely response will be an increase in saving and investment as intertemporal distortions are removed. Second, because a consumption tax removes capital income from the tax base, it will lower the administrative and compliance costs of taxation. Most of the complexity of the income tax stems from efforts to define, measure, and tax capital income; the measurement of depreciation allowances in particular (aside from expensing) introduces enormous complexities in the tax code. Because a consumption tax does not tax capital income, these difficulties are eliminated, an especially important advantage in an inflationary environment.

Advocates of the consumption tax also sometimes argue that a consumption tax will be more equitable than an income tax. Two reasons are cited in support. First, following Thomas Hobbes, they argue that it is more equitable to tax an individual on what he or she takes out of the common pool than on what he or she contributes to it. Second, they argue that an equitable tax should treat individuals with equal incomes equally, but that this equal treatment should be over the lifetimes of the individuals, not over a single year. Seen in this life-cycle perspective, a consumption tax is an equitable tax because the present values of a flat rate consumption tax for two individuals with equal incomes (who consume all of their incomes) are the same. In contrast, the present values of an income tax will be different if the pattern of saving differs, because interest income is taxed under an income tax.

The main argument that has been made against any consumption tax is that it imposes a heavier burden on low-income families than on high-income ones. Because the tax base is consumption, and because the fraction of annual income spent on consumption tends to be higher for low-income than for high-income families, a consumption tax is necessarily regressive. Put differently, any consumption tax effectively exempts from taxation capital and capital income, taxing them only when they are consumed. Such a system will reduce the tax burden on high-income families while increasing the burden on low-income families. A consumption tax will also redistribute tax burdens across generations. Those who are or will soon be retired (whose income is almost entirely consumed) will experience a significant increase in tax liabilities. Note, however, that lifetime income may be more relevant than annual income in calculating the average tax rate by income class. There is some evidence that consumption as a proportion of lifetime income is roughly the same at all income levels, which would make even a retail sales tax or a VAT more or less proportional.

In the context of current debate in Puerto Rico, there is general agreement among local entrepreneurial and professional associations that there should be tax reform in Puerto Rico and that this reform should include a new broad-based consumption tax, should include the repeal of the 5 percent general excise tax, and should reform the income tax and the various excises. However, there is no agreement about the specifications for any broad-based consumption tax or about the details of the income and excise tax reform. One of the issues in the debate is whether the broad-based consumption tax should be a retail sales tax (RST) or a value added tax.

The question fundamentally centers on two issues. One is that the VAT is regarded as more efficient than the RST in its ability to control tax evasion. The other is that administration and compliance costs are generally considered higher for the VAT than for the RST. However, any debate on these two issues misses two other points: which tax is more efficient in avoiding the taxation of inputs and which is more efficient in taxing services.

Taxing services under a consumption tax is always a difficult task. Even so, it is important to tax services, in order to avoid distorting relative prices and consumers' choices and to ensure adequate buoyancy in tax revenues over time. International experience tends to indicate that the VAT is more effective than the RST in taxing services; indeed, the practice with the retail sales tax in the United States is that most services are excluded from the RST base.

A consumption tax should tax consumption and nothing else. A consumption tax that taxes inputs is something other than a true consumption tax. The experience in the United States indicates that the RST has some significant limitations in avoiding the taxation of intermediate inputs.[42]

The Current System Is an Outdated and Ad Hoc System

Puerto Rican tax policy has apparently and increasingly become focused on accommodating the requests of specific individuals and of specific sectors of the economy. A move away from a transparent and rule-based approach to one with many preferential treatments has harmed the fairness of the system, increased its complexity, and increased the burden on taxpayers and tax administrators alike.

It is tempting to assume that favored tax treatments result from pressure from special interest groups. While some of this may occur, the Puerto Rico government is also likely—for good reasons—to reduce the tax on certain items of neces-

42. Ring (1999).

sary consumption in order to help the poor or other target groups or to reduce the tax on certain types of investments to encourage investments the government considers worthwhile. Regardless of the motivation, however, these policies affect the fairness of the tax system, lead others to clamor for favorable treatment, make the system less transparent and more complex, and lead to unintended and unforeseen consequences. They also cause a revenue loss that must be made up by higher taxes on other sectors of the economy, and they may well generate corruption.

More fundamental, however, is that the Puerto Rican tax system has failed to evolve to reflect the changing economic circumstances of governments in small, open economies. Back in the 1940s and the 1950s, when the current system of Puerto Rican taxation largely emerged, the tax systems of most isolated governments were originally designed for a world in which production and consumption were primarily of *tangible goods,* the sale and consumption of these goods generally occurred in the *same location,* and the factors of production used to make the goods were for the most part *immobile.* In such a world, taxation was a fairly straightforward exercise. Sales and excise taxes could be imposed on the tangible goods that were consumed, by the government in the jurisdiction in which consumption (or production) occurred. Similarly, income and property taxes could be imposed on factors (residents and businesses) where they lived and worked without fear that taxes would drive those factors elsewhere. In making tax decisions, a government in one jurisdiction had no need to consider how its actions would affect the governments in other jurisdictions, because tax bases were largely immobile.

There is little doubt that, in principle, the current economic environment changes things, and changes them dramatically. First, tax bases are significantly more mobile. With integrated national and world markets, factors of production are obviously able to move more easily from one jurisdiction to another. For example, businesses have more flexibility in choosing where to locate because communication and transportation costs have been slashed. Some forms of production activity require little in the way of traditional capital and labor, so that physical location becomes less important. Labor, especially skilled labor, becomes more mobile in this environment, and financial capital is able to flow quickly across local, state, and national boundaries.

Clearly, if factors of production can move easily from one location to another, then the ability of a government to tax these factors is greatly diminished. A government that raises its tax rates above those of other jurisdictions risks losing its tax base to these areas. Particularly in the case of income from capital, there is much speculation that taxation will become increasingly problematic.[43] In fact, some empirical evidence suggests that factors of production are responding to these types of tax considerations.[44]

43. Mintz (1992).
44. Grubert (1998); Hines (1999).

Increased mobility is not limited to factors of production. Consumers are also able to plan their consumption according to tax considerations, and consumption does not necessarily occur in the jurisdiction in which a taxpayer resides. A jurisdiction that attempts to tax, say, gasoline more heavily than in surrounding areas will find that consumers will purchase gas elsewhere. Similarly, individuals can now purchase most types of products over the Internet and thereby avoid paying some (or even all) sales taxes. Additionally, there has been increased consumption of services and intangible goods, both of which are much more difficult to tax than tangible goods. Services contribute a minor role in international trade (about 20 per cent), but they contribute a great deal to domestic GDP and GNP. The once-tight link between the location of sales and the location of consumption is now quite loose.

Second, the measurement, identification, and assignment of tax bases are much more difficult than they once were.[45] Consider a typical multinational business. The product that the firm makes may be designed in one or more jurisdictions; the firm may use inputs purchased in multiple jurisdictions; the product may be produced in several places and assembled in yet a different location; and the final good may be sold in multiple locations. Because the business operates in multiple jurisdictions, the firm has considerable leeway to manipulate prices to minimize its tax liabilities. This latter problem is well known, especially in the context of the section 936 credit, but its severity has increased with the enormous expansion in the number of firms operating in multiple jurisdictions like Puerto Rico.

Similarly, consider an individual whose income comes from multiple sources. A global income tax requires that income from these sources be aggregated. However, it is easy for an individual to hide, say, interest income from multiple areas. In the absence of information sharing across governments, the ability of any government to identify incomes from other jurisdictions is quite limited.

Consider, finally, a consumer who can purchase goods and services in several different ways: from traditional local merchants or from company websites. In the former case, identification, measurement, and assignment of the tax base are straightforward. In the latter case, they are not. Application of sales taxes in this new environment poses considerable problems for governments.

How will governments respond to these various pressures, especially in their tax choices? Most important, globalization implies that the ability of any government to choose its tax policies independently of those in other jurisdictions is greatly curtailed. In the presence of mobile tax bases, a single government's choice of tax policies will have effects beyond its own borders and will be affected by the actions of other jurisdictions. In short, tax competition will

45. McLure (1997).

increase, and this increase will have a number of effects: on the level of taxation, the composition and form of taxes, and the general strategies that a government can pursue in setting its taxes.[46]

Overall, these compositional changes imply that the tax systems of smaller governments, such as state governments and federal governments in small, open economies, will most likely become more regressive than at present. If taxes on capital and skilled labor decline, if excise and sin taxes increase, if income taxes on all forms of labor, especially immobile unskilled labor, increase, and if marginal income tax rates flatten, then governments will find it quite difficult to maintain any progressivity in their tax systems. The ability of governments to redistribute income to lower-income individuals will most likely diminish.

Reforming the Puerto Rican Tax System

The current fiscal system of Puerto Rico has some significant strengths. Nonetheless, improvements can still be made. These reforms should be in the direction of

—changing the tax structure, not increasing tax effort

—changing the composition of taxation toward more reliance on indirect taxation

—simplifying the tax system, especially in the ways in which tax incentives are used

—expanding the bases of the various taxes, especially those of the individual and the corporate income taxes, thereby reducing the burden on wage earners in the formal sector, allowing reductions in the marginal tax rates, and reducing the distortions now present in the tax system

—improving tax administration, thereby reducing tax evasion

On the expenditure side, reforms should attempt to improve the provision of governmental services. Given the large and increasing budget deficits of recent years, reforms must also address overall fiscal balance.

In this regard, the Tax Reform Committee established by Governor Acevedo Vila recommended in May 2005 a comprehensive tax reform, the centerpieces of which were a 10 percent flat rate tax for all income taxes (both individual and corporate) and a 10 percent general consumption tax designed to replace the current general excise tax. Under the flat rate individual income tax, single adults with annual income of less than $15,000 and married couples with annual income of $30,000 or less would be exempt; there would also be tax credits of $500 per individual for families with income of less than $100,000 a year, and each retiree would receive an income tax credit of $1,000. Under the

46. Alm, Holman, and Neumann (2003).

corporate income tax, there would be limited use of tax credits and incentive schemes, although the details have not been fully spelled out. The details of the 10 percent general consumption tax, including the list of exemptions, also remain to be specified. The intention is that this tax would be a hybrid of a sales tax and a value added tax, with the tax imposed on products as they enter Puerto Rico from overseas (for example, a VAT) or at the point of domestic sale (for example, an RST). There would also be reimbursements to low-income individuals and families, intended to reduce their burdens from the consumption tax.

Overall, the commission expects that the burden on individuals will decline, while corporations will most likely pay more. To the extent that revenues from the flat rate individual and corporate income tax decline, the increased rate of taxation under the flat rate consumption tax is expected to offset the income tax revenue loss.

If this reform package is fully implemented, I believe that the reforms are more or less in line with broadly accepted tenets of suggested directions for reform; that is, the proposed Puerto Rico reforms are likely to

—change mainly the tax structure, not the overall level of taxation

—change the composition of taxation toward more reliance on indirect taxation

—simplify the tax system, mainly by reducing the number of tax brackets and also by eliminating some of the deductions, credits, and, especially, tax incentives

—expand the bases of the individual and corporate income taxes and reduce marginal tax rates, thereby reducing the burden on wage earners and improving incentives

Of course, many details have yet to be specified, and the reform seems some distance from enactment. There is also little information on ways in which tax administration is to be improved, including specific actions to limit tax evasion.

Most reforms typically achieve some goals but fail on others, and the proposed Puerto Rico tax reform is likely to be no exception. For example, an increase in indirect taxation will quite likely impose greater burdens on low-income individuals and families, who consume a higher proportion of their incomes than those with higher income. It is not known whether the reimbursements under the general consumption tax would fully compensate these individuals and families for the higher burden of the general consumption tax; it is also not known whether the exemption levels in the flat rate (individual) income tax, by removing many individuals and families from the income tax net, would offset a potentially higher indirect tax burden. Similarly, the flat rate income tax represents a considerable simplification of the current income tax system, especially if incentive schemes are largely eliminated. However, the hybrid consumption tax may well complicate, not simplify, the tax system because it combines two approaches to consumption taxes and because it moves

Puerto Rico somewhat away from the indirect taxation used by most U.S. states (for example, a retail sales tax). The considerably lower marginal tax rates under the flat rate income tax would almost certainly improve individual and firm incentives to engage in productive activities and would also reduce the many distortions generated by the current tax system. However, the elimination of many investment incentives may well lower economic growth, at least in the affected sectors. The reform plan is largely silent on administrative reforms that would reduce tax evasion.

There are trade-offs in any reform, and the government must recognize these and set priorities. I hope that this chapter helps in this process of identifying the trade-offs and highlighting the ways in which the government can address them.

Table 7A-1. *Distribution of State and Local Government Taxes, United States, by State and by Type, Fiscal Year 2002*

Percent, except as indicated

State	Individual income[a]	Corporate income[a]	Sales and gross receipts[a]	Property[a]	Motor vehicle[a]	Other[a]	Total taxes	
							As share of gross state product	Per capita (dollars)
Alabama	21.88	3.32	49.39	15.16	2.13	5.94	7.74	2,169.87
Alaska	n.a.	13.01	15.00	40.10	2.29	27.82	6.97	3,229.19
Arizona	14.50	2.40	49.10	29.50	1.06	2.61	8.39	2,650.31
Arkansas	24.24	2.74	51.71	15.52	1.66	1.57	8.98	2,387.11
California	27.44	4.43	34.51	25.11	1.45	3.78	8.80	3,440.25
Colorado	25.01	1.48	38.14	29.94	1.32	3.20	7.75	3,088.21
Connecticut	24.37	0.99	29.86	39.64	1.59	2.47	9.13	4,372.63
Delaware	28.41	9.36	12.14	14.88	1.19	6.16	5.70	3,333.87
Florida	n.a.	2.72	51.15	35.13	2.13	7.49	8.61	2,686.34
Georgia	26.97	2.36	39.05	27.60	1.12	1.97	7.87	2,815.82
Hawaii	26.22	1.24	52.94	14.50	3.15	1.19	9.64	3,416.24
Idaho	25.60	2.33	34.50	29.13	3.51	1.55	8.54	2,450.55
Illinois	17.97	3.33	33.38	38.18	3.51	2.25	8.55	3,302.84
Indiana	24.26	4.18	32.51	35.18	1.77	1.63	8.29	2,758.91
Iowa	21.78	1.06	34.65	34.55	4.54	1.55	8.48	2,837.33
Kansas	23.26	1.53	38.45	31.66	1.82	2.18	8.91	2,940.63
Kentucky	32.43	2.80	36.57	18.34	1.98	4.64	8.82	2,635.88
Louisiana	14.68	2.17	57.04	15.93	0.97	5.92	9.26	2,721.64
Maine	23.63	1.70	27.35	42.11	2.31	1.37	11.63	3,506.68
Maryland	38.46	1.81	25.03	27.23	1.00	5.28	9.84	3,645.99
Massachusetts	33.11	3.40	22.44	36.50	1.13	2.45	8.29	3,733.08
Michigan	21.53	6.74	33.41	31.96	2.91	2.13	8.72	3,051.30
Minnesota	29.49	2.89	32.06	28.25	2.69	2.60	9.23	3,672.92

Mississippi	15.10	3.00	49.90	25.24	1.71	2.14	9.44	2,275.45
Missouri	25.98	1.99	39.96	25.66	1.64	2.91	8.06	2,667.27
Montana	24.24	3.19	17.52	39.92	5.96	5.78	8.98	2,346.35
Nebraska	21.70	2.02	34.22	32.90	1.96	5.13	8.72	3,076.59
Nevada	n.a.	n.a.	59.70	26.46	2.02	7.02	7.92	2,968.42
New Hampshire	1.98	10.48	16.82	60.28	2.13	5.30	7.75	2,824.85
New Jersey	19.83	3.18	25.42	46.35	1.07	2.45	9.11	4,038.34
New Mexico	20.15	2.55	47.55	15.50	2.45	10.69	9.11	2,633.70
New York	33.99	5.71	25.30	30.18	0.91	3.48	11.22	4,645.04
North Carolina	32.18	2.96	34.78	24.02	1.94	2.03	7.52	2,718.09
North Dakota	11.55	2.89	39.83	30.79	3.02	8.99	8.74	2,726.74
Ohio	32.61	2.10	29.77	29.43	1.99	1.49	9.32	3,169.88
Oklahoma	26.03	1.98	39.24	16.88	6.49	6.48	9.23	2,516.30
Oregon	40.82	2.18	9.87	34.86	3.06	6.65	7.82	2,557.74
Pennsylvania	25.27	3.19	30.01	29.00	2.05	7.01	8.77	3,051.88
Rhode Island	22.74	0.78	32.15	40.36	1.47	1.42	9.79	3,391.61
South Carolina	24.09	1.64	35.12	31.75	1.13	4.02	7.97	2,376.15
South Dakota	n.a.	2.20	50.50	36.28	3.60	2.43	7.36	2,422.96
Tennessee	1.13	3.88	57.50	26.62	2.64	3.62	6.82	2,240.72
Texas	0.00	n.a.	48.56	41.57	2.19	2.94	7.63	2,713.37
Utah	26.64	1.84	43.45	23.56	1.42	2.06	8.26	2,598.60
Vermont	20.75	1.90	29.15	41.91	2.09	2.52	10.02	3,190.15
Virginia	30.32	1.39	29.56	30.32	2.02	5.34	7.70	3,036.67
Washington	n.a.	n.a.	61.37	29.67	1.73	5.57	8.38	3,216.33
West Virginia	22.29	4.74	42.66	19.41	1.89	7.12	10.20	2,571.38
Wisconsin	26.73	2.39	30.62	34.75	1.69	1.61	9.76	3,420.94
Wyoming	n.a.	n.a.	38.03	38.07	3.45	18.06	8.96	3,644.02
Total	22.41	3.11	35.81	30.85	1.87	5.95	8.63	3,140.48

Source: Data from U.S. Census Bureau, State and Local Government Finances (http://www.census.gov/govs/www/estimate.html).
a. As share of total taxes.

Table 7A-2. Distribution of State and Local Government Expenditures, United States, by State and by Type, Fiscal Year 2002

Percent, except as indicated

State	Public education[a]	Highways[a]	Welfare[a]	Health and hospitals[a]	Police and fire protection[a]	Administration[a]	Insurance trust[a]	Utility and liquor store[a]	Other[a]	Total expenditures	
										As share of gross state product	Per capita (dollars)
Alabama	29.16	5.85	14.59	14.31	3.47	3.35	6.19	7.57	17.92	22.72	6,370.13
Alaska	22.42	9.74	11.01	2.80	3.72	5.56	7.07	3.08	35.20	31.63	14,660.58
Arizona	28.10	6.11	10.50	3.86	5.57	5.25	6.18	13.17	19.99	18.23	5,754.12
Arkansas	32.83	8.97	17.79	6.28	3.78	4.61	6.23	4.08	17.70	20.26	5,384.42
California	26.27	3.92	12.16	7.17	4.90	5.35	8.93	9.56	17.49	21.38	8,354.16
Colorado	28.26	8.89	8.85	6.40	4.69	4.58	7.55	7.46	24.86	17.78	7,085.25
Connecticut	28.46	4.44	12.58	6.90	4.25	4.92	9.29	3.00	25.17	16.65	7,976.77
Delaware	32.56	7.81	11.09	5.49	3.61	6.87	6.18	3.73	22.10	12.61	7,378.84
Florida	25.98	6.77	12.59	7.54	6.29	4.92	5.07	7.24	23.73	19.08	5,949.38
Georgia	33.20	5.62	11.77	9.24	4.19	4.59	5.96	8.11	18.76	17.10	6,122.44
Hawaii	24.01	4.45	12.14	6.93	3.81	5.62	8.10	3.58	31.09	21.37	7,576.18
Idaho	32.03	8.17	13.68	8.00	4.27	5.54	7.40	2.66	18.84	19.62	5,632.67
Illinois	29.69	6.49	11.28	5.95	5.25	4.75	10.00	5.54	22.58	17.98	6,944.36
Indiana	33.59	5.59	14.63	7.92	3.85	5.25	4.75	4.91	19.42	17.71	5,896.12
Iowa	33.52	9.13	13.90	9.77	3.21	4.34	6.32	4.38	18.25	19.64	6,571.45
Kansas	32.90	9.14	11.98	7.36	3.99	5.64	6.03	4.99	20.12	18.68	6,164.49
Kentucky	27.69	7.86	19.39	5.82	3.26	4.07	8.29	4.79	20.52	20.31	6,073.12
Louisiana	28.90	5.53	12.15	13.09	4.51	5.06	8.32	3.78	17.71	21.02	6,180.45
Maine	28.71	7.12	20.65	5.76	3.06	4.88	6.21	1.78	21.19	22.23	6,700.47
Maryland	34.13	5.21	13.31	4.19	5.22	4.62	7.52	3.10	21.03	17.62	6,526.66
Massachusetts	26.28	6.37	11.21	6.21	4.48	4.01	10.02	6.83	26.08	17.75	7,990.32
Michigan	34.15	4.63	14.15	7.69	3.82	4.11	8.59	3.99	16.42	19.79	6,923.58

Minnesota	27.81	6.62	18.45	4.85	3.17	4.30	8.82	4.96	21.57	20.25	8,062.82
Mississippi	29.51	7.15	18.72	12.38	3.67	3.67	6.60	4.40	14.56	25.00	6,028.88
Missouri	31.95	7.48	16.71	7.37	4.52	3.94	7.48	4.59	16.02	17.62	5,826.52
Montana	31.91	9.66	11.95	6.73	3.78	5.96	7.88	2.17	22.85	23.62	6,171.75
Nebraska	30.40	7.40	13.63	4.86	3.15	3.48	3.41	18.46	16.88	20.49	7,229.24
Nevada	26.33	9.10	8.02	6.60	6.69	6.51	6.71	9.02	21.47	17.21	6,447.00
New Hampshire	34.52	7.14	14.58	2.60	4.68	5.10	5.21	5.02	20.82	15.21	5,546.24
New Jersey	31.95	4.61	10.28	4.26	4.85	4.36	10.58	4.70	23.79	16.91	7,497.31
New Mexico	32.91	9.01	16.37	6.53	4.38	4.93	6.86	3.01	15.97	23.71	6,851.27
New York	24.04	3.56	16.37	6.55	4.62	3.76	9.83	8.70	20.73	25.07	10,376.08
North Carolina	29.44	5.82	14.77	11.74	4.01	3.36	6.95	7.12	17.31	17.27	6,241.10
North Dakota	31.29	10.99	15.84	2.47	2.47	4.29	5.13	2.13	29.10	21.19	6,609.61
Ohio	29.54	5.12	15.35	6.82	4.52	5.82	12.52	3.64	17.05	20.60	7,009.52
Oklahoma	33.23	7.43	15.36	6.28	4.16	4.16	7.18	5.24	18.16	21.84	5,953.01
Oregon	27.20	4.32	14.59	7.91	4.14	5.73	11.09	6.01	16.64	24.09	7,878.18
Pennsylvania	28.16	6.13	16.79	5.97	3.40	3.97	9.34	5.26	20.05	20.11	6,996.67
Rhode Island	27.50	4.18	21.02	3.77	5.40	4.69	11.62	2.75	17.45	21.43	7,423.24
South Carolina	29.82	5.30	15.56	11.18	3.39	4.59	7.15	8.10	15.64	22.97	6,848.38
South Dakota	31.81	13.57	14.15	3.99	3.32	4.66	5.30	3.85	24.62	17.10	5,626.03
Tennessee	25.84	4.84	17.63	9.01	3.82	3.40	5.12	15.85	14.71	19.27	6,327.82
Texas	35.19	5.80	11.48	7.78	4.02	3.47	7.06	7.01	17.75	16.79	5,974.78
Utah	33.47	6.55	10.28	5.53	3.79	5.89	5.58	11.57	18.40	21.27	6,693.95
Vermont	34.62	8.59	17.94	2.07	3.02	6.04	4.25	5.31	18.30	21.52	6,847.58
Virginia	34.68	7.10	10.70	7.29	4.42	5.15	5.91	4.21	18.38	15.19	5,994.44
Washington	25.51	4.71	12.29	7.96	3.48	3.45	9.91	13.43	18.34	21.65	8,312.39
West Virginia	29.50	8.72	17.93	4.33	2.12	5.33	15.26	2.19	16.78	26.21	6,609.35
Wisconsin	32.00	7.61	14.16	5.30	4.49	3.95	10.24	3.16	20.24	20.59	7,217.24
Wyoming	29.45	11.00	8.79	11.90	3.78	5.61	6.90	4.25	21.87	21.38	8,692.20
Total	29.04	5.64	13.65	7.15	4.42	4.53	8.29	6.98	19.65	19.68	7,110.69

Source: Data from U.S. Census Bureau, State and Local Government Finances (http://www.census.gov/govs/www/estimate.html).

a. As share of total taxes.

Ronald Fisher

James Alm has provided a helpful summary that encompasses both explanation and clarification of what turns out to be a difficult issue—examining and assessing fiscal policy in Puerto Rico. The work and issues considered in his chapter are unexpectedly complicated for at least three reasons: First, data and factual information about some aspects of the fiscal sector in Puerto Rico are not as easily available as for some other jurisdictions, for example, the U.S. states. Second, it is difficult to put the information that is available in context because what constitutes the appropriate comparison governments is not always clear or the same for different questions. Third, assessing policy is sometimes difficult because the underlying objectives of government policymakers are not explicitly known.

Tax Structure

That the overall tax structure in Puerto Rico is exceptionally nonneutral—riddled with special exclusions, exemptions, credits, rate reductions, and other targeted incentives—is the overriding and dominant finding in this chapter. The author convincingly documents the difficulties with efficiency, equity, and administration created by such a tax structure. But he is unable to determine just why such a structure came about. Sometimes he seems to suggest that the development of Puerto Rico's tax structure was the result of a conscious, well-intentioned but unsuccessful attempt to stimulate economic development. At other times, Alm seems to imply that the structure reflects pork-barrel politics run amok, with a variety of groups seeking and achieving special treatment. Of course, the Puerto Rican tax structure may reflect some of both.

Alm recommends tax reform that broadens the base of the personal and corporate income taxes (presumably permitting lower marginal tax rates), increases reliance on consumption taxes (what he calls "indirect taxation"), and improves tax administration, both directly and as a result of the first two reforms. Indeed, he comes close to endorsing a proposal by the governor's Tax Reform Committee for a combination of a flat-rate comprehensive income tax and consumption taxation composed of both value added and retail sales taxes.

Rather than simply following general prescriptions and practices, however, policymakers in Puerto Rico may want to think about how the economic and social structures of the island and its people influence design of the best tax structure for the situation. Tax structures differ dramatically among U.S. states, even among states that are geographic neighbors, as is demonstrated by the data in Alm's table 7A-1. There is some strong evidence that in developing their tax structures states have sought to take advantage of special economic circumstances. Florida (the state that is geographically closest to Puerto Rico and shares some other characteristics, as well) has a tax structure essentially opposite Puerto Rico's—with no personal income tax and heavy reliance on general and selective sales taxes. Mississippi (the state closest to Puerto Rico in per capita income) also has a revenue structure quite different from Puerto Rico's—one that relies heavily on revenues from user fees, property tax, and general sales tax, with relatively low reliance on income taxes. Perhaps unexpectedly, the U.S. state whose overall revenue structure is most similar to that of Puerto Rico is Oregon, which has the highest reliance on income taxation of any U.S. state.

What economic and social characteristics of Puerto Rico might be important in designing an optimal revenue structure for its particular situation (as opposed to trying to replicate a theoretically "best" or a "typical" revenue system)? The research for this book seems to support a view that there has been less real growth in manufacturing and more in services and technology in Puerto Rico than is sometimes perceived. If this view is true, then a revenue and tax structure focused on providing incentives for manufacturing may be less important than one that reflects the growing importance of services in the economy (in both production and consumption). The documented low rates of labor force participation and saving among the island's population suggest not only a possible role for broad tax bases and low marginal tax rates but also the possible benefit of using the tax structure to create work incentives, perhaps through an earned income tax credit (now used by seventeen states and the District of Columbia). The island seems to have a substantial number of part-time residents—both Puerto Ricans who spend a substantial amount of time in the United States and residents of other places who have second homes in Puerto Rico. This may suggest an important role for consumption taxes and user fees (similar to the practice in Florida), as well as reform of the property tax system.[1]

The specifics of these perspectives are less important than the general message. Certainly, the general prescription of broad tax bases and low tax rates is a valuable and powerful one. But it does not necessarily follow that any jurisdiction, including Puerto Rico, will benefit from trying to mimic the "average" or "typical" comparable government. The economic structure of the society may well determine the best revenue structure, rather than the revenue structure determining the direction of economic activity and growth.

---

1. User fees seem to be relied upon relatively less in Puerto Rico than in many U.S. states. For instance, see the discussion about the funding of higher education in chapter 5 of this volume.

Fiscal Imbalance

Regarding the aggregate public sector, the author makes four key observations: First, central and municipal government spending has remained relatively constant at 22–23 percent of GNP for the past twenty years, although below its peak in the middle 1970s (see figure 7-3). Second, recent years have seen a pattern of substantial operating-budget deficits for both the central and municipal governments that have been covered, at least to some degree, by additional borrowing. Third, public sector employment has continued to rise in absolute numbers (see figure 7-5) and has remained essentially constant relative to total employment in the past decade (see figure 7-6), while government consumption expenditure as a fraction of GNP has declined over the same period. Fourth, the relative importance of state enterprises has declined since the late 1980s, partly owing to privatization of some entities (telephone service in 1999, for instance).

The falling government consumption share coupled with the continued importance of public employment reflects an apparent fundamental problem with public sector service provision: government services are not growing or improving, but spending and government employment are. An example is provided in chapter 5 of this volume, which shows a relatively low student-teacher ratio but seemingly not a corresponding level of improvement in student achievement. This general perspective is reinforced by the fact that the government employment share has remained constant even with privatization of some state enterprises. Unfortunately, Alm is not able to provide additional specific examples or offer any convincing explanations for why this seems to be occurring.

The more relevant issue is whether this decline in public sector productivity is related to the structural deficits that seem to have been prevalent for both the central and municipal governments in recent years. Of course, a number of state governments in the United States have faced problems of continuing operating deficits in recent years, so that situation is certainly not unique to Puerto Rico. The magnitude of the problem in Puerto Rico seems particularly substantial, however, as public sector debt has risen substantially relative to GNP to levels that greatly exceed the typical situation for U.S. states. The main policy recommendation Alm offers is reform of the Puerto Rican tax system, without increasing what he calls "tax effort." It seems likely, however, that the continuing government deficits are not so much a problem of tax structure as an issue of the appropriate role for government in Puerto Rico.

The public sector apparently is providing a source of employment for a substantial number of Puerto Ricans, but the society is not willing to generate sufficient current revenue to fund that level of public sector service. There is an important question of causation here that deserves further attention. One possibility, which the author seems to favor, is that the nonneutral tax structure, which was most likely selected for specific reasons such as stimulation of economic development, caused the structural deficits. The alternative view is that the lack of public support for public sector spending has contributed to the development of a tax structure with substantial base erosion (and possibly evasion as well). This is important because of the difference in prescriptions. If the first is true, then reform of the tax system may well improve confidence in the public sector and help to reduce deficits. If the latter is true, however, attempts to reform the tax structure seem doomed to failure unless there is simultaneous improvement in public sector productivity or control of government spending.

Putting Puerto Rico in Context

Alm presents a substantial amount of data comparing fiscal practices and structure in Puerto Rico with that in U.S. states and in other nations, including other small nations in the Caribbean region. These comparisons lead the author to a number of conclusions, including the following:

—Tax levels relative to GDP in Puerto Rico are about average compared with all nations, a bit lower than in other small nations in the Caribbean area, and higher than the U.S. states (including state and local taxes).

—Puerto Rico relies more on income taxes and less on sales taxes than other nations or U.S. states and localities.

—The distribution of spending by the Puerto Rican central government is similar to that of the aggregate state and local government sector in the United States. The unusual political and fiscal structure of Puerto Rico limits the value of such comparisons, however. The issue about income tax reliance is instructive. The data in tables 7-5, 7-6, 7A-1, and 7A-2 regarding U.S. states reflect the aggregate situation for state and local governments in each state. But the data for Puerto Rico (in tables 7-3 and 7-7) reflect the situation for only the central government and do not include municipalities. Tables 7-3 and 7-7 show zero reliance on property taxes for 2000 and 2002, for instance, because that revenue source funds municipalities rather than the central government. As a consequence, relative reliance on income tax in Puerto Rico appears higher than it is. In fact, reliance on personal income taxes by the Puerto Rican central government (39 percent in 2002, table 7-3) is only slightly higher than for U.S. state governments (35 percent in 2002). This comparison excludes local governments in both instances (both of which have heavy reliance on property taxes).

The position of Puerto Rico within the U.S. federal governmental structure should also be considered. Given that Puerto Rican residents are not liable for U.S. federal income taxes, one might expect that the Puerto Rican central government would elect to use personal income taxes to a greater degree than do most U.S. states. Personal income taxes (not including Social Security payroll taxes) account for about 43 percent of total government revenue in the United States (including the federal government). By that comparison, the 39 percent reliance in Puerto Rico does not seem unusual. Indeed, the data in table 7-7 show that Puerto Rico's reliance on personal income, payroll, and corporate income taxes combined is roughly the same as that of the United States, although greater than in many other nations. The explanation for the high rate relative to other nations rests principally, one would think, on the use of payroll taxes in the United States to fund basic retirement security (Social Security) and on Puerto Rico's relatively high reliance on corporate income taxes compared with both other nations and the U.S. states.

The commonwealth status of Puerto Rico with respect to the United States would also seem to be important for comparisons of its fiscal policy and practices with those of other nations. The government of Puerto Rico does not face the spectrum of international issues—including security, immigration, trade, and finance—that other independent nations, even small ones, must deal with. And as Alm documents, Puerto Rico receives substantial fiscal support in transfers from the U.S. federal government, which represented more than 20 percent of central government revenue in Puerto Rico in 2002. Most other small nations that may be comparable in other characteristics are different in this important one.

Property Taxation

The author focuses his discussion mostly on the tax structure of the Puerto Rican central government, but the property tax, which provides about one-third of revenue for municipal governments, is one of the most interesting fiscal policy issues for the island. As Alm notes, the property tax in Puerto Rico is characterized by three important features, two of which are uncommon. First, property taxes on real estate are based on historical or, for more recently constructed properties, imputed 1958 values. There is an exemption of $15,000 of assessed value for owner-occupied homes. Second, tax rates vary little among municipalities, with a maximum tax rate of 8 percent (except for a small allowed surcharge to cover debt service for neighborhood public investments). I suggest that these characteristics imply that the "property tax" on real estate in Puerto Rico is not a property tax at all, at least not in the conventional way that economists think of property taxes. The real estate "property tax" in Puerto Rico seems more accurately identified as a lump-sum tax that is constant from year to year. The amount of the tax is independent of any changes in the value of the property, and because rates are additionally fixed, the tax amount essentially remains constant. So a property owner might owe a constant "property tax" of $100 or $500 a year.[2]

Apparently, there has been discussion of converting to a tax based on current market prices, and a process to do that has been adopted but not implemented. The economic effects of such a change may be very different from those envisioned, however. Because the tax is no longer related to property value and the effects of the past or current tax are most likely fully capitalized, any new property tax based on current values should be thought of as adoption of a property tax in an economy where no such tax existed previously. Those effects are expected to include a decline in the rate of return to investment in capital in Puerto Rico and a decline in land values. These effects are predicted to arise even if the "new" property tax (that is, the shift to a market value system) is structured to raise the same amount of revenue as the current tax.

The easiest way to think of this tax change is to imagine it happening in two steps. First, the current "property tax" is repealed. Essentially, this provides a lump sum or windfall gain to current property owners that is not necessarily related to the current status of the property. This gain effectively increases the income of current owners but is not expected to have a substantial effect on property values. In economic terms, the repeal of the current tax has an income effect but no price or substitution effect.[3] Second, a true property tax based on current market values is adopted. Whatever tax rates are used, the new tax is a true ad valorem tax—that is, related to value. Owners and consumers of capital now face a price incentive related to capital that is expected to affect (reduce) prices or values. So transition to a true property tax based on market values is expected to do much more than simply reallocate tax burdens among different properties.

One option related to property taxation that might be considered (although not discussed in the Alm chapter) is a land value tax. There are at least three ways that Puerto Rico might proceed in that direction. One possibility is to maintain the current property tax structure (which provides little revenue growth) and augment it with a new property tax on land values only. In essence,

2. Data about changes in property values in Puerto Rico over time are not readily available. For the United States, average consumer prices have increased by about a factor of seven since 1958. If property values in Puerto Rico changed similarly, an owner-occupied home with a $100,000 market value today would be expected to have an assessed (1958) value of slightly more than $14,000. Because of the exemption, no tax would be owed. A $150,000 property would be expected to have an assessed value of about $21,500, implying a constant tax of $520 for an owner-occupied home or $1,720 otherwise.

3. The only possible substitution effect is on the decision whether to own property in Puerto Rico at all, rather than on the amount of property. Essentially, the tax is owed if one owns property, regardless of its current value. The magnitude of the tax seems too small to affect locational decisions between Puerto Rico and elsewhere to any substantial degree.

this would create a two-tier system, with land and structures taxed differently. A second option is to replace the current property tax completely with a tax on land value only (so that structures are taxed at zero rate effectively). A third possibility is to formally adopt a two-tiered tax that taxes land value at one rate and structures and equipment at a different rate. There has been substantial research about the potential advantages of land value taxes and some work about the practical implementation issues. If Puerto Rico is interested in considering a move in this direction, the work of Claudia M. De Cesare and colleagues may be helpful.[4]

Policy Choices

This chapter shows convincingly how important the public sector and public sector fiscal policies are in Puerto Rico. Alm highlights the variety of fiscal policy choices that the island faces and the implications of many of those choices. What seems most clear is that some change in direction is necessary. As a public policy economist, I hope that the extensive information and analysis presented in this book will be a valuable guide to beginning that change process.

COMMENT
William Lockwood Benet

In my comment on James Alm's chapter, I would like to provide a review of Puerto Rico's recent fiscal management practices. Such a review is essential to understanding the implications of the chapter and conveying the magnitude of the fiscal challenges the government faces. It is also a necessary prologue to the pursuit of credible negotiations with investors, the Puerto Rican legislature, and interest groups regarding reform of the fiscal system to advance the key financing strategies of the island's next development phase.

Reestablishing Puerto Rico's fiscal stability is crucial to maintaining investor trust. Puerto Rico has the lowest credit rating and the highest level of net tax-supported debt per capita in the United States. Its debt was downgraded by both Moody's and Standard and Poor's in May 2005.[5] If the commonwealth

---

4. Claudia M. De Cesare and others, "Analyzing the Feasibility of Moving to a Land Value–Based Property Tax System: A Case Study from Brazil," Lincoln Institute of Land Policy, 2003 (www.lincolninst.edu/pubs/pub-detail.asp?id=1050 [February 2006]).

5. Moody's downgraded the general obligation rating to Baa2, and Standard and Poor's lowered its rating to BBB; see Moody's Investors Service (2005a, 2005c); Standard and Poor's (2005).

receives one further downgrade, $4.3 billion in appropriation debt will be below investment grade, and all $36.5 billion in total debt will be negatively affected, further postponing access to capital markets.

Puerto Rico's current fiscal plight is the result of continued use of non-recurrent revenues and debt to finance increased investment and recurrent spending within a weakly administered fiscal system, as Alm documents. In addition to such overheating of the economy, pre-2001 policies allowing for collective bargaining agreements for central government employees, as well as the additional cost to the central government of financing managed health care and repaying Puerto Rico Aqueduct and Sewer Authority debt, increased the rigidity and political costs of expenditure reduction. The fiscal system is characterized by a lack of analysis on the quality of program expenditures, heavy reliance on special tax provisions to attract external investment and steer local capital to preferred areas, and significant amounts of tax evasion. In their present form, the main tax components are very regressive. The failure to address these issues adversely affected the budget proposed by the executive branch for fiscal year 2006. That budget sought to postpone significant reduction in expenditures, presented unrealistic proposals that increased expenditures through early retirement provisions and the consolidation of some agencies, and increased taxes.

In prior years, the central government's fiscal executives increased spending in response to both the 2001 recession and the steady loss of manufacturing jobs arising from the phase-out of section 936 of the U.S. Internal Revenue Code. (From 1996 to 2003, 41,300 jobs were lost, representing 26 percent of total manufacturing employment.) They added to the economy's cyclical and structural risk by financing the outlays with nonrecurrent revenue and debt. None of these measures addressed the profound shift in Puerto Rico's external competitiveness that resulted from the elimination of section 936 provisions and a slowing of growth in the biopharmaceutical industry.[6] The fragmentation between fiscal management and monitoring of economic development strategies grew further during this period.

Four mechanisms have been used to cover the imbalances. First, starting in 2003, the $800 million level of intrayear borrowing from the Government Development Bank (GDB) was increased through approvals under Law 183 of 1974. The higher borrowing ceiling facilitated spending increases, allowed for lax collection of federal grants, and postponed the need for accountability by department heads. Second, year-end loans from the GDB in excess of $1 billion

6. With more than 50 percent of its corporate taxes coming from biotechnology and pharmaceutical companies, Puerto Rico has had a decade to readjust its fiscal system and infrastructure to the ten-year phase-out of the section 936 provision. The change presents a major competitive challenge to Puerto Rico. The biopharmaceutical group accounts for thirty thousand direct jobs, making the cluster one-third larger than that of Ireland or New Jersey.

were used to balance the 2003, 2004, and 2005 budgets and repay intrayear borrowings. These loans reflected the weakness of the cash management, budgeting, tax administration, and information systems controls. The loan advances against delayed or uncollected federal grants and the weak institutional opposition to and oversight of costly new tax incentive programs adopted in 2001 are two examples.

Third, debt service, operational programs, capital expenditures, and a cash injection to the Puerto Rico Aqueduct and Sewer Authority were financed with $1.2 billion in new debt, to be repaid out of future tobacco settlement proceeds, as well as more than $700 million in additional transfers from a variety of sources, including the liquidation of the Housing Bank and use of reserves from the lotteries and the Municipal Revenues Collection Center. Fourth, in addition to $2.1 billion borrowed since 2001 through the issuance of general obligation bonds, capital expenditures have been accelerated by borrowing from the GDB, repayable from future government obligation bond issues. Such advances and the 2003, 2004, and 2005 year-end loans represent an amount equal to more than 25 percent of GDB assets. Financing an ongoing central government deficit with debt is highly risky and unsustainable. I believe that the implications of the internal fiscal policy response since 2001, given the changing external economic environment and the magnitude and political costs of the required fiscal restructuring, have not yet been fully understood by policymakers, labor leaders, and private leaders.

The fiscal policies have also placed at risk the interim financing role, earnings stream, and liquidity of the GDB. Consequently, despite controls adopted in 2001, there are questions about the pace of repayment of the more than $3 billion lent to the central government to fund operational deficits since 2003 and capital advances repayable from future government obligation bond issuance.[7] In addition, the GDB made a special $500 million dividend distribution to the Special Communities Perpetual Trust, and the central government receives annual transfers from the GDB annual net operating income. Therefore, the degree of future fiscal flexibility to provide stimulus and reform along with much needed conditionality has been further impaired by the central government's fundamental shift on the independence of the GDB.

A simple summary of the growth in central government finances conveys the consequences of these policies. Central commonwealth government outlays increased by 20 percent from fiscal year 2001 to fiscal year 2004, from

---

7. Fiscal controls imposed under Law 164 of 2001 restricted GDB loans repayable from future appropriations and authorized the issuance of an additional $2.6 billion in appropriation debt, starting in 2001, to finance the current and previous years' operating deficits financed by the GDB, reimbursing $1.7 billion to the bank and requiring an annual debt service of $317 million by the central government.

$12 billion to $14.4 billion, while revenues increased only by 8 percent, from $11.2 billion to $12.1 billion.[8] No effective spending controls were adopted at agencies incurring budget overruns (Department of Education, the Police and the Corrections Department), while accounts payable continued to accumulate throughout the central government without monitoring. From 2001 to 2005, the number of central government employees increased by 29,600, or 14 percent, for a total of 235,400, in contrast to a reduction of 17.3 percent over the preceding eight years. Previously frozen positions created by the 2000 early retirement program were filled. Before the 2004 elections, 16,000 temporary employees were granted permanent posts, and salary increases were approved.

The accumulated deficit for the central government increased from $8.5 billion in fiscal year 2001 to $13.7 billion in fiscal year 2004, an increase of $5.1 billion (60 percent) over the period. During fiscal year 2004 the deficit increased by $1.0 billion to reach $2.8 billion, compared with the $1.8 billion to $1.9 billion deficit registered in the previous two years.[9]

Pre-2001 Structural Imbalances

The origins of structural budget imbalances and the lack of spending flexibility can be traced to several program initiatives adopted during the Rossello administration (1993–96 and 1996–2000) and the adoption of the New Economic Model in February 1994, which envisioned a reduction in the role of the public sector. However, central government revenues benefited from the economic cycle, growing from $4 billion in fiscal year 1993 to $6.8 billion in fiscal year 2000, and thus supported the expenditure initiatives. The key fiscal challenge was to accommodate the annual payment of more than $1 billion in insurance premiums for managed health care. The Rossello administration also added rigidity to government labor costs by granting union representation to central government employees (Law 45 of 1998), entering into agreements with compensation increases, and adopting specific procedures for hiring and firing.

---

8. After 2001, payments to component units were reported as expenditures by function, as called for under Governmental Accounting Standards Board Statement 34. For comparison purposes, the expenditure figures reported here are adjusted to include interfund transfers for both 2001 and 2004. The expenditure figures exclude repayment of debt principal. See Commonwealth of Puerto Rico, "Comprehensive Annual Financial Report, Fiscal Year Ending April 8, 2005" (www.hacienda.gobierno.pr). The reports are audited by KPMG, L.L.P.

9. Although the accumulated deficit is principally the result of the commonwealth's practice of issuing debt and transferring such funds to its discretely presented component units in order to carry out the corresponding construction programs, the increase in fiscal year 2004 is a result of increases in operational spending. See Commonwealth of Puerto Rico, "Comprehensive Annual Financial Report, Fiscal Year Ending June 30, 2004" (www.hacienda.gobierno.pr), p. 14.

Since 1994, the General Fund's payment on the debt of the Aqueduct and Sewer Authority has grown to represent as much as $200 million in fiscal year 2005 outlays. This new central government commitment was part of an unsuccessful attempt to privatize management of the agency. As a complementary plan to finance the Aqueduct and Sewer Authority's future capital investment, all the interest received by the Puerto Rico Infrastructure Financing Authority from the sale of the controlling equity stake in Puerto Rico Telephone Company to GTE International Telecommunications in 2000 was pledged to repay a bond issue of $1.04 billion.

Other key elements of fiscal and economic policy during the Rossello administration included the 1994 and 1999 tax reforms and the adoption of agricultural and tourism investment tax credits. The period was also marked by construction of the *tren urbano* light-rail mass transit system, the coliseum, and the Convention Center—all financed, at a cost of $2 billion, outside central government debt capacity but partially reliant on its revenue stream base, and their required operating subsidies thereby placed an additional burden on the General Fund.[10]

Pensions

The Rossello administration failed to address a problem of a growing unfunded liability within the public pension plans. According to the most recent actuarial valuation of the Employees Retirement System and the Judiciary Retirement System, as of June 30, 2003, the total pension benefit obligations were $11.2 billion and $167 million, respectively; the unfunded obligations were $9.2 billion and $105 million, respectively, representing funding ratios of 17.4 percent and 37.1 percent. The high level of the unfunded liability is the result of legislatively approved increases in benefits without corresponding increases in contributions, unpaid central government contributions to fund early retirement programs, postponements in central government contributions after the 1976 recession, and imprudent investment decisions. Limited research has been conducted on these matters.

A defined contribution plan was established in 2000 that covers all new government employees, in order to limit further growth of the Employees Retirement System's defined benefit plan. Improved returns and some temporary measures kept the pension crisis at bay until the post-2001 equity market decline.

The proposed issuance of $2 billion in taxable pension obligation bonds to secure a positive interest spread, now at risk given fiscal and credit constraints,

10. The Port of the Americas project, with an approved commonwealth guarantee of up to $250 million, will be an additional burden on the General Fund.

was the main transaction devised by Citigroup advisers to the Calderón administration during 2004. The bonds would allow the Employees Retirement System to cover its pension obligations without disposing of investment assets and to revise its portfolio allocation policies. A second phase entails the future sale of the remaining 28 percent equity holding of the local exchange carrier, the Puerto Rico Telephone Company, now a Verizon majority–owned and Verizon-operated firm. The pension fund continues to represent a major financial problem that needs to be addressed.

The Changing External Situation

The government's fiscal system and the development programs it funds must continually interact with and adjust to changes in the economy, particularly those on the external side. Recent examples are provided by the changing structure of the global pharmaceutical industry and the profound shift in U.S. tax policy as it affects Puerto Rico.[11] These are the key external elements that should be considered in a program of fiscal reform. The changing situation within the biopharmaceutical industry with respect to the development of new products has been evident since 2001, and the phase-out of the section 936 tax provision was approved by the U.S. Congress by 1996.

Puerto Rico needs a comprehensive policy, which includes cooperation and reform across government, to stabilize and anchor a changing pharmaceutical industry. By 2001, investment promotion was acknowledged as a priority concern in response to the phase-out of section 936. The local response included the amendment of the Industrial Incentives Act of 1998 to create a new 0–2 percent corporate tax rate for the "core pioneer industries" category, defined as companies using innovative technology not used in Puerto Rico before January 1, 2000. Significant incremental investments by Amgen, Lilly, Abbott, and Merck came about from this new incentive. However, the Treasury, the Puerto Rico Industrial Development Company, public utilities, and the university system have all exhibited an inability to manage the fiscal consequences of the erosion of tax revenue and a pressing need for improved power and water costs and reliability, among other aspects of their relationship with the drug companies. Investment and tax negotiations need to be redirected in order to better understand corporate investor needs, to improve risk management, and to expand the expertise within the academic community on newly emerging issues in the industry, such as oral drug–manufacturing

11. Starting in 1976, Puerto Rico's development strategy was subsidized by section 936 of the U.S. Internal Revenue Code, possibly one of the largest subsidy programs in the world. The phase-out period for section 936 was approved as part of the Omnibus Act of 1996 and ended December 2005. The American Jobs Creation Act of 2004 allowed for dividends repatriation from Puerto Rico but excluded the island as a location for reinvestment.

automation and productivity, bioprocess manufacturing, and the implications of the manufacture of smaller batches within the upcoming personalized medicine era.[12]

Beyond manufacturing, the university system also must undertake highly targeted investments to understand and support critical scientific and technical tools—including assays, standards, genomic records, computer-modeling techniques, biomarkers, drug delivery innovation, and clinical trial endpoints—to make the development, scale-up process, and intellectual property roles of Puerto Rican manufacturing operations more efficient and effective. This is particularly critical given the patent expiration schedule of the Puerto Rico drug portfolio, pharmaceutical companies' product life extension strategies, and the prospect for a limited introduction of new drugs in the near future. With the expansion of U.S. research and development spending on pharmaceuticals from $12 billion in 1995 to $30 billion in 2004, the number of drugs in early-stage testing has increased substantially, but the number in the later stages of clinical trials has remained essentially constant.[13] The changing biopharmaceutical industry environment and technology innovation since 2001 should have alerted economic development and higher education policymakers to the need to reform higher education financing and strengthen the management, scale, and capabilities of biosciences research teams.

Conclusion: A Stronger Fiscal Reform Framework

Fiscal reform efforts started in 2005 by the Puerto Rico Treasury, under the guidance of a team led by Harvard economics professor Stephen A. Marglin, will be based solely on individual return simulations and modeling developed by Bearing Point in 2004. (Critical modeling of corporate tax returns, particularly biopharmaceutical returns, has yet to be conducted, and the development and optimal sequencing of scenario simulations, balanced policies, and the legitimacy of the process are therefore limited.) The initiative is unfortunately subject to pressure for immediate delivery of more than $1 billion in incremental revenues starting in fiscal year 2007 to avoid expenditure cuts. It seeks to reduce income tax rates through the adoption of a consumption-based tax, the elimination of most deductions to households, and the taxation of passive income at ordinary rates.

Consensus building between the executive and legislative branches, which are controlled by opposing parties, is critical for a successful shared vision and implementation. In that regard, my comments highlight several issues that are

12. The plans to finance the new Science, Technology, and Research Trust, a key private sector–governed trust created by law in 2004, have also been affected by central government fiscal constraints.

13. The number of drugs in phase-1 and phase-2 clinical tests has increased from 1,010 in 1995 to 1,931 in 2004. The number of phase-3 drugs rose from 376 to just 399.

critical to comprehensive fiscal reform: the unsustainable current level of expenditures; the need for debt management controls, performance-based budgeting, management accountability, and strategic investments in the knowledge economy; and the need to rethink the role of the state and adjust investment priorities in light of the island's current stage of economic development. There are significant questions about whether improved governance controls can be achieved without greater institutional autonomy from party politics and authority to recruit and strengthen the management teams.

In the short run, the central government must focus directly on what it can accomplish independently. Better management of the existing cash flow and reengineering to reduce expenditures will need to replace exclusive reliance on fiscal reform negotiations with the legislature to generate the necessary increments to revenues. Policies that might further that end would include proposals that improve the investment climate, reduce the regressivity to low-income households, and cautiously address the use and values of real estate, which has been the preferred savings and financing mechanism, given the tax regime to date, and the main source of refinancing, given prevailing interest rates.

Priority should be granted to a comprehensive reform package consisting of a review of corporate tax deductions, credits, and exempt activities as well as expenditure cuts, including the firing of recent hires according to strict criteria of how recently they were appointed (starting with all temporary employees granted permanence during 2004); agreements with unions on reengineering; a hiring freeze; and sale of noncore assets. Debt service reserves should be enhanced, and short-term debt paid off. Such measures, along with a temporary pledge of new consumption tax revenues to debt service, would allow the time needed to improve the quality of the tax reforms and reduce systemic risk.

For realistic innovation to occur, the government should focus on certain processes and management talent in a rather small number of key institutions while embarking on policy reform. Short-term coordination and initial integration efforts are also achievable and essential to deliver immediate budget and cash management controls. Treasury, Office of Management and Budget, and GDB information systems should be strengthened and integrated to improve payroll and other expenditure controls and to monitor intragovernment debt. Plans to address the increasing operating losses that encumber more than a third of the seventy-eight municipalities are required.[14] Reducing property assessment

---

14. Jobs lost in electronics, apparel, footwear, and other labor-intensive operations after the phase-out of section 936 have contributed to municipal fiscal deficits, since outlying municipalities typically rely on a small number of corporate taxpayers. Furthermore, under the Industrial Incentives Act of 1987 and all previous versions of it, corporations could obtain higher tax benefits by locating farther away from urban areas. This policy exposed poorer municipalities to labor-intensive operations. A regional transition fund to address these disparities was never established.

backlogs at the Municipal Revenues Collection Center would allow for higher property tax revenues and afford needed changes in the regressivity of the existing property tax regime identified by Alm. Such basic governance controls and early successes may increase credibility with investors and the financial system and gain time to build comprehensive, strategic fiscal reform with essential shared political successes.

Subject to a successful first phase of fiscal stabilization, integrated plans should be developed with the investment community and private sector and labor leaders in the following areas: new utilities regulatory schemes; competition and privatization with employee participation and aligned operating incentives; pilot programs to explore synergies and savings, leading to fewer and more robust regional government units; and regional program consolidation and the delegation of central government services to such regions, particularly the decentralization of education, security, and other services. The revenues derived from these plans could be used to fund strategic investments and pensions and to repay the GDB.

In addition to raising the standards for government fiscal performance and innovation to improve the quality of long-term social investments such as higher education and research infrastructure, there is a need to reexamine the private sector and the desirable mix of reliance on markets and government intervention. More effort should be made to promote growth by broadening the entrepreneurship infrastructure, revisiting regulatory impediments to competition and private sector growth, facilitating pension portability, and welfare reform to speed the entry of participants into the labor force and the formal economy.

The integrity of Puerto Rico's fiscal affairs and credibility for future economic development deserves the fullest level of disclosure and the shrewdest policy and decisional acumen by a leadership committed to transparency, quality decisions, and execution. I hope these comments will convey the extent of the challenge the island faces and the need for a significantly higher level of institutional expertise and autonomy.

COMMENT
Fuat Andic

James Alm has done an excellent job of analyzing the issues surrounding the fiscal problems of Puerto Rico and putting them in an international perspective. The diagnostic of the problems and the conclusions reached are scientifically sound, and the recommendations drawn from their conclusions are strategically correct. I disagree with some specific tax issues, but not with the strategies proposed.

The chapter's most important contribution is to bring to light the urgent need for expenditure reform together with tax reform within overall fiscal reform. In the past, fiscal reform was equated with tax reform, and the need for expenditure reform was essentially ignored. In this regard I would like to share my own personal experience with the tax reform endeavors in Puerto Rico.

In 1968, after a long period of PDP (Popular Democratic Party) administration, the PNP (New Progressive Party) came into power. One of the actions of the new government was to set up a tax reform committee to which a group of mainland and local economists, lawyers, and certified public accountants were appointed as members. I was honored to be among those appointed. The committee's mandate was pure and simple: find ways to increase government revenues. The committee completed its work within six months, and its report was presented to the governor. The report did not, however, have much effect.

In 1973 the guards at the helm of the government changed once again. At the request of the new governor, a law was enacted that created a new tax reform commission. I again had the honor to serve, this time as its chief economic adviser. Several commission members presented a thorough analysis (ten volumes in total) of every tax levied in the island; at ten volumes, this study was perhaps the most comprehensive examination ever done of Puerto Rico's tax system.[15] The commission's mandate was once again to explore what changes would need to be made to increase tax revenues and at the same time encourage economic growth, enhance equity, simplify the tax structure, and close the loopholes of evasion. Regrettably, the petroleum crisis of the mid-1970s resulted in recession and stagflation, and the measures taken as a result of the commission's recommendations were limited to revenue enhancement and addressed little else.

Several other reform proposals, and even actions, followed the 1973–75 tax reform efforts.[16] The 1987 reform resulted in a reduction of government revenues (owing to several rate and base changes), did not bring greater equity, and failed to control tax evasion. In 1994 an additional attempt was made to reform the tax system. This reform proposal paid special attention to tax administration. It did not succeed in influencing the government to restructure the tax system, but as a result of the reform report some serious attempts

---

15. It is lamentable that these studies remain in the hands of some private individuals and cannot be found in the library of the Treasury.

16. See Andic and Cao (1986, 1996); Cao (2004).

were made to control evasion. There was some increase in tax collections thanks to administrative measures that were essentially designed to finance current expenditures.

All the reform efforts were directed toward improving revenue performance, although current expenditures consistently grew faster than tax revenues between 1955 and 1990, and the tax system did not keep pace with economic growth. Between 1985 and 1990, the average annual growth of current government expenditures was 7.6 percent, while tax revenues grew by only 6.5 percent. The overall buoyancy of the tax system was 1.13. The buoyancy of the three major taxes—personal income tax, corporate taxes, and general excises (*arbitrios*)—was 1.00, 1.76, and 1.18, respectively. From 1993 to 2001 the buoyancy of the individual income tax fell from 1.76 to −0.02, and that of *arbitrios* fell from 2.71 to −0.47. These two taxes are the major revenue sources of the government. As Alm notes, the individual income tax base has been narrowed by exemptions and deductions, in violation of the basic tenets of taxation, rendering it inadequate. Another potentially appreciable revenue-yielding tax, a consumption tax—be it a value added tax or a general sales tax, which essentially are broad based—is also absent in Puerto Rico. The *arbitrios* are far from satisfactory, not only from the standpoint of yielding revenue but also in terms of neutrality and resource allocation. Conversely, government expenditures continued to increase faster than GNP, leading to today's serious budget deficit. The government is consistently spending more than it is collecting.

The tax system of Puerto Rico today is in such a state that the revenue collection capacity of the government has eroded. The personal income tax has become not much more than a payroll tax riddled with exemptions; the corporate income tax does not fare any better; excise taxes do not correspond to the structure of the economy; and the property tax has become an insignificant source of revenue. The tax system has lost its internal coherence and has become too complex and therefore difficult to administer.

Policymakers need to think seriously about public expenditures, and I hope this volume makes an impression. Clearly, reform in public expenditures will have to come first. Public expenditures are only the means of securing the collective welfare, providing public goods, correcting flagrant inequalities, and stimulating economic development. They should not be used for strictly political purposes, to provide employment, or to satisfy the interests of particular groups. Decisions should not be made to increase expenditures and then seek revenue sources to finance them without paying due attention to the incidence of additional revenues.

Yet the government of Puerto Rico, going against trends elsewhere, is ever expanding. It is the island's biggest employer, providing today about one-quarter of total employment. (It could be argued, moreover, that for many of these employees, their marginal productivity is zero.) About three quarters of public sector outlays consist of wages and salaries. Precious little remains for investment expenditures. This is a dangerous trend, indeed.

While public expenditures are rising, the quality of the services the government provides is declining appreciably. A great deal is spent on maintaining law and order, yet private protection is on the rise. Many urban developments are fenced in, protected by private guards. Education expenditures are also increasing, yet parents complain of poor quality of education, from the primary to the university level. The solution is found in private schools. Those who can afford to do so supplement electricity services with their own generators and sewage services with private septic tanks. In other words, people pay for public services twice: they pay their taxes (though, admittedly, not all of them) and additionally buy those services privately.

If the government is serious about fiscal reform it must take a firm, hard look at the expenditure side. Puerto Rico can no longer simply raise taxes in response to ever growing expenditures; it must at the same time find ways and means to reduce government expenditures, provide the services efficiently, and reduce superfluous employment in the public sector. Moreover, a number of extra-budgetary outlays riddle the general budget, an issue that requires immediate attention. One of the major contributions of this chapter is to call attention to the expenditure side of the budget.

The chapter's analysis is perfect on the revenue side, as well. The author expounds the ills of the present system and bases prescriptions on sound tenets of public finance. In principle, I agree with most of them. My disagreements with two issues are essentially tactical. One involves the question of the value added tax, and the other is the property tax.

The value added tax is perhaps the best indirect tax, but only in certain circumstances. To begin with, the value added tax is more difficult to administer than a retail sales tax; it requires excellent tax administration and a fairly sophisticated private sector. Moreover, given the present tendency among municipalities to impose a municipal sales tax, a general sales tax—presupposing the elimination of *arbitrios*—with a municipal revenue–sharing clause is preferable. It is my understanding that some 80 percent of total retail purchases originate in shopping malls; hence compliance may be rather easy to verify. A general sales tax with a zero rate on a few necessities—medicine, food, schoolbooks, for example—should yield more than 20 percent of total government revenues, an amount equivalent to what *arbitrios* yield today. Additionally, the government might consider some specific excises—such as one on luxury items—that tax high-income groups, as well as taxes on alcohol, cigarettes, and the like for social and public health reasons.

Another tax that requires serious consideration is the property tax, which yields about 0.1 percent of total tax revenues. The tax is antiquated. It is based on the 1958 valuation. There is a $15,000 deduction from the base for owner-occupied residences. Obviously, the tax base is ridiculously narrow. But the tax rate is equally ridiculous for those who are caught in the tax net. The rate varies according to municipalities; in San Juan it is more than 8 percent. It is high time for an upward assessment of property values and a reduction in rates to a realistic level. It is said time and again—by governors, senators, representatives, and mayors—that the property tax is a political issue and cannot be tackled. But the time has long since come to bite the bullet and reform the property tax.

The final point I would like to address is just as essential, tax evasion and tax administration. It is well known that Puerto Rico suffers from widespread tax evasion. Estimates on the underground economy vary, but it is said to be around 30 percent. The individual income tax alone is estimated to be more than 15 percent of the potential tax revenue. To reduce tax evasion will require much better tax administration, not to mention taxpayer education. The Treasury (Departamento de Hacienda) suffers from a lack of qualified personnel and failure to use modern compliance methods. One piece of information is quite eye opening, for it indicates the serious shortcomings in the system: only 1.7 percent of tax returns are filed electronically. A recent study finds that some 30 percent of posts in the Treasury are continuously vacant.[17] Auditors represent no more than 8 percent of the total Treasury workforce. Yet in practically all countries with reasonably good tax administration, audit staffing ranges from 20 to 35 percent of total tax administration staff. Moreover, six hundred Treasury employees, about 20 percent of the agency's workforce, are classified as temporary. This is a serious shortcoming, since it is inconceivable that corporate culture is absorbing such employees.

Dealing with auditors is a costly proposition for taxpayers. Those who are audited spend, on average, two full days in Treasury offices to put the record straight. Often, it appears at the end that the auditor made a mistake or that some document—although filed by the taxpayer—was inadvertently lost. I am told by several public accountants that in about 90 percent of the cases, the taxpayer is found innocent of wrongdoing. But the transaction cost of proving innocence is very high.

Owing to other shortcomings in the organizational structure, Treasury administration is not state of art for our time. There is neither time nor space to enter into discussion of all of them. The research firm Bearing Point has carried out an instructive analysis that should be studied seriously, and its recommendations should be implemented as soon as possible.[18] As it is, the Treasury is not sufficiently professional to cope with the complexities of the economy.

17. See Bearing Point (2004).
18. Bearing Point (2004).

Alm notes the need not only for tax reform to remedy the existing ills but also, perhaps foremost, the need for expenditure reform. A tax reform is only as good as its administration. Even a perfectly designed tax system cannot overcome the effects of poor administration. I appeal to decisionmakers to consider taking measures that will not simply increase revenues to finance ever rising government expenditures but will instead rationalize the expenditure system in order to reform the taxes, with the view not only to collecting more revenues but also to making the system more equitable and conducive to economic development.

References

Agosto, Alicea J. 1987. *Informe del secretario de hacienda sobre reforma contributiva.* San Juan: Department of Housing.

Alm, James, Jill Ann Holman, and Rebecca M. Neumann. 2003. "Globalization and State/Local Government Finances." In *State and Local Finance under Pressure,* edited by David L. Sjoquist, pp. 276–98. Cheltenham, U.K.: Edward Elgar.

Alm, James, and Janet L. Rogers. 2005. "Do State Fiscal Policies Affect Economic Growth?" Working Paper. Atlanta: Georgia State University, Andrew Young School of Policy Studies.

Andic, Fuat M., and Arthur J. Mann. 1976. "Secular Tendencies in the Inequality of Earnings in Puerto Rico." *Review of Social Economy* 34, no. 1: 13–32.

Andic, Suphan, and Ramón Cao Garcia. 1986. *Evaluación del sistema contributivo de Puerto Rico.* Estudio Efectuado para el Senado de Puerto Rico. San Juan (December).

Andic, Suphan, and Ramón Cao Garcia, eds. 1996. *Reforma contributiva en Puerto Rico.* San Juan: Editorial de la Universidad de Puerto Rico.

A. T. Kearney Management Consultants. 2003. *Puerto Rico 2025 Project Assessment: Current Status of Economic, Social, Environmental, and Infrastructure Development in Puerto Rico.* Report prepared for the Puerto Rico Industrial Development Company. San Juan (December).

Bahl, Roy W., Jr. 1971. "A Regression Approach to Tax Effort and Tax Ratio Analysis." *IMF Staff Papers* 18, no. 3: 570–612.

Barro, Robert J. 2000. "Inequality and Growth in a Panel of Countries." *Journal of Economic Growth* 5, no. 1: 5–32.

Bearing Point. 2004. *Tax Reform Impact Assessment Project.* Report submitted to the Puerto Rico Treasury Department, San Juan.

Berry, Dan M., and David L. Kaserman. 1993. "A Diffusion Model of Long-Run State Economic Development." *Atlantic Economic Journal* 21, no. 4: 39–54.

Bird, Richard M. 1989. "The Administrative Dimension of Tax Reform in Developing Countries." In *Tax Reform in Developing Countries,* edited by Malcolm Gillis, pp. 301–22. Duke University Press.

Blumenthal, Marsha, and Joel Slemrod. 1992. "The Compliance Cost of the U.S. Individual Income Tax: A Second Look after Tax Reform." *National Tax Journal* 45, no. 2: 185–202.

———. 1996. "The Income Tax Compliance Cost of Big Business." *Public Finance Quarterly* 24, no. 4: 411–38.

Cao Garcia, Ramón J. 1992. "Reforma municipal y finanzas de los municipios." Serie de Publicaciones de la Unidad de Investigaciones Económicas. University of Puerto Rico, Río Piedras.

———. 2004. *Impuestos en Puerto Rico: Treinte años de experiencia y estudios.* San Juan: University of Puerto Rico Press.

Cao Garcia, Ramón, and Suphan Andic, eds. 1996. *Reforma contributiva en Puerto Rico.* San Juan: Editorial de la Universidad de Puerto Rico.

Chattopadhyay, Saumen, and Arindam Das-Gupta. 2002a. *The Income Tax Compliance Cost of Indian Corporations.* New Delhi: National Institute Public Finance and Policy.

———. 2002b. *The Personal Income Tax in India: Compliance Costs and Compliance Behavior of Taxpayers.* New Delhi: National Institute Public Finance and Policy.

Desai, Mihir, and James R. Hines Jr. 2004. "Old Rules and New Realities: Corporate Tax Policy in a Global Setting." Working Paper. Cambridge, Mass.: National Bureau of Economic Research.

Estado Libre Asociado de Puerto Rico, Comisión de Reforma Contributiva. 1975. *Informe final.* San Juan.

Fisher, Peter. 2002. "Tax Incentives and the Disappearing State Corporate Income Tax." *State Tax Notes* 23, no. 8: 36–45.

Friedlander, Ann F. 1967. "Indirect Taxes and Relative Prices." *Quarterly Journal of Economics* 81, no. 2: 125–39.

Gillis, Malcolm. 1985. "Micro and Macroeconomics of Tax Reform in Indonesia." *Journal of Development Economics* 19, no. 3: 221–54.

Goode, Richard. 1981. "Some Economic Aspects of Tax Administration." *IMF Staff Papers* 28, no. 3: 249–74.

Gruber, Harry. 1998. "Taxes and the Division of Foreign Operating Income among Royalties, Interest, Dividends, and Retained Earnings." *Journal of Public Economics* 68, no. 2: 269–90.

Grubert, Harry, and Joel Slemrod. 1998. "The Effect of Taxes on Investment and Income Shifting to Puerto Rico." *Review of Economics and Statistics* 80, no. 3: 365–73.

Gugl, Elisabeth, and George R. Zodrow. 2005. "International Tax Competition and Tax Incentives in Developing Countries." In *The Challenges of Tax Reform in a Global Economy,* edited by James Alm, Jorge Martinez-Vazquez, and Mark Rider, pp. 167–91. New York: Springer Science and Business Media.

Hall, Robert E., and Alvin Rabushka. 1995. *The Flat Tax.* 2nd ed. Stanford, Calif.: Hoover Institution Press.

Hexner, J. Tomas, and Glenn P. Jenkins. 1995. "Puerto Rico and Section 936: A Costly Dependence." *Tax Notes International* 10, no. 235: 23–39.

Hines, James R., Jr. 1999. "Lessons from Behavioral Responses to International Taxation." *National Tax Journal* 52, no. 2: 305–22.

———. 2004. "Do Tax Havens Flourish?" In *Tax Policy and the Economy,* vol. 19, edited by James M. Poterba, pp. 65–99. MIT Press.

International Monetary Fund. 2003. *Government Finance Statistics.* Washington.

Levine, Ross, and David Renelt. 1993. "A Sensitivity Analysis of Cross-Country Growth Regressions." *American Economic Review* 82, no. 4: 942–63.

Liard-Murient, Carlos F. 2003. *The Effectiveness of Tax Incentives in Attracting Investment: The Case of Puerto Rico.* Ph.D. dissertation, University of Massachusetts–Amherst.

Marrero Velasquez, Wanda Ivelisse. 1989. *The Effects of Tax Exemption on Industrial Location: The Case of Puerto Rico.* Ph.D. dissertation, University of Texas–Austin.

McLure, Charles E., Jr. 1997. "Tax Policies for the 21st Century." In *Visions of the Tax Systems of the XXIst Century,* pp. 9–52. The Hague: Kluwer Law International, International Fiscal Association.

Meade, James E. 1972. "Poverty in the Welfare State." *Oxford Economic Papers* 24, no. 3: 289–326.

Mendoza, Enrique G., Gian Maria Milesi-Ferretti, and Patrick Asea. 1997. "On the Ineffectiveness of Tax Policy in Altering Long-Run Growth: Harberger's Superneutrality Conjecture." *Journal of Public Economics* 66, no. 1: 99–126.

Mintz, Jack M. 1992. "Is There a Future for Capital Income Taxation?" *Canadian Tax Journal* 42, no. 6: 1469–1503.

Moody's Investors Service. 2005a. "Special Comment: Moody's Downgrades Commonwealth of Puerto Rico G.O. Bonds to Baa2." New York (May 23).

———. 2005b. "Special Comment: 2005 State Debt Medians." New York (May).

———. 2005c. "Rating Update: Moody's Downgrades Puerto Rico G.O. Rating to Baa2." New York (May 19).

Morisset, Jacques, and Neda Pirnia. 1999. "How Tax Policy and Incentives Affect Foreign Direct Investment: A Review." Working Paper 2509. Washington: World Bank and Foreign Investment Advisory Service.

Organización de Estados Ameicanos. 1974. *La Tributación al Consumo: Analisis y Recomendaciones: Estuodio Preparado para la Comisión de Reforma Contributiva de Puerto Rico.* Oficina de Finanzas Publicas, Misión a Puerto Rico, Washington, D.C.

PricewaterhouseCoopers. 2004. *Individual Taxes 2003–2004: Worldwide Summaries.* New York: John Wiley and Sons.

Rivera-Batiz, Francisco, and Carlos E. Santiago. 1996. *Island Paradox: Puerto Rico in the 1990s.* New York: Russell Sage Foundation.

Rider, Mark. 2004. "Corporate Income Taxation in Jamaica." Working Paper 3. Jamaica Tax Reform. Atlanta: Georgia State University, Andrew Young School of Policy Studies.

Ring, Raymond J. 1999. "Consumers' Share and Producers' Share of the General Sales Tax." *National Tax Journal* 52, no. 1: 79–90.

Sandford, Cedric, ed. 1995. *Tax Compliance Costs: Measurement and Policy.* Bath, U.K.: Fiscal Publications.

Sandford, Cedric, Michael Godwin, and Peter Hardwick. 1989. *Administrative and Compliance Costs of Taxation.* Bath, U.K.: Fiscal Publications.

Schneider, Friedrich, and Dominik H. Enste. 2002. *The Shadow Economy: An International Survey.* Cambridge, U.K.: Cambridge University Press.

Standard and Poor's. 2005. "Puerto Rico's G.O. Debt Rating Lowered to BBB; Growing Structural Imbalance Cited." New York (May 24).

Surrey, Stanley S. 1958. "Tax Administration in Underdeveloped Countries." *University of Miami Law Review* 12, no. 2: 158–88.

Thirsk, Wayne. 1991. "Jamaican Tax Incentives." In *The Jamaican Tax Reform,* edited by Roy Bahl, pp. 701–25. Cambridge, Mass.: Lincoln Institute of Land Policy.

Toledo, Wilfredo, and Wilfredo Camacho. 1997. *Análisis de opiniones y percepciones de los contribuyentes sobre la labor del Departmento de Hacienda.* San Juan: Statistics and Economics Consulting Group.

Yu, Wei, Myles S. Wallace, and Clark Nardinelli. 1991. "State Growth Rates: Taxes, Spending, and Catching Up." *Public Finance Quarterly* 19, no. 1: 80–93.

Zee, Howard, Janet Stotsky, and Eduardo Ley. 2002. "Tax Incentives for Business Investment: A Primer for Policy Makers in Developing Countries." *World Development* 30, no. 9: 1497–1516.

8

Financing Economic Development

RITA MALDONADO-BEAR AND INGO WALTER

Some sixty years ago, John G. Gurley and Edward Shaw discussed the importance of the financial sector in the economic development process, although the causality of the relationship was not directly addressed.[1] A decade later, in a well-developed conceptual construct, Rondo Cameron and his colleagues argued that, as historical experience has demonstrated, financial institutions represent leading sectors in the process of economic development and actually induce growth through direct industrial promotion and proactive

We would like to acknowledge the Office of the Commissioner of Financial Institutions of Puerto Rico, which supplied most of the data used to construct the tables in this chapter and the associated appendix. The commissioner himself was helpful in clarifying complexities in data classification and legal and tax issues pertaining to the data. Data were also obtained from Puerto Rico's Office of the Commissioner of Insurance, the Government Development Bank and its Office of Economic Research, and several private sector institutions and consultants, including Banco Popular, Banco Santander, the law firm Pietrantoni, Mendez, and Alvarez, and Generans Bioventures. We are particularly grateful to William Lockwood for his assistance in obtaining data and for his thoughtful comments while at Generans Bioventures. We would also like to thank Alejandro Lopina for his invaluable help in putting together the tables and charts. Finally, we want to acknowledge the editorial assistance of Professor Susan Collins, as well as Starynee Adams and Gabriel Chodorow-Reich, from Brookings, and Professor Larry Alan Bear, of the Stern School of Business of New York University.

1. Gurley and Shaw (1955); how the interaction of the real economy and the financial sector takes place within the authors' context is summarized in Maldonado-Bear (1970).

finance.[2] Raymond Goldsmith subsequently suggested that financial deepening, the level of financial intermediation, grows along with the level of economic development. Clearly, the direction of the relationship—whether financial deepening induces economic development or economic development spurs financial deepening—had still not been determined.[3] In a recent review of the literature, Marco Terrones concludes that the evidence does appear to support the view that a more developed financial sector helps to induce economic growth.[4] Equally, there is a consensus that well-designed processes of financial liberalization, a well-developed legal system, and a high degree of financial transparency are crucial for the economic development process to take hold.

Most of these conditions appear to be present in Puerto Rico. Whether financial intermediaries in the private sector and government financial agencies follow Cameron's model of direct industrial promotion and proactive finance to maximize the benefits of economic growth in Puerto Rico is one of the questions explored in this chapter.

More recently, key drivers of economic development that have grown in prominence are the structural and functional properties of financial intermediation and the impact of such mediation on the production function. Capital formation is a key component of economic growth under most circumstances and finds its source either in domestic savings or in capital inflows to the local economy. In local financial intermediation, an important issue is how effectively financial institutions gather assets, predominantly from the household sector, and allocate funds to investments that have a positive risk-adjusted net present value (NPV). The objective is to minimize the cost of intermediation, so that more projects can become NPV-positive and lead to higher rates of capital formation. The same objective applies in cross-border intermediation, where financial institutions have an important role in stimulating local capital formation by tapping foreign savings.

Financial institutions are also at the center of the payments process, which is a key driver of transactions costs in the economy and also ameliorates information asymmetries. Banks, in particular, play a central role in lowering transactions and information costs that otherwise would have adverse effects on economic efficiency and growth, showing up over time in total factor productivity.

Beyond this, financial intermediaries have other important properties. They should be innovative with respect to their own products and processes, contributing to technological change as a source of growth in a key sector of the economy. In a dynamic context, they serve a catalytic role in feeding capital to nascent sectors of the economy in the form of private equity, venture capital,

---

2. Cameron and others (1967).
3. Goldsmith (1969).
4. Terrones (2004).

and early-stage high-risk debt financing to assure that industries and firms with good competitive and growth prospects have opportunities to obtain financial resources. At the same time, they assume a critical role in denying capital to industries and firms that are losing competitive advantage and have poor growth prospects. Since structural adjustment is a key facet of economic growth, financial institutions and markets serve a critical allocative function in this regard.

In short, the state of the financial system and its development touches each element of the production function—the labor force, capital formation, and total factor productivity—and therefore serves as a key driver of economic growth. Beyond this, the financial sector itself represents a major industry in terms of output, income, growth, and the generation of tax revenue. A healthy, innovative, and competitively vibrant financial services sector is therefore in the interest of Puerto Rico's economic development as much as that of any major industry, quite apart from the "specialness" of financial intermediation, payments, and financial risk management. In this respect, the Puerto Rican financial sector has several unique dimensions.

First, Puerto Rico does not have its own currency or central bank, so key functions normally carried out by financial institutions are absent. This fact has both positive and negative dimensions. Theoretically, on the positive side it aligns the Puerto Rican inflation rate to that of the United States, which is low by emerging market standards, and to the extent that price level stability is associated with higher growth, this is a good thing. In addition, the absence of a central bank imposes financing constraints on the Puerto Rican public sector, preventing debt monetization, one of the roots of emerging market financial crises. On the negative side, absence of the normal tool of monetary policy deprives Puerto Rico of the principal technique of macroeconomic control, and the island is limited to fiscal measures only.

Second, Puerto Rico is part of the U.S. payments system centered on Fedwire and the Clearing House Interbank Payments System and does not have to maintain the domestic payments infrastructure of stand-alone financial systems. This lowers the cost of transactions in the banking system as well as the cost of financial intermediation and should be a positive factor in economic development.

Third, banks operating in Puerto Rico are regulated (depending on their charter) by the Federal Reserve System as the lender of last resort, the U.S. Comptroller of the Currency, and the Federal Deposit Insurance Corporation (FDIC), as well as the Puerto Rico banking authorities, the Office of the Commissioner of Financial Institutions of Puerto Rico, under the Puerto Rico Department of the Treasury. Exposure to bank-specific risks, as well as to Puerto Rican sovereign risk, is eliminated (for qualified deposits) by FDIC deposit insurance. This applies both to local depositors in Puerto Rico and to sources of brokered deposits on the mainland and elsewhere. To the extent that lender-of-last-resort services are unpriced and FDIC insurance is underpriced given the risks associated with Puerto Rican banks, this represents a potentially valuable subsidy from the U.S. mainland. So do other regulatory services, notably rigorous safety and soundness standards and professional bank examinations that cannot be taken for granted in an emerging market context. Although it is difficult, perhaps impossible, to quantify the regulatory costs and risks that fall to the Puerto Rican banking system because of its association with the U.S. regulatory infrastructure, they are doubtless significant, and the efficiency and stability of the system constitute a valuable subsidy on the part of U.S. taxpayers.

Fourth, the operations of securities firms in Puerto Rico are regulated by the U.S. Securities and Exchange Commission as well as Puerto Rican "blue sky" laws, which are similar to those applied in the fifty U.S. states though they rarely deviate materially from national norms. The rules of various U.S. self-regulatory organizations such as the New York Stock Exchange and the National Association of Securities Dealers also apply in Puerto Rico. Again, the regulatory infrastructure governing the securities industry does not have to be replicated in Puerto Rico, and the commonwealth thereby realizes commensurate savings and lower risks in this domain of financial intermediation.

In contrast, the Puerto Rican insurance industry is regulated solely by the Office of the Commissioner of Insurance of Puerto Rico, since the United States has no national insurance regulator. If there are failures of insurance companies regulated by Puerto Rico, and particularly if insurance forms a significant channel for financial intermediation, bailouts may ultimately have to be organized, and the Puerto Rican economy therefore bears the risk of a potentially significant contingent liability.

On balance, regulatory commonality in the areas of banking and securities probably generates significant savings and lower risks in creating and maintaining Puerto Rico's financial infrastructure compared with stand-alone financial systems. On the other hand, the one-size-fits-all nature of the U.S. financial and regulatory infrastructure may also limit the degree to which that system can be adapted to some of Puerto Rico's unique developmental aspects. Moreover, because there are far fewer distortions, inefficiencies, and regulatory shortcomings in the U.S. infrastructure than in that of many developing countries, there are fewer obvious ways of improving the conditions under which financial intermediation takes place and hence the size of the financial system as a whole.

This chapter begins with a broad overview of financial intermediation dynamics—that is, how financial intermediaries are structured to serve the various key functions connecting sources and users of funds, risk management, payments transactions, and so on. This framework allows us to identify a set of benchmarks that can be used to evaluate the contribution of the financial sector in Puerto Rico to economic development in the island.

We proceed from the overview framework to a specific focus on the contribution of the financial sector in Puerto Rico to the economic development of the island. After describing the Puerto Rican financial sector and analyzing its growth over the past ten years, we consider the following:

—the evolution of assets and liabilities of commercial banks and how these proxies for sources and uses of funds relate to economic growth

—international banking entities (IBEs) in the island and their potential for stimulating economic growth

—insurance companies and their role as financial intermediary

—the significant growth of investment companies and their impact on the financial intermediation process

—the evolution of specialized financial institutions

—the key role of the Government Development Bank

—supervisory and regulatory institutions

—an assessment of Puerto Rico's financial sector relative to selected benchmarks

To evaluate the Puerto Rican financial sector, we conduct a comparison of key financial ratios in Puerto Rico with those the World Bank has developed as indicators of financial sector maturity and effectiveness in economic development. We then compare key metrics of the Puerto Rican banking system with those of the United States as a whole and two regional comparators, Florida and Hawaii. We end this chapter with conclusions and recommendations aimed at financial institutions and their role in improving the rate of economic growth of Puerto Rico.

An Overview of the Financial Sector

The central component of any model of a modern financial system is the conduits through which the financial assets of the ultimate savers flow to the liabilities of the ultimate users of finance, both within and between national economies. This involves alternative and competing modes of financial intermediation, or "contracting," between counterparties in financial transactions. A guide to thinking about financial contracting and the role of financial institutions and markets is summarized in figure 8-1. The diagram depicts the financial process (flow of funds) among the different sectors of the economy.

The ultimate source of funds in financial systems—household, government, and corporate savings—may be held in the form of deposits or alternative types of claims issued by commercial banks, savings organizations, insurance companies, or other types of financial institutions that finance themselves by placing their liabilities directly with the general public (denoted as "banks" in figure 8-1). Financial institutions ultimately use these funds to purchase assets issued by nonfinancial entities such as households, firms, and governments. These can be described as fully intermediated financial flows. Savings

Figure 8-1. *Financial Intermediation*

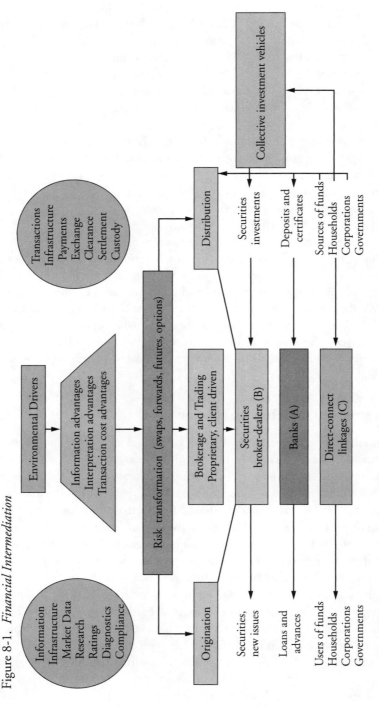

Source: Smith and Walter (1997).

may be allocated directly or indirectly, through fiduciaries and collective invest-ment vehicles, toward the purchase of securities publicly issued and sold by vari-ous public and private sector organizations in the domestic and international financial markets (denoted as "users of funds" in figure 8-1). These can be described as investment banking and securitized intermediation.

Funds can also come from direct-connect mechanisms between ultimate borrowers and lenders. Savings surpluses may be allocated to borrowers through various kinds of direct-sale mechanisms, such as private placements, usually involving fiduciaries as intermediaries. Ultimate users of funds make up the same three segments of the economy—the household or consumer sector, the business sector, and the public sector. Consumers may finance purchases by means of personal loans from banks or through loans secured by purchased assets (hire-purchase or installment loans). These may appear on the asset side of the balance sheets of credit institutions for the duration of the respective loan contracts on a revolving basis, or they may be sold off into the financial market in the form of various kinds of securities backed by consumer credit receivables. Corporations may borrow from banks in the form of unsecured or asset-backed straight or revolving credit facilities, or they may sell debt obliga-tions (for example, commercial paper, receivables financing, and fixed-income securities of various types) or equities directly into the financial market. Simi-larly, governments may borrow from credit institutions (sovereign borrowing) or issue securities directly.

Borrowers such as corporations and governments also have the possibility of privately issuing and placing their obligations with institutional investors, thereby circumventing both credit institutions and the public debt and equity markets. Consumer debt can also be repackaged as asset-backed securities and sold privately to institutional investors.

In the first mode of financial contracting, shown as "A" in figure 8-1, deposi-tors buy the "secondary" financial claims or liabilities issued by credit institu-tions and benefit from liquidity, convenience, and safety through the ability of financial institutions to diversify risk and improve credit quality by means of professional management and monitoring of their holdings of primary financial claims (both debt and equity). Savers can choose from among a set of standard-ized contracts and receive payments services and interest.

In the second mode of financial intermediation, shown as "B" in figure 8-1, investors can select their own portfolios of financial assets directly from among the publicly issued debt and equity instruments on offer. This may provide a broader range of options than standardized bank contracts and permit larger investors to tailor portfolios more closely to their objectives while still achiev-ing acceptable liquidity through rapid and cheap execution of trades—aided by linkages with banks and other financial institutions that are part of the domes-tic payments mechanism. Investors may also choose to have their portfolios professionally managed, for a fee, through various types of mutual funds and pension funds—designated in figure 8-1 as collective investment vehicles.

In the third mode of financial intermediation ("C" in figure 8-1), institutional investors buy large blocks of privately issued securities. In doing so, they often face a liquidity penalty—owing to the absence or limited availability of a liquid secondary market—for which they are compensated in the form of a higher yield. On the other hand, directly placed securities can be specifically tailored to more closely match issuer and investor requirements than can publicly issued securities. Market and regulatory developments (such as the Securities and Exchange Commission's rule 144A in the United States) have added to the liquidity of some direct-placement markets.

Value to ultimate savers and investors, inherent in the financial processes described here, accrues in the form of a combination of yield, safety, and liquidity. Value to ultimate users of funds accrues in the form of a combination of financing cost, transactions cost, flexibility, and liquidity. This value can be enhanced through credit backstops, guarantees, and derivative instruments such as forward rate agreements, caps, collars, futures, and options captured under "risk transformation" in figure 8-1. Furthermore, markets can be linked functionally and geographically, both domestically and internationally. Functional linkages permit bank receivables, for example, to be repackaged and sold to nonbank securities investors. Privately placed securities, once they have been seasoned, may be able to be sold in public markets. Geographic linkages make it possible for savers and issuers to gain incremental benefits in foreign and offshore markets, thereby enhancing liquidity and yield or reducing transaction costs. The intermediation process is heavily influenced by the economics of information production and dissemination, as well as transactions systems, depicted in the two circles at the top of figure 8-1.

Shifts in Intermediary Market Shares

Developments over the past several decades in intermediation processes and institutional design both across time and geography are striking. In the United States, commercial banks—institutions that accept deposits from the public and make commercial loans—have seen their market share of domestic financial flows to end users of the financial system decline from about 75 percent in the 1950s to less than 25 percent today. In Europe the change has been much less dramatic, and the share of financial flows running though the balance sheets of banks continues to be well over 60 percent, but declining nonetheless. In Japan, as well as much of the rest of Asia, banks continue to control in excess of 70 percent of financial intermediation flows. Most emerging market countries cluster at the highly intermediated end of the spectrum, but in many of these economies there is also factual evidence of declining market shares of traditional banking intermediaries. Classic banking intermediation functionality, in short, has been in long-term decline more or less worldwide.[5]

Where has all the money gone? Disintermediation as well as financial innovation and expanding global linkages have redirected financial flows through the securities markets. Figure 8-2 shows developments in market share in the United States from 1970 to 2004, highlighting the extent of commercial bank losses and institutional investor gains. Although this may be an extreme case, even in highly intermediated financial structures, financial disintermediation of the core deposit-gathering and commercial-lending functions of banks has been significant.

Ultimate savers increasingly use the fixed-income and equity markets directly and through fiduciaries, which, through vastly improved technology, are able to provide substantially the same functionality as classic banking relationships—immediate access to liquidity, transparency, safety, and so on—coupled with a higher rate of return. The one thing they cannot guarantee is settlement at par, which in the case of transactions balances (for example, money market mutual funds) is mitigated by portfolio constraints mandating high-quality, short-maturity financial instruments. Ultimate users of funds have benefited from enhanced access to financial markets across a broad spectrum of maturity and credit quality, using conventional and structured financial instruments. Although market access and financing cost normally depend on the current state of the market, credit and liquidity backstops can be easily provided.

Within the fiduciary sector, open-end mutual funds (both in defined-contribution pension plans and as savings, investment, and transactions vehicles) have turned out to be one of the most successful financial innovations of all time—in 2004 totaling some $7.4 trillion in the United States alone. More recently, closed-end vehicles in the form of hedge funds have had a spectacular run, with close to $1 trillion invested at the end of 2004 worldwide.

Hedge funds, along with an array of alternative investments, including those linked to real estate, emerging markets, commodities, private equity and venture capital, and other asset classes, have added a richness to the capital markets that has served investors well in modern financial markets. At the same time, a broad spectrum of derivatives overlays the markets, making it possible to tailor financial products to the needs of end users with increasing granularity, further expanding the availability and reducing the cost of financing, on the one hand, and promoting portfolio optimization, on the other. Interest-rate and currency swaps, for example, bridge both monetary units and fixed-income pricing conventions, making it possible to optimize the

5. See Walter (1993, 2003, 2004).

Figure 8-2. *U.S. Financial Market Shares, 1970–2004*

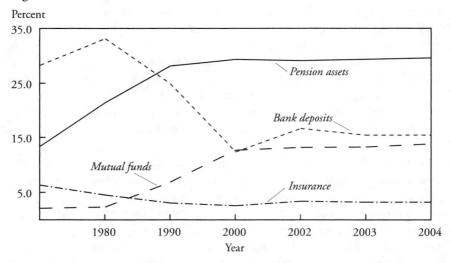

Source: Data from Federal Reserve (www.federalreserve.gov/releases/Z1/Current/data.htm [August 2005]).

comparative financial market advantage of both borrowers and investors. Wherever there is market risk or credit risk, as well as other risk such as natural catastrophe or the weather, derivative contracts have emerged to efficiently transfer that risk to those best able to bear it—progressively covering the entire state-space of potential end users, from risk-tolerance to return objectives—through exchange-traded as well as over-the-counter contracts. Much of the innovation in derivatives (and regulatory concern) has focused on over-the-counter contracts.

As the financial markets have developed, the end users of those markets have themselves been forced to become more performance oriented in the presence of much greater transparency and competitive pressures. It has become increasingly difficult to justify departures from highly disciplined financial behavior on the part of corporations, public authorities, and institutional investors. In the process, two important and related differences are encountered in this generic financial-flow transformation: intermediation shifts—in the first place, from book-value to market-value accounting and, in the second place, from more intensively regulated to less intensively regulated channels, generally requiring less oversight and less capital; regulation shifts from the institutions themselves to the financial markets and practices in those markets. Both have clear implications for the efficiency properties of financial systems and for their transparency, safety, and soundness.

The Puerto Rican Financial Sector

From its beginnings in the early twentieth century, the financial sector in Puerto Rico consisted primarily of nonlocal commercial banks and insurance companies. As of 1967 the sector had evolved to include many domestic (that is, Puerto Rican) private sector and governmental financial institutions. The total assets of all Puerto Rican financial institutions as of 1967 amounted to slightly more than $3 billion. Commercial banks accounted for approximately 53 percent of assets, government financial institutions about 24 percent, and nonbank private financial institutions about 23 percent. Within this last group, the largest institutions were savings and loan, insurance, and finance companies.

In early 2005 the financial sector in Puerto Rico is quite different. There are approximately ten different types of financial institutions with considerable presence in financial intermediation, and at least one previously important type of financial institution, the savings and loan company, no longer exists. The total assets of these ten groups of institutions as of June 2004 amounted to $218 billion, representing an annual rate of growth of 12 percent since 1995 (see tables 8-1 and 8A-1).

Ranked by asset size as of 2004, the largest component is the banking sector, holding 47 percent of total assets (table 8-1). The banking sector includes fourteen private commercial banks with 43 percent of total asset footings, while the two government banks account for 4 percent. The second largest group consists of thirty-five international banking entities (IBEs), which account for 31 percent of total assets in the system. The rest are relatively small and specialized institutions in terms of the proportion of the financial sector's assets, though many showed remarkable growth during the previous decade. Insurance companies account for 6 percent of total assets, investment companies (mutual funds) 5 percent, mortgage companies 4 percent, credit unions 3 percent, finance companies 2 percent, broker-dealers and leasing companies each 1 percent, and small-loan companies less than 1 percent. It should also be noted that venture capital companies, the smallest of all groups, also record less than 1 percent of total assets.[6]

Among all these institutions, the IBEs appear to have the least connection with the local economy, since all their financial activity is outside the island. They exist exclusively to conduct transactions with nonresidents, as do similar institutions in other areas of the world, such as Ireland and Singapore. However, these institutions show considerable promise for the development of Puerto Rico as a niche international financial center, while contributing to local

---

6. In terms of size, venture capital companies represent less than 0.0001 percent of the total financial sector and thus are left off tables 8-1 and 8A-1. Their compound annual growth rate over the period has equaled almost exactly that of the sector as a whole.

Table 8-1. *Financial Sector Assets as Share of Total Financial Sector Assets, Puerto Rico, Selected Years, 1995–2004*[a]

Percent, except as indicated

Institution type	1995	2000	2004	CAGR[b]
Small-loan companies	2.7	1.6	0.6	−5.5
Leasing companies	1.3	0.9	1.0	8.7
Broker-dealers	4.7	3.6	1.1	−4.6
Finance companies	2.3	3.3	2.2	11.4
Credit unions	4.1	3.2	2.8	7.6
Mortgage companies	1.6	3.3	3.8	23.2
Investment companies	0.6	1.7	5.4	43.7
Insurance companies	9.0	8.1	5.5	6.1
International banking entities	23.5	31.1	30.6	15.4
Banking sector	50.3	43.3	47.1	11.2
Total financial sector	100	100	100	12.0
Total financial sector (billions of dollars)	78	143	218	...

Source: Data from the Offices of the Commissioner of Financial Institutions and the Commissioner of Insurance of Puerto Rico.

a. Assets of insurance companies and credit unions were estimated as of June 2004, as the data were not available.

b. Cumulative annual growth rate, 1995–2004.

economic and employment growth. It is interesting to note that the U.S. trend among commercial banks toward diminished importance as the dominant form of financial intermediation from 1970 to 2003—shown in figure 8-2—is reflected in Puerto Rico as well, but at a much more moderate pace. Although the Puerto Rican data do not include pension funds and are therefore not fully comparable, the evolution shows the banking sector declining from 50 percent of all financial sector assets in 1995 to 43 percent in 2000 and then increasing to 47 percent by June 2004 (see tables 8-1 and 8A-1).[7] Earlier data for 1967 show that commercial banks held 53 percent of the assets of all financial institutions in Puerto Rico, excluding pension funds.[8] During the entire period from 1967 to 2004, banking sector assets as a proportion of financial sector assets in Puerto Rico declined by only 6 percent, whereas the data in figure 8-2 show that their decline on the mainland was 15 percent over a period four years shorter than that covered in Puerto Rico.

7. Pension funds in Puerto Rico have not grown much. Funds in the private sector pension plan are owned primarily by large manufacturing firms established in the mainland United States, and the funds are kept there, not on the island. The island's government pension plans, which are several and rather large, are currently heavily underfunded. Practically speaking, this component of the financial sector in Puerto Rico is nonexistent at the moment.

8. Maldonado-Bear (1970).

The growth in assets experienced by the Puerto Rican financial sector from December 31, 1995, to June 30, 2004, can be seen from table 8A-1. It is clear that the banking sector and the IBEs, in that order, have dominated the Puerto Rican financial sector over the entire period. The table gives the dollar volume in assets of each of these groups of financial intermediaries for each year during the period. Note that the growth in assets for the entire financial sector over the ten-year period runs at a compound annual rate of 12 percent. Those institutions experiencing the highest annual growth rates are investment companies, at 44 percent, and mortgage companies, at 23 percent. The largest players, the IBEs and the banks, grew at 15 percent and 11 percent, respectively, over the period. All financial institutions except broker-dealers and small-loan companies experienced positive growth rates.

Table 8-1 shows the proportion of the total financial sector assets that each group of financial intermediaries held in selected years during the period. The banking sector experienced a decline in its share of total assets from 50 percent in 1995 to 47 percent in 2004. On the other hand, the IBEs increased their share from 23 percent to 31 percent over the same period. Insurance companies experienced a decline from 9 percent to 6 percent, while investment companies increased from 1 percent to 5 percent, and mortgage companies from 2 percent to 4 percent. Finance companies held their share, and all other intermediaries experienced a reduction in their proportionate share of total Puerto Rico financial sector assets.

Financial institutions operating in Puerto Rico are supervised and regulated by two local agencies—the Office of the Commissioner of Insurance, which regulates and supervises all the insurance companies on the island, and the Office of the Commissioner of Financial Institutions, which oversees and regulates all depository institutions as well as all other financial institutions operating in Puerto Rico. As noted earlier, commercial banks are also subject to the FDIC, the Federal Reserve Bank, and the U.S. Comptroller of the Currency.

The Banking Sector

Banking sector growth is illustrated in figure 8-3. This sector includes sixteen banks, of which two are government banks (the Government Development Bank and the Economic Development Bank) and fourteen are commercial banks. The commercial banks are broken down as follows: two national banks (chartered under the Office of the Treasury of the United States), an international bank (operating as a branch of a foreign bank), and eleven domestic banks (operating under the laws of Puerto Rico).

The assets of these sixteen banks have grown from $40 billion to $102 billion during the ten-year period from 1995 through 2004. This is an 11 percent compound annual rate of growth. By far the most rapid growth was

Figure 8-3. *Total Assets of the Banking Sector in Puerto Rico, 1995–2004*[a]

Billions of dollars

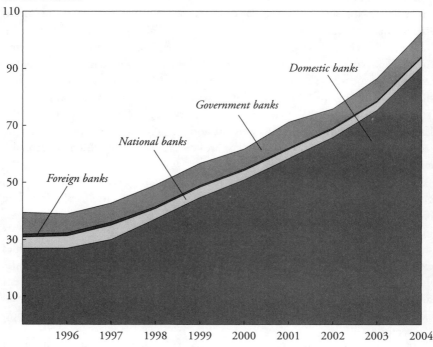

Source: Data from the Office of the Commissioner of Financial Institutions of Puerto Rico.
a. Data as of December of each year.

experienced by the eleven private domestic banks. The other categories in the figure—government banks, foreign banks, and national banks—show virtually no growth at all and in some cases a decline. This is particularly true of the foreign banks, as is clear from their virtual disappearance in figure 8-3.[9]

Commercial Banks

Twenty-two commercial banks were operating in Puerto Rico in 1995. By 2004, mergers and acquisitions had reduced the number to fourteen. The data

9. We tried to classify commercial banks as domestically owned (that is, Puerto Rico–owned) and foreign owned in order to compare the Puerto Rican data with data from the World Bank, which covers national financial systems. Under the World Bank definitions, a bank is classified as domestically owned if more than 50 percent of its shares are owned by local residents; otherwise, the bank is classified as foreign owned. Almost all the commercial banks in Puerto Rico are traded on the New York Stock Exchange and the NASDAQ. It appears that the grouping of shareholders, for shares that trade in the exchanges, are classified in three major groups: institutional investors,

presented in this chapter pertain to the fourteen banks that are still in operation. As noted, two of these, Banco Popular NA and Citibank, are national banks, and one, Nova Scotia Bank, is an international bank. Banco Cooperativo is chartered and supervised by the International Association of Cooperatives; it is also supervised by the Office of the Commissioner of Insurance. All others are domestic banks. The fourteen banks are listed below by volume of assets as of 2004, from highest to lowest:

—Banco Popular de Puerto Rico (domestic)
—Firstbank of Puerto Rico (domestic)
—Doral Bank (domestic)
—Westernbank of Puerto Rico (domestic)
—Banco Santander Puerto Rico (domestic)
—R-G Premier Bank of Puerto Rico (domestic)
—Banco Bilbao Vizcaya Argenta (domestic)
—Oriental Bank and Trust (domestic)
—Citibank (national)
—Eurobank (domestic)
—Scotia Bank de Puerto Rico (domestic)
—Banco Cooperativo (Credit Cooperatives Bank) (domestic)
—Nova Scotia Bank (international)
—Banco Popular NA (national)

The asset composition of all the commercial banks during the period 1995–2004 is presented in tables 8-2 and 8A-2. The annual growth in total assets was 13 percent, fueled by increases in security holdings by the banks, which grew by 16 percent a year (table 8A-2). Other significant categories growing at an above-average rate were the two real estate loan categories, with growth rates of 17 percent and 16 percent, respectively. Commercial and industrial loans grew at a rate of only 10 percent, well below the 13 percent average growth of total assets, and loans to individuals grew a mere 1 percent a year. Loans to individuals include credit card debt—about $1.4 billion in 2004.

Table 8-2 shows the proportionate composition of assets, presenting a clearer view of the reality that investments in securities have been the largest component of assets, with 31 percent of the total in 1995 and 41 percent in 2004. Real estate loans are the second largest component, with 23 percent in 1995 and 31 percent of total assets in 2004. Commercial and industrial loans declined

---

insiders (mainly management), and other individuals. We contacted the investor relations officer for each of the local banks, some of whom reported that for most local banks in Puerto Rico, ownership averaged 55 percent institutional investors, 20 percent insiders, and the remainder individuals. Some of the investor relations officers were willing to provide estimates about the share of each of these three groups representing Puerto Rican residents, but we did not find that approach reliable or critical for the study.

Table 8-2. *Asset Composition of Commercial Banks as Share of Total Assets,*
Puerto Rico, Selected Years, 1995–2004
Percent, except as indicated

Item	1995	2000	2004	CAGR[a]
Investments and securities	31.3	39.7	41.1	16.2
Loans secured by residential real estate	13.8	15.4	19.0	16.8
Loans secured by other real estate	9.2	10.0	11.6	15.7
Commercial and industrial loans	17.8	15.1	14.1	9.8
Other assets	5.6	3.9	3.7	7.8
Cash and interest-bearing placements	5.0	3.5	3.6	8.9
Other loans and leases, net	0.2	1.0	0.5	23.3
Loans to individuals	17.1	11.4	6.4	1.1
Total assets	100	100	100	12.8
Total assets (millions of dollars)	31,969	54,785	94,330	. . .

Source: Data from the Office of the Commissioner of Financial Institutions of Puerto Rico.
a. Cumulative annual growth rate, 1995–2004.

from 18 percent of total assets in 1995 to 14 percent in 2004, and the share of loans to individuals dropped from 17 percent to 6 percent. In short, commercial banks have allocated their funds to security investments and real estate lending at the expense of commercial and industrial loans and loans to individuals.

Commercial and industrial lending represents precisely the type of financial intermediation that creates the greatest traction in the process of economic development, and when reflected in investment spending, it exerts a multiplier effect on the local economy. For economic development purposes, it would be ideal to see more loans in this category than in any other. To the extent that Puerto Rican bank deposits have been intermediated to the purchase of securities issued outside Puerto Rico (mainly by U.S. government and other mainland issuers), this local intermediation gain has arguably been absent. Similarly, real estate lending can be considered inferior to commercial and industrial lending in terms of its impact on income and growth. Asset allocation by Puerto Rican banks may be explained in part by the island's internal revenue laws, which provide exemptions from taxes on specific types of investments. The liabilities and equity of these banks are presented in tables 8-3 and 8A-3. As shown, there was relatively little growth in traditional deposits, with increased debt accounting for most of the growth in bank liabilities. Local private sector deposits (total deposits, excluding section 936 and brokered deposits) grew at only 7 percent annually, outdistanced by advances from the Federal Home Loan Bank (57 percent growth), the issuance of preferred stock (37 percent),

Table 8-3. *Liability and Equity Composition of Commercial Banks as Share of Total Assets, Puerto Rico, Selected Years, 1995–2004*
Percent, except as indicated

Item	1995	2000	2004	CAGR[a]
Liabilities	92.7	93.6	93.4	12.9
Brokered deposits	0.0	8.0	13.5	40.9
Advances from the Federal Home Loan Bank	0.0	8.5	7.4	57.0
Section 936 deposits	15.4	3.2	0.0	−100.0
Total deposits (excluding section 936 and brokered)	58.3	47.7	36.1	6.9
Long-term debt	4.4	3.9	12.0	26.0
Short-term debt	12.4	19.9	19.4	18.6
Other liabilities	2.3	2.6	4.9	22.9
Equity	7.3	6.4	6.6	11.5
Preferred stock	0.1	0.2	0.4	37.2
Other equity	7.2	6.2	6.2	10.8
Total liabilities and equity (percent)	100	100	100	12.8
Total liabilities and equity (millions of dollars)	31,969	54,785	94,330	. . .

Source: Data from the Office of the Commissioner of Financial Institutions of Puerto Rico.
a. Cumulative annual growth rate, 1995–2004, computed using first nonzero entry.

brokered deposits (41 percent), long-term debt (26 percent), other liabilities (23 percent), and short-term debt (19 percent).[10]

All of these growth rates are rather startling, but perhaps more significant were the main sources of funds in 2004 compared with 1995. In 1995 total deposits including section 936 funds were about $24 billion, or 74 percent of total liabilities and equity, whereas in 2004 total deposits including brokered deposits were $46.8 billion, or 49 percent of total liabilities and equity— a decline of 25 percent. This could be interpreted as an unexpected and unhealthy relationship in a developing economy, where deposits—particularly domestic deposits from the general public and business—should be the key to channeling savings into productive investments. Even in the mature economy of

10. Section 936 funds are funds deposited by U.S. companies manufacturing on the island to take advantage of the exemptions offered by the Tax Reform Act of 1976, section 936, which exempted earnings from U.S. mainland companies from federal taxes as long as the funds remained in deposits in local institutions or were reinvested in Puerto Rico. The objective of this law was to stimulate the creation of jobs on the island. The section 936 exemptions were gradually eliminated, beginning in 1996, and came to an end during 2005. Many companies are eligible and are switching their status to controlled foreign corporations. Brokered deposits are deposits made by financial brokers on the U.S. mainland to Puerto Rican banks because of higher interest rates on the island.

the United States, we find that in 2004 deposits were about 65 percent of total bank liabilities and equity, significantly higher than the 50 percent in Puerto Rico. The situation with respect to total debt held by banks on the island is of some concern, not only from an economic development point of view but also in light of what is generally accepted as a strong balance sheet position. In 1995 total debt of banks in Puerto Rico, excluding deposits, was $6.1 billion, or 19 percent of total liabilities and equity, while in 2004 it was $41.3 billion, or 44 percent of total liabilities and equity. In the United States, total debt excluding deposits was only 25.2 percent of total liabilities and equity in the same year.[11]

How long this weak balance sheet position can be sustained is an issue. During the decade analyzed here, it appears that some of the banks began to aggressively sell preferred stock to increase equity and reduce reliance on debt. This category grew dramatically over the period, at a compound rate of 37 percent annually. Although the monetary volume is not significant based on the preferred stock outstanding in 2004, it is noteworthy that preferred stock is 7 percent of total equity in Puerto Rico's banks, as opposed to less than 1 percent in the United States. For example, Moody's views preferred stock, even if it is noncumulative and perpetual, as rather expensive debt rather than as equity.[12]

There is an interesting observation as well with respect to the equity composition of Puerto Rico's banks. Generally, commercial banks need to maintain 8 percent of their assets in equity capital—primarily in common stock and retained earnings but also in preferred stock. From table 8-3, where the components of liabilities and capital appear as a percentage of total assets, we find that adding preferred stock to other equity results in a total equity capital component of 7 percent as of 2004, about the same as in 1995. Although not shown here, in 1995 the preferred stock component was only 1 percent of total equity, whereas in 2004 it was 7 percent of total equity, or $421 million. The 2004 balance sheets of bank holding companies, which were not available for use in this chapter, contained more than $2.5 billion dollars in preferred stock.[13] In light of these data as well as Moody's conservative views about preferred stock, we believe that in this respect the state of the Puerto Rican banks' balance sheets was weaker in 2004 than it was in 1995, with too much preferred stock relative to equity as a component of total capital.

This is particularly true given more recent preferred stock flotations by domestic banks through trusts incorporated in Delaware and sold in the United States as cumulative preferred stock. This means their presence in the banks'

11. All U.S. data cited in this paragraph are from the Federal Deposit Insurance Corporation (www2.fdic.gov/SDI.asp).
12. All U.S. data cited in this paragraph are from the Federal Deposit Insurance Corporation (www2.fdic.gov/SDI.asp).
13. "Negocios del Domingo," *El Nuevo Dia,* January 15, 2005.

equity makes the equity portion more risky than if these issues were noncumulative or common stock. Preferred stocks have a special tax treatment that enables investors to reap a 10 percent return while costing borrowers between 6.40 and 8.35 percent.[14] The differential is absorbed by taxpayers, and the banks profit. Finally, we note that while regulatory guidelines permit noncumulative preferred stock in tier I capital without limitations, the regulation states that "it is desirable from a supervisory standpoint that voting common equity remains the dominant form of Tier I capital."[15]

Commercial banks as well as mortgage companies in Puerto Rico sell a large volume of mortgage loans in the U.S. market. Most of those mortgage and real estate loans are made to individuals, which means that the real estate loan portfolio observable in the balance sheet of Puerto Rican banks and mortgage companies would most likely include only commercial real estate loans and new mortgages to individuals. The servicing of the sold mortgage loans remains in the local market. Most banks and mortgage companies arrange with the buyers of these loans to service them locally, that is, to act as intermediaries between the debtors (local individuals) and the creditors (mainly investors in the United States). The loan servicing provides banks with a source of fee income that is not reported separately from other income in the accounting statements provided by the banks to the Office of the Commissioner of Financial Institutions. Therefore, we were unable to obtain these data separately. The volume of mortgages served by commercial banks and mortgage companies appears in table 8A-4. The total volume of mortgages serviced is significant, growing at a compound annual rate of 9 percent, from $15.9 billion in 1995 to $34.3 billion in 2004. However, most of the growth was experienced by mortgage companies, whose assets grew at an annual compound rate of 15 percent, from $6.3 billion in 1995 to $22.8 billion in 2004. Still, mortgages serviced by commercial banks were about 12 percent of their total assets as of 2004—$11.6 billion in mortgage accounts relative to $94.3 billion in assets.

A summary of the income statements of Puerto Rican commercial banks as well as selected profitability ratios are presented in table 8A-5. The data for the entire 2004 year were extrapolated utilizing the first two quarters' data. Total net income of banks over the ten-year period increased at a respectable compound annual rate of 18 percent, whereas total revenue increased by only 7 percent. It appears that interest revenue declined proportionately from 89 percent of total revenues in 1995 to 83 percent in 2004. However, the banks were able to reduce interest costs proportionately from 46 percent in 1995 to 35 percent

14. "Negocios del Domingo," *El Nuevo Día,* January 15, 2005. The commissioner of financial institutions in Puerto Rico told us (in correspondence) that dividends on banks' preferred stock yield about 10 percent to investors and that the issued preferred stock may have varying maturities, which may or may not be cumulative.

15. Slack and Klock (2004, p. 6).

in 2004 so that the proportionate net interest income increased from 43 percent in 1995 to 49 percent in 2004.

The ratio of net interest income to gross interest income increased from 48 percent in 1995 to 58 percent in 2004. The ratio of net income to assets at the beginning of the period increased as well, from 0.9 percent in 1996 to 1.6 percent in 2004; and the ratio of net income to equity at the beginning of the period increased, with minor fluctuations, from 12.5 percent in 1996 to 21 percent in 2004. The income performance of commercial banks appears to be quite healthy, indeed.

The eight largest commercial banks in Puerto Rico had combined net income of $1.71 billion in 2004, an increase of $382.3 million, or 28.7 percent, over 2003. These banks, in order of income earned, are Banco Popular, Banco Santander, Eurobank, Doral Bank, Firstbank, Oriental Bank and Trust, R-G Premier Bank, and Westernbank.[16] A comparison of figures reported in the press with those in table 8A-5 suggests that some banks must have incurred losses.

Another approach to analyzing and evaluating the commercial banks in terms of their presence in the economy and their importance in the economic growth of Puerto Rico is to relate their assets to gross national product and compute other ratios, as has been done by the World Bank in analyses of the financial sector in the economic development of various national economies.[17] It should be noted that in the case of Puerto Rico there is a large discrepancy between GNP and GDP.[18] Gross national product measures the value of the production of a country that accrues to residents of that country, whereas GDP indicates the total production that took place inside that country, irrespective of how much of the income generated accrues to its residents. In some countries the value of the GDP is greater than GNP, and in others it is the opposite. However, these two measures are most commonly found to be the same or very close. In the case of Puerto Rico, GDP has through the years become larger than GNP because a good portion of the value produced in Puerto Rico—principally by manufacturing firms and more specifically by pharmaceutical companies operating on the island—is repatriated as profit to the U.S. mainland and does not remain on the island. In Puerto Rico, GDP per capita yields a much larger number than GNP per capita, although the lower figure is more meaningful. Consequently, for many types of analysis it is better to use the GNP measure in the case of Puerto Rico. With the passage of time, the commonwealth's GNP has become smaller as a percentage of GDP, falling from roughly 100 percent of GDP in 1963 to about 64 percent in 2004—a significant difference.

16. "La banca en Puerto Rico," *San Juan El Vocero,* January 31, 2004, p. 51.
17. Beck, Demirgüç-Kunt, and Levine (2000).
18. See Curet Cuevas (2003).

Figure 8-4. *Commercial Bank Assets, Puerto Rico, 1995–2003*
Percent

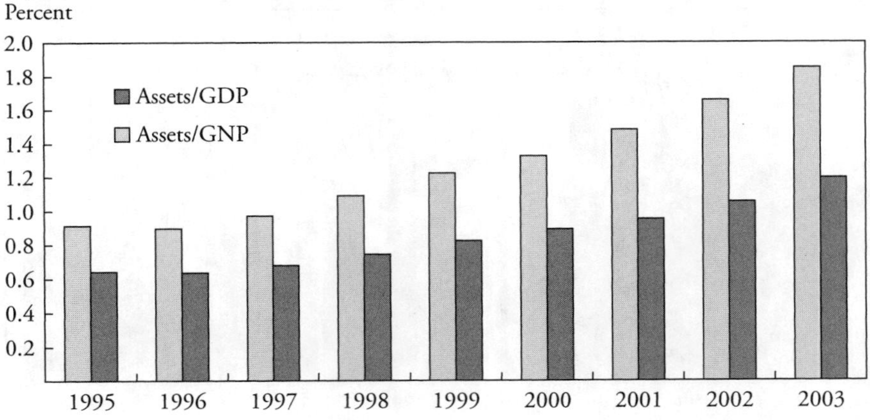

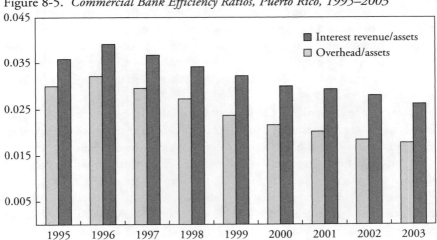

Source: Data from the Office of the Commissioner of Financial Institutions of Puerto Rico.

Figure 8-5. *Commercial Bank Efficiency Ratios, Puerto Rico, 1995–2003*

Source: Data from the Office of the Commissioner of Financial Institutions of Puerto Rico.

Figure 8-4 presents commercial bank assets as a percentage of GDP and GNP. It is clear that these assets have increased quite dramatically relative to total economic activity. In this respect the banking industry is doing quite well, and Puerto Rico is comparable to the high-income group of countries presented in the World Bank study cited earlier.

The efficiency of commercial banks as measured by the ratio of net interest margin or interest revenue to assets is quite impressive (see figure 8-5). Equally

Figure 8-6. *Commercial Bank Competitiveness Ratios, Puerto Rico, 1995–2003*

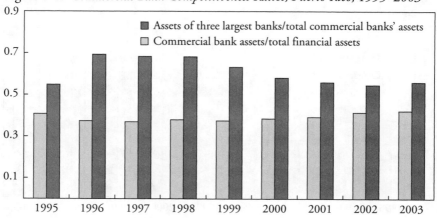

Source: Data from the Office of the Commissioner of Financial Institutions of Puerto Rico.

impressive is the relationship of overhead costs to assets in the same figure. Normally, one would expect these margins to decline, reflecting increased efficiency in the market—for example, profit margins drop with competition and the ratio of operating costs to assets declines because of the better technologies and management controls induced by competition and perhaps by larger-size institutions.

Other important indicators of the sophistication of the banking sector on the island are concentration ratios and diversification of financial intermediary presence, shown in figure 8-6. Both indicators are positive in the sense that the former, the three-firm concentration ratio (assets of the three largest commercial banks as a percentage of assets of the Puerto Rican banking sector), has declined back to its 1996 level, after increases in the late 1990s. This decline, although not significant, indicates an improvement in the competitiveness of the industry and suggests that more efficient banking has emerged, which ultimately benefits consumers.

Finally, commercial bank assets as a percentage of the assets of all financial institutions (figure 8-6) shows a slight decline from 1995 to 1996 but a slight overall increase from 1995 to 2003, indicating that this group of financial intermediaries is holding its ground. Table 8-1 shows a similar relationship, including the government banks.

This discussion is based on the World Bank approach to analyzing and evaluating financial institutions' performance. We believe, however, that the commercial banks in Puerto Rico could have played a more effective role in development if they had undertaken a more aggressive approach in lending to commerce and industry as opposed to investing in securities and real estate lending. We conclude that commercial banks have not been able to allocate funds to economic development through commercial and industrial loans as much as would seem appropriate for a developing economy. Nor have they been able to generate significant savings and checking deposits from the household sector to stimulate domestic savings to help in the creation of self-sustained economic development, as discussed in chapter 1 of this book.

Moreover, the high leverage of commercial banks may represent a serious concern for Puerto Rico and may constrain the ability to book commercial and industrial loans. The trade-off between using funds for development and using them in more liquid forms is not easily resolved.

International Banking Entities

International banking entities were allowed to engage in offshore activity in Puerto Rico by Law 16 of July 1980. The intent of the law was to develop in Puerto Rico a major international banking center. However, the international business entities did not begin to flourish until 1996, after a major amendment to the original 1980 law.[19] Since 1995 there have been forty-four licensed IBEs in Puerto Rico, although they may not all have been in operation in any given year during the decade. As of September 30, 2004, thirty-five IBEs were operating in Puerto Rico. Most of them are controlled by a local commercial bank. Others are owned by foreign banks that do not operate in Puerto Rico as commercial banks, and still others are owned by manufacturing corporations— for example, pharmaceutical companies. The two largest IBEs have between $11 billion and $21 billion in assets each; one other institution has more than $5 billion, and eight institutions have between $1.5 billion and $3 billion each. Of these major IBEs, only one is not affiliated with a commercial bank operating in Puerto Rico. Over the past decade, IBEs more than tripled their assets, and they are now the second largest player among island financial institutions (see table 8A-1).

The expectation was that the IBEs would significantly increase employment as well as attract real investors to Puerto Rico. This did not materialize, and the Office of the Commissioner of Financial Institutions developed a proposal to amend the law once again to establish a 10 percent income tax rate on all IBEs in order to increase government revenues. To evaluate this proposal, the commissioner ordered a review of the IBE sector by outside consultants, resulting in several well-reasoned conclusions.[20]

The first was that the Puerto Rico Internal Revenue Code be amended to provide that all income derived from activity in Puerto Rico in relation to off-

19. It is interesting to note that this amendment to the 1980 law coincided with the elimination of the federal tax exemption to all U.S. corporations that earned income in the island (section 936 of the federal Tax Reform Act of 1976).

20. See Lockwood (2003, including app. 4 therein).

shore operations should be exempt from Puerto Rico income tax. Offshore activity would be defined to require that both the source and the use of the funds generating the income be derived and applied outside Puerto Rico. In addition, all of the other tax benefits accorded to IBEs would be retained and specified in the tax law.

The logic for this recommendation was twofold. First, the law that applies to IBEs specifically does not ensure the needed transparency and leaves room for the wide discretion of the Office of the Commissioner of Financial Institutions, as well as for "secret tax rulings or the ability of persons to negotiate a separate and particular tax rate, unique unto itself," whereas a law included as part of the Internal Revenue Code will be uniform and consistent. Second, "In the modern world of globalization, foreign trade becomes increasingly important for a jurisdiction's economy to survive and grow."[21] The report notes:

> Cross-border trade and investment has grown substantially over the past decade. International investment, and the encouragement of enticing international investors into a jurisdiction, plays an important role in the effort to survive and grow. Under a system of taxation whereby only income derived in the taxing jurisdiction is taxed, it is conceivable that that jurisdiction is in a position to better attract more investment capital and increase its share in the marketplace of international finance. A government's tax policies affect the likelihood of successful importation of capital and make it available for growth by its own residents. . . . [In] general, increased capital formation increases labor and its productivity. Accordingly, any increase in foreign investment in Puerto Rico can be expected to enhance the welfare of the Puerto Rico labor force, while enticing the exiting of that investment can have the opposite effect. The unhindered flow of investment, be it domestic or foreign, in Puerto Rico with a view to convert Puerto Rico into a major international banking center, if properly addressed, can lead to additional productive resources in Puerto Rico. . . . [Furthermore, it can facilitate] the realization of cost-efficient scales of business if operations currently conducted in other offshore banking centers are transferred to Puerto Rico because of its new attractiveness.[22]

The second recommendation was that an IBE, or any other entity claiming the tax benefits established in Law 16, must not have a minimum employment level but "must have a permanent establishment ('PE') in Puerto Rico. The PE would conform to the requisites provided by the OECD [Organization for Eco-

21. Lockwood (2003, app. 4, pp. 93, 3).
22. Lockwood (2003, app. 4, p. 93).

nomic Cooperation and Development] in this respect. That is, the PE must, in essence maintain a place of business the operations of which play a major factor in the production of the offshore income." This permanent establishment must meet a series of other OECD requirements but in particular, adequacy of capital, transparency of assets used, and transparency of risks assumed. "The interrelationship between the IBE and the PE nexus would encourage job creation since the mere booking of transactions would not conform to the modernized concepts of an offshore banking operation; rather, the requirement of substantial presence would serve to generate the job creation that Puerto Rico seeks."[23]

The third recommendation was that the relevant Puerto Rican authorities attempt to participate in U.S. tax treaties with other countries as well as in tax information exchange agreements. These treaties, as well as information exchange agreements, create an environment that is more attractive to cross-border investors. The United States has administrative tax agreements, which minimize double taxation from income earned by companies that do business in both locations, with approximately sixty countries. These agreements stimulate trade and cross-border economic and financial transactions in general. Puerto Rico, not being a state, does not participate in these agreements; however, many of the countries with whom the United States engages in such agreements include in their agreements their territories and possessions. It would be important for Puerto Rico to try to reach the appropriate channels to discuss and change the current conditions with respect to tax treaties. If this were accomplished, it would make Puerto Rico a more attractive environment for investors as well as for IBEs as envisioned for the future. Even an established IBE may well be able to begin paying a share of taxes in Puerto Rico, as they do in Ireland and other areas where the "offshore" entities have a high reputation and abide by many of the recommendations of the OECD, the International Monetary Fund, the Basel Committee on Banking Supervision, and other worldwide international organizations that promote an equal playing field for countries to promote development and increase worldwide welfare.

Finally, it was recommended that Puerto Rico set up a special organization to announce to the world that the government of Puerto Rico supports the establishment of IBEs and to advertise the myriad conditions that make Puerto Rico an ideal location for "offshore" activities such as the following:

—political stability

—an excellent communication system, including the two most commonly used languages in cross-border activity, English and Spanish

—excellent and worldwide banking facilities

—nonmonetary exchange controls

—withholding-tax exemptions on most interest and dividend payments

23. Lockwood (2003, app. 4, p. 94).

—a commercial legal system based on well-established U.S. law

—a regulatory environment in accordance with international watchdog organizations such as the OECD, the International Monetary Fund, and the Basel Committee of bank regulators

—a competitive wage structure

—freedom to locate operations anywhere on the island

—availability of a young, well-educated workforce

These recommendations were made to help Puerto Rico attract not only IBEs but also industrial investment from various sources and increase the creation of jobs in new manufacturing and service industries, specifically, in the new back-office service industry needed by the IBEs and other outsourcing companies on the U.S. mainland. This could help materially in absorbing Puerto Rico's well-educated labor force.

The balance sheet items as a percentage of total assets of the IBEs are presented in table 8-4. (See also tables 8A-6 and 8A-7.) As shown, the assets of these institutions grew at a compound growth rate of 15 percent a year over the period 1995–2004. Their principal assets were securities holdings, balances due from related parties, and loans and leases; major liabilities included external and related-party borrowings. Net income increased from 3 percent of total revenues in 1995 to 28 percent in 2004, while net interest income as a percentage of total interest income grew from 16 percent in 1995 to 48 percent in 2004. Net income as a percentage of total assets was 0.2 percent in 1996 and 1.2 percent in 2004, and net income relative to equity was 1.9 percent in 1996 and increased to 6.6 percent in 2004 (table 8A-7). Clearly, these institutions were growing not only in assets but in profitability as well.

Insurance Companies

Insurance companies were founded in Puerto Rico during the period 1892–1921, emerging at the beginning of the Spanish-American War.[24] The Office of the Commissioner of Insurance, created in 1921 as the Bureau of Insurance and later called the Superintendent of Insurance, is today the supervisor and regulator of the insurance industry on the island. The only recent significant change in the industry was induced by the 1999 U.S. Gramm-Leach-Bliley Act, which brought to an end the separation of insurance and banking. All local laws had to be amended to take into account the new federal legislation, and by 2000 several banks had established or acquired insurance subsidiaries. As of 2003 there were approximately 312 insurance companies in Puerto Rico, of which only 50 were domestic or local.

Although local insurance companies are a distinct minority, they do have by far the largest premium share of the market. In 2003 their share was 87 percent,

24. The interesting history of this industry may be found in Ferrao (2003).

Table 8-4. *International Banking Entities' Balance Sheet as Share of Total Assets, Puerto Rico, Selected Years, 1995–2004*

Percent, except as indicated

Item	1995	2000	2004	CAGR[a]
Total assets	100	100	100	15.4
Cash	0.2	0.6	0.7	36.0
Banks' placement	74.5	0.2	1.2	−27.2
Securities	16.3	21.0	42.4	28.3
Loans and leases	3.3	20.1	27.1	45.8
Federal funds sold	3.0	0.5	0.7	−1.8
Due from related parties	0	55.5	23.4	150.7
Other assets	2.7	2.1	4.5	22.3
Total liabilities and stockholders' equity	100.0	100.0	100.0	13.9
Total liabilities	92.1	85.5	81.9	13.9
Deposits	71.9	13.9	13.5	−4.2
Demand deposits	. . .	1.7	1.3	45.9
Time and savings deposits	. . .	12.3	12.2	37.7
Liabilities	20.2	71.5	68.4	13.9
Federal funds purchased	4.2	3.3	2.5	8.6
Borrowings	13.8	16.0	41.4	30.4
Due to related parties	0	51.5	23.4	−1.6
Other liabilities	2.2	0.7	1.1	7.4
Stockholders' equity	7.9	14.5	18.1	26.4
Total assets (millions of dollars)	18,404	44,255	66,751	15.4

Source: Data from the Office of the Commissioner of Financial Institutions of Puerto Rico.
a. Cumulative annual growth rate, 1995–2004, computed using first nonzero entry.

up from 78 percent in 1991 (see table 8A-8). Note that the data show the breakdown by domestic insurers and international insurers, as well as by type of insurance.

As shown in tables 8-1 and 8A-1, insurance companies accounted for $7.1 billion of the total $78.5 billion financial sector assets in 1995, and for $12.0 billion of the total $218.0 billion in June 2004.[25] Proportionately, insurance companies are a smaller player in the financial system than they were ten years ago, with 9.0 percent of the total sector in 1995 and 5.5 percent in June 2004, a decline of 3.5 percent. Their compound annual growth rate was only 6 percent over the period. However, this is not true of the domestic insurers, as shown in

25. Office of the Commissioner of Insurance for the Commonwealth of Puerto Rico (1993–2001) shows the total global assets of international insurance companies operating on the island. To estimate the portion of the assets in Puerto Rico, we first computed the average premiums-to-assets ratio for the top five insurance companies in the world for each type of insurance (that is, life, and property and casualty). We then divided the premiums of the international insurers active in Puerto Rico by the corresponding insurance-type ratio to arrive at an estimated figure for assets of these insurers in Puerto Rico.

Table 8-5. *Selected Aspects of Insurance Companies' Income Statement,*
Puerto Rico, 2003
Units as indicated

Item	Number of companies reported	Premiums earned (millions of dollars)	Net income (millions of dollars)	Net income/ premiums (percent)
Domestic	50	4,279	231	5.4
HMO	12	1,321	39	3.0
Property and casualty	22	1,101	125	11.4
Life, accident, and health	16	1,857	67	3.6
Foreign	237	400	27	6.9
Property and casualty	121	128	11	8.7
Life, accident, and health	116	271	16	6.1
Total domestic and foreign	287	404	27	6.9

Source: Data from the Office of the Commissioner of Insurance of Puerto Rico.

table 8A-8, which increased their assets from $1.7 billion to $5.0 billion, at an annual compound growth rate of 9.4 percent; and their proportionate share of the total financial sector declined by only 1.2 percent, from 3.5 percent in 1995 to 2.3 percent in 2003. Insurance companies as well as commercial banks grew in total assets, but other financial intermediaries grew at a faster rate, so that both of these institutions' assets were a smaller proportion of the total financial sector assets in 2003 and 2004 than they had been in 1992 and 1995.[26] The only income data made available to us by the Office of the Commissioner of Insurance, which were provided by reporting companies for 2003, are in reference to the income earned relative to the premiums issued by domestic and foreign insurers and by category, as shown in table 8-5.

Evaluating the insurance industry in Puerto Rico, we observe that the density ratios of insurance companies on the island increased over the period (see figure 8-7) and are rather high and comparable to the high-income countries as classified by the World Bank database.[27] Consequently, the dollar premiums per inhabitant in Puerto Rico are rather high. Similarly, the assets-to-GNP ratio and the penetration measure (premiums-to-GNP ratio) show trends similar to those experienced by the high-income, high–economic development group of countries in the World Bank classification. Comparable trends can be observed for domestic and foreign insurers in figure 8-8. It is interesting to note that

26. The major missing aspects in assessing the insurance sector are their investments, distributed by type of financial asset and whether those investments are in island securities or external market securities. Also missing are data from the income statements for the period covered in this chapter, which would permit an analysis of profitability and efficiency of this important subset of financial intermediaries in Puerto Rico.

27. Beck, Demirgüç-Kunt, and Levine (2000).

Figure 8-7. *Insurance Industry Indicators, Puerto Rico, 1991–2003*

Dollars per inhabitant

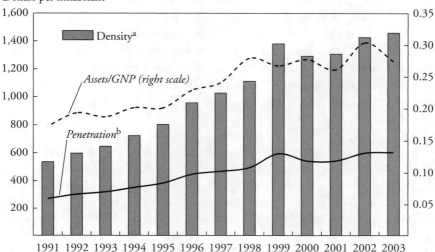

Source: Data from the Office of the Commissioner of Insurance of Puerto Rico.
a. Premiums per population (left scale).
b. Assets/GNP (right scale).

Figure 8-8. *Insurer Density Ratios, Domestic and Foreign Insurers, Puerto Rico, 1991–2003*[a]

Dollars per inhabitant

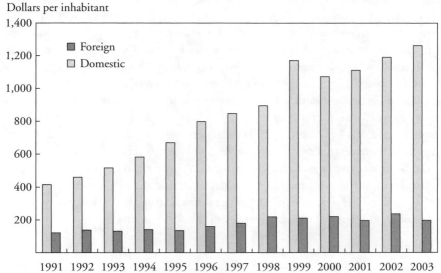

Source: Data from the Office of the Commissioner of Insurance of Puerto Rico.
a. Premiums per inhabitant.

domestic insurers have performed better than foreign insurers in the measures that we were able to obtain from the Office of the Commissioner of Insurance in Puerto Rico. Although the domestic firms are fewer in number (fifty firms, or 17 percent of the total), their premiums have accounted for the larger proportion of the total premiums and have grown at a much faster pace—accounting for the relatively large increase in their density. The penetration measure of the domestic firms (not shown) is also relatively superior to the total sector of insurers in figure 8-7.

Investment Companies

There are approximately forty-one investment companies (mutual funds) in Puerto Rico today, compared with only ten in 1995. Most of them are owned by five major players such as UBS AG, Banco Popular, Banco Santander, Citigroup Smith Barney, and Oriental Securities. By far the largest player is UBS, followed by Banco Popular. The managed assets of this group of institutions grew at a compound annual rate of 44 percent (see table 8-1), from $500 million in 1995 to $11,800 million in 2004. From table 8A-9, it is evident that the larger portion of their asset allocation is in Puerto Rican domestic securities, followed by investments in U.S. securities. Their major source of funds is individuals and companies, followed by loans. The rapid growth experienced by these institutions is an indication that individuals are channeling their savings to mutual funds. This would tend to run counter to the negative savings reported in the Puerto Rican national income accounts, so that some of these funds may be part of the underground economy discussed in chapter 1. Since most of their investments are in local financial instruments, and since most of their funds come from individuals, these dynamic organizations are essential in the savings-investment process that helps develop a much-needed local capital market in Puerto Rico. Unfortunately, they are still a rather small component of the island's financial sector, especially relative to commercial banks.

Table 8A-10 shows that the net interest income of investment companies grew from $54 million in 1997 to $414 million in 2004, at a compound annual growth rate of 34 percent. In 2004 net interest income as a percentage of total revenue increased from 39 percent in 1997 to 47 percent, and net interest income as a percentage of interest revenue increased from 65 percent to 84 percent. Net income as a percentage of total assets and net income as a percentage of total equity experienced significant swings during the period but averaged around 4 and 6 percent, respectively, over the entire period.

Mortgage Companies

Today there are some fifty mortgage companies operating in Puerto Rico. This is a significant increase over the twenty-eight operating in 1995. The growth in the number of companies has been matched by growth in the assets of these institutions, as well. Table 8A-11 shows that the annual growth of the assets of this group of institutions was 23 percent for the period 1995–2004. Their assets grew from $1.3 billion in 1995 to $8.3 billion in 2004. Their primary activity is to lend funds for real estate, especially home purchases—which accounted for between 23 and 44 percent of total assets during the period. Shorter-term loans showed an increasing trend as a percentage of total assets, with 3 percent at the beginning of the period and 29 percent at the end of the period. The relative importance of securities varied considerably during this period, from 16 to 53 percent of total assets. Mortgage companies' main sources of funds are loans from banks, parent companies, and others, which account for between 29 and 79 percent of total assets. Equity is the other major source of funds, which showed a steady upward trend (from 16 percent to 37 percent of total assets) during the period. Total revenue increased at an annual rate of 23 percent. Net income as a percentage of total revenue, shown in table 8A-12, increased from 20 percent in 1995 to 54 percent in 2004. All other profitability measures presented in the table show a healthy increasing trend.

The economic activity revealed in their financial statements is not the only type of transactions mortgage companies perform. They also service significant volumes of mortgage loans for investors on the U.S. mainland whose mortgages are backed by properties owned by local residents in Puerto Rico. Table 8A-4 shows that mortgage companies serviced almost 65 percent of the total $217.2 billion in mortgages servicing outstanding for the period 1995–2004. The income generated by mortgage companies from providing this service appears in the income statement in table 8A-12 as "other fee revenue" and shows increasing annual revenues, from $66 million in 1995 to $118 million in 2004, growing at 7 percent annually, whereas the volume of mortgages shown in table 8A-4 grew at 15 percent annually over the same period. Other fee revenue from mortgage service in table 8A-12 represents around 40 percent of total revenue for the period 1995–98, whereas for the period 2000–04 this revenue source is only between 11 and 20 percent of total revenue, clearly a declining trend.

Credit Unions

Credit unions or credit cooperatives, as they are also called, have been operating in Puerto Rico since the late 1950s. Although they have grown in volume of assets from $3.2 billion in 1995 to $5.9 billion in 2004, which represents an annual growth of 7 percent over the ten-year period (see table 8A-13), they have diminished in number. In 1995 there were 197 credit unions operating in Puerto Rico; in 2004 there were only 140. Individuals buy shares in these institutions, which entitles them as members to place deposits at relatively high interest rates and obtain loans at relatively low rates. The credit unions' objective is to stimulate savings and make low-cost financing available to members. Their major source of funds is member deposits, which represented an increasing trend with 67 percent to 73 percent of total assets for the period 1995 to 2004. The second major source of funds is capital (mostly member shares), which fluctuated between 26 and 31 percent of total assets for the period. Funds are used mainly for loans to individual members of the cooperative, for automobile financing, personal loans, credit card loans, mortgages, and other consumer uses of finance. Loans represented between 58 and 71 percent of total assets over the period covered and have been declining since 2000. Total revenues increased at an annual rate of 6 percent (see table 8A-14). Net income as a percentage of total revenue moved erratically between 7 and 14 percent over the period but shows an upward trend over the last five years. Net income as a percentage of assets shows no trend during the period and has fluctuated between 0.6 and 1.2 percent. Finally, net income as a percentage of equity, with an increasing trend during the last five years of the period, shows variability between 2.3 and 3.9 percent. Although these institutions are technically nonprofits, whatever profit is made is paid out in dividends to member shareholders.

Finance Companies

The number of finance institutions increased from twenty firms in 1995 to forty-six firms in 2004. Their asset growth over the period was 11 percent, as shown in table 8A-15. The major sources of funds for these companies were loans from banks, parent companies, and others, which fluctuated between 66 and 75 percent of total assets. Finance companies provide funds primarily for equipment leasing for businesses and individuals, shown as net loans and leases in table 8A-15. Their income has grown at an annual rate of 9 percent, from $255 million in 1995 to $570 million in 2004 (see table 8A-16). Net income has been between 10 and 19 percent of total revenue over the period.

Broker-Dealers

About thirty-seven broker-dealers were licensed to operate in Puerto Rico during the period from 1995 to 2004, though not all were operating in any single year. In 1995 only eleven were active, and in 2004 only nineteen. In 1995 nineteen broker-dealers submitted financial statements to the Office of the Commissioner of Financial Institutions, but in 2004 only nine.[28] Table 8A-17 shows that assets of all broker-dealers reporting over the period 1995–2004 declined from $3.7 billion to $2.4 billion. The decline in reporting institutions can partially explain the overall decline. Table 8A-17 also shows broker-dealers' sources and uses of funds, and table 8A-18 shows their income statement.

---

28. The criteria that determine which broker-dealers are required to submit financial statements are determined by the Office of the Commissioner of Financial Institutions and they are mainly related to asset size. Only the broker-dealers with significant levels of assets are required to submit. For the report of customer assets under control, all broker-dealers having customers' assets under their control are required to supply these data.

All operating broker-dealers who have customer assets under control are required to show the funds they are managing on behalf of their customers. Table 8A-19 shows that the volume of funds managed by these institutions is very large. In 1995 assets of $8.5 billion were under the management of broker-dealers in Puerto Rico; at the end of December 2004, that number had more than tripled, to $26.2 billion. These institutions are much more important than their total assets would suggest. By collecting savings and investing them into equities and fixed-income investments, these institutions perform an important intermediary function. Of the total amount of funds managed in 2004, 41 percent were invested in equities and 59 percent in fixed-income securities. These funds were invested mainly in the Puerto Rican and U.S. capital markets; the proportions invested in each are not available.

What is clear is the volume of local funds saved by individuals and companies—a total of $26.2 billion in 2004. This is a remarkable amount for an island that supposedly has negative savings. Perhaps a significant proportion of these funds originated in the underground economy, but they nonetheless represent a form of savings. There might also be some double-counting, since some of the funds reported in table 8A-19 may be included in the balance sheets of the investment companies as well as those of the broker-dealers. In the opinion of the Office of the Commissioner of Financial Institutions, this duplication is not large, and currently the office is in the process of making sure that there is no double-counting, correcting data as necessary. It would seem that the intermediation function performed by broker-dealers is more in line with the economic development function of financial intermediation, for example, transferring household and business savings to ultimate users of funds for use in real capital formation. Still, the total volume of funds these institutions command is not as large as the funds that commercial banks handle.

Leasing Companies and Small-Loan Companies

Nineteen leasing companies were active in Puerto Rico in 2004, up from twelve institutions in 1995. Their assets grew from $986 million in 1995 to $2 billion in 2004, an 8 percent compound annual growth rate (see table 8A-20). Their main activity is to provide loans and leases to customers. Net loans and leases receivable represent between 76 and 82 percent of total assets during the period. The major sources of leasing companies' funding were current liabilities during the first seven years and long-term liabilities during the last three years. Income from operations, shown in table 8A-21, increased from $183 million in 1995 to $333 million in 2004. The ratio of net income to total revenue over the period was a healthy 10 to 14 percent. The profitability ratios are also presented. Clearly, though declining in the number of institutions leasing companies have been increasing in size and profitability.

There were seven small-loan companies operating in Puerto Rico at the end of 2004, down from fourteen in 1995 and many more before that. As table 8A-22 shows, small-loan companies' total assets declined from $2.1 billion in 1995 to $1.3 billion in 2004; the major component of the assets was net loans and leases receivable, ranging from 47 to 83 percent of total assets. The most important source of funding came from bank loans. Income declined from $308 million to $284 million between 1995 and 2004 (see table 8A-23), and profitability has been erratic.

Venture Capital Firms

In 2004 twelve venture capital firms were operating in Puerto Rico, one fewer than in 1995, and their assets grew from $68.1 million in 1995 to $142.9 million in 2004 (see table 8A-24). Although the number of firms is not large, this type of institution is vital for economic development because of its role in assuming high risks while investing long term in new ventures. Small in size, these firms appear to focus on leading-edge industries such as biotechnology, disseminating important operational and market skills. Accordingly, securities portfolio investments in new innovative companies dominate venture capital firms' assets—between 50 and 84 percent during the ten-year period under consideration. Their major source of funds is equity, which consisted of 86 to 99 percent of total assets. Their profitability in Puerto Rico has been erratic, as shown in table 8A-25.

Stock Market

There is no stock market in Puerto Rico. However, in August 1995 the Government Development Bank contracted Wilshire Associates to develop a stock market index for Puerto Rico so as to capture the total return history of all publicly traded stocks of corporations headquartered on the island. The economic objective of this index was to encourage the growth of a private, equity-oriented capital market structure, attract capital investment, and create a measure of the economic success of companies operating and investing in the commonwealth. The index was created using a Wilshire-accepted computation methodology for ten companies headquartered on the island that had been trading in the U.S. equity markets.[29] In terms of market value, in 1995 the financial sector represented 78.7 percent of these companies, 7.7 percent of materials and services, and 13.6 percent of utilities.

Today the index is still in use as an indicator of the financial health of the nine companies that are included therein. Eight of the nine are financial institu-

29. Wilshire Associates (1995). The ten companies included were BanPonce Corporation, Cellular Communications of Puerto Rico, First Financial Caribbean Corporation, Firstbank of Puerto Rico, Interstate General Corporation, Margo Nursery Farms, Oriental Bank and Trust, Ponce-Bank, Puerto Rican Cement, and Westernbank of Puerto Rico.

tions, and one is the tropical plant grower, Margo Nursery Farms. No longer in the index are Puerto Rican Cement, as it was sold to Mexico's Cemex, and Cellular Communications of Puerto Rico, and some of the finance companies have been replaced by others, mainly as a result of acquisitions. The companies included originally had headquarters on the island, but whether all the companies in the index today have their headquarters in Puerto Rico is not clear. The index continues to be used primarily as an indicator of the banking sector, whose recent performance has shown an increase of 38 percent in 2004 from 14,637.32 at the beginning of the year to 20,207.81 at the end of the year. This increase was four times that of the S&P 500, which increased only 9.3 percent, and five times that of the Nasdaq (8.4 percent). However, from January to April 2005 the Puerto Rican stock market index dropped by 42 percent to 11,700, reflecting the performance of the banking sector.

The Government Development Bank

The Government Development Bank (GDB) was created in 1942 as the Development Bank of Puerto Rico.[30] At that time, Puerto Rico was a very poor economy that had recently acquired local political autonomy and had a cadre of honest, creative, and dedicated professionals in government and its agencies, institutions that began the task of developing the island. The GDB was empowered to serve as fiscal agent for the government, and legislative appropriations were made to provide the bank with its initial capital of $500,000, raised to $20 million in 1945. In addition to fiscal agency, the GDB served as depository and trustee of government funds, lender to the government and the private sector—although not in competition with private sector financial institutions—and financial adviser to the governor and public agencies, corporations, and instrumentalities, including the municipalities.[31]

In its beginning, the GDB financed several large industrial projects that were owned directly by the government. These included a cement plant, a glass-bottle manufacturing plant, construction of the Caribe Hilton Hotel in San Juan, and others. In 1948 the GDB undertook its first bond issue on behalf of the government of Puerto Rico for improvements to the island's electricity infrastructure. This marked the beginning of the bank's effort to create a market on the U.S. mainland for the debt obligations issued by the island government in order to secure access to short- and long-term funds. From the beginning, one of the main tasks of the GDB was to maintain the flow of economic information about Puerto Rico for the benefit of the U.S. and international investment community. In the 1950s the bank changed its role in the development process

30. See *Anotadas Leyes de Puerto Rico,* Titles 6 and 7, and Cumulative Supplement to Be Used during 2004, 2000 ed. (San Juan, 2004).

31. To avoid competition with private banks, the GDB undertook novel projects regarded as too risky by the private sector. Some of these risky projects were successful; others were not.

from hands-on projects, owned by the government, to promoter of private enterprises and financial facilitator. By 1959 most of the loans granted by the bank went to local private enterprises that could not secure funding from private financial institutions. But its major role has been to operate successfully in the dynamic and competitive financial markets in the United States.

As fiscal agent as well as adviser to the government of Puerto Rico, the GDB responsibilities, beyond fundraising, include serving as a watchdog regarding the way public funds are expended. It advises the Office of the Governor, with, among others, the island's Office of Management and Budget and Department of Treasury, in developing economic initiatives and assisting in the formulation and implementation of financial solutions that facilitate the execution of public policy. In these multiple capacities the GDB has experienced conflicting roles.

Financial Statements. The GDB's balance sheet and income statement data for the period from 1995 to 2004 are presented in tables 8-6, 8A-26, and 8A-27. The balance sheet is strong, as should be that of an institution that serves as a fiscal agent of the government, particularly one that serves as the transaction agent in the international capital markets for all securities issued by the Commonwealth of Puerto Rico, its instrumentalities, corporations, and municipalities. The largest share of the bank's assets consists of commercial and industrial loans. Originally, these were granted to local private industry, as well as to government industrial projects undertaken by the various government agencies. Today, virtually all GDB loans are made to Puerto Rico government units of one type or another. Loans in this category amounted to $5.1 billion, 68 percent of its total assets, in 2004. Most of the rest of the bank's assets are held in investments and securities. It is interesting to note that the bank has grown at about the same rate as the economy as a whole, with a compound annual growth rate of 2 percent over the period 1995–2004.

The major components of the other side of the balance sheet are deposits of government institutions—constituting between 43 and 58 percent of total assets during the ten-year period. Equity, which fluctuated over the period, ranging from $1.1 billion to $2.2 billion, represented between 18 and 35 percent of total assets (see table 8A-26). The GDB's income statement (see table 8A-27) reflects declining total revenue from $229 million in 1995 to $170 million in 2004. The profitability of the GDB from year to year was erratic in terms of the four basic profitability measures;—the bank is financially healthy but not very profitable, which is consistent with its status.

Bond Flotations by the GDB. Between April 1993 and June 2004, the GDB raised a total of $51.7 billion in U.S. and international capital markets, of which $34.4 billion was new money to be invested in projects and the remainder, $17.2 billion, was to be used in refunding outstanding debt (table 8A-28). Total savings realized in refunding operations amounting to $204.5 million during this period. In addition, through one of its affiliates (the Puerto Rico Industrial, Tourist,

Table 8-6. *Government Development Bank's Balance Sheet as Share of Total Assets, Puerto Rico, Selected Years, 1995–2004*

Percent, except as indicated

Item	1995	2000	2004	CAGR[a]
Total assets	100	100	100	2.0
Cash and interest-bearing placements	0.3	1.8	0.2	−2.7
Investments and securities	56.3	26.2	12.2	−13.9
Federal funds sold and securities purchased	0.0	0.0	7.1	0
Loans and leases, net, including commercial, industrial, and agricultural	35.1	57.1	68.1	9.8
Other assets	8.3	14.9	12.5	6.7
Total liabilities and equity	100	100	100	2.0
Total liabilities	82.5	72.0	75.1	1.0
Total deposits	55.6	45.5	58.1	2.5
Liabilities	26.9	26.5	17.0	−3.0
Long-term debt	23.8	4.4	n.a.	−17.5
Short-term debt	1.8	21.1	n.a.	30.6
Other liabilities	1.3	1.0	17.0	35.5
Equity	17.5	28.0	24.9	6.1
Total assets (millions of dollars)	6,329	6,057	7,585	2.0

Source: Data from the Office of the Commissioner of Financial Institutions of Puerto Rico.
a. Cumulative annual growth rate, 1995–2004.

Educational, Medical, and Environmental Control Facilities Financing Authority, AFICA) the bank raised an additional $5.9 billion from May 1978 to August 2004—primarily for private-sector firms operating in Puerto Rico (table 8A-29).

Financing the Government Deficit. The GDB's performance has declined in stature owing to its loss of independence as a fiscal agent and economic adviser to the government. This is reflected in several forms such as the increasing size of the government bureaucracy, the growing proportion of government employment in Puerto Rico, and the increasing fiscal deficit. In recent years, the government budget has been able to meet the legal requirement that it be balanced only by borrowing large sums at ten-year terms from the GDB, raising questions about future debt service and crowding out of commercial and industrial financing. This problem finally emerged in late 2004, with a warning to the bank by Moody's Investors Service that its bond rating could be in jeopardy. On May 19, 2005, Moody's downgraded the Commonwealth of Puerto Rico general obligation bonds to Baa2 from Baa1 and kept the rating outlook negative. On May 24, 2005, Standard and Poor's ratings service lowered its rating on the Commonwealth of Puerto Rico general obligation bonds to BBB from A—in response to weakening credit quality caused primarily by a growing general fund structural imbalance. Their outlook is negative, as well.[32]

The President's Term of Office. To illustrate the bank's loss of independence from the political process, we can examine the historical term of its presidents. From 1942 to 2004 inclusive, a period of sixty-three years, there have been eighteen presidents, who have served an average of 3.5 years. This is not a particularly long term of office, yet it becomes shorter with time. The first twenty-eight years (1942 to 1969) saw only four presidents, each of whom served, on average, 7 years. Adding the presidency of Julio Pietrantoni, which lasted for 8 years (from 1978 to 1985), increases the average tenure of the president to 7.2 years. However, during the last thirty-five years there have been fourteen presidents, with an average of 2.5 years in office, and during the final six years there were four, with an average tenure of only 1.5 years. It is unlikely that an institution of such importance as the GDB can successfully carry out its mandate with a leadership that is changing every two and a half years or even more frequently. It appears that if the president of the bank were to disagree with what the Puerto Rican government's executive branch wants—for example, to balance the commonwealth budget by borrowing from the GDB—the presidential tenure could come to an abrupt end.[33]

The GDB is a sizable financial institution in the Puerto Rican context. With more than $7.5 billion in assets as of June 2004, it is Puerto Rico's fourth largest bank. Moreover, given the amount of funding and the operations of its five subsidiaries, four affiliates, and the many other commonwealth corporations to which it supplies assistance in various forms, particularly in securing funding, the impact of the bank in the Puerto Rican economy is significant indeed.[34]

Official Subsidiaries of the GDB. The Government Development Bank has five direct subsidiaries. The Puerto Rican Housing Finance Authority emerged in the latter part of 2004 from the merger of GDB's subsidiary, the Puerto Rico

32. See Moody's Investors Service (2005) and Standard and Poor's (2005).

33. The data used in this analysis come from Government Development Bank for Puerto Rico (1993–2003, 2002) and personal communication with former presidents of the Government Development Bank during December 2004. The former presidents referred to were in office only one or two years and bear no responsibility for our stated conclusions here.

34. The data presented in this section pertaining to the GDB subsidiaries, affiliates, and other commonwealth institutions with which the bank is closely related come from two sources: a series of pamphlets covering each subsidiary and affiliate, prepared by the GDB Office of Economic and Finance Studies, and the documents accompanying Commonwealth of Puerto Rico (2004, app. I). The latter document, issued for the bond flotation of the Puerto Rican commonwealth government, was prepared and revised by a multitude of lawyers, economists, and other executives and individuals at the GDB, the Office of the Treasury, the Office of Management and Budget of the Commonwealth of Puerto Rico, and the lead managers of the consortium issuing the bonds. This document was made available to us at GDB offices.

Housing Finance Corporation (created in 1977), and the commonwealth's Banco de la Vivienda (Bank for Housing Finance). It appears that U.S. regulators forced the closing of the Banco de la Vivienda, owing to financial discrepancies, and that the commonwealth sold the Banco de la Vivienda to the GDB and used the proceeds for capital investments. The result of these transactions is the Puerto Rico Housing Finance Authority, operating as a subsidiary of the GDB. The authority administers state and federal programs to finance the development and preservation of housing for low- and moderate-income families. It also provides financing at favorable interest rates to assist low- and moderate-income families in acquiring, building, or improving their homes. It has helped the Puerto Rico Department of Housing to promote the creation and rehabilitation of fifty thousand social-interest homes for the neediest families. During 2003 the housing authority had total investments of $921 million in its various programs, and its outstanding debt as of June 30, 2004, was $826.3 million.

Puerto Rico's Tourism Development Fund was created in 1993 to promote the development of the island's tourist industry by making partial or total guarantees available to secure payment of private financing used for new hotel development projects. It is also authorized to make capital investments and provide direct financing to tourism-related projects. As of June 30, 2004, the fund had outstanding loans and guarantees covering the financing of fourteen hotel and tourism-related projects, totaling some $562.5 million. Projects it has promoted or has helped establish include the Westin Río Mar Beach Resort and Casino, the Ritz-Carlton San Juan Hotel and Casino, and the Wyndham Old San Juan Hotel and Casino. The Tourism Development Fund has made payments under its guarantees and letters of credit in the aggregate amount of approximately $216.7 million with respect to several projects, including repayment in full of the bonds of three projects in which bonds had been declared due and payable at the fund's direction, owing to the failure of the borrowers to comply with their obligation under the related reimbursement agreements. After taking these payments and all related recoveries into consideration, the tourism fund's unrestricted net assets as of June 30, 2004, were approximately $92.4 million, and its allowance for loan losses on guarantees, loans, and letters of credit approximately $6.4 million.[35] This fund is managed by a GDB executive and operates out of the offices of the bank.

The Puerto Rico Development Fund, created in 1977, undertakes capital investments through the issuance of common or preferred stocks in enterprises that cannot obtain funds from other private financial institutions and are judged to be contributors to Puerto Rico's economic growth. The fund can

35. Commonwealth of Puerto Rico (2004, app. I, pp. 30, 31).

invest up to 30 percent of the total capital of individual businesses. It can also grant conventional loans or participate in loans issued by other institutions to qualifying enterprises, and it can be a guarantor in financing provided by private sector financial institutions. A GDB executive runs this fund within the bank's headquarters. In 2004 the fund financed or invested approximately $17 million.

The Capital Fund was created in 1992 to facilitate investment activities at the GDB. Its main objective is to diversify and increase the yield of the GDB's portfolio. It trades in debt obligations and shares of domestic and foreign corporations. An executive of the GDB oversees this fund, which, like the Capital Fund, is administered at GDB headquarters.

A final GDB subsidiary is the Puerto Rico Public Finance Corporation, which was created in 1984 to provide alternative financing options to agencies and instrumentalities of the government. It has the capacity to borrow money and issue debt through its own bond issues and other obligations. Some issues are intended for refinancing current debt of other government entities at lower interest rates, while others are for new money raised for the same instrumentalities. As of June 30, 2004, the corporation had $4.333 billion in bonds outstanding. Most of these had been issued to purchase debt of agencies and instrumentalities of the commonwealth and are payable from commonwealth appropriations. An executive at the GDB oversees this operation.

In addition to its direct subsidiaries, the GDB has four affiliated organizations. The Puerto Rico Industrial, Tourist, Educational, Medical, and Environmental Control Facilities Financing Authority (AFICA). This affiliate was created in 1977 and has periodically issued revenue bonds to finance industrial, educational, medical, and environmental control facilities for the use of private companies, nonprofit entities, and government agencies. Since its inception, it has issued more than $5.9 billion in bonds (see table 8A-29), of which approximately $2.2 billion were outstanding as of June 30, 2004. The authority lowers the cost of financing for its clients by forming large baskets of obligations of multiple firms and institutions before issuing a single large flotation, effectively securitizing the debt. Once the funds are acquired in the capital markets, AFICA then distributes them to the clients. The bonds are payable by AFICA from payments from the client institutions. The debt issued by AFICA is not direct debt of the commonwealth or any of its other public corporations or municipalities, although the attractive interest rates it commands in the market suggest an implied guarantee. For example, AFICA has financed the construction of a multipurpose coliseum in San Juan with a line of credit provided by the GDB. The coliseum was recently completed at a cost of approximately $350 million and was transferred to the Convention Center District Authority. This organization is under the direction of a GDB executive and operates from the bank's headquarters.

A second affiliate is the Puerto Rico Infrastructure Financing Authority, established in 1988 with two purposes: to provide financial, administrative, technical, or other assistance to public agencies that develop infrastructure projects, and to provide an alternative means of financing public sector infrastructure development. This affiliate is authorized to issue bonds and provide loans, grants, and other financial assistance for the construction, acquisition, repair, maintenance, and reconstruction of infrastructure projects by public corporations and instrumentalities of the commonwealth. It also administers the Puerto Rico Infrastructure Development Fund, funded annually from the first proceeds of federal excise taxes imposed on rum and other products procured in Puerto Rico and sold in the United States and transferred to Puerto Rico pursuant to the U.S. Internal Revenue Code of 1986. This amount is currently $70 million, and it will increase to $90 million for fiscal years 2007 to 2052. The authority draws on these funds to provide financial support for water and sewer projects. As of June 30, 2004, its total debt was $936.7 million.

The Puerto Rico Infrastructure Financing Authority provides assistance to the Aqueduct and Sewer Authority, for example, and also acts as the custodian and administrator of the Infrastructure Development Fund, a permanent trust fund to be used by the authority for the purpose of financing infrastructure projects. The Infrastructure Development Fund was initially financed in March 1999 with $1.2 billion of proceeds received by the Telephone Authority from the sale of a controlling interest in the government-owned Puerto Rico Telephone Company, funds intended to remain permanently in a segregated, perpetual account to be invested exclusively in U.S. government or U.S. government-backed obligations. The income may be used only to finance infrastructure projects related to the commonwealth's water and sewer systems. In October 2000 the Puerto Rico Infrastructure Financing Authority issued $1.093 billion in bonds payable from, and secured by a pledge of the interest received by the authority from, the investment of the Infrastructure Development Fund.[36]

The Puerto Rico Municipal Finance Agency, a third GDB affiliate, was created in 1972 to facilitate access to capital markets for the municipalities of Puerto Rico, in order to bolster their economic self-sufficiency and reduce their dependence on central government funding while enabling them to borrow at attractive interest rates. The agency became a (de facto) municipal "bond bank." "It is authorized to issue its own bonds and use the proceeds to purchase general obligation bonds and notes of Puerto Rico municipalities and to fund a debt service reserve. Debt service on the Agency's bonds is payable from payments on municipal bonds held by the Agency and from the debt service reserve. The Commonwealth has agreed to pay such amounts to the debt service reserve as

---

36. Commonwealth of Puerto Rico (2004, app. I, p. 34).

may be necessary to maintain its required level, subject to appropriation by the legislature. To date, no such payments have been required. As of June 30, 2004, the Agency had $1.323 billion of bonds outstanding."[37] Interestingly, the Public Finance Corporation, a GDB subsidiary established in 1984, also is mandated to provide alternative means of financing to municipalities in Puerto Rico, including issuing bonds on their behalf, arguably an unnecessary expansion of bureaucracy inside the GDB itself.

A fourth affiliate is the Caribbean Basin Projects Financing Authority, created in 1991 to finance projects geared toward promoting economic development in neighboring Caribbean jurisdictions. It lends funds raised by its own bond issues to borrowers to finance development-related projects throughout the Caribbean.

In addition to its subsidiaries and affiliates, the Government Development Bank assists at least thirteen other corporations of the commonwealth with bond issues, interim financing, and other services, including, at least in one instance, a grant from its own equity:

—The Puerto Rico Aqueduct and Sewer Authority, the sole institution that provides the Puerto Rico population with water and sewer services, created in the early 1940s, is an important element in the economic development of the island. In 2004 it had outstanding debt of $717 million, and it has had critical infrastructure, union, and other operating problems, with operating losses every fiscal year from 2000 to 2003, totaling $470.8 million. Recent legislation provides for the full restructuring of the authority.

—In October 2002, the Children's Trust, a nonprofit corporation created in 1999 to improve the health, education, and general welfare of children, issued $1.171 billion bonds (through the GDB) secured by the statutory pledge of payments under the Tobacco Litigation Master Settlement Agreement.[38]

—The Convention Center District Authority was created in September 2000 to own, develop, finance, design, build, operate, maintain, administer, and promote the Convention Center in Puerto Rico.

—The Electric Power Authority, in operation since the 1940s, supplies electrical power in the island but is experiencing significant operating problems.

—The Health Insurance Administration was created in 1993 to implement health reform by negotiating and contracting for the provision of comprehensive health insurance coverage for qualifying (generally low-income) Puerto Rico residents and currently covers some 1.5 million people. The total cost of the health insurance program for fiscal year 2004 has been estimated at $1.354 billion, and earlier years saw a similar level of expenses.[39]

37. Commonwealth of Puerto Rico (2004, app. I, p. 35).
38. See Commonwealth of Puerto Rico (1999).
39. Commonwealth of Puerto Rico (2004, app. I, p. 32).

—The Highway and Transportation Authority is responsible for highway construction intended to be financed by debt, revenues of the authority, and federal and commonwealth grants.[40]

—The Puerto Rico Industrial Development Company participates in the commonwealth-sponsored economic development program by providing physical facilities, general assistance, and special incentive grants to manufacturers, financed by revenue bonds.[41]

—The Maritime Shipping Authority, which began operations in 1974 upon the acquisition of three shipping lines serving Puerto Rico and the U.S. mainland, was later sold to a private investor group. Liabilities in the form of bonds for this project are still outstanding and are payable by legislative appropriations.

—The Ports Authority owns and operates the major airport and seaport facilities in Puerto Rico.

—The Public Buildings Authority is authorized to construct, purchase, or lease office, school, health, correctional, and other facilities for lease to departments, public corporations, and instrumentalities of the commonwealth.[42]

—The Special Communities Perpetual Trust is an irrevocable and permanent trust created in November 2002 as a public corporation with original funding of $1.0 billion to be financed by the GDB. The trust's principal purpose is to fund development projects that address the infrastructure and housing needs of underprivileged communities.

—The Telephone Authority was created in July 1974 when the commonwealth purchased the Puerto Rico Telephone Company from International Telephone and Telegraph Corporation. The telephone company operates the principal telephone system in Puerto Rico. In March 1999 the Telephone Authority sold a controlling interest in the Puerto Rico Telephone Company to a consortium led by GTE International Telecommunications, which was acquired by Verizon Communications; $1.2 billion of the proceeds from the sale were transferred to the Puerto Rico Infrastructure Financing Authority to

40. Debt service on the Highway and Transportation Authority's revenue bonds constitutes a first lien on its gross revenues, which consist currently of all the proceeds of the gasoline tax; one-half of the proceeds of the tax on gas oil or diesel oil; all the proceeds of the excise taxes on crude oil, unfinished oil, and derivative products, up to $120 million per fiscal year; highway toll revenues; and the gross receipts of $15.00 per vehicle a year from certain motor vehicle license fees. Such revenues (except for toll revenues) may be applied first to the payment of debt service on general obligation bonds and notes of the commonwealth and payments required to be made by the commonwealth under its guarantees of bonds and notes to the extent that no other revenues are available for such purpose. The commonwealth has never applied such revenues for such payment. In April 2004 the authority issued approximately $140 million of bonds secured solely by federal highway aid grant revenues. As of June 30, 2004, the authority's total debt was $5.799 billion.

41. Commonwealth of Puerto Rico (2004, app. I, pp. 32, 33).

42. Commonwealth of Puerto Rico (2004, app. I, p. 35).

pay for outstanding bonds of that authority and to pay benefits, among other items, to the Puerto Rico Telephone Company.[43]

—The University of Puerto Rico, with 68,627 students in the academic year 2003–04, is by far the largest institution of higher education on the island. Government appropriations are the principal source of university revenues, but additional revenues are derived from tuition, student fees, auxiliary enterprises, interest income, federal grants, and other sources. In December 2000 AFICA issued about $87 million in educational facilities revenue bonds. The university total debt was $425.2 million as of June 2004.[44]

Other public corporations had outstanding debt in the aggregate amount of $793.6 million as of June 30, 2004. The commonwealth is not obligated to cover debt service, although legislative appropriations can be made to enable them to cover their operating expenses.[45] This broad array of institutional affiliations illustrates the ubiquitous presence of the GDB, the role it plays in actual long-term financing through the issuing of bonds, and part of the liquidity function it provides through its outstanding lines of credit and other loans in three forms: the bank's lending to the government, as reflected in its balance sheet; the bank's facilitating of funds, through bond flotations; and the intertwined activity between the bank and the many government appendages described above.

The volume of public sector debt was $33.9 billion in June 2004 (see table 8-7), at which time the ratios of debt to GDP and debt to GNP were 45.4 percent and 71.7 percent, respectively, suggesting the need for public sector debt restructuring as a priority issue. Arguably, a good portion of the island's government debt was facilitated by the GDB. Table 8A-28 shows that $51.7 billion in debt from the U.S. and international capital markets was raised by the GDB from 1993 to 2004. In addition, as of June 2004 the bank had outstanding loans to the Puerto Rico central government and government appendages of another $4.1 billion. This debt burden weighs heavily on the future economic development of the commonwealth. It can be argued that development depends on sharpening human resources and technological skills, local manufacturing and agriculture for import substitution, and eventual export creation by local industry.

Three issues related to the Government Development Bank deserve special mention here. As the official fiduciary and fiscal agent of the commonwealth government, the GDB participates in the preparation of the commonwealth government's annual budget and oversees several of the pension or retirement plans of the government.[46]

---

43. Commonwealth of Puerto Rico (2004, app. I, p. 35).
44. Commonwealth of Puerto Rico (2004, app. I, pp. 35, 36).
45. Commonwealth of Puerto Rico (2004, app. I, pp. 35, 36).
46. See Government Development Bank (2004).

Table 8-7. *Public Sector Debt, Puerto Rico, June 2004*
Millions of dollars

Debt type	Amount
Puerto Rico direct debt[a]	8,519
Municipal debt	2,046
Public corporations' debt	23,377
Puerto Rico guaranteed debt[b]	652
Debt supported by Puerto Rico tax appropriations[c]	14,971
Other nonguaranteed debt[d]	7,754
Total public sector debt	33,943

Source: Data from the Government Development Bank as presented in Commonwealth of Puerto Rico (2004, app. I, p. 24).

a. Includes general obligation bonds, tax and revenues anticipation notes, and lines of credit provided by the GDB. Includes $10 million of certain indebtedness originally issued by the Urban Renewal and Housing Corporation that was transferred to the commonwealth by virtue of Act 134 of the Legislature of Puerto Rico, approved on December 13, 1994 (such indebtedness is referred to as "Transferred CRUV Debt"). Excludes certain commonwealth general obligation bonds that have been refunded with proceeds that were invested in guaranteed investment contracts or other securities not eligible to effect a legal defeasance, even though such bonds will be considered outstanding under their respective authorizing resolutions and for purposes of calculating the commonwealth's constitutional debt limitation.

b. Consists of $499.9 million of bonds issued by the Aqueduct and Sewer Authority and $152.5 million of State Revolving Fund Loans, incurred under various federal water laws. Excludes Public Buildings Authority bonds in the principal amount of $2.898 billion as of June 30, 2004, and $267 million of Government Development Bank bonds payable from available moneys of GDB.

c. Represents bonds and notes issued by the Aqueduct and Sewer Authority, the Highway and Transportation Authority, the Housing Finance Authority, the Infrastructure Financing Authority, the Public Buildings Authority, and the Public Finance Corporation, among others.

d. Excludes $1.066 billion of Infrastructure Financing Authority bonds, which are payable solely from the investment income of funds on deposit in the Infrastructure Development Fund consisting of proceeds from the sale of a controlling interest in Puerto Rico Telephone Company. Excludes $1.155 billion of Children's Trust bonds, which are payable solely from the payments to be received pursuant to the tobacco litigation settlement. Excludes the $660 million of Housing Finance Authority bonds, which are payable from Puerto Rico Housing Administration's annual allocation of Public Housing Capital Funds from the U.S. Department of Housing and Urban Development.

First, the weakening of the GDB input in the budget process of the commonwealth government would seem to be clear, given that for at least a decade the government has been borrowing against future tax revenues.[47] Only recent data are available that indicate the amounts borrowed by the central government directly from the GDB to satisfy the legal requirement that the budget be balanced. These amounts appear to be $233 million for fiscal year 2003, $370 million for 2004, and $550 million for 2005, all at ten-year terms, debt to be paid by taxes receivable. In addition, to finance the new Special Communities

47. "Commonwealth Unable to Balance Budget," *San Juan Star,* January 29, 2005, p. 1.

Perpetual Trust, a line of credit of $500 million was made available to the trust, of which $90.9 million was outstanding as of June 2004. An additional grant is to be made by the GDB whenever the line of credit is extinguished. The grant of $500 million is to be financed from the bank's equity, which, in turn, is to be replenished by GDB future earnings.[48]

Willingly or not, the GDB is contributing to a fiscal problem that has been emerging through time. The bond issues for the commonwealth government and its various instrumentalities that the GDB has undertaken in the U.S. capital market have helped finance fiscal deficits and have ultimately facilitated a large government debt. In effect, it can be argued that the Puerto Rican fiscal picture has contributed to the crowding out of local private sector borrowers, and to the extent that the GDB has contributed to the financing of the deficit, it may have contributed to a crowding-out phenomenon as well. Although net inflows from the U.S. financial system should counteract this effect, it is useful to note that Moody's earlier warning that a possible bond rating downgrade might be on the horizon seems justified by three factors: public expenditures' growing faster than the economy; government spending in excess of revenues, covered by borrowing; and government assignment of nonrecurrent funds to key investment projects. Moody's warnings, echoed by Standard and Poor's and various others, have materialized.[49] As mentioned earlier in this chapter, in May 2005, Moody's downgraded the Commonwealth of Puerto Rico's general obligation bonds from Baa1 to Baa2, and Standard and Poor's lowered its rating from A– to BBB. Both maintained a negative outlook.

Second, there is also the issue of tax policy, which in Puerto Rico seems to favor investments in securities issued by the local government or the U.S. government and loans to certain sectors such as tourism and real estate. To the extent that such tax incentives distort capital allocation in Puerto Rico, they will tend to have an adverse effect on economic growth. The GDB advisory function has been at best weak in this respect.

Third, the Commonwealth Employees Retirement System covers all public employees in Puerto Rico through five retirement systems: the Retirement System of the Commonwealth and Its Instrumentalities, the Annuity and Pension System for the Teachers of Puerto Rico, the Commonwealth Judiciary Retirement System, the Retirement System of the University of Puerto Rico, and the Employees Retirement System of Puerto Rico Electric Power Authority.[50] The commonwealth government is not directly responsible for making contributions to the latter two systems; but a large proportion of university revenue consists of

48. Commonwealth of Puerto Rico (2004, app. I, pp. 30, 43, 52, 54).

49. Manufacturers Association of Puerto Rico (2005). See also Carlos A. Colon de Armas, "El déficit: Implicaciones y Soluciones," *San Juan El Vocero,* January 28, 2005, p. 40.

50. Commonwealth of Puerto Rico (2004, app. I, 36–39).

legislative appropriations. During the 1990s there were several changes in the Commonwealth Employees Retirement System. Some were increases in the future postretirement system benefits; others were amendments to reduce the pension liability of the system and changes from defined benefits to defined contributions. A cash shortfall for fiscal years 2002 and 2003 was covered with a portion of the proceeds from the sale to Verizon of the 15 percent stock ownership in the Puerto Rico Telephone Company.[51] The Commonwealth Employees Retirement System anticipates that its future cash flow needs for disbursement of benefits to participants may exceed the sum of the employer and employee contributions received and its investment and other recurring income. The system expects to cover this cash flow imbalance in the next few fiscal years with the proceeds from the sale of the remaining shares of telephone company stock. The Commonwealth Employees Retirement System is currently evaluating other measures to increase its revenues.[52] As in many countries, the public pension system in Puerto Rico faces further strains going forward.

The liabilities and assets of these three systems for two periods, as viewed by independent actuarial experts contracted by the systems' managers, are presented in table 8-8. The underfunding of the retirement systems translates into more debt to the commonwealth government if it is indeed going to meet its commitments to the beneficiaries. The commonwealth's $33.9 billion public debt outstanding would be higher yet if the actuarial liabilities that will eventually have to be met by the commonwealth government were added. This is difficult to estimate, but based on the difference between the latest data presented on liabilities and assets in table 8-8, the debt could be another $3.9 billion—for a total public debt of $37.8 billion. Other estimates suggest that the actuarial retirement deficit is $11.2 billion, raising the overall public debt to $45.1 billion.[53] Either of these two estimates substantially elevates the future ratio of public debt to GNP or to GDP. It is clearly a critical situation, and as the fiscal agent of the commonwealth, the GDB has been incapable of overcoming or influencing the direction of the pressures that have driven Puerto Rico's public finances to a perilous state.[54] All of these factors also contributed to the bond ratings downgrade in May 2005.

Without question, the Government Development Bank has been a venerable and praiseworthy institution, without which neither the industrial and commercial development of the island nor the enhancement of the standard of living would have been possible. However, it is also clear that the GDB, perhaps

51. The Puerto Rico Telephone Company was wholly owned by the government until sold to a consortium led by GTE International Telecommunications (subsequently acquired by Verizon Communications).

52. See Commonwealth of Puerto Rico (2004, app. I, p. 38).

53. For actuarial retirement deficit estimate, see Manufacturers Association of Puerto Rico (2005, p. 17).

54. See the earlier discussion of presidential tenure problems at GDB.

Table 8-8. *Employee Retirement System Balance, Puerto Rico, 2001 and 2003*
Billions of dollars, except as indicated

Retirement system	Liabilities	Assets	Funding ratio (percent)
As of June 2001			
Employees	9.9	7.5	25
Judicial	162.2	92.1	43
Teachers	3.7	2.3	62
As of June 2003			
Employees	11.3	9.3	17
Teachers	3.9	2.1	55

Source: Data from Commonwealth of Puerto Rico (2004, app. I, pp. 36–37).

unwillingly, has contributed to the increase in government bureaucracy, the high concentration of employment in the government sector, and the large government debt that could render further development more difficult. The bank needs to become politically independent if it is to carry out its mandate effectively, particularly in light of the current financial crisis.

The Puerto Rico Economic Development Bank

The Puerto Rico Economic Development Bank (EDB) was created in 1985 by the Puerto Rico Development Bank Act to provide financing to small and medium-size businesses that, owing to their particular circumstances, fail to meet the strenuous credit and capital requirements of private banks. The act set forth several objectives, such as having the EDB serve as a facilitator offering financing, capital, guarantees, and other assistance, with emphasis on projects that help create and retain jobs, establish new companies, and diversify and strengthen the Puerto Rican economy. The EDB was intended to back projects that increase exports, reduce the need for imports, encourage companies to reinvest on the island, and expand the entrepreneurial community in Puerto Rico.

Arguably, the Economic Development Bank was created to separate lending to emerging industry enterprises that could not secure funding from private financial institutions or from the GDB from lending to risky ventures. The GDB could thus maintain a strong balance sheet to carry on with its goal of facilitating funds raised in the U.S. capital markets, serving as fiscal agent and adviser to the government and its instrumentalities. The financial statements of the Economic Development Bank appear in tables 8A-30 and 8A-31. The bank has experienced an annual rate of decline in assets of 2 percent, from $1.2 billion in 1995 to $0.96 billion in 2004, and an increase in net income of 7 percent a year over the same period. The EDB profitability indicators were erratic but positive over the decade, and its ability to lend to local entrepreneurs has declined with its decline in assets. A governmental bank dedicated to economic development should be financially solid, and the condition of the EDB, in short, is not good. It has been suggested in recent annual reports of the Economic Development Bank that it should become another subsidiary of the GDB.[55]

Nevertheless, the EDB did make an effort to finance local entrepreneurs who could not get financing from the private sector in manufacturing, service, tourism, commerce, and agriculture. An economic development bank could play a significant role in financing local high-risk entrepreneurs if it were managed effectively and without the likelihood of its top management's changing every time the political term of the executive branch changes, which has proved to be the case with the EDB as well as with the GDB.

Supervision and Regulation

Two institutions supervise and regulate the financial sector in Puerto Rico. The Office of the Commissioner of Financial Institutions is in charge of all the financial institutions in Puerto Rico except the insurance companies, which are under the authority of the Office of the Commissioner of Insurance. Both commissioners are appointed by the governor of Puerto Rico and are organized as part of the Puerto Rico Department of the Treasury.

The primary responsibility of the Office of the Commissioner of Financial Institutions is to supervise and regulate Puerto Rico's financial sector (except for the insurance companies) to ensure its safety and soundness as well as to oversee a strict adherence to all applicable laws and regulations. For this purpose, the office collects all relevant data and makes them available to the general public upon request. The Office of the Commissioner of Insurance has the same responsibility with respect to the insurance companies operating on the island and provides data as well, but not in as free a form as the Office of the Commissioner of Financial Institutions.[56] The Federal Deposit Insurance Corporation, the Federal Reserve Bank, and the Office of the Treasury of the United States also have jurisdiction in Puerto Rico, as noted earlier in this chapter.

Benchmarking Puerto Rico's Financial Sector

The financial sector in Puerto Rico can be favorably compared with that in the United States using the contributions of finance, insurance, and real estate (FIRE) to economic activity during the period 1947 to 2004 (figure 8-9). The United States maintains data for the FIRE sector in the national income

55. See Economic Development Bank of Puerto Rico (1992–2003).

56. For more information about these two important "regulators," see their respective websites (www.ofi.gobierno.pr and www.ocs.gobierno.pr). Most of the statistical data used in this chapter come from the Office of the Commissioner of Financial Institutions. A somewhat less full set of data comes from the Office of the Commissioner of Insurance.

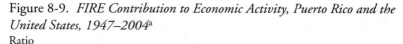

Figure 8-9. *FIRE Contribution to Economic Activity, Puerto Rico and the United States, 1947–2004*[a]

Ratio

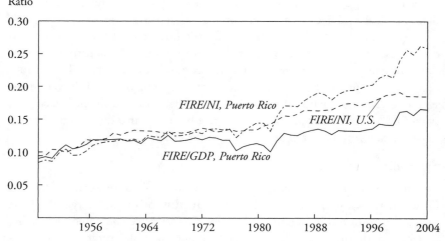

Source: Data from U.S. Bureau of Economic Analysis, except data points for 1947 and 2004, which were estimated to complete series; Puerto Rico Planning Board, Program for Social and Economic Planning, Subprogram for Economic Analysis.

a. FIRE is finance, insurance, and real estate; NI is national income.

accounts, while for Puerto Rico these data are available in the commonwealth GDP accounts. The data series NI (national income and GDP) are not strictly comparable, although they are useful in terms of the contribution of the FIRE sector to overall economic activity. The FIRE contribution to NI in the United States increased from 9 percent to 19 percent over the period, while in Puerto Rico it increased from 8 percent to 26 percent (FIRE's contribution to GDP in Puerto Rico increased from 9 percent to 17 percent). Puerto Rico's financial sector has kept pace with the U.S. financial sector in terms of overall economic activity. Throughout the period, the differential between the two data series was between 0 and 8 percentage points.

Another way to assess the Puerto Rican financial sector is to compare commercial banking, its most important dimension, with its counterparts in the United States as a whole and with comparable states. Florida and Hawaii were selected because they appear to be roughly comparable to Puerto Rico in terms of population ethnicity, multilingualism, climate, and, at least in one case, political history—although Hawaii actually chose to become a state in the relatively recent past (1959). All the data used in this section come from the Federal Deposit Insurance Corporation website, available to the general public.

We first compare the average of bank balance sheet and income statements for Puerto Rico and the three benchmarks for the nine years from 1995 to

2003. The data for Puerto Rico exclude two relatively small banks that do not have FDIC insurance, although their absence does not yield a significant difference from the data used in the analysis in the rest of this chapter, which are based on data from the Office of the Commissioner of Financial Institutions in Puerto Rico and include all fourteen commercial banks active in 2004.

Our interest lies in examining any significant differences in the uses and sources of funds and in profitability or efficiency between the twelve FDIC-insured banks in Puerto Rico and those in the United States, Florida, and Hawaii. To examine these potential differences, we first computed an average of the nine-year balance sheet and income statements and then computed the proportionate relationships of the balance sheet components to total assets and those of the income statement components to total revenue. Table 8-9 shows average balance sheet figures as a percentage of total assets as well as the change in percentage points over the period. (See also table 8A-32.) Please note that the figures have not been adjusted for inflation, thus more weight is given to the most recent observations.

Investments in securities among banks in Puerto Rico are proportionately much higher (37 percent) than in the United States (18 percent), Florida (18 percent), and Hawaii (21 percent), and their value increased by 16 percentage points annually over the period compared with 7.5 percentage points in the United States as a whole, a decrease of 6.5 percentage points in Florida, and an increase of 2.8 percentage points in Hawaii. Total deposits accounted for a smaller proportion of assets in Puerto Rico than in the other regions—61 percent versus 68 percent in the United States as a whole, 80 percent in Florida, and 71 percent in Hawaii. Although deposits grew more rapidly in Puerto Rico than on the mainland or in the two comparator states, the proportion of assets funded by deposits declined by 19 percentage points in Puerto Rico over the period, as against declines of 4 points in the United States and 2 points in Florida and an increase of 9 points in Hawaii. There was a significant increase in Puerto Rican banks' debt relative to that of the benchmarks—debt was 32 percent of total assets, as against 24 percent in the United States, 11 percent in Florida, and 19 percent in Hawaii. Debt finance increased by 19 percentage points in Puerto Rico over the nine-year period as against 3 percentage points in the United States as a whole and 1 percentage point in Florida, whereas Hawaii actually experienced a decline of 13 percentage points in bank assets financed by debt. Banks in Puerto Rico have a lower proportion of equity to total assets (7 percent versus 9 percent in both the United States as a whole and in Florida, and 10 percent in Hawaii); the ratio has declined in Puerto Rico but increased in all of the benchmark regions.

Table 8A-33 presents the averaged income statement for all the banks in each of the sectors over the nine-year period as well as the compound annual growth rate over the period for each category of the income statement presented.

Table 8-9. *Commercial Banks' Average Balance Sheet for Puerto Rico, the United States, Florida, Hawaii, and the Five Most Aggressive Banks in Puerto Rico, 1995–2003*

Units as indicated

Item	As share of total assets (percent)					Change in percentage points				
	Puerto Rico	United States	Florida	Hawaii	Five banks	Puerto Rico	United States	Florida	Hawaii	Five banks
Total assets	100	100	100	100	100					
Cash and interest-bearing placements	4.1	6.2	6.1	6.6	3.0	-1.9	-2.0	-1.7	-4.4	-1.8
Investments and securities	36.6	18.0	18.4	21.0	43.4	10.4	0.2	2.0	2.4	15.2
Other loans and leases, net	0.6	6.4	2.9	3.9	-0.2	0.5	-0.6	-0.6	-0.5	2.0
Commercial and industrial loans	17.0	15.0	10.9	16.7	6.0	-2.8	-3.9	0.0	-7.1	1.0
Loans to individuals	11.6	10.5	8.5	6.8	9.5	-10.0	-2.2	-6.9	0.4	-22.4
Loans secured by residential real estate	15.7	16.0	24.7	21.5	22.9	3.9	2.6	-9.3	2.4	-0.7
Loans secured by other real estate	10.0	10.9	19.3	14.1	11.9	1.8	2.3	17.9	-0.6	7.7
Other assets	4.4	17.1	9.3	9.3	3.4	-1.9	3.6	-1.5	7.3	-0.9
Total liabilities and equity	100	100	100	100	100					
Liabilities	92.8	91.3	91.2	89.9	93.3	0.1	-1.0	-0.9	-4.4	0.2
Deposits	61.1	67.5	80.2	70.6	51.9	-19.4	-3.9	-2.1	8.5	-16.8
Debt	31.7	23.9	11.0	19.3	41.4	19.5	2.9	1.2	-12.9	17.0
Equity	6.9	8.7	8.8	10.1	6.7	0.1	1.0	0.9	4.4	-0.2
Perpetual preferred stock	0.3	0.1	0.0	0.0	0.5	0.7	0.0	0.0	0.0	0.5
Other equity	6.5	8.6	8.8	10.1	6.2	-0.6	1.0	0.9	4.4	-0.7
Total assets (millions of dollars)	50,698	5,790,978	96,479	23,324	17,178	11.9	7.3	-7.7	1.5	29.5

Source: Data from the Federal Deposit Insurance Corporation (www2.fdic.gov/hsob/SelectRpt.asp?EntryType=10 [May 2005]).

Table 8A-34 presents a risk analysis of the return on equity for all the banks in each of the sectors for two periods, the reported period 1995–2003 and a longer thirty-six-year period, 1967–2003. This table depicts the mean return as well as standard deviation and coefficient of variation of return on equity. Banks in Puerto Rico have been more profitable in terms of most of the relevant metrics, and they appear to be more efficient than banks in the comparison areas— noninterest expense was 40 percent of total revenue ($1,899 million/$4,788 million) compared with 53 percent in the United States, 52 percent in Florida, and 54 percent in Hawaii. The mean, standard deviation, and coefficient of variation of return on equity during the nine-year period did not show any dramatic differences, although the standard deviation for Puerto Rico was much lower, at 1 percent, over the nine-year period than over the longer period (7 percent)—a difference that does not appear in the other areas considered here.[57]

The overall picture seems to indicate that Puerto Rico's banks are comparatively less engaged in the typical banking functions of collecting deposits and lending to business and individuals than in financing securities positions with borrowed funds. It is true that U.S. banks also finance securities positions with borrowed funds, but they have maturity risk management strategies in place even though their mismatch positions appear to be relatively lower. Puerto Rican banks, particularly the most aggressive ones, do not appear to have such strategies in place. Their equity funding is lower and has been declining over the period relative to the U.S. benchmarks. On the other hand, the profitability of banks in Puerto Rico is higher than that in these other areas, and noninterest expense is lower. These could be a reflection of lower wages and lower tax burden relative to banks on the U.S. mainland.

The lower tax burden of Puerto Rican banks appears to be the primary reason why commercial banks on the island are more profitable than commercial banks in the United States or in any of its states. In addition, it appears that the asset allocation of the banking sector on the island is also affected (induced) by the tax exemptions that the island government has established.

Puerto Rican banks are subject to income taxes that are higher than federal taxes. For example, the highest federal tax rate in the United States is 35 percent, and it applies at the income level equal to or above $10 million, whereas income taxes to banks in Puerto Rico are 39 percent and apply at the income level of only $275,000. Still, the tax burden on island banks is significantly less than that on their counterparts in the states of the United States, because federal taxes are not applicable to certain types of income derived by banks organized under the laws of Puerto Rico (which are considered foreign banks for federal income tax purposes). For instance, the income derived by these banks from

57. See also Brean Murray Research (2002); Diamond and Rajan (2005); Lang and Wetzel (1998).

investments in U.S. Treasury bills, notes, or bonds and that from obligations issued by the Federal Home Loan Bank are not subject to federal taxation if the bank is organized in Puerto Rico and such income is not attributable to U.S. business conducted by said bank. However, in the case of banks located in any of the states of the United States, the income derived from the aforesaid federal obligations would be subject to federal taxation when received by these stateside institutions. Moreover, the quantity of available exemptions from island taxes on income from investments and loans is significantly greater than exemptions from state taxes on income from these investments and loans in any state in the United States. Although this is a complex matter, as exceptions can vary from state to state, island banks in the aggregate have a much larger amount of tax-exempt income than do any group of state banks. For example, Ginnie Mae (Government National Mortgage Association) mortgage pools on local properties of new construction after June 31, 1997, are exempted from island income taxes. It would be hard to find a state with a similar tax exemption. Also exempt from island income taxes are, to name a few, income from investments in island government securities or securities of its agencies and corporations, income from the U.S. Federal Home Loan Bank securities, income from projects related to industrial and commercial loans for tourism, income from loans for new hospital construction, and income from loans to workers' cooperatives.[58]

Securities held by Puerto Rican banks have maturity terms of up to ten years, whereas their debt has a maximum maturity of five years—a possible mismatch that creates an exposure to market risk in the absence of a well-developed interest rate hedging strategy. We conclude that, indeed, over the thirty-six-year period the risk is reflected in variations in return on equity (see table 8A-34) and is likely to be reflected in bank stock prices. We know that several of the more aggressive banks on the island—defined in terms of their high annual growth rate of assets—have seen significant declines in stock prices recently, possibly reflecting this market risk (see figure 8-10).

From our examination of the individual bank data, we suspect that these five aggressive banks account for most of the differences between the Puerto Rican banks and the benchmarks.[59] We conducted a separate analysis of these five banks, to be compared with the Puerto Rican banks as a whole and those of the three benchmark areas. The results are shown in tables 8-9, 8A-32, 8A-33, and 8A-34. The five most aggressive banks maintain disproportionately large securities holdings, lower deposit funding, higher debt levels, and lower equity capitalization than the aggregate of all banks in the island and, of course, those in

58. The authors are grateful to Edgar Rios Mendez, from the Puerto Rican law firm Pietrantoni, Mendez, and Alvarez, for an extensive discussion on how the law applies to the banks. See also *Puerto Rico Taxes*, Tax Law, 13LPRA §8422 (PRIRC §1022), 100,731-100,733.

59. These five banks are Firstbank, Doral Bank, R-G Premier Bank, Oriental Bank and Trust, and Westernbank.

Figure 8-10. *Puerto Rico Banks' Stock Prices, December 31, 2004, to April 20, 2005*
Dollars

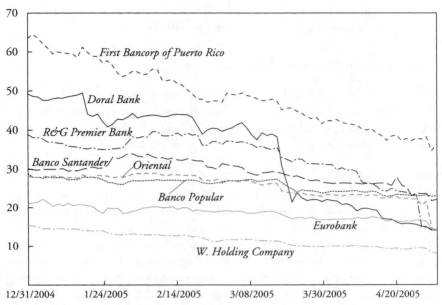

Source: Data from *Factset*, March 10, 2005.

Florida, Hawaii, and the United States in general. In addition, the return on equity for these five banks, according to the data in table 8A-34, was significantly higher than for the rest of the banks on the island as well as the other three comparable groups of banks. However, as table 8A-33 reveals, net income as a percentage of total revenue for these five aggressive banks was lower than that for all the other banks in the island, lending support to our observation that their equity financing is lower than that of the average bank on the island. Furthermore, as indicated by the risk analysis data presented in tables 8A-34 and particularly 8A-35, these five banks are significantly more risk tolerant in their investments than the rest of the banks on the island. This higher level of risk is confirmed by the stock price behavior portrayed in figure 8-10, which shows a significant decline in the first four months of 2005. The more mature banks on the island, such as Banco Popular and Banco Santander, barely show a decline in their stock prices over the same period.

Bringing Puerto Rican banks more in line with those of the United States as a whole and the two comparison states of Florida and Hawaii in particular would involve allocating a significantly larger proportion of assets to commercial and industrial lending, more-intensive deposit taking from the general public as against funding through securities markets, and an increase in equity funding beyond the regulatory minimums. It appears that if the five aggressive banks were to adopt these recommendations rigorously, the entire banking sector in Puerto Rico would pretty much fall in line with its counterparts in Florida, Hawaii, and the United States in general.

Summary and Recommendations

Puerto Rico has accomplished a great deal in terms of the architecture of its financial system but also has much to be concerned about in terms of the contemporary structure and functioning of the financial system. Improvements must be undertaken if Puerto Rico is to realize its economic potential.

Commercial Banks

Commercial banks appear to have failed to allocate funds to economic development through commercial and industrial loans as much as would seem desirable in an economy such as Puerto Rico's. Moreover, they have not generated sufficient asset gathering in the form of savings and checking deposits from the household sector to underwrite the capital formation needed to create the kind of self-sustained economic development described in chapter 1 of this book.[60] Moreover, the somewhat fragile financial structure of the commercial banks is a concern that needs attention from the institutions themselves and from the supervisory institutions.[61] As shown in this chapter, most of the fragility and deficiencies of the island banking sector vis-à-vis the comparable sectors of Florida, Hawaii, and the United States could be corrected if the five most aggressive Puerto Rican institutions were to adopt the necessary measures. However, what does apply to all the banks on the island is the need to invest less in securities and instead to lend for commercial and industrial purposes at longer maturities, because doing so is more conducive to economic development, even though it is less liquid and hence more risky. The trade-off between dedicating funds for development and for more liquid investments—securities issued mainly outside Puerto Rico—is a necessity if the banks are indeed going to do their job to stimulate development. In the long run this will prove a sound investment for the banks as the industrial and business sectors of the island develop and strengthen.

60. It may be, however, that the low savings rate in Puerto Rico is not quite as bad as public statistics indicate. On this issue see the discussion of investment companies and broker-dealers earlier in this chapter, where it is suggested that there may be relevant savings taking place in Puerto Rico through these institutions.

61. See the discussion on the large percentage of commercial bank sources of funds coming from debt, other than deposits, and the discussion on preferred stocks, which portray a potential risk with the equity-type capital that some of the banks are using increasingly as equity. More important, see the discussion on benchmarking Puerto Rico's financial sector, where the analysis of the five most aggressive banks is presented.

Puerto Rico's tax laws exempt from island taxes the interest earned from investments in securities from the U.S. government and local government. It also exempts interest earned on loans to tourism development projects, hospital construction, and the like. We believe that these tax exemptions have played a key role in the current allocation of assets by the banks. Although this allocation has enriched the banks, it has done little to stimulate the island's economic growth. It is therefore of utmost importance that the tax code be amended to eliminate or significantly reduce the current tax exemptions, in order to reduce the misallocation of bank assets on the island and to bring their high profitability more in line with banks on the U.S. mainland.

International Banking Entities

With respect to IBEs in Puerto Rico, the review ordered by the Office of the Commissioner of Financial Institutions concludes with four recommendations, with which we concur:

—amending the island's Internal Revenue Code in relation to exemptions for offshore activity

—requiring a "permanent establishment" in Puerto Rico of all IBEs conducting business there

—participation of Puerto Rico in U.S. tax treaties with other countries

—establishment of an organization dedicated to encouraging IBEs to conduct their offshore business on the island

Other Financial Institutions

The financial intermediation process as undertaken by most nonbank financial institutions in Puerto Rico seems appropriate when evaluated from the perspective of economic development. This conclusion emerges from our examination of the major activities performed by investment companies, broker-dealers, and venture capital funds. Their asset gathering, essential for investment in the real economy as exemplified by their investments in stocks and bonds, to some degree does not take place in Puerto Rico but goes instead to the U.S. mainland and perhaps other countries. Nevertheless, the major portion of the funds that these three institutions gather do appear to be used for investments on the island. It is important that their function be better understood by the authorities, and perhaps special efforts might be made, particularly in educating the public, so that more savings might be channeled to them, especially to venture capital funds.[62]

62. For example, for particular public and private sector institutions, such as local entrepreneurial development, efficient public services training, venture capital and biotechnology training, attracting outsourcing services, and the like.

The Government Development Bank and the Economic Development Bank

The GDB and the EDB play a key role in the financial development of Puerto Rico and therefore should be subject to key reforms. The term of the president and the board of directors of the GDB and its subsidiaries should be changed to a full term of seven years; the same change should be applicable to the EDB. On each bank board, there should be at least two representatives of the major commercial banks active in Puerto Rico and one representative of each group of financial institutions making up the island's financial sector. We believe that the perpetually at-risk and often brief terms of office of government bank presidents subject to executive and legislative branch pressures can have negative consequences. These are made manifest through financial determinations subject more to political pressures than to sound economic analysis and risk-return assessments.

Unsound financial decisions can place at risk the entire economic development of Puerto Rico. We believe there is a need to divorce the GDB (as well as the EDB) from the political process—as is done in the United States through the Federal Reserve System. Even though the GDB has no monetary policy functions, it can and does exercise considerable influence on the level of economic activity in Puerto Rico by undertaking key bond flotations in U.S. capital markets. Proceeds are, of course, applied in Puerto Rico by government agencies and private businesses in infrastructure or in industrial projects for local development and export creation.

This is not to suggest that financial policymaking be diverted from the executive branch or the legislature. Rather, it is to recommend that the GDB president be, in fact, a positive, expert source of guidance and recommendation to these branches without fear of political retribution. The better the background, experience, and integrity of the GDB president in any new, more independent organizational administrative structure, the more positive will be the effect on the market for Puerto Rican debt.

The GDB should be empowered to issue and sell its own shares, on its own behalf, restricting their sale to commercial banks and other financial institutions in a well-developed and prorated form so that the private sector has part ownership in the bank. Private sector participation in equity ownership and monitoring, we believe, will improve its operations as a fiscal agent for the government and as a development finance agency. Shares of the private sector should not exceed 40 percent of the total outstanding, so that 60 percent remains in the hands of the government.

We also believe that the bureaucracy in the bank and outside the bank must be reduced. A good place to begin would be with internal examples, such as consolidating the Puerto Rico Municipal Finance Agency (created in 1972) with the Puerto Rican Public Finance Corporation (created in 1984), which performs similar tasks.

The five government retirement systems—all of which are, to one degree or another, in financial difficulty (underfunded, experiencing cash-flow problems, or both)—should be brought to financial health by revenue allocations from the legislature, with the assets to be invested in securities in diverse industries and geographical locations. Private lenders, primarily banks, should be induced to provide industrial loans for development for new or developing firms, such loans guaranteed by the sound assets of the government's various retirement systems. This measure, together with the amendments to the tax code suggested in this chapter, which should eliminate the multitude of exemptions on selected investments, is likely to result in significant direct lending by banks and other financial institutions to local businesses. This technique has been successfully utilized in a number of developing countries. Lower rates and better terms of payment could thus be provided for local industries. When the health of the Puerto Rican retirement systems is assured, perhaps other forms of incentives to financial institutions could be devised to induce more lending for industrial and service-sector development.

The quality of statistics must be improved, as must technology for gathering, storing, and disseminating information. Such information, in addition to substance, must be made effectively and efficiently available, not just to government but to researchers and the public alike. At the moment, such is not always the case.

Conclusion

As in any serious overview of a national financial system, various recommendations could be made with regard to the strengthening of those components of the system requiring improvement or change. Puerto Rico is no different, in this broad sense, from any economic aggregation. Geographically, Puerto Rico is a small body of land that is heavily populated. It has had to cope with many changes, from its political structure to its accommodation to rapid social, economic, and technological developments around as well as within it. Broadly speaking, this tiny island, through its own strength and purpose—and the great help of the United States—has accomplished a great deal in a part of the world where progress in many social, political, and economic domains has never come easily. Today it faces a new challenge in discarding the obsolete and embracing the new if it is truly to realign itself on its path toward the level of a modern economy. Aligning its financial system to these challenges is a key task that should be addressed as a matter of priority.

Table 8A-1. *Financial Sector Assets in Puerto Rico, 1995–2004*

Billions of dollars, except as indicated

Institution type	1995	1996	1997	1998	1999	2000	2001	2002	2003	2004	CAGR (percent)[a]
Small-loan companies	2.1	2.4	2.5	2.5	2.1	2.3	1.5	1.2	1.3	1.3	−5.5
Leasing companies	1.0	1.2	0.9	0.9	1.0	1.2	1.3	1.4	1.8	2.1	8.7
Broker-dealers	3.7	5.4	5.9	7.9	7.4	5.2	3.9	3.3	2.6	2.4	−4.6
Finance companies	1.8	2.7	3.0	3.7	5.0	4.7	5.0	5.2	4.7	4.7	11.4
Credit unions[b]	3.2	3.5	3.8	4.4	4.4	4.5	5.0	5.4	6.0	6.2	7.6
Mortgage companies	1.3	1.5	2.2	3.3	4.2	4.7	5.6	6.2	7.0	8.3	23.2
Investment companies	0.5	0.8	1.6	1.7	2.2	2.4	2.6	5.6	8.8	11.8	43.7
Insurance companies[b]	7.1	8.3	9.0	10.8	10.8	11.5	11.0	12.7	11.7	12.0	6.1
International banking entities	18.4	22.0	26.4	30.2	37.0	44.3	51.5	50.5	56.5	66.8	15.4
Banking sector	39.5	39.1	42.8	49.1	56.8	61.8	71.2	75.9	86.6	102.9	11.2
Total financial sector	78	87	98	114	131	143	159	167	187	218	12.0

Source: Data from the Offices of the Commissioner of Financial Institutions and the Commissioner of Insurance of Puerto Rico.

a. Cumulative annual growth rate, 1995–2004.

b. Assets for 2004 were estimated, as the data were not available.

Table 8A-2. *Asset Composition of Commercial Banks, 1995–2004*
Millions of dollars, except as indicated

Asset type	1995	1996	1997	1998	1999	2000	2001	2002	2003	2004	CAGR (percent)[a]
Investments and securities	10,002	8,707	10,672	14,387	17,646	21,723	23,141	27,760	32,853	38,728	16.2
Loans secured by residential real estate	4,416	4,857	5,116	6,124	7,425	8,435	10,023	11,437	13,926	17,933	16.8
Loans secured by other real estate	2,936	3,069	3,252	3,433	4,714	5,493	6,494	7,466	8,661	10,947	15.7
Commercial and industrial loans	5,703	6,547	7,097	7,591	8,556	8,268	10,752	11,297	11,864	13,267	9.8
Other assets	1,785	1,939	2,067	2,121	2,110	2,150	2,474	2,555	2,865	3,518	7.8
Cash and interest-bearing placements	1,599	1,462	1,838	1,761	2,188	1,921	2,838	2,456	2,444	3,432	8.9
Other loans and leases, net	70	−255	22	333	495	536	474	552	579	459	23.3
Loans to individuals	5,459	6,078	6,143	5,925	5,911	6,260	5,924	5,762	5,600	6,046	1.1
Total assets	31,969	32,404	36,207	41,676	49,045	54,785	62,120	69,284	78,791	94,330	12.8

Source: Data from the Office of the Commissioner of Financial Institutions of Puerto Rico.
a. Cumulative annual growth rate, 1995–2004.

Table 8A-3. *Liability and Equity Composition of Commercial Banks, 1995–2004*
Millions of dollars, except as indicated

Liability type	1995	1996	1997	1998	1999	2000	2001	2002	2003	2004	CAGR (percent)[a]
Long-term debt	1,417	1,680	1,590	1,443	1,559	2,112	4,259	7,120	10,186	11,361	26.0
Brokered deposits	0	0	0	1,626	2,860	4,358	6,114	8,691	11,112	12,716	40.9
Advances from the Federal Home Loan Bank	0	189	678	1,692	3,526	4,638	5,628	6,098	6,536	7,000	57.0
Short-term debt	3,954	2,957	5,303	6,968	9,827	10,890	10,553	7,580	9,467	18,307	18.6
Other liabilities	726	1,109	1,802	2,392	1,374	1,412	1,855	3,667	4,059	4,643	22.9
Other equity	2,316	2,277	2,629	2,865	2,815	3,382	3,804	4,502	5,201	5,837	10.8
Preferred stock	24	45	45	115	81	135	213	314	610	421	37.2
Section 936 deposits	4,909	4,382	3,222	2,773	2,362	1,742	957	0	0	0	…
Deposits (excluding section 936 and brokered)	18,623	19,709	20,938	21,802	24,641	26,116	28,737	31,311	31,620	34,045	6.9
Total liabilities and equity	31,969	32,347	36,207	41,676	49,045	54,785	62,120	69,284	78,791	94,330	12.8

Source: Data from the Office of the Commissioner of Financial Institutions of Puerto Rico.
a. Cumulative annual growth rate, 1995–2004; computed using first nonzero entry.

Table 8A-4. *Mortgage Loans Servicing, 1995–2004*
Units as indicated

Year	Commercial banks		Mortgage companies		Total
	Billions of dollars	*Share of yearly total (percent)*	*Billions of dollars*	*Share of yearly total (percent)*	
1995	9.6	60.1	6.3	39.9	15.9
1996	4.7	38.9	7.4	61.1	12.2
1997	5.2	36.1	9.2	63.9	14.4
1998	5.3	30.8	11.9	69.2	17.2
1999	6.0	31.7	12.9	68.3	18.8
2000	6.6	31.4	14.6	68.6	21.2
2001	7.8	32.4	16.3	67.6	24.1
2002	9.9	35.0	18.3	65.0	28.2
2003	10.4	33.7	20.5	66.3	30.9
2004	11.6	33.7	22.8	66.3	34.3
Total	77.1	35.5	140.2	64.5	217.2
CAGR (percent)[a]	2.1	. . .	15.3	. . .	8.9

Source: Data from the Office of the Commissioner of Financial Institutions of Puerto Rico.
a. Cumulative annual growth rate, 1995–2004.

Table 8A-5. *Commercial Banks' Income Statement, 1995–2004*

Millions of dollars, except as indicated

Item	1995	1996	1997	1998	1999	2000	2001	2002	2003	2004	CAGR (percent)[a]
Interest revenue	2,383	2,488	2,674	2,909	3,337	4,017	3,921	3,683	3,591	3,991	5.9
Interest expense	1,237	1,220	1,345	1,476	1,760	2,379	2,103	1,749	1,535	1,667	3.4
Net interest income	1,146	1,268	1,329	1,433	1,576	1,638	1,818	1,934	2,056	2,325	8.2
Noninterest revenue	305	304	346	413	423	421	478	529	693	797	11.2
Noninterest expense	1,172	1,279	1,344	1,473	1,508	1,565	1,707	1,707	1,853	1,899	5.5
Net noninterest income	(867)	(975)	(999)	(1,060)	(1,085)	(1,144)	(1,229)	(1,178)	(1,160)	(1,103)	n.a.
Net income	279	293	330	373	491	494	589	756	896	1,222	17.8
Total revenue	2,688	2,792	3,019	3,322	3,760	4,438	4,399	4,212	4,284	4,788	6.6
Net interest income/interest revenue (percent)	48.1	51.0	49.7	49.2	47.2	40.8	46.4	52.5	57.2	58.2	…
Net income/total beginning assets (percent)	n.a.	0.9	1.0	1.0	1.2	1.0	1.1	1.2	1.3	1.6	…
Net income/beginning equity (percent)	n.a.	12.5	14.2	14.0	16.5	17.1	16.7	18.8	18.6	21.0	…
Net income/total revenue (percent)	10.4	10.5	10.9	11.2	13.1	11.1	13.4	17.9	20.9	25.5	…

Source: Data from the Office of the Commissioner of Financial Institutions of Puerto Rico.
a. Cumulative annual growth rate, 1995–2004.

Table 8A-6. *International Banking Entities' Balance Sheet, 1995–2004*
Millions of dollars, except as indicated

Item	1995	1996	1997	1998	1999	2000	2001	2002	2003	2004	CAGR (percent)[a]
Cash	28	144	6	252	262	280	357	761	323	449	36.0
Banks placement	13,719	14,744	2,330	113	668	92	29	54	592	790	–27.2
Securities	3,007	4,240	5,964	6,198	7,071	9,301	14,149	15,594	20,057	28,328	28.3
Loans and leases	609	1,348	1,246	4,291	7,441	8,880	11,425	13,061	15,770	18,104	45.8
Federal funds sold	549	775	342	276	121	203	246	262	486	465	–1.8
Due from related parties	4	5	16,053	18,379	20,532	24,549	23,897	18,708	17,051	15,617	150.7
Other assets	489	760	428	679	930	951	1,408	2,018	2,255	2,998	22.3
Total assets	18,404	22,016	26,368	30,188	37,025	44,255	51,510	50,458	56,535	66,751	15.4
Deposits	13,228	14,242	929	3,322	6,514	6,165	6,802	7,059	7,113	9,029	38.4
Demand deposits	n.a.	n.a.	61	393	702	743	716	741	792	860	45.9
Time and savings deposits	n.a.	n.a.	868	2,929	5,812	5,422	6,087	6,318	6,321	8,169	37.7
Federal funds purchase	781	1,551	519	1,614	1,086	1,480	1,347	1,388	1,587	1,638	8.6
Borrowings	2,532	4,000	5,732	3,835	6,041	7,088	12,818	14,680	21,128	27,604	30.4
Due to related parties	n.a.	n.a.	17,533	19,077	20,249	22,797	22,299	17,516	16,537	15,646	–1.6
Other liabilities	401	732	63	127	300	310	343	365	221	762	7.4
Total liabilities	16,943	20,525	24,776	27,975	34,190	37,840	43,609	41,008	46,586	54,678	13.9
Stockholders' equity	1,461	1,492	1,592	2,212	2,835	6,415	7,901	9,450	9,949	12,073	26.4
Total liabilities and stockholders' equity	18,404	22,017	26,368	30,188	37,025	44,255	51,510	50,458	56,535	66,751	15.4

Source: Data from the Office of the Commissioner of Financial Institutions of Puerto Rico.
a. Cumulative annual growth rate, 1995–2004; computed using first nonzero entry.

Table 8A-7. *International Banking Entities' Income Statement, 1995–2004*
Millions of dollars, except as indicated

Item	1995	1996	1997	1998	1999	2000	2001	2002	2003	2004	CAGR (percent)[a]
Interest revenue	366	392	1,404	1,876	2,007	2,629	2,562	2,045	1,809	2,094	21
Interest expense	307	336	1,225	1,593	1,593	2,140	1,865	1,278	986	1,099	15
Net interest income	59	55	179	282	414	489	697	767	822	995	37
Noninterest revenue	–6	0	5	138	140	153	204	293	361	293	–255
Noninterest expense	42	28	123	292	391	408	419	501	598	628	35
Net noninterest income	–48	–28	–118	–154	–251	–255	–215	–208	–237	–334	n.a.
Net income	11	28	62	128	163	235	483	559	585	661	58
Total revenue	360	392	1,409	2,014	2,147	2,782	2,766	2,338	2,170	2,387	23
Net interest income/interest revenue (percent)	16	14	13	15	21	19	27	37	45	48	…
Net income/total beginning assets (percent)	n.a.	0.2	0.3	0.5	0.5	0.6	1.1	1.1	1.2	1.2	…
Net income/beginning equity (percent)	n.a.	1.9	4.1	8.1	7.4	8.3	7.5	7.1	6.2	6.6	…
Net income/total revenue (percent)	3.0	7.1	4.4	6.4	7.6	8.4	17.5	23.9	27.0	27.7	…

Source: Data from the Office of the Commissioner of Financial Institutions of Puerto Rico.
a. Cumulative annual growth rate, 1995–2004.

Table 8A-8. *Assets and Premiums of Insurance Companies Operating in Puerto Rico, 1991–2003*[a]

Millions of dollars, except as indicated

Series	1991	1992	1993	1994	1995	1996	1997	1998	1999	2000	2001	2002	2003	CAGR (percent)[b]
Domestic	1,707	1,848	2,082	2,387	2,768	3,015	3,034	3,390	3,570	3,889	4,258	4,556	4,996	9.4
Health organizations and associations	109	131	148	160	184	203	281	231	219	199	236	295	345	10.1
Life and disability	433	531	610	721	826	949	1,014	1,252	1,246	1,318	1,366	1,444	1,586	11.4
Property and casualty	1,165	1,187	1,324	1,506	1,758	1,863	1,740	1,908	2,106	2,372	2,656	2,817	3,065	8.4
International	3,793	4,349	4,118	4,452	4,295	5,272	5,987	7,418	7,197	7,616	6,740	8,178	6,710	4.9
Life and disability	2,851	3,203	2,806	2,798	2,636	3,915	4,325	5,739	5,500	6,249	5,184	6,076	4,384	3.7
Property and casualty	942	1,147	1,313	1,654	1,658	1,358	1,662	1,679	1,697	1,366	1,557	2,103	2,327	7.8
Total assets	5,500	6,198	6,201	6,839	7,062	8,287	9,021	10,809	10,767	11,504	10,998	12,734	11,706	6.5
Domestic	1,462	1,632	1,850	2,106	2,448	2,951	3,165	3,366	4,433	4,078	4,250	4,579	4,881	10.6
Health organizations and associations	684	777	852	566	643	880	1,030	781	784	711	822	1,130	1,327	5.7
Life and disability	212	243	266	704	883	1,084	1,174	1,452	2,534	2,064	2,021	1,856	1,887	20.0
Property and casualty	566	612	731	836	922	987	961	1,133	1,114	1,303	1,408	1,592	1,667	9.4
International	423	487	465	507	491	589	671	825	801	840	750	914	762	5.0
Life and disability	304	342	300	299	282	418	462	613	587	667	554	649	468	3.7
Property and casualty	119	145	165	209	209	171	210	212	214	172	196	265	293	7.8
Total premiums	1,885	2,118	2,315	2,613	2,938	3,540	3,836	4,191	5,234	4,918	5,000	5,493	5,642	9.6

Source: Data from Office of the Commissioner of Insurance of the Commonwealth of Puerto Rico (1993–2001). Additional data supplied by the same office.

a. Annual reports from the Office of the Commissioner of Insurance show global assets of international insurance companies. Assets of those companies in Puerto Rico were estimated as follows: A ratio of average premiums to average assets was computed for the top five insurance companies in each type of insurance (that is, life, property and casualty). The premiums of these international insurers in Puerto Rico were divided by the corresponding insurance-type ratio to arrive at an estimated figure for assets of these insurers in Puerto Rico.

b. Cumulative annual growth rate, 1991–2003.

Table 8A-9. *Investment Companies' Balance Sheet, 1997–2004*
Millions of dollars, except as indicated

Item	1997	1998	1999	2000	2001	2002	2003	2004	CAGR (percent)[a]
Cash and current accounts	4	4	4	8	13	10	12	24	34.7
U.S. investments	513	542	689	759	808	2,382	3,039	4,161	38.0
Puerto Rican investments	1,052	1,164	1,464	1,607	1,729	3,278	5,616	7,452	35.2
Foreign assets	n.a.	n.a.	n.a.	n.a.	4	6	10	11	43.4
Other assets	17	21	12	18	9	(33)	133	147	38.8
Total assets	1,582	1,728	2,165	2,384	2,551	5,643	8,810	1,795	36.2
Accounts payable	10	11	14	12	14	87	236	376	74.4
Borrowed funds	723	707	856	924	918	2,015	3,577	403	−8.6
Other liabilities	5	8	5	32	33	56	9	4,512	186.7
Total liabilities	738	727	875	969	965	2,159	3,822	5,291	35.4
Stockholders' net worth	847	1,004	1,295	1,423	1,598	3,485	4,988	6,504	36.8
Total liabilities and stockholders' net worth	1,585	1,731	2,170	2,392	2,563	5,643	8,810	11,795	36.2

Source: Data from the Office of the Commissioner of Financial Institutions of Puerto Rico.
a. Cumulative annual growth rate, 1997–2004; computed using first nonzero entry.

Table 8A-10. *Investment Companies' Income Statement, 1997–2004*

Millions of dollars, except as indicated

Item	1997	1998	1999	2000	2001	2002	2003	2004	CAGR (percent)[a]
Interest	83	95	32	130	134	212	367	491	29.0
Dividends	0	1	0	2	4	5	9	18	92.4
Other	6	16	6	25	21	31	20	18	17.3
Total operating income	89	112	38	157	159	248	396	528	29.0
Interest paid	29	37	12	53	43	43	54	77	15.1
Management fee	0	0	0	0	0	11	29	0	10.1
Transactions fees	0	0	0	0	0	0	0	0	n.a.
Other	10	13	4	17	19	21	25	76	34.3
Total operating expense	38	51	16	70	62	74	108	153	21.9
Total recurring income	51	61	23	87	97	174	288	360	32.3
Net capital gain	0	0	1	-23	2	-31	-134	29	-325.9
Pretax income	51	61	24	65	99	143	153	403	34.5
Distributions to shareholders from income	14	15	3	21	29	163	256	4	-15.6
Distributions to shareholders from capital gains	n.a.	n.a.	n.a.	n.a.	n.a.	n.a.	n.a.	n.a.	n.a.
Total distributions	14	15	3	21	29	163	256	4	-15.6
Net interest income	54	58	21	77	92	169	313	414	33.7
Total revenue	140	172	61	244	256	422	683	888	61.3
Net interest income/interest revenue (percent)	65.4	60.7	64.1	59.2	68.3	79.9	85.4	84.4	...
Net interest/total beginning assets (percent)	n.a.	3.8	1.4	3.0	4.1	5.6	2.7	4.6	...
Net interest/beginning equity (percent)	n.a.	7.2	2.4	5.0	6.9	8.9	4.4	8.1	...
Net interest/total revenue (percent)	38.8	33.5	33.8	31.5	35.8	40.1	45.8	46.6	...

Source: Data from the Office of the Commissioner of Financial Institutions of Puerto Rico.

a. Cumulative annual growth rate, 1997–2004; computed using first nonzero entry.

Table 8A-11. *Mortgage Companies' Balance Sheet, 1995–2004*
Millions of dollars, except as indicated

Item	1995	1996	1997	1998	1999	2000	2001	2002	2003	2004	CAGR (percent)[a]
Current assets	564	804	1,198	1,789	1,253	1,428	1,852	3,812	3,733	5,179	27.9
Cash in hand and banks	57	65	47	47	41	28	66	72	281	865	35.3
Net loans and leases receivable	463	540	965	1,431	993	1,167	1,478	1,783	1,824	1,875	16.8
Other current assets	44	199	186	311	219	233	308	1,958	1,628	2,438	56.2
Securities (A – 1)	571	489	822	960	2,155	2,505	2,336	980	1,799	1,343	10.0
Other assets	127	157	221	518	745	791	1,438	1,361	1,506	1,762	34.0
Total assets	1,262	1,450	2,242	3,267	4,152	4,724	5,626	6,153	7,037	8,283	23.2
Current liabilities	1,056	1,144	1,863	2,586	3,017	3,440	3,527	3,012	3,241	3,655	14.8
Accounts payable and accrued liabilities	57	82	124	392	359	418	379	471	645	1,210	40.5
Loans from banks, parent companies, and others	999	1,061	1,693	2,193	2,657	3,021	3,147	2,539	2,592	2,434	10.4
Other current liabilities	0	1	45	0	0	0	1	2	3	12	65.6
Long-term liabilities	8	69	75	72	368	374	489	1,144	1,113	1,537	78.4
Total liabilities	1,064	1,214	1,938	2,658	3,384	3,814	4,016	4,156	4,353	5,193	19.3
Common stock	20	20	30	55	55	57	65	89	128	132	23.0
Preferred stock	1	1	2	2	4	7	6	10	36	34	46.0
All other equity	176	215	272	552	709	846	1,539	1,898	2,520	2,925	36.6
Total capital	198	236	304	609	768	910	1,610	1,997	2,684	3,091	35.7
Total liabilities and capital	1,262	1,450	2,242	3,267	4,152	4,724	5,626	6,153	7,037	8,283	23.2

Source: Data from the Office of the Commissioner of Financial Institutions of Puerto Rico.
a. Cumulative annual growth rate, 1995–2004.

Table 8A-12. *Mortgage Companies' Income Statement, 1995–2004*

Millions of dollars, except as indicated

Item	1995	1996	1997	1998	1999	2000	2001	2002	2003	2004	CAGR (percent)[a]
Interest revenue	83	73	118	184	205	265	247	311	316	330	16.5
Interest expense	59	65	80	139	158	244	172	157	147	140	10.1
Net interest income	25	8	38	45	46	21	74	154	169	190	25.4
Other fee revenue	66	87	90	156	126	99	124	121	167	118	6.6
Net gains on sale of loans	14	28	38	58	145	190	243	327	515	599	52.2
All other revenue	0	0	1	0	0	1	0	1	1	0	0.1
Noninterest expense	73	108	124	151	194	194	239	287	410	344	18.9
Net noninterest income	8	7	5	63	78	96	129	162	273	373	53.8
Net income	33	15	43	108	124	116	203	316	442	563	37.3
Total revenue	164	188	248	398	476	555	614	760	999	1,047	22.9
Net interest income/interest revenue (percent)	29.7	11.1	31.9	24.4	22.7	7.8	30.1	49.4	53.5	57.7	…
Net income/total beginning assets (percent)	n.a.	1.2	3.0	4.8	3.8	2.8	4.3	5.6	7.2	8.0	…
Net income/beginning equity (percent)	n.a.	7.5	18.3	35.5	20.4	15.2	22.3	19.6	22.1	21.0	…
Net income/total revenue (percent)	19.9	7.9	17.4	27.1	26.1	21.0	33.0	41.6	44.3	53.8	…

Source: Data from the Office of the Commissioner of Financial Institutions of Puerto Rico.

a. Cumulative annual growth rate, 1995–2004.

Table 8A-13. *Credit Unions' Balance Sheet, 1995–2004*

Millions of dollars, except as indicated

Item	1995	1996	1997	1998	1999	2000	2001	2002	2003	2004[a]	CAGR (percent)[b]
Cash	515	568	605	1,032	893	854	160	1,569	1,864	1,820	16.0
Investment in securities	335	328	301	263	262	248	226	208	320	421	2.7
Loans											
Personal	629	1,525	1,670	1,658	1,678	1,688	1,719	1,810	1,966	n.a.	15.3
Credit cards	38	49	75	91	101	110	116	111	109	n.a.	14.0
Auto financing	195	240	285	339	420	463	479	459	386	n.a.	8.9
Mortgage	498	497	559	604	663	744	796	831	830	n.a.	6.6
Other	808	124	136	144	144	155	166	197	236	n.a.	−14.3
Total loans	2,168	2,435	2,724	2,836	3,007	3,160	3,276	3,407	3,527	3,430	5.5
Other assets	185	190	206	227	231	231	1,347	254	270	229	2.6
Total assets	3,203	3,520	3,836	4,358	4,394	4,493	5,009	5,439	5,982	5,900	7.4
Deposits	2,162	2,404	2,618	3,108	3,085	3,143	3,615	3,932	4,329	4,281	8.4
Other liabilities	63	79	93	71	108	98	71	76	82	72	1.7
Total liabilities	2,225	2,482	2,710	3,179	3,193	3,242	3,686	4,008	4,411	4,353	8.2
Shares	894	948	1,007	1,045	1,067	1,088	1,125	1,203	1,305	1,283	4.3
Regular reserve	45	59	71	87	103	120	145	166	193	191	18.5
Investment valuation reserve	(2)	(9)	(3)	(0)	(8)	(4)	0	1	(0)	0	n.a.
Other reserves	4	7	13	12	13	16	15	16	21	22	20.4
Undivided earnings	38	32	37	35	26	32	38	44	51	51	3.5
Total capital	979	1,038	1,126	1,179	1,201	1,252	1,323	1,431	1,570	1,547	5.5
Total liabilities and capital	3,203	3,520	3,836	4,358	4,394	4,493	5,009	5,439	5,982	5,900	7.4

Source: Data from the Office of the Commissioner of Financial Institutions of Puerto Rico.

a. Second quarter.

b. Cumulative annual growth rate, 1995–2004:2; computed using last nonzero entry.

Table 8A-14. *Credit Unions' Income Statements, 1995–2004*

Millions of dollars, except as indicated

Item	1995	1996	1997	1998	1999	2000	2001	2002	2003	2004	CAGR (percent)[a]
Interest revenue	225	254	269	299	325	345	354	379	391	397	6.5
Interest expense	86	101	109	122	137	148	146	158	147	134	5.0
Net interest income	139	152	160	177	188	197	208	221	244	263	7.4
Noninterest revenue	18	22	23	26	28	27	28	28	29	29	5.3
Noninterest expense	122	136	144	163	184	196	196	205	222	235	7.5
Net noninterest income	–104	–115	–121	–138	–155	–169	–168	–177	–193	–206	n.a.
Net income	35	38	39	39	33	27	40	44	51	57	5.7
Total revenue	243	276	292	325	354	372	382	407	420	426	6.4
Net interest income/interest revenue (percent)	62	60	59	59	58	57	59	58	62	66	...
Net income/total beginning assets (percent)	n.a.	1.2	1.1	1.0	0.8	0.6	0.9	0.9	0.9	1.0	...
Net income/beginning equity (percent)	n.a.	3.9	3.7	3.5	2.8	2.3	3.2	3.3	3.6	3.7	...
Net income/total revenue (percent)	14.4	13.7	13.2	12.1	9.3	7.4	10.4	10.7	12.1	13.5	...

Source: Data from the Office of the Commissioner of Financial Institutions of Puerto Rico.

a. Cumulative annual growth rate, 1995–2004.

Table 8A-15. *Finance Companies' Balance Sheet, 1995–2004*

Millions of dollars, except as indicated

Item	1995	1996	1997	1998	1999	2000	2001	2002	2003	2004	CAGR (percent)[a]
Cash in hand and banks	14	41	65	43	146	143	107	217	381	587	51.6
Net loans and leases receivable	1,638	2,437	2,666	3,368	4,511	4,266	4,521	4,717	4,277	4,207	11.0
Other current assets	43	71	89	95	100	85	98	111	122	129	13.1
Total current assets	1,695	2,549	2,820	3,506	4,757	4,494	4,727	5,044	4,780	4,923	12.6
Other assets	82	149	190	192	219	210	288	173	(94)	(227)	n.a.
Total assets	1,777	2,698	3,010	3,698	4,976	4,704	5,015	5,217	4,686	4,696	11.4
Loans from banks, parents, and others	1,166	1,893	2,238	2,694	3,696	3,367	3,410	3,504	3,522	3,499	13.0
Other current liabilities	67	121	96	214	403	431	501	673	418	400	22.0
Total current liabilities	1,233	2,013	2,334	2,908	4,099	3,798	3,912	4,177	3,940	3,899	13.6
Long-term liabilities	55	76	93	77	79	128	172	156	195	193	15.0
Total liabilities	1,288	2,089	2,427	2,985	4,179	3,926	4,084	4,332	4,135	4,091	13.7
Total capital	489	608	583	713	797	778	931	885	551	605	2.4
Total liabilities and capital	1,777	2,698	3,010	3,698	4,976	4,704	5,015	5,217	4,686	4,696	11.4

Source: Data from the Office of the Commissioner of Financial Institutions of Puerto Rico.

a. Cumulative annual growth rate, 1995–2004.

Table 8A-16. *Finance Companies' Income Statement, 1995–2004*

Millions of dollars, except as indicated

Item	1995	1996	1997	1998	1999	2000	2001	2002	2003	2004	CAGR (percent)[a]
Interest revenue	213	342	376	418	528	490	523	536	477	464	9.0
Interest expense	57	98	112	139	200	213	188	167	158	134	10.0
Net interest income	156	243	264	279	328	277	336	369	318	330	8.7
Noninterest revenue	41	89	107	105	105	102	69	63	104	106	11.1
Noninterest expense	150	262	315	327	366	286	309	371	359	353	10.0
Net noninterest income	–109	–173	–209	–222	–261	–184	–241	–308	–256	–247	9.5
Net income	48	70	55	57	67	93	95	61	63	84	6.4
Total revenue	255	431	483	522	634	592	592	599	580	570	9.4
Net interest income/interest revenue (percent)	73.3	71.2	70.2	66.8	62.2	56.6	64.2	68.9	66.8	71.1	...
Net income/total beginning assets (percent)	n.a.	3.9	2.1	1.9	1.8	1.9	2.0	1.2	1.2	1.8	...
Net income/beginning equity (percent)	n.a.	14.3	9.1	9.7	9.5	11.7	12.2	6.6	7.1	15.2	...
Net income/total revenue (percent)	18.8	16.3	11.5	10.8	10.6	15.8	16.1	10.2	10.8	14.6	...

Source: Data from the Office of the Commissioner of Financial Institutions of Puerto Rico.

a. Cumulative annual growth rate, 1995–2004.

Table 8A-17. *Broker-Dealers' Balance Sheet, 1995–2004*
Millions of dollars, except as indicated

Item	1995	1996	1997	1998	1999	2000	2001	2002	2003	2004	CAGR (percent)[a]
Cash	2	10	19	15	16	16	20	16	20	31	36.1
Securities purchased under resell agreements	2,101	2,763	3,433	3,189	4,190	2,169	1,534	1,879	1,744	1,685	–2.4
Receivables from brokers, customers, and noncustomers	159	5	47	530	593	78	293	59	41	66	–9.3
Securities owned	1,414	2,608	2,344	4,071	2,507	2,823	1,982	852	697	561	–9.8
Other assets	29	46	67	71	85	82	76	66	68	80	11.9
Total assets	3,705	5,433	5,909	7,876	7,391	5,167	3,906	2,873	2,571	2,423	–4.6
Securities sold under repurchase agreements	2,932	3,525	3,734	5,057	4,287	4,624	2,977	2,226	1,630	1,422	–7.7
Accounts payable	393	1,497	1,716	2,343	2,292	194	626	280	462	440	1.3
Notes, mortgages payable, and bank loans	2	4	20	14	291	93	6	12	15	26	36.4
Subordinated liabilities	189	3	8	1	28	60	60	65	91	96	–7.2
Total liabilities	3,516	5,029	5,478	7,416	6,897	4,972	3,668	2,582	2,198	1,984	–6.2
Total capital	189	404	431	448	494	196	237	290	373	439	9.9
Total liabilities and capital	3,705	5,433	5,909	7,864	7,391	5,167	3,906	2,873	2,571	2,423	–4.6

Source: Data from the Office of the Commissioner of Financial Institutions of Puerto Rico.
a. Cumulative annual growth rate, 1995–2004.

Table 8A-18. *Broker-Dealers' Income Statement, 1995–2004*

Millions of dollars, except as indicated

Item	1995	1996	1997	1998	1999	2000	2001	2002	2003	2004	CAGR (percent)[a]
Commission revenue	4	2	5	37	18	79	89	120	155	158	51.3
Interest revenue and other revenue	69	68	88	352	104	309	159	96	78	78	1.3
Other revenue	14	−16	−21	−40	−14	9	72	32	31	27	7.7
Interest expense	54	39	50	228	74	253	137	58	43	45	−2.0
Noninterest expense	26	15	19	93	26	121	132	129	148	149	21.5
Total expense	80	54	69	320	100	374	270	187	191	194	10.4
Net income	7	0	3	29	9	23	51	61	73	68	29.5
Total revenue	87	54	72	350	109	397	320	248	265	262	13.1
Net interest income / interest revenue (percent)	21.8	42.7	42.6	35.3	29.0	17.9	13.8	40.1	45.1	41.8	…
Net income / total beginning assets (percent)	n.a.	0	0.1	0.5	0.1	0.3	1.0	1.6	2.6	2.7	…
Net income / beginning equity (percent)	n.a.	0	0.8	6.8	2.0	4.6	25.9	25.6	25.3	18.3	…
Net income / total revenue (percent)	7.7	0.1	4.6	8.3	8.1	5.8	15.8	24.5	27.7	26.0	…

Source: Data from the Office of the Commissioner of Financial Institutions of Puerto Rico.

a. Cumulative annual growth rate, 1995–2004.

Table 8A-19. *Assets under Management Control by Broker-Dealers Operating in Puerto Rico, 1995–2004*
Millions of dollars

Institution	1995	1996	1997	1998	1999	2000	2001	2002	2003	2004
UBS Financial Services of Puerto Rico	3,305	3,417	4,474	4,886	5,162	5,487	6,250	7,603	10,271	12,143
Santander Securities	n.a.	3	674	791	985	2,956	2,979	3,148	3,727	4,543
Popular Securities	n.a.	n.a.	610	992	1,276	1,508	1,772	1,971	2,640	3,271
Smith Barney, retail branch	1,820	1,700	2,000	2,200	2,200	2,691	2,311	2,474	2,355	2,141
Oriental Financial Services	n.a.	369	554	761	852	829	906	805	1,004	1,026
Charles Schwab	111	185	420	340	460	615	540	n.a.	641	709
Wachovia Securities (Prudential)	526	499	504	489	541	602	698	553	558	523
Morgan Stanley Dean Witter Reynolds	n.a.	n.a.	n.a.	n.a.	n.a.	n.a.	564	692	749	517
R&G Investment	n.a.	n.a.	n.a.	n.a.	n.a.	n.a.	n.a.	43	n.a.	515
BBVA Securities	n.a.	n.a.	n.a.	n.a.	n.a.	77	139	138	216	323
Merrill Lynch, Pierce, Fenner, and Smith	2,485	2,286	2,639	2,940	2,989	n.a.	n.a.	n.a.	50	195
RD Capital Group	17	22	64	62	53	50	53	54	68	80
Samuel Ramírez	n.a.	n.a.	n.a.	127	99	108	86	n.a.	74	80
Sydney Prevor and Company	43	43	42	65	69	50	7	26	53	50
Tower Square Securities	n.a.	n.a.	n.a.	n.a.	n.a.	n.a.	n.a.	n.a.	29	39
Raymond James Financial Services	n.a.	n.a.	n.a.	n.a.	n.a.	n.a.	n.a.	13	23	33
World Group Securities	n.a.	n.a.	n.a.	n.a.	n.a.	n.a.	n.a.	1	2	14
Jefferson Pilot	n.a.	n.a.	n.a.	n.a.	1	1	3	n.a.	11	13

	n.a.	n.a.	n.a.	n.a.	n.a.	n.a.	n.a.	3	4	6
Axa Advisors	n.a.	n.a.	n.a.	n.a.	n.a.	n.a.	n.a.	n.a.	n.a.	n.a.
Chase Securities Puerto Rico	140	288	145	n.a.	n.a.	n.a.	n.a.	n.a.	n.a.	n.a.
Marketing One Securities	22	151	n.a.	n.a.	n.a.	n.a.	n.a.	n.a.	n.a.	n.a.
Smith Barney	21	59	n.a.	58	n.a.	n.a.	n.a.	n.a.	n.a.	n.a.
Linsco Private	1	3	3	7	12	15	n.a.	n.a.	n.a.	n.a.
Citicorp Financial Services	n.a.	221	272	736	1,123	1,858	2,285	2,969	n.a.	n.a.
Doral Securities	n.a.	n.a.	74	138	227	286	303	35	n.a.	n.a.
T.D. Waterhouse Investor	n.a.	n.a.	n.a.	n.a.	n.a.	n.a.	n.a.	n.a.	n.a.	n.a.
Rizek Investment	n.a.	n.a.	n.a.	19	n.a.	n.a.	n.a.	n.a.	n.a.	n.a.
Booksheet Securities	n.a.	n.a.	n.a.	n.a.	n.a.	45	n.a.	n.a.	n.a.	n.a.
All America Investment	n.a.	n.a.	0	0	0	0	n.a.	n.a.	n.a.	n.a.
Liberty Securities	n.a.	n.a.	n.a.	5	n.a.	n.a.	n.a.	n.a.	n.a.	n.a.
Dean Witter Reynolds	n.a.	217	712	546	993	597	n.a.	n.a.	n.a.	n.a.
Smith Barney Puerto Rico Capital Market	n.a.	n.a.	59	70	n.a.	n.a.	n.a.	n.a.	n.a.	n.a.
R. K. Grace	n.a.	n.a.	n.a.	n.a.	n.a.	n.a.	n.a.	n.a.	n.a.	n.a.
Clark Melvin Securities	n.a.	203	n.a.	n.a.	n.a.	n.a.	n.a.	n.a.	n.a.	n.a.
The Capital Market	n.a.	16	19	13	35	n.a.	n.a.	n.a.	n.a.	n.a.
Total	8,490	9,681	13,265	15,244	17,077	17,775	18,897	20,527	22,475	26,221

Source: Data from the Office of the Commissioner of Financial Institutions of Puerto Rico.

Table 8A-20. *Leasing Companies' Balance Sheet, 1995–2004*
Millions of dollars, except as indicated

Item	1995	1996	1997	1998	1999	2000	2001	2002	2003	2004[a]	CAGR (percent)[b]
Cash in hand and banks	16	7	10	13	26	31	15	14	14	21	2.8
Net loans and leases receivable	750	990	696	744	796	982	1,040	1,130	1,386	1,630	9.0
Other current assets	49	28	34	36	55	56	51	49	68	96	7.6
Total current assets	816	1,026	740	792	878	1,069	1,106	1,193	1,467	1,747	8.8
Personal property held for lease	74	72	65	75	81	92	90	143	177	175	10.0
Other assets	96	108	67	73	60	74	83	105	107	108	1.4
Total assets	986	1,206	872	940	1,019	1,235	1,279	1,441	1,751	2,030	8.4
Loans payable from banks, parent companies, and others	619	930	612	667	713	912	934	257	387	311	−7.4
Other current liabilities	179	56	63	76	87	81	80	81	80	75	−9.2
Total current liabilities	798	986	675	743	800	993	1,014	338	467	386	−7.8
Long-term liabilities	71	29	29	16	13	14	14	849	953	1,260	37.6
Total liabilities	869	1,015	704	759	813	1,007	1,028	1,187	1,420	1,646	7.4
Total capital	116	191	168	181	206	228	250	254	331	384	14.2
Total liabilities and capital	986	1,206	872	940	1,019	1,235	1,279	1,441	1,751	2,030	8.4

Source: Data from the Office of the Commissioner of Financial Institutions of Puerto Rico.
a. Third quarter.
b. Cumulative annual growth rate, 1995–2004:3.

Table 8A-21. *Leasing Companies' Income Statement, 1995–2004*

Millions of dollars, except as indicated

Item	1995	1996	1997	1998	1999	2000	2001	2002	2003	2004[a]	CAGR (percent)[b]
Interest revenue	106	110	89	94	97	110	119	126	141	152	4.2
Interest expense	51	57	41	43	46	59	57	52	54	55	0.8
Net interest income	55	53	47	51	50	51	62	75	87	98	6.7
Noninterest revenue	78	116	86	79	114	131	126	133	175	180	9.8
Noninterest expense	112	146	114	111	135	156	159	174	228	235	8.6
Net noninterest income	-34	-30	-28	-32	-21	-26	-33	-40	-54	-55	n.a.
Net income	20	23	19	19	29	25	29	34	33	43	8.6
Total revenue	183	226	174	173	211	240	245	260	316	333	6.9
Net interest income/interest revenue (percent)	51.7	47.9	53.5	54.2	52.1	46.4	52.2	59.0	61.5	64.1	…
Net income/total beginning assets (percent)	n.a.	2.3	1.6	2.2	3.1	2.5	2.4	2.7	2.3	2.5	…
Net income/beginning equity (percent)	n.a.	19.4	10.1	11.2	16.2	12.3	12.8	13.7	13.0	13.0	…
Net income/total revenue (percent)	11.2	10.0	11.1	10.8	13.9	10.5	11.9	13.2	10.5	12.9	…

Source: Data from the Office of the Commissioner of Financial Institutions of Puerto Rico.

a. Extrapolated.

b. Cumulative annual growth rate, 1995–2004.

Table 8A-22. *Small-Loan Companies' Balance Sheet, 1995–2004*
Millions of dollars, except as indicated

Item	1995	1996	1997	1998	1999	2000	2001	2002	2003	2004	CAGR (percent)[a]
Cash in hand and banks	2	1	3	(1)	10	10	6	5	9	6	16.1
Net loans and leases receivable	1,641	1,889	1,928	1,471	1,158	1,056	1,041	1,006	1,031	1,048	–4.9
Other current assets	5	21	29	362	201	346	46	111	19	19	17.1
Total current assets	1,648	1,911	1,960	1,831	1,369	1,411	1,093	1,122	1,058	1,073	–4.7
Other assets	456	469	581	626	750	848	360	133	208	193	–9.1
Total assets	2,104	2,380	2,542	2,458	2,119	2,259	1,453	1,255	1,267	1,266	–5.5
Loans from banks, parent companies, and others	1,248	1,530	1,684	1,751	1,448	1,421	744	609	621	652	–7.0
Other current liabilities	35	44	42	35	31	32	63	52	47	52	4.6
Total current liabilities	1,283	1,574	1,725	1,786	1,479	1,453	808	661	668	704	–6.4
Long-term liabilities	577	517	491	316	279	317	307	270	282	273	–8.0
Total liabilities	1,860	2,091	2,217	2,102	1,759	1,770	1,115	931	950	978	–6.9
Total capital	244	289	325	356	361	489	338	323	316	288	1.9
Total liabilities and capital	2,104	2,380	2,542	2,458	2,119	2,259	1,453	1,255	1,267	1,266	–5.5

Source: Data from the Office of the Commissioner of Financial Institutions of Puerto Rico.
a. Cumulative annual growth rate, 1995–2004.

Table 8A-23. *Small-Loan Companies' Income Statement, 1995–2004*
Millions of dollars, except as indicated

Item	1995	1996	1997	1998	1999	2000	2001	2002	2003	2004	CAGR (percent)[a]
Interest revenue	300	383	426	425	348	293	303	294	281	274	–1.0
Interest expense	101	127	136	132	100	78	67	49	43	46	–8.4
Net interest income	200	256	291	293	248	214	236	246	238	228	1.5
Noninterest revenue	8	16	16	21	20	26	18	11	16	10	2.2
Noninterest expense	189	245	303	642	229	171	213	347	232	223	1.9
Net noninterest income	–181	–228	–287	–621	–210	–145	–194	–336	–216	–213	1.9
Net income	19	27	3	–328	38	69	42	–90	22	15	–2.8
Total revenue	308	399	442	447	367	319	321	305	297	284	–0.9
Net interest income/interest revenue (percent)	66.5	66.8	68.2	68.9	71.3	73.2	77.9	83.4	84.7	83.4	…
Net income/total beginning assets (percent)	n.a.	1.3	0.1	–12.9	1.6	3.3	1.8	–6.2	1.8	1.2	…
Net income/beginning equity (percent)	n.a.	11.2	1.1	–100.8	10.7	19.1	8.5	–26.7	6.8	4.7	…
Net income/total revenue (percent)	6.2	6.9	0.7	–73.4	10.4	21.6	12.9	–29.5	7.4	5.2	…

Source: Data from the Office of the Commissioner of Financial Institutions of Puerto Rico.
a. Cumulative annual growth rate, 1995–2004.

Table 8A-24. *Venture Capital Funds' Balance Sheet, 1997–2004*
Thousands of dollars, except as indicated

Item	1997	1998	1999	2000	2001	2002	2003	2004	CAGR (percent)[a]
Cash	2,945	4,243	4,752	9,545	3,730	17,574	16,981	22,697	33.9
Securities and portfolio investments	54,367	68,149	89,960	100,263	67,289	94,941	64,058	100,101	9.1
Other assets	10,827	15,856	12,060	9,896	14,950	16,360	48,143	20,082	9.2
Total assets	68,139	88,248	106,772	119,704	85,969	128,875	129,182	142,880	11.2
Liabilities									
Current liabilities	5,925	6,577	1,524	707	860	5,258	1,323	1,334	–19.2
Long-term liabilities	3,554	5,767	3,488	80	9,940	8,759	17,289	16,705	24.7
Total liabilities	9,479	12,344	5,012	787	10,800	14,017	18,612	18,039	9.6
Eligible contributed capital	n.a.	n.a.	n.a.	n.a.	n.a.	118,222	104,438	121,845	n.a.
Noneligible contributed capital	n.a.	n.a.	n.a.	n.a.	n.a.	12,132	12,132	n.a.	n.a.
Retained earnings	n.a.	n.a.	n.a.	n.a.	n.a.	(15,496)	(6,000)	2,996	n.a.
Total equity	58,660	75,905	101,760	118,917	75,169	114,858	110,570	124,841	11.4
Total liabilities and capital	68,139	88,249	106,772	119,704	85,969	128,875	129,182	142,880	11.2

Source: Data from the Office of the Commissioner of Financial Institutions of Puerto Rico.
a. Cumulative annual growth rate, 1997–2004.

Table 8A-25. *Venture Capital Funds' Income Statement, 1997–2004*

Thousands of dollars, except as indicated

Item	1997	1998	1999	2000	2001	2002	2003	2004	CAGR (percent)[a]
Operating	n.a.	n.a.	n.a.	n.a.	n.a.	833	3,271	4,611	n.a.
Dividends	63	29	577	1,841	2,094	1,192	0	233	n.a.
Interest	705	657	432	290	200	479	291	610	-2.0
Gains on the sale of investments	n.a.	n.a.	n.a.	n.a.	n.a.	-3,907	3,152	11,044	n.a.
Other	996	1,819	10,508	-571	53	-725	299	134	-24.9
Total revenues	1,764	2,505	11,517	1,560	2,347	-2,128	7,013	16,632	37.8
Operating	n.a.	n.a.	n.a.	n.a.	n.a.	746	2,347	2,728	n.a.
General and administrative	n.a.	n.a.	n.a.	n.a.	n.a.	2,197	2,084	2,414	n.a.
Total expenses	3,931	4,908	7,674	756	3,646	2,943	4,431	5,142	3.9
Pretax income	-2,167	-2,403	3,843	804	-1,299	-5,071	2,582	11,490	n.a.
Gains on the sale of assets and investments	0	7,553	-8,346	-1,599	1,328	n.a.	n.a.	n.a.	n.a.
Income taxes	0	8	33	0	0	0	0	0	n.a.
Net income	-2,167	5,142	-4,536	-795	29	-5,071	2,582	11,490	-226.9
Net income/total beginning assets (percent)	n.a.	7.5	-5.1	-0.7	0	-5.9	2.0	8.9	…
Net income/beginning equity (percent)	n.a.	8.8	-6.0	-0.8	0	-6.7	2.2	10.4	…
Net income/total revenue (percent)	-122.8	205.3	-39.4	-51.0	1.2	238.3	36.8	69.1	…

Source: Data from the Office of the Commissioner of Financial Institutions of Puerto Rico.

a. Cumulative annual growth rate, 1997–2004.

Table 8A-26. *Government Development Bank's Balance Sheet, 1995–2004*

Millions of dollars, except as indicated

Item	1995	1996	1997	1998	1999	2000	2001	2002	2003	2004	CAGR (percent)[a]
Cash and interest-bearing placements	18	47	285	789	225	108	113	54	45	14	-2.7
Investments and securities	3,565	2,413	2,038	1,696	2,007	1,586	3,039	2,257	1,812	924	-13.9
Federal funds sold and securities purchased	n.a.	n.a.	n.a.	n.a.	n.a.	n.a.	n.a.	845	662	535	n.a.
Loans and leases, net, including commercial, industrial, and agricultural	2,219	2,953	2,662	2,943	3,378	3,459	3,774	1,929	3,357	5,165	9.8
Other assets	526	574	674	802	851	905	661	800	940	946	6.7
Total assets	6,329	5,987	5,660	6,230	6,462	6,057	7,587	5,884	6,816	7,585	2.0
Total deposits	3,518	2,899	2,635	3,382	2,773	2,753	3,577	2,763	3,177	4,408	2.5
Short-term debt	115	69	1,212	895	1,788	1,279	1,366	624	1,274	n.a.	-100.0
Long-term debt	1,504	1,684	365	354	267	267	519	267	n.a.	n.a.	-100.0
Other liabilities	84	119	89	98	68	63	218	194	128	1,290	35.5
Total liabilities	5,221	4,772	4,301	4,728	4,897	4,363	5,680	3,847	4,579	5,697	1.0
Equity	1,108	1,214	1,359	1,502	1,565	1,695	1,907	2,037	2,237	1,888	6.1

Source: Data from the Office of the Commissioner of Financial Institutions of Puerto Rico.

a. Cumulative annual growth rate, 1995–2004.

Table 8A-27. *Government Development Bank's Income Statement, 1995–2004*

Millions of dollars, except as indicated

Item	1995	1996	1997	1998	1999	2000	2001	2002	2003	2004	CAGR (percent)[a]
Interest revenue	203	177	172	155	156	193	240	111	141	141	-4.0
Interest expense	156	126	105	112	112	118	79	58	42	57	-10.6
Net interest income	47	51	67	44	45	75	161	53	100	84	6.6
Noninterest revenue	26	26	33	40	10	3	30	35	21	29	1.4
Noninterest expense	19	16	19	20	34	31	16	22	23	520	44.8
Net noninterest income	7	11	14	20	-25	-27	14	13	-2	-491	…
Net income	55	62	80	64	20	48	175	66	98	-407	-225.0
Total revenue	229	203	205	196	166	197	270	146	162	170	-3.3
Net interest income/interest revenue (percent)	23.2	28.9	38.8	28.2	28.7	38.8	67.0	47.8	70.6	59.7	…
Net income/total beginning assets (percent)	n.a.	1.0	1.3	1.1	0.3	0.7	2.9	0.9	1.7	-6.0	…
Net income/beginning equity (percent)	n.a.	5.6	6.6	4.7	1.3	3.1	10.3	3.4	4.8	-18.2	…
Net income/total revenue (percent)	23.8	30.4	39.2	32.5	12.2	24.3	64.8	45.1	60.3	-238.9	…

Source: Data from the Office of the Commissioner of Financial Institutions of Puerto Rico.

a. Cumulative annual growth rate, 1995–2004.

Table 8A-28. *Total Debt Facilitated by the Government Development Bank on Behalf of the Commonwealth of Puerto Rico, April 1993 to June 2004*

Year	New money		Refunding		Total
	Millions of dollars	As share of yearly total (percent)	Millions of dollars	As share of yearly total (percent)	
1993	1,199	25	3,530	75	4,728
1994	1,140	80	287	20	1,428
1995	1,461	52	1,357	48	2,818
1996	2,209	90	242	10	2,451
1997	3,379	80	825	20	4,204
1998	3,946	73	1,447	27	5,393
1999	1,058	78	293	22	1,351
2000	4,209	98	71	2	4,280
2001	4,088	78	1,175	22	5,263
2002	6,526	73	2,457	27	8,983
2003	3,842	59	2,689	41	6,531
2004	1,385	33	2,845	67	4,230
Total	34,441	67	17,218	33	51,659

Source: Data from the Office of the President of the Government Development Bank of Puerto Rico.

Table 8A-29. *Total Debt Issued by AFICA, 1978–2004*

All new money in millions of dollars

Year	Amount	Year	Amount
1978	35	1992	135
1979	52	1993	188
1980	74	1994	164
1981	268	1995	280
1982	336	1996	87
1983	887	1997	48
1984	64	1998	429
1985	307	1999	508
1986	155	2000	668
1987	124	2001	197
1988	174	2002	174
1989	141	2003	17
1990	67	2004	7
1991	265		
1978–2004	5,852		

Source: Data from the Office of the President of the Government Development Bank of Puerto Rico, January 2005.

Table 8A-30. *Economic Development Bank's Balance Sheet, 1995–2004*

Millions of dollars, except as indicated

Item	1995	1996	1997	1998	1999	2000	2001	2002	2003	2004	CAGR (percent)[a]
Cash and interest-bearing placements	56	8	33	44	59	120	213	235	359	253	18.3
Investments and securities	1,031	550	679	864	914	458	957	327	507	500	–7.7
Federal funds sold and securities purchased	n.a.	n.a.	n.a.	n.a.	n.a.	n.a.	n.a.	100	95	35	n.a.
Commercial and industrial loans	73	118	178	236	264	338	352	147	163	179	10.5
Other loans, net	(9)	(10)	(18)	(39)	(37)	(39)	(39)	(38)	(35)	(34)	15.5
Other assets	45	43	55	63	64	51	34	32	31	30	–4.2
Total assets	1,195	708	928	1,168	1,264	928	1,516	802	1,121	964	–2.4
Total deposits	337	365	403	502	374	427	544	331	509	321	–0.5
Short-term debt	676	185	364	492	657	234	738	152	27	107	–18.5
Long-term debt	96	72	42	48	107	130	. . .	101	368	413	17.6
Other liabilities	13	10	41	38	35	20	126	11	12	10	–2.4
Total liabilities	1,122	631	850	1,080	1,173	810	1,407	595	917	851	–3.0
Equity	74	78	78	89	91	118	109	107	109	113	4.8

Source: Data from the Office of the President of the Government Development Bank of Puerto Rico.

a. Cumulative annual growth rate, 1995–2004.

Table 8A-31. *Economic Development Bank's Income Statement, 1995–2004*

Millions of dollars, except as indicated

Item	1995	1996	1997	1998	1999	2000	2001	2002	2003	2004	CAGR (percent)[a]
Interest revenue	33.0	38.9	25.8	35.9	34.8	40.7	18.7	11.7	15.0	18.8	–6.1
Interest expense	26.0	29.7	19.1	28.7	27.8	33.3	11.4	6.7	9.4	12.6	–7.8
Net interest income	7.0	9.2	6.7	7.2	7.0	7.4	7.3	5.0	5.6	6.2	–1.4
Noninterest revenue	1.5	2.2	5.0	5.4	5.5	27.5	3.7	2.7	2.5	4.1	12.1
Noninterest expense	6.3	6.2	8.4	6.9	7.3	9.3	6.1	5.6	6.0	6.3	–0.1
Net noninterest income	–4.9	–4.0	–3.3	–1.5	–1.8	18.2	–2.4	–2.9	–3.5	–2.2	n.a.
Net income	2.1	5.2	3.4	5.6	5.2	25.5	4.9	2.1	2.1	4.1	7.4
Total revenue	34.5	41.1	30.8	41.2	40.3	68.1	22.4	14.4	17.5	22.9	–4.5
Net interest income/interest revenue (percent)	21	24	26	20	20	18	39	43	37	33	…
Net income/total beginning assets (percent)	n.a.	0.4	0.5	0.6	0.4	2.0	0.5	0.1	0.3	0.4	…
Net income/beginning equity (percent)	n.a.	7.0	4.4	7.2	5.9	28.1	4.2	1.9	2.0	3.7	…
Net income/total revenue (percent)	6.2	n.a.	n.a.	13.6	13.0	37.5	22.1	n.a.	12.0	17.7	…

Source: Data from the Office of the President of the Government Development Bank of Puerto Rico.

a. Cumulative annual growth rate, 1995–2004.

Table 8A-32. *Commercial Banks' Average Balance Sheet for Puerto Rico, the United States, Florida, Hawaii, and the Five Most Aggressive Banks in Puerto Rico, 1995–2003*
Units as indicated

Item	Amount (millions of dollars)					CAGR (percent)[a]				
	Puerto Rico	United States	Florida	Hawaii	Five banks	Puerto Rico	United States	Florida	Hawaii	Five banks
Cash and interest-bearing placements	2,056	359,588	5,865	1,543	516	5.4	3.0	-11.2	-6.9	21.0
Investments and securities	18,543	1,043,037	17,794	4,903	7,456	16.0	7.5	-6.5	2.8	35.6
Other loans and leases, net	312	370,639	2,753	903	-36	30.3	6.0	-11.3	-0.3	0
Commercial and industrial loans	8,630	866,122	10,512	3,894	1,037	9.6	3.4	-7.7	-4.9	33.1
Loans to individuals	5,896	605,283	8,240	1,588	1,638	0.3	4.7	-19.3	2.2	4.0
Loans secured by residential real estate	7,973	927,703	23,793	5,026	3,939	15.4	9.4	-12.1	2.9	29.0
Loans secured by other real estate	5,057	629,608	18,593	3,296	2,043	14.5	10.2	2.3	1.0	42.7
Other assets	2,230	988,999	8,930	2,171	585	6.1	10.2	-9.7	11.5	25.1
Total assets	50,698	5,790,978	96,479	23,324	17,178	11.9	7.3	-7.7	1.5	29.5
Total deposits	30,956	3,907,593	77,344	16,467	8,916	7.7	6.5	-8.0	3.0	24.6
Debt	16,067	1,381,599	10,602	4,511	7,115	22.3	9.0	-6.2	-7.0	37.2
Total liabilities	47,023	5,289,192	87,946	20,979	16,031	12.0	7.1	-7.8	0.8	29.5
Perpetual preferred stock	176	3,414	32	0	84	49.5	16.0	-4.5	-100.0	51.9
Other equity	3,310	498,373	8,500	2,346	1,063	10.6	8.8	-6.5	7.0	27.8
Total liabilities and equity capital	50,692	5,790,978	96,479	23,324	17,178	11.9	7.3	-7.7	1.5	29.5

Source: Data from the Federal Deposit Insurance Corporation.

a. Cumulative annual growth rate, 1995–2003.

Table 8A-33. *Commercial Banks' Average Income Statement for Puerto Rico, the United States, Florida, Hawaii, and the Five Most Aggressive Banks in Puerto Rico, 1995–2003*
Units as indicated

Item	Income (millions of dollars)					CAGR (percent)[a]				
	Puerto Rico	United States	Florida	Hawaii	Five banks	Puerto Rico	United States	Florida	Hawaii	Five banks
Interest revenue	3,991	353,304	6,337	1,513	1,024	5.3	1.3	-12.4	-4.7	20.0
Interest expense	1,667	159,186	2,632	626	563	2.7	-5.4	-16.9	-16.9	20.2
Net interest income	2,325	194,119	3,705	887	461	7.6	5.7	-9.9	1.4	19.9
Noninterest revenue	797	135,202	1,317	372	105	10.8	10.7	-10.6	3.2	22.1
Noninterest expense	1,899	259,769	3,961	1,014	360	5.9	7.0	-10.1	1.1	16.7
Net noninterest income	-1,103	-124,567	-2,643	-642	-255	n.a.	n.a.	n.a.	n.a.	n.a.
Net income	1,222	69,551	1,062	245	206	15.7	9.7	-10.0	4.4	26.8
Total revenue	4,788	488,506	7,654	1,884	1,130	6.0	3.9	-12.1	-3.1	20.3
Net interest income/interest revenue (percent)	58.2	54.9	58.5	58.6	45.0	9.2	20.6	14.4	32.6	-0.6
Net income/total beginning assets (percent)	1.1	1.3	1.0	1.1	1.6	1.3	0.2	0	0.4	-0.1
Net income/beginning equity (percent)	16.1	15.1	11.3	11.2	23.5	18.6	0.2	-2.6	-2.1	-4.1
Net income/total revenue (percent)	25.5	14.2	13.9	13.0	18.2	n.a.	n.a.	n.a.	n.a.	n.a.

Source: Data from the Federal Deposit Insurance Corporation.
a. Cumulative annual growth rate, 1995–2003.

Table 8A-34. *Return on Equity Risk Analysis, Puerto Rico, the United States, Florida, Hawaii, and the Five Most Aggressive Banks in Puerto Rico, 1995–2003 and 1967–2003*

Percent

Region	1995–2003			1967–2003		
	Mean	Standard deviation	Standard deviation/ mean	Mean	Standard deviation	Standard deviation/ mean
United States	15	1	4	13	3	22
Florida	11	3	28	12	3	27
Hawaii	11	2	15	15	3	20
Puerto Rico	17	1	9	14	7	48
Five banks[a]	24	3	12	. . .	. . .	. . .

Source: Data from the Federal Deposit Insurance Corporation.

a. The five most aggressive banks are relatively new and did not exist for the first ten to twenty years of the period.

Table 8A-35. *Risk and Return on Equity for Selected Banks in Puerto Rico and for All FDIC-Insured Puerto Rican Banks, 1995–2003*

Percent

Bank	Mean	Standard deviation	Standard deviation/mean
Twelve Puerto Rican insured banks	16.7	1.4	8.6
Oriental Bank and Trust	22.7	9.3	41.1
R-G Premier	17.9	5.4	30.3
Doral Bank	27.6	8.1	29.4
Firstbank	24.5	4.4	18.1
Westernbank	23.8	3.0	12.6

Source: Data from the Federal Deposit Insurance Corporation.

Arturo Estrella

Economic progress in every nation in the world, from the most advanced industrial powers to the least-developed emerging economies, depends on the availability of financial capital for business and government. This capital may be internally or externally generated, may be supplied directly or intermediated, may take the form of debt or equity, and may be denominated in local or foreign currencies. In whatever form, it is an essential component for economic growth.

Thus the chapter written by Rita Maldonado-Bear and Ingo Walter addresses a topic that is important both to understanding the past economic development of Puerto Rico and to exploring the prospects for future economic growth on the island. Not many researchers have chosen previously to tackle this topic, very likely because of difficulties such as lack of adequate data and the complications of a financial sector that is locally diverse, externally open, and unique.

Earlier Literature

More than three decades ago, following a period of strong economic growth in the 1950s and 1960s, there was a flurry of serious academic work on the role of the financial sector in the economic development of Puerto Rico. Jorge Freyre, Raúl Asón, and Rita Maldonado-Bear all completed doctoral dissertations on this topic, and their work was widely circulated within Puerto Rico and, to some extent, more broadly.[1] In each case, an analytical model encompassing the financial sector of Puerto Rico was formulated and estimated empirically, and the conclusions were generally supportive of an important role for the financial sector in the rapid growth experienced in the preceding years.

More recently, Leandro Colón and Francisco Martínez (1999) discuss financial flows in the island's economy, taking a broad perspective that ranges from local financial institutions to the balance of payments.[2] As do most researchers in this field, they lament the lack of relevant financial data and recommend that steps be taken to improve the situation. They also provide a useful review of intervening research on the financial sector in Puerto Rico, a review that is particularly helpful because many of the works cited are not currently readily accessible.

---

1. Freyre (1969), Asón (1970), and Maldonado-Bear (1970).
2. Colón and Martínez (1999).

Contributions of the Chapter

Maldonado-Bear and Walter's chapter brings together a wealth of relatively inaccessible information about financial institutions in Puerto Rico. The sources of this information are generally public, but they are not easily available from either print or electronic sources, and certainly not from a single coherently organized source. The chapter provides a comprehensive view of the development of various financial sectors in the island over the past decade. The information is up to date (annual data range from 1995 to 2004) and covers a broad range of financial intermediaries.

The picture that emerges from these data is one of domination by the banking sector over other types of financial institutions. As of 2004, the banking sector accounted for 78 percent of aggregate assets of financial institutions on the island. Traditional commercial banking institutions represent 47 percent of the total. Remarkably, another 31 percent is attributable to international banking entities, special purpose institutions with a narrow role made possible by a local statute passed in 1980 and amended in 1996.

Based on this information, the chapter identifies several features of the financial sector in Puerto Rico that may be problematic in terms of fostering economic growth. Two fairly straightforward examples are the low volume of commercial and industrial loans (as a proportion of bank assets) and relatively high debt levels of banks. When compared with other benchmark jurisdictions, commercial banks in Puerto Rico seem to hold unusually high levels of securities, crowding out commercial loans. Low levels of equity capital associated with significant debt financing may be detrimental to the continued health of the banking sector in the event of local or international problems with asset quality.

Some other problems identified in the chapter are not as clear-cut, such as the term of office of the head of the Government Development Bank (GDB) and the level of funding of government pension systems. The authors argue that there is a need for greater stability and independence in the management of the GDB. Although these goals might be constructive, it is not certain that an extension of the term of office would have the desired effect. If anything, incumbents have demonstrated a proclivity to stay on the job for much less time than the current limits allow, and not to test those limits.

The issue of funding of government pension systems is quite problematic. It would doubtless be beneficial if that funding were currently adequate by acceptable actuarial standards. However, if unfunded liabilities have grown over decades to large proportions, how quickly is it advisable to close those gaps? U.S. regulation for private pension plans allows for lengthy periods to amortize unfunded liabilities. Any attempt to fix this problem too quickly is likely to have visible contractionary effects on the economy. That being said, the authors are to be commended for pointing to this real problem and for arguing that it should not be ignored.

Some Difficult Questions

The absence of long, consistent data series makes it all but impossible to address certain types of important questions. The bulk of the data used in the chapter's analysis is of annual frequency for the period from 1995 to 2004. Thus there is little to say about conditions in the more distant past or about comparisons of that past with current experience. How important was the financial sector for the "economic miracle" of the 1950s and 1960s? Is the current state of the financial sector more or less favorable than in those periods? What, has been the significance, if any, of the explosive development of financial derivatives in the United States since the 1980s?

The last question is suggestive of another type of difficulty. Can we unscramble the effects of development in the U.S. financial sectors from the effects of local financial development in Puerto Rico? Because of the island's political status, interaction between the Puerto Rican and U.S. economies is very open in terms of trade, monetary conditions, and factor mobility. U.S. corporations have extensive operations on the island, and local firms operate in the United States, as well. This means that financial capital for local projects may just as easily be obtained in the United States as in Puerto Rico. Recent empirical estimates suggest that U.S. financial development may explain Puerto Rican economic growth as well as or better than does the development of the local financial sector.[3]

For similar reasons, data on financial capital raised by local firms could be misleading. For instance, the largest number of public debt issues by firms domiciled in Puerto Rico in any one year is thirteen, observed in both 2002 and 2004, and the largest aggregate dollar volume is $1.4 billion in 1999 (table 8-10). These figures are quite modest compared with the volume of commercial loans extended by local banks. Are they truly representative of total public debt issuance to finance projects in Puerto Rico? How much public debt is issued in the United States and elsewhere?

One caveat about table 8-10 is that it compares a flow with a stock, which may overstate the volume of commercial lending. However, commercial loans are typically short term, so the volume outstanding should provide at least a rough benchmark for the flows. Moreover, even the net changes in loans outstanding tend to surpass debt issuance, much of which is issued by banks and not by end users (76 percent in 1999). A second caveat is that the financial sectors of most countries tend to be dominated by banking, with public debt

3. Estrella (2005).

Table 8-10. *Public Debt Issuance and Commercial Loans, Puerto Rico, 1995–2004*[a]

Units as indicated

	Public debt		
Year	Number of issues	Amount raised (millions of dollars)	Commercial loans (millions of dollars)
1995	2	224	5,703
1996	7	270	6,547
1997	5	220	7,097
1998	2	160	7,591
1999	5	1,400	8,556
2000	0	0	8,268
2001	8	85	10,752
2002	13	270	11,297
2003	5	45	11,684
2004	13	798	13,267

Source: SDC database from Thomson Financial.

a. Public debt represents issues by firms domiciled in Puerto Rico. Commercial loans are outstanding at banks domiciled in Puerto Rico, as given in chapter 8 text.

issuance playing a major role only in countries such as the United States and the United Kingdom. Nonetheless, Puerto Rico's access to the U.S. financial system would suggest that public debt might play an important role.

It is unlikely that the foregoing issues can be definitively addressed with the current state of economic and financial data. Even if data availability improves substantially in the future, some of the identification issues are likely to persist and to require great analytical ingenuity. More generally, and regardless of the status of data availability, there is a need to bring more formal theoretical and statistical models to the analysis of the financial sector in Puerto Rico. That approach was adopted in the three dissertations cited earlier from around 1970 but seems absent from much of the more recent literature.

Chapter's Recommendations and Economic Policy

I end with a brief review of some of the article's key recommendations. Focus in the text is on economic goals to be achieved, not so much on why policy intervention is needed or on the policy tools that would be required to achieve the goals.

I have mentioned the recommendations that banks place a greater proportion of their assets in commercial and industrial loans and that they hold less debt on their liabilities side. Real GDP growth in the time period examined is

Table 8-11. *Real Gross Domestic Product, Puerto Rico, 1950–2004*
Percent

Period	Real GDP growth
1950–59	5.4
1960–69	7.0
1970–79	5.3
1980–89	3.3
1990–99	4.1
1995–2004[a]	3.6

Source: Data from Puerto Rico Planning Board.
a. Matches years of data sample in chapter 8.

lower than it was in the 1950s and 1960s, but not as low as in the 1980s (see table 8-11). It would be interesting to have bank data for these earlier periods. For instance, the case for more commercial loans would seem prima facie more or less compelling, depending on whether the trend toward higher security holdings was already in place in the 1980s.

From a policy perspective, commercial loans are socially desirable if they finance productive projects. If these loans are crowded out by other assets, we need to look more closely at whether those other assets are less socially desirable, in particular, whether the extent of those other holdings is driven by market imperfections. This type of policy analysis would dictate whether intervention is required and, if so, the right policy tools to be used.

The issue of bank capital in general is extensively addressed in the financial literature, and existing policy tools already apply to banks in Puerto Rico.[4] Perhaps it is useful to ask whether special conditions require that different tools be in place for Puerto Rican banks.

The chapter's recommendations with regard to international banking entities are adopted from a study prepared for the Office of the Commissioner of Financial Institutions in Puerto Rico and are largely technical in nature. They pertain mainly to means of encouraging the development of these entities and not to the policy reasons for developing the sector. Given the phenomenal growth of international banking entities during the past decade, further analytical work focused on this sector seems highly desirable.

Maldonado-Bear and Walter make one recommendation that is virtually unassailable: the development of better data sources for the Puerto Rican economy and financial sector. Shortcomings in the existing data, identified in any number of studies of the financial sector, should be examined to determine whether the costs of data collection are warranted by the benefits of more exten-

4. See Santos (2001) for a review of the literature.

sive public data. Great benefits might even be derived from simply organizing the existing data and posting them in accessible sites.

All in all, this chapter is a welcome addition to the literature on a topic of great importance for local economic development. It brings us a step closer to an understanding of the role of the financial sector in Puerto Rico, and it points clearly and convincingly to the pressing need for more analysis.

COMMENT
James A. Hanson

The association between finance and economic development is well established, but there remains a question of whether finance leads or lags economic development or simply reflects underlying factors that support both economic development and finance. Alexander Gerschenkron, following Joseph Schumpeter, suggested more than forty years ago that finance should be a leader in development and that state banks should act as entrepreneurs.[5] However, recent econometric research suggests that state banks have had a negative effect on economic development.[6] Casual empiricism suggests that this effect may relate to their financing of "white elephants" and government deficits. The state banks' large nonperforming loans and the unfavorable distributional effects of their subsidies led to their privatization, closure, or conversion to explicit, transparent parts of the treasury in many countries in the 1990s.[7]

Work by Ross Levine and his colleagues suggests a different view of the role of finance: that across countries, large banking deposits and large credit to the private sector (relative to GDP), as well as liquid stock exchanges, tend to precede economic growth, even taking into account differences in legal systems.[8] Their explanation is that banks, other financial intermediaries, and capital markets allocate scarce savings to activities with the best combination of risk and return. Of course, the question is how to generate such a financial system. As Levine and his colleagues notes, large volumes of credit to the private sector and subsequent growth may reflect common underlying factors such as the rule of law and property rights.[9] Moreover, this cross-country relationship is an average one. Some countries, notably China, have grown very fast, albeit at high cost in terms of investment and low rates of consumption. Its state-owned financial

5. Gerschenkron (1962).
6. LaPorta, Lopez-de-Silanes, and Shleifer (2002).
7. World Bank (2005).
8. See Levine and others (2003) and works cited therein.
9. Levine and others (2003).

system mobilized substantial deposits, but these went mainly to the state-owned enterprises, not the private sector. In distortion-riddled financial systems, the work of Levine and his collaborators would suggest liberalization. However, the recent crises in East Asia have raised concerns regarding external borrowing by banks and private corporations to finance credit to the private sector in an environment of weak governance and overextended institutions.[10]

What is the implication of this work for Puerto Rico and its development? Rita Maldonado-Bear and Ingo Walter's chapter attempts to answer this question in various ways. I focus here on three areas: the special characteristics of Puerto Rico, the role of the Government Development Bank, and the risks that the banking system and government borrowing entail for Puerto Rico's development.

Puerto Rico differs in many fundamental ways from most developing countries, two of which help its financial and economic development but also limit the range of policies that the government of Puerto Rico can use. First, Puerto Rico is completely open to capital and goods flows and uses the U.S. dollar, the implications of which are not discussed much by Maldonado-Bear and Walter. The result is low inflation. Second, Puerto Rico, unlike other countries that use the dollar, has the Federal Reserve as a lender of last resort, deposit insurance from the U.S.'s Federal Deposit Insurance Corporation (FDIC), and banking regulation and supervision from the FDIC and the U.S. Comptroller of the Currency, in addition to its own Commissioner of Financial Institutions, as the authors point out. The latter arrangements reduce the cost of regulation, among other benefits. These characteristics restrict Puerto Rico's ability to carry out monetary policy and adjust its financial regulatory system. Yet these restrictions are probably a good thing, given the problems with inflation and with bank regulation and supervision in most developing countries.

I would also suggest that these two characteristics effectively fix the size of Puerto Rico's banking system, which is the main element of the financial system, as it is in most developing countries.[11] Puerto Rico cannot do much to

---

10. World Bank (2005).

11. This discussion of the banking system ignores Puerto Rico's international banking entities, whose total assets are nearly as large as those of the domestic banking system. However, international banking entities have little to do with the economy, particularly in terms of providing resources. The international banking entities do provide some employment, but probably not much. Management of the funds typically would take place offshore. The success of these intermediaries is probably the result of Puerto Rico's reputation for governance, compared with other locales. Attempts to increase intermediaries' role in the economy are likely to reduce returns to the investors in them and reduce the funds that pass through Puerto Rico. Finally, just how fast these institutions can grow in the future remains a question; Puerto Rican offshore banking is likely to be squeezed by enforcement of anti–money laundering rules, which will push the activities back to the United States or to entities where such rules are not well enforced.

increase the size of its financial sector, although there are a few actions it could take, such as raising taxes on the financial sector, that would have negative effects on financial activity. To put it another way, Puerto Rico already has a liberalized and well-regulated banking sector; it cannot do much to increase its size. In particular, the volume of resources that Puerto Rican banks mobilize is not restricted by interest rate controls that could be lifted. Rather, interest rates are set freely, and the amounts of funds that are mobilized depend on the savings of Puerto Ricans ("home country" bias), the attraction of Puerto Rico to foreign savers, Puerto Rican banks' ability to intermediate funds to borrowers both locally and offshore, and domestic and foreign governmental interventions that channel funds to the banks and affect their use.

These two characteristics also help explain some features of the Puerto Rican banking system observed by Maldonado-Bear and Walter. On the funding side, the banks have relatively low local deposits by international standards, perhaps reflecting Puerto Ricans' low savings rates but also a result of competition for local deposits from mainland institutions and instruments. Brokered deposits and short-term debt, both probably from the mainland, represent a large share of bank liabilities, as do advances from the Federal Home Loan Bank, a U.S. government program to which Puerto Rico has access. The growth of banks' long-term borrowing since 2000 probably reflects their ability to raise money from U.S. investors who have been searching for higher yields than are available in the United States. This process has occurred in many developing countries recently. On the asset side, the major companies in the largest economic sectors in Puerto Rico, chemicals and hotels, usually raise money offshore, where intermediation costs are less. Hence Puerto Rican banks need to look elsewhere for borrowers.

Puerto Rican banks have a lot of mortgage loans, some of which presumably are back-to-back with funding from the Federal Home Loan Bank and do not absorb local deposits. The mortgage banking industry on the island has also grown. The origination of mortgages is mainly a local activity. In modern financial markets, once a mortgage loan is made, it can be sold or securitized, in which case it will no longer appear on the bank's books, though the originating bank may continue to handle the servicing of the mortgage. Thus the volume of mortgage lending originating in Puerto Rico is probably much larger than shown on the banks' balance sheets. According to Maldonado-Bear and Walter, the handling of these loans is a profitable banking business in Puerto Rico. From a developmental standpoint, mortgage lending, though it does not directly contribute to large-scale industrial development, generates jobs in construction and industrial activity in producers of building supplies while satisfying demand for housing by consumers. It is worth noting that in the work by Levine and his colleagues, housing loans would certainly count as credit to the private sector and thus would show up as a factor in growth.

Consumer credit has not grown along with mortgage lending in Puerto Rico as it has in most countries. Perhaps the slow growth of consumer credit reflects differences between the legal framework for mortgages and credit cards.

Other bank assets include a lot of investments and securities. Presumably, some of these are Puerto Rican government securities, the supply of which has grown substantially because of deficits. From a developmental standpoint, the funding of these deficits represents a risk of crowding out bank credit to the private sector. Of course, Levine's work identifies private credit as an explanation of growth. Thus the Puerto Rican government must decide whether its deficits contribute more to longer-run growth than would the same credit allocated to the private sector by the banks.

Finally, we come to Puerto Rican banks' commercial and industrial loans, which are perhaps the most obvious factor in economic growth. These loans have grown nearly 10 percent annually since 1995, on average. No doubt there has been some crowding out from deficits. Nonetheless, commercial and industrial loans have grown at a higher rate than nominal GDP, so it is hard to say finance has been a constraint to growth. It is true that the share of these loans in total bank assets has declined, but this is a result of the potential crowding out by government paper and of the fast growth of mortgages, many of which were financed from abroad, not the slow growth of commercial and industrial loans. More complex, but difficult, questions are whether the banks have done enough with this type of lending, in terms of finding businesses that can contribute to Puerto Rico's growth, and how the government can help such financial activities.

Information may be one area where improvements can be made. For banks and other institutions to lend well and stimulate development, they need to have a good system of compiling information on potential borrowers; a legal system that allows easy execution of collateral and an agile treatment of bankruptcy, as a threat to nonpayers; and good underlying accounting systems. To some extent, these obviously exist in Puerto Rico, but there is probably room for improvement. For example, the lack of credit cards may indicate some issues. Resolving these issues could help finance small businesses—credit cards are one way that small businesses can finance working capital—and help in their accounting. The active mortgage market in Puerto Rico is a good feature for new businesses—a classic way that new entrepreneurs finance their businesses is to mortgage their homes.

Banks inherently are not good at venture capital. The characteristic of venture capital is that it takes a share of the equity in a venture; many ventures fail, but high profits in those that succeed more than make up for the failures. Banks, lending at fixed rates, are simply not good at this activity. So the question is whether government restrictions limit the activities of the venture capital funds that exist and prevent the entry of new firms. It might be useful to survey them and see how their activities can be improved.

Puerto Rico, like many developing countries, has attempted to use a government bank as a venture capital firm. The Government Development Bank (GDB) was founded in 1942 as a fiscal agent of the government but also acted as a depository of government funds and lender to the private and public sector. It has served Puerto Rico well as a fiscal agent, a creator of a market for government debt in the United States, and a fiscal adviser to the government. Currently, almost all loans on its balance sheet are to government institutions, financed largely by deposits of government institutions. In addition, the GDB makes loans and guarantees to public sector entities through its many subsidiaries and affiliated organizations. It also assists public sector entities in obtaining finance. Since the GDB is government owned, its deposits and borrowing represent something of a contingent liability, but assessing the importance of this liability is complicated by the fact that the deposits belong to the government and government agencies. Hence losses on loans show up, nontransparently, as lower returns on government and public sector entities' deposits.

The GDB's lending activities in the private sector are now enacted largely through three of its subsidiaries and one of its affiliated organizations, according to Maldonado-Bear and Walter. The Tourism Development Fund has outstanding loans and guarantees of some $500 million. In some cases these loans and guarantees have been to well-known international firms, and in some cases loans have not been serviced or guarantees have had to be paid by the fund. The Puerto Rico Development Fund and the Capital Fund also invest in private businesses, but they are relatively small. The Puerto Rico Industrial, Tourist, Educational, Medical, and Environmental Control Facilities Financing Authority, an affiliate, issues bonds to finance loans to private firms, nonprofit entities, and government agencies. It has more than $2 billion in outstanding loans. The bonds are serviced from the repayments of the loans, in effect securitizing them. However, there may be legal issues in that the holders of the bonds may not suffer losses if loans are not repaid. Although the bonds are not direct debt of the government, the market probably considers them to have a government guarantee, and the politics of any crisis situation would probably mean that the obligation would be taken over by the government.

The question is whether these activities are effectively and transparently conducted by the GDB and to what extent they represent a contingent liability to the government. As noted earlier, empirical evidence suggests that a large state bank presence has tended to reduce countries' growth rates. Whether this is true in Puerto Rico is hard to assess; the GDB is large, but state enterprises, which have often been linked with low productivity investments, are small. At the same time, the GDB has been involved, directly or indirectly, in financing municipal and quasi-governmental activities like infrastructure and stadiums, according to Maldonado-Bear and Walter. In other countries, these types of loans have often become nonperforming. Exactly how losses on these loans would be covered remains an open question.

Loans of GDB subsidiaries and affiliates to the private sector also raise issues. Generally speaking, public sector banks make poor venture capitalists. Maldonado-Bear and Walter note that these loans are to firms that were unable to get funds from the commercial banks and other parts of the nongovernment financial sector. However, this is always hard to judge in practice. Perhaps the borrowers preferred to borrow from the GDB because the terms offered were better. Perhaps the alternative sources of funding required borrowers to give up some equity. Perhaps the GDB puts less collection pressure on firms and accepts losses more easily. Finally, it is hard to see how funding for tourism to major hotel companies, mentioned by Maldonado-Bear and Walter, classifies as lending to firms that were unable to raise funds. More likely it was a nontransparent subsidy to attract the investment.

These questions are part of the general issue of efficiency and transparency in a public sector bank.[12] As experience in other countries shows, a public sector bank's loans and guarantees, at best, run the risk that scarce funds are allocated to inefficient investments, using the government's borrowing capacity; at worst, the bank runs the risk of requiring an eventual large government bailout. Exactly how a loan or guarantee is allocated to one borrower or another is always unclear, but, at least in the case of a private bank, it is the overall goal of the bank to take the best combination of risk and return and ensure that it is the owners who are risking their capital. In the case of a public bank, experience suggests that other elements can often enter, such as political connections or a desire to offer nontransparent subsidies, which would be better done, more transparently done, through the budget.

In the case of the GDB, transparency is also complicated by the multiplicity of subsidiaries, affiliates, and other relationships. The GDB is probably in part a victim of its own success and competent staff, which has led successive governments to expand its role. Perhaps it would be desirable to have an independent evaluation of the GDB and its various subsidiaries and affiliates, to judge how much its lending has contributed to Puerto Rico's development and at what cost; how much of its activity would be better put within the budget, for reasons of transparency; and how the GDB could be streamlined and better focused on its most important tasks and held more accountable for its activities.

Issues of risk have been at the forefront of many discussions of the financial system since the crises in many developing countries that began in the mid-1990s. If the financial system collapses and brings the economy down with it, then it certainly is not helping development. In looking at risks that face Puerto

---

12. See Hanson (2004) for a discussion of these issues in various countries and ways to transform public sector banks.

Rico, it is useful to discuss separately the risks in the financial system and the risks in its fiscal policy and the GDB.

Banking crises were major problems in many developing countries in the 1990s, but commercial banking problems are likely to be of little consequence to Puerto Rico's government finances and its economy. The reason is Puerto Rican banks' attachment to the Federal Reserve as lender of last resort and to the FDIC. Puerto Rican banks, particularly the rapidly growing ones, may be getting riskier, as Maldonado-Bear and Walter point out; but in the context of the regulatory and supervisory arrangements mentioned earlier, this poses little risk to the economy. As with a bank in a state of the United States, a Puerto Rican bank that chooses to adopt a more risky strategy faces discipline from financial markets to some degree. Market discipline places some limits on expansion by raising the cost of market borrowing and, perhaps, brokered deposits.

However, if most Puerto Rican banks suffer a run, they can borrow from the U.S. Federal Reserve system—there is no Puerto Rican central bank that by lending to distressed banks will put its international reserves in danger. If Puerto Rican banks start to lose too much capital because of bad loans, then the FDIC tries to intervene well before capital is exhausted. (Only two small banks in Puerto Rico operate outside of this system.) Intervention means no loss to the depositors, however, because of the FDIC guarantee of deposits. This is probably true even for many of the brokered deposits, since the brokers often use computers to break down the deposits being brokered into units that are fully protected by the FDIC. Usually, the FDIC bailout of the depositors is through an arranged merger of the weak bank with another bank. In the rare cases in which this is not possible, the covered depositors are paid off, and the worst that occurs is a brief disruption. Perhaps most important, and in great contrast to what happened in the crisis countries in the 1990s, all this occurs at no cost to the Puerto Rican government.

The issues are more complex with financial institutions other than commercial banks, notably cooperative banks and insurance companies. These institutions are not protected by U.S.-based insurance of depositors and investors. A crisis in one or more of these institutions could lead to pressures on the government to bail out the depositors or investors and, by leading to an issue of government debt to provide the institutions with earning assets, could compromise government finances. Thus the local regulatory agencies must take a tough view of these institutions' activities to limit the government's contingent liabilities.

Although the banking system appears to present little risk to the economy, the fiscal accounts raise a number of issues. According to Maldonado-Bear and Walter, a history of government deficits implies that future tax revenues are being mortgaged to pay for today's expenditure. The key question is whether today's expenditure is contributing to future growth, in order to cover those taxes. At the moment, Puerto Rico appears to have a relatively high ratio of public debt to GNP, which in market-borrowing countries is often an indicator of risks. Moreover, the government pension systems, according to the authors, are significantly underfinanced. Finally, some of the activities of the GDB represent potential contingent liabilities of the government of Puerto Rico. A fiscal crisis in Puerto Rico could have a major impact on economic activity, as occurred in numerous Latin American economies in the 1980s and 1990s.

Recognizing these and other risks, both Moody's and Standard and Poor's have recently downgraded Puerto Rico's bond ratings. The government responded with an attempt to reduce the fiscal gap. This is an appropriate response, even given the low interest rates prevailing in world markets. Even if interest rates are low, a high debt-to-GNP ratio may require a reduction in borrowing. Indeed, a reduction in excessive debt is probably politically easier in the benign environment of low interest rates than when higher rates prevail. The reason is that the lower costs of debt permit governments to reduce their interest payments and their budget deficits without the need to cut noninterest spending as much. Thus the government needs to implement fully its program of fiscal tightening. It can also take advantage of current market conditions by converting its debt to long-term, fixed-rate obligations to reduce the risks of future fiscal problems. Finally, the underfunding of the pension system also needs to be corrected.

References

Asón, Raúl. 1970. "An Econometric Model of the Puerto Rican Banking Sector." Ph.D. dissertation. University of California, Berkeley.

Beck, Thorsten, Asli Demirgüç-Kunt, and Ross Levine. 2000. "A New Database on Financial Development and Structure." *World Bank Economic Review* 14, no. 3: 597–605.

Brean Murray Research. 2002. *Financial Institutions of Puerto Rico: The Investment Opportunity: Equity Outperformance with Modest Valuations.* New York (November 6).

Cameron, Rondo, and others. 1967. *Banking in the Early Stages of Industrialization.* Oxford University Press.

Colón, Leandro A., and Francisco E. Martínez. 1999. "Los flujos financieros en Puerto Rico: Una visión panorámica." In *Futuro económico de Puerto Rico,* edited by Francisco E. Martínez, pp. 287–313. Río Piedras: Editorial de la Universidad de Puerto Rico.

Commonwealth of Puerto Rico. 1999. *La ley para crear el "Fideicomiso de los niños."* Law 173 of July 30.

———. 2004. "General Obligation Bonds of 2005," Series A, including Appendix I: Financial Information and Operating Data Report (August 1). San Juan.

Curet Cuevas, Eliécer. 2003. *Economía política de Puerto Rico: 1950–2000.* San Juan: Ediciones M.A.C.

Diamond, Douglas W., and Raghuram Rajan. 2005. "Liquidity Shortages and Banking Crises." *Journal of Finance* (April): 615–47.

Economic Development Bank of Puerto Rico. 1992–2003. *Annual Reports.* San Juan.

Estrella, Arturo. 2005. "Financial Dependence and Economic Growth in Puerto Rico." Federal Reserve Bank of New York.

Ferrao, Luis A. 2003. "Historia de los seguros en Puerto Rico: 1898–2002." San Juan: Comisionado de Seguros de Puerto Rico.

Freyre, Jorge F. 1969. *External and Domestic Financing in the Economic Development of Puerto Rico.* Río Piedras: Editorial de la Universidad de Puerto Rico.

Gerschenkron, Alexander. 1962. *Economic Backwardness in Historical Perspective.* Harvard University Press.

Goldsmith, Raymond. 1969. *Financial Structure and Development.* Yale University Press.

Government Development Bank for Puerto Rico. 1993–2003. *Annual Reports.* San Juan.

———. 2002. "Strength, Performance, and Innovation for Puerto Rico." San Juan. (Orig. pub. 1992.)

———. [Banco Gubernamental de Fomento]. 2004. "Informe sobre la deuda pública, año fiscal 2003 y primeros seis meses año fiscal 2004." Report presented to the Commission of the Treasury of the Legislative Assembly. San Juan (March 5).

Gurley, John G., and Edward S. Shaw. 1955. "Financial Aspects of Economic Development." *American Economic Review* (September).

Hanson, James. 2004. "The Transformation of State-Owned Banks." In *The Future of State-Owned Financial Institutions,* edited by Gerard Caprio and others, pp. 13–50. Brookings.

LaPorta, Rafael, Florencio Lopez-de-Silanes, and Andrei Shleifer. 2002. "Government Ownership of Banks." *Journal of Finance* 57, no. 1: 265–301.

Levine, Ross, and others. 2003. "More on Finance and Growth: More Finance, More Growth?" *Federal Reserve Bank of St. Louis Review* 85, no. 4: 31–46.

Lockwood, William, and others. 2003. "Análisis de la situación de las EBIs en Puerto Rico y evaluación de las propuestas de modificación de la ley." Report prepared for the Commissioner of Financial Institutions of Puerto Rico. San Juan: Econometrica, Lockwood Financial Advisors Corporation, and Sierra/Serapion PSC (May).

Maldonado-Bear, Rita M. 1970. *The Role of the Financial Sector in the Economic Development of Puerto Rico.* Washington: Federal Deposit Insurance Corporation.

Manufacturers Association of Puerto Rico. 2005. "Situación fiscal de Puerto Rico: Escenario actual y necesidad de reforma." Presentation at the Bankers Club, San Juan (January 26).

Moody's Investors Service. 2005. Global Credit Research. "Special Comment: Moody's Downgrades Commonwealth of Puerto Rico's G.O. Bonds to Baa2" (May 2005).

Office of the Commissioner of Insurance of the Commonwealth of Puerto Rico. 1993–2001. *Annual Reports.*

Santos, João A. C. 2001. "Bank Capital Regulation in Contemporary Banking Theory: A Review of the Literature." *Financial Markets, Institutions, and Instruments* 10, no. 2: 41–84.

Slack, Bain, and Brian Klock. 2004. "Puerto Rico Field Trip 2004." New York: Keefe, Bruyette, and Woods (December 14).

Smith, Roy C., and Ingo Walter. 1997. *Global Banking.* Oxford University Press.

Standard and Poor's. 2005. "Puerto Rico's GO Debt Rating Lowered to 'BBB'; Growing Structural Imbalance Cited." New York (May 24).

Terrones, Marco. 2004. "Are Credit Booms in Emerging Markets a Concern?" *IMF World Economic Outlook* (April): 147–66.

Walter, Ingo. 1993. "High Performance Financial Systems: Blueprint for Development." Singapore: ASEAN Economic Research Unit, Institute for Southeast Asian Studies.

———. 2003. "Strategies in Financial Services, the Shareholders, and the System: Is Bigger and Broader Better?" In *Financial Conglomerates,* edited by Robert Litan and Richard Herring. Brookings.

———. 2004. *Mergers and Acquisitions in Banking and Finance: What Works, What Doesn't, and Why.* Oxford University Press.

Wilshire Associates. 1995. "Government Development Bank for Puerto Rico: Puerto Rico Stock Index" (August).

World Bank. 2005. "Financial Liberalization: What Went Wrong, What Went Right." In *Economic Growth in the 1990s: Learning from a Decade of Reform,* pp. 207–39. Washington.

9

Trade Performance and Industrial Policy

ROBERT Z. LAWRENCE AND JUAN LARA

Trade performance is of interest for three distinct reasons. The first relates to the external constraint. For most economies, external adjustment has both monetary and real dimensions. Countries need imported components and capital to grow. Although these purchases can temporarily be financed through borrowing, in the long run they have to be paid for by exporting. If exports fail to grow fast enough to meet import needs, relative price adjustments brought about through changes in the real exchange rate may be required.

Puerto Rico has a fixed exchange rate and is part of the U.S. monetary system. The dollar is both its domestic and its foreign currency. This means that exchange rate adjustment plays a relatively minor role in external adjustment.[1] If Puerto Ricans have unsustainable spending patterns, they will eventually be forced to adjust. Such adjustments might involve not only changes in income and spending by private citizens and the commonwealth govern-

We are grateful to Magali Junowicz for excellent research assistance, to the Center for the New Economy and Brookings for their help and assistance, and to participants in the project conference held in San Juan for their comments.

1. To be sure, Puerto Rico's external trade is influenced by changes in the dollar, but 80 percent of its trade is with the United States.

ment but also shifts in relative prices. These will occur directly, through product and factor price adjustments, rather than through changes in the exchange rate.

The second reason trade performance is of interest is its relationship to domestic performance—in particular, employment and growth. Puerto Rico has had a high and persistent unemployment rate—in December 2004 unemployment stood at 11.2 percent—and low labor force participation rates. Employment growth in Puerto Rican manufacturing, which is closely linked to trade performance, has been especially weak. Between 2000 and December 2004, for example, Puerto Rican manufacturing employment declined by almost 20 percent.[2] The labor market appears to be in long-run disequilibrium, and it is difficult to reduce real wages to clear the market because of U.S. welfare, minimum wage, and immigration policies. Given these constraints, it is natural to think of measures that could shift the demand curve for labor outward—something improved trade performance might do.

The third dimension of domestic performance relates to growth. Trade and economic growth are strongly correlated, with causal linkages running both ways, and thus trade performance may be particularly important not only in generating more employment but also in stimulating investment and productivity growth.

This chapter first investigates the adjustment issue. The regression analysis of Puerto Rican trade behavior presented in this chapter suggests that relative price adjustments are not required to maintain external balance. Indeed, the analysis suggests that even if Puerto Rican GDP were to grow 60 percent more rapidly than on the mainland, import growth would equal export growth. With the relatively slower growth differential Puerto Rico has actually recorded, the trade surplus has increased.

However, there are concerns about the data on which this analysis rests. Tax considerations provide international firms with incentives to overstate their Puerto Rican activities. This means that the export data may not give an accurate picture of the value that is actually added in the commonwealth; in particular, the data could distort the employment implications of trade flows. We explore this issue by adjusting exports for foreign profits and directly examining employment growth. We find that the positive impressions of trade performance survive these adjustments. Indeed, over the past four years, Puerto Rican export performance has outperformed that of most U.S. states.

---

2. In the United States over the same period, manufacturing employment fell by 17 percent.

Our analysis of the microeconomic dimensions of export performance points to the overwhelming role U.S. tax policy has played in determining Puerto Rico's comparative advantage. The commonwealth has become increasingly specialized in high-tech products, such as pharmaceuticals, that when produced in the United States are intensive in skilled labor, capital, and research and development (R&D). Puerto Rico sells these products in astounding volumes both to the United States and to other developed economies. Whatever may have been the original reasons for locating in Puerto Rico, the high-tech sectors have now established a firm footing in the commonwealth. Despite the repeal of section 936 tax provisions, growth in these sectors has been sustained—indeed, it has accelerated. The process appears to have become self-reinforcing, even if the connections with the rest of the economy are not deep. In particular, there has been robust employment growth in the pharmaceuticals sector since section 936 was repealed. There is also evidence of smaller but rapidly growing services exports that are more closely linked to Puerto Rican factor endowments.

Our analysis of Puerto Rican industrial policies suggests that they should be concentrated on stimulating growth. The challenge is how to focus on cases in which reliance on private market activities is likely to be inadequate—so-called market failures—but to do so in a precise fashion that avoids providing financial support for private sector activities that would be undertaken in any case. Policies that simply stimulate all types of a particular activity (foreign investment, exports, import substitution) or sectors (pharmaceuticals, electronics) are likely to be wasteful. Rather, the focus should be on stimulating learning and innovation, providing coordination, and investing in infrastructure and public goods throughout the economy.

Some analysts have expressed deep dissatisfaction with the Puerto Rican model of growth and trade because it has emphasized foreign investment and exports and failed to involve large parts of the population. They advocate a more active policy of import substitution. It is by no means obvious, however, that such a policy focus can succeed. It seems more reasonable to think instead about policies that promote innovation, learning, and coordination throughout the economy. Some of these would entail assisting activities that predominate in tradable goods and could build on two distinct opportunities: the dynamic high-tech sector clusters in Puerto Rico and services exports both to the United States and to the Western Hemisphere. However, opportunities in sectors that are not involved in trade should not be neglected.

Recent Puerto Rican industrial policies have emphasized promotion of clusters, particularly in the high-tech sector and in exports more generally. In some cases, policy does seem to be aimed at dealing with market failures and improving public infrastructure, but in others the approach remains undeveloped or lacks focus.

Exploring the External Constraint

The traditional approach to explaining the behavior of trade in goods markets is to estimate equations in which the volume of exports (or imports), Q, is a function of income, Y, and the relative price of domestic and foreign goods, P—that is, $Q = F(Y, P)$. This approach can be rationalized as estimating a demand function under the (extreme) assumption that supply is infinitely elastic and domestic and foreign goods are imperfect substitutes, but it is probably more likely that in the case of a small economy like Puerto Rico, the income variable, which has a strong trend, captures both supply- and demand-side effects. It is, therefore, probably more reasonable to consider this approach as a historical statistical summary of the relationships between three endogenous variables rather than as a well-identified structural model.

With this caveat in mind, we have estimated a pair of trade equations using annual data from 1975 to 2003 to explain Puerto Rican exports and imports of goods. In the case of exports, we use U.S. GDP to capture the market—since more than 80 percent of exports go to the United States—and for the relative price of exports we used a ratio of the implicit Puerto Rican export price deflator and the U.S. import price index. For imports we use Puerto Rican GDP as the income variable and the ratio of the Puerto Rican implicit import price deflator to the personal consumption expenditure deflator. The equations are estimated in logarithms, so the coefficients can be interpreted as elasticities. Table 9-1 presents the results for 1975–2003.

The results we obtain are reasonable. The import equation has a mean-squared error of 4.76 percent, and the coefficients are correctly signed and statistically significant. The export equation is less precise, with a mean-squared error of 8.24 percent, but it too has significant and correctly signed coefficients. The price elasticities on both exports and imports are close to unity, suggesting a fairly low elasticity of substitution between Puerto Rican exports to the United States and those of other countries and also between Puerto Rican imports and domestically produced goods. Each 1 percent growth in real U.S. GDP results in a 2 percent rise in Puerto Rican export volumes. By contrast, each 1 percent increase in Puerto Rican GDP results in a 1.26 percent rise in the volume of Puerto Rican imports. Interpreted structurally, therefore, this pair of equations suggests that if these historic relationships held, if Puerto Rican GDP growth was 58 percent faster (that is, $2/1.26 = 1.58$) than GDP growth in the United States, exports would rise as rapidly as imports. In fact, from 1993 to 2002, Puerto Rican and U.S. GDP grew at 4.1 and 3.2 percent respectively, a ratio of 1.28. These coefficients imply that if relative prices remained constant, with these growth rates there would be a strong trend toward a trade surplus, since

Table 9-1. *Puerto Rican Trade Equations*[a]

Independent variable	Imports	Exports
Constant	−2.07	−22.35
	(−8.31)	(9.36)
Puerto Rican GDP[b]	1.26	...
	(42.1)	
U.S. GDP[c]	...	1.99
		(12.34)
R price imports[d]	−0.99	...
	(−4.1)	
R price exports[e]	...	−1.2
		(4.1)
Summary statistic		
R^2	0.99	0.95
RMSE[f]	0.048	0.083

Source: U.S. national income accounts; Puerto Rico national income accounts.
a. All variables in logarithms; *t* statistics in parentheses.
b. 1954 dollars.
c. Chain weighted.
d. Ratio of Puerto Rico import price deflator to personal consumption expenditure deflator.
e. Ratio of Puerto Rico export price deflator to U.S. imports price index.
f. Root mean-squared error.

Puerto Rican exports and imports would grow at 8.2 and 4.0 percent a year, respectively.

The rising trends in the Puerto Rican balances in merchandise trade and goods and services and the relationships between these variables are apparent in figure 9-1, in which they are depicted as a share of GDP. The dominant source of changes is clearly the trade balance, which has a strong upward trend after 1997. As table 9-2 shows, by 2003 Puerto Rico had a large merchandise trade surplus in goods of almost 20 percent of GDP, with merchandise exports alone equal to 75.7 percent of GDP and imports 57.2 percent. Yet the deficit in the tradable services accounts was even larger than the surplus in goods—amounting to 36.5 percent of GDP. The dominant reason was that the services account includes profits earned by foreign investors, which in 2003 amounted to $29 billion—or 39 percent of GDP. Conceptually, the earnings of foreign corporations do belong in the balance of trade in goods and services—indeed, when not repatriated to the United States they show up as services (debit) and a capital inflow (credit).

Puerto Rican exports have grown especially rapidly. Compared with the mainland states and Washington, D.C., Puerto Rico's performance from 1999 to 2003 was extraordinary. The 44 percent growth in Puerto Rican exports to countries outside the United States was recorded in a period when total U.S.

Figure 9-1. *Balance of Payments, Puerto Rico, 1989–2003*
Percent

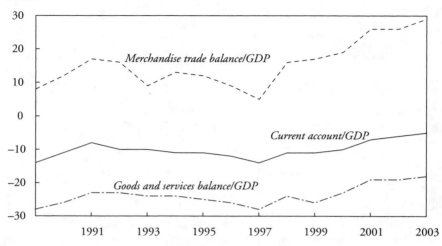

Source: Data from U.S. Department of Commerce; Puerto Rico Planning Board.

Table 9-2. *Balance of Payments, Puerto Rico, 2003*

Category	In millions of current dollars	As share of GDP (percent)	Growth rate, 1998–2003 (percent)
Exports of goods and services	62,742.6	84.4	65.6
Merchandise, adjusted	56,301.0	75.7	73.1
Transportation	495.5	0.7	−34.3
Visitors' expenditures	2,676.6	3.6	19.9
Income on investments	1,007.8	1.4	−7.3
Net operating expenditures of federal agencies in Puerto Rico	1,154.2	1.6	48.8
Miscellaneous services	1,108.5	1.5	112.0
Imports of goods and services	76,196.9	102.5	49.3
Merchandise, adjusted	42,512.8	57.2	61.1
Transportation	2,067.5	2.8	25.0
Travel expenditures	985.2	1.3	12.7
Income on investments	29,024.6	39.0	39.3
Miscellaneous services	1,606.8	2.2	26.1
Balance on goods and services transactions	(13,454.4)	−18.1	...

Source: Data from Puerto Rico Planning Board, Program of Economic and Social Planning, Sub-program of Economic Analysis.

exports increased by just 4 percent (table 9-3). Only the District of Columbia (96 percent), Nevada (90 percent), South Carolina (65 percent), and the Virgin Islands (63 percent) recorded faster growth over that period. Similarly, the $3.6 billion increase in Puerto Rican exports was outmatched only by Texas ($15.7 billion), Ohio ($4.9 billion), and South Carolina ($4.6 billion). In a period in which most U.S. exporters were hurt by the strong dollar and slow global economic growth, this was a particularly impressive performance.[3]

The growth rates from 1999 to 2003 also indicate the rapid increases in merchandise exports (up 73.1 percent) and even more rapid growth in exports of miscellaneous services, which increased by 112.0 percent over the period (table 9-2). Although they represented just 1.5 percent of GDP, miscellaneous services have clearly been a dynamic component of recent Puerto Rican export performance. By contrast, visitors' expenditures (tourism), while still a large share of GDP (3.6 percent), increased by just 19.9 percent. Merchandise imports also expanded rapidly, up 61.1 percent over this period, as did the profits earned by foreign corporations in Puerto Rico (up 39.3 percent).

Puerto Rican Exports: Tiger or Just Paper Tiger?

The increase in payments on foreign investments in Puerto Rico raises questions about the links between exports and foreign profits that need to be answered to provide an accurate picture of what is actually happening. Between 1976 and 1995, foreign direct investments in Puerto Rico were governed by section 936 of the U.S. tax code. This provision allowed corporations qualifying as "U.S. possessions corporations" to remit their profits on a current basis free of corporate income tax. Although these profits were in principle subject to federal income taxes, as long as a significant portion of income was earned from the "active conduct of a trade or business," an offsetting tax credit (the "possessions tax credit") was provided—effectively making Puerto Rican profits free of tax liabilities.[4]

This provision was ended effective October 1995, although companies operating under this section of the tax code were given a ten-year transition period.[5] Nonetheless, there remain tax benefits from operating in Puerto Rico. Firms can incorporate themselves as "controlled foreign corporations" and receive the benefits accorded to U.S. firms operating abroad. Until repatriation, firms can

3. See Baily and Lawrence (2004) for an analysis of U.S. exports from 2000 to 2003.
4. For a more complete description, see Dietz (2003, chap. 5). See also chapter 2 in this volume.
5. These companies were allowed temporarily to operate under section 30A of the code, which allowed firms to claim 60 percent of wages and capital investment as allowances against their federal tax liability on repatriated profits during the phase-out. Dietz (2003, p. 150, table 5.1) reports a decline in revenues from the possessions tax credit from $4.6 billion in 1993 to $1.49 billion in 1999 and an increase in U.S. income tax collected from zero in 1992 to $2.15 billion in 1999.

Table 9-3. *U.S. Merchandise Exports, by State or Territory, 1999–2003*[a]
Millions of dollars, except as indicated

Rank	State	1999	2000	2001	2002	2003	Change, 1999–2003 Dollars	Change, 1999–2003 Percent	Change, 2002–03 Dollars	Change, 2002–03 Percent
1	Texas	83,177	103,866	94,995	95,396	98,846	15,669	19	3,450	1
2	California	97,920	119,640	106,777	92,214	93,995	-3,925	-4	1,781	4
3	New York	37,067	42,846	42,172	36,977	39,181	2,113	6	2,204	2
4	Washington	36,731	32,215	34,929	34,627	34,173	-2,558	-7	-454	6
5	Michigan	31,086	33,845	32,366	33,775	32,941	1,855	6	-834	-1
6	Ohio	24,883	26,322	27,095	27,723	29,764	4,881	20	2,041	-2
7	Illinois	29,432	31,438	30,434	25,686	26,473	-2,959	-10	786	7
8	Florida	24,155	26,543	27,185	24,544	24,953	799	3	409	3
9	Massachusetts	16,805	20,514	17,490	16,708	18,663	1,857	11	1,955	2
10	Louisiana	15,842	16,814	16,589	17,567	18,390	2,548	16	823	12
11	New Jersey	15,354	18,638	18,946	17,002	16,818	1,463	10	-184	5
12	Indiana	12,910	15,386	14,365	14,923	16,402	3,492	27	1,479	-1
13	Pennsylvania	16,170	18,792	17,433	15,768	16,299	129	1	531	10
14	Georgia	13,749	14,925	14,644	14,413	16,286	2,538	18	1,874	3
15	North Carolina	15,007	17,946	16,799	14,719	16,199	1,192	8	1,480	13
16	Arizona	11,824	14,334	12,514	11,871	13,323	1,500	13	1,452	10
17	Tennessee	9,868	11,592	11,320	11,621	12,612	2,744	28	990	12
18	South Carolina	7,150	8,565	9,956	9,656	11,773	4,623	65	2,117	9
19	Wisconsin	9,673	10,508	10,489	10,684	11,510	1,837	19	826	22
20	Minnesota	9,373	10,303	10,524	10,402	11,266	1,893	20	863	8
21	Virginia	11,483	11,698	11,631	10,796	10,853	-630	-5	57	8
22	Kentucky	8,877	9,612	9,048	10,607	10,734	1,857	21	127	1
23	Oregon	10,471	11,441	8,900	10,086	10,357	-114	-1	271	1
24	Alabama	6,192	7,317	7,570	8,267	8,340	2,148	35	74	3
25	Connecticut	7,231	8,047	8,610	8,313	8,136	905	13	-177	1
26	Missouri	6,059	6,497	6,173	6,791	7,234	1,175	19	443	-2

27	Colorado	5,931	6,593	6,125	5,522	6,109	178	3	587	7
28	Iowa	4,094	4,465	4,660	4,755	5,236	1,143	28	482	11
29	Maryland	4,009	4,593	4,975	4,474	4,941	931	23	467	10
30	Kansas	4,669	5,145	5,005	4,988	4,553	-116	-2	-435	10
31	Utah	3,134	3,221	3,506	4,543	4,115	981	31	-428	-9
32	Arkansas	2,177	2,599	2,911	2,804	2,962	785	36	159	-9
33	Alaska	2,564	2,464	2,418	2,516	2,739	175	7	222	6
34	Nebraska	2,096	2,511	2,702	2,528	2,724	627	30	196	9
35	Oklahoma	2,987	3,072	2,661	2,444	2,660	-327	-11	216	8
36	Vermont	4,023	4,097	2,830	2,521	2,627	-1,396	-35	106	9
37	Mississippi	2,216	2,726	3,557	3,058	2,558	343	15	-500	4
38	West Virginia	1,893	2,219	2,241	2,237	2,380	487	26	143	-16
39	New Mexico	3,133	2,391	1,405	1,196	2,326	-808	-26	1,129	6
40	Maine	2,014	1,779	1,812	1,973	2,188	174	9	215	94
41	Idaho	2,191	3,559	2,122	1,967	2,096	-96	-4	129	11
42	Nevada	1,067	1,482	1,423	1,177	2,033	965	90	856	7
43	New Hampshire	1,930	2,373	2,401	1,863	1,931	2	0	68	73
44	Delaware	2,287	2,197	1,985	2,004	1,886	-401	-18	-118	4
45	Rhode Island	1,116	1,186	1,269	1,121	1,177	61	5	56	-6
46	North Dakota	699	626	806	859	854	155	22	-5	5
47	South Dakota	495	679	595	597	672	178	36	75	-1
48	Wyoming	458	502	503	553	582	124	27	28	13
49	Hawaii	274	387	370	514	368	95	35	-145	5
50	Montana	427	541	489	386	361	-65	-15	-24	-28
	District of Columbia	412	1,003	1,034	1,066	809	397	96	-257	-6
	Puerto Rico	8,301	9,735	10,573	9,732	11,914	3,613	44	2,182	-24
	Virgin Islands	155	174	187	258	253	98	63	-5	22
	Unallocated	59,578	58,454	41,506	34,468	35,168	-24,410	-41	700	-2
	U.S. total[b]	692,821	780,419	731,026	693,257	723,743	30,923	4	30,486	2

Source: Data from U.S. Department of Commerce, International Trade Administration, Office of Trade and Economic Analysis.
a. States are ranked by 2003 dollar value of exports.
b. Includes territories.

retain the difference between their U.S. tax liabilities and the taxes they pay to a foreign (or, in this case, the Puerto Rican) government. This treatment still gives firms located in the United States an incentive to shift their profits to their Puerto Rican subsidiaries.

Traditionally, concerns about international profit shifting have focused on the transfer pricing of intrafirm cross-border sales of goods. These have led to efforts to ensure that intrafirm transactions are conducted at arm's-length prices. However, intrafirm transfers of knowledge may offer even more opportunities for profit shifting. It is difficult to price know-how and the costs associated with its production, and this provides an opportunity for firms to transfer the know-how from high- to low-tax regimes at less than its true cost. The federal tax code has a complex set of rules that governs the treatment of intangible assets, but there are reasons to suspect that these are not neutral with respect to location decisions.[6] In particular, firms with intangible assets appear able to take advantage of the income-shifting incentives these opportunities provide. In particular, they allocate high-cost activities, such as R&D spending, to the parent company and highly profitable production activities (that benefit from the R&D) to the foreign (or Puerto Rican) subsidiary.

This practice helps explain the huge share of Puerto Rican GDP that is represented by foreign profits and the overwhelming presence in Puerto Rico of firms in R&D-intensive industries such as pharmaceuticals, instruments, and electronics.[7] If profits recorded in Puerto Rico are heavily influenced by this activity and actually depict value that is really added elsewhere, a better picture might be obtained by subtracting these profits from the value of exports. (To be sure, this measure still remains a crude reflection of value added in Puerto Rico because exports include imported components and profits are earned by foreign companies in services as well as goods.) In 2003 undertaking this adjustment did alter the picture: profit-adjusted merchandise exports minus imports recorded a deficit. However, exploring this measure's behavior over time leads to a more optimistic conclusion: that the share of profit-adjusted value added in Puerto Rican GDP has been rising. In 1998, for example, profit-adjusted exports amounted to 21.6 percent of Puerto Rican GDP; in 2003 they were 36.7 percent. Moreover, as indicated in figure 9-1, these upward trends are evident not only in the balance on merchandise trade but also in the balances on goods and services and the current account, which take account of profits earned by nonresidents.

6. For a description of these rules, see Grubert and Slemrod (1998). The authors conclude that "in the presence of these rules, U.S. companies have apparently been able to shift substantial amounts of intangible asset–related income to Puerto Rico" (p. 368).

7. For a study finding that location in Puerto Rico is particularly profitable for firms with higher expenditures on R&D, see Hill (1990).

Table 9-4 presents 1997 Census Bureau data for manufacturing in both Puerto Rico and the United States, allowing some insights into the nature of manufacturing production in Puerto Rico. The industries are ranked by average worker compensation—a proxy for the skills and human capital of workers employed by each industry. The data indicate that manufacturing employment in Puerto Rico is highly concentrated in chemical products (basically pharmaceuticals), electrical equipment, apparel, and manufactured foods. Together, these industries accounted for 63 percent of overall employment, and chemicals alone for almost a quarter. These are much higher shares than these industries have in the United States. Compensation per worker in Puerto Rico was, on average, about 60 percent of that in the United States, ranging from 50 percent of U.S. levels in electronics to 71 percent in food. With the exception of electronics, which employs lower-skilled workers (compared with the economy average) in Puerto Rico than in the United States, all industries, in both economies, have similar rankings in terms of average compensation. In both countries the lowest earnings are in apparel, and the highest earnings are in chemicals. The most striking difference is the very low share of overall value added accounted for by payroll in value added. In the chemicals, industrial machinery, and food industries, the payroll shares of value added in Puerto Rico are just 5, 4, and 10 percent, respectively. By contrast, in the United States these shares are 23, 52, and 36 percent, respectively. Clearly, operations in Puerto Rico are extremely "profit intensive"—reflecting a much higher share in production of both tangible and intangible capital.

The data in table 9-5 allow us to explore changes in the employment of production workers in Puerto Rican manufacturing from 1997 to the end of 2002 (the latest data we have available). Overall in this period, there was a precipitous decline from 121.7 to 101.5 thousand. (This 16.6 percent decline is actually quite similar to the 15 percent drop in the employment of workers in manufacturing production recorded on the U.S. mainland over the same period). However, it is striking that production worker employment in chemical products actually increased by 21.6 percent, while production worker employment in industrial machinery and instruments remained constant. (Over the same period, on the mainland, production worker employment in chemicals, industrial machinery, and instruments declined by 5.3, 23.0, and 8.5 percent, respectively, while employment in drugs production increased by 16 percent.)[8] Clearly, the employment mix in manufacturing has shifted strongly to the high-skill sectors, particularly pharmaceuticals, supporting the notion that high-tech export and output growth, while heavily concentrated in profits, has also boosted employment.

8. U.S. Department of Labor, Bureau of Labor Statistics, *Current Employment Statistics* (www.bls.gov/ces/home.htm [November 2005]).

Table 9-4. *Manufacturing, Puerto Rico and the United States, 1997*

	Puerto Rico		United States			Ratio	
Industry[a]	*Employment share*	*Compensation per worker*[b] *(1)*	*Payroll/ value added (2)*	*Compensation per worker*[b] *(3)*	*Payroll/ value added (4)*	*Compensation per worker*[b] *(1)/(3)*	*Payroll/ value added (2)/(4)*
Chemical products	23.17	30.32	0.05	45.40	0.23	0.67	0.23
Industrial machinery	2.63	24.84	0.04	37.69	0.52	0.66	0.08
Instruments	7.49	20.79	0.17	n.a.	n.a.	...	...
Food	11.06	19.40	0.10	27.50	0.36	0.71	0.28
Electrical equipment	15.24	18.28	0.16	36.82	0.35	0.50	0.45
Apparel	13.33	10.67	0.34	18.57	0.59	0.57	0.58
Total	100.00	20.28	0.09	33.93	0.43	0.60	0.21

Source: Data from U.S. census 1997.

a. Industries are ranked by compensation per worker in Puerto Rico.

b. Thousands of U.S. dollars.

Table 9-5. *Manufacturing Employment and Trade in Puerto Rico, 1997 and 2002*

	1997		2002		Change, 1997–2002
	Employment				
Industry	Thousands of people	Share (percent)[a]	Thousands of people	Share (percent)	In employment (percent)
Chemical products	19.9	16.3	24.2	23.8	21.6
Industrial machinery	2.5	2.0	2.5	2.4	0.1
Instruments	13.0	10.7	13.1	12.9	0.6
Food	11.7	9.6	8.5	8.3	−27.9
Electrical equipment	21.2	17.4	14.2	14.0	−32.9
Apparel	17.6	14.5	11.5	11.3	−35.0
Total	85.9	70.5	73.8	72.7	−14.0
Other	35.9	29.5	27.7	27.3	−22.7
Total manufacturing	121.7	100.0	101.5	100.0	−16.6

| | Trade[b] | | | | | | |
	Exports	Imports	Net trade	Exports	Imports	Net trade	In net trade
Chemicals	3,490	5,416	−1,926	33,318	12,343	20,976	22,902
Industrial machinery	3,490	1,370	2,120	3,738	1,686	2,052	−68
Instruments	1,626	902	724	2,283	1,043	1,240	516
Food	3,386	2,193	1,194	3,699	2,410	1,289	95
Electrical equipment	2,204	2,424	−219	1,881	2,027	−147	73
Apparel	696	445	251	546	672	−126	−377
Total	14,893	12,750	2,143	45,465	20,181	25,285	23,142
Other	8,945	7,782	1,162	1,588	7,979	−6,391	−7,554
Total manufacturing	23,837	20,532	3,305	47,053	28,160	18,893	15,588

Source: Data from U.S. Bureau of Labor Statistics; Puerto Rico Planning Board.

a. The data presented here and in table 9-4 differ slightly because of classification and reporting differences between the Bureau of Labor Statistics and the U.S. Census.

b. Millions of dollars.

These are not simply paper profits. It appears, therefore, that despite the phasing down of section 936 incentives, Puerto Rico has continued to be an attractive location for high-tech investments, particularly in the pharmaceuticals sector.[9] In the five-year period, the value of chemicals exports increased more than ninefold, while chemicals imports doubled and exports of instruments increased by 40 percent. Over this period, employment growth in the high-tech

9. A. T. Kearney Management Consultants (2003, slide 135) estimates that in 1996, the last year in which section 936 was in effect, investment in the pharmaceutical sector was $86 million. Between 1997 and 2002 this investment averaged $238 million annually.

sectors was more rapid in Puerto Rico than in the United States, and particularly in these two sectors, trade played an important role. By contrast with the performance in the high-tech sectors, there were major declines in employment in food (−28 percent), electrical equipment (−33 percent), and apparel (−35 percent). According to A. T. Kearney Management Consultants, these basic industries export more than half their output.[10] As shown in table 9-5, from 1997 through 2002, exports and imports in food and electrical equipment behaved quite similarly, rising in the case of food by 9 and 10 percent and falling in the case of electronics by 15 and 16 percent, respectively. In apparel, exports fell by 22 percent, and imports increased by 51 percent. Thus trade performance appears to have contributed to the drop in basic manufacturing employment, and it has boosted employment in the high-tech sectors.

Made in the USA: Puerto Rican Comparative Advantage

The balance of payments statistics of Puerto Rico treat the commonwealth as a separate economy, and from a Puerto Rican standpoint a dollar earned by selling in the United States is just as valuable as a dollar earned from selling to the rest of the world. Nonetheless, an interesting issue is whether Puerto Rico sells the same kinds of products to the United States as it does to the rest of the world.

Economic theory is ambiguous on this question. In some economic models, for example, a country with an intermediate factor intensity endowment might have very different comparative advantages vis-à-vis different trading partners. If Puerto Rico is, for example, less capital intensive than the United States and more capital intensive than developing countries, one might expect to find it exporting more labor-intensive goods to the United States (and other developed economies) and more capital-intensive goods to the developing countries. However, it could also be the case that Puerto Rico is fully specialized vis-à-vis the world as a whole and exports similar goods to all its trading partners.

It could also be the case that the intrafirm transaction between U.S. firms on the mainland and their Puerto Rican subsidiaries give U.S.–Puerto Rican trade a very different character from Puerto Rican trade to the rest of the world. On the other hand, the relationships could be quite similar if Puerto Rico tax advantages make the commonwealth an attractive location to manufacture certain goods and then sell them in both U.S. and world markets. Knowing which of these views is correct could be useful for policymakers seeking to promote Puerto Rican exports. If the exports are very different, different approaches might be called for.

---

10. A. T. Kearney Management Consultants (2003, slide 113).

Table 9-6. *Main Puerto Rican Exports, 2003*
Percent

Description	HTS code	Share of exports to the United States	Share of exports to the rest of the world
Pharmaceutical products	30	56.9	40.2
Nuclear reactors, boilers, machinery, and mechanical appliances	84	7.8	21.5
Organic chemicals	29	8.2	13.1
Optical, photographic, cinematographic, measuring, checking, precision, medical, and surgical instruments	90	9.3	4.2
Total		85.7	79.0

Source: Data from Puerto Rico Planning Board.

In fact, we find that the goods exported by Puerto Rico to the United States are similar to those exported to the rest of world. Using the U.S. International Trade Commission's harmonized tariff schedule (HTS) data, at the two-digit level (which divides merchandise trade into ninety-eight categories) we find a high and statistically significant correlation between the value of goods exported by Puerto Rico to the United States and the value of goods exported to the rest of the world. The coefficient of correlation is 0.92.

We also developed a similarity index by summing the absolute differences in shares of Puerto Rican exports to the United States with shares in exports to the world.[11] If all exports categories had identical shares in both types of exports, the sum of the absolute differences in shares would be zero; if they were all different, the sum divided by two would be one hundred. We obtain an index of 31.57, which suggests considerable similarity. Indeed, exports (like output generally) are highly concentrated in just a few categories. As we can see from table 9-6, just four product categories account for 86 percent of all exports from Puerto Rico to the United States and 79 percent of Puerto Rican exports to the rest of the world.

11. The methodology can be described as follows: We first calculated the share (Sus_i) for each of the ninety-eight categories of exports to the United States—that is, $Sus_i = Xus_i / Xus$, where Xus_i is the value of exports to the United States of commodity i and Xus is the total value of exports to the United States. Next, we do the same for the shares of exports to the rest of the world ($Srow_i = Xrow_i / Xrow$). We then calculate the absolute difference of Sus_i minus $Srow_i$ for each set of values, sum these up, and divide by two. If the shares are identical, the resultant similarity index will equal zero; if they are completely different, it will equal 100.

A third approach is to consider unit values. These are derived using measures such as units (for example, dozens of shirts) or weight to obtain average prices. (If goods are close substitutes, they should sell for similar prices and thus have similar unit values.) Both value and quantity measures are available for most Puerto Rican trade. We drop categories in which there is no trade either to the United States or to the rest of the world and find that the remaining trade accounts for 72 percent of Puerto Rican exports to the rest of the world and 82 percent of Puerto Rican exports to the United States, indicating, again, how similar this trade is. We then compute the ratio of the unit values at the most disaggregated level possible (UTS ten-digit code) and sum these ratios weighted by the value of trade in each category.[12] We find that the ratio of unit values of goods exported by Puerto Rico to the United States to those exported to the rest of the world is 2.62. Apparently, Puerto Rico actually exports more-expensive products to the United States than it does to the rest of the world.

We are unable to distinguish the reasons why the goods exported to the United States are relatively more expensive. These goods could show up as relatively expensive because there is a particular incentive to overprice them to transfer profits to Puerto Rico or because they are of higher quality and are thus in greater demand by U.S. consumers, who have higher incomes (or more generous health insurance). But the hypothesis that Puerto Rico might specialize more in relatively low-tech types of goods in its trade with the United States than it does with the rest of the world is not confirmed. If anything, the opposite is true. Puerto Rico appears to export more-sophisticated products to the United States.

We have done a similar calculation for the ratio of Puerto Rican exports to the United States and Puerto Rico's imports from the United States. Again, we find the weighted sum is 1.28, suggesting that Puerto Rican goods sold to the United States tend to have higher prices (and quality) than Puerto Rico goods bought from the United States, although in this case the differences are small. There also appears to be close integration in the goods markets of Puerto Rico and the United States: similar types of products are produced in the commonwealth and on the mainland.

Thus it does not appear that firms make their relatively cheap products in Puerto Rico and sell them in the United States—indeed, the opposite is the case. If there were strong tax advantages to recording profits in Puerto Rico, this is exactly what we would expect to find: firms choose to produce in Puerto Rico

12. Using HTS data at the ten-digit level, we calculated the unit values by dividing total value of exports by total quantity for each commodity. Next, we calculated the ratio of unit values of exports to the United States to unit values of exports to the rest of the world for each product (considering only those products that were exported to both the United States and the rest of the world). We then weighted these ratios by the total value of trade for each product and summed these weighted measures. We used the same methodology to obtain ratios of import unit values.

precisely those products (for example, blockbuster drugs) on which profit margins (and prices) are the highest. Thus the evidence suggests that the tax bias has stimulated Puerto Rican production in the highest-margin activities and that these products enjoy a particularly strong demand in the United States.

We have also calculated measures of revealed comparative advantage vis-à-vis the United States and the rest of the world.[13] We find a measure of 0.67 in organic chemicals, whereas with the rest of the world it is 0.87. Thus we find that with respect to the rest of the world, Puerto Rico is a heavy importer but not an exporter of these chemicals, whereas it is a moderate exporter to the United States.

Characteristics of Puerto Rican Manufactured Exports

We have analyzed the products that Puerto Rico sells to the United States and to the rest of the world in terms of unit values. We are also interested in the characteristics of Puerto Rican exports in terms of production inputs. The workhorse model in international trade, the Heckscher-Ohlin model, explains trade patterns on the basis of relative factor endowments. It also assumes that products have unique production characteristics, so we can associate products with particular factor intensities. We can use U.S. data to provide measures of the factor inputs that are used to produce these products in the United States. To undertake this exercise, we have collected U.S. data for 2000 on average worker compensation in manufacturing, which would give us a measure of labor skills; profits as a share of value added, which indicates (tangible and intangible) capital intensity; and the share of scientists and engineers per 1,000 employees, which indicates R&D intensity.[14]

As reported in table 9-7, in 2000 the average annual compensation in U.S. manufacturing was $53,807. However, weighting compensation within each manufacturing sector (as categorized by the three-digit North American Industry Classification System) by the value of its exports yields an average compensation of $64,539, suggesting that workers in U.S. manufactured exports are 20 percent more skilled than in manufacturing as a whole. Aggregating the U.S. compensation measures using Puerto Rican exports of manufactured goods for 2000 as weights leads to an estimate of $66,427, suggesting that, based on U.S.

13. Revealed comparative advantage is defined as the ratio between the trade balance (exports minus imports) for each commodity and the total value of trade (exports plus imports) in that commodity—that is, $RCA = (X - M) / (X + M)$.

14. Using the measures described earlier in this chapter, we calculated factor intensities (labor, capital, and R&D) for each U.S. manufacturing sector, as defined by the North American Industry Classification System. We used these measures to weight the value of Puerto Rican and U.S. exports (and imports), thereby obtaining the weighted average factor intensities for U.S. and Puerto Rican exports (and imports).

Table 9-7. *Measures of Input Intensity of Puerto Rican Exports, 2000*[a]

Units as indicated

Sector	Skill[b]	Capital[c]	R&D[d]
(1) U.S. manufacturing weights	53,807	0.37	45
(2) Puerto Rican export weights	66,427	0.47	83
(3) U.S. exports weights	64,539	0.31	87
Ratios			
(2)/(3) Puerto Rican exports/U.S. exports	1.03	1.52	0.96
(2)/(1) Puerto Rican exports/U.S. manufacturing	1.23	1.27	1.83
(3)/(1) U.S. exports/U.S. manufacturing	1.20	0.83	1.92

Source: National Science Foundation, *Annual Survey of Manufactures*, IO tables.

a. In each case, 2000 U.S. input measures are weighted by the indicated sectoral output.

b. Skill refers to average compensation per worker, in U.S. dollars.

c. Capital refers to the share of profits in value added.

d. R&D refers to the number of scientists and engineers per 1,000 employees.

input coefficients, Puerto Rican exports of manufactured goods are actually more skill intensive than U.S. exports of manufactured goods. Remarkably, however, if they were produced using U.S. input ratios, Puerto Rican exports would be only slightly less concentrated in R&D-intensive sectors than U.S. exports. This is particularly remarkable since we also find that U.S. exports are much more highly concentrated in R&D intensive sectors (1.92) than U.S. manufacturing output. We also find that Puerto Rican exports have much higher capital intensity measures (as measured by the share of profits in value added). In sum, compared with U.S. exports, Puerto Rican exports are slightly more skill intensive, slightly less R&D intensive, and far more capital intensive. All in all, we would conclude on the basis of export factor contents that compared with the mainland, Puerto Rico was about as intensively endowed in skills and R&D inputs as the United States, and even more intensively endowed with capital.

Given the goods it exports, we would expect to see that Puerto Rico is a strong performer of R&D (that is, relatively intensively endowed with R&D). Yet Puerto Rico itself performs only a modest amount of R&D. In numerous dimensions the science and engineering profile of Puerto Rico compiled by the National Science Foundation does not look like that of the United States. It is useful to keep in mind that Puerto Rico ranks twenty-seventh in population among a sample of the fifty U.S. states, Puerto Rico, and the District of Columbia. However, in 2001 it ranked forty-ninth in terms of the number of doctoral scientists and forty-seventh in the number of engineers with doctorates, and in 2002, forty-fourth in the number of doctorates awarded and thirty-third in the number of graduate students in doctorate-granting institutions. Puerto Rico ranked last in the sample in the number of utility patents granted to state residents and last in small business innovation research grants received. Indeed, its firms received only 3 of the 19,383 such grants awarded between 1995 and 2000. Puerto Rico also ranked last in terms of federal R&D grants to industrial firms and forty-seventh as a recipient of federal R&D funding obligations.[15] Taken together, these data suggest that although it has begun to train more scientists and engineers, Puerto Rico is not a substantial location for R&D. Data on R&D expenditures provide a similar picture. In the late 1990s Puerto Rico spent an estimated 0.24 percent of GDP on R&D; by 2001 this figure had declined to just 0.14 percent.[16] Yet the goods Puerto Rico produces are highly R&D intensive. Clearly, the R&D is undertaken in the United States, while the manufacturing is done in the commonwealth.

The particular form in which the tax incentives have been structured helps explain some important features of this activity. On the one hand, firms have selected their leading-edge and highest-margin products for production in Puerto Rico. On the other hand, however, though the products are R&D intensive, the R&D itself is not carried out in Puerto Rico. Again, this should not be a surprise. It is the other side of the coin: just as they create incentives to record profits in the low-tax region (Puerto Rico), tax considerations also create incentives for firms to record their R&D expenses in the high-tax location (the United States).

To Whom Does Puerto Rico Export?

In 2003 Puerto Rico's largest export markets outside the United States were Belgium (16.6 percent), Canada (10.2 percent), the United Kingdom (7.9 percent), Netherlands (9.6 percent), and France (6.5 percent). Among its top ten markets, which together accounted for 75 percent of exports, only one—the Dominican Republic (6.1 percent)—was a developing country in the Caribbean. In addition, chemical manufactured products accounted for almost all exports to Canada and Belgium and 77 percent of exports to the Dominican Republic. All told, Puerto Rican exports are overwhelmingly concentrated in high-tech products and are sold in developed-country markets.

It is also not surprising, given the product composition of its exports, that in the U.S. market Puerto Rico is not a major competitor with developing countries. With the exception of Miscellaneous Edible Preparations (for example, rum), which account for 4.3 percent of its exports, almost all other Puerto Rican exports compete mainly with developed countries. Pharmaceutical products account for 56.9 percent of all Puerto Rican exports to the United

15. National Science Foundation (www.nsf.gov/statistics/nsf02318/pdf/pr.pdf).
16. A. T. Kearney Management Consultants (2003, slide 141).

States. If the commonwealth were an independent country, the $27.4 billion would make it by far the top pharmaceuticals exporter to the United States. Indeed, U.S. imports of these products from Puerto Rico were actually larger than its imports from the rest of world and more than five times greater than imports from Ireland (5.6 percent), the next largest source of U.S. imports. The other major exporters of pharmaceuticals to the United States are the United Kingdom ($4.5 billion), Germany ($3.6 billion), and France ($2.5 billion). In fact, U.S. imports of pharmaceuticals from Puerto Rico are equal to between 30 and 70 percent of value added by that industry. Puerto Rico would also rank as a major exporter of optical instruments (which would make it the fourth-largest exporter to the United States), organic chemicals (second largest), and miscellaneous edible preparations, especially rum (the largest). In organic chemicals its major competitors are Ireland, Japan, and the United Kingdom, and in edible preparations, Canada, Mexico, and Thailand. Table 9-8, which shows the destinations of Puerto Rican merchandise exports, indicates that they are highly concentrated and concentrated in developed-country markets.

Are Puerto Rican Exports to the United States Vulnerable to U.S. Trade Liberalization?

The U.S. economy generally has low tariffs. Indeed, it is among the most open in the world, with the notable exception of some labor-intensive and some agricultural products. At the same time, U.S. trade policy has been reducing tariffs for countries that sign free trade agreements.[17] An important issue for Puerto Rico is how vulnerable it is to further tariff reductions by the United States. We have calculated average tariff protection by using the ratio of tariff revenues to imports. This measure captures the effects of variations both in product tariff rates and in trade preferences. If Puerto Rican exports to the United States were heavily influenced by the advantages that Puerto Rico obtains from having tariff-free access to the U.S. market, we would find a positive relationship. However, when we relate Puerto Rican exports to the United States to the tariff variable, we obtain a negative correlation of 0.19.[18] If anything, it would appear that Puerto Rican exports to the United States are associated with low external tariffs. This suggests that Puerto Rican exports to the United States are unlikely to be affected much by additional U.S. liberalization either in free trade agree-

17. See Schott (2004).
18. First, we calculated the average U.S. tariff protection for each of the two-digit HTS categories by dividing the value of import duties by the total value of imports. Then we correlated the vector of average tariff protection by category with the vector of Puerto Rican exports to the United States for the same two-digit HTS categories. The result was a coefficient of correlation of −0.19.

Table 9-8. *Top Ten Puerto Rican Exports and Main Destinations, 2003*
Percent

Description	HTS code	Share of Puerto Rican total exports	Main partners and their shares
Pharmaceutical products	30	56.9	United States (87.7); Netherlands (2.9); Belgium (2.0); France (1.8)
Nuclear reactors, boilers, machinery, and mechanical appliances	84	10.2	United States (63.2); Singapore (12.2); Germany (9.1); Netherlands (8.8)
Organic chemicals	29	9.1	United States (75.0); Belgium (12.4); Netherlands (4.4); Japan (1.9)
Optical, photographic, cinematographic, measuring, checking, precision, medical, and surgical instruments	90	8.4	United States (91.4); Netherlands (2.9); Dominican Republic (1.5); Japan (1.0)
Miscellaneous edible preparations	21	4.3	United States (95.0); Israel (1.7); Malaysia (0.9)
Electrical machinery and equipment; sound and television image recorders and reproducers	85	3.3	United States (79.2); Dominican Republic (8.6); Germany (3.8); Singapore (1.7)
Miscellaneous chemical products	38	1.9	United States (48.7); India (28.6); Germany (8.9); Belgium (3.0); France (1.8)
Mineral fuels, mineral oils, and products of their distillation; bituminous substances, mineral waxes	27	0.8	United States (43.1); Dominican Republic (31.7); Bahamas (13.6); Antigua and Barbuda (2.6)
Special classification provisions	98	0.7	United States (98.6); Dominican Republic (0.4); Kuwait (0.2)
Essential oils and resinoids; perfumery, cosmetic, and toilet preparations	33	0.6	United States (94.7); United Kingdom (0.8); Mexico (0.7)
Total		96.1	

Source: Data from Puerto Rico Planning Board.

ments or in the World Trade Organization's trade negotiations. Puerto Rican exports to the United States are not dependent on tariff preferences.

All told, we have been able to develop a consistent picture of Puerto Rican comparative advantage. Foreign firms that operate in Puerto Rico have been attracted not by the traditional advantages that the Commonwealth might have been expected to provide (or that it might once have provided), such as a relatively abundant labor endowment or duty-free access to the U.S. market. Instead, the real benefits stem from being able to enjoy the advantages that the United States tax code provides to U.S. corporations that operate in the commonwealth and the agglomeration economies that these activities appear to have created. These advantages are greatest where firms have the ability to take advantage of transfer pricing opportunities to undervalue the transfer of intellectual property obtained in the United States. They also confer an advantage on capital-intensive operations. The result is that Puerto Rico is competitive in products that paradoxically reflect mainland comparative advantages in high-technology activities. The result is also an export sector that is made up of large foreign-owned firms and is not deeply integrated into the local economy. At the same time, however, as indicated in the previous section, this is clearly a dynamic activity that has continued to flourish in recent years despite the elimination of the even more favorable treatment that was provided under the section 936 provisions.

Are Services the Future?

In contrast to Puerto Rican exports of goods, Puerto Rican services exports— which, as reported above, have recently been growing rapidly—appear more grounded in the island's factor endowments. To be sure, the commonwealth has provided some modest tax incentives to stimulate this activity, but it appears to have arisen more organically from developments in the domestic economy. A large number of well-educated Puerto Ricans earn substantially less than their U.S. counterparts. In addition, Puerto Rico has a particularly dynamic domestic financial sector that enjoys participation in an economy based on the U.S. dollar and is subject to U.S. regulatory oversight. The Spanish language also gives Puerto Rican services providers a natural advantage in Central and Latin America.

Puerto Rican Imports: Ripe for Substitution?

We now turn our focus from Puerto Rican export characteristics and performance to the import side.[19] A significant share of Puerto Rican imports consists of

19. The methodologies we used to analyze the import side were the same ones used for the export side.

Table 9-9. *Main Puerto Rican Imports, 2003*
Percent

Description	HTS code	Share of imports from the United States	Share of imports from the rest of the world
Organic chemicals	29	4.1	58.3
Pharmaceutical products	30	19.8	9.8
Electrical machinery; sound and television image recorders and reproducers	85	12.4	2.3
Nuclear reactors, boilers, machinery, and mechanical appliances	84	9.0	1.6
Vehicles, other than railway or tramway rolling stock	87	8.5	3.7
Optical, photographic, cinematographic, measuring, checking, precision, medical, and surgical instruments and thereof	90	5.9	1.4
Total		59.7	77.1

Source: Data from Puerto Rico Planning Board.

capital goods and inputs into imports. The goods imported from the United States are very different from those imported from the rest of the world and for the most part are also quite different from goods produced in and exported from the commonwealth. Whereas the overwhelming majority of Puerto Rican exports (86.4 percent in 2003) go to the United States, a much smaller share of merchandise imports (48.9 percent) come from the United States.[20] The largest imports from the United States are pharmaceutical products (19.8 percent) and electrical machinery (12.4 percent) (table 9-9). Imports from the rest of the world are also more highly concentrated. Just two categories, organic chemicals and pharmaceutical products, account for two-thirds of all goods imported from the rest of the world. Together with machinery, transportation equipment, and instruments, the total is 76 percent. This leaves some $3.3 billion that is imported from a wide variety of countries, the principal suppliers being the Dominican Republic, China, Mexico, and Canada. The bulk of Puerto Rican imports, it appears, are basically raw materials, intermediate inputs, and capital goods.

Although there is some overlap in the broad product categories, Puerto Rican imports from the rest of the world are very different from the goods imported

20. Government Development Bank for Puerto Rico (2004).

Table 9-10. *Measures of Input Intensity of Puerto Rican Imports, 2000*[a]
Units as indicated

Sector	Skill[b]	Capital[c]	R&D[d]
(1) U.S. manufacturing weights	53,807	0.37	45
(2) Puerto Rican import weights	60,865	0.44	63
(3) U.S. import weights	61,317	0.31	77
Ratios			
(2)/(3) Puerto Rican imports/U.S. imports	0.99	1.45	0.82
(2)/(1) Puerto Rican imports/U.S. manufacturing	1.13	1.19	1.38
(3)/(1) U.S. imports/U.S. manufacturing	1.14	0.82	1.69

Source: National Science Foundation, *Annual Survey of Manufactures*, IO tables.
a. In each sector, 2000 U.S. input measures are weighted by the indicated sectoral output.
b. Skill refers to average compensation per worker, in U.S. dollars.
c. Capital refers to the share of profits in value added.
d. R&D refers to the number of scientists and engineers per 1,000 employees.

from the United States. The similarity index for import shares to the United States and the rest of the world is 64.13, suggesting that these goods are twice as different as are Puerto Rican exports to the United States and the rest of the world (the similarity index for exports is 31.51, and the coefficient of correlation is just 0.28). The goods are so different that for many import categories we do not find imports coming both from the United States and from the rest of the world. After dropping those commodities for which there are no imports both from the United States and from the rest of the world, we are left with only 30 percent of imports. For these overlapping categories, we find that unit values of goods imported from the United States are much higher than those imported from the rest of the world.

The weighted sum of relative unit values of Puerto Rican exports to the rest of the world is 5.21 times as high as Puerto Rican imports from the rest of the world, showing that Puerto Rico is exporting much more expensive products than those it imports from the world. This again suggests rather low substitutability between the goods Puerto Rico sells to the rest of the world and those that it buys. Indeed, in our import equation we estimated the import price elasticity of demand at approximately unity.

In the case of exports, we saw that Puerto Rico has specialized in goods that reflect the U.S. comparative advantage. We computed the factor content of imports, again using U.S. input coefficients for both Puerto Rico and the United States; the results are given in table 9-10. We find that weighting each industry's input coefficients by Puerto Rican import weights suggests that the goods Puerto Rico imports are relatively more skill intensive (13 percent), capi-

Table 9-11. *Top Ten Puerto Rican Basic Manufactured Imports, 2003*
Percent

Description	HTS code	Share of imports from the rest of the world
Miscellaneous edible preparations	21	4.3
Mineral fuels, mineral oils, and products of their distillation; bituminous substances and mineral waxes	27	0.8
Essential oils and resinoids; perfumery, cosmetic, and toilet preparations	33	0.6
Articles of apparel and clothing accessories, knitted or crocheted	61	0.3
Tobacco and manufactured tobacco substitutes	24	0.3
Beverages, spirits, and vinegar	22	0.3
Plastics and articles thereof	39	0.3
Articles of apparel and clothing accessories, not knitted or crocheted	62	0.2
Preparations of meat, fish or crustaceans, mollusks or other aquatic invertebrates	16	0.2
Sugars and sugar confectionery	17	0.2
Total		7.6

Source: Data from Puerto Rico Planning Board.

tal intensive (19 percent), and especially R&D intensive (38) than U.S. manufacturing as a whole.[21] Imports to both Puerto Rico and the United States are produced with quite similar compensation levels, but Puerto Rican imports tend to be substantially more capital intensive (ratio of 1.45) and less R&D intensive (ratio of 0.82) than U.S. imports. This profile might suggest that Puerto Rico is about as skill intensive as the United States, less capital intensive, and more R&D intensive; but because of the high level of aggregation at which this exercise is carried out, these results should be taken with a large grain of salt. It also suggests, however, that Puerto Rico might need considerable investment in skills, capital, and R&D to accomplish a significant amount of import substitution. As can be seen in table 9-11, Puerto Rico imports a relatively small share of more basic commodities.

Policies for Growth: Some Basic Principles

As noted in the introduction to this chapter, three concerns generally motivate the focus of policies on trade: meeting the external constraint, reducing

21. U.S. imports tend to be more skill intensive (14 percent), less capital intensive (82 percent), and very much more intensive in R&D (69 percent).

unemployment and encouraging labor force participation, and stimulating economic growth. For Puerto Rico, as we have shown, the external constraint is not a problem because of the dollarization of the economy and because the current account has tended toward a surplus and the island has enjoyed rapid export growth in recent years. In any case, Puerto Rico does not have the ability to implement an independent trade policy, even if it wanted to. As part of the United States Customs Area, the commonwealth has essentially no independent trade policy instruments. It has no border barriers with respect to U.S. products that constitute most of its trade, and its barriers with respect to non-U.S. trade and its access to foreign export markets are both essentially determined in Washington. In addition, because Puerto Rico's currency is the U.S. dollar, both labor and capital move freely. In these respects, therefore, Puerto Rico is best thought of as a U.S. state rather than a country. Although it is certainly affected by trade policy, Puerto Rico has a small impact on its own trade policy. Puerto Rico may need a development strategy in which tradable goods may play some part, but it cannot have a trade policy in the traditional sense. Import protection is simply not an instrument that is available, and export subsidies are constrained by the general disciplines imposed by World Trade Organization rules. This suggests that for our purposes, the principal concerns of policy relate to employment and growth.

The demand generated by exports or increased import substitution could certainly help reduce unemployment in the short run, but we believe that Puerto Rico's employment problems are primarily attributable to structural problems in the Puerto Rican labor market that are more appropriately dealt with directly, through labor market policies that remove the constraints on clearing the labor market. These supply-side policies need to deal with problems that are generally associated with low-skilled workers. In particular, it appears that the cost of unskilled labor on the island is relatively high while the cost of skilled labor is relatively low. This suggests that policies seeking to raise the demand for labor by stimulating international trade are more likely to increase the relative demand for skilled workers and therefore less likely to mitigate the problems facing low-skilled workers.

Our analysis therefore concentrates on how to stimulate growth. In thinking about growth, it is a useful discipline to assume full (or a constant level of) employment. This is a useful framework because it reminds us that resources added in one activity subtract from resources added elsewhere. If there are unutilized resources in an economy—for example, high unemployment—there is a wide range of policies that might generate positive social returns. Indeed, almost any policy—even paying the unemployed to dig ditches and refill them—may be justified on the grounds it creates jobs. The crucial issue with respect to growth, however, is whether an additional dollar spent in promoting one activity would be more beneficial than a dollar spent elsewhere.

Thus the question for those who believe a particular activity should be promoted—for example, import substitution or increasing exports—is why they believe the social returns to such an activity will be higher than elsewhere in the economy.

In this regard, there are good reasons to be wary of industrial policy approaches that emphasize the promotion of entire industries rather than particular activities. These are unlikely to be precisely targeted. Indeed, policies designed to promote particular activities are often called industrial policies. This is an unfortunate moniker because it is sometimes taken to mean that such policies should emphasize manufacturing (that is, industry) or that they should promote specific industries or sectors. The case for government policies should rest on the likelihood that private markets alone are unable to achieve optimal outcomes and not the favorable consequences that are believed to result from particular sectors or industries.

The Wrong Way

Broad-based expenditures encouraging particular industries or "all exports" or "all firms substituting for imports" are bound to be wasteful. To be sure, the pharmaceutical industry, for example, has the desirable attribute that it spends a lot on R&D. But this does not imply that at the margin a public grant of the next R&D dollar that is spent in pharmaceuticals will yield a higher return than spending that dollar elsewhere. Indeed, it is just as plausible that at the margin the return could be higher in the low-tech sectors that spend far less on R&D. Similarly, just because many firms that export have relatively rapid productivity growth does not imply that additional export promotion will enhance productivity growth. In fact, there is considerable evidence that faster productivity growth leads to exports rather than the other way around.[22]

Trying to encourage import substitution wherever possible may have similar problems. Some analysts have argued that for Puerto Rico, high-tech exports, despite their dynamic character, have not been an ideal driver of economic development. They complain that by being able to rely on foreign firms for exports (as well as other palliatives such as U.S. transfers and the ability to migrate to the United States), Puerto Rico has forgone the opportunity to develop the institutions and policies necessary for sustaining its long-run growth and development.[23] Local entrepreneurs, by contrast, are not heavily engaged in merchandise exports—indeed, according to A. T. Kearney Management Consultants, locally owned firms account for just 3 percent of all exports.[24] It is therefore possible that an explicit import-substitution strategy might have led to

---

22. Bernard and Jensen (1995).
23. See, for example, Padin (2003) and Dietz (2001).
24. A. T. Kearney Management Consultants (2003, slide 96).

superior trade linkages with the domestic economy and generated a more indigenous growth path.[25]

It is unquestionably the case that the transition from an agrarian economy to an industrial one is likely to entail some element of import substitution in addition to the development of export capabilities. Indeed, Rivera Figuera has documented such development in Puerto Rico, and it is likely that Puerto Rican firms in the future will be able to expand by increasing their market shares in products that Puerto Rico currently imports.[26] In addition, for a sizable segment of the economy (nontradables), local production will be essential. Again, it is important to be clear why, *at the margin,* growth in import substitution is likely to be better than growth in activities that service the domestic market.

A focus on import substitution at all costs would inevitably encounter problems. First, as has been pointed out, because it is part of the United States Customs Area, Puerto Rico cannot use trade protection to achieve this goal. Instead, it would have to rely on fiscal incentives and perhaps selective government procurement. Fundamentally, therefore, under the assumption of full (or constant) employment, a dollar spent on diverting resources toward import substitution would divert resources from either export production or nontradables, and there are reasons for caution in favoring domestic procurement. In particular, the domestic market may well be too small to support efficient production of many of the goods Puerto Rico imports. A second problem relates to the relatively high cost of Puerto Rican labor. A substantial share of Puerto Rican consumer imports comes from developing countries. It is likely that expansions of these activities will be not be viable without permanent government assistance.

It is by no means obvious that the economy is necessarily better off making a product at home than buying it abroad. The case for subsidizing import substitution is the same as that for infant industry protection more generally. It must rest on the view that there are market failures that currently prevent firms from producing these products profitability and that in the long run, the cost savings from domestic production of these products will be sufficiently large to offset the higher costs that are imposed in the short run. There may well be some activities in which these conditions are met, but a policy that provides incentives for all types of this activity is bound to be wasteful.

Similar caution is warranted with respect to export promotion, particularly by small firms. It is tempting to argue that there are large unexploited opportunities for small firms to become exporters, but the evidence does not actually support this as a blanket generalization, particularly for manufactured goods. Most of the manufactured goods exported by the United States, for example,

25. For an argument in favor of import substitution, see Weisskoff (1985).

26. Cited in Dietz (2001). See also Imbs and Wacziarg (2003) for evidence that economic growth is associated with increasing diversification.

are actually produced by very large firms. According to the Small Business Administration, in 2002 just 26.4 percent of all U.S. exports of manufactures came from firms with fewer than five hundred workers, and much less from firms with fewer than one hundred employees. In Puerto Rico in 2002, small and medium-sized enterprises accounted for 11.2 percent of exports.[27] This suggests that, particularly in manufacturing, exporting in sizable quantities is fundamentally a large-firm endeavor.[28]

The Right Way

Nonetheless, there is a case for the government to assist in economic development. But this assistance needs to be applied carefully. The mere fact that a product is being purchased from a domestic source rather than imported does not make this purchase preferable. Similarly, the mere fact that money is being given to small rather than large firms, or the mere fact that money goes to one particular sector rather than another, does not make it preferable. The crucial issue is whether an activity that is being promoted is likely to have social benefits beyond those the individual entrepreneur can capture. In principle, the government could have a role to play in three crucial areas: stimulating innovation and social learning, aiding in the collective coordination of investments, and providing public goods and infrastructure; these are activities unlikely to be provided in optimal quantities by private individuals acting alone. Industrial policy would thus be best implemented by promoting these activities throughout the economy. But it is also important that the government be able to apply such policies effectively. Government failure could be worse than market failure.

Stimulating Innovation and Learning. Successful innovation by some brings with it opportunities for others. The traditional view of innovation focuses on new products and technologies and the evidence that the social returns from these activities are much higher than the private returns. Particularly for developing countries, however, a key dimension relates to searching for and discovering new profitable activities.[29] Successful innovation is accomplished not only by discovering new technologies and inventing new products but also by determining which products and technologies can actually make money in a particular setting. In a seminal study, Edwin Mansfield and his colleagues have found that though an overwhelming majority of R&D projects succeed from a

27. U.S. Department of Commerce, International Trade Administration, "Small and Medium-Sized Exporting Companies: A Statistical Handbook" (www.ita.doc.gov/td/industry/otea/docs/SMEstat-hbk2002.pdf [November 2005]).

28. Taking other trade into account, the shares of firms with fewer than 500 and 100 employees were 29.5 and 19.9 percent, respectively. Seven hundred and eight Puerto Rican firms were identified as exporters in 1992. Of these, 186 employed more than 500, and another 282 between 19 and 499.

29. See Hausmann and Rodrik (2003).

technological standpoint, a much smaller percentage turn out to be profitable.[30] This implies that simply supplying more R&D inputs is not sufficient; attention must also be paid to the market's demands.

Moreover, in addition to the inherent risk in undertaking new activities, pioneers often have reason to be wary. The first firm that establishes a successful call center, for example, and shows that this is a profitable activity, may find that the workers it trains are hired away by new competitors. Although the benefits of such training may be enjoyed by the broader economy, they are not all captured by the initial firm, and indeed, firms will be reluctant to shoulder training from which they may not benefit. These types of considerations point to a possible government role in helping to offset the costs that are borne by first movers, particularly for activities that have the potential to demonstrate opportunities that may be emulated by others. By contrast, there is no need to subsidize second and third movers, who have the benefit of being able to copy.[31] This suggests the need for selectivity and discretion in the activities that government promotes. Such activities are unlikely to be isolated by making grants automatically to all investments in a particular sector or subsidizing all types of exports or using domestic inputs. But there could be a role for special assistance to the pioneers who first try to break into new export or domestic markets.

Coordination. The second crucial area for policy lies in the coordination of activities, both private and public, where a multiplicity of measures is required for success. A classic example is tourism. Establishing a successful tourist industry requires appropriate international and domestic transportation facilities, public safety, public health, a clean environment, an abundant choice of restaurants, nightclubs, shopping opportunities, and sporting facilities, trained workers with language skills, and so on. No single entrepreneur can supply them all, but a critical mass of these activities is required for any to succeed. Identifying the key complementary components required for particular activities and helping to ensure that they are all present (through measures such as loan guarantees) could be a legitimate government activity.

Public Goods. The third key dimension, also evident in the tourism example, is supporting institutions and infrastructure. Education (training), regulation, and the provision of public services are areas in which public roles are crucial. Similarly, transportation and communications facilities are particularly important for an island economy and are an area in which the government obviously has an important role to play. Again, a sense of where the

---

30. Reporting on a study of R&D programs, Mansfield and others (1977, p. 10) state, "It is much more likely that a project will achieve its technical aims (this probability being about 0.60 in these firms) than that, if it achieves these aims, it will earn an economic profit (this probability being about 0.2 in these firms)."

31. Paradoxically, entry barriers to second movers may actually encourage innovation. See Bailey and Lederman (2004).

most important growth nodes in the economy are likely to be located is important so that government spending on complementary public goods can be appropriately focused.

Bringing It All Together. Simply informing the government that it needs to encourage discovery and learning, coordinate investments, and provide public goods does not, however, constitute a policy. There is considerable disagreement about how the government should prioritize its spending in each of these dimensions. What types of knowledge are best promoted? Where is policy coordination most needed? Which public goods should be provided? It is here that some idea of the likely developments in the economy is required, not necessarily to promote all activities in particular sectors but rather to promote these three types of activities. As Dani Rodrik has emphasized,

> The right model for industrial policy is not that of an autonomous government applying Pigovian taxes or subsidies, but of strategic collaboration between the private sector and the government with the aim of uncovering where the most significant obstacles to restructuring lie and what type of interventions are most likely to remove them. We need to worry about how we design a setting in which private and public actors can come together to solve problems in the productive sphere, each side learning about the opportunities and constraints faced by the other. . . . Hence the right way of thinking of industrial policy is as a discovery process—one where firms and the government learn about underlying costs and opportunities and engage in strategic coordination.[32]

Puerto Rican Policies Examined

In light of the theoretical considerations laid out above, it is useful to reexamine three current aspects of Puerto Rican policy: the focus on clusters, the use of tax incentives, and export promotion activities. In some cases the policies do appear to focus on market failures, but in many other cases they are likely to subsidize activities that would take place anyway.

Strategic Clusters: Puerto Rico's New Approach to Industrial Policy

The demise of section 936 tax credits ended the period of comparatively easy industrial promotion in Puerto Rico. Since the turn of the century, therefore, the commonwealth has been trying to refocus its economic development strategy to provide a stable foundation for future industrial promotion policies, stimulate greater linkages between the local economy and the export-oriented manufacturing sector, and increase the science and technology

32. Rodrik (2004).

content of economic activity. A new policy orientation has taken shape, one that emphasizes the development of innovation-driven "strategic clusters."

A cluster may be defined as a sectoral or geographic concentration of firms engaged in the same activities or activities closely linked in a value added chain, exchanging between them inputs, services, knowledge, and technology and together generating and using external and agglomeration economies in a flexible and dynamic structure that fosters innovation.[33] A cluster is not the same as an industry grouping, since it typically includes firms from different industrial classifications as well as related institutions such as universities and even regulatory entities. It is this sort of definition that the Puerto Rico Industrial Development Company (PRIDCO) has adopted as a framework for its industrial policy strategy. The concept emphasizes input-output linkages and puts a premium on innovation as part of the expected outcomes.

The clusters approach adopted by PRIDCO overlaps two government administrations, each headed by one of the island's two major political parties. Thus the strategy appears to enjoy bipartisan support. In the late 1990s, PRIDCO hired the U.S. consulting firm Arthur D. Little to help it devise a strategy to promote science and technology activities. In 2001–02 PRIDCO, now under a new government administration, asked McKinsey & Company, another U.S. consulting firm, to produce a plan to promote the communications and information technology sector. These two projects eventually led to the identification of eight strategic clusters to become the focus of the government's promotion program:
—pharmaceutical products
—biotechnology
—plastics
—electronic and communications products
—medical instruments and devices
—personal and health care products
—optical products
—construction services and materials
With the exception of personal and health care products and construction services and materials, the clusters selected by PRIDCO are all made up of high-technology activities. Most of these industries already have a significant presence in Puerto Rico, and the key players in each are mostly subsidiaries of U.S. manufacturing multinationals.

The clusters strategy was not invented by PRIDCO or its consultants. Indeed, Puerto Rico may be a latecomer to a strategy that other countries have already been pursuing for years, which in itself may entail some disadvantages.

---

33. Organization for Economic Cooperation and Development (1999) and Porter (2002).

According to a study conducted by the Organization for Economic Cooperation and Development, clusters development is "the most common and more viable strategy" for countries hoping to become more competitive on the world scene. Similarly, the United Nations Industrial Development Organization stresses that development of the industrial sector based on innovation and knowledge is now "the global tendency."[34]

In Latin America, a similar approach is being championed by one of the older development think tanks, the Economic Commission for Latin America and the Caribbean. Recently, the commission's documents have been emphasizing the importance of the "systemic competitiveness" that results from the positive externalities created by economic agents interacting through production linkages.[35] The message also stresses the importance for economic development of innovations and the associated learning processes.

A key question is whether Puerto Rico is well prepared to pursue this strategy successfully. Given the large high-tech manufacturing base already existing on the island, PRIDCO's own studies have concluded, the initial conditions are favorable for the development of the desired clusters. While this does not guarantee success, it does mean that Puerto Rico is at a much better starting point than many other developing economies. Using the United Nations Industrial Development Organization index of competitive industrial performance for 1998, PRIDCO's consultants have compared Puerto Rico with eighty-eight countries, including a number of newly industrialized countries and developed industrial economies. Puerto Rico ranked second on the list, bested only by Singapore.[36] To be sure, this does not mean that Puerto Rico is a stronger industrial power than, say, the United States or Japan, but it does indicate the strong presence of high-technology manufacturing in the Puerto Rico economy.

The index averages four indicators to measure competitive industrial performance: manufacturing value added per capita, manufactured exports per capita, the share of high-tech industries in manufacturing value added, and the share of high-tech products in manufactured exports. Our analysis in the previous sections gives reasons why Puerto Rico might be expected to show up strongly in all of these indicators, but it also suggests reasons to be wary of these measures because much of the recorded value added in Puerto Rico may well reflect activities that are actually performed on the mainland. Thus though Puerto Rico may excel on the basis of this index, the index in no way measures an economy's capacity to generate competitive industrial performance endogenously; it only measures the actual level of performance at a given time.

34. Organization for Economic Cooperation and Development (1999); United Nations Industrial Development Organization (2004).

35. See, for example, Ocampo (2001, p. 33).

36. Estudios Técnicos (2003).

In another study, PRIDCO's chief economist, John Stewart, calculates location quotients for industries in Puerto Rico vis-à-vis the U.S. mainland.[37] A location quotient greater than 1 indicates that a particular industry has a relatively larger presence in Puerto Rico than on the mainland; a value of less than 1 indicates the opposite. Stewart finds fourteen industries with quotients greater than 1, six of which are high-tech industries belonging to one or more of the clusters targeted by PRIDCO: pharmaceutical products, power distribution equipment, medical instruments and devices, instruments and related products, electronic components, and electronic and electric equipment. The location quotient for pharmaceutical products is 10.5, meaning that this industry has a presence in Puerto Rico 10.5 times larger than its presence on the mainland.

Stewart also finds, however, that some of the industries in PRIDCO's clusters have a smaller presence in Puerto Rico than on the mainland. Such is the case with communications products (0.9) and health services (0.7). A glaring difference was found in transportation equipment, which had the lowest quotient value of all the industries examined (0.1).[38] These results point the way to needed investments and provide a guide for priority rankings of promotion activities.

The same consultants also interviewed top executives in key industries in Puerto Rico to identify industrial promotion priorities. In essence, the executives interviewed gave their opinions as to what are the "holes" in the input-output matrix presenting the best investment opportunities for cluster development. The top ten on the list are as follows:

—blow-molded plastic products
—personal computer board manufacturing in small quantities with flexible production schedules
—products to replace human tissue
—testing of products to repair bone fractures
—auto parts
—insulating construction materials
—specialty chemicals for pharmaceutical plants
—food-processing technologies
—software development
—additional airfreight routes

Identifying growth nodes is a useful exercise, but in and of itself it does not constitute a complete policy strategy. Although it should be particularly helpful in identifying areas in which measures to improve coordination and remove bottlenecks could be useful and in helping government investments in comple-

37. Stewart (2003).
38. Stewart (2003).

mentary public goods and infrastructure, there remain additional implementation challenges.

A key issue is what instruments are needed or available to promote activities at the more aggregate level of the eight strategic clusters. The commonwealth already offers generous tax incentives for manufacturing, so there is little more that can be provided in this direction. On the U.S. side, it is best to assume that no new federal tax incentives will be forthcoming, at least within a reasonable planning horizon. As a general principle, PRIDCO is shifting to a strategy of providing focused, even tailor-made, incentives to new businesses, including outright cash grants and help financing specific investments. It should be noted, however, that this critical dimension of the clusters strategy is still being worked out, and, in the light of the earlier discussion, the key focus should be on dealing with market failures rather than simply funding projects that appear to be viable (and could therefore simply substitute for private funds).

It is early to expect results from a strategy still in its beginning stages of implementation, but there have been some encouraging developments in the past two years. Major firms in some of key cluster industries have announced expansions or added new products to their production lines in Puerto Rico. Amgen, one of the larger biotechnology firms in the world, is building capacity that will make Puerto Rico its largest production location. Top pharmaceutical names like Eli Lilly and Abbott are also expanding their local operations with a view to supplying larger segments of U.S. and foreign markets. In the communications and information technology cluster, PRIDCO has provided substantial assistance to support a major expansion of Hewlett-Packard's operation in Aguadilla, on the island's western coast.

There have also been several other initiatives related to the clusters strategy. A consortium of local government, university, and business entities recently set up INTECO (the Center-East Techno-Economic Initiative) to promote investment in cluster-related activities, especially those intensive in R&D. A similar organization, the Techno-Economic Corridor, was set up by private, academic, and public entities on the western side of the island a few years ago. The thrust of initiative in these two cases has come from the private and academic sectors, not the government, and accords with the notion that cooperative activities can play an important role in supplementing private activity.

A major challenge for this strategic approach is to provide the required supporting infrastructure and institutions. It is generally agreed that Puerto Rico needs to lower the cost of electric power for industrial users and to improve the transportation infrastructure. It is also generally acknowledged that the government's permitting and regulatory functions need to be modernized and refocused. Not least is the need for Puerto Rico's universities to become more research oriented. Excellence in teaching is a necessary but not sufficient contribution of academia to a development strategy emphasizing science and technology.

Puerto Rico now has an opportunity to develop major pieces of infrastructure that could have a significant impact on future industrial development on the island. These are the Puerto of the Americas, on the southern coast, the former U.S. Navy base in Ceiba, on the eastern coast, and the former U.S. Air Force base in Aguadilla, on the western coast. Each of these can provide enormous transportation capacity to support a highly developed trade-oriented industrial base while enabling Puerto Rico to become a hub for regional or even hemispheric trade. These projects are still in their early stages of definition and implementation but could become significant factors for Puerto Rico's development within a decade. In sum, the cluster approach could provide a useful focus for industrial policy activities, but it remains to be seen whether policies will be able to focus on stimulating discoveries with potential applications by other firms rather than crowding out private activities.

Tax Incentives: Do They Really Identify Pioneers?

A special tax incentive program is provided by PRIDCO for "pioneer industries" to assist with these policies. It defines these as "operations that are deemed to have a novel or innovative technology not utilized in Puerto Rico before January 1, 2000, and that will have a significant impact on the economic and industrial development of Puerto Rico."[39] Firms in pioneer industries "may qualify for corporate income tax rates between 2% and 0%, compared with the regular tax rate of 7 percent."[40] In addition, a range of deductions and credits is offered to firms. These include deductions for payroll, training (200 percent), R&D (200 percent of expenses), and accelerated depreciation for buildings, machinery, and equipment. There is a 25 percent tax credit for increased purchases of locally manufactured goods, a 35 percent credit for locally recycled goods, and a tax credit for withheld royalty payments. "Operations of designated services for external markets will also be eligible for a tax rate of 7% on their industrial development income, 90% of their property taxes and 60% on municipal license taxes and fees."[41]

39. Commonwealth of Puerto Rico, "Corporate Income Tax Incentives" (www.pridco.com/english/tax_and_business_incentives/tax_incentives/3.12corp_tax_incentives.html).

40. Commonwealth of Puerto Rico, "Corporate Income Tax Incentives" (www.pridco.com/english/tax_and_business_incentives/tax_incentives/3.12corp_tax_incentives.html). Eligibility for these benefits will depend on such factors as "the nature of the employment to be created[,] development of high levels of technical, scientific and managerial expertise in the employees[,] the investments to be made in plant, machinery and equipment[,] a substantial concentration of production for global markets to be located in Puerto Rico[, and] the integration of research, development and technological improvements as part of the industrial operation." "Corporate Income Tax Incentives."

41. Commonwealth of Puerto Rico, "Corporate Income Tax Incentives" (www.pridco.com/english/tax_and_business_incentives/tax_incentives/3.12corp_tax_incentives.html).

The emphasis on new technologies in this approach is sensible, but the danger is that firms could use these benefits simply to buy new plant and equipment—an essentially private market activity. In addition, though they attempt to focus on novel technologies, the provisions do not distinguish between first movers and those that simply copy what others have done. The virtue of tax breaks is that they can be applied by firms independently; the problem, however, is that this makes it difficult to use the needed discretion to ensure that the funds actually yield additional social benefits. The danger is that a broad reading of the eligibility requirements could allow firms to take advantage of these tax breaks to subsidize activities they would undertake anyway.

Export Promotion Strategies

There is a Puerto Rico government agency dedicated to export promotion, a branch of the Commerce and Exports Corporation (COMEX, by its Spanish acronym). This corporation operates under the umbrella of the Department of Economic Development. Over the past twelve years, this agency has changed names and personality—it started as Fomexport and was later called Promoexport—but its function has remained the same: helping Puerto Rican firms sell their products abroad.

In 1995 the External Trade Board, a public and private advisory body appointed by the governor, produced what is probably the first comprehensive export promotion strategy ever drafted on the island. The "Strategic Plan for External Trade," as it was called, was meant as a blueprint for Promoexport, the trade promotion agency that had just discarded its original name, Fomexport.[42] Although the plan is already ten years old, it still provides a good idea of the government's approach to export promotion policies.

The consultants working for the External Trade Board evaluated the legal, infrastructure, and economic aspects of Puerto Rico's external trade and recommended several strategies to improve the export performance of local-capital firms. Before examining the most significant of these, it is worthwhile to review the researchers' findings regarding the export promotion programs existing at the time (which are mostly the same ones in existence today).

For years, there have been several programs and incentives designed to stimulate exports from Puerto Rico. Most of these have been written into the industrial incentives legislation, while others apply to specific sectors, such as agriculture and transportation. The commonwealth's Industrial Incentives Act provides for a 90 percent tax exemption on income arising from the export of manufactured products or services from Puerto Rico to foreign countries (other than the United States). The legislation providing incentives to agriculture

42. Arthur D. Little and others (1995).

includes provisions for the promotion and marketing abroad of Puerto Rico's agricultural products. There is also a tax exemption for up to ten years for commercial producers of ornamental flowers for the local market and for export. In addition, a 1986 law provides for the creation of a register of exporting firms to help focus government assistance with the promotion and marketing of their products. However, the consultants to the External Trade Board found in 1995 that "these laws have not been used to any great extent and have not provided the anticipated boon to Puerto Rico's export capability."[43] That conclusion is still valid today. It also appears that Puerto Rican firms seldom use the services of U.S. government agencies and programs such as the Export-Import Bank (EXIMBANK) and the U.S. Commercial Service.

Why haven't these programs been more successful? One simple reason is that many firms are apparently unaware of their existence. More vigorous promotion of the programs themselves is therefore needed. In addition, the External Trade Board has found that some of the existing legislation imposed accounting and reporting requirements that firms found difficult to comply with—for example, the requirement of separate bookkeeping for local market and export activities. In addition, agencies like Fomexport did not have enough budget resources and staff to carry out their export promotion activities effectively.

A survey of 1,166 manufacturing firms in Promoexport's client base conducted by the External Trade Board in 1995 produced the following interesting results:[44]

—Nearly half of the companies were exporters. However, only 30.3 percent of Puerto Rican–owned companies in the group were exporters, as opposed to 86.3 percent of United States–owned and 72.1 percent of foreign-owned firms.

—Exports accounted for 20.4 percent of total sales among the Puerto Rican–owned companies.

—Besides the United States, markets in the Caribbean, Central America, and Mexico were the most important destinations for exports of Puerto Rico-owned firms.

—Only 17.8 percent of local firms were willing to pay for trade-support services, as opposed to 32 percent of U.S. subsidiaries and 35 percent of foreign firms.

—The type of support most frequently requested was provision of market information and training about "things to consider" in international markets.

The sample of local firms in the survey—766—was fairly large. This was not, however, a random sample, and since it was taken from Promoexport's client list, exporters were most likely overrepresented. That said, it is interesting that Puerto Rico exporters tend to concentrate their efforts in the United States and

43. Arthur D. Little and others (1995, p. 21).
44. Arthur D. Little and others (1995, pp. 50–51).

the Greater Caribbean area; they have a more regional focus than either U.S. or foreign firms, who export all around the world. This is a point to bear in mind in regard to the potential effects of regional trade agreements in the Caribbean and Central America.

The Strategic Plan identified sixteen market segments, the product of four types of exporters or exports and four market destinations. The exporters-exports categories are products of U.S. subsidiaries, local products, local services, and general trading. The latter category encompasses all products that may be traded through Puerto Rico, even if not produced here. The four market destinations are the Expanded Caribbean Basin, which comprises the Caribbean proper plus Central America, Mexico, and the northern part of South America; the U.S. market; other Latin America; and Europe and Asia. The plan selected the following as high-priority segments:

—local products to the Expanded Caribbean Basin and U.S. regional markets

—local services to the Expanded Caribbean Basin markets

—local services to other Latin America

These are still likely to be the market segments presenting the most potential for export generation by local firms. Puerto Rican products can be sold competitively in U.S. regional markets with large Hispanic populations and may also find attractive markets in the Greater Caribbean. The latter will be harder to penetrate, owing to the competition from low-cost domestic production and the transactions costs related to foreign contracts, customs procedures, and foreign exchange risk. None of these is an insurmountable obstacle, however; rather, these are precisely the areas in which an effective export promotion agency would prove helpful, providing market intelligence and how-to assistance.

As for specific industries and products, the plan recommends an initial strong focus on the following:

—manufactured products: processed foods and beverages, high-fashion clothing, furniture, plastics, and printing and publishing products

—services: design and engineering, management and consulting, data processing, health care, education, financial services, telecommunications, cinematography (including feature production and technical support services), and television programming and production services

—agriculture: mangoes, coffee, citron, ornamental plants, flowers, pineapple, organic fruit, tropical fruits and vegetables, and poultry table

These are still likely to be the industries and products in which Puerto Rico either already has or can quickly develop comparative advantages (other than the high-tech U.S. subsidiary industries). One wonders, then, how much progress there has been in implementing the plan over the past ten years. An evaluation and, if necessary, reassessment of the plan is probably overdue, and now, while the Chile–United States Free Trade Agreement and the Central

America–Dominican Republic–United States Free Trade Agreement are about to go into effect, is probably the best time to do it.

Conclusion

The clusters approach to industrial promotion and some related initiatives have begun to shift the focus of government policies to three dimensions of development: stimulating learning and innovation, coordinating public and private investment, and providing fundamental public goods. The very concept of clusters emphasizes the coordination of investment opportunities to maximize interactions within a network of interindustry and intraindustry linkages. The Puerto Rico Industrial Development Company is increasingly assuming the role of facilitator in this process, working jointly with companies and private sector organizations to identify investment priorities. The large investments involved in the expansions at Hewlett-Packard and Amgen in recent years are two examples of this approach at work. In addition, PRIDCO is now more inclined to provide selective and targeted incentives, as required by a specific venture, rather than rely exclusively on a standard package of incentives offered to all potential investors on essentially the same terms, which has been the traditional practice. The move in this direction is a rather recent development, but in time it may become the new way of doing business for PRIDCO. It is to be hoped that these incentives are applied using a "market failure" perspective, with a view to promoting benefits that are enjoyed beyond those that the firms themselves can capture.

It is also encouraging that while the government refocuses its promotions strategy and practices, nongovernmental entities are becoming more actively involved in economic development initiatives. The Techno-Economic Corridor on the western coast and the INTECO initiative in the center-east region are two examples of privately launched projects designed to stimulate innovation-inducing collaborations among industry, academia, and government. Although PRIDCO and some local governments have been involved in these initiatives from the beginning, the organizing force came primarily from private businesses and universities. This is a welcome change from the traditional attitude in the private sector of relying entirely on government leadership and guidance in all matters pertaining to economic development strategies and policies. To be sure, these initiatives are recent, and there is no guarantee that they will be successful; but they do provide an indication of willingness and readiness to embrace a new model in the post-936 era.

There is room for improvement in the provision of adequate infrastructure and public goods by the government in Puerto Rico, a fact most government officials readily accept. The island is better stocked with transportation, communications, power, and water infrastructure than most developing countries, but it still does not measure up to developed-country standards in many respects. The water and sewage system, in particular, is severely hampered by underinvestment and poor labor-management relations. The supply of electric power is generally reliable but at a higher cost that on the mainland and in many other countries. A network of roads and highways crisscrosses the whole island, but it is deteriorated and severely congested in many areas. These problems impose costs on productive activities and restrictions on future development, which means that every dollar invested in their solution is likely to generate substantial private and social returns.

As for the provision of public goods, a top concern of Puerto Rico authorities is to improve public safety. This is not only a priority social objective but also a necessary condition for the maintenance of an attractive business environment. Like most countries, Puerto Rico is afflicted with a rising crime rate, largely related to drug trafficking and drug addiction. Reversing that trend is a significant challenge for the authorities and for Puerto Rican society in general. It is also necessary to strengthen the education system, especially at the basic and middle levels and particularly in areas serving lower-income groups.

In the area of export promotion, government policy has also been trying to play the role of facilitator rather than picking winners. Correctly, in our view, the export promotion agency has emphasized the provision of market intelligence to actual and potential exporters, which may be seen as providing a public good. The agency also devotes a good deal of its resources to helping local firms participate in trade fairs and trade missions, thus performing a necessary coordination function. A more controversial practice—and probably also more uncertain as to potential outcomes—is the targeting and nurturing of local firms to help them become exporters, which has been frequently advocated by both business and government leaders. This has not been the main thrust of the export promotion agency; the practice has emerged more in response to budget constraints than from choice of strategy. Some of the policies and practices currently favored by the government of Puerto Rico fit the criteria described above, and some do not.

It can be argued that industrial and export promotion policies are increasingly moving in the direction we have called "the right way," but elements of "the wrong way" still play an important role. For example, in recent years local authorities have been stressing preferential government procurement practices to stimulate local-capital businesses. Legislation was enacted in 2002 to set aside a portion of public sector purchases exclusively for local suppliers, and more recently the administration of Governor Aníbal Acevedo Vilá has expressed its support for the law and its intention to ensure that it is faithfully enforced. This is a form of import substitution that could run afoul of regional trade agreements between the United States and several Caribbean and Latin American countries.[45] Even if such legal problems could be avoided, there is still danger that automatic preferences for local suppliers may lead to rent seeking instead of promoting new investment and to expenditures that are wasteful.

The government has also found it difficult to break with the decades-old practice of relying on local and U.S. tax exemptions to attract investment by U.S. manufacturing multinationals, no matter what they do in Puerto Rico. In the years from 2001 to 2003, local authorities tried to persuade the U.S. Congress to enact special tax incentives under section 956 of the U.S. tax code for U.S. corporations operating in Puerto Rico. These incentives were meant to go into effect before the definitive phase-out of the benefits provided under section 936, scheduled for year-end 2005. Faced with an unreceptive Congress, the Puerto Rico government eventually abandoned the initiative, but the hope of reviving some version of section 936 dies hard. As we see it, the central challenge for Puerto Rico is devising government policies that can focus on supplementing rather than substituting for market forces.

---

45. By contrast, unlike the federal government, several U.S. states do not adhere to the World Trade Organization's Government Procurement Agreement.

COMMENT
James L. Dietz

Trade has been central to the Puerto Rican economy since the Spanish conquest. After all, the extraction of raw materials or the production of otherwise unavailable or expensive products was the economic raison d'être, if not the sole motivation, for a "mother" country's interest in any particular colonial possession. To some, Puerto Rico remains a colony, though technically it is an unincorporated territory of the United States, and an understanding of the significance and contribution of trade to economic growth, incomes, and employment remains as pressing as ever.

Robert Lawrence and Juan Lara provide clues about the structure and dynamics of trade and center our attention on what might distinguish Puerto Rico's export and import sectors from those of the mainland United States—an essential focus, given the virtually complete integration of product, financial, and factor markets between the two economies. They make a number of points worth reiterating:

—The economy of Puerto Rico exhibits a high degree of openness, with total trade equal to about 125 percent of GDP, and about 200 percent of gross national product (GNP), in 2002; merchandise exports alone equaled 70 percent of GDP.

—Although there is a surplus on unadjusted merchandise trade, there is an overall current account deficit owing to a large net outflow of factor service payments that equaled 39 percent of GDP in 2003.

—The chemical-pharmaceutical sector saw substantial absolute and relative growth in both trade and employment over the 1998–2003 period despite the phasing down of preferential federal tax treatment for U.S. corporations that began in late 1995.

—Other significant trade sectors (for example, food, apparel, and electrical equipment), however, suffered slow or negative growth after 1996 such that the net effect of trade on employment has been negative, despite positive changes in nominal GDP and GNP (real GNP dipped 0.3 percent, in 2001–02, and both real per capita GNP and GDP fell after 2001, by −0.9 and −0.2 percent, respectively).

—Puerto Rican labor had an extremely low share in value added in key export industries, particularly chemicals (predominately pharmaceuticals), compared with U.S. firms—a finding that echoes that in chapter 2 of this volume—owing to substantial transfer pricing on intangible capital.

—Traditional trade theory does not predict well what is exported. Exports tend to be of high value with substantial skill, R&D, and capital content, reflecting locational decisions of U.S. corporations responding to federal tax incentives rather than local factor endowments; most exports are destined for the United States and other developed countries.

—Puerto Rico's exports appear to be as endowed in human capital and R&D inputs as U.S. exports, and more intensive in capital inputs. Although this may seem surprising, it is less so when it is realized that Puerto Rico's exports are heavily concentrated in just one export category—pharmaceuticals, intensive in these inputs—whereas U.S. exports are substantially diversified.

—Locally owned Puerto Rican firms are less likely than U.S. firms to export (30 and 86 percent, respectively), less knowledgeable about exporting, and less willing to (or at least less willing to admit to wanting to) pay for information about exporting. Only about 3 percent of total Puerto Rican exports originate from local firms.

Trade and Growth

Trade is often considered to be an important engine of growth; this may be one of those relatively few truths shared by most economists.[1] Since the beginning of Puerto Rico's industrialization program, the manufacturing sector, particularly export-oriented manufacturing, has been targeted for incentives—both local and federal—designed to distort U.S. corporate decisions to favor production in Puerto Rico. The Puerto Rican strategy of a poorer economy linking with a richer nation through unrestricted trade flows and nonlocal investment was marketed around the world for the supposed gains in income and employment such integration promised. Barry Bosworth and Susan Collins, in chapter 2 of this volume, closely examine the puzzle of Puerto Rico's growth and income experience; other chapters consider the long-standing quandary of less-than-perfectly-functioning labor markets and high official unemployment levels.

What do Lawrence and Lara—and the data—tell us about the specific impact of Puerto Rico's manufactured goods trade on the commonwealth's economic growth and employment? Has trade been as critical as economic theory might predict and as supporters of the Puerto Rican strategy have claimed? Is Puerto Rico more than the export platform for U.S. corporations that many critics claim it to be?

The first three columns of table 9-12 show annualized changes in Puerto Rico's nominal GDP, nominal GNP, and merchandise exports over various periods. The last two columns measure the percentage change in GDP or GNP

1. Dollar and Kraay (2004).

Table 9-12. *Economic Growth and Exports, Puerto Rico, 1970–2003*

Period	%ΔGDP (1)	%ΔGNP (2)	%ΔGoods X (3)	GDP sensitivity to X growth (1)/(3)	GNP sensitivity to X growth (2)/(3)
1970–80	11.14	8.97	16.70	0.67	0.54
1980–90	7.77	6.93	9.67	0.80	0.72
1990–98	7.38	6.25	5.84	1.26	1.07
1998–2003	6.57	6.17	11.61	0.57	0.53
1970–90	9.44	7.94	13.13	0.72	0.60
1990–2003	7.07	6.22	8.02	0.88	0.77
1970–2003	8.50	7.26	11.09	0.77	0.65

Source: Data from Puerto Rico Planning Board (1989, 2000, 2004, tables 1 and 18 in each report).

associated with a 1 percent increase in merchandise exports ("sensitivity"). Since 1970, there has been a 0.77 percent increase in nominal GDP when goods exports rise 1 percent and a smaller 0.65 percent connection to GNP.[2] The sensitivity of GDP (or GNP) to export growth was lower than the average in the 1970s and again after 1998; it was largest from 1990 to 1998.[3]

Of course, none of this "proves" that Puerto Rico's GDP or GNP growth was more rapid when export growth was faster. Lawrence and Lara do not test that hypothesis, and this constitutes an important gap in their analysis. Nor is the link between export growth and employment seriously investigated, though the authors do state that "employment growth in Puerto Rican manufacturing . . . is closely linked to trade performance," though weakly. Since the end of the tax incentives provided by section 936 of the U.S. tax code, decreases in trade in basic manufacturing have led to lower levels of employment, while high-tech export expansion has resulted in modest employment gains. Overall, however, manufacturing employment has trended downward.

Lawrence and Lara do find that Puerto Rican exports rise by about 2 percent for each 1 percent increase in GDP in the United States, which is the market for more than 80 percent of Puerto Rican export sales. So what has driven Puerto Rico's export trade, apparently, is U.S. GDP and not some internal dynamic (such as productive efficiency or technological change) particular to the local economy. We do not discover much, unfortunately, about the importance of export trade in and of itself to Puerto Rico's income growth and employment, though, admittedly, Lawrence and Lara's stated focus is on trade and policy, not the links between trade, income, and employment.

2. Looking at the impact of exports on GNP this way is equivalent to the profit-adjusted export calculations of Lawrence and Lara.

3. For comparison, the sensitivity of U.S. GDP to exports over the 1970–2003 period was 0.83. Council of Economic Advisers (2005, tables B-1 and B-103).

Table 9-13. *U.S. Economic Growth and the Impact on Puerto Rican GDP and Exports, 1970–2003*

Period	%ΔUSGDP (1)	%ΔPRGDP (2)	%ΔGoods X (3)	Δ(2)/Δ(1) (4)	Δ(3)/Δ(1) (5)
1970–80	10.39	11.14	16.70	. . .	. . .
1980–90	7.60	7.77	9.67	1.21	2.52
1990–98	5.26	7.38	5.84	0.17	1.64
1998–2003	4.70	6.57	11.61	1.42	−10.21

Source: Data from Council of Economic Advisers (2005, table B-1); table 9-12 above.

Table 9-13 shows changes in U.S. GDP for the same periods as table 9-12. The positive, roughly two-to-one relationship between changes in Puerto Rican export growth and changes in U.S. GDP growth identified by Lawrence and Lara seems to hold fairly well until 1998. Before that date, the growth rate of GDP in Puerto Rico fell with lower annual growth in U.S. GDP and the lower rate of growth of Puerto Rican exports, suggesting a positive link between these variables, too. However, over the 1998–2003 period, despite a lower U.S. GDP growth rate compared with the previous period, Puerto Rico's merchandise export growth rate doubled compared with the previous period, thus breaking the historically positive relationship between U.S. GDP and Puerto Rican exports. The growth rate of Puerto Rican GDP also declined relative to the previous period, despite the doubling of export growth. This switching at least raises a question about the reliability of presuming a positive export-income nexus. More modeling is sorely needed in this area to sort out the relevant independent variables driving the relationship between Puerto Rico's exports and income, as these discrepancies suggest.

The surge in exports over the 1998–2003 period occurred despite the phase-out of section 936. This is precisely when an adverse impact on manufacturing growth and manufactured exports might have been predicted, given the predominance of U.S. corporations in total exporting, firms that had benefited heavily from section 936 tax exemptions. Although this export expansion may turn out to have been an anomaly over the longer term, the need for a well-identified structural model describing Puerto Rico's export and income growth nexus is once again underscored by this unexpected outcome.

The Chemical-Pharmaceutical Sector

The real story of Puerto Rico's recent export performance may, in fact, be found within one sector alone. Among manufactured exports, chemicals, especially prescription drugs, have grown steadily in importance, rising from 44 percent of the total in 1996 to 72 percent in 2003.[4] Lawrence and Lara note that "Puerto Rico sells these products in astounding volumes"; in fact, Puerto Rico is the number one source of U.S. legal drug imports. Moreover, though it is true that employment in this sector was responsible for almost one-quarter of all manufacturing employment in 2002, a figure often cited by government officials, only 2.5 percent of total employment was generated directly by the chemicals-pharmaceuticals industry, despite its being almost the only manufacturing sector with positive employment growth since 1996.[5] It is this sector, too, that has benefited most over the past three decades from federal tax exemption; pharmaceuticals have received roughly half of all section 936 tax savings by section 936 corporations, benefits equal to three times the wages paid per employee.

The dynamics of the pharmaceutical industry in the United States most likely provide a better explanation for the trajectory of Puerto Rico's manufacturing employment and exports over the 1998–2003 period, and perhaps before, than does total U.S. GDP. On the mainland, employment in the pharmaceutical industry rose by 16 percent at the same time that overall manufacturing employment fell 15 percent. Given the large and rising manufactured goods export share derived from chemicals and pharmaceuticals in Puerto Rico, transactions that are typically intrafirm, an understanding of this sector and its specific growth path in the United States could allow better conceptualizing of the variables affecting Puerto Rico's exports in general, at least given the current productive structure.

Such a high concentration of exports in any one industry—now nearly three-quarters in pharmaceuticals—is both good news and bad news. The bright side has been modest employment expansion. Still, the growth of chemicals-pharmaceuticals at the expense of other manufacturing industries, local and nonlocal, is not something to be celebrated unconditionally.[6] For one thing, the pharmaceutical industry has the lowest output multiplier among all manufacturing, equal to 1.12, reflecting its low degree of integration with the local economy. The limited contribution of the sector to total employment has already been noted.[7]

It may seem paradoxical that the industry that nearly everyone hypothesized to be most sensitive to the changes in federal tax exemptions has been the leader

4. In 2003 manufactured exports constituted about 90 percent of merchandise exports, and merchandise exports about 90 percent of total exports (up from 83 percent in 1990).

5. Since 1996, annual investment in pharmaceuticals has grown threefold, according to Lawrence and Lara, once again confounding the expectation of an adverse effect from the phasing out of section 936.

6. It is also eerily reminiscent of earlier days in Puerto Rico's history, when sugar production occupied an equally dominant role in total exports before the push to industrialize in the late 1940s.

7. Ruíz (1994, p. 63).

in manufacturing and export growth since the gutting of section 936. Lawrence and Lara's explanation, citing the agglomeration effects of many firms' operating in one relatively small location, rings true.[8] If this is the case, then maintaining these agglomeration economies and the viability of this sector has to be a short- and medium-term priority, regardless of whatever else might be on the longer-run agenda for economic transformation.

Future Policies on Industry and Trade

The government agency charged with overseeing industrial promotion, PRIDCO, is probably doing the best it can, given its limited resources and its own history.[9] Its new emphasis on promoting clusters and encouraging competitiveness may help target the agency's limited resources to high-technology, knowledge-intensive sectors, where Puerto Rico's large, latent pool of ostensibly well-trained human capital might best be utilized.[10] However, as the authors correctly note, most of these clusters are already dominated by U.S. firms (construction services and materials are a partial exception), so the pattern of depending on nonlocal investment, R&D, and other inputs is not severely challenged by this new thrust. Furthermore, the authors note compelling reasons for thinking that the defining characteristics for choosing these clusters based on their supposed competitiveness was severely biased by the existence of rampant transfer pricing.

Unlike the East Asian economies, Puerto Rico's own promotion efforts have not enforced any quid pro quo policies on nonlocal firms that might have resulted in greater positive externalities to local factors of production, particularly through backward linkages, in exchange for the fiscal incentives received. The result is that foreign factors of production have substituted for, and not complemented, local inputs. That has removed some of the essential internal

8. U.S. tax laws still provide incentives for firms to organize themselves as controlled foreign corporations and earn and hold profits offshore, a factor that probably complements and strengthens the agglomeration effects.

9. Dietz (1993).

10. That the apparently highly educated labor force is not being used fully is evident from the high levels of unemployment and low labor force participation rates discussed in other chapters in this volume, an indication that the economy is operating significantly inside its production possibilities frontier. However, as Lawrence and Lara note, the export profile of Puerto Rico as intensive in human capital, physical capital, and R&D is contradicted by the low ranking of the economy compared with U.S. states on indicators of the stock and flow of these inputs. This suggests that the stock of productive human capital may not be as qualitatively large as the raw numbers about college graduates might indicate, that is, the stock of human capital may be severely overestimated when adjusted for quality. This fact leads Lawrence and Lara to believe that this resource gap may necessitate significant investment if Puerto Rico is to be able to do any significant import substitution.

dynamic to economic development that has characterized other more successful late developers, like South Korea and Taiwan, that relied more on internal financing, local entrepreneurs, and local initiative.

Lawrence and Lara question, as have others, the value of import substitution, but it is here that local entrepreneurs might best be able to thrive. It is difficult to disagree with their conclusion that any activity that the government promotes should be expected "to have social benefits beyond those that the individual entrepreneur can capture." However, any assumption of full employment and of trade-offs at the margin do not apply in Puerto Rico. It is true, of course, that the impact of any government spending targeted at import substitution must be weighed against that of some other use, such as export expansion. But given the long history of excessive unemployment of resources, particularly labor, the cost of not promoting import substitution should be compared with doing nothing to mobilize human resources and speed up the process of learning by doing.

It is critically necessary to try to measure the potential long-run benefits of promoting local factors of production. Static, short-run benefit-cost analyses that miss the potential transformative effects on local inputs of "doing" production and eventually achieving world-class efficiency, even if through initially inefficient import substitution, tip the balance of future development efforts toward the existing actors, primarily U.S. firms, who now dominate.

Conclusion

It is difficult to understand how the Puerto Rican experience can be termed a success when such an enormous waste of human resources has been a deep-seated characteristic of the economy for more than four decades. Many believe that the problem is with labor markets that cannot clear owing to federal transfers, U.S. minimum wage laws, and unfettered migration. These institutional facts are not going to change, however, and it is quite likely that labor markets *are* clearing, given the employment arbitrage opportunities open to workers vis-à-vis the U.S. labor market. The cause of the employment problem is more likely found in insufficient demand and less in factors on the supply side that are argued to push reservation wages up.

It is necessary to find the means to reduce official unemployment and increase labor force participation, including shrinking the informal sector. The employed labor force is still not optimally distributed. The gains in output and income in the early years of Operation Bootstrap, Puerto Rico's development program, that contributed to income convergence up to 1970 were to a great degree the product of low-productivity labor being shifted from agriculture to higher-productivity pursuits in industry and services. That transformation is still not completed, as Bosworth and Collins point out in table 2-5, so income gains are still possible by a more optimal distribution of labor that can also move the economy toward its production possibilities curve.

One issue left mostly untouched by this volume is the vexing problem of Puerto Rico's status in relation to the United States. This political question has undeniable economic consequences in that attention to the problems raised by Lawrence and Lara, as well as in other chapters in this volume, is compromised by insular politics. Valuable resources from the municipal to the commonwealth level are squandered in a nearly continuous struggle for political advantage, resources that definitely could be better used for the common good achieving structural change, selective promotion, and other areas of the sorts these valuable studies delineate. This volume may not have been the forum in which to raise such issues, but it should be clear that all the good intentions and constructive policies contained here will have a better chance of success once the status issue is resolved.

COMMENT
Daniel Lederman

Robert Lawrence and Juan Lara have written an informative paper about Puerto Rico's trade trends and structure and its emerging industrial policies since the phase-out of the U.S. tax code's section 936 provisions. But they and other authors in this volume do not fully appreciate the significance of the Puerto Rican development experience. As a development specialist, I am deeply interested in learning about this experience, especially from a Latin American perspective.

In the following paragraphs I raise several issues concerning the island's economic performance that seem to be more interesting when viewed from an economic development perspective than from the narrow focus on Puerto Rico's economy. First, there are several important issues regarding the island's economic performance in terms of productive capacity and income generation for its population. The debate, which permeates several other chapters in this volume, seems to have focused too much on the impact of the tax incentives and not enough on the island's dramatic experience with "deep" integration with the U.S. mainland. With the advent of the North American Free Trade Agreement in 1994, which institutionalizes a milder form of integration between Mexico and the United States than Puerto Rico's commonwealth status, and subsequent similar agreements among several other Latin economies and the United States, the island's experience might be a beacon of things to come for these emerging economies. Second, the island's experience with tax incentives to attract foreign (or U.S. mainland) investment can be viewed as an extreme form of tendencies already apparent throughout Latin America, where governments of various stripes are experimenting with different types of tax incentives, including those pertaining to export-processing zones. But the issues emerging from the twenty-year experience with the section 936 incentives are distinct from the lessons that can be drawn from Puerto Rico's broader experience with economic, social, and institutional integration with the U.S. mainland.

My focus on these broad topics comes at the expense of commenting on minor questions concerning the chapter's methodologies and policy discussion. For example, I do not raise econometric issues concerning the estimation of the trade equations (which are probably unreliable) or engage in discussion concerning the relationship between productivity improvements and labor demand (which is clearly incomplete, since technical change can be labor saving). My main goal is not to quibble with technicalities but rather to highlight the relevance of Puerto Rico's experience for Latin American development economics more generally.

Puerto Rico's Economic Performance: The Future for Latin America?

A common theme that runs through this chapter and most of the others in this volume concerns the measurement of the island's economic performance. Barry Bosworth and Susan Collins (in chapter 2) make adjustments to the GDP numbers to correct for profit repatriation by the pharmaceutical industries. Lawrence and Lara adjust the export data for the same reason, although their conclusion—"these are not simply paper profits"—is a bit more optimistic than those of other contributors. In our discussions in the workshop on which this book is based, I was criticized for using GDP data instead of GNI (gross national income) data. Hence the measurement issues seem central in the debate over Puerto Rico's development model.

Perhaps more important, this debate raises profound issues about what it means to be a successful economy in a world of open economies, where goods, services, people, and capital are allowed to move freely across political jurisdictions. In this context, there are at least three points worth clarifying. First, no matter how it is measured, Puerto Rico's experience is a case of successful development, given its origins from a Spanish colony: its performance has been stellar when compared with other Latin American economies. Figure 9-2 shows the evolution of per capita GNI (adjusted for purchasing power parity) of exemplar Latin economies measured with respect to the Puerto Rican GNI. By 2001, the island had become the richest Latin American economy, even when measured by GNI, which subtracts net factor payment flows from GDP. As Bosworth and Collins note (in chapter 2), this might be a result of the island's avoidance of the

Figure 9-2. *Relative Gross National Income per Capita, Selected Latin American Countries, Five-Year Moving Average, 1979–2001*[a]

Index (Puerto Rico = 1.00)

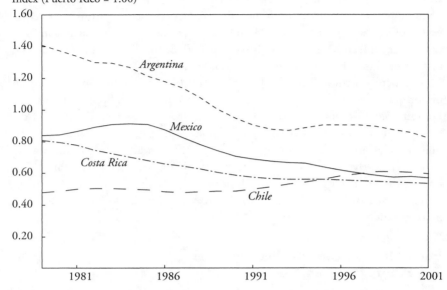

Source: Data from World Bank, World Development Indicators database (econ.worldbank.org [May 15, 2005]).

a. Data given are for the final year of each five-year period. Data are adjusted for purchasing power parity.

recurrent macroeconomic crises that have led Argentina, for example, to experience a continuous decline relative to Puerto Rico. But by 2001, even the best-performing economies of Latin America, such as Chile, Costa Rica, and Mexico, were far from the Puerto Rican benchmark. (Argentina's most recent crisis, during 2001–02, pushed this nation further down.)

A second point concerns the gap between GNI and GDP. Figure 9-3 plots the ratio of GDP to GNI for the same four Latin American economies and Puerto Rico. Although all the economies in this sample have ratios above one for most of the period shown (1975–2001), it is obvious that Puerto Rico is an outlier. The conventional wisdom in this volume seems to be that the island's GDP is over-estimated owing to section 936 tax incentives that lead pharmaceutical companies to underreport value added in the mainland and overreport value added in Puerto Rico. This might be true; but if so, why has this not also occurred in other countries, such as Costa Rica and other Caribbean and Central American economies, that offer handsome tax incentives to foreign investment? Even Mexico and economies from the Andean countries use export-processing zones and tax incentives to attract foreign firms. One argument that appears in Lawrence and Lara's

Figure 9-3. *Ratio of GDP to Gross National Income, Selected Latin American Countries, 1975–2001*

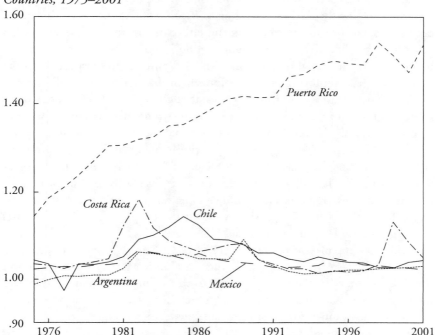

Source: Data from World Bank, World Development Indicators database (econ.worldbank.org [May 15, 2005]).

chapter as well as others in this volume is that the pharmaceutical industry is special, owing to its reliance on R&D investments. But most multinational firms also spend a lot of money in advertising, which supports the value of their trademarks. The Nike and Adidas logos seem to be worth quite a bit, at least from a consumer's standpoint, but their value is also supported by the now well-known research by John Sutton on the theoretical and empirical effects of marketing expenditures on industrial organization.[11] How do we know that price shifting does not occur in most "footloose" industries? How big are R&D costs in the pharmaceutical industry relative to marketing costs in textiles and apparel or in any industry? These are questions that would need to be answered in order to be sure that observed differences between Puerto Rico's GDP and GNI are due to the accounting practices of the pharmaceutical industry, and I remain unconvinced.

Nevertheless, it might be the case that the pharmaceutical industry located in Puerto Rico on a scale not witnessed in other developing economies. This could

11. Sutton (1991).

have occurred because of the magnitude of the tax incentives. Do other countries offer zero taxes on corporate profits? In fact, before Harry Grubert and Joel Slemrod's frequently cited work on Puerto Rico, the literature on the impact of tax havens had previously found strong effects in Ireland and several Asian economies.[12] The extent of this phenomenon in Puerto Rico might also be a function of institutional integration with the United States, especially in the areas of intellectual property and its enforcement that make the island so attractive for pharmaceutical companies. Hence though tax incentives can obviously play an important role, it might also be that the strong pharmaceutical presence in Puerto Rico is the result of the institutional regime. This would explain the continued growth in the industry's employment and exports after the announcement of the phase-out of the section 936 provisions. Of course, as the authors argue, it is also possible that tax incentives succeeded in creating an industrial cluster that has now grown up and no longer requires such incentives. But I doubt this would be possible without the deep integration that exists between the island and the mainland.

A third point concerns the measurement of GNI in the context of dramatic migration flows from the island to the mainland. María Enchautegui and Richard Freeman, in their contribution to this volume (chapter 4), cite data indicating that the emigration rate of Puerto Rican men is about 37 percent. This is a huge number. Hence it is possible, depending on how remittances are accounted for in the island's national accounts, that the GNI data are underestimated. Consider, for example, two immigrants living on the U.S. mainland. One is an illegal immigrant from Mexico, the other a Puerto Rican who resides legally in New York City. When they send money home to support their families, the transfer by the latter is reported as a capital flow from the mainland to the island, whereas in the case of the former it is reported as a repatriation of factor payments. The only difference lies in the legal status of the migrant. In other words, if remittances sent by Puerto Ricans on the mainland to the island were reported as factor payments, the island's GNI would be higher than reported by the current statistics. Some evidence presented in this volume points to an important role of this type of capital or factor-payments flows. Bosworth and Collins report incredibly high average current-account deficits for Puerto Rico, exceeding 10 percent of GDP (which is allegedly overestimated). If remittances were being counted as factor payments, these numbers would be smaller. Another piece of evidence comes from the discussion, in chapter 4, of labor market participation. Enchautegui and Freeman estimate that remittances might be one of the important explanations for the low labor participation rates on the island, especially among low-skilled workers. This is consistent with evidence from Mexico provided by Gordon Hanson, which suggests that remit-

12. Grubert and Slemrod (1998); Harris and others (1993).

tances in Mexico are associated with reductions in labor participation among men and possibly also among women.[13] Consequently, it is likely that the big gap between Puerto Rico's GDP and GNI results partly from an underestimation of the commonwealth's GNI, and it is unclear whether this is a more important factor than the overestimation of its GDP owing to the price shifting accounting of profits by the pharmaceuticals.

Thus we can agree that Puerto Rico is the richest Latin American economy, regardless of the definition of output or income used. But we really cannot be sure that the gaps between GDP and GNI are larger than in other developing countries purely because of the tax incentives. We also cannot be sure that the growth of the pharmaceutical industry on the island has been a result only of tax incentives. Perhaps more interesting, the case of Puerto Rico might be the light at the end of tunnel for developing countries in the Americas that are more slowly moving toward greater and deeper forms of integration with the United States through legal and illegal migration and comprehensive trade agreements (for example, the North American Free Trade Agreement, the Central America–Dominican Republic–United States Free Trade Agreement, and other free trade agreements) that cover a substantial number of nontraditional commercial issues, such as intellectual property rights and investor rights. Traditional definitions of national accounts might be too rigid to be helpful in understanding the progress of nations.

Tax Incentives and Industrial Policies

Tax incentives are widely used throughout the developing world to attract foreign investment and often in industrialized countries to stimulate certain types of investments, including R&D. The policy issues for Puerto Rico seem to revolve around the disappearance of the "big carrot" that was section 936, and there are concerns about what other instruments can be used to help the island's economy grow faster while avoiding the alleged problems caused by the enclave economy that resulted from the establishment of the pharmaceutical industry. My own view is that Lawrence and Lara got it right on at least two counts: I agree both with their more optimistic assessment of the lingering effects of section 936 and with their focus on disciplining industrial policies so that the public sector targets market failures.

The latter, however, is easier said than done. Indeed, the programs currently in place in Puerto Rico, as described by Lawrence and Lara, are worrisome. The focus on clusters of industries that are already profitable on the island, for example, seems redundant. Most of the economic models of market failures

13. Hanson (2005).

that justify government involvement to spur specific industries are variants of the textbook infant-industry argument. In a nutshell, in the presence of market failures in credit markets (a reality in most countries), subsidies to below-optimal-sized firms are justified in the presence of sunk costs. That the clusters approach has identified sectors with an existing comparative advantage is worrisome, however counterintuitive this might sound. Lawrence and Lara are probably right in urging policymakers to focus on the public investments that would solve bottlenecks in public goods, inhibiting the further development of the clusters. But subsidies to firms in this context are likely to be wasteful.

Another policy being pursued by PRIDCO in Puerto Rico concerns attracting "new" businesses as part of the clusters strategy and through tax incentives for "pioneer" industries. According to PRIDCO's tax incentive guidelines as described by Lawrence and Lara, the main characteristic of pioneer industries is the use of "novel or innovative" technology not utilized in the island before January 1, 2000. These ideas are interesting, especially in light of the theory paper written by Ricardo Hausmann and Dani Rodrik and cited by the authors.[14] The market failure presented in this paper is, in practical terms, similar to the failures in the markets of ideas and innovation. That is, the possibility of imitation of business strategy (or technical innovations) produces less than optimal investment in testing new products or business plans, since imitators can drive down profits either by driving down the prices of new products (in a closed economy) or by driving up the costs of (nontraded) factors or inputs required by the new production process. Hence it is theoretically plausible that without government intervention, private sector investment in experimentation will be suboptimal.

In the context of technical innovations, patent laws aim to strike a balance by providing monopoly rents to investors for a given period of time (for example, twenty to thirty years) in exchange for the technical information that might feed subsequent innovations. But patent grants are an imperfect instrument for the protection of intellectual property rights, because they tend to raise the cost of imitation that brings about the social benefits and because firms and inventors will not patent innovations that have the potential of producing a large number of future spin-offs. Hence most industrialized countries provide tax incentives or subsidies (or both) for R&D. The empirical evidence, which is never bulletproof, suggests that the returns to R&D are huge, at least in the United States.[15] However, the evidence on the effects of tax incentives and subsidies on private R&D suggests that in most cases one dollar given translates into one dollar invested.[16] If Puerto Rico's efforts were to have the same effect as those in high-

14. Hausmann and Rodrik (2003).
15. For example, Jones and Williams (1998).
16. Hall and van Reenen (2000).

income economies, then such efforts would not necessarily be justified; a one-to-one ratio between subsidies and private effort implies that market failures are not being resolved, since that would entail ratios in excess of one. Again, Lawrence and Lara are probably right to stress that public subsidies need to go beyond financing activities that the private sector would undertake on its own.

The overall picture that emerges from the international evidence is thus consistent with Lawrence and Lara's cautious optimism about the potential role of industrial policies that explicitly target market failures or the provision of public goods. One can easily come up with solid arguments in favor of policy experimentation; but the empirical evidence concerning the policies that can be pursued is quite limited or leaves us sitting on the fence. Thus I would have liked the authors to provide us with some guidelines about how to monitor and evaluate any of the policies that the government of Puerto Rico wishes to pursue. Without a rigorous monitoring and evaluation program, it is unlikely that any policies pursued will lead this economy to a path of fast-paced growth or productive diversification. And, as in the rest of Latin America, the failures of such policies will be overshadowed by the debate about the alleged failures of the dramatic experiment in deep integration with the mainland.

References

Arthur D. Little and others. 1995. *A Strategic Plan for External Trade.* Report prepared for the Puerto Rican External Trade Board. San Juan (August).

A. T. Kearney Management Consultants. 2003. *Puerto Rico 2025 Project Assessment: Current Status of the Economic, Social, Environmental, and Infrastructure Development in Puerto Rico.* Report prepared for the Puerto Rico Industrial Development Company. San Juan (December).

Bailey, Klinger, and Daniel Lederman. 2004. "Discovery and Development: An Empirical Exploration of New Products." Working Paper 3450. Washington: World Bank (November).

Baily, Martin N., and Robert Z. Lawrence. 2004. "What Happened to the Great U.S. Job Machine? The Role of Trade and Electronic Outsourcing." *Brookings Papers on Economic Activity,* no. 2: 211–84.

Bernard, Andrew, and J. Bradford Jensen. 1995. "Exporters, Jobs, and Wages in U.S. Manufacturing: 1976–1987." *Brookings Papers on Economic Activity: Microeconomics 1995,* pp. 67–120.

Council of Economic Advisers. 2005. *Economic Report of the President.* U.S. Government Printing Office.

Dietz, James L. 1993. "La reinvención del subdesarrollo: Fallos fundamentales del proyecto de industrialización en los 50." In *Del nacionalismo al populismo,* edited by María Elena Rodríguez Castro and Silvia Alvarez Curbelo, pp. 179–205. Río Piedras: Ediciones Huracán.

————. 2001. "Puerto Rico: The 'Three Legged' Economy." *Integration and Trade* 5, no. 15: 247–73.

————. 2003. *Puerto Rico: Negotiating Development and Change.* Boulder: Lynne Rienner.

Dollar, David, and Aart Kraay. 2004. "Trade, Growth, and Poverty." *Economic Journal* 114, no. 493: F22–F49.

Estudios Técnicos. 2003. *Investment Opportunities in Puerto Rico's Strategic Clusters.* Report prepared for the Puerto Rico Industrial Development Company. San Juan (March).

Government Development Bank for Puerto Rico. 2004. *Puerto Rico Fact Sheet.* San Juan: Office of Economic Studies and Analysis (June).

Grubert, Harry, and Joel Slemrod. 1998. "The Effect of Taxes on Investment and Income Shifting to Puerto Rico." *Review of Economics and Statistics* 80, no. 3: 365–73.

Hall, Bronwyn H., and John van Reenen. 2000. "How Effective Are Fiscal Incentives for R&D? A Review of the Evidence." *Research Policy* 29, nos. 4–5: 449–69.

Hanson, Gordon H. 2005. "Emigration, Remittances, and Labor Force Participation in Mexico." University of California, San Diego (May). Mimeograph.

Harris, David, Randall Morck, Joel Slemrod, and Bernard Yeung. 1993. "Income Shifting in U.S. Multinational Corporations." In *Studies in International Taxation,* edited by Alberto Giovannini, R. Glenn Hubbard, and Joel Slemrod, pp. 277–302. University of Chicago Press.

Hausmann, Ricardo, and Dani Rodrik. 2003. "Economic Development as Self-Discovery." *Journal of Development Economics* 72, no. 2: 603–33.

Hill, Marianne T. 1990. "Tax Incentives and Manufacturing Profitability in Puerto Rico." *Atlantic Economic Journal* 18, no. 2: 66–73.

Imbs, Jean M., and Romain T. Wacziarg. 2003. "Stages of Diversification." *American Economic Review* 93, no. 1: 63–86.

Jones, Charles I., and John C. Williams. 1998. "Measuring the Social Return to R&D." *Quarterly Journal of Economics* 113, no. 4: 1119–35.

Mansfield, Edwin, and others. 1977. *The Production and Application of New Industrial Technology.* New York: Norton.

Ocampo, Jose Antonio. 2001. "Raul Prebisch y la agenda del desarrollo en los albores del siglo XXI." *Revista de la CEPAL,* no. 75: 25–40.

Organization for Economic Cooperation and Development. 1999. *Innovative Clusters: Drivers of National Innovation Systems.* Paris.

Padin, Jose A. 2003. "Puerto Rico in the Post War: Liberalized Development Banking and the Fall of the 'Fifth Tiger.'" *World Development* 31, no. 2: 281–301.

Porter, Michael E. 2002. "Regions and the New Economics of Competition." In *Global City-Regions: Trends, Theory, Policy,* edited by Allen J. Scott, pp. 139–57. Oxford University Press.

Rodrik, Dani. 2004. "Industrial Policy for the Twenty-First Century." Paper prepared for the United Nations Industrial Development Organization (September). Mimeo.

Ruíz, Angel L. 1994. "The Impact of Transfer Payments (Federal and Others) to Individuals and to Government on the Puerto Rican Economy." *Ceteris Paribus* 4, no. 1: 55–72.

Schott, Jeffrey J. 2004. *Free Trade Agreements: U.S. Strategies and Priorities.* Washington: Institute for International Economics.

Stewart, John. 2003. "Competitive Clusters for Puerto Rico." San Juan: Puerto Rico Industrial Development Company.

Sutton, John. 1991. *Sunk Costs and Market Structure: Price Competition, Advertising, and the Evolution of Concentration.* MIT Press.

United Nations Industrial Development Organization. 2004. *Industrial Development Report, 2002–2003: Competing through Innovation and Learning.* New York.

Weisskoff, Richard. 1985. *Factories and Food Stamps: The Puerto Rico Model of Development.* Johns Hopkins University Press.

10

Restoring Growth: The Policy Options

BARRY P. BOSWORTH AND SUSAN M. COLLINS

In the middle of the twentieth century, Puerto Rico emerged as one of the world's fastest-growing economies, drawing comparisons with the rapidly industrializing countries of East Asia. Over the past several decades, however, while the economy has continued to grow, it has done so at a greatly reduced rate. Since 1980, there has been no further convergence of living standards with those of the U.S. mainland. Income per capita is currently only 30 percent of the U.S. average, and 58 percent of all children live below the U.S. poverty level.

Identifying the causes of Puerto Rico's deteriorating economic performance has been a primary objective of this project, and it is an important backdrop for designing a turnaround strategy. Drawing on the prior chapters, we argue in the following section that in terms of providing an environment conducive to growth, Puerto Rico can be characterized as a glass that is only half full. Furthermore, while its unique position vis-à-vis the United States provides it with valuable opportunities and advantages, this position also creates constraints and disincentives that are particularly intransigent. From this perspective, we summarize our assessment of the main factors behind the island's growth slowdown. These factors are clearly interrelated and interact in complex ways. Thus it would be extremely difficult to pin down the relative importance of each, and it is not our objective to do so.

Similarly, in developing a growth strategy we argue against seeking a single answer, proposing instead a program that addresses each of the major problem areas. That strategy is outlined in some detail in the second section. Its primary focus is a set of measures aimed at addressing Puerto Rico's most evident problem, a low employment rate for its adult population. The proposals include greater incentives to seek employment and actions to expand the range of private sector job opportunities. Puerto Rico must also act quickly to shore up its education system—an area of previously strong performance that has begun to experience greater problems. If it is to succeed in the future, prosperity will be built on the structure of a well-educated and productive workforce. Finally, there is an important need to improve governance by increasing the transparency of government decisions and reducing the tendency to use government powers to restrict competition and promote rent-seeking behavior.

Puerto Rico has few if any natural resources, and any advantages it has realized from a special relationship with the United States are quickly being eroded. It is also important to recognize that neither traditional tourism nor low-wage manufacturing offers a viable way forward. Puerto Rico requires a dynamic, modern, outward-oriented economy that attracts international businesses and the job opportunities that they offer.

Diagnosing the Growth Slowdown

This section provides the context for the policy prescriptions that follow. We begin by summarizing what we believe to be the main lessons about economic growth that can be distilled from the economics literature. We then assess how Puerto Rico's economy measures up from this vantage point. Given the prior decades of successful performance, understanding what went wrong in the past quarter century is critical. Thus the final part of the section takes a somewhat broader historical perspective so as to outline why growth slowed.

Basic Growth Determinants

The effort to understand the determinants of economic growth has generated an enormous volume of economic research. Even a casual perusal of this work makes clear that views about the economic (and other) characteristics that are most critical for growth have evolved over time. Furthermore, neither the theoretical nor the empirical studies point to a simple, cookie-cutter listing of necessary or sufficient conditions. Nonetheless, emerging from this work is an underlying core set of policy objectives that most analysts believe can create an environment conducive to both accelerating and sustaining economic growth. That core set can be divided into four broad policy groupings of: macroeconomic stability, openness, institutions and the business climate, and physical and human capital.

Macroeconomic stability refers to an integrated mix of a sustainable fiscal program and sound monetary policies. On the fiscal side, budget deficits should be small enough to ensure manageable levels of debt and required debt service; tax revenues should be adequate to provide the government with the resources to achieve its expenditure goals; and spending allocations should be consistent with those goals. With an increased awareness of the distorting effects of high tax rates on economic decisions, emphasis is placed on the combination of a broad tax base and low rates. Monetary policy should focus on maintaining low inflation and a competitive exchange rate.

Openness involves the interaction with the external global economy, with a particular emphasis on openness of the trade regime. Openness is particularly important to small economies, such as Puerto Rico, because of the opportunities that it offers to specialize in particular economic activities and to avoid the diseconomies of small-scale production. Competition in a larger economic arena also promotes efficiency and exposure to a wider range of innovations and other ideas. Openness includes financial interactions, such as inflows of foreign direct investment, that reduce the cost of capital for new investment and provide a channel for the spread of technology.

The importance of institutions for economic development has long been recognized. Their role was emphasized in the eighteenth-century writings of Adam Smith and more recently in the awarding of a Nobel Prize to the economist Douglass North. They have been a particular focus of research over the past decade aimed at determining which types of institutions are most important and the process through which they affect economic growth. In this literature, institutions are defined as the "rules of the game" that govern political, social, and economic interactions. Good institutions are those that create an incentive structure that reduces uncertainty and promotes economic efficiency. They protect individual initiative, promote trust by ensuring that promises will be kept, and constrain self-seeking political groups with rules that are enforced equally on everyone. Extensive efforts have been made to develop indicators of the quality of institutions of governance that focus on measures of corruption, political rights, regulatory burdens, and public sector efficiency.[1]

Finally, increases in physical capital per worker have long been seen as a major means of raising workers' productivity and incomes. The importance of capital has been further increased by a growing awareness of the need to define it broadly to include gains in educational attainment of the workforce and the development of new ideas that take the form of intangible capital. In the early stages of development, countries can make progress by simply using the technology of others: but as growth continues, reliance on external sources of capital and technology will yield diminishing returns in a world oversupplied with unskilled labor.

1. Kaufmann, Kraay, and Zoido-Lobatón (2002).

While these four factors can go a long way toward explaining the extraordinarily wide divergence of growth experiences over the past half century, the timing of the growth is more difficult to explain: What initiates a period of sustained growth? Why did countries like Ireland and the countries of East Asia, long mired in economic stagnation, achieve a transition to buoyant growth? Why did growth in Puerto Rico suddenly surge in the 1950s after many decades of abysmal poverty? Questions such as these are notoriously difficult to answer. However, the good news is that sustained increases in growth do not appear to be rare events. That growth accelerations appear to be much more common than typically recognized implies that they are achievable.[2]

Strengths and Concerns for Puerto Rico

At first blush, Puerto Rico looks extremely strong in terms of the four criteria discussed above, and its disappointing recent performance appears quite puzzling. The economy possesses many of the attributes that have emerged as key to fostering growth. The left side of table 10-1 lists a variety of ways in which the economy measures up favorably. In the macroeconomic arena, Puerto Rico operates completely within the U.S. monetary and financial system. In dealings with the mainland economy there are no risks of currency revaluations.

Furthermore, Puerto Rico is among the most open economies in the world. Located next to the world's largest market, it enjoys the unconstrained bilateral movement of goods, capital, and people. Trade in goods and services operates within the U.S. customs union. Puerto Ricans are U.S. citizens and can travel and work freely on the mainland and change residence without restriction. Puerto Rico is also well situated to be a center for economic transactions within the Western Hemisphere and with Europe.

Third, the economic institutions of Puerto Rico are largely those of the United States. Economic activities in Puerto Rico are heavily guided by the U.S. legal and regulatory system. The commonwealth controls its own internal affairs, except where its authority is superseded by federal law.[3] As Rita Maldonado-Bear and Ingo Walter note, in chapter 8 of this volume, Puerto Rican enterprises and individuals have full access to U.S. financial markets, and its financial institutions are subject to the same supervisory oversight as mainland institutions. Thus in

2. Hausmann, Pritchett, and Rodrik (2004).

3. Puerto Rico is treated as a state for purposes of all federal legislation, with three important exceptions: income taxes, income support and welfare programs, and federal health care programs. In terms of economic affairs, federal legislation applies in all the important areas: agricultural standards, antitrust, aviation, banking, bankruptcy proceedings, food and drug regulation, interstate commerce, environmental laws, intellectual property, international trade, labor standards, maritime issues, securities, telecommunications, and so on. However, Puerto Rico differs from the states in terms of its local economic institutions. Specifically, areas such as business permits, contract law, mortgage law, professional regulation, real property transactions, and zoning reflect a strong influence from the Spanish civil law system.

Table 10-1. *Strengths and Concerns for Puerto Rican Growth*

Factor	Strength	Concern or constraint
Macroeconomic	Stable currency Low inflation	Fiscal difficulties High and rising debt Lack of transparency No monetary independence

Openness	Access to U.S. markets,
	   including financial markets
	Free flow of labor and capital
	Participant in U.S. open
	   trade regime with rest of
	   world
	Potential gateway to Latin
	   American countries
		U.S. law and treaties
		   not designed for or by
		   Puerto Rico
		Jones Act restrictions on
		   trade with United States
		Exports poorly diversified

Institutions and
   business climate
	Financial system
	   Access to mainland
	   FDIC regulation of banks
	Legal system (including U.S.
	   protection of intellectual
	   property rights)
	U.S. social safety net
		Complex and inconsistent
		   tax policies
		Difficult regulatory
		   procedures
		Political seesaw and policy
		   uncertainty
		Poor incentive structure of
		   transfer programs
		U.S. minimum wage
		U.S. dependency issues

Physical and human capital	High educational attainment
	English-speaking workforce
	Strong infrastructure for the
	   region
		Low investment, especially
		   in the 1980s
		Concerns about school
		   quality
		Weaknesses of the
		   infrastructure compared
		   with United States and
		   Ireland
		Environmental degradation

its economic affairs Puerto Rico is similar to a U.S. state, except for its exemption from the Internal Revenue Code. This provides a high degree of institutional certainty for doing business in Puerto Rico. In fact, Puerto Rico scores well on various international competitive indexes that aim to measure the quality of institutions.[4]

Finally, as discussed in several of the prior chapters, Puerto Rico has achieved remarkable gains in the educational attainment of its population. The education level of the workforce today is comparable to that of the industrialized countries

4. See chapter 6 in this volume for further discussion.

of the Organization for Economic Cooperation and Development. In the 2000 census, average years of schooling for the Puerto Rican population aged sixteen to sixty-four was 12.2 years compared with 13.8 years for the United States. Puerto Rico has a bilingual workforce, and the quality of its physical infrastructure is high compared with other countries in the region and relative to those with similar levels of income per capita.

However, as shown on the right side of table 10-1, an equal number of concerns may be constraining growth. In recent years, the government has had frequent fiscal problems. The public debt has been a rising percentage of revenues, and its bond ratings have been sharply lowered. Unlike many countries, Puerto Rico cannot use a currency devaluation to strengthen its competitive position. In addition, U.S. trade policies are not designed from the perspective of Puerto Rico's needs, and the island finds itself disadvantaged by laws that force it to use high-cost American shipping. Puerto Rico's trade is distorted and overly concentrated in a few areas in which American manufacturing was drawn to the island in pursuit of tax advantages that have now been eliminated. Futhermore, concerns have been raised that the downside of access to U.S. resources may be promotion of a culture of dependency.

Internally, the government's interactions with citizens and businesses lack transparency. Its tax policies are complex and inconsistent, and information on budget expenditures is difficult to obtain. In chapter 6, Steven Davis and Luis A. Rivera-Batiz observe that the regulatory system appears to be particularly complex and is a contributor to what is perceived as a difficult business environment. The balance of voting strength between the two main political parties has led to a focus on politics as opposed to economics and a lack of continuity in government economic policies. In addition, many current transfer programs are structured so as to provide disincentives for work. This issue is stressed by both Gary Burtless and Orlando Sotomayor in chapter 3, and by María Enchautegui and Richard Freeman in chapter 4. The U.S. minimum wage (currently $5.15 an hour) applies to Puerto Rico; but given wage rates that average only half those of the mainland, the minimum wage has a much larger constraining effect on job opportunities for lower-skilled workers. There is also evidence, presented by Helen Ladd and Francisco Rivera-Batiz in chapter 5, that the quality of a once enviable education system is deteriorating.

Legacy of the Past

In chapter 2, Barry Bosworth and Susan Collins have provided a detailed review of Puerto Rico's past growth performance. That analysis suggests a break in economic performance in the 1970s, with much lower rates of economic growth in succeeding decades. In that and later chapters on more specific aspects of the economy, the contributors to this volume have suggested that several changes in the economic environment and policies contributed to the slowdown. By the early 1970s the process of shifting workers out of low-productivity agriculture into industry and services was complete, and growth became more dependent on improving productivity within the major sectors. Most strikingly, the industrialization program known as Operation Bootstrap ran out of steam after 1970. It was always a program that relied heavily on large multinational companies headquartered on the mainland, and it did little to build links with local supplying firms. As a result, Puerto Rico did not develop a large cadre of dynamic local entrepreneurs like that which emerged in the East Asian economies, nor was there significant transfer of know-how from the multinationals to Puerto Rican firms.

Chapter 2 argues that the expansion of the section 936 tax program shifted the focus away from developing activities in which Puerto Rico had a comparative advantage toward those with significant tax advantages to U.S. corporations. Growth was narrowly focused around a few manufacturing industries with large inputs of intangible capital (patents) that benefited from Puerto Rico as a tax shelter. The narrowing of the base of industrialization was also reflected in a sharp decline in capital investment during the 1980s.

The 1970s and early 1980s also witnessed a significant drop in rates of labor force participation. Chapter 3 argues that the expansion of the U.S. transfer programs in Puerto Rico during that period was a significant contributing factor to the decline in the participation rate. The level of benefits provided by those programs was more attractive in Puerto Rico, with its lower average wage rates, than in the United States. As Burtless and Sotomayor show, there was a large increase in the proportion of Puerto Ricans receiving benefits from the various means-tested programs in the 1970s and 1980s. The introduction of the U.S. minimum wage in Puerto Rico in the 1970s also played a role in reducing job opportunities for the least educated portion of the population.

Today, Puerto Rico has an unusual industrial structure. As measured by the distribution of employment, it has a very small private sector; and within the private sector, the service-producing industries are underdeveloped. The missing jobs in Puerto Rico are largely in industries that would employ the least educated workers. At the same time, Puerto Rico has not generated growth in medium-sized enterprises, based locally, to offset the declining role of the large mainland firms. In a variety of ways, such as occupational licensing and control of location decisions, the government has restricted competition and the entry of new enterprises. The result is extensive rent-seeking behavior by those with links to the government. In several respects, rather than fulfilling its earlier role of promoting innovative change, the government of Puerto Rico has evolved over the years to become an impediment to growth.

With the cancellation of the section 936 tax provisions, the relaxation of U.S. trade barriers against other countries, and the emergence of numerous other tax havens around the globe, Puerto Rico no longer has a significant competitive advantage in the production of most manufacturing products for the global market. In the area of pharmaceuticals, the buildup of a large manufacturing infrastructure will continue to yield some advantages in future years; but it is also a sector of rapid technological change in which future manufacturing advantages are hard to predict.

However, Puerto Rico's economy is not in a state of collapse. The concern is that growth is insufficient to achieve progress in narrowing the income differences between Puerto Rico and the U.S. mainland and that poverty remains far too high. It also seems clear that the old strategy of attracting large offshore corporations has been exhausted. Puerto Rico needs a new approach to promoting convergence with mainland living standards.

Prescriptions for Restoring Growth

The preceding chapters present a number of policy actions that the authors believe have the potential to raise incomes in Puerto Rico. We will not repeat all of their suggestions; but we do identify five major policy areas that need to be addressed, and we discuss a number of specific policy proposals within each. The major issues are as follows:

—raising the employment rate of adult Puerto Ricans
—promoting a more dynamic private sector that would create additional job opportunities
—improving the skills of the workforce
—investing greater resources in the economic infrastructure
—reforming government with a more efficient tax system and targeted expenditure programs

Creating Employment

A large portion of the differences in income between Puerto Rico and the United States is the result of differences in the employment rate between the island and the mainland—that is, too few Puerto Ricans are actually working and earning income. The differences are particularly large for the least educated members of the population, but they remain substantial even for those with a tertiary level of education. If the employment rate of Puerto Rico could be increased to that of the mainland, while average wage rates were maintained, per capita income would rise by 50 percent.

The causes of the low employment rate among adults in Puerto Rico are not fully understood. In particular, not enough is known about the economic situation of individuals who report that they are not currently employed. Much could be learned if the monthly household employment survey were expanded on a temporary basis to ask more questions of individuals who report their status as out of the workforce. Why are they not seeking employment? Do health problems keep them from working? Do they believe that no job exists? Are they engaged in other activities?

Achievement of a goal of parity with the employment rate of the mainland is a challenging but achievable task. Over the next quarter century, Puerto Rico will experience a sharp deceleration of growth in the population of labor force age, to an average growth rate near zero. Over a twenty-five-year horizon, employment would need to grow by about 1.7 percent a year to raise Puerto Rico's labor force participation rate from its current 46 percent to the mainland average of 66 percent and to lower the unemployment rate from 10 percent to 6 percent of the labor force. If the goal were to be achieved over a fifteen-year period, employment growth would need to be 3 percent a year. As shown in table 10-2, employment grew at a 2.4 percent rate in Puerto Rico over the last twenty-five years of the century, and growth rates in excess of 3 percent were achieved in fast-growing regions of the United States as well as in countries such as Ireland, Korea, and Singapore. Admittedly, these growth rates benefited from rapid growth in the underlying population, but they suggest that the proposed target for employment growth is feasible.

The current low employment rate reflects long-standing problems on both the supply side, in terms of incentives to seek employment, and the demand side, in the form of limited job opportunities. Specifically, as argued by the authors of both chapter 3 and chapter 4, the design of the public transfer system in Puerto Rico discourages work effort. These disincentives are magnified for those with the lowest expected earnings: the young, the old, and those with the least education. The structures of the transfer programs, with the emphasis on means-testing of benefits, result in a situation in which many families would receive little additional net income if one more adult member obtained a job. Means-tested programs also have work-disincentive effects on the mainland. But these effects are considerably more problematic in Puerto Rico, where they influence a much larger proportion of the working population.

Puerto Rico needs to reform its social protection programs to promote efforts by individuals to seek employment. Enactment of an earned income tax credit, similar to that available on the mainland, is one reform that has been proposed for the island.[5] Unlike transfer programs whose benefit level declines as an individual's earnings rise, the earned income tax credit rises in step with earnings up to a ceiling amount. Beyond the ceiling, the credit is gradually phased out. It is a proven effective program that has been used to assist low-income working families on the mainland. The program should be financed by scaling back the benefits paid under other transfer programs, such as the Nutritional Assistance Program, that currently impose no work requirement.

Other transfer programs that are administered by the commonwealth government should also be reviewed with the objective of maximizing incentives to maintain employment. Puerto Rico operates an extensive social safety net,

5. Enchautegui (2003).

Table 10-2. *Employment Growth, Puerto Rico and Selected States and Countries, 1976–2001*[a]

Region	Employment in 2001 (thousands)	Average annual percent change, 1976–2001
Puerto Rico	1,136	2.4
United States	131,826	2.0
Arizona	2,265	4.5
Florida	7,171	3.9
Wisconsin (median state)	2,814	2.0
Korea	18,721	5.3
Ireland	1,533	4.6
Singapore	2,047	3.5

Source: Data for U.S. states from U.S Bureau of Labor Statistics, *Current Employment Survey,* various years; for Puerto Rico, Puerto Rico Planning Board; for Korea and Ireland, Organization for Economic Cooperation and Development; for Singapore, the International Labor Organization.

a. Data are for total nonfarm employment. Data for Korea are for 1972–97, and for Ireland, 1990–2000.

with public provision of housing, food, and medical care assistance. It needs to make access to that assistance network conditional on employment or strong efforts to obtain employment and to limit the duration of benefits that are not linked to employment.

The Social Security retirement program is administered by the federal government, and its rules cannot and should not be modified to the special circumstances of Puerto Rico, since it is vital that workers remain free to move between the island and the mainland without complication. However, as highlighted in chapters 3 and 4, rates of disability are much higher in Puerto Rico than on the mainland. It would be appropriate for the Social Security Administration to review this experience to ensure its consistency with overall program requirements.

In addition, Puerto Rico needs to follow the lead of many U.S. states in developing a network of training and education programs to meet the occupational education needs of potential labor force entrants into the local economy.[6] Workforce development programs combine secondary vocational training, community colleges, welfare-to-work programs, regional development agencies, and employer organizations to provide a full range of training and related employment services. An integrated approach helps increase employers' access to a skilled workforce and helps individuals to find career jobs. It also ensures that the educational system is responsive to changing labor market conditions;

6. Puerto Rico has introduced some elements of a workforce development program with its Council on Human Resources and Occupational Development.

it goes beyond learning to assist in preparing individuals to enter or reenter the labor market.[7]

Private Sector Development

We believe that much of the problem of too few individuals working originates on the demand side of the market in the form of limited job opportunities. This aspect is stressed in chapter 6 of this volume. Measured by jobs, Puerto Rico has a very small private business sector. In its pursuit of large multinational corporations from the mainland, the Puerto Rican government has stifled the development of the local business economy and discouraged the development of linkages between foreign-based and local firms that normally makes the pursuit of foreign direct investment a desirable part of a progrowth strategy. For example, because the government imposed local employment quotas on the multinationals, the companies were unwilling to outsource even the simplest of support services, an important channel through which local firms in other countries learn from the multinationals.

There is no simple answer to the problem of an underdeveloped local business sector because the factors that contribute to it are deeply embedded in an overly complex tax system, a stifling regulatory regime, and a political process that is heavily dominated by competing rent-seeking interest groups. In past years, the government has initiated numerous economic development programs; but follow-up efforts have been unfocused, and the programs are often cast aside with the next shift of administration.

Puerto Rico needs to create and sustain a comprehensive program to promote the development of island-based businesses that can provide the job opportunities that are currently lacking. That effort will require a greater focus on small and medium-sized enterprises, and it should be coordinated by a government agency dedicated to promoting the interests of those firms. The program should address five major problem areas by eliminating excessive regulatory burdens, ensuring access to financial capital, improving training for entrepreneurs and their employees, increasing access to the research and development network, and developing core business areas of sufficient size to generate significant synergies.

Davis and Luis Rivera-Batiz emphasize the importance of reforming the regulatory environment surrounding the entry of new business firms and their development. Previous attempts to change an administrative regime that is viewed as inhospitable to business, however, have met with limited success. Efforts have been made to transfer the permitting process to municipalities and grant them greater authority to institute reforms. However, as the authors point

---

7. Robert Giloth (1998) provides a range of perspectives on workforce development programs with case studies. A wide range of information on the role of community colleges is available at the website of the Community College Research Center, Columbia University (ccrc.tc.columbia.edu/Home.asp [February 2006]).

out, this is not a practical solution for an economy comprising seventy-eight municipalities. Reform needs to be concentrated at the commonwealth level with the elimination of unneeded regulations and licensing requirements that suppress new business and the streamlining of the permit process in a single, one-stop coordinating office.

Financing is always a problem for small and medium-sized companies. However, it is not evident that it is the major barrier in Puerto Rico. Enterprises on the island are eligible for the loan guarantee and other support programs of the federal Small Business Administration. The agency operates a district office in Puerto Rico, and local firms appear to be active participants in the loan guarantee program, according to data for fiscal year 2005. The volume of loans ($163 million), scaled by personal income, is above the national average and even above fast-growing states such as Florida. Arguments are made, however, that new firms do not have the benefit of a program of active support from venture capitalists and peer-to-peer networks that can assist start-up firms. As noted in chapter 8, twelve venture capital funds are known to operate in Puerto Rico, but the amount of funding appears to be low. It is difficult to determine whether this lack of funding of innovative business activities represents a financing problem or is a reflection of limited entrepreneurial activity.

Puerto Rican firms are also eligible for the Small Business Innovative Research program, which reserves a small portion of federal R&D grants for small business. The program funds the critical start-up and development stages, and it encourages the commercialization of new technologies, products, and services. While Puerto Rican firms have received such grants, the magnitude of the grants between 2000 and 2004 has been very small. Over the period, Puerto Rico ranks below all the U.S. states both in terms of total dollar amount of such grants and in total amount of grants as a percentage of total personal income.[8]

Within Puerto Rico, the need to improve educational programs in the area of business and entrepreneurial skills is often mentioned as a barrier to the growth of local businesses. For example, the government's recent visioning exercise, "Puerto Rico 2025," emphasizes the need to strengthen business training, promote a closer link between the universities and the local business community, and encourage the formation of business networks among local small and medium-sized enterprises. Such activities are also closely related to the expansion of workforce development programs discussed in the prior section.

While R&D and linkages between the research institutions and local business are often mentioned as a priority for economic development in Puerto Rico, the available data suggest it is currently an area of considerable weakness. As noted earlier, Puerto Rico is underrepresented in the federal Small Business

---

8. Data on grant activity by state are available from the Small Business Administration (www.sba.gov/sbir/indexsbir-sttr.html [February 2006]).

Innovative Research program. In addition, the island ranks below all the U.S. states as a recipient of federal research funds and in the category of academic R&D expenditures, even when the measures are scaled by personal income of the state.[9] Furthermore, the number of scientists and engineers as a percentage of the labor force is below that of the states. Puerto Rico has much to do to build a significant R&D base for future economic activities.

In chapter 9, on trade and industrial policy, Robert Lawrence and Juan Lara suggest that Puerto Rico should focus on a development strategy that concentrates on a few industrial clusters, such as pharmaceuticals manufacturing, in which Puerto Rico might expect to develop a strong comparative advantage. The concept emphasizes linkages among private firms, research centers, and government agencies. It is similar to the approach adopted by the Puerto Rico Industrial Development Company. But at present, research and development is not a high priority within the university system, and few private firms are engaged in such activities. Thus the government would have to do much more than at present to fund a local research program.[10] In addition, the list developed by the Puerto Rico Industrial Development Company is too extensive for an economy of Puerto Rico's size.

Puerto Rico is likely to do better as a regional center for finance and business services. It is well located relative to the United States, Latin America, and Europe. It has a strong banking sector and a pool of bilingual educated labor to work in key areas of business services. It also has a fairly strong base in information and communications technologies. At present, however, most professional service firms are small, with a limited amount of activity outside of Puerto Rico. Thus the island would need to expend considerable effort to promote the sector and improve the underlying infrastructure. There is much to learn from the related experience of Singapore as a business center in Southeast Asia, and Ireland's development of business links with the rest of Europe.

U.S. regulations handicapped Puerto Rico in any effort to become a business logistics center. Nearly all goods trade between the island and the mainland is subject to the Jones Act, which requires that the goods move in U.S.-built, U.S.-owned, and U.S.-manned ships. This constitutes a significant cost barrier for Puerto Rico as it competes with Mexico, which has equivalent access to the U.S. markets under the North American Free Trade Agreement but is not subject to the provisions of the Jones Act. The issue will take on increased importance with implementation of the Central American Free Trade Agreement, which will further isolate Puerto Rico. Furthermore, Puerto Rico is considered

9. Data from National Science Foundation, Division of Science Resources Statistics, *Science and Engineering State Profiles, 2001–2003,* 2005 (www.nsf.gov/statistics/nsf05301/ [February 2006]). Information could not be obtained on the magnitude of industry R&D in Puerto Rico.

10. Actions were taken in 2005 to begin construction of a biotechnology center under the sponsorship of the University of Puerto Rico and the Puerto Rico Industrial Development Company.

to be part of the United States for purposes of international agreements on air transport, restricting travel between the United States and Puerto Rico to U.S.-flagged airlines. As a result of these measures, Puerto Rico's ability to act as a transportation hub serving the United States, Latin America, and the rest of the world is constrained. The United States could assist the island's development as a regional business center by exempting it from these transportation restrictions.

Finally, actions should be taken to modify the application of the minimum wage in Puerto Rico. Under pressure from U.S. trade unions looking to restrict competition with the mainland, the federal minimum wage was imposed on Puerto Rico in the 1970s. Because prevailing wages are only half those of the mainland, however, the U.S. minimum on the island constitutes a far larger barrier to the employment of low-skilled workers than in the states. The current U.S. minimum of $5.15 is equivalent to a $10.00 minimum wage on the mainland. According to the 2000 census, 37 percent of Puerto Rican workers report hourly earnings of less than $6.00, compared with only 14 percent on the mainland. While the minimum wage may raise the earnings of some workers, it eliminates job opportunities for low-skilled workers. Employers will not hire workers whose productivity is less than the minimum wage. The system is particularly constraining on the employment of young first-time entrants to the job market. Puerto Rico needs to regain the right to impose minimum wage rates in line with its own prevailing wage structure.

Education Reform

A dramatic gain in educational attainment stands out as a major contributor to Puerto Rico's past economic growth. However, as highlighted by Ladd and Rivera-Batiz, there is evidence that this area of former strength is now encountering significant problems. Families that can afford to do so are abandoning the public school system in response to problems of violence, perceptions of declining quality, and a lack of accountability at all levels. These problems are similar to those faced by many large urban systems on the mainland, but the rate of deterioration seems more rapid in Puerto Rico.

Like all U.S. states, Puerto Rico is subject to the test-based accountability provisions of the federal No Child Left Behind Act of 2001. The provisions of the act can be useful in developing meaningful measures of performance and in establishing stronger accountability standards. The test-based assessments can help guide the reallocation of education resources to the areas of greatest need. In strengthening accountability, Ladd and Rivera-Batiz also suggest, Puerto Rico can learn from the experience of mainland school systems, such as Chicago, that faced similar problems but have made progress in recent years. Given the failure of the education reform efforts of the 1990s and a highly politicized education system, Puerto Rico may have to consider some of the extreme management changes that were made in Chicago.

Puerto Rico faces different problems within its system of higher education. Both the proportion of the population aged eighteen to twenty-four that is enrolled and the proportion of enrollees who receive a degree are similar to the U.S. average; but there are concerns about the quality of the education. For example, the proportion of students receiving graduate degrees is low, faculty salaries are low, and research and development activity is limited. The cost per student in the public system is again similar to the U.S. average; but the proportion paid for by tuition is far below that in the United States, and the system's dependency on public funds is far greater. In effect, Puerto Ricans pay a much larger proportion of their taxes to subsidize the university system, with no evidence of comparable returns.

The result, as Ladd and Rivera-Batiz point out, is a substantial public subsidy to high-income families, who are more likely to have a member attending the university. A more efficient system would use public funds to provide financial assistance, in the form of grants and loans, directly to students and let them chose among the available institutions. The result would be greater competition among the higher-education institutions to provide a quality education. At the same time, more needs to be done to promote R&D activities and interactions between the institutions and the local economy. In effect, Puerto Rico needs to use its university system to strengthen its comparative advantage in knowledge-based industries and to promote its efforts to become a regional center for business services.

The Physical Infrastructure

The quality of Puerto Rico's physical infrastructure needs to be improved. As documented in chapter 2, on growth performance, the island suffers from a congested road system, inefficient provision of electrical energy, and a communications system that lags behind that of the mainland. Overall, the quality of the infrastructure is superior to that of most industrializing countries, but it falls short of the higher-income countries with which Puerto Rico is trying to compete.

The need for reform is most urgent in the area of electric energy. The high cost of energy is a significant barrier to the expansion of the island's industrial base. As documented by Sergio Marxuach, the cost of electric power is far above that on the mainland, and the Puerto Rico Electric Power Authority is highly inefficient relative to other comparable utilities.[11] The government should begin immediately to restructure this public enterprise, with the ultimate objective of increasing the availability of high-quality, reliable, and cost-efficient electric power in Puerto Rico. In addition, an independent regulatory board should be created to provide oversight of both the generation and distribution of electric-

---

11. Marxuach (2005).

ity. Exposure to the international energy market is high, however, as the island has few internal sources.

The Puerto Rico Telephone Company has been effectively privatized. Verizon Corporation holds a controlling interest, and the government is a minority stockholder. Despite substantial investment in recent years, Puerto Rico lags behind other advanced economies in many dimensions of communications use. In part, the low usage, as measured by indicators such as the number of Internet connections, can be explained by the current industrial mix; but if Puerto Rico hopes to become an important regional center for business services, it will need a superior communications system. A study aimed at accounting for the low usage of information and communications technologies would have considerable value.

In addition, Puerto Rico needs to improve the quality of what are at present deteriorating transportation and water and sewer systems. These are all areas of importance in expanding the island's economy and improving the quality of life; but they will require better management and substantial public investment. Given the government's fiscal problems, it is imperative that these efforts be financed by greater reliance on user fees.

Government Reform

The government of Puerto Rico is faced with growing fiscal problems. In recent years it has experienced substantial budget deficits that would be even larger were it not for the use of nonrecurring income and other temporary actions to cover the shortfalls. The public debt is rising as a proportion of income, and the government is faced with a large unfunded liability in its employee pension system. These problems, together with the lack of a plan to deal with them, have resulted in a deteriorating bond rating that by 2005 was at the lowest investment grade.

The general trends in Puerto Rican revenues and expenditures are shown in figure 10-1. Expenditures as a share of the island's income have been slowly declining in recent years; but the decline in revenues has been even more rapid, owing largely to the erosion of the tax base. Federal government payments are also a major revenue source, about 30 percent of the total (not shown).

As James Alm reports in chapter 7, the size and composition of government expenditures in the major program areas is similar to that of the U.S. states. It is difficult to make a detailed comparison because of the greater importance of government enterprises that operate outside of the General Fund. Some enterprises supply services that are often provided by the private sector in the United States, but others represent activities that would normally be classified as government activities.[12] Moreover, it matters greatly whether the comparison is

---

12. Examples of enterprises that operate outside the governmental funds are the Puerto Rico Electric Power Authority, the Government Development Bank, and the University of Puerto Rico. We have focused on the governmental funds, which report only the net payments to government enterprises (excluding their other sources of revenue).

Figure 10-1. *General Fund Revenues and Expenditures as Share of Gross National Income, Puerto Rico, 1990–2004*

Percent of GNI

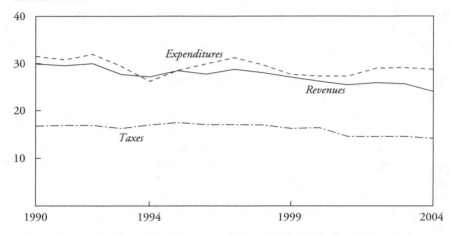

Source: Data are from Puerto Rico Department of Treasury (1990–2004), "Statistical section."

based on gross domestic product (income produced in Puerto Rico) or gross national income (the net income of residents). According to Alm, U.S. state and local taxes have averaged about 9 percent of gross state product in recent years. In Puerto Rico, taxes are a similar share of gross domestic product but a larger 14 percent share of gross national income.[13] On an employment basis, public administration is 30 percent of nonagricultural employment, compared with 14 percent in the states.[14]

Puerto Rico has an extraordinarily complex tax system, as Alm notes, with numerous layers of conflicting tax preferences. The problems are particularly severe with the taxation of business activities. The commonwealth imposes a hefty tax on corporate income, with rates rising to 39 percent, but it exempts large numbers of both domestic and foreign-based firms from the tax. Many of these exemptions are negotiated between individual corporations and the government, with effective tax rates as low as zero. In today's global economy, the taxation of business activities at rates above those of competitive locations can easily lead to a diversion of business, particularly of those businesses aimed at the export market.

13. Puerto Rico does not regularly publish aggregate data on the tax revenues of municipal governments, but they are less significant than in the average state. Employment in the municipalities is about 20 percent of total public administration, compared with more than 60 percent in the states. Revenues are obtained from a property tax, construction fees, and transfers from the central government.

14. Again, however, it is important to remember that the share of the population working in public administration is much more similar to that in the United States. As noted in several prior chapters, Puerto Rico has a very low employment-to-population ratio.

However, Puerto Rico's current approach of negotiating special deals with foreign-based corporations can easily disadvantage its own Puerto Rican businesses.

The individual income tax has also accumulated a significant number of special provisions and exemptions that have eroded the effective tax base. With exemptions for many forms of capital income and underreporting of self-employment income, the tax is largely a wage tax. Despite a range of marginal tax rates from 7 to 38 percent, the effective tax on total personal income is less than 6 percent. Such a large difference between average and marginal rates implies the potential for major tax distortions. Puerto Rico also imposes a number of excise taxes and a sales tax on manufactures and imports.

There is a growing recognition of the need to reform the tax system, but a consensus on the characteristics of the new system has not emerged. We would suggest, first, that attention be paid to the importance of combining a broad tax base with low rates, as the available tax research highlights. High tax rates are the primary cause of the economic distortions and incentives to evade the tax. Second, in a highly competitive global economy, Puerto Rico needs to be made an attractive base for international business. That calls for a simple and highly transparent system of business taxation with low rates. Third, Puerto Rico could reduce many of it problems with tax evasion and disincentives toward work by placing greater reliance on a broad-based consumption tax. Fourth, Puerto Rico needs to reform what has become an absurd system of property taxation.

In the past, Puerto Rico could rely on its special appeal for U.S. corporations that took advantage of section 936 of the U.S. tax code. But with the elimination of that provision and the conversion of U.S. subsidiaries to controlled foreign corporations (CFCs), Puerto Rico must compete with other countries as a base for those CFCs engaged in export-based production. It can no longer maintain a system of cross-subsidization in which large business taxes support subsidies to the resident population.

As Alm observes, many of the problems of the current tax regime could be reduced by shifting to a greater emphasis on a broad-based consumption tax. There are basically two alternatives: a retail sales tax, such as that used in the U.S. states, or a value added tax (VAT). We believe that in the case of Puerto Rico, there are clear advantages to the VAT. The retail sales tax is employed in the United States largely because the individual states do not have information on the volume of cross-border transactions.[15] A VAT generally imposes the tax on imports and rebates it on exports. However, as an island economy, Puerto Rico can easily introduce such a system for transborder transactions. Second, Puerto Rico is said to have a severe problem with tax avoidance and a growing

15. The retail sales tax is also encountering increased problems with the growth of Internet sales. There have been ongoing discussions of a national VAT, with a state allocation of the proceeds on the basis of state income or population, but it is hard to reach any agreement among such a large group of diverse interests.

underground economy. Those problems are aggravated by the retail sales tax but minimized under a VAT. If an enterprise does not pay the tax on its sales, it cannot deduct the tax paid on its purchased inputs. Each firm has an incentive to ensure that its suppliers have paid the tax in order to claim it as a credit. The VAT has been the overwhelming choice of countries that have enacted consumption-based tax regimes.

A broad-based consumption tax will fall more heavily on low-income households because they spend a larger portion of their income in the local economy. However, efforts to deal with that problem by exempting some items, such as food and medicine, are quite ineffective because the exemptions are not closely correlated with income, and the special provisions greatly complicate the tax system. It is more effective to focus instead on the distributional concerns in designing the income tax system, which can be tailored more closely to the economic situation of individuals and can easily be made more progressive as an offset to a regressive consumption tax.

The continued reliance on 1958 property values in the determination of property tax assessments makes no sense. A rational system of property taxation is an important means of diversifying the government's revenue base, and the tax helps ensure the efficient use of a valuable resource. Ideally, the tax should apply only to the value of the underlying land so as not to discourage improvements in the accompanying structures, but the assessment of land independently of the structures is a difficult undertaking. A property tax also works best when the total amount of the tax is maintained at a relatively modest level.

The problems of the government sector, however, go beyond a need for reform of the tax system. The operations of the government lack transparency, with far too great a reliance on special administrative, tax, and regulatory actions tailored to the interests of individual groups. Like many states, Puerto Rico has a constitutional requirement for a balanced budget, but the requirement is consistently circumvented by reliance on short-term borrowing from the Government Development Bank or other funds or by reliance on one-time revenue inflows. The lack of fiscal discipline has created a serious threat that Puerto Rico could lose its access to debt markets.

Concluding Thoughts

Puerto Rico has made many impressive economic achievements, and its citizens enjoy a standard of living above that of any economy of Latin America. Yet, equally relevant, it is poorer than the poorest American state by a substantial margin, and more than half of its children live below the U.S. poverty line. Furthermore, the narrowing of the income gap between Puerto Rico and the mainland has stalled. In this chapter we examine the economic issues from the perspective that Puerto Rico can and should do better. We have argued that its highly skilled population and its physical and social infrastructure provide the requisite base from which to launch rapid economic growth in future years. Persistence of the currently high rates of poverty should be unacceptable—both to Puerto Rican residents and to their fellow citizens on the mainland.

Participants in the project on which this volume was based uncovered a fascinating set of economic puzzles in struggling to understand why Puerto Rico's economic growth faltered recently, despite strong performance before the 1970s. Why does the income gap with the mainland persist in the presence of a common set of economic, legal, and social institutions and a population that has made such remarkable strides in educational attainment? The chapters in this volume, we believe, offer insights that can account for key dimensions of Puerto Rico's economic performance. They also outline a set of proposals that we think would help restore higher rates of economic growth and improve the standard of living relative to that of the mainland.

However, we would be remiss if we did not emphasize that Puerto Rico is at an important crossroads as it seeks to develop and implement a strategy for future growth. Evolution of the global economy and developments within its own region dictate that the policies it pursued in the past will not work for the future. Puerto Rico cannot continue to rely on tax advantages as the primary attraction for multinational firms. Instead, Puerto Rico must diversify and strengthen its economy by developing its own dynamic private businesses and the jobs that they will bring.

References

Enchautegui, María E. 2003. *Reaping the Benefits of Work: A Tax Credit for Low-Income Working Families in Puerto Rico.* San Juan: Center for the New Economy (www.grupocne.org/ [February 2006]).

Giloth, Robert P., ed. 1998. *Jobs and Economic Development: Strategies and Practice.* Thousand Oaks, Calif.: Sage Publications.

Hausmann, Ricardo, Lant Pritchett, and Dani Rodrik. 2004. "Growth Accelerations." Working Paper 10566. Cambridge, Mass.: National Bureau of Economic Research (June).

Kaufmann, Daniel, Aart Kraay, and Pablo Zoido-Lobatón. 2002. "Governance Matters II: Updated Indicators for 2000–01." Policy Research Working Paper 2772. Washington: World Bank.

Marxuach, Sergio M. 2005. "Restructuring the Puerto Rico Electricity Sector." White Paper 3. San Juan: Center for the New Economy (August 11).

Puerto Rico Department of Treasury. 1990–2004. *Comprehensive Annual Financial Report*, annual reports (www.hacienda.gobierno.pr/estados_fin/index.html [April 2006]).

Contributors

JAMES ALM
Georgia State University

FUAT ANDIC
United Nations Adviser

MARINÉS APONTE
University of Puerto Rico

DAVID AUDRETSCH
Indiana University

WILLIAM J. BAUMOL
New York University

BARRY P. BOSWORTH
Brookings Institution

GARY BURTLESS
Brookings Institution

SUSAN M. COLLINS
*Brookings Institution and
    Georgetown University*

STEVEN J. DAVIS
University of Chicago

JAMES L. DIETZ
University of California–Fullerton

MARÍA E. ENCHAUTEGUI
University of Puerto Rico

ARTURO ESTRELLA
Federal Reserve Bank, New York

RONALD FISHER
Michigan State University

RICHARD B. FREEMAN
Harvard University

JAMES A. HANSON
World Bank

ALAN B. KRUEGER
Princeton University

HELEN F. LADD
Duke University

JUAN LARA
University of Puerto Rico

ROBERT Z. LAWRENCE
Harvard University

DANIEL LEDERMAN
World Bank

WILLIAM LOCKWOOD BENET
*Lockwood Financial Advisors and
   Center for New Economy*

RITA MALDONADO-BEAR
New York University

BELINDA I. REYES
University of California–Merced

FRANCISCO L. RIVERA-BATIZ
Columbia University

LUIS A. RIVERA-BATIZ
University of Puerto Rico

CARLOS E. SANTIAGO
University of Wisconsin

EILEEN V. SEGARRA ALMÉSTICA
University of Puerto Rico

MIGUEL A. SOTO-CLASS
Center for the New Economy

ORLANDO SOTOMAYOR
University of Puerto Rico

KATHERINE TERRELL
University of Michigan

JOSÉ J. VILLAMIL
University of Puerto Rico

INGO WALTER
New York University

Index